GREAT BATTLES
OF THE 20TH CENTURY

IWM

Grosset & Dunlap

A Filmways Company
Publishers • New York

in association with Phoebus

INTRODUCTION

Massed armies and new weapons of vast destruction have ceased to make war the prerogative of a few belligerent aristocrats and their followers. Waging war has now become a decision of awesome political importance taken only as a last resort — yet war has always fascinated men.

This animal game of destruction or survival, of hunting and escaping is the ultimate test of the individual and the group, beside it all other forms of human endeavour are insignificant. In the 20th Century this test has reached new proportions — the battles of the First World War which stretched over weeks and months were a grim contrast to Napoleonic actions which could be over in a day. In the Second World War, Stalingrad, Kursk, Alamein and Midway were the turning points of a war which at its start seemed to herald the triumph of a new totalitarianism. After these battles the war moved slowly in favour of the Allies — as one German commentator said "After Stalingrad we knew that we would not win the war, but after Kursk we knew that we would lose."

The postwar years have seen battles of no lesser importance. Dien Bien Phu and the Tet offensive of 1968 were two actions which were militarily indecisive — Tet was ultimately a defeat for the Viet Cong, while the French losses at Dien Bien Phu were not great when compared to their total forces in Indo-China — yet both had a political and prestige effect greater than their military importance.

For despite the endless agony of the First World War and the world-wide destruction of the Second, wars do not exist in isolation. They are born of political ambition and national arrogance, characteristics fostered by the people in their leaders, and so we must accept that ultimately this responsibility lies with us.

EDITOR BARRIE PITT

This edition © 1977
Phoebus Publishing Company
BPC Publishing Limited
169 Wardour Street
London W1A 2JX

Library of Congress Catalogue Card Number: 77-78750

This material first appeared in *History of the First World War*
© 1971 BPC Publishing Limited, *History of the Second World War* © 1966/1972/1975 BPC Publishing Limited and *History of the 20th Century* © 1968 BPC Publishing Limited © 1973 Phoebus Publishing Company

First Grosset & Dunlap Edition 1977

Made and printed in Great Britain by
Waterlow (Dunstable) Limited

ISBN 0-448-14458-1

CONTENTS

SPION KOP

The shock of the British defeat at Spion Kop affected not only the army but also the nation who believed that the largely civilian Boer forces would be defeated in a short victorious campaign. The after-effects were a Royal Commission and changes in training and officer selection which dragged the British Army into the 20th Century and prepared it for the First Great European War.

The Second Boer War began on October 11, 1899, the culmination of a century of growing enmity between British and Boer settlers in South Africa. After the annexation of the Cape by Great Britain in 1814, the Great Trek took many of the Boers north into Zulu and Basuto territory. There they established the republics of the Orange Free State, finally granted independence by the British in 1854, and the Transvaal, which declared itself the South African Republic two years later. After the discovery of diamonds at Kimberley in 1867, however, the British began to expand their claims over southern Africa. In 1871 Basutoland was annexed, followed in 1877 by the Transvaal. But after reconstituting the republic in 1880 the Boers fought for and won their independence, granted by the Treaty of Pretoria in 1881. The discovery of gold at Witwatersrand in 1886 further unified the Boers, and with the two republics allied, British settlers found themselves exploited economically and were secure only in Cape Colony. Great Britain opened negotiations on behalf of her settlers, but neither side showed any willingness to compromise: territorial rivalry had gradually hardened into hatred.

Finally, Paul Kruger, President of the Transvaal and the man who had led the republic to victory over the British in 1881, issued an ultimatum. He demanded that all British troops in Cape Colony be withdrawn from the borders of the Transvaal, all new reinforcements leave South Africa and no more be allowed to land. The British government, forced by public opinion to protect the British colonists, rejected the ultimatum. General Sir Redvers Buller was appointed Commander-in-Chief of the British forces in South Africa, and he left London to an impressive send-off: the war was to be over by Christmas.

But by Christmas the war was far from over. The Boers had invaded Natal and Cape Colony, annexed British territory and laid siege to Mafeking, Kimberley and Ladysmith. In the second week of December they defeated Gatacre at Stormberg and Methuen at Magersfontein. And that same week – 'Black Week' – Buller himself was defeated at Colenso, with the loss of 145 men killed and 1,200 wounded and missing,

Left: Louis Botha, the farmer lawyer who commanded the Boers at Spion Kop

in an attempt to cross the Tulega River and relieve Ladysmith. Astonishingly, he then heliographed General White, commander of the 13,000 men bottled up in Ladysmith, advising him to fire off the remainder of his ammunition and surrender. This action, on top of the series of defeats, prompted London to relieve Buller of his command. He was, however, retained as commander of the Natal Field Force.

In this context, a signal from Buller received in London on January 22, 1900 aroused considerable interest. It read: 'Spion Kop is to be attacked tonight.' An otherwise insignificant hill in the heights above the Tulega River, Spion Kop – 'lookout hill' in Afrikaans – had great strategic significance, for it commanded the roads to Ladysmith. Victory there would be welcome not only as a success in its own right, it would also bring a new chance of relieving White and his men.

At his headquarters south of the Tulega, Buller had every reason to expect victory. One of the few British commanders of the day to show real concern for the welfare of his men, he enjoyed their complete loyalty, and even affection. A soldier's soldier, known to his troops as 'old fighting Buller', he had fought in Canada, in the Ashanti War and in the abortive expedition to relieve Gordon at Khartoum. His Victoria Cross was won in the Zulu War, and he had gone on to be chief of staff to General Wood during the First Boer War and head of the Intelligence Department in Egypt. Now he commanded an impressive force: over 30,000 men, including the newly arrived 5th Division under Lieutenant-General Sir Charles Warren, were disposed along the Tulega River, supported by eight batteries of field artillery as well as cavalry and engineers. All were regular troops, subject to harsh discipline but undoubtedly courageous. A significant question mark hung over Buller, however, one he expressed himself to the Secretary of War when he was appointed to lead the South African forces: "I was better as a second in a complex military affair than as an officer in chief command."

By contrast, the commander of the Boers in the heights on the other side of the river was a natural leader of men. Louis Botha had grown to his position by the force of his personality and the natural brilliance of his leadership. His troops were not

regular soldiers but consisted of locally raised commandos which enjoyed considerable autonomy and made their decisions at democratic councils of war. They were heavily outnumbered by the British forces, though their artillery – mainly 94-pdr Creusots, 65-mm Krupps and 1-pdr Maxims – was efficient enough. However, years of battling for their lives in a hostile wilderness had made them crack shots, and their Mauser rifles were at least the equal of the British Lee-Enfields and Lee-Metfords. Botha's plan, therefore, was to remain in the heights with their natural defensive positions and wait until the British could be drawn into a confined space and contained. He was to have his opportunity sooner than he could have hoped.

When Botha arrived at the Tulega heights on January 18, the first part of the British force had already crossed the river, the cavalry swimming with their horses and the infantry and artillery following on pontoon bridges. During the 18th the main part of the force to attack the heights, commanded by Warren, followed, and by the 20th, after some unwieldy manoeuvring and two days of hard fighting, the British troops were in position for the attack, some 2,000 yards below the Spion Kop itself. Meanwhile, a cavalry reconnaissance led by Lieutenant-General the Earl of Dundonald had surprised a Boer patrol at Acton Homes Farm, on the Boer right flank, and captured the outpost. From here the road to Ladysmith behind the Boer positions could be commanded and rapid consolidation could have opened the way for an advance on the besieged town. But Warren sent only token reinforcements and then ordered Dundonald to return to his headquarters.

Finally the attack on Spion Kop began. General Woodgate was in command of the spearhead force, and the advancing columns were headed by Lieutenant-Colonel Thorneycroft and Lieutenant-Colonel Bloomfield. At 2030 on January 23, a starless and rainy night, they began the climb towards their objective. No Boer sentries were encountered until 0330, when a brief skirmish forced a small party of Boers to withdraw. By 0430, as dawn began to break, Spion Kop had apparently been captured. Under the cover of thick mist the troops began to dig in among the

dry scrub and boulders.

However, Botha was informed of the British advance and immediately began to dispose his forces. The artillery was brought up on to the neighbouring hills, and reinforcements were moved to the summit. By the time the mist had cleared, the British realised they had made a terrible mistake; what they thought was the peak of the hill was only the upper part of the plateau immediately below the summit, and their position now was precarious indeed. Boer riflemen occupied the highest part of the hill, and from the adjacent peaks—Green Hill, Conical Hill, Aloe Knoll and Twin Peaks—rifle and artillery fire was directed on to the exposed British positions. Woodgate's immediate response was to ask for artillery to be

brought up, and for Twin Peaks to be attacked.

It was now that the fatal flaws in the British preparations were revealed. No reconnaissance had been carried out of the Spion Kop area, there was no mountain artillery in the vicinity and the command structure was muddled and indecisive. Because of the lack of maps, the answering fire from the British batteries was short, causing many casualties among their own troops. Moreover, no preparations had been made to move the artillery to more effective positions on higher ground, and by the time the lighter battery of mountain guns arrived, it was too late to send them forward. And while Buller remained aloof at his headquarters and Warren dithered at the foot of the hill,

Woodgate was fatally wounded, opening the way for confusion about who was in command on the plateau.

When Buller was wounded, at 0830, Lieutenant-Colonel Bloomfield assumed command, only to be wounded himself almost immediately. Next Lieutenant-Colonel Crofton took over, and asked Warren for more reinforcements—probably the last thing that was needed on the cramped fire-trap that the plateau had become. Nevertheless, they were despatched under Major-General Coke, whom Warren also appointed to take over command at the summit. Meanwhile, however, Buller had been watching the fighting and, impressed by the fearless leadership of Thorneycroft, suggested that Warren place him in command. Warren complied,

Left: A Boer Commando poses by a waggon. The men are armed with Mauser rifles and wear their working clothes from their farms or stores. *Above:* British dead litter the field following the battle of Spion Kop. *Below:* More losers. (Left) General Sir Redvers Buller C-in-C in South Africa. (Right) Colonel A.W. Thorneycroft who led and inspired the soldiers on the hill but, after he had withdrawn with battle fatigue, became the scapegoat at the Royal Commission on the War in South Africa which was held in 1903. Recommendations by the Commission did much to improve and modernise the army

making Thorneycroft an acting Brigadier-General. Unfortunately, he omitted to inform Coke of this latest move.

Thorneycroft had been an inspiration to his men throughout the savage fighting during the morning, in spite of a sprained ankle, maintaining order in the lines and organising counter-attacks against the Boer positions. At one point, when some 200 men of the Lancashire Fusiliers attempted to surrender, he forced them back as the Boers were starting to take them away—reportedly telling the would-be captors: "You may go to hell. I am in command here and allow no surrender."

By noon, however, there was total confusion over who was in command. Coke was still under the impression that he was to take over, while many of the officers thought that one or other of the various Lieutenant-Colonels who were senior to Thorneycroft should be in charge. For the rest of the day the confusion remained.

Meanwhile, Botha, although in a commanding position, was far from certain of victory. Sustained British attacks against the neighbouring hills would be too much for his outnumbered forces, so, hopeful of a rapid victory, he mounted an attack round the side of the hill against Thorneycroft's left. This produced a second action, as vicious as the main battle on the lower part of the plateau. For yet more reinforcements, sent by Major-General Lyttleton, were making their way towards the summit. With no clear plan for reinforcing the summit, they were diverted to the lower plateau, where they met the Boer force coming round the hill.

In the ensuing action, though no one involved realised it was anything but an extension of the main fighting, the Boers were driven back, and Thorneycroft's position was kept intact. At the same time, Botha had suffered another setback: one of his outlying positions, that on Twin Peaks, had been taken.

The officer responsible for the attack on Twin Peaks was Major-General Lyttleton. His troops had been in action after the crossing of the river and were in reserve when the assault on Spion Kop was mounted. But after sending the reserves which successfully held the lower plateau, he decided to take the initiative himself. Realising what Botha already knew—that

Mary Evans

not only Spion Kop but the whole of the ridge of which it was part would have to be taken if the road to Ladysmith was to be secured – he saw that Twin Peaks, a mile to the east of Spion Kop, was the weakest Boer position. Accordingly, he despatched a battalion of the King's Royal Rifle Corps to attack the hill.

Two coloumns, under Lieutenant-Colonel Buchanan-Riddell and Major Bewick Copley, stormed the hill, charged the Boer defences and drove out the defenders. But having occupied the two summits of the hill, Buchanan-Riddell fatally over-extended his lines: he himself was killed, and the occupiers were ordered by Buller to withdraw.

Had there been any plans for fighting there, it might have been possible to reinforce the riflemen on Twin Peaks, consolidate their victory, and launch a new offensive to drive the Boers out of the other hills. However, the only plan had been to capture Spion Kop, there had been no preparations to reinforce any other positions, and it was too late in the day to provide the necessary support for such an action. The troops on Twin Peaks had no alternative but to obey Buller's order.

By now it was almost nightfall. The troops with Thorneycroft on the upper plateau of Spion Kop had been fighting all day in blistering heat, caught in a murderous cross-fire from rifles and artillery. They were exhausted, almost without water and short of ammunition. The trenches were filled with corpses, the dead and dying were everywhere: the casualties

Lieutenant General Sir Charles Warren who commanded the 5th Division. A Sapper with no field experience he became the scapegoat for the disaster at Spion Kop

amounted to 40 per cent of the original force. Winston Churchill, then a young war correspondent, had made his way to the upper plateau and, realising that the men there could not be expected to hold the hill for the night and fight again in the morning, decided to make his own report to General Warren.

Thorneycroft had already signalled to Warren that the hill could not be held without fresh troops. Coke, however, who had not been to see for himself, reported that no more men were needed and sent an order to Thorneycroft – his own commanding officer – instructing him not to attempt any further advance. Back at Warren's headquarters, Churchill insisted on seeing the commander and told him of Thorneycroft's plight. After ordering the correspondent to be arrested, Warren changed his mind, and sent Churchill back with a message that fresh troops, plus the mountain battery which had finally arrived, would be sent up during the night, and that more artillery would follow when the engineers had prepared a road.

But it was already too late. Thorneycroft had finally decided that his men could stand no more and ordered a withdrawal. The bizarre ending to a day of savage fighting was under way. For, on the other side of the hill, the Boers too had begun to withdraw.

When Churchill arrived back at the plateau he found the withdrawal had begun. In spite of protests from the men and some of the officers, Thorneycroft was convinced it was the only course open to him, and refused to change his mind. Botha, on the other hand, when he found his men preparing to leave, persuaded them to remain, and by nightfall they had returned

The battle as recorded by the Germans who were pro-Boer. The commanding position of the hill and the excellent shooting of the Boers made withdrawal very difficult

to their positions. Not realising that the British had pulled back, a small patrol crept forward from the Boer lines under cover of darkness to retrieve their wounded. No one challenged them: the hill was deserted except for the British wounded; the Boers had won the Battle for Spion Kop.

The immediate scapegoat for the disaster at Spion Kop was General Warren, who was roundly criticised in Buller's report. Thorneycroft, too, was singled out for reprobation – though his withdrawal was perfectly understandable in the circumstances, and in any case should never have been left to the judgement of an officer who had begun the day as a Lieutenant-Colonel then been left to fight largely unsupported. The real inquest, however, came with the Royal Commission on the War In South Africa in 1903.

The Commission's report was a thoroughly damning indictment of virtually every aspect of the British Army and its conduct of the war. The quality of the officers, from the Commander-in-Chief, Viscount Wolseley, down; the organisation of supplies and communications; the standard of rifles and ordnance; the lack of proper maps; the basic strategy and planning: all were found to have been inadequate. Spion Kop had been the most glaring symptom of a fundamentally outdated army. Fortunately, by 1914 the recommendations of the Commission had caused a radical improvement in training, equipment and efficiency, or the BEF would have been hopelessly unprepared to fight the Great War.

TSUSHIMA

The naval action fought between the Empires of Japan and Russia in the straits of Tsushima was the first major battle of the 20th Century. It also marked the rise of Japan as an international power and the beginning of the decline of Tsarist Russia. For naval officers throughout the world it was a fascinating trial of the tactical theories of speed and gun power. For the Royal Navy it was a test of their training methods and doctrine which had been adopted by the Japanese.

13

The great sea battle that was fought on May 27, 1905 in the straits dividing Tsushima island from Japan ended with the complete destruction of a first-class European battle squadron by the navy of a country with only 50 years of modern industrial and organisational experience. In those 50 years warship design had progressed from wooden sailing-ships firing cannon broadsides to steel steam-powered battleships, equipped with wireless, fire-control systems and mounting guns capable of engagement at ranges over five miles. When the battle came it was a clash of design ideas and tactical doctrines, but above all of two different social systems' will to win. As the Japanese commander, Admiral Togo, wrote after the battle, "The *Mikasa* (Togo's flagship) and the eleven others of the main force had taken years of work to design and build, and yet they were used for only half an hour of decisive battle. We studied the art of war and trained ourselves in it, but it was put to use for only that short period. Though the decisive battle took such a short time, it required 10 years of preparation..."

On January 30, 1902 Japan announced the conclusion of an alliance with Great Britain. The Royal Navy's tactical doctrines and British shipbuilding practice had already permeated the thinking of those directing Japan's emergence as a world naval power. Japan's transformation from a medieval to a modern state had proceeded at breakneck speed. They had imported two hundred years of Europe's industrial revolution wholesale, but in choosing their military mentors – Germany for the army, and Britain for the navy – they had chosen well. There had even been a modern naval action for Japan to test and show her efficiency at sea.

In 1894 the Chinese Empire seemed on the verge of breaking up. Korea and the vast Manchurian hinterland were tempting targets for Japanese military ambition. The Japanese successfully convoyed a large army to Korea in August, 1894, until the Chinese Admiral Ting sought battle off the mouth of the Yalu River.

When the time came, however, the contest was not so clear; Admiral Ting adopted outdated tactics, throwing away his advantage in gunpower, and the Japanese Admiral Ito decided the action by out-manoeuvring and encircling the Chinese line of battle. Four Chinese ships were sunk by gunfire and one by collision, but their battleships proved the value of armour against hits from smaller guns. Ito's flagship, the *Matsushima*, was hit three times by 12-in and once by 10-in shells, causing great damage and over a hundred casualties. Both fleets retired, but Japan was left in command of the Yellow Sea and free to continue her military adventure in Korea.

The prize of the Liaoutang Peninsula, with the ice-free port Port Arthur at its base, was snatched away when the European powers put on diplomatic pressure to 'protect' China. The wound to Japanese pride was deepened when, as soon as Port Arthur had been returned to China, ·Russia bullied the ailing Empire into allowing the Trans-Siberian Railway to be completed to Vladivostok across Manchuria. By March 1898 the Russians were in Port Arthur itself and developing an ice-free naval base to complement Vladi-

vostok, 300 miles to the north. The Japanese, however, had already started a programme of naval expansion which would bring their fleet up to six new battleships, six armoured cruisers, and eight light cruisers by 1903.

Russia watched with alarm and commenced production in Baltic yards of eight battleships. In contrast to the Anglophile Japanese, these ships were strongly influenced by French practice, with pronounced tumblehome and high freeboards (high hulls bellying out at the waterline), long waterline armour belts, and massive masts and built-up superstructures.

The Russo-Japanese War began on the evening of February 8, 1904. Japanese destroyers in two waves made a precision night attack against the Russian First Pacific Squadron lying in the roadstead of Port Arthur. Seven battleships, six cruisers, and 25 destroyers lay anchored in the harbour, their lights blazing and their defences woefully ill-prepared. Only three torpedoes found their mark, but they crippled three battleships. The *Tsarevitch, Retzivan* and *Pallada* settled on the shallow bottom, stranded without dry-dock facilities, and for a vital month the Japanese controlled the Yellow Sea and began the transfer of their armies to the mainland.

When the dynamic Admiral Makarov arrived in March to take command of the dispirited Russian fleet, the squadron was roused from its somnolence and the damaged battleships were raised in coffer-dams. As the new spirit and the renewed threat to their lines of troop transports became evident to the Japanese, they redoubled their efforts to block the harbour. Admiral Togo was forced to use his ships in close blockade, with its wear and tear on his vessels (although keeping the crews combat trained), and face the increasing hazards of Russian minefields. However, on their few sorties out of harbour, the lack of skill of the Russian commanders was painfully obvious. Coming out in the battleship *Petropavlovsk* to cover the return of a disastrous destroyer sortie, Makarov led his whole squadron over a freshly laid minefield. There was a muffled explosion under the flagship, then suddenly two vast explosions threw a great chunk of the battleship's superstructure into the air. The big ship heeled over and slid to the bottom, her propellers still turning, taking Makarov with her.

His ability had been the Pacific Squadron's hope, and with his death the offensive power of the fleet, even to stop a landing on the peninsula behind the port, collapsed. 'The squadron went back to slumber in the basins of the inner harbour,' wrote an observer.

The Japanese, however, had their problems. Togo's repeated attempts to block the harbour with suicide assault blockships had failed. The battleships *Habuse* and *Yashima* were claimed by mines. The Vladivostok cruisers were harrying troop transports. It was clear that the Russians were gathering a fleet in the Baltic to come to the aid of embattled Port Arthur, and Togo was still forced to keep his fleet concentrated should the new if reluctant Russian commander, Admiral Vitgeft, attempt a breakout.

It was not Togo, however, who had to make the first move. Vitgeft received direct orders from the Tsar to take the

squadron to Vladivostok and, led by minesweepers, the fleet left harbour on August 10, 1904. There was little hope aboard the Russian ships and already Japanese scouts were signalling the news of the attempted break-out to Togo's battle-squadron, now steaming north to engage. Togo had hoped the Russian fleet could be kept inside harbour where it would be destroyed or captured by the besieging army. Now his Combined Fleet, the entire battleship strength of Japan, would have to accept battle, with the threat of the Baltic Fleet still to come. He could afford to lose no more ships.

The Japanese purpose would be served by barring the way out, if not destroying the Pacific Squadron in battle. Suitably the opposing heavy squadrons opened fire at extreme range, with the Russian gunnery surprisingly accurate. As the long daylight action continued and the opposing fleets manoeuvred for the best position, the Japanese were taking serious punishment. Mutual destruction would bring Togo a tactical victory but would lose him the strategic object.

Then suddenly, with darkness beginning to fall, two 12-in shells struck the Russian flagship *Tsarevitch*, killing every man on the bridge. Of Vitgeft only a bloody piece of one leg remained, and the battleship lurched out of control, turning the battle-line into a milling throng. After minutes of utter disorder, Admiral Prince Uhtomski, flying signals from the bridge-rails of *Pereviet* (the signalling masts had been shot away), led the squadron back to Port Arthur as *Retzivan* and *Pobieda* put up a gallant rearguard. Japanese destroyers closed in for the kill, but in the darkness the Russian stragglers managed to regain the harbour they had so recently left. The crippled *Tsarevitch*, hit by over fifteen 12-in shells, was interned in German Kiau-Chow, and two cruisers suffered similar fates. The sortie had been a fiasco, but until the hit on *Tsarevitch* the Russians had held their station. With their leadership gone, their fighting ability collapsed. The Vladivostok squadron was brought to action on August 14, but again this resulted in a Russian defeat. The cruiser *Rurik* was sunk and the cruiser *Gromoboi* ran aground. All that was left was the cruiser *Rossiya* and three Russian admirals, unable to reach Port Arthur, where the leaderless Russian battleships had retired to lick their wounds.

The humiliations in the East made the despatch of reinforcements inevitable. The Russian confidence of 1904 that the 'yellow monkeys' would be crushed had been shattered by Admiral Togo Heiacho and his British-built battleships. In the Baltic a force of new first-class battleships were under construction, while older cruisers and battleships were undergoing refits. If Port Arthur held out, and a powerful new fleet could come to the rescue, Japan might still be denied her mainland ambitions.

The man appointed to command this 'Second Pacific Squadron', Rear-Admiral Zinovei Petrovitch Rozhdestvenski, faced immense problems in even getting his ships ready for sea. Food and clothing had to be procured for the fleet's 12,000 seamen, and machinery prepared for an ordeal beyond any design endurance. In the brief periods of manoeuvres nothing had gone

皇國興廢在此一戰各員一層奮勵努力

Above: The battleships of the Japanese fleet in perfect line astern at Tsushima. *Left:* Count Heihachiro Togo, the victorious Japanese Admiral

right, with ships colliding and wildly inaccurate gunnery. The overriding problem, however, was coal. Great Britain, with her virtual monopoly of high-grade smokeless Welsh coal, had declared it contraband, but not before the Japanese had built up large stockpiles. The Royal Navy's dominance in the world's oceans was maintained by a strategic chain of coaling stations. Russia had none and only a fitfull access to 'neutral' French and German colonial ports. The Baltic Fleet would have to cover 19,000 miles of sea, round the Cape and across the Indian Ocean, consuming 17,000 tons of coal per 1,000 miles. The bunkering capacity of the most modern Russian battleship was 1,063 tons. The solution was a fleet of 60 German colliers despatched in succession to meet the slow-moving fleet at pre-arranged rendezvous between Libau in the Baltic and Port Arthur on the other side of the globe.

On October 15, 1904 Rozhdestvenski raised his flag on *Kniaz Suvorov* and, with flags waving and bands playing, the fleet steamed out of Libau to avenge the humiliations in the East. It comprised seven battleships – the recently completed *Suvorov, Aleksandr III, Borodino, Orel* and *Oslyaba,* and the *Sissoi Veliki* and *Navarin,* with two armoured cruisers, *Admiral Nakimoff* and *Dmitri Donskoi,* four light cruisers, *Aurora, Svietlana, Zhemtchug* and *Almaz,* plus seven destroyers and nine transports. The modern battleships mounted four 12-in and seven 6-in guns in paired turrets and had complete waterline armour belts 10 in thick. The pronounced tumblehome and built-up superstructures, following French design practice, made them bad seakeepers. The overloading of coal and stores added to the miseries of the voyage.

Once at sea, the morale and incompetence of the fleet was revealed to the world when fantastic rumours of a Japanese torpedo attack were taken seriously. To the men on the bridges who remembered the surprise night attack on Port Arthur, however, an attack from British bases did not seem that fantastic. In the North Sea the repair ship *Kamchatka* lost contact with the main fleet, and her frantic signals of sighting torpedo-boats (in fact a Swedish steamer) reached the line of battleships just as they ran into British trawlers working off the Dogger Bank. Wild alarm seized the Russians and equally wild gunnery tore into the trawlers. The voyage had opened in fiasco, and meanwhile Britain seemed on the brink of war.

At Tangier the fleet divided. Admiral Velkerzam was ordered to take the older shallow-draught ships through the Suez Canal and rendezvous at Nossi Bé on the northern tip of Madagascar. At a halting pace the main squadron crawled around the coast of Africa. Ships got lost. Engines broke down. Sailors went mad in the heat, cursing the back-breaking ritual of coaling from the faithful German colliers. Inside the ships coal was piled everywhere, 'not up to the neck but over the ears', as an officer wrote, blinding and choking, but, worst of all, making any combat training impossible.

At Nossi Bé the divided squadron rejoined and learned the news that Port Arthur had fallen. Worse still, the coaling arrangements had broken down and the Fleet was stuck. All the Russian Admiralty could do was despatch a 'Third Pacific Squadron' under the command of Rear-Admiral Nebogatov. The fleet did manage an epic crossing of the Indian Ocean, coaling at sea from lighters, until on 9 May, off the coast of French Indo-China, Nebogatov's 'tubs' caught up to further embarrass Rozhdestvenski.

On May 23, the Russians coaled off the China coast for what was going to be the last time. The force heading into the battle-zone was organised in four divisions. The first, led by Rozhdestvenski's flagship *Suvorov,* comprised the battleships *Aleksandr II, Borodino,* and *Orel.* The Second Division was commanded by Admiral Velkerzam aboard the *Oslyaba.* The unfortunate admiral had succumbed to a tropical disease on the day of the last coaling, but Rozhdestvenski kept this information from the fleet. The *Sissoi Veliki, Navarin,* and *Admiral Nakhimoff* followed the dead admiral's flagship. In *Nicolai I* Nebogatov led the Third Division, *Apraxin, Seniavin* and *Ushakoff,* while Admiral Enquist, in the *Oleg,* commanded the eight cruisers.

On board the *Mikasa,* flagship of the Combined Fleet lying in the anchorage of Masan on the Korean mainland, Togo directed the operations to meet Rozhdestvenski's ships, now heading for Vladivostok. The most likely route, the Tsushima Strait separating the island of that name from Japan, was divided into boxes, each patrolled by Japanese cruisers. The Tsugau Strait and the northern route around the top of Japan itself was left thinly protected, but it was a gamble that would pay off. The Russian crews prayed for fog to conceal the seven miles of the ships under their black smoke haze until they reached the safety of Vladivostok, which now seemed like the promised land. But for Rozhdestvenski merely to evade Togo and take refuge in another Port Arthur might merely repeat the fate of the First Pacific Squadron. The Russian admiral had at least to inflict some damage on the enemy, so the squadron's speed was adjusted so that it would enter the zone of maximum danger at daylight on May 27, 1905.

A Japanese armed merchant cruiser, the *Shinano Maru*, made the first contact at 0330. The wireless message reached Togo in the *Mikasa* – 'The enemy sighted in section 203, he seems to be heading for the eastern channel.' Ninety minutes later Togo led the battleships of the First Division out of Masan, the *Mikasa, Shikishima, Fuji,* and *Asahi,* the armoured cruisers *Kasuga* and *Nisshin*. Vice-Admiral Kanimura led the Second Division, the armoured cruisers *Izumo, Azuma, Tokira, Yagumo,* and *Iwate*. The cruisers *Naniwa, Takachino, Tsushima* and *Akashi* made up the Third Division. Every ship was fuelled and armed for maximum combat efficiency and able to make 18 knots, in contrast to the worn-out Russian ships' nine or ten. Togo's fleet could bring to action sixteen 12-in guns, and a hundred and twelve 8-in and 6-in guns. The Russians had twenty-six 12-in, seventeen 10-in and a hundred and twenty-one 8-in and 6-in. Any disparity in gunpower mattered little, however; it was how the rivals used their gunpower that would decide the battle.

Togo's operations officer, Commander Akiyama, had set a seven-stage trap for the Russians to sail into. The battle would open with torpedo and destroyer attacks and the third phase would be the direct fleet engagement. The remaining stages envisaged the piecemeal destruction of any survivors who might break through towards Vladivostok. The Russian fleet was detected too late for torpedo attacks, but shadowing cruisers forced Rozhdestvenski into weakening his formation. Fearing an attack, he ordered a manoeuvre designed to give him the advantage of crossing the 'T' of the main Japanese force that must be waiting somewhere ahead. When the shadowing cruisers disappeared, the Russian admiral ordered the First and Second Battleship Division to make an eight-point turn to starboard to bring the ships in line abreast. As *Suvorov* began the turn, the Japanese cruisers reappeared and the order to the Second Division was contradicted. The Russian captains could not execute the change with any kind of precision and, as Nebogatov wrote, 'The enemy continued to turn to port and lay parallel to our mob, since this is the only word ω describe our formation.' Thus the Russians were suddenly steaming towards Togo's battlefleet at a closing speed of 24 knots in a ragged battle formation exposed on the port side.

It was not Togo's intention to make a north-south broadside pass which, although it might damage the weaker Russian ships,

would leave them travelling in the direction of Vladivostok. At 1355 the Japanese line swung to port, following the *Mikasa* in line ahead. Rozhdestvenski meanwhile had ordered the First Division to increase speed and come out from behind the weaker line to his left and take up battle formation in one line ahead. Then, as Togo reached the chosen position, the battle ensigns were unfurled, and in a breathtaking manoeuvre the whole Japanese line swung round 180°, turning in succession, with the *Mikasa* leading. At the moment of the turn they were helpless targets, but only the lighter Russian shells were making hits. Coming out of their turn, one after the other, the Japanese ships opened a slow deliberate fire at a range from five to six thousand yards. Then they put on speed, sprinting north-east at 15 knots across the head of the labouring Russian column. The classic manoeuvre that the pirates of the Inland Sea had known for centuries, crossing the 'T', had been achieved.

As the Japanese gunners found the range, the leading Russian ships were subjected to a fearful battering. *Suvorov* and *Oslyaba* were soon set ablaze, while, on board, stunned Russian seamen struggled with primitive damage-control procedures. At 1455 *Suvorov* fell out of line on fire. At 1505 *Oslyaba* sank, throwing the following ships into chaos. *Aleksandr III* turned to port to escape under the smoke haze and slip behind the stern of the Japanese line, all steaming in perfect formation at 15 knots, all guns in action. As they looped back to intercept them, only the *Suvorov* was left in sight, still fighting back with one remaining 12-in gun and a few remaining 12-pdrs. From the shattered bridge the severely wounded Rozhdestvenski was carried to a gun turret.

An hour later the missing Russian main body was resighted and forced to turn away south-east as Togo's ships poured fire into them at a range of 1,000 yards. *Aleksandr III* was forced out of formation until, at 1800, it capsized and sank. The *Orel* was raked with fire and the *Borodino* burned until her exploding magazines ripped the ship apart. At the same time the gallant *Suvorov* was being finished off with torpedoes. The agony of the battleships could not relieve the cruisers *Oleg* and *Zhemtchug*, set ablaze, and the sinking of several auxiliary ships.

At darkness, with Vladivostok still 300 miles away, Admiral Nebogatov, in the old *Nicolai I*, attempted to achieve some sort of order from the decimated survivors of the First and Second Divisions and his still largely intact Third Division. The gathering darkness, however, brought the torpedo-boats. Pressing home vicious attacks at ranges under 300 yards, the Japanese sank *Navarin* and *Sissoi Veliki*. Admiral Enquist, in the *Oleg*, led *Zhemtchug* and *Aurora* away from the slaughter out by the southern exit of the Tsushima Strait, but the cruisers *Admiral Nakhimoff* and *Monomakh* were scuttled on the island of Tsushima itself.

At dawn the next day Nebogatov's shattered fleet was found again by the Japanese battlefleet. The tragic Rozhdestvenski lay critically wounded in the destroyer *Bedovi*. By 1115 the Japanese had formed a great circle around the Russian ships. There was no other choice. A white tablecloth was run up on *Nicolai I*,

but Togo did not cease fire until the Russians had stopped their engines. Victory was complete when the unconscious Admiral Rozhdestvenski was carried into captivity. Of the 12 Russian ships that had made up the battle-line, eight had been sunk and four captured. Four cruisers had been sunk, three scuttled and Enquist's three escaped to the Philippines and were interned in Manila. One cruiser, the *Almaz*, and two destroyers reached Vladivostok. The Russians lost 4,830 men killed, 7,000 prisoners and more interned. The Japanese lost three torpedo boats, 117 killed and 585 wounded.

What had happened? How had two battlefleets – on paper, at least, evenly matched – met and fought with such an uneven outcome? The reports of the British naval attachés who had gone into action with the Japanese fleet were eagerly studied, and they indicated several things: that Russian gunnery had been surprisingly accurate at long range but had rapidly deteriorated as soon as the Russian ships themselves took damage; high-explosive shells had caused the most damage, and a high proportion of Russian shells found their target but failed to explode; that shells, not torpedoes, were the deciders; that both sides had fought bravely, but that the Japanese were vastly more competent than their opponents. All this was true, and the reports strongly influenced naval thinking up to the start of the First World War and beyond, however the Second Pacific Squadron had been disadvantaged from the very start.

The ships were worn out by the voyage from across the world. Of the men themselves, many were sick. Ironically, after the repeated stops and the backbreaking task of coaling, the Russians had gone into action with too much, some of it stacked on the decks in bags. The Japanese, taking the advice of a Royal Navy report by Admiral Fisher, had actually dumped coal, losing weight to fighting trim and giving them the crucial speed advantage which allowed Togo's in succession turn and the foiling of Russian evasive manoeuvres. The Japanese had concentrated fire on the Russian flagships, and as soon as they had been battered out of line, their squadrons' formation and fighting qualities fell to pieces.

Finally, the initiative and competence of the Japanese commanders and seamen was something that could not be quantified in the reports drafted by naval attachés. As they had closed for action, Admiral Togo had been urged to take cover as he stood on the exposed bridge. He shook his head. 'I am getting on for sixty, and this old body of mine is no longer worth caring for. But you are all young men with futures before you, so take care of yourselves and continue living in order to serve your country'. The Imperial Japanese Navy was a curious mixture of Royal Navy traditions of understatement and Oriental determination to triumph. Togo had signalled to the Fleet: "The rise and fall of the Empire depends upon the result of this engagement. Do your utmost, every one of you."

Japanese torpedo-boats in action against Russian warships

MONS

The crew of an 18-pounder in action at Mons. The sheer professionalism of the tiny BEF came as a surprise to the advancing Germans

As the French forces fell back from the frontiers, the British Expeditionary Force found itself defending the canal between Mons and Condé. The resulting battle against the numerically superior German forces was the first fought in western Europe by the British since the battle of Waterloo. Although vastly outnumbered, the speed and accuracy of the British marksmen forced the Germans to abandon their unsupported massed infantry attacks

'Before the week is over, the greatest action the world has ever heard of will have been fought,' wrote Major-General Henry Hughes Wilson in his diary on August 21, 1914. These four battles which formed the 'greatest action' were known as 'The Battle of the Frontiers'. They were linked to each other like a party of roped mountaineers. The first, Lorraine, affected Ardennes, which influenced the outcome of Charleroi, which in turn had a serious impact on Mons. This was to be the setting of the first battle since the Crimean War that British troops had fought on European soil.

As a result of Germany's violation of Belgium's neutrality the BEF, commanded by General Sir John French, began its channel crossing on August 12. It consisted of two Army Corps, I and II, commanded by Generals Sir Douglas Haig and Sir Horace Smith-Dorrien (who hurried out to France to replace General Grierson, who died on August 17). The supporting cavalry division consisted of four brigades and was led by Major-General Sir Edmund Allenby (known as 'the Bull'). The four brigades of this division included dragoons, hussars, lancers and the composite Household Cavalry.

The first British troops to disembark at Boulogne were the 2nd Battalion of the Argyll and Sutherland Highlanders. Kilts swinging and bagpipes playing, they received an ecstatic welcome before setting off for the Belgian frontier.

The first British troops in action were the 4th (Royal Irish) Dragoon Guards under Lieutenant-Colonel Robert Mullen. Captain Hornby led 'C' squadron into the village of Soignies on a skirmishing reconnaissance, killing an enemy cycle patrol and eight *Uhlans* (German heavy cavalry) of the *9th Cavalry Division*.

It was already August 21 when the BEF began advancing into the actual line of battle. Allenby's cavalry were in the lead, followed by Smith-Dorrien's II Corps with Haig's I Corps at the rear. Reconnaissance aircraft and cavalry reconnaissance units discovered strong enemy forces between Enghien and Charleroi, and German cavalry in the area around Nivelles.

The French armies on the British right had run into large German formations and had suffered heavily, and this, plus the reported strength of the opposing German forces, made it abundantly clear that the BEF's first action would be defensive. The French staff had once hoped optimistically to break the German attack along the Charleroi-Mons line and then counterattack, assume the offensive, pivot around Namur, raise the siege, liberate Brussels and link the British left wing with the Belgian army which they expected would be advancing from Antwerp.

The BEF infantry marched through the sweltering heat of August 22 and spent most of the night digging in. Originally they had hoped to defend the high road from Charleroi through Binche to Mons, but this was obviously impracticable after the German success and the French withdrawal on the British right. Sir John French, therefore, positioned his men along the line of the Mons Canal with II Corps on the left behind the canal and I Corps extending as far as Villers St Ghislain on the right – a total of 27 miles.

A dangerous salient

Curving up in a distorted semi-circular bulge to the north and east of Mons lay the area known as 'the Salient' – as welcome strategically to the defenders as a malignant wart, which it resembled on the map. If the Germans were to be kept out of Mons for the maximum possible time, the Salient had to be defended; and this defence was allocated to II Corps. Before moving out to protect the flanks, the cavalry was ordered to act as a screen for the salient's defenders, to provide reconnaissance patrols and to fill the gap between the two corps.

Lanrezac, commanding the French Fifth Army, had quarrelled with Sir John French at their first meeting on Monday August 17. Subsequently, when Lanrezac asked for a British attack to ease German pressure on his army, he received only a promise that the BEF would hold its line for at least 24 hours.

In round figures, the BEF would have to hold its line with 75,000 men and 300 guns. The British army, in defiance of the decimal system, maintained that a corps was the sum of two divisions, and that a division contained 18,073 men, 5,592 horses, 76 guns and 24 machine guns. A British cavalry division, however, consisted of 9,269 men with 9,815 horses. The BEF were opposed by at least 200,000 men and 600 guns belonging to Kluck's *First Army* and elements of the right wing of Bülow's *Second Army*. A German army corps was made up of two infantry divisions each containing 17,500 men, 4,000 horses, 72 guns and 24 machine guns, in addition to heavy artillery, bridging trains, supply columns, field hospitals and bakeries.

The French Fifth Army consisted of approximately 300,000 men: the I, III, X and XI Corps, the 37th and 38th Divisions, two reserve Divisions – the 52nd and 60, and cavalry. It was French practice to organise their divisions as units of 15,000 men, 36 guns and 24 machine guns, with either two or three divisions making up a corps.

Lanrezac's men had been attacked not only by Bülow but by Hausen's formidable Saxons of the *Third Army* who had driven a wedge into the extended French line and struck alternately at Lanrezac's right and the left of de Langle de Cary's Fourth French

The BEF arrives at Le Havre on August 14, 1914. The troop convoys used the western channel ports, rather than the shorter straits crossing, for fear of German naval intervention. In fact the Germans, unimpressed by the BEF's size, made no attempt to interfere

BUCKINGHAM PALACE

My message to the Troops of the Expeditionary Force. Aug 12ᵗ 1914

You are leaving home to fight for the safety and honour of my Empire.

Belgium, whose country we are pledged to defend, has been attacked and France is about to be invaded by the same powerful foe.

I have implicit confidence in you my soldiers. Duty is your watchword, and I know your duty will be nobly done.

I shall follow your every movement with deepest interest and mark with eager satisfaction your daily progress, indeed your welfare will never be absent from my thoughts.

I pray God to bless you and guard you and bring you back victorious.

The King's message to his troops. Although Britain went to war to guarantee Belgian neutrality, her army moved in accordance with plans previously made in concert with the French

Army. The ghost of the humiliating defeat at Sedan in the Franco-Prussian War of 1870 haunted French military thinking in 1914. Lanrezac later wrote of it as 'that abominable disaster'. Anything, even the retreat of the Fifth Army, was preferable to another Sedan. He is also reported to have said: 'We have been beaten, but the evil is reparable. As long as the Fifth Army lives, France is not lost.'

Mons was by no means an easy place to defend. The main features of the district were small hamlets to the north, rows of cramped houses, factories and sprawling slag heaps. It was a drab area of bogs and mists, coalmines and railway embankments. The canal was 7 feet deep, 60 feet wide and crossed by 18 bridges in 16 miles. It represented practically no obstacle to the German advance.

General Sir Hubert Hamilton, a veteran of the South African War, knew that his 3rd Division was mainly responsible for the defence of the salient. Because of the serious disadvantages of the position, a second line of defence was prepared behind Mons. If it became necessary to occupy these second positions the line would straighten out automatically, disposing of the awkwardly exposed salient.

Dawn attack

Brigadier-General Beauchamp Doran was in command of the 7th Regiment of Foot, the Royal Fusiliers, who were predominantly Londoners. Their 4th Battalion was led by Lieutenant-Colonel Norman McMahon and it was against his sector of the salient that the brunt of Kluck's first attack fell. Dawn and the first shell greeted the fusiliers more or less simultaneously on the morning of August 23. After a short sharp bombardment had killed and wounded 20 men, there was a pause followed by the appearance of a German cavalry patrol.

The fusiliers' first volley unseated most of them, and Lieutenant von Arnim of the Death's Head Hussars was brought in swearing profusely with a bullet in the knee.

The Germans next attacked the salient frontally with four infantry regiments. This was largely because Kluck had not been able to make the best use of his superior numbers by going round the British left flank, as Bülow had ordered him to remain on

hand for support. Kluck's two central corps, *III* and *IV*, suffered drastically from this head on meeting. One German reserve captain of *III Corps* discovered he was the only officer left alive in his company and the only surviving company commander in his battalion. It appeared to the defenders that a solid mass of field grey was advancing in columns of four. They moved unhurriedly, like a football crowd or a civic parade. This formation was apparently based on the idea that losses were compensated for by having every available rifle in the firing line at the earliest possible moment.

Watching the slowly-rolling, grey ocean of men, Captain Ashburner of the 4th Battalion's 'C' Company asked Captain Forster to pinch him in case he was dreaming. The Germans were 600 yards off when Ashburner gave his fire order. It would have been difficult to miss the enemy infantry and few did. The Lee Enfield rifle fired a flat trajectory up to 600 yards and machine gunners added substantially to the heavy German casualties.

Subsequent German attacks, however, were preceded by long, accurate artillery bombardments, machine gun and small arms fire. The 4th Battalion offered stiff resistance, but an eventual withdrawal was unavoidable. Lieutenant Dease and Fusilier Godley both earned a VC for their machine gun work—the former posthumously, the latter in a prisoner-of-war camp.

Also predominantly of London origin was the 4th Battalion of the Middlesex Regiment, commanded by Lieutenant-Colonel Charles Hull. They were positioned to the right of the Fusiliers and shared with them the brunt of Kluck's attack on the salient. Their war diary for August 23 read simply: 'Battle commenced 10.15 am, retirement started 3 pm.' Like the Royal Fusiliers, the Middlesex soon found that the Germans abandoned their suicidal close order advance and began to move carefully, supported by heavy artillery, machine gun and rifle fire which gouged into the hastily dug British trenches with deadly results. The Middlesex also had to withdraw. Their machine gun section, which was in action for the first time, distinguished itself under Lieutenant Lawrence Sloane-Stanley, who refused to be evacuated, despite severe wounds, until the final withdrawal.

The Royal Fusiliers lost 200 men, the Middlesex 700.

Further east, the 1st Battalion of the Gordon Highlanders defended the right flank of the salient, and the 2nd Battalion of the Royal Scots extended the line towards Haig's I Corps. In response to a request for reinforcements, Lieutenant-Colonel John Cox, commanding the 2nd Battalion Royal Irish Regiment (which was in reserve), sent forward two companies to assist the Gordons. Not many days earlier Scots and Irish had gone for each other vehemently in a brawl in Devonport which had put nearly a dozen of them in hospital. Now, however, with the defenders in serious difficulties, Company Quartermaster-Sergeant Thomas Fitzpatrick, a Dubliner, organised a mixed group of Royal Irish batmen, cooks, drivers and latrine orderlies into a useful fighting reinforcement.

Jemappes, to the west of the salient, was held by the 1st Battalion of the Royal Scots Fusiliers. With only one machine gun to supplement their rifle fire, and with only ruined buildings and slag heaps for cover, these 210 Royal Scots held back over 2,000 German troops and prevented the encirclement of the salient.

Sir Horace Smith-Dorrien, commander of II Corps which took the left wing at Mons

Sir Douglas Haig, commander of I Corps of the BEF on the right at Mons

Adjacent to Jemappes, near the Mariette bridge, the line was held by the 1st Battalion of the Northumberland Fusiliers. Captain Brian St John of 'B' Company ordered his men to hold their fire when a dozen Belgian schoolgirls emerged from a house and raced for shelter. The Germans, who had driven the girls forward as cover, were close behind. When withdrawal from Jemappes and Mariette became due it was found that the bridges could not be destroyed. Captain Wright of the Royal Engineers made a daring but unsuccessful attempt at Mariette which won him the VC, while Lance-Corporal Jarvis and Private John Heron were awarded the VC and DCM respectively for their successful attempt at Jemappes. So far neither of Kluck's flanking Corps, IX on his left and II on his right, had been used.

At 1700 hours French received a telegram from General Joffre, Commander-in-Chief of the French Armies, renowned for his imperturbability and known to French soldiers as 'Papa' or 'Le Grandpère'. Three German army corps, a reserve corps plus the *IX* and *IV Corps,* and two cavalry divisions were moving against the British front. The German *II Corps* was turning on the left from Tournai. This meant that the BEF was outnumbered six to one, and Lanrezac's Fifth Army was dropping back. Sir John French ordered the BEF to retreat before dawn on the 24th to a new line stretching from Jerlain, south-east of Valenciennes, to the Maubeuge fortress which covered its right flank. Bavai was the dividing point between I and II Corps.

Smith-Dorrien's corps' headquarters was situated in the Château de la Roche at Sars-la-Bruyère and had neither telegraph nor telephone. The château was difficult to find in the dark and Smith-Dorrien did not receive the retreat orders until 0300 hours. Haig, on the other hand, received his by telegraph an hour earlier and his I Corps was able to start pulling out well before dawn.

A defiant last stand

The II Corps began its retreat under fire and as part of the fighting retreat along the Elouges-Audregnies road, Lieutenant-Colonel Dudley Boger's 1st Battalion of the Cheshire Regiment was to all intents and purposes wiped out after a defiant last stand during a rearguard action against vastly superior numbers.

Despite the hard German pressure on the centre and left of II Corps and the cavalry divisions, by the morning of the 24th most of the BEF, weary but more or less intact, stood along their line on either side of Bavai. Kluck did not press on immediately, because he believed that the British would stand and fight again as they had done at Mons, and by the time he realised they were continuing the retreat it was too late for the German forces to carry out an effective encirclement.

In retrospect the Battle of Mons developed a peculiar mystique. Legends of supernatural intervention on the allied side — 'The Angels of Mons' — gained currency. In some romantic British minds it began to rank with Hastings and Agincourt. It cannot be denied that the British at Mons fought with great courage, skill, discipline and tenacity. A German officer in the Brandenburg Grenadiers wrote: 'curse them, they seem to understand war, these English.' But these qualities were also demonstrated by the Belgians at Haelen, and the French brigade under General Mangin at Onhaye.

The Battle of Mons lasted nine hours prior to the retreat and engaged 35,000 British soldiers of whom 1,600 became casualties. The advance of Kluck's army was held up for one day. During the four days from August 20 to 24 the French had lost 140,000 men. For the Germans, Mons was both a victory and a lost opportunity: for the allies it represented a fortunate escape from really grave military disaster.

German machine gunners.
Because of its size and weight the machine gun was still almost entirely a defensive weapon. Consequently the attacking Germans were unable to match the fire power of the British

Ullstein

VERD

UN THE STORM BREAKS

At dawn on February 21 the German bombardment of Verdun and its defences began, a bombardment so massive that it was heard as a steady rumbling 100 miles away. The Germans, superior in the air, in artillery and in numbers of fighting men, seemed poised for a stunning victory, and the fall of Fort Douaumont, the largest of the forts guarding Verdun, was seen as the beginning of a major French catastrophe. Yet the Germans let their opportunity slip, largely owing to caution from above. Fighting desperately under the inspiring leadership of Pétain, the French began to slow the German advance. *Below:* The effect of the massive German bombardment — the devastated entrance of Fort Souville, one of the forts guarding Verdun

It was chance—even bad luck—that in the early morning of February 12, 1916, the day fixed for the German assault on Verdun, there was a ferocious blizzard. At dawn deep snow lay everywhere, the storm still raged and mist lay across the whole countryside, concealing all the meticulously pin-pointed targets for the German artillery, on whose accuracy success depended absolutely. So their opening bombardment had to be postponed.

This initial postponement did in fact prevent immediate disaster for the French. On that morning, two newly-arrived French divisions, the 51st and the 14th, were not yet in position. If the Germans had attacked then, with their blanketing artillery and their battalions of chosen assault troops, they would have found the French in half-completed positions—the French 72nd Division alone facing the six German attacking divisions, and the other four French divisions, including the two newly-arrived, spread about through the citadel and the rest of the Verdun salient. Some of the French troops holding the front line were elderly Territorials.

While the Germans waited for the stormy weather to abate, the French settled into their new dispositions. There were now three French divisions—making up General Chrétien's XXX Corps—facing the Germans between the Meuse and the railway to Etain. Of these, the 72nd and 51st Divisions, with 20 battalions, manned the north-eastern curve of the salient, which was to be the sector of the main German attack; and there were 14 further battalions on the French flanks or in close reserve. An elderly gunnery officer, General Herr, was in immediate command of the French troops in Verdun and the salient; but having lost a large part of his fortress artillery to Joffre's recent purges of fixed emplacements, Herr felt himself at a loss in a world of trenches, infantry, wire and chronic lethargy. As a fortress commander, Herr was directly responsible, not to a field army headquarters, but to General de Langle de Cary, commanding the Central Group of Armies.

Opposite these 20 French battalions, the main German attacking force was made up of 72 battalions, or six divisions. On the German right, from the Meuse at Consenvoye eastwards to Flabas, was *VII Reserve Corps* under General von Zwehl—Westphalians. Next, on a short sector opposite the Bois des Caures, was *XVIII Corps* under General von Schenck—mostly Hessians. On the left, from Ville to Azannes, was *III Corps*: these were the famous Brandenburgers, and their commander, General von Lochow, had already gained a reputation for aggressive action—in particular, against Pétain's thrust towards Vimy Ridge in the previous spring. Supporting troops of *V Reserve Corps* and *XV Corps* were on the German left.

But the principal feature of the German line-up was the concentration of guns—over 1,200 for an assault frontage of barely eight miles. There were 654 'heavies', including 13 of the 42-cm mortars, the 'secret weapon' of 1914 that had shattered the Belgian forts, and two 38-cm long-range naval guns earmarked to interrupt communications behind Verdun. There were 21-cm howitzers to pulverise the French front lines, and 15's to seek out and destroy the French batteries. Two and a half million shells had been

Ullstein

24

Left: A German 21-cm short howitzer. A sudden thaw on February 28, following the long spell of cold weather, turned the surface into a sea of mud and made it difficult for the German artillery to advance

Above: A French soldier is hurled violently back by the impact of a German bullet. By the end of March, 81,607 Germans and 89,000 French had been killed—not only France, but Germany too, was being bled white

brought up to supply this greatest concentration of artillery yet seen on any battlefield.

To preserve secrecy, the Germans had deliberately restricted their front and not included the eastern side of the salient for their attack; for the Woëvres Plain on that side was overlooked by the French-held Meuse Heights. Of much greater significance, however, was the German decision not to attack at the same time on the left, or western, bank of the Meuse. This limitation, and the later German efforts to rectify it, were to be among the terrible hall-marks of the Battle of Verdun.

For nine days bad weather held up the opening of the German bombardment which was to precede the attack of their assault troops. There was snow again; a thaw with fog, rain and gales; more rain and gales; wind and snow squalls; mist and cold. The French troops at least were accustomed to a rough life in poorly finished trenches and improvised dug-outs, with shelter for some in the forts, now largely deprived of their guns, which ringed the inner fortress of Verdun. The Germans probably suffered more in these harsh days of waiting, keyed up as they were for the attack. The concrete *Stollen* in which they assembled expectantly each day were not meant as a permanent shelter for these large bodies of troops; so most of them had a seven-mile march each night and morning to and from their billets through freezing sleet or snow.

On February 19 and 20 the weather improved. So at dawn on the 21st, the massive German bombardment started—heralded by a poor shot from one of the two long-range, long-barrelled 38-cm (15-inch) naval guns which, instead of destroying the Meuse Bridge in Verdun, exploded in the courtyard of the Archbishop's Palace, knocking off a corner of the cathedral. The other naval gun, aiming at Verdun Station, had more success. The ordeal of the salient had begun.

The bombardment of the French lines and rear quickly rose to a shattering peak of intensity, and continued without abatement for nine hours. In all the great artillery barrages of 1915, nothing compared with this concentration of high-explosive shells, with this appalling weight of flying, disintegrating metal. From left to right, from front to rear and back again in the narrow sector of the impending German infantry attack, everything was methodically bombarded. Gas and tear-gas shells were included too, with the aim of incapacitating the French artillery. The French trenches, poorly prepared, were quickly obliterated and many of the troops manning them were buried.

Lieutenant-Colonel Driant, whose warning voice had first drawn attention to the deplorable state of the Verdun defences, was now in the front line in the Bois des Caures, with his *Chasseurs*, as a detachment of 72nd Division—in the very centre of the German attack sector, opposite *XVIII Corps*. They experienced the full intensity and horror of the shelling. It seemed to them as if the wood was being swept by 'a storm, a hurricane, a tempest growing ever stronger, where it was raining nothing but paving stones'. Through the din of the explosions came the splintering crash as the great oaks and beeches of the forest were split or uprooted by the shells. The bombardment was heard nearly 100 miles away on the Vosges front as a steady rumbling.

Unpreparedness played as much a part as the German gas-shells in upsetting the French artillery. Their counterbattery work was generally ineffective from the start: their fire was spread rather aimlessly, and ceased to count as visibility decreased and contact with the infantry broke down. All telephone communication with the French front line had been cut by the shelling within the first hour, and runners often found it impossible to get through the avalanche of shells. As a result, effective command rapidly broke down. There was no question of sending up reinforcements; and in Verdun itself the shelling from the 38-cm naval guns had already dislocated the unloading of trains.

About mid-day there was a sudden pause: the shelling stopped and the French troops emerged from the debris of their line, ready to face the expected onslaught of the German infantry. But it was a trick. The Germans quickly took note of those parts of the French line which were still manned, and then at once took up the bombardment again, concentrating their short-range heavy mortars on the sections where the French had shown themselves, and shelling every part with the same unrelenting fury. To the German infantry, after long days in and out of the flooded *Stollen*, the sight of the French trenches disintegrating was intoxicating.

Even so, the Germans were taking no risks. When the bombardment at last finished at 1600 hours, they cautiously sent forward powerful fighting patrols who, making skilful use of the ground, probed for the sectors of least resistance. True to Falkenhayn's directive for a controlled but insistent advance, the Germans were here evolving a new method of approach and attack, which was quickly to become characteristic of the fighting at Verdun on both sides; and, paradoxically, by prolonging individual survival, these tactics also prolonged the duration and suffering of this inhuman battle.

On this first day at Verdun, however, German caution from above, and their unreadiness to follow up the probing, infiltrating patrols at once with assault troops, lost them their opportunity. For once, the massed waves of attacking infantry, which until now had been the ultimate weapon all along the Western Front, incurring always suicidal losses—for once, these disciplined lines of infantry, coming over immediately while the French were still stunned and shattered from the immensity of the bombardment, could have given the Germans a quick breakthrough and a clear road to Verdun. As it was, two of the corps' commanders stuck rigidly to orders and held back their main bodies of infantry until the next morning, leaving their patrols to do no more than explore French weaknesses. Only Zwehl, commanding *VII Reserve Corps* on the German right, obstinately improved on his orders and sent in his first wave of storm-troops hard on the heels of the patrols, and at once achieved an important success. They managed to occupy the whole of the Bois d'Haumont before dusk and so effect the first breach of the main French defences.

Elsewhere on the French 72nd Division front, and to the east on the 51st Division front, the German patrols, even without support, did damage enough to the French line, exploiting the gaps made by the shell-fire and using their new weapon of horror, the flame-thrower, with terrifying effect, causing panic through the French ranks. There still remained stubborn and heroic pockets of French resistance, flaring out even into disconcerting counterattacks.

None of this, however, was the easy success the Germans had expected. The concentration of shell-fire from the unprecedented opening bombardment had been planned to destroy all life in the French front-line trenches and block-houses. But somehow men had survived. Driant's sector, for example, in the Bois des Caures had consisted of a complex network of redoubts and small strongholds, quite unlike the usual continuous trench lines. Here and elsewhere the German troops were therefore disconcerted to meet intense machine gun and rifle fire from defenders who ought to have been buried in the wreckage of the uprooted forest.

Full-scale attack

By nightfall, Knobelsdorf, Prince Wilhelm's Chief-of-Staff, had become impatient of this cautious progress, and ordered a full-scale attack for the morning after another softening-up bombardment. It was the French, however, who surprisingly took the initiative at dawn on the 22nd, attempting several counterattacks with

△ One of the *Stollen* (concrete bunkers) which the Germans built near the French line to permit first-wave troops to concentrate safely
▽ Douaumont after the German bombardment

A German shell explodes and the 'mincing machine' grinds on. Making skilful use of the ground, the Germans sent out powerful fighting patrols probing for the sectors of least resistance

the spirit and dash typical of their army's tradition. But the means were not there, nor the organisation and communications: many attacks failed to get going, others were soon swamped.

Even though Knobelsdorf now placed no limits on corps' objectives the *XVIII Corps,* opposite the Bois des Caures, was still a model of caution, faced as it was with the verve and flexibility of Driant's *Chasseurs,* which masked the absurdly small size of the French opposition; and it took the Germans all day, with the help of their comrades on either flank, to silence Driant's valiant resistance. Zwehl's *VII Reserve Corps* had captured the village of Haumont on Driant's left, after a hard fight lasting into the afternoon, and now the Brandenburgers of *III Corps* came round on Driant's right through the Bois de Ville, split up by the cross-fire from the surviving French machine guns, but relentless with their flame-throwers and overwhelming in their numbers. They surrounded the French positions and picked off their strong-points one by one. Driant himself and a handful of men tried to hold out in the last strong-point, in vain; and as they broke out to the rear, they were mown down by enfilading fire.

The German losses in silencing the Bois des Caures had been unexpectedly heavy, and the confidence of their assault troops was shaken. Above all, their offensive had been held up during one whole day by Driant's resistance in the very centre of the German attack. Nor was Driant alone in this. The anchor position on the left of the French line at Brabant on the Meuse was still held by other elements of 72nd Division; and on the right, 51st Division continued to fight bitterly in Herbebois, holding up the advance of the Branden-

burgers. These delays, though seeming small in the overall picture, robbed the German assault of its required momentum.

Earlier on this day, the French artillery had improved their shooting, and had been reinforced. Fire from French batteries on the left (western) bank of the Meuse onto the Germans' flank was starting to cause trouble. Falkenhayn's parsimony in keeping back reserves for Verdun had deprived the German *VI Reserve Corps,* holding the line on the left bank, of adequate artillery, and this weakness prevented them from silencing the French guns on this side. But on the right bank, behind the battlefield itself, the French field guns were being knocked out one by one by the fire of the long-barrelled 15's.

Once more on the next day, February 23, the Germans made surprisingly little progress, even though they were still held only by the remnants of 72nd and 51st Divisions, whose losses continued at a terrible rate. Brabant had been evacuated, but mixed elements managed to hold out all day in Beaumont, on a rise behind the Bois des Caures. Infantry of the German *XVIII Corps* pressed forward against this position in dense formations, one wave pushing in closely behind another, in the established style of the Western Front, to be scythed down in turn by the French machine guns. At the same time, the French heavy guns under XXX Corps' command had found the range of the advancing Germans, who were suffering too from their own shells falling short. Official German records speak of this as a 'day of horror'.

The French infantry were also starting to get the measure of the dreaded flame-throwers. They were learning to pick off the German pioneers who wielded them, as they moved clumsily under the heavy bur-

den of their equipment, before they came within flame-throwing range. So 51st Division on the right were still able to cling tenaciously to Herbebois. On the other side of the sector, 72nd Division managed to hold up Zwehl's corps at last in front of Samogneux on an 'intermediate line', which de Castelnau had ordered to be constructed in January. When this line was broken, a battalion still held out in Samogneux itself till late into the night, when it was suddenly wiped out by a barrage of French 155's, firing across from the left bank in the belief that the village had already fallen to the Germans.

With this final tragedy, 72nd Division virtually ceased to exist. The two first-line French divisions, 72nd and 51st, with an original combined establishment of 26,523, had together lost 16,224 officers and men.

The Germans, despite their rebuffs, felt that Verdun was now theirs for the taking. So it was. They overran the whole French second position, inadequately prepared to start with, and now pounded out of existence, in three hours on February 24. But following the unexpected and savage opposition which they had experienced in the previous two days and the serious losses they had suffered, the Germans were no longer poised to exploit the situation fully, and their cautiousness had increased. Once more, they missed the opportunity of breaking right through.

The gap in the French lines left by the decimation of 72nd Division was now filled by 37th African Division—the Zouaves and Moroccan *Tirailleurs.* But the bitter, freezing weather, which had returned once the German offensive was launched, and was causing suffering enough to European troops, had cowed the temperamental North Africans. Furthermore, in an attempt to plug the disastrous holes in the French defences, they were being split up into small units under strange officers—survivors of the 72nd and 51st. The incessant bombardment, the horror of which was beyond their comprehension, was the last straw. When the North Africans saw the great grey carpet of German infantry rolling out towards them, some of them lost their nerve and fled.

Crumbling morale

By the night of February 24, French morale was crumbling seriously. Their guns were silent, their clearing stations overflowing with casualties, untended, their wounds often frozen by the intense cold. Only a fraction could be got out: the German 38's, firing with 'diabolical precision', had cut the one full-gauge railway out of the Verdun salient. Chrétien's XXX Corps was finished. Balfourier's XX Corps from the Lorraine front was to relieve them, but only the vanguard had reached Verdun, cold, hungry, and exhausted. Despite every protest, Chrétien insisted on throwing them into the battle at once; but it seemed doubtful if they would hold till the corps' main body, en route in a desperate forced march, could arrive.

It was on the following day that the French Command took decisions which committed them finally to the defence of Verdun, whatever the cost.

On the evening of February 24, de Langle de Cary obtained permission from Joffre to shorten the line in front of Verdun drastically on the still unthreatened Woëvres Plain side of the salient, and to withdraw from the Woëvres Plain to the Meuse Heights east and south-east of the city. Later that night, with the news desperate, Joffre, against all orders and precedent, was rudely wakened from his routine allocation of sleep. One authority says that it was de Castelnau who insisted on waking him; another that it was the Prime Minister himself, Briand, who had driven over from Paris to General Headquarters at Chantilly; a third merely states that Joffre rose to the occasion. The consequence, in any case, was of supreme importance. Joffre sent de Castelnau off to Verdun that night with full powers to do whatever was needed. De Castelnau, as the recently-appointed Chief-of-Staff at French General Headquarters and Joffre's closest colleague (and rival), was the obvious choice for such a critical mission. But the very choice of de Castelnau made certain that the decision over Verdun would be a firm one. He was still very much a 'fighting general', as well as being outstandingly intelligent, quick-witted and flexible; and he had a way of inspiring staff officers and front-line soldiers alike.

De Castelnau reached Verdun at breakfast-time on February 25. He found Herr, who was still in command of Verdun and its salient, 'depressed' and 'a little tired'. He then went straight to the battle-torn right bank, made rapid and accurate appreciations, and effected miracles in reanimating the defence, with his experience and insight and his boundless energy: 'wherever he went, decision and order followed him'. He saw that Verdun could be saved, that an effective defence could be maintained on the remaining cross ridges of the right bank. He telephoned his conclusions to Joffre's headquarters that afternoon, and without waiting for agreement gave orders that the right bank of the Meuse should be held at all costs, and that there must be no retreat to the left bank.

On the previous evening, Joffre had already agreed that General Pétain, the tenacious commander of the French Second Army, should be brought over to defend the left bank at Verdun. Now de Castelnau recommended that Pétain should be put immediately in total command at Verdun, of both sides of the river, and despatched the necessary order without waiting for Joffre's approval. Pétain enjoyed a considerable reputation as a master of the defensive: he had been one of the first to recognise the full implications of firepower. He was also a very able commander, meticulous in his preparations for action, with a real concern for his troops, who therefore trusted him. He had shown his mettle in attack at Vimy Ridge and, less successfully, in the Champagne. Austere, aloof, distrustful of politicians, he was a dedicated soldier.

De Castelnau, by insisting on the defence of the right bank, had accepted the challenge of the German assault on Verdun: without knowing it, he was acting as Falkenhayn wished and expected, allowing the French army to be drawn inexorably into the Verdun salient, to be bled there by the remorseless German pressure. And in appointing Pétain, de Castelnau was ensuring that his decision to defend Verdun would be carried out.

The French, in theory, need not have taken up the challenge. They could have withdrawn to the left bank, eliminating the dangerous salient and shortening their line considerably. Verdun and its ring of forts were no longer of practical defensive value: their guns had by now mostly been withdrawn to augment the French artillery barrages for Joffre's hopeful offensives, and the forts stood there imposing and toothless. In the hilly country behind the Meuse, the French could have conducted a fighting withdrawal with advantage, exhausting the attacking Germans and overstraining their lines of supply. As Winston Churchill wrote at the time: 'Meeting an artillery attack is like catching a cricket ball. Shock is dissipated by drawing back the hands. A little "give", a little suppleness and the violence of the impact is vastly reduced.' Yet de Castelnau's decision to hold was based not only on his own aggressive spirit, but on an intuition of a greater truth: that perhaps, after 18 months without success, the French army was not capable of a controlled, fighting retreat in the face of superior forces. Nor, as Briand was aware, would the French nation or his government have easily survived the shock of abandoning a fortress with the immense symbolic value which Verdun held for the French, a factor of which Falkenhayn in laying his plans was conscious.

Brutal shell-fire

On the ridges before Verdun, whose great forests were being rapidly torn down by the brutal weight of shell-fire, there was still some French resistance on the left, facing *VII Reserve Corps*. But elsewhere in the salient on the morning of February 25 —while de Castelnau was appraising the terrain with his quick, experienced eye— the Germans had before them only the forts which ringed Verdun, sinister guardian monsters which the Germans thought were still fully manned and armed. Fort Douaumont was the first that lay in their path, and the strongest. From every angle its great tortoise hump stood out, stark, menacing, fascinating. It was, in fact, occupied by only a small detachment of territorial gunners, manning the 155-mm turret gun which had survived Joffre's purge; its approaches were inadequately covered by the French infantry. Small bodies of Brandenburgers, heroically defying a powerful garrison existing only in their imagination, managed to edge into the fort unobserved during the afternoon of the 25th and to capture its elderly occupants.

The reaction to the fall of Fort Douaumont was electric. In Germany church bells rang; a newspaper declared, 'Victory of Verdun. The Collapse of France'. In Verdun itself morale went to pieces. An officer ran through the streets crying 'Sauve qui peut', and civilians poured out of the city, jamming the vital roads. Worse still, the commander of the 37th African Division, on hearing the news, blew up the unthreatened Meuse bridge at Bras and withdrew his battered troops, quite needlessly, back to the last ridge before the city itself.

Pétain took over command at midnight and set up his headquarters in the village of Souilly, on the main road into Verdun from the south-west. His journey in the rigours of winter weather had been long and tiring, and the last stage, through the distracted rear of the French army in defeat, harrowing. He received his instructions briefly from de Castelnau, who then left. Pétain contacted his corps' commanders by telephone, and spent the night huddled

Risking the shell-fire, French stretcher bearers attempt to reach a fallen comrade

Südd Verlag

28

in an armchair in an unheated room. Next morning he had contracted double pneumonia; but the secret was strictly guarded – with reason, for the mere knowledge of his arrival, that he was now in command at Verdun, had stiffened the French resistance and given new heart to every man, from General Balfourier down to the exhausted troops holding out in the front line, so high was Pétain's reputation in the army.

In the defence lines themselves the turning-point came at the same time with the arrival of the main body of Balfourier's seasoned XX Corps, the 'Iron Corps'. All troops in the salient were now regrouped under four corps' commanders, responsible to Pétain and his Second Army staff. I Corps was coming in from reserve, and others were on their way. Haig too had at last agreed to relieve the French Tenth Army, which was sandwiched between the British First and Third in the area of Arras.

Pétain, on his sick-bed, took up the threads of command with remarkable vigour. He realised that the loss of Fort Douaumont did not mean final disaster, that the other forts remained, and could be manned and linked into a formidable defence perimeter. He issued orders accordingly: from this line there must be no withdrawal. With his profound understanding of the defensive power which guns could provide, he now had the artillery round Verdun reorganised into one concentrated and effective weapon. From this moment, says the German official history, 'began the flanking fire on the ravines and roads north of Douaumont that was to cause us such severe casualties'.

It was the precarious supply route into Verdun which was Pétain's next concern. The full-gauge railway had been rendered useless by the German long-range shelling. The only substitute was motor transport on the one road in, the narrow second-class road from Bar-le-Duc, just 21 feet wide. Pétain and his able transport officer, Major Richard, threw all their energies and organising ability into making this road a life-line for Verdun. Richard went out requisitioning lorries throughout France, and gangs of Territorials were detailed to devote themselves entirely to the upkeep of the road. It was their tireless labour which kept the road intact and the lorries moving when a sudden thaw on February 28, following the long spell of hard weather, turned the surface to a sea of mud. The road was reserved strictly for the ceaseless flow of motor traffic in both directions. Any lorry that broke down was heaved aside into the ditch. With their solid tyres and top-heavy weight, many skidded on the bad surface; others caught fire. Drivers were inexperienced, and always fatigued.

At night, the procession of dimly lit vehicles resembled 'the folds of some gigantic and luminous serpent which never stopped and never ended'. It is astonishing that the Germans never thought of bombing the road, which would so easily have been blocked: they had the aeroplanes to do it – C-class aircraft – and Zeppelins. Eventually vehicles were passing along the road at a daily average of one every 14 seconds, and for hours on end at a rate of one every five seconds; and the equivalent of more than a division of soldiers was kept mending it. The road was the artery through which the life-blood of France was pumped into Verdun. Maurice Barrès gave it the immortal name of the *Voie Sacrée*.

The tide, for the moment, had turned. By February 28, as the German official history says, 'the German attack on Verdun was virtually brought to a standstill'. The French now were fresher and more determined. Their original divisions had been replaced and the numbers greatly reinforced. The German formations, on the other hand, had not been relieved at all and their troops were feeling the strain of a week's intensive fighting: promised reserves were not forthcoming.

Behind this shifting balance between attacker and defender can be seen a change in the balance of artillery; and it was the artillery's positioning and fire-power which were to rule the battlefield – no longer as a prelude, an opening barrage to clear the path, but as the constant and most demanding element of the battle. Now the German guns were flagging: they were having extreme difficulty in moving forward over the ground which they themselves had so violently cratered; and the sudden thaw turned the clay to deep mud. Worse still, the French had increased their heavy guns in the salient from 164 to more than 500, and they were shelling the German infantry with continuous and effective flanking fire from the left bank of the Meuse, in particular from the Bois Bourrus ridge.

The left bank had therefore become an immediate problem to the Germans, and pressure to open an attack on it intensified in the Crown Prince's *Fifth Army*. The commanding height in this western sector, le Mort Homme, was the obvious objective; for its capture would also neutralise the Bois Bourrus ridge, behind which much of Pétain's artillery was dug in. As late as February 26, with the right bank apparently within the Germans' grasp, Falkenhayn had again refused permission for an attack

on the left bank; but the next few days changed his mind, and he let Knobelsdorf have his agreement on February 29, at the same time sending up reinforcements behind *VI Reserve Corps* holding the left bank trenches – *X Reserve Corps*, two further divisions and 21 batteries of heavies.

Prince Rupprecht of Bavaria, one of the most responsible of German commanders, noted at his headquarters in northern France: 'I hear that at Verdun the Left Bank of the Meuse is to be attacked now, too. It should have been done at once; now the moment of surprise is lost.' These German reserves – quite apart from those held immobilised opposite the currently inactive British front in the north – would have ensured a German breakthrough on the right bank to Verdun itself.

Before the new German offensive could be launched, the increasing weight of French guns on the left bank was already taking a terrible toll. Many of these guns were old 155's, firing visually into the German ranks; and *VII Reserve Corps*, which had done so well initially on the Meuse flank, suffered prohibitive losses. The German wounded streaming back were 'like a vision in hell'. Franz Marc, the painter, wrote in a letter from the Verdun front on March 3: 'For days I have seen nothing but the most terrible things a human mind can depict.' He was killed next day by a French shell.

The French at this time were slowly wresting back air superiority over the battlefield. The dramatic step had been taken of assembling some 60 of the French air aces, including Brocard, Nungesser, Navarre and Guynemer, and banding them together into the famous *Groupe des Cigognes* (the Storks). Altogether the French brought in 120 aeroplanes over

Carrying their few bits and pieces, French prisoners move away from the Verdun front

Verdun, to set against the Germans' 168 planes, 14 observation balloons and four Zeppelins. Poor German tactics and French verve tipped the scales, and in the next two months, while the German balloons were shot down in flames, French observation planes were to contribute greatly to the success of their artillery, who once more had eyes. The German aces, Boelcke and Immelmann, failed to upset the French supremacy, which the new Nieuport plane later helped to consolidate.

It was clear to the French that the Germans would attack on the left bank now; but the first days of March slipped by, and the French were given time to assemble four divisions on that side and one in reserve, under General Bazelaire, the French VII Corps commander. As the German attack still failed to materialise, Pétain was heard to remark, 'They don't know their business.' All the same, when it came, on March 6, starting with a bombardment comparable to that of February 21, the Germans at first had considerable success. They took the Meuse villages of Forges and Regnéville and advanced towards the ridge of the Mort Homme on its north-eastern slope; but their attack on the northern side was held by a wall of fire from the French guns.

The French 67th Division, defending the north-eastern approach to the Mort Homme had given ground too readily following the terror of the German bombardment, and over 3,000 of its men had surrendered by the end of the second day. It took a brilliant bayonet charge by a superbly disciplined regiment at dawn on March 8 to hold the Germans on this flank of the hill and force them to delay the final assault. In fact, the front now established on this north-eastern approach barely shifted for the next month.

The Germans had planned a simultaneous attack on the right bank of the river, with Fort Vaux as their objective. The difficulties of bringing up ammunition to the guns over the bogged and cratered ground delayed them for two days. They then blundered in thinking the fort had been taken and marched up in column of fours straight into the French machine gun fire.

The 'mincing machine'

The terrible frontal assault on the Mort Homme from the north began on March 14. With German reserves flowing in more freely, there seemed no limit to the men and shells they were willing to expend to gain possession of this desolate hill. Attack and defence were evenly matched and the fighting swayed forward and back, until a deadly pattern of combat was established. It continued in this sector for the next two months. There would first be several hours of German bombardment; then their assault troops would surge forward to carry what remained of the French front line, which was no longer trenches but clusters of shell-holes. When the German attack had exhausted itself, ground down by the barrages from the French guns on the Bois Bourrus ridge to the south-east, the French would counterattack within 24 hours and drive the surviving Germans back again. But each flow and ebb of the tide brought the German high water mark a little further forward. The cost was terrible: by the end of March, 81,607 Germans had been killed and 89,000 French; and in this compressed and shelterless battle area a high proportion of the casualties were senior commanding officers.

Here, on the bare slopes of the Mort Homme, there were no woods or ravines to favour infiltration, so that the Germans had lost the advantage they had gained elsewhere by their expert use of these tactics. Their flame-throwers had become suicide weapons, for the pioneers were easy targets in open country; and the French flanking fire was even more crippling on these naked hill-sides.

The Germans, in attacking the Mort Homme with the object of eliminating the threat to their exposed Meuse flank, now found their new right flank on the Mort Homme itself a target for crippling French shell-fire—this time from the neighbouring hill on the west side, Côte 304. So this too would have to be attacked and taken. The German army, even more reluctantly than the French, was being sucked into this ever expanding battle in the Verdun salient. The German Command was still not facing the full implications of its extended attack. Replacements were not being provided: the divisions were being kept too long in the line, and the gaps in the ranks merely filled with unseasoned youths. The French, in contrast, accepting the German challenge in its entirety, were committed to a scheme of rapid rotation of units at Verdun. Pétain, facing this same problem of exhaustion, was insisting, through his *Noria* system of reliefs, that no division remained more than a few days under fire. As a result, two-thirds of the French army was to be fed through the 'mincing machine' of Verdun, and its reserves drained. This was what Falkenhayn had hoped and expected—but he had not anticipated that the German army would also be 'bled white'.

A key position at the base of Côte 304 fell to the Germans on March 20, after French deserters had given them information on the defences. But this success brought no further advantage, only staggering losses under the French machine gun fire. Signs of exhaustion and unwillingness to attack were increasing in the German ranks.

The German *Fifth Army* command structure was now simplified in preparation for a final assault. Mudra, a corps commander from the Argonne front, was put in command of the right bank, and Gallwitz, a gunner, fresh from successes in the Balkans, in command of the left bank. On April 9 a massive simultaneous attack was mounted on Côte 304 and the Mort Homme. The Germans reached only a secondary crest of the Mort Homme; and on Côte 304 the French guns kept up their relentless, devastating fire on the exposed German flank. Pétain, recognising that an extremely dangerous attack had been held, issued next day his famous Order No 94, which he ended with the exhortation: *'Courage! On les aura!'* ('We'll get them!').

Further Reading
Falkenhayn, E. von, *General Headquarters, 1914-1916* (London 1960)
Horne, A., *The Price of Glory, Verdun 1916* (London 1962)
Joffre, Marshal, *The Memoirs of Marshal Joffre* (London 1932)
Palat, Gen. B. E., *La Grande Guerre sur le Front Occidental*, Vols. X-XII (Paris 1925)
Romains, Jules, *Men of Good Will*, Vols. 15-16 (London 1926)

VERDUN
Nivelle takes over

Throughout April, the fighting on the hills around Verdun continued. Casualties on both sides were very high, but on the French side, Pétain's policy of constant replacement of tired troops had yielded some success, and by April 19 the Crown Prince was resigned to abandoning his dreams of hope and victory. It was at this point that Knobelsdorf replaced Mudra and Joffre manipulated the impetuous Nivelle into Pétain's position. Both the new commanders believed in fighting to the end.

This page: Rocks and debris are thrown up as a German mortar bomb bursts near Verdun

Since early March 1916, the Germans had been attacking the dominant height on the left bank of the Meuse, the Mort Homme, where the fighting had swayed backwards and forwards near the hill crest in a futile and devilish rhythm. On April 9, they had launched a massive combined attack on the heights of both Mort Homme and Côte 304, further west. But without decisive conclusion: the fighting line was merely stretched out a little wider, its burden of horror increased.

At this crisis, as in the grave days at the end of February, there was little to hold the exhausted French except the inspiring leadership of Pétain, who was in command of the Verdun salient. He fully recognised the immense danger of this new German assault and threw in fresh units as quickly as the French Army Staff could send them up along the one road into Verdun, the *Voie Sacrée*.

The German troops who had fought their way so heroically up the slopes of Mort Homme on April 9 had reached a crest which their maps showed as the summit of the hill. Their discouragement was bitter when they saw ahead of them, a few hundred yards distant, another summit, 100 feet higher. It was between these two summits—Point 265 held by the Germans and Point 295 still held by the French—that a long-drawn battle of desperation now developed on Mort Homme, and the artillery of both sides turned the hill into a smoking volcano. A participant remembers: *The trench no longer existed, it had been filled with earth. We were crouching in shell-holes, where the mud*

Südd Verlag

thrown up by each new explosion covered us more and more. The air was unbreathable. Our own soldiers, the wounded and the blinded, crawling and screaming, kept falling on top of us and died drenching us with their blood. Suddenly the enemy artillery lengthened its fire, and almost at once someone shouted: 'The Boches are coming!' As if by magic, every one of us, exhausted only a moment ago, immediately faced the enemy, rifle in hand.'

It was only by a slender thread that the French had held the Germans on Mort Homme on April 9. A company commander, facing the German tide with ten men, would be told, 'There are no reinforcements.' And the Germans, throwing in their men recklessly, suffered terrible losses: one division alone had to leave 2,200 men on the blood-soaked northern slopes of the hill.

A young French officer, Second-Lieutenant Jubert, describes how he moved his company up from the rear to recapture Mort Homme ridge – which they had just lost: *I have rarely seen less hesitation, greater calm. We assembled without a word. Having put down our knapsacks, we took an ample supply of cartridges, as well as one day's extra rations. To gain time, my company, ignoring the communication trench, moved up over open ground in single file. Passing the first crest (Point 295, the southern summit) we descended towards the ravine where, as in a crucible, the deadly explosions and gas were concentrated in a roaring inferno. Another 30 yards and we were in the danger area. The German shells were raining down all round us, and the men were silent. They kept marching forward, grim-faced and in good order, towards the barrier of fire and steel that rose before us.* He and his men then recaptured half a mile of what had once been trenches, and held them under unceasing bombardment for 36 hours.

It was typical of Mort Homme, and of Verdun as a whole, that soldiers of both sides suffered appalling slaughter without ever seeing the enemy infantry, such was the devastating power of the massed artillery. After being relieved from Mort Homme Captain Cochin wrote: *I have returned from the toughest trial I have ever been through – four days and four nights – 96 hours – the last two days soaked in icy mud – under terrible bombardment, without any shelter other than the narrowness of the trench, which even then seemed too wide; not a hole, not a dug-out, nothing, nothing. The Boches did not attack, naturally, it would have been too stupid. It was much more convenient for them to carry out excellent firing practice on our backs. I arrived there with 175 men, I returned with 34, several half mad.*

As soon as this battle was joined on Mort Homme, rain added to the misery and degradation. It rained solidly for 12 days following the attack of April 9. The German official history describes the consequences: 'Water in the trenches came above the knees. The men had not a dry thread on their bodies; there was not a dug-out that could provide dry accommodation. The numbers of sick rose alarmingly.'

The German commander on the left bank, Gallwitz, was under no illusions. On taking over, before Mort Homme attack, he had noted: 'Too great a task, undertaken with inadequate reserves.' He soon had cause to complain of the methodical slowness of his subordinate, Falkenhayn's elder brother, who was commanding *XXII Reserve Corps* on Mort Homme: 'We shall be in Verdun at the earliest by 1920.' Now, with his troops held, and even pushed back, on Mort Homme, exposed on its bleak northern slopes to the shattering, relentless bombardment of the French guns on the unconquered Côte 304, Gallwitz told Knobelsdorf with some force that it would be pointless to pursue the attacks on the Mort Homme until Côte 304 was finally taken.

See-saw battle

By the end of April, despite the mud and the misery, the French, with persistent, dogged counterattacks, had recaptured the whole crest of Mort Homme and had wiped out virtually all the German gains of April 9.

Meanwhile, as the focus of battle stretched ever westward in its vain outflanking attempts, the forces on the right bank of the Meuse, in the hills above Verdun itself, were still locked in fruitless combat, little different in character from the greater conflict on Mort Homme. Zwehl's *VII Reserve Corps* was engaged during most of April in a see-saw battle for one small feature, the stone quarries at Haudromont, a mile or so to the west of Fort Douaumont. Throughout April, the right bank front never shifted as much as 1,000 yards – a bitter contrast for the Germans to the five miles they had advanced in the first four days of the offensive.

Here, before Verdun itself, as much as on Mort Homme, the murderous artillery blanket laid down by both sides never lifted. In all, there were now nearly 4,000 guns in the salient. In April, casualties had risen by about 50%: on the German side to 120,000, on the French side to 133,000.

The French High Command was the first to react to the anxiety caused by these casualties. Joffre, with his mind permanently tuned to the offensive, to the expectation of the masterly break-through which would end the war, found these great losses in Pétain's army at Verdun, with no attack launched to justify them, nor even planned, hard to accept. It was not long before he was regretting his choice of Pétain as commander at Verdun. This mistrust was aggravated by Pétain's insistence on an unusually rapid turn-round of divisions in the line in the salient. By May 1, 40 French divisions had passed through Verdun, as against only 26 German divisions. Because of this, the French were able to maintain their miraculous resistance with ever fresh troops, so that the Germans, at all levels, constantly asked themselves where the French were getting their fresh men from. Increasingly demoralised by their enemy's resources, and themselves exhausted by their long spells in the fighting line, the Germans were unable to carry their massive attacks through to any semblance of success. Despite the overall correctness of the French plan, its sponsor, Pétain, carried it through only from the narrow tactical standpoint of saving his men in the field, with little thought of where this drain on reserves would be leading French strategy. Joffre, on the other hand, was more conscious of the failure of his plans for a mighty breakthrough on the Somme than of the great and constant danger to France at Verdun: 'the whole French Army would have been absorbed in this battle,' he wrote in his Memoirs.

But to replace Pétain was not a thing Joffre could now easily do. Pétain was already the idol of France, the saviour of Verdun. But eventually in mid-April the opportunity presented itself of promoting Pétain out of Verdun to command the Central Group of Armies, and to put in the ambitious and confident General Nivelle, who had made an impression as commander of III Corps on the right bank opposite Fort Douaumont, as commander at Verdun, under the overall but remote direction of Pétain.

Pétain was deeply disturbed at this change and feared that all his careful nursing of the French troops in the salient would be thrown to the winds by the impetuous Nivelle. He saw ahead of him the constant, negative task of keeping Nivelle in check. Even Joffre noted: 'he was not pleased'. On taking up his command on May 1, Nivelle declared with his usual bold assurance, 'We have the formula!' A few days later, Joffre renounced Pétain's *Noria* system of quick replacements to the Verdun front.

It had been on April 19, in the midst of the slaughter and anxiety on Mort Homme, that Pétain had been told of the impending change in the command. It was during the next few days that doubts and differences shook the generals of the German *Fifth Army*. Mudra, commanding on the right bank, one of the ablest German corps commanders, let Knobelsdorf know of his misgivings about the whole future of the Verdun offensive. Knobelsdorf at once got rid of him, sending him back to his corps in the Argonne on April 21; but first, Mudra had been able to express his doubts in a memorandum to the Crown Prince. As a result, the Crown Prince, on this same day, reached the irrevocable conclusion that the attack on the Verdun salient had failed, and should be called off altogether. He wrote later of this change of heart: *I was now convinced, after the stubborn to-and-fro contest for every foot of ground which had continued throughout the whole of April, that although we had more than once changed our methods of attack, a decisive success at Verdun could only be assured at the price of heavy sacrifices, out of all proportion to the desired gains. I naturally came to this conclusion only with the greatest reluctance; it was no easy matter for me, the responsible commander, to abandon my dreams of hope and victory!*

A master plan

Knobelsdorf was the one member of the Crown Prince's staff who was not of this opinion, and he now clung to the reins of power in the *Fifth Army* even more tenaciously. In Mudra's place he put the Brandenburgers' ardent corps commander, Lochow, a general who believed in attack to the utmost limit; and Knobelsdorf himself set out to oppose any further weakening of the Crown Prince's resolve.

On each side now, the original champions, Pétain and the Crown Prince, with their horror of senseless carnage, had lost control to their ruthless subordinates, Nivelle and Knobelsdorf, both of them determined to fight to the bitterest end.

By the beginning of May, Gallwitz, on the left bank, had put all his personal expertise in gunnery into a master plan to subdue the French bastion on Côte 304 at last. The new attempt would be a pure artillery exercise; it would blast the French off the hill; and this time it would succeed.

On May 3, over 500 German heavy guns opened fire on Côte 304, a front just over a mile wide. The bombardment continued for two days and a night. The French, lacking deep shelters after weeks of heavy shelling, suffered frightful casualties: it seemed to them 'as if to finish things off the Germans had decided to point a gun at each one of us.' Of one battalion, only three men survived. One by one the French machine guns were destroyed. For over two days no food or supplies could be got through, nor any wounded evacuated. Reinforcements got lost, the units were all jumbled together. The French command 'had pushed up men on top of men and set up a living wall against the monstrous German avalanche.' Even when the Germans had managed to obtain a foothold on the summit, it took three more days of bitter close combat before Côte 304 was finally theirs. About 10,000 Frenchmen had been killed there.

The capture of Côte 304 made the first breach in the defence perimeter, the 'Line of Resistance', which Pétain had laid down on taking up his command at Verdun at the end of February. The stage was now set for the final German attack on Mort Homme itself. The Crown Prince watched the opening of the assault from a position well forward: 'Mort Homme flamed like a volcano, and the air and the earth alike trembled at the shock of thousands of bursting shells.' By the end of May the Germans had taken the whole of Mort Homme and the village of Cumières at its foot by the Meuse. The Bois Bourrus ridge, from which the French artillery had menaced the German positions across the river on the right bank since the last days of February, was now itself overlooked by the Germans on Mort Homme and effectively neutralised.

This small clearing action on the left bank, as it had initially appeared to the Germans, had in the end taken three months and cost them as many lives as all the fighting on the right bank so far; and there were signs that the German losses might now be exceeding those of the French. Nevertheless, with this success the margin of retreat for the French had become very narrow indeed, and now the full weight of the German forces could be thrown against the defences ringing Verdun itself on the right bank of the Meuse.

The month from mid-March to mid-April had seen a return of German dominance in the skies, when their new ace, Boelcke, who was also an imaginative organiser of air fighting, temporarily drove the French *Cigognes* pilots from the skies. This led to an immediate improvement in German artillery spotting, which contributed greatly to their successes in the left bank fighting. By mid-April, however, the tables had turned again. In this sphere, the French capacity for organisation was no less than that of Boelcke, and 226 French aircraft were now assembled over Verdun. The French were starting to fly their planes, too, in concentrated groups, though loosely controlled – an important step forward towards later co-ordinated interception techniques. Boelcke noted: 'They were sending out as many as 12 fighters to protect two observation machines. It was seldom that we could get through this protecting screen to reach the observation aircraft.' Furthermore, the new French 107-mph Nieuport fighter was appearing at Verdun, to challenge the long supremacy of the German Fokker. Boelcke's reply to these new tactics, his so-called 'Flying Circus', though planned for Verdun, in fact made its principal appearance over the Somme battlefield.

To the infantry creeping in the mud and debris beneath them the airmen seemed to be men of another world. 'They are the only ones,' thought an infantry lieutenant, 'who in this war have the life and death of which one dreams.' The contrast was indeed extreme. On the ground, the battlefield stretched on in limitless horror, its landmarks erased, its objectives nearly forgotten. Yet from the air it looked absurdly small to contain such magnitude of suffering: the long-range guns and their distant targets were always simultaneously visible. With the noise of battle drowned by the aircraft's engine, it was 'a weird combination of stillness and havoc'. The airman, almost alone, had the detachment to view the battleground in all its concentrated defilement: *there is only that sinister brown belt, a strip of murdered nature. It seems to belong to another world. Every*

sign of humanity has been swept away. The woods and roads have vanished like chalk wiped from a blackboard; of the villages nothing remains but grey smears. During heavy bombardments and attacks I have seen shells falling like rain.

The artillery, the big guns especially, were indeed masters of the battlefield. Fresh troops approaching Verdun heard sounds 'like a gigantic forge that never stopped, day or night'. To be under constant, remorseless sentence of death or mutilation, not from enemy soldiers you could see, fight, and hope to outwit, but from guns remote, hidden, all-powerful, was to know an unrelenting fear. 'Verdun is terrible because man is fighting against material, with the sensation of striking out at empty air.'

As the men, advancing up the communication trenches, approached the front line, the parapets grew steadily lower, eroded away by shell fire, until the trench became little deeper than a roadside ditch. The relief columns, coming up in the darkness, stumbled over the wounded. Suddenly the trench became 'nothing more than a track hardly traced out amid the shell holes'. In the mud, which the shelling had turned to a consistency of sticky butter, troops stumbled and fell repeatedly, cursing in low undertones. Heavily laden men fell into the huge water-filled shell craters and remained there until they drowned, unable to crawl up the greasy sides. With all reference points long since obliterated, relieving detachments got lost and wandered hopelessly all night; only to be

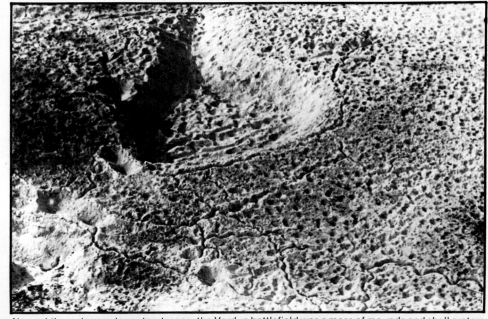

Above: Like a strange lunar landscape, the Verdun battlefield was a mass of mounds and shell craters

Roger Viollet

massacred by an enemy machine gunner as dawn betrayed them.

In the front line, the troops spent each night laboriously scraping out holes in which they might find the illusion of shelter and protection; all day long the enemy guns worked at levelling them. There was no chance and no longer any will to bury the dead: the stench of putrefaction throughout the Verdun battlefield was unbearable. Dead comrades were slung over

the parapet into the nearest shell hole; and the guns churned up the mounting corpses into endless dismembered limbs. 'You found the dead embedded in the walls of the trenches, heads, legs and half-bodies, just as they had been shovelled out of the way by the picks and shovels of the working party.' The highly compressed area of the battlefield had become a reeking open cemetery. The French writer, Duhamel, serving as an army doctor, wrote: 'You

Below: French engineers move into the ruins of a village near Verdun to repair communications

Above: By the middle of April, German positions held earlier in the month had been shattered

eat, you drink beside the dead, you sleep in the midst of the dying, you laugh and sing in the company of corpses.'

There were few heroes' deaths, instead, 'those small painful scenes, in obscure corners, of small compass, where you cannot possibly distinguish if the mud is flesh or the flesh mud'. A German soldier wrote that 'the torture of having to lie powerless and defenceless in the middle of an artillery battle' was 'something for which there is nothing comparable on earth'; a Frenchman wrote, 'to be dismembered, torn to pieces, reduced to pulp, this is a fear that flesh cannot support'.

The artillery came to be hated, their own included, even more than the enemy infantry. The gunners always seemed to have an easy life, remote from the battle, with snug shelters and motor transport. Yet in reality, counter-battery firing on both sides was remorseless and accurate: 'Nobody escapes; if the guns were spared to-day, they will catch it tomorrow.' If death came from the long-range counter-battery guns, it came with frightening suddenness; and in action the gunners had even less cover than the infantry. The few roads which could carry the nightly French munition columns out of Verdun city, creeping up head to tail, were a fixed target for the German gunners.

Perhaps the bravest of all were those who were the least prepared for bravery, the runners, the ration parties, the stretcher-bearers. 'Many would rather endure hunger than make these dangerous expeditions for food,' wrote a German soldier in April. The French *'hommes-soupe'*, or *'cuistots'*, often made a round trip of 12 miles every night, returning with a dozen heavy flasks of wine lashed to their belt, and a score of loaves strung together like a bandolier; in many places having to crawl through the glutinous mud. They arrived with the flasks punctured by shell splinters, the bread coated with filth; or they never came back. Returning at dawn through machine gun fire, they declared they would never do it again; yet the evening saw them 'starting off again on their erratic journey across the fields and gulleys'. The stretcher-bearers' lot was the worst, and volunteers were always few: the French troops at Verdun came to recog-

nise that their chances of being picked up, let alone taken back for medical attention, were extremely slim. And even if they arrived at a casualty clearing station, their ordeal was not over. Many were just labelled 'untransportable'—their wounds too hopeless or too complex to deal with—and were laid outside, where before long a German shell would find the helpless pile and save the doctors some work. Inside, the surgeons, surrounded by dustbins filled with lopped-off limbs, did the best they could to patch up the ghastly wounds caused by the huge shell splinters.

At the same time as Côte 304 was finally falling to the Germans, a terrible explosion occurred on the right bank in Fort Douaumont on May 8. Bavarian soldiers had been brewing up coffee on upturned cordite cases, using explosive scooped out of hand grenades as fuel—a reflection of the generally careless attitude to life which conditions at Verdun had engendered. A small explosion resulted, which detonated a store of hand grenades. These in turn ignited flame-thrower fuel, which flowed burning through the fort and set off a magazine full of 155-mm shells. Those Germans who were not blown to pieces or asphyxiated emerged from the fort through the smoke and chaos with uniforms shredded and faces blackened, to be mown down by their own comrades outside who mistook them for the most feared of enemies, the French African troops. In all, 650 Germans perished. But the tragedy had more significant consequences: it strengthened the Crown Prince in his resolve not to pursue the assault on Verdun, thus widening the rift between him and Knobelsdorf; and it induced the French to launch an important attack on Douaumont, which they had so easily lost in February.

By now Nivelle was well set in the saddle as commander of the French Second Army at Verdun. He in turn was driven forward by two close subordinates, both of them reckless of the cost of victory. On the one hand Nivelle had his Chief-of-Staff, Major d'Alençon, a man dying of consumption, who possessed the ruthless disregard for lives of one who knows himself condemned; on the other hand was General Mangin, commanding the 5th Division in front of Douaumont who was known as Mangin 'the

butcher', a tough, uncompromising ex-colonial officer, technically one of the most competent generals in the French Army, and every bit as self-confident as Nivelle himself. Of Mangin, Churchill wrote that he was 'reckless of all lives and of none more than his own, charging at the head of his troops, fighting rifle in hand when he could escape from his headquarters, he became on the anvil of Verdun the fiercest warrior-figure of France.'

From the very day of the arrival of 5th Division in the sector opposite Fort Douaumont at the beginning of April, Mangin had engaged in frequent small but costly counter-attacks. Admittedly they contributed to the dislocation of German plans for a resumed offensive on the right bank, but probably less effectively than the stubborn defensive battle being maintained by Pétain on the Mort Homme. From his headquarters in Fort Souville, Mangin would peer at the great dome of Douaumont two miles away, until it became as much an obsession to him as it had once been to the Brandenburgers. He could think of nothing but its recapture. The fort was indeed a thorn in the French side. It housed large numbers of fresh and rested German troops in immediate proximity to the fighting line. But above all it provided the finest observation point on the whole front. One of Mangin's machine gunners described its impact on the fighting in April and May: 'They dominate .us from Fort Douaumont; we cannot now take anything without their knowing it, nor dig any trench without their artillery spotting it and immediately bombarding it.'

Mangin had already made one attempt on the fort, on April 22. His men had reached the superstructure before they were driven off by machine guns. Now, as the scale of the explosion in the fort on May 8 filtered through to him, Mangin realised that a superb opportunity of recapturing it had been presented to him. He quickly obtained Nivelle's consent to an attack on May 22, though Pétain, now a distant voice at Bar-le-Duc, would have preferred to wait until more troops were available.

Security was bad, and the Germans had time to make full defensive preparations. The opening artillery bombardment, from 300 guns for five days, including four new 370-mm mortars, was the most powerful French concentration yet seen at Verdun; but it was considerably less than this tough old fort could stand, and only one breach in the concrete was made.

'Thick hide'
When the French infantry rose from their trenches for the assault, the German guns already had their range and they were decimated. Nevertheless, what remained of the 129th Regiment charged fearlessly and magnificently through the hail of shot and reached the fort in 11 minutes. Within half an hour, the greater part of the fort's superstructure was in French hands. The Crown Prince admitted, it 'seemed likely at one time that the fort itself must be lost'. But the French artillery, even the 370-mm mortars, could not touch the inner workings through its thick hide.

The French, however, never had a firm enough hold on the superstructure, and from dawn on the next morning, May 23, the Germans were able to hem in the French force, and then destroy it with a heavy mine-thrower. Mangin was hurling in fresh units, but they reached the fort cut to pieces or not at all. A French company commander watched these attempts to relieve the hard-pressed 129th Regiment: *Two companies of the 124th carried the German trenches by assault. They penetrated them without firing a shot. But they were insufficiently supplied with handgrenades. The Boches counterattacked with grenades. The two companies, defenceless, were annihilated. The 3rd Battalion, coming to their aid, was smashed up by barrage fire in the approach trenches. Altogether nearly 500 killed or wounded. The dead were piled up as high as the parapet.*

That night a few remnants of the French spearhead crept back to their lines in ones and twos. Their losses had been terrible, and they had left over 1,000 prisoners in German hands. Mangin's 5th Division did not have even a single company in reserve, and for a time there was a dangerous hole in the front, 500 yards wide.

Before the disastrous French attack on Douaumont, Falkenhayn, always indecisive, might have been persuaded to share the Crown Prince's misgivings over Verdun. At a *Fifth Army* conference on May 13, Knobelsdorf too had seemed to fall in with the Crown Prince's wish to put off any further offensive. But when Knobelsdorf saw Falkenhayn immediately afterwards, his stubborn determination to wrest victory from Verdun had reasserted itself. Côte 304 and most of Mort Homme had now been captured, he pointed out; all could yet be won at Verdun if only the offensive were continued on the right bank. Finally Falkenhayn was convinced and

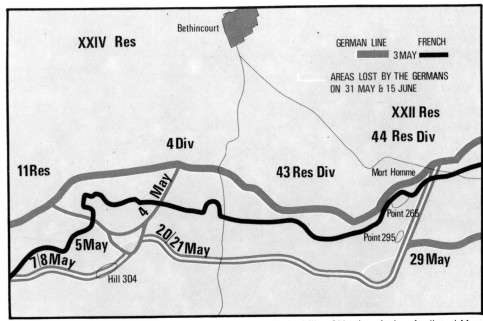

Above: French gains during the fighting on and around the hills of Verdun during April and May

gave his permission for the new attack, even allocating a fresh division for it. When the Crown Prince received Falkenhayn's order, he was in despair.

Preparations for this operation, 'May Cup', to be launched on June 1, went quickly ahead. Three corps, *I Bavarian, X Reserve,* and *XV Corps,* were to attack with a total of five divisions, on a front only three miles wide. The objective was to gain jumping-off points for a final thrust on Verdun itself—the Thiaumont stronghold, the Fleury ridge, Fort Souville, and above

all, the north-eastern bastion of the French line, Fort Vaux.

To Knobelsdorf, success seemed assured. His artillery was now more numerous than the French, with 2,200 pieces against 1,777. This time his confidence might not be misplaced, for French morale had slumped badly following the failure at Douaumont, Mangin had been temporarily disgraced, ominous cases of 'indiscipline' were beginning to be reported. And now the French were to face the fiercest onslaught the Germans had yet made at Verdun.

Below: Piles of ammunition in the street—by 1916 a familiar sight in villages behind the line

By midsummer 1916, the Germans had changed their line of attack to the right bank of the Meuse. Now the most important obstacle in the line to Verdun was Fort Vaux, garrisoned by a French unit whose heroic resistance and survival won them the admiration of their attackers

VERDUN
The surrender of Fort Vaux

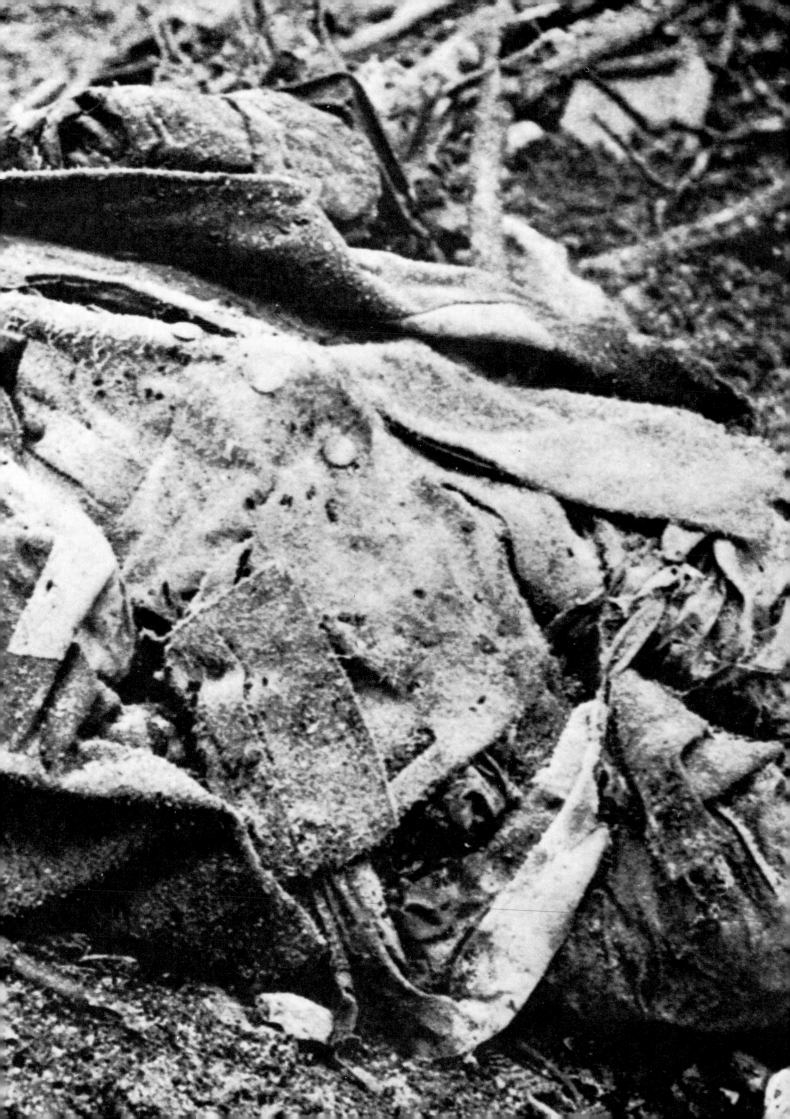

In history there is no example known of a battle which lasted as long and was as violent as that which went on for five months around Verdun. Towards the end of February 1916, a sudden attempt to break the French line was followed, in March and in April, by a series of battles for the positions necessary to a new assault. This lapsed into a battle of attrition which might have continued over many months, but at the beginning of May, indications of offensive preparations from the Allies prompted the Germans to new action. On May 15, an offensive launched by Austria-Hungary against the Italian army having failed, Falkenhayn was forced to draw important reinforcements from the German armies in Galicia. On the Russian front, Brusilov was preparing a new attack and Britain, it was rumoured, had begun preparations for another offensive. In Falkenhayn's mind the only way out of these difficulties was to hasten the collapse of France which he considered to be the 'main sword of England'.

But Germany realised that a new attempt to break through had to be made, and the Kronprinz accordingly received the order to push forward towards the ridges of the River Meuse. His troops were exhausted by their fierce preparatory attacks on Hill 304, on Mort-Homme and on Thiaumont, but morale was still high after their success in the defence of Douaumont from May 22 to May 25. Their new mission was to complete the advance towards the points necessary to cover the

Above: An occupied German trench near Verdun. By June 1916 the ground was scarred beyond recognition. *Below:* German troops work forward behind a barrage of gas shells

main attack that would take Verdun.

At this stage in the fighting, the strengths of the two opponents were approximately the same. Their front lines were manned according to different methods, making comparison difficult, but it can be estimated that there were about 20 divisions on each side. Their value was identical, their courage equal, but the Germans, more methodical and disciplined, had a tactical advantage over the French. They succeeded in avoiding losses by digging shelters, driving saps and opening trenches. But even more significant was their supply of heavy artillery which gave them the mastery of the battlefield. In all, they had 2,200 guns, out of which 1,730 were heavy guns, whereas the French could line up only 1,200 field-guns, including 570 heavy guns. Relying on this superiority, they had worked out plans for a major breakthrough.

Right bank attack

In spite of General von Gallwitz' success on the left bank of the river Meuse, General von Knobelsdorf, leading operations at Verdun himself, on May 30 reverted to the German Staff's original plan: to decide the issue on the right bank. Gallwitz was accordingly ordered to slow down his action but did so unwillingly. The French were in a temporary state of confusion having just lost Mort-Homme and Hill 304, and a determined attacker might well have gained a decisive victory against them on the hills south of Esnes and Chattancourt.

Gallwitz felt bitter enough to write: 'the result of this plan is that we will be stopped on both banks'.

Twenty-six German mortars and 24 heavy howitzers were withdrawn from the left bank and Gallwitz' successes declined accordingly. He managed to complete the capture of Hill 304, and the *XXII Reserve Corps* which had already taken Mort-Homme, managed to seize Chattancourt. But the same units were used continually in these actions, the *38th* and *51st Divisions* in particular, and their strength was declining.

On the French side, General Delétoile (XXXI Corps) succeeded General Berthelot and from the River Meuse to the La Hayette ravine, the 65th and 19th Divisions were managing to hold the line. On June 15, a fierce attack on Mort-Homme by the 65th Division inflicted heavy casualties on the Germans and managed to recapture the trenches south of this position. But the fighting on this bank was gradually fading, and on July 1 the Allied offensive was launched on the Somme; thereby precluding the chance of further operations on the left bank. General von Gallwitz was transferred to take command over the endangered front of the Somme and was succeeded by General von François at Verdun.

His transfer signalled the end of one of the most bloody episodes at Verdun. Mort-Homme and Hill 304 are still wrapped in dark horror.

The Germans now concentrated their efforts on the area occupied by III and XII

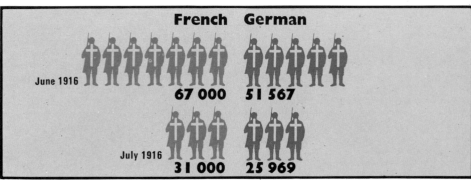

Above: German and French casualties in the latest stage of the Verdun fighting. Both sides believed that this bloody sacrifice was necessary for ultimate victory

Below: Fighting in the east sector of Verdun during June and early July 1916. The capture of Fort Vaux by the Germans meant that they could press on towards Souville and Verdun

Corps; the sector occupied by III Corps, under command of General Lebrun, included the sector of Tavannes and the sector of Souville. In the centre of XII Corps' sector, under General Nollet, was Poivre ridge and on the right was Thiaumont farm, held by the 151st Division.

Whitsunday attack
At the end of May, the French front line included the Damloup village salient, Fort Vaux, the north-east edge of Fumin Wood, and the Vaux pond dam which crosses half way up Caillette Wood, stretches north of Thiaumont farm, then across Dame ravine and Nawé Wood and cuts the road Bras-Douaumont, west of Haudromont quarry.

To implement their operation on the

right bank of the Meuse, the Germans first had to get hold of Fort Vaux in order to advance towards Verdun and set foot on Fort Souville.

On Whitsunday, June 1, three corps from von Lochow's army rushed forward, jumping off from a line running from Nawé Wood on the west, and to Damloup on the east. The *1st Bavarian Division, X Reserve Corps* and *XV Corps* made some headway, and the attack was the most violent in the Thiaumont and Vaux sectors where three divisions, about 60,000 men, made a dash between the Cailette woods and Damloup. At the same time the *50th Division* was attacking the fort itself. Through a clever pincer movement the Germans were able to attack both ends of this salient: in the

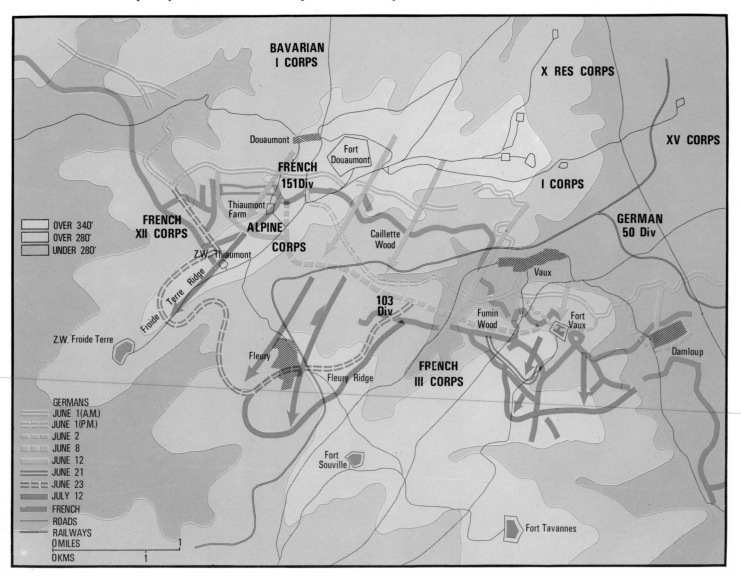

An aerial view of Fort Vaux, one of the key forts on the right bank of the Meuse

February by a direct 420-mm hit and the fort could therefore be used only as an observation post and as a garrison for no more than 250 men. Observation was possible from the front but not the rear.

As early as June 1, the Germans seized Caillette Wood, the Bazil ravine and infiltrated into Fumin Wood. On June 2, they attacked the fort itself. It was not long before they had taken a foothold on the flanks, and then on the top. Shortly afterwards, the *50th Division* overcame French resistance at Damloup village and was able to complete the encirclement of the fort and sever its communications.

French counterattacks, launched immediately, lacked artillery support and failed; but the Germans had not succeeded completely in breaking down the resistance of the fort. The situation in the garrison, however, was critical. Hundreds of soldiers, looking for shelter in the confusion, had now raised the strength of the garrison to six companies.

Poison gasses then invaded the fort through breaches on the flanks and the situation in the overcrowded underground barracks became untenable. The successive bombardments had damaged the pipes and water was scarce. By June 4, the water tank level had come down to six or seven cubic yards and the water ration had to be reduced to half a pint per man per day. Many volunteers for water-carrying missions never came back.

In order to save water and supplies, Major Raynal, the commander of the fort,

Fort Vaux. The French, deprived of water and supplies, finally surrendered it on June 8

west at the Hardaumont works and in the east at Damloup.

Fort Vaux had been rebuilt in concrete in 1911, surrounded by ditches ten yards wide and supported on the flanks by two casemates, each of them equipped with two 75-mm guns. The central turret with another 75-mm gun had been destroyed in

decided to evacuate a large proportion of his men. During the night of June 4, under command of a volunteer, Second-Lieutenant Buffet, the approximate strength of a company succeeded in escaping and reaching the rear headquarters near Tavannes. Buffet came back the following night to meet his besieged fellows and to

Below: German troops with supply cart on the slopes of Mort Homme—Dead Man's Ridge

French troops on the vast, outer walls of Fort Vaux a few days before it fell to the Germans

signals received by Fort Souville testified to the desperate struggle these men were undergoing: 'Enemy working—western side of the fort—digging mine chamber to blow up vault; pound quickly with artillery.' And later, 'Are attacked by gas and flame-throwers, close to collapse.'

By the evening of June 6, there remained only 12 gallons of water for several hundred men, most of which had to be kept for the wounded.

The operation ordered by General Nivelle to relieve the fort was carried out by Colonel Savy's brigade, but it failed dismally on June 8 with heavy losses. The attempt served only to promote distrust and hostility among the troops who knew it was too late to send in reinforcements. General Kurst von Reden granted the garrison the honours of war. The French soldiers came out of the smoking ruins under arms, while two platoons of Prussian soldiers presented arms. Major Raynal, as a prisoner of war, was allowed to keep his sword.

Consolidation

Having mastered the fort, the German staff immediately drove home their attack. Taking advantage of their initial success, they were aiming to widen the breach and gain a foothold on the Fleury Ridge. Knobelsdorf's plan consisted of a frontal thrust against the line Souville-Tavannes: the first advance on Souville was to be made from the west; it was designed to open the way to Froide-Terre Ridge, the last key position at the junction

The Kronprinz to his father: 'We must have a higher pile to see Verdun'

of the roads going north and east.

Knobelsdorf spurred his divisions into action, reinforcing them with fresh troops of the *III Bavarian Corps* and the famous *Alpine Corps*.

They resumed the assault on June 8. The crack Bavarian regiments of *I Corps* surged against the French positions, but from

bring orders for a combined operation planned to relieve the fort.

Inside the fortress, the situation was becoming worse and worse. The last carrier-pigeon was sent off, bearing the message: 'We stand fast, but are suffering heavy gas attacks. We need urgent relief. This is our last pigeon.' The last visual

Nawé Wood to Thiaumont farm, the French 151st Division stood its ground in spite of heavy casualties in the 293rd and 337th Regiments. The Germans succeeded in taking the Thiaumont works from the 52nd Division but were forced to pause in their attack at this point due to exhaustion.

General Nollet, commanding the sector, was now able to send reinforcements and during the night, the French reoccupied the Thiaumont works. Under cover of darkness the Germans had withdrawn; they had found their positions untenable and prefered withdrawal at this point to suffering heavy losses. But the French had evacuated Thiaumont farm and the Germans were able to establish a position there.

The companies were already reduced to half their strength. Many soldiers had been buried under landslides caused by the explosion of 305-mm guns. Pungent smoke and thick dust poisoned the air, the soil was torn up and covered with debris. At night time, the Germans sapped their way forward and at 0400 hours the fearful crash of the bombardment was resumed. The soldiers of Vendée expected the final assault after such a violent burst of fire. Some of them began to pray.

At 0600 hours the Germans rushed forward but an immediate counterattack, supported by machine gun fire, dislodged them. The French troops were able to advance up to the trenches of the 137th Regiment, but the ground there was torn up; most of the long trench had been smothered by earth and only a few bayonets emerged, showing the place where the soldiers had died at their combat posts.

This is one of the most tragic episodes of the days at Verdun. Two battalions had been utterly destroyed, after awaiting death for 50 hours with patience and resignation, in a nerve-shattering bombardment, during which they had neither supplies nor water. 'These people from Vendée, they were tough guys,' said Major Dreux, a survivor of the second battalion.

No withdrawal

As early as the beginning of June, Pétain reported that 'the Germans want a quick decision at Verdun and give battle on the right bank of the River Meuse with all means available and a real superiority in heavy artillery; we cannot afford any withdrawal. At all costs we must stand on a front line marked by the Bourru Woods on the left bank and on the right by the intermediate line Froide-Terre-Souville-Tavennes. To lose this position would mean to place bridges over the River Meuse under German artillery fire and to be forced to retire from the right bank.' He stressed the great moral and material advantage the Germans would gain if they could seize Verdun and insisted upon a quick start of the British offensive.

The C-in-C, nevertheless, gave priority to the immediate offensive on the River Somme; he had rightly estimated that the German staff were worried by this imminent threat and therefore threw their last resources into the battle: on the right, the *Bavarians,* in the centre, the *Alpine Corps,* the *103rd Division* at Souville and the *50th Division* at Tavannes.

General Nivelle had reorganised the Second Army into seven sectors: on the left bank A sector (VII Corps), B sector (XV Corps), C sector (XXXI Corps), and on the right bank, D sector (XI Corps with

General Nollet and later General Mangin), E sector (VI Corps with General Paulinier and the 130th and 12th Divisions in particular) and sector G (II Corps). A new standard gauge railway line was ready for service on June 20 and would help bring constant supplies to the French divisions.

The German attack began on June 21, with a bombardment concentrated from Nawé Wood to south of Damloup, followed by two preparatory attacks. At Nawé Wood and north-west of the Thiaumont works, where so much blood had already been spilled, the attack failed. The other one, south-west of Fort Vaux, disrupted the front line of the 12th Division and infiltrated between Fumin Wood and La Vaux-Regnier Wood.

The following day and the rest of the night the German guns increased their fire, pounding the French positions with gas shells from Froide-Terre to Tavannes, and making untenable the low ground where the men were forced to make a stand somewhat-may.

At 0600 hours on June 23, the German divisions began their major attack on Fleury. The French held their positions, despite the fierceness of the blow. Both sides had equal experience and skill in fierce hand-to-hand fighting, and on the left, on the south edge of Nawé Wood and on Hill 321 the French managed to beat off the onslaught. But on the right the French were outnumbered; the *Bavarians* carried the Thiaumont works by storm. The 129th Division was submerged, the 121st Battalion of Chasseurs wiped out.

On the right the French 130th Division, outflanked on the east and on the west, was forced to withdraw from Fleury after a desperate street fight at the south end of the village. In the centre, the Alpine Corps was unable to break out from the railway ravine and the heroic 307 Brigade (General Bordeaux), stood up alone against the *103rd German Division.* The 407th Regiment put up a gallant defence to cover Souville and stemmed the enemy's advance. On June 21 the regimental strength was 2,800 men; five days later only 1,200 men returned from the front line. The French 129th Division had withdrawn to the Froide-Terre Ridge; the Germans had seized the transversal ridge of Fleury south of Nawé Wood and had infiltrated between Mangin and the Paulinier Army Corps. At 1200 hours, General Pétain telephoned to the Chantilly HQ stating that: 'the situation is bad; if the Germans reach the reverse slope, we must be prepared to withdraw on the left bank'. Bearing in mind the fact that one-third of the French artillery was concentrated on the right bank, we understand Pétain better when he writes: 'June 23 was a particularly critical day. The situation was very serious, our last position from Fort Souville was nearly invested. If we had lost it, Verdun itself would have emerged undefendable in the centre of a vast circle, the edges of which were held by the Germans. Our positions on the right bank would have then been condemned.'

At the beginning of the afternoon, the German advance was stopped but the French line was not continuous, and a large gap had been opened between the Souville and Tavannes sectors. In the afternoon, the Germans tried to exploit their initial success, and the last French reserves were thrown into the battle.

From Souilly, General Nivelle, always self-confident, reported that the situation was 'serious' but well in hand and that he did not foresee any withdrawal. In the afternoon Pétain made his report to Chantilly and reiterated his daily request: 'we must advance the time of the British offensive'; clamouring for reinforcements, he obtained four fresh divisions.

At this point, Joffre retained the remarkable self-possession as he had shown on the Marne. General Claudel, the assistant to the major-general, had drawn his attention to the dangers of loosing men and equipment by putting up a resistance on the right bank without any chance of withdrawal. 'But Joffre, already bent in a familiar attitude to sign the order for reinforcements, his left arm resting on the table, his back stooped, his pen close to the paper, slowly raised his head and showed perhaps a slight hesitation in his eyes. Then having recovered all his serenity, Joffre signed: "There it is, my dear Claudel," he said, "I have already signed so many others."'

The night of June 23 was relatively quiet. With fresh units, General Nivelle was able to stop the German advance and even to launch several counterattacks in order to clear the positions suitable for a withdrawal. On the Froide-Terre Ridge and around the Thiaumont works, severe fighting took place over the strong points which changed hands several times. The French counterattacks on June 24 and 25, brought little result. A more important one, launched by two brigades on June 27, failed also.

After ten days, the French still faced a difficult situation on the right bank of the Meuse. In spite of eight attacks, the Thiaumont works remained in German hands and the French feared a renewed attack by the Germans.

But on July 1, the Battle of the Somme began and the Germans, from now on, started to lose the initiative. Their present offensive against Verdun had no longer much significance, but to ease suddenly their pressure on this key point would have underlined before world opinion the failure of German hopes. Furthermore, it was important to prevent the French from transferring to the Somme battlefield part of their resources at Verdun.

After the capture of the Thiaumont works on July 1, General Nivelle planned a new operation and reorganised the front line, 'in order to bring all means available in the hands of a single commander'. General Mangin, commanding D sector up to Fleury, led this operation but the Germans took the initiative. On July 11 they launched the last large-scale attack—the final episode that was not entirely revealed by French official reports of the time, in order not to disclose how close they were to losing the battle.

Further Reading
Beumelburg, Wermer, *Combattants Allemands à Verdun* (Payot)
Bordeaux, H., *Verdun* (Plon)
Pétain, Maréchale, *La Bataille de Verdun* (Payot)
Raynal, Commandant, *Journal du Fort de Vaux* (Albin Michel)
Romains, Jules, *Les Hommes de Bonne Volonté* (Paris)

COUNTERATTACK AT VERDUN

The opening on July 1 of the Anglo-French attack on the Somme served notice of closure on the Germans' offensive at Verdun, as their High Command was quick to recognise. For, great though German strength was, it fell short of what was necessary to conduct large-scale operations on two widely separated sectors of the front; and the need to defend their lines on the Somme far outstripped in importance any that the capture of Verdun might once have had. By the beginning of July, moreover, most of the High Command was ready to welcome an excuse to abandon the exercise in self-flagellation which Verdun had become. Falkenhayn's concept of the battle as a 'bleeding-white' of the French army at virtually no cost to the German army had been proved unfeasible after the first few days; latterly, the Germans' daily losses had risen as high, perhaps even higher than those of the French. It was with resignation, therefore, perhaps almost with relief that Falkenhayn brought himself to order, after the failure of the last attack on Fort Souville on July 11, that Crown Prince Wilhelm's armies would in future 'adopt a defensive posture'. Verdun was to be allowed to revert to the status of a 'quiet sector'.

But it takes two sides to make a quiet sector, and the French commanders were not prepared to co-operate. Indeed, two less pacifically inclined generals than Nivelle, GOC Second Army, and his subordinate Mangin, GOC XI Corps, would have been hard to find. Nivelle, a cavalryman turned gunner but above all a devotee of the Grandmaison school of the offensive, whom two years of war had left uncon-

By July 1916 the Franco-British offensive on the Somme was beginning to place a great strain on German resources, and Falkenhayn was ready to declare the Verdun sector a 'quiet zone'. But German gains had been such a blow to French pride that there was to be little respite. As autumn followed summer, the French launched repeated counterattacks, as if determined to follow the logic of attrition to its bitter conclusion.
Below: In an advance trench, Nivelle's *poilus* await the signal to advance and retake Fort Douaumont

vinced of any need to moderate his fundamental ideas, was bursting to find an opportunity of recapturing the ground yielded to the Germans since February. And Mangin, the trap-jawed colonial warrior, had a temperamental revulsion for defensive tactics. It was certain, therefore, that as soon as the Germans relaxed their efforts, Nivelle and Mangin would move over to the attack.

At what point on the perimeter they would do so was clear to all: it had to be in Mangin's XI Corps' sector, between the Meuse and Damloup, where the Germans had won their most important prizes—Fort

Douaumont, lost on February 25, and Fort Vaux, lost on June 7—and had pushed their lines closest to Verdun. Indeed, if allowed as much as another inch on these slopes the Germans would have the city under observation and be able to direct fire onto the nerve centres of the French defence. Thiaumont and Fleury were therefore to be the scenes of some lively French counterattacks in the weeks following Falkenhayn's abandonment of the defensive —a decision at which the French could guess but of which they had not, of course, been informed and on the finality of which they could not therefore count.

Dazy

45

The counterattacks of the following weeks were thus delivered with a frequency and ferocity better suited to a more desperate situation. On July 15/16, the 115th Regiment recaptured Battery C and Command Post 119 near Thiaumont; and on July 20 the adjoining powder-mill was retaken. On August 1 both CP 119 and Battery C were overrun by the Germans again, but they were both recaptured next day. The village of Thiaumont was recaptured, as a result of and during the course of the same operation, on August 4. The Germans, however, defending stubbornly and even counterattacking frequently, retook Thiaumont on August 8 – the sixteenth time it had changed hands since their great push of June 23 – and it was not firmly secured by the French until August 18, after the splendid *Regiment di d'Infanterie Coloniale du Maroc* (Moroccan Colonials) had driven its German garrison out, this time for good. The French continued to make step-by-step advances, all very costly, between September 3 and 13. It was on that day that Poincaré, the French President, arrived in Verdun, together with representatives of the major Allies, to decorate it with the *Legion d'Honneur*. Before an audience which included the four generals most responsible for its successful defence, Joffre, Pétain, Nivelle and Mangin, he paid tribute to the inviolability of the place 'against whose walls', he proclaimed, 'the highest ambitions of Imperial Germany have broken'.

Of far greater moment within the perimeter of Verdun itself, however, was an occurrence, a little over a week earlier, of which no word had been allowed to penetrate to the outside world: the explosion in the Tavannes railway tunnel.

This narrow-gauge tunnel, which carried the line from Verdun to Etain, in the plain of the Woëvres, beneath the ridge known as the Côte St Michel, had naturally been adopted from early on in the siege as a place of refuge from bombardment, and eventually as the main staging point for reliefs and supply columns making their way forward to the sector of the line between Damloup and Fort Vaux. Besides these transients, it also provided permanent shelter for the headquarters of a brigade, two engineer battalions and three labour regiments, and the staff of four field dressing stations (including whatever wounded were under treatment). All these, amounting to a population of between 1,000 and 2,000 men, were accommodated in a string of shacks and platforms which had been built along the right-hand side of the tunnel, filling it to the roof (which was only 15 feet high) and leaving a gangway less than four feet wide on the left. The walls of the gangway were festooned with telephone wires and naked power cables carrying current from a (fortunately rather inadequate) generator. At the tunnel's mid-point, 500 yards into the hill, was situated a large store of grenades and Verey lights, which had to be restocked constantly as its contents were distributed to troops on the line.

Minor accidents with explosives were frequent, though less concern was felt for that hazard than for those threatened by the indescribably filthy condition to which five months of continuous occupation had reduced the interior (it possessed only one source of water and a single ventilating shaft). And, in any case, small explosions within seemed to count for little in the scale of risk when measured against the constant racket of shellfire playing round the tunnel mouth.

Late in the evening of September 4, however, one of these explosions, caused it has been suggested, but never definitely established, by a mule stumbling under its cargo of grenades, or by a member of a carrying party brushing a power cable with a rocket, or even by the detonation of one of the tunnel's demolition charges – set off a petrol fire, which in turn exploded other small stores of explosives and so on until, the shacks and platforms taking light, the interior of the tunnel was quickly turned into an inferno. Many, perhaps the majority of those inside at the time, were unable to reach an exit ahead of the flames and some who did were forced back by shell-fire. When, after three days' helpless inactivity, rescue parties were at last able to penetrate within, they found, of the 1,000 who had perished, almost nothing recognisable as human remains. Beneath the single airshaft, it is true, the first rescuers saw a pile of what appeared to be bodies. But at a touch they fell into dust.

The Tavannes tunnel disaster was a scarcely propitious omen for the attack which Nivelle had now begun to plan to recover ground in that sector. His intention was to recover a strip of territory four miles wide by one and a half deep, between Damloup on the right and the Côte de Poivre, the ridge the left of which abutted onto the Meuse above Verdun. It was a nightmare landscape which he planned to recapture, a wilderness of water-logged shell holes so close together that the advancing infantry would scarcely be able to find a way between. But it gave onto the two lost strongholds of the French defence (and symbols of French humiliation), Forts Douaumont and Vaux, which were Nivelle's real objectives. Moreover, the dreadful condition of the battlefield made it very unlikely that the Germans would have been able to organise anything but the most sketchy sort of positions in the semi-liquid soil, the condition of which was further to deteriorate during the heavy rains of early October.

4,000 tons per mile

Whatever defences the Germans had constructed, Mangin counted on being able to destroy them with the very powerful artillery which Nivelle had allotted him for this attack: 289 field and 314 heavy guns, which included some 370-mm mortars and two 400-mm Schneider-Creusot railway guns, the heaviest yet produced by the French armament industry. Fifteen thousand tons of shells were being dumped to feed the batteries, nearly 4,000 tons for each mile of the front to be attacked.

German artillery strength amounted to between 400 and 500 pieces, of which a far smaller proportion were of heavy calibre than in the French artillery. They would thus be at a dangerous disadvantage in the gun duel preceding the assault.

And that boded ill for the seven German divisions, all tired and understrength, in the line: the *13th* and *25th Reserve, 34th, 54th, 9th, 33rd Reserve* and *50th Divisions*. Almost all had been at Verdun for long periods without relief and had suffered heavy losses. The *13th Reserve* had taken part in the opening attack in February; the *54th* had been at Verdun since May; the *25th Reserve* since July; the *9th* had been thereabouts, either at Verdun or at such equally wearing spots as Les Eparges or the Calonne Trench, since September 1914. Only one of the divisions could be rated as really first class, the *50th*, a wartime formation but one composed of Active regiments of the peacetime army, one of which, the *158th Regiment*, had captured Fort Vaux on June 4. It was still holding the same sector in October.

Most of the divisions, moreover, were holding their fronts with only three battalions in line, the rest being in support and reserve; and while this was a perfectly safe method when support and reserve positions were strong, with good, secure communications to front and rear, the current condition of the Germans' defences made it distinctly dangerous. For Nivelle's 'creeping barrage', the artillery technique which he had done so much to perfect, was designed to cut sectors of the defence off from one another, allowing them to be dealt with in detail by the advancing infantry, enclosed within this moving curtain of shellfire.

The French attackers were, on paper, fewer than the German defenders, for Nivelle had allotted only three divisions to the assault, the 38th, 133rd and 74th. All, however, were excellent fighting formations and had been heavily reinforced for this operation. The 38th, one of the two divisions raised in the French North African *départements,* was composed of the 4th Zouaves, a white regiment, the 8th Tirailleurs, a Moslem regiment, the 4th Mixte (Zouaves and Tirailleurs) and the Moroccan Colonial Infantry Regiment. They

French troops move up for the final assault on Fort Douaumont

Sirot

were to be reinforced for the occasion by the 11th Infantry Regiment. The two other divisions had had seven infantry regiments added to their strengths, a Senegalese battalion, one of those raised on the West Coast of Africa, and nine battalions of Chasseurs, the élite light infantry units of the French army. In all, 29 battalions would jump off at zero hour. In the preparatory period, they were rehearsed over a fullscale model of the terrain, until they knew it blindfold.

On the afternoon of October 22 every German gun on the front opened up to quell what looked like the first onrush of the French assault. It was in fact a carefully organised feint, designed to establish the position of all the German batteries which, in the two days remaining before the assault, were brought under a final counterbombardment so heavy that, by French calculation, only 100 German guns remained operational by zero hour. Also bombarded with increasing severity during these days was the fortress of Douaumont itself. Its interior, though badly damaged by an accidental explosion and fire, similar to that which had gutted the Tavannes tunnel, had never been penetrated by shellfire. Indeed it was believed by the garrison that its concrete and earthwork skin was impenetrable. Under the constant erosion of casual shellfire, however, the outer earthwork layer of the fort's carapace had been reduced imperceptibly but significantly, and the new projectiles of the French 400-mm guns had sufficient terminal velocity to carve through the inner concrete layer. Exploding beneath the eight-foot concrete roofs,

in steady succession, these enormous shells quickly reduced much of the interior to a shambles, killed many of the garrison and started a fire of threatening dimensions. On the night of October 23, the German commander of Fort Douaumont ordered it to be evacuated.

Next morning dawned misty. Visibility was limited to 20 yards and the gunners were blinded, at least on the German side. In consequence their SOS barrages did not come down until 12 minutes after the attack had begun, and it was by then too late to try breaking up the French attacking waves, which had already crossed into the German lines. It was a desolation they found there. The ground had been harrowed by shellfire, a French officer who took part wrote, 'and its surface littered with broken relics; German haversacks, rifles, helmets, webbing, boots, human remains; an arm – a leg – a hand. Everything has been chopped to pieces.'

Yet, he also recorded, the troops went forward with 'their rifles slung'. This manoeuvre, which it had been promised them they would be able to perform on numerous occasions before, was for once a reality. Almost everywhere the Germans gave up or were found to have run away before the French appeared. This was to be true even of Douaumont. Abandoned by its official garrison, just as the French had left it abandoned in February, the handful of battlefield strays who had crept for protection into its cellars on the morning of October 24 rendered up its ownership to the first French soldier who asked them for it. The urgent demand for reinforcements sent rearward by the leader of the

party, when he found the fort abandoned and the fire burnt out, had never been answered, perhaps never received. The *Regiment d'Infanterie Coloniale du Maroc* thus entered and took possession almost unopposed and unscathed. During the whole day the French had taken 6,000 prisoners, and most of the ground lost in the fighting of May and June.

On October 26 the Germans sent in four violent counterattacks, and another the day following, but despite these the Moroccan Colonials continued to advance their line, eventually consolidating a firm position 400 yards west of Fort Douaumont. Fort Vaux, heavily bombarded by the French from October 28 to November 2, was abandoned that evening by the Germans and reoccupied next morning by a company of the 298th Regiment. Nivelle, it seemed, had indeed hit upon a secret of tactical success. He was to have his next chance to prove it in December.

Further Reading
Falkenhayn, E. von, *General Headquarters, 1914-1916* (London 1960)
Horne, A., *The Price of Glory, Verdun 1916* (London 1962)
Joffre, Marshal, *The Memoirs of Marshal Joffre* (London 1932)
Palat, Gen. B. E., *La Grande Guerre sur le Front Occidental*, Vols. X-XII (Paris 1925)
Pétain, H., *Verdun* (London 1930)
Romains, Jules, *Men of Good Will*, Vols. 15-16 (London 1926)
Ryan, S., *Pétain the Soldier* (London 1969)
Der Weltkrieg 1914-1918, Vol. X – *Die Operationen des Jahres 1916*

Below: French soldiers in a German communications trench

VERDUN THE END

For months the convulsion around Verdun had continued, costing the Germans and the French the lives of hundreds of thousands of their troops. But now the end was at hand. Forts Vaux and Douaumont had been recaptured by the French. All that they now needed was the line of hills to the east of the city of Verdun, as these hills dominated the whole of the battle field and made French movement impossible, for the moment the Germans detected any activity below them, they caused a storm of shells to descend on the river valleys. Now in one last climacteric offensive, the French hurled the Germans off the heights with heavy losses in dead and prisoners. The mincing machine had finally ground to a halt. *Right:* A French machine gun team waits in one of the ruins which littered the Verdun area so liberally

In the aftermath of the offensive of October 24, which had restored Forts Douaumont and Vaux to French possession, an outward calm descended on the ravaged slopes of the Meuse valley at Verdun. The Germans, on the defensive here since July, had neither the men nor the heart to attempt to recapture any of those 'points of major tactical importance' which it had cost them so dear to win in the spring and early summer of the year. The French, also desperately worn by the cumulative effort of two and a half years of war, were content for the moment to consolidate what they had regained and to repair some of the ravages which the battle had wrought in the rear areas of the 'fortified zone'.

The regiments of territorials – those over-age reservists who house-maided for the French army – now moved into the recaptured forts and began to clear them of debris and to repair their ventilation, lighting and communication systems. Further back they undertook the reconstruction of the rail network and, to supplement it, laid spurs to the 60- and 40-centimetre light railway tracks which were of such enormous assistance in getting supplies forward over the shell-pocked ground.

The French high Command – Nivelle, whose 'victory' of October 24 had served to convince him more strongly than ever that he 'had the secret' and who, as commander of the Second Army, also had the power to decree local offensives in the Verdun sector, and Mangin, his ferocious subordinate, commanding II Corps, responsible for the right bank of the Meuse – were neither of them wholly satisfied with the results of the battle in October. Though it had won back much ground, it still left the Germans in possession of an important circle of observation points from which they could overlook many of the French defended positions and approach routes. Most of these points were known by their elevation: Hills 378, 347 and 380. Besides these, the Germans also continued to control a complex of small valleys and broken ground between the heights and the new French front line – the ravins des Houyers, de Fond-du-Loup, de Hassoule and du Helly – and by possessing these they kept the French under a constant threat of raiding and minor attack. Nivelle had therefore proposed to Joffre very soon after the conclusion of the October battle that he be allowed to make one more effort in the same sector to drive the Germans further away and consolidate an easily defensible line on the high ground the Germans at present occupied. On November 18, Joffre, overriding the objections of his Operations Section, gave his assent to this proposal. Nivelle at once directed Mangin to complete detailed planning.

The sector to be attacked was six miles in length and ran from the Meuse at

Vacherauville, a riverside village which was to be recaptured, to Damloup, just north-east of Fort Vaux. It was garrisoned by five German divisions in the front line, from left to right, the *14th Reserve 39th*, *10th, 14th* and *39th Bavarian Reserve*, and four in support, the *Guard Ersatz, 5th, 30th* and *21st Reserve*. This was a mixed bag. The *39th Bavarian Reserve* was a formation of the lowest grade, composed of *Landwehr* regiments, which had not previously been committed to an active sector of the front. The *39th Division* was one of the four recruited in the *Reichsland* (occupied Alsace-Lorraine), and composed, therefore, of the rejects from other recruiting areas. The *10th* was another 'colonial' division, recruited among the Poles of Upper Silesia, and these fought with something less than a will. The *14th Reserve* had been a good division, but having occupied the same sector on the Côte de Poivre since the first day of the battle in February, was now badly worn down in body and spirit. Only the *14th*, a Rhineland division which had been on the Verdun front since June was really fit to withstand a major French attack. The four divisions in support were of much higher quality, the *5th* in particular, and could be counted upon to halt a breakthrough. But since the French aimed at no more than the seizure of ground, they might not be able to intervene quickly enough to aid their stricken comrades in the first line.

The French themselves were intending to employ five divisions in the first wave of the assault, the 22nd, 126th, 133rd and the 37th and 38th. The latter, forming XIX Corps, represented the contribution made by the French settlers in North Africa to the army of the Motherland – and also that of some of the subject peoples. These, the *Tirailleurs indigenes* or Turcos, and the Zouaves, their white brothers-in-arms, were among the finest fighting troops on the Allied side.

They were to be supported, as on October 24, by an immensely powerful artillery element, including batteries of 220-mm and 370-mm mortars. These were unable to 'shoot in' onto their targets until later than planned in the fire programme, because of the execrable weather which made all aerial observation impossible. On December 11, however, the skies cleared, aeroplanes were able to take off and the first shots were fired in the bombardment which would isolate the former German positions from sources of reinforcement and resupply.

Flanks soon secured

The attack began on December 15 at 0950 hours. The German positions were battered but fundamentally sound and, unlike those taken by the French in October, had been in German hands long enough for the latter to prepare them thoroughly; they were cleverly adapted to take advantage of the many corners of dead ground in that broken area of ravines and reverse slopes. The Germans were therefore ready for the French. Nevertheless, on both flanks the French quickly seized all their objectives: to the left the 126th Division took possession of Vacherauville – though failing to secure the Côte de Poivre, which remained in German hands until the following day – and beat off the counterattacks which the Germans immediately launched. The 38th Division, which had taken Douaumont in

October, also got quickly onto its objectives, took considerable booty and 3,500 prisoners; but its most distant objective attained had to be evacuated after a bombardment from the French 155-mm guns had dropped short onto it. The division suffered few casualties, but among these was Nicolai, commander of the battalion of the Moroccan Colonials which had captured Douaumont fort itself and a genuine hero to his brother officers and men in the Verdun area.

On the right, the 133rd Division, moving faultlessly behind the creeping barrage at a pace of 100 yards every four minutes, advanced steadily onto its assigned positions, though some of those were not wholly cleared of Germans until the following day. Nevertheless, its attack was generally successful and as planned. It was in the centre of this, and particularly on 38th Division's sector, that the Germans offered their fiercest resistance. Consequently the advance was most costly in that area and the fighting most confused. A soldier of the 2nd Zouaves, Dufournay, has left this gripping and authentic memoir of the day's events:

Day is beginning to break, and it is turning very cold. A crust forms on the surface of the mud and a thin sheet of ice on the puddles. There is an arctic wind from the north and big snow clouds are building up. The sergeant-major points out to me on the right beyond the Germans' lines, the dark mass of the Bois D'Hardaumont silhouetted on the crest. 'Take a good look at it,' he said, 'we're advancing in that direction and the 5th Battalion have got to take that wood.'

Towards 0800 hours the bombardment begins again, just as terrible as yesterday. I am thinking to myself that I've been in this place for 100 years when the sound of voices makes me turn my head. It is some machine gunners looking for a hole. At that moment I realise that the bombardment has stopped. Behind us the slope which descends from Douaumont is covered by Zouaves who, line by line, halt and disappear into craters. An order is passed along the trench: '42nd Company, fix bayonets.' One wants to be brave, one wants to look calm, one is quite unable to stop shaking. I check that my grenade-cup is clean, slide a grenade in and out again. Everything all right? I am ready. '42nd Company, advance.' With an uncertain step, we emerge. The company commander is already out. Sixty mud-covered bundles follow him, sliding and falling on the slope. Snow suddenly begins to fall, more heavily than before. The slope flattens, and we can pick out a slight scrape in the earth, running parallel to our line of advance. It must be the German front trench.

Someone shouts, 'The Boches are running away. They're scared, they're beating it.' We can just make out vague shapes disappearing through the curtain of smoke. 'Forward – we've got them.'

It is just about at this moment that the first hostile fire reaches us. The note of a machine gun rises violently. Slanting in from the right, bursts of fire strike us in a hail, scything down half the assaulting wave. We jump from shell-hole to shell-hole, our numbers growing smaller at each leap. We arrive at the lip of the trench. But, by the worst of bad luck, it turns out to be only a shallow ditch, not much more than 15 inches deep. We flatten ourselves into it,

trying to be swallowed by the earth.

Another machine gun has joined in now. I just catch a glimpse of the one in front. If I could throw a grenade I could just reach it, but from here it's impossible. A yard behind me there is a deep shell-hole. I chuck my rifle into it, and follow it in a bound. But when I try to put a grenade into the cup, I find it full of mud, wipe it out with my scarf, and finally discharge it. I follow the grenade with my eyes, and scorning the risk, rise to watch it fall. A puff of smoke billows in front of the machine gun post. Too short. I hastily let fly a second. Too long. I have now been observed and the gun concentrates its fire on me. I only just manage to get another grenade away. I don't see where it lands but the machine gun falls silent.

Then all around me, there is a sudden rush and shouts of, 'Forward – this time we'll have them.' The right-hand machine gun has stopped firing. We push on for some yards and arrive at the German position. Large, round helmets emerge from the ground, arms wave in the air. 'Kamerad! Kamerad! Don't shoot.'

The captain, left behind by the suddenness of our charge, arrives whirling his cudgel. 'Don't kill them, don't kill them,' he shouts, but too late. Several have already been knocked flat, their heads battered in.

A great ox of a man, apparently an officer, rushes up and asks what troops we are. I haven't time to reply, for the captain is shouting, 'Come on, boys.' We leap across the captured trench. The bottom is full of empty cartridge cases. They had gone on firing until the last moment. The ground is rising. I pass close by the machine gun which I'd silenced. A man lies beside it. He is dead, his head resting on a heap of empty cartridge cases. Men without weapons emerge from every shell hole; comically, all show the same expression as they shout, 'Kamerad! Kamerad!'

We arrive on a plateau. The captain orders us to halt. The support companies are now going to pass through and continue the advance. Our part in the battle is over. In front of us the ground drops steeply into a ravine, the far slope of which is covered by the Bois D'Hardaumont, which is the other battalion's objective.

The Bois d'Hardaumont was taken the following day according to plan. All in all, Mangin's men had captured 11,387 prisoners, 115 pieces of artillery, 44 trench-mortars and 107 machine guns. The new front which it had established had deprived the Germans of all their points of observation over the city and fortress of Verdun. It also restored the French tactical situation to a very satisfactory footing.

Nivelle, who had remained on the Front only to see this final stage of his programme of limited offensives through, left Verdun on the evening of December 15 to 'take charge of the Armies of the North and the North-West', as the communiques put it, but in fact to replace Joffre as Commander-in-Chief. Mangin followed him on December 22 to take command of the Sixth Army. With their departure, the Battle of Verdun was brought to a close. It had cost both sides between 300,000 and 350,000 men each. At the end of the battle in December the lines stood very much where they had done before the battle had begun in February, and the German war machine finally ground to a halt.

THE SOMME BARRAGE

British and French tactics for the Somme offensive hinged upon a massive and prolonged artillery barrage. Despite recent examples to the contrary, it was hoped that an intense seven-day bombardment would destroy all German resistance and leave the way open for easy infantry penetration. Accordingly, the British and French marshalled over 1,300 heavy guns and more than 2,000,000 shells, and began to pound the German line. By the seventh day most of the shells had been fired with an effect so stunning that nearly all present were convinced that there could be nobody left alive in the German trenches.

The Somme barrage gets under way—British howitzers in action

So much tragedy, so much emotion now pervades our view of the First World War that we tend to overlook the perspective of the men involved, not least of those engaged in the direction of the war. For example, at the end of 1915 the British cabinet was appalled that they were not a whit nearer victory despite a year of hard fighting and a casualty list exceeding 500,000. But whenever they talked of an armistice, their debate was frustrated by an intolerable fact: Germany, the aggressor, the invader, occupied almost all Belgium and a rich tract of France. So, on December 28, the cabinet approved a paper of intention prepared by its war committee, which included this paragraph:

Every effort is to be made for carrying out the offensive operations next spring in the main theatre of war (France and Flanders) in close co-operation with the Allies, and in the greatest possible strength.

Yet within a week their apprehensions of mass slaughter persuaded them to hesitate. At the end of this paragraph, the following was added:

although it must not be assumed that such operations are finally decided on.

Weekly—sometimes daily—until April 1916, Mr Asquith and his cabinet colleagues, severally and collectively, discussed ways and means of defeating the Germans without heavy loss; all the while agreeing jointly with the French that 'we have to destroy the morale of the German Army and nation'. At length, with the crocuses bursting through the grass in St James's Park, with all prospect of a spring offensive past, the decision had to be taken. On April 7, the Chief of the Imperial General Staff, Sir William Robertson, was able to telegraph to General Haig in France that the government approved a combined offensive with the French in the summer.

The planning staffs of the Allied commanders-in-chief in France had not of course been waiting on this authority. Since February, Joffre and Haig had struck a form of bargain: they would

△ A British shell explodes in the German trenches prior to the attack on La Boiselle, half way along Fourth Army's front
◁ The lanyard is pulled, and one of the 1,732,873 shells expended by the Allies in the preliminary bombardment is fired from a British 8-inch Mk V howitzer

jointly undertake a major assault on the German defences on either side of the River Somme. They do not appear to have been attracted to this sector by any special strategic prize. It was more a matter of convenience: along the river the British and French armies joined together. When the bargain was made, Joffre believed that a common action round this junction point would make it easier for him to retain control of the timing and direction of the offensive. Haig's agreement was qualified by private reservations. While General Rawlinson and the headquarters of the newly created Fourth Army studied the Somme lines, preparations for offensive operations in other British sectors continued. Haig's preference was for a summer campaign in Flanders; but he was not anxious to be drawn into the battles of attrition which Joffre believed to be necessary. But while the planners of both nations were still busy at their maps and sums, their chiefs were reminded that the initiative did not lie with them alone. At 0430 hours in the morning of February 21, 1916, the Germans fired the first shot of their opening barrage at Verdun. After drenching the

French defences with high explosive for eight hours, the German and French infantry locked in a dreadful struggle.

The events at Verdun soon put the British and French at variance in the matter of timing for their summer offensive. As more and more French divisions were drawn in to bolster the crumbling French line across the Meuse—from which they emerged exhausted and depleted after a period of days—it was only reasonable from the French point of view that the British should be asked to hasten the date of the Allied offensive. A little after 11 o'clock on the morning of Friday, May 26, Joffre came to Haig's headquarters to ask directly for an opening date. 'The moment I mentioned August 15,' Haig wrote in his diary, 'Joffre at once got very excited and shouted that "The French Army would cease to exist if we did nothing till then". The rest of us looked on at this outburst of excitement, and then I pointed out that, in spite of August 15 being the most favourable date for the British Army to take action, yet in view of what he had said regarding the unfortunate condition of the French Army, I was prepared to commence operations on July 1 or thereabouts. This calmed the old man, but I saw he had come to the meeting prepared to combat a refusal on my part, and was prepared to be very nasty.'

In the previous winter, the French offensive had been conceived as a massive venture employing 40 divisions from the Somme southward to Lassigny. It was hoped that the British would employ 25 divisions to the north of the river. Now on the last day of May, the French President, Prime Minister and Minister for War came from Paris to see Haig with the brief that 'one can and one must foresee the eventuality of the British army conducting the offensive'. The change of view had already been recognised by Haig. Recounting the events of the meeting in his diary, he remarked: 'The slow output of French heavy guns was pointed out and the need for supplying Verdun with everything necessary was recognised, and I said that *in view of the possibility of the British having*

Joffre misconstrued Haig's reluctance; the question in the latter's mind was not 'whether?' but 'where?' When Joffre wrote blandly on June 3 to ask what notice Haig required to open the offensive on July 1, he obtained a straight answer—'12 days' notice for an attack on July 1 or later,' and a direct question, 'how many French divisions will be taking part?' Since Joffre's staff had been quite unable to find 20 divisions, the reply was vague: General Fayolle's Sixth Army would attack astride the Somme 'to support the British'. Now they had it. Fayolle had but 12 divisions and his assault frontage was limited to about eight miles. This contribution, necessarily diminished by the demands of Verdun, was but a fragment of the original scheme; but it was enough to ensure that the British would fight also on the Somme that summer.

The trenches of the British Fourth Army ran for 20 miles from the village of Hébuterne south across the Ancre to the Willow Stream by Fricourt, then east to the Bois

all the high ground to the valley of the Somme and south again across the Flaucourt plateau. Most importantly, the first line of German trenches had been cunningly dug amongst the many outcrops of the main ridge line, so as to command every approach from the west.

Aware of their enemy's advantages in observation, the British and French took care during their preparations, confining much of their movement and construction work to the night. They used wire netting, hessian and paint in camouflage successfully by day but had not the means or as yet the skill to deny all their activity to the air observers in aircraft or balloons. The very fact that the allied flying corps concentrated progressively to deny access to German aircraft and intensified their attacks on balloons confirmed that something of importance was happening to the west. The sightings of new roads, railways and hutments in rear, the glimpses of new battery positions, were more than enough

Joffre—he was anxious for a British effort to relieve pressure on the French at Verdun

General Rawlinson (left), Commander of the Fourth Army (the striking force), and Haig

Robertson, CIGS. On April 7 he passed on the government's approval of the offensive

to attack alone, it was most desirable to bring to France the Divisions which the Allies held at Salonika. Beat the Germans here and we can make what terms we like!'

Haig was now in difficulty. Having agreed to attack on the Somme so as to combine directly with the French it was now clear that France might not participate. There was a British plan for an independent attack in the sector but it showed little promise. Flanders beckoned Haig strongly still.

'D' day agreed

Joffre was aware from the reports of his liaison staff at the British headquarters that Haig was not enthusiastic for the Somme project. He feared that, lacking a French presence, the British might withdraw altogether from offensive action in 1916. The Russians had achieved nothing in their assaults round Lake Narotch and were asking urgently for heavy ordnance to help them in a new operation. The Italians were calling similarly for help after their defeat in the Trentino. The needs of these allies might offer a ready excuse for British inactivity in France. But

de Maricourt. The wood was held by the French, Maricourt village just behind was shared by British and French companies. Two miles to the south lay the left bank of the Somme. The country here, both north and south of the river, is downland, open grazing above rolling chalk hills with a scattering of woods. It had been a quiet sector. The woods and villages were mostly unbroken, the trees in full leaf; patches of the grassland were bright with larkspur.

Opposite both Rawlinson's and Fayolle's armies lay the *Second Army* of General Fritz von Below, comprised of three corps and, depleted by the removal of forces for the attack on Verdun, lacking any appreciable army reserve. In May, Below and his Chief-of-Staff, Grünert, became convinced that they were about to be attacked. From about Hébuterne to the Ancre, Below's regiments were on ground generally overlooked by the British though often hidden by woods and re-entrants. The Serre knoll was an important exception, offering an excellent view north-west to Hébuterne, west to the copses amongst the British trenches and south along the road to Beaucourt. Below the Ancre, the Germans held

to suggest what all this presaged.

While preparing to open the onslaught at Verdun, Falkenhayn had warned all army commanders that they must expect Allied relief attacks elsewhere. Since he would be unable to send reinforcements to any other point along the German line, he advised— and they would have needed very good reasons for ignoring his 'advice'—that each regimental front should be held in strength as far forward as possible. They should not surrender a metre of ground. If a section of trench should be lost it must be retaken immediately. The officers and men forward must understand that the order was to defend their position to the last man, to the last round; orders which would surely persuade them to fight tenaciously from the outset since they would realise that there was no hope of being told to fall back if pressure became intense. The consequences of this policy were twofold. First, as the majority of each division was within the range of the Allied field artillery, it was necessary to provide them with adequate shelter. Deep shafts were sunk into the chalk below the trenches and galleries were run out on either side, providing safe living quarters in dormitories for the soldiers and separate rooms for the officers. Fresh air was pumped in; stocks of bottled water, biscuits and tinned food were cached against emergencies when fresh rations could not be brought up daily. Secondly, surface strong points were provided a little in rear of each front trench to house medium machine guns and many of these positions were constructed in reinforced concrete by the end of June. In certain areas, the strong points were connected by tunnels to form enclosed fortresses. Throughout the second line of defence – on average 4,000 yards behind the first – there were deep dugouts and a number of deep shafts and galleries. When Below warned Falkenhayn of his expectations, he was sent an additional detachment of 8-inch howitzers, captured from the Russians, and a reinforcement of labour units to speed the development of the third line, five miles behind the first. Between mid-March and the beginning of June, the

ground and the lie of the trenches, it is quite conceivable that he will attempt only to pin the front of 26th Reserve Division *by artillery fire (that is, the ground immediately north and south of the Ancre valley), but he will not make a serious attack. To oppose (the French south of the Somme),* XVII Corps *is too weak, both in infantry and guns. Even against an enemy attack on a narrow front made only as a diversion the* Guard Corps *(on the extreme left of his line) is also too thin; it is holding 36 kilometres with 12 regiments, and behind it there are no reserves of any kind.*

It was on this day, June 6, that Haig accepted that he was committed to the Somme offensive. Perhaps due to the uncertainty, he had not given Rawlinson precise orders during the long preliminaries of reconnaissance and preparation, an omission which had inhibited Fourth Army commander. Yet, whatever his task was to be, Rawlinson was very clear by June that the enemy defences were formidable; any

went well, the cavalry under Gough should exploit any full breach of the enemy defence lines by passing through into the open country in the enemy rear while the infantry attack swung north towards Arras up the line of the enemy trenches. Alternatively, Haig's orders continued, 'after gaining our first objective as described we may find that a further advance eastwards is not advisable. In that case, the most profitable course will probably be to transfer our main efforts rapidly to another portion of the British front but leaving a sufficient force on the Fourth Army front to secure the ground gained, to compel the enemy to use up all his reserves and to prevent him from withdrawing them elsewhere.'

Between January and June, 19 divisions were sent to France to join the British Expeditionary Force. Eleven had seen active service before – some were Gallipoli veterans – the remainder were from the New Armies formed by Kitchener. By May, Rawlinson had 16 divisions in his army, in-

Fayolle, Commander of the French Sixth Army which played a much-reduced rôle in the attack

Roger Viollet

Below, Commander of the German *Second Army* which was understrength and lacking in reserves

Ullstein

General Horne, Commander of the British XV Corps facing the corner stone of the German line

German wire was consistently thickened in front of the forward defences.

Despite the progress made in preparations against enemy attack, Below and Grünert remained anxious. In each divisional area, almost all the infantry were committed to the first line; even the corps reserves had been tapped to man trenches at critical points between divisions. On May 25, Grünert proposed to Supreme Headquarters that they should make a preventive attack on the British front. He asked tentatively for more infantry. With the battle at Verdun at its height, there were none, though Falkenhayn made no objection to a local venture within their own resources. As encouragement, he sent two more batteries of artillery. By June 6, Below was more sanguine about the British threat but still very anxious about the French below the Somme. He reported that: *The preparations of the British in the area Serre-Gommecourt, as well as the increase of 29 emplacements of artillery in the past few days, detected by air photographs, lead to the conclusion that the enemy thinks first and foremost of attacking the projecting angles of Fricourt and Gommecourt. In view of the*

attempt to breach the two main lines would be costly. Imaginative and shrewd, he was also an ambitious man. In April, it is probable that he hoped to cover himself against failure by suggesting that: *It does not appear to me that the gain of 2 or 3 more kilometres of ground is of much consequence, or that the existing situation is so urgent to demand that we should incur very heavy losses in order to draw a large number of German reserves against this portion of our front. Our object rather seems to be to kill as many Germans as possible with the least loss to ourselves, and the best way to do this appears to me to be to seize points of tactical importance which will provide us with good observation and which we may feel certain the Germans will counterattack under disadvantages likely to conduce heavy losses.*

Haig rebuked him for this limited view but it was June 16 before the strategic concept was finally made clear, when the principal objectives were issued to Fourth Army and subsidiaries to First, Second and Third, acting in support. In brief, Rawlinson was to seize the main feature in front of him between the Ancre and Montauban. If all

cluding a share of those recently arrived, and had allocated three to each of his five corps headquarters. His plan envisaged an assault by two divisions in each corps with the third ready to exploit or reinforce. In retrospect, there is an ominous similarity in the orders issued within each formation for the first assault, even though the ground and the enemy in front of each division was markedly different. But it is easy to criticise, to forget that an operation was developing on a scale never attempted before by the British army. Its professional commanders still had much to learn in the handling of vast numbers of men; their communications were inadequate for the type of operation envisaged; many of the subordinate commanders and staffs were amateurs, the majority of the regimental officers and men raw. None knew this better than Haig. It may sometimes be said of him that he was overconfident in himself but he was seriously concerned to keep matters simple for the assault forces, without inhibiting the enterprise of the junior commanders. Stage by stage he discussed the tactics to be employed with Rawlinson, and with Allenby whose right flank corps was to attack Gommecourt as Rawlinson's men went forward.

Along the whole front from mid-June onwards there were to be local attacks and raids: no hint was to be given that one sector was more important than another. A barrage of some days' duration was to be fired by the Royal Artillery with the aim of breaking the enemy wire and destroying the other defences; eroding the strength of the German troops in the first line; reducing to as great an extent as possible their guns, howitzers and mortars by a great weight of counter battery fire; and striking the enemy's routes forward into the battle area. Because telephone lines were so often cut, all British artillery fire for the assault was to be controlled by time. At a given time, zero hour, the guns would lift to let the infantry cross No-Man's Land into the first of the enemy trenches. After a time judged to be adequate to complete the subjection of these, the fire would lift again to permit a second advance. Provided the Germans knew and obeyed the rules of this theory, the general plan must succeed.

were directed to pass through both the first and second lines to capture the Flaucourt plateau. To support this attack, the French artillery was to fire for eight days beforehand, 117 heavy batteries supplementing the many field and medium guns.

The British artillery support for the offensive was unique. The preliminary bombardment was to be fired over five days, U, V, W, X and Y. On U and V days the gunners were to register and cut enemy barbed wire; on W, X and Y the shells were to rain on enemy defences while wire-cutting continued. Counter-battery fire would feature on every day. There would be checks and pauses to deceive the enemy, to persuade them that an assault had begun so that they would hasten up the steep ladders from their shelters to man the fire strips only to be raked with shellfire. When these stratagems no longer tricked the foe, gas would be fired to persuade them that an assault had begun at last. The programme for Z day, the day of assault, was so arranged that the usual 80-minute bombardment at that time should be fired for only 65

Joffre suggested, for Z day. After some demur, the 29th was accepted at GHQ. At 0700 hours on June 24, therefore, the first of the heavy guns was loaded and the gun position officer cried 'Fire'. The bombardment had begun.

Sunday the 25th was a fine warm day in contrast to two preceding days of summer storms. The Royal Flying Corps scouted or spotted for the guns. They found 102 enemy batteries and began early the counter-bombardment. But this was the last day of good weather for some time. Morning mist, low cloud and bursts of heavy rainfall hampered observation on the ground and in the air. Numbers of dud shells or fuses delayed still more the gunners' work. The high rate of fire wore seriously the buffer springs and smoothed those gun barrels which had already once been relined. On Wednesday, it was decided to go on firing until the 1st and assault on that day. Forward, the infantry trenches were manned by skeleton forces while the bulk of each battalion rested in such billets as could be found immediately in rear. On the Friday night, June 30,

Loading one of the 305-mm guns, part of the massive French barrage

A mine explodes under the Hawthorne Redoubt ten minutes before zero

Imperial War Museum

In the French sector, General Fayolle had borne with good humour the many visits paid to him. The British called periodically and a valuable friendship developed with Rawlinson and his headquarters. Amongst the French, Foch appeared often. As Commander of the northern group of armies it was his task to distil practical directions from the high sounding but vague orders issued by Joffre's staff for the offensive. Foch wished to delay the attack of Fayolle's army for at least several days after the British attack, believing that the French divisions would gain the advantage of surprise. Understandably, Rawlinson did not agree; one of Fayolle's corps, XX, was directly on his right on the north bank of the river. Any delay by the French here would uncover his flank. Foch continued to argue doggedly for his proposal and won eventually the concession that the I Colonial and XXXV Corps south of the river might attack a little after zero but on the same morning. The objective of XX Corps was Hem, where they expected to breach the enemy first line. The other two

minutes. It was hoped that the enemy would be sufficiently used to the former to stay below while the British infantry crossed.

This mass of shells and mortar bombs, high explosive, shrapnel and phosphorus gas was to fall upon a frontage of attack of 25,000 yards. 1,010 British field guns and howitzers, 427 heavies and 100 French pieces fired for Rawlinson's army. 2,000,000 shells and bombs lay stacked ready for their use.

Vague orders

As all the preparations went forward, there were a series of final crises among the Allied chiefs as to Z day. On June 12 the Germans renewed the assault at Verdun and Clemenceau sought to bring down Briand's government in Paris. Joffre urged Haig to bring forward the opening date to June 25. Haig agreed. On the evening of the 16th came a telephone call to say that Verdun was secure and Briand's government had won a vote of confidence. June 29, even July 1, would now be preferable,

commanding officers consulted with their brigade commanders and there were some disquieting reports that long stretches of enemy wire remained uncut. Still the boom and bang of the bombardment, faithfully maintained by the weary gunners after a week, raised many hopes.

Early on the Sunday morning, July 1, the clouds cleared. Breakfast was eaten in the dark, kit was packed and dumped. Company guides began to lead their fellows forward across the dark wet ground. The German lines were quiet as the soldiers marched heavily into the foremost trenches, weighed down with full marching order: rifle and ammunition, grenades or bombs, a digging tool and perhaps some other special load. Below ground, the miners waited, sweating in the heat of the narrow tunnels leading to the mine chambers they had cut under the enemy positions.

The warm sun rose dispelling the mist. It was Z day. Zero hour approached.

Right: The guns at work – a painting by Hamlyn Reid entitled *Barrage on the Somme*

The date is agreed. Early on Sunday morning the clouds cleared. It was Z day, Zero hour

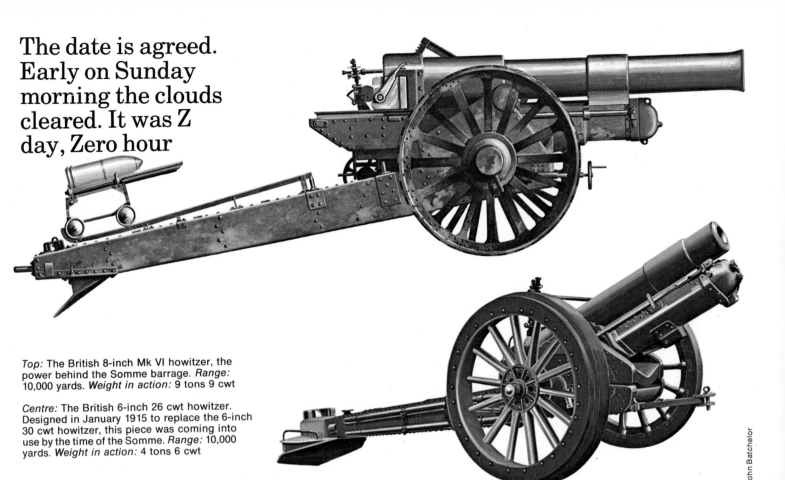

Top: The British 8-inch Mk VI howitzer, the power behind the Somme barrage. *Range:* 10,000 yards. *Weight in action:* 9 tons 9 cwt

Centre: The British 6-inch 26 cwt howitzer. Designed in January 1915 to replace the 6-inch 30 cwt howitzer, this piece was coming into use by the time of the Somme. *Range:* 10,000 yards. *Weight in action:* 4 tons 6 cwt

John Batchelor

Imperial War Museum

A GENERATION SACRIFICED

At 0730 hours on July 1 the greatest barrage ever fired by the British army lifted, and the first wave went 'over the top'. Never had so many men walked so confidently to a certain death — for the barrage had not done its job of destroying all resistance. Innumerable German machine-gunners emerged unscathed from their deep dugouts and began to mow down the heavily-laden attackers. The blood-bath of the Somme had started

Over the top

Imperial War Museum

July 1 dawned under a cloudless sky. The German lines, visible through patches of low-lying mist, seemed very quiet. The British and French gunfire was intense from the early hours of the morning and rose to a furious climax shortly before zero hour, when trench mortars joined it with a rapid bombardment of 30 rounds a minute. At that point the German batteries also opened up strongly. During the night the assault troops had quietly moved up to their action stations, and the wire in front of their trenches had been cleared away. At 0730 hours on July 1, 1916, the Allied guns lengthened their range, and within seconds whistles blew, and along the whole 25-mile front north of the Somme the Allied infantry, with bayonets fixed, went over the top as one man.

The attack on the German first line (disregarding for the moment the French supporting action south of the Somme, which commenced two hours later) had been planned as a coherent operation, and neither in the weight of the bombardment nor the timing and tactical methods of the initial attack had any distinction been made between the weaker and stronger parts of the German defence line. However, the very uneven effect of the bombardment and other factors had increased the diversity of fighting conditions in different sections of the front, so that from the earliest stage

the operation dissolved into a number of separate battles, the outcome of which ranged from full success to disastrous failure. They must, therefore, be considered one by one.

We will begin with the southern sector containing, on the German side, the villages of Montauban, Hardecourt and Curlu. The British XIII Corps, commanded by General Congreve, V.C., started from a position facing north, between Carnoy and Maricourt, on the lower slopes of the Montauban ridge. On its right the French XXII Corps advanced simultaneously from a line between Maricourt and the river—the first time in the war that British and French units were joined in action. On this sector the bombardment had done its work well. Moreover, the Germans had not expected that this part of the front would be included in the first assault; in fact, they had planned the overdue relief of their tired *109th Reserve Regiment*, which was holding the line opposite the British corps, for the morning of that day. In these comparatively favourable circumstances it was possible for the assault forces to carry out their tasks more or less according to plan, and despite determined German resistance they did so with great dash.

The XIII Corps was composed of the 30th, the 18th (Eastern), and the 9th Divisions; the last-named was in reserve two miles

behind the front and did not take part in the day's fighting. The objectives of the 30th Division were to be reached in two stages, the first being the capture of Dublin Trench, which, about 1,000 yards behind the German front line, connected the two strongpoints of Dublin Redoubt at the eastern, and Glatz Redoubt at the western end. At Dublin Redoubt contact was to be re-established with the left wing of the French corps. The second stage was the capture of Montauban, the heights lying immediately beyond it, and a trench, Nord Alley, which ran east of the village down to Dublin Redoubt and was to protect the right flank.

The advance on Dublin Trench was the work of the 89th Brigade, whose two leading battalions, the 17th King's and 20th King's, crossed the 500 yards of No-Man's Land with but few casualties, and found the barbed wire well cut. They overran the feebly defended front trenches easily, leaving it to special mopping-up parties to take prisoner the 300 or more Germans who were still in their dugouts. The second line of trenches was also quickly reached and taken; so quickly, in fact, that further progress was delayed for a short time because the artillery barrage covering the advance had not yet lifted from the position which the brigade was about to attack. For, consistently with the rigid tactical planning of the offensive, the British batteries were under orders to keep to their fixed time-table and 'lanes' of fire: the alternative system of 'creeping' barrages, that is, series of short lifts more closely adapted to the actual movements of the infantry, had been rejected as involving too great a risk of error and confusion. However, as soon as the barrage had lifted, the 89th Brigade pressed on and at 0830 hours they arrived at Dublin Trench, which was deserted and battered almost out of existence, so that the two battalions had no further task for the day but to repair the trench and consolidate their positions generally. At the same time, another unit entered Dublin Redoubt to link up with the French, who had already arrived there.

The 21st Brigade had to fight harder and suffered heavier casualties before reaching their objective, Glatz Redoubt. Its leading battalion also had no difficulty in getting beyond the German front trenches, but their subsequent advance was held up by raking machine gun and rifle fire from 'The Warren', a network of German trenches which, though for the greater part situated in the area of the 18th Division, protruded slightly into that of the 30th. The battalion affected, the 18th King's Liverpool, lost nearly three-quarters of its effectives in this engagement before the survivors were able to scatter the German party. After that the advance was rapid. At 0835 hours the 21st Brigade entered the redoubt and linked up with the 89th Brigade in Dublin Trench. The 30th Division had therefore fully attained the first objective in just over an hour.

Screened by a smoke barrage

The 90th Brigade, which had been waiting in a sheltered valley west of Maricourt, now moved from its assembly trenches in order to mount the attack on Montauban through the new positions of the 21st Brigade. The 18th Manchesters and the 17th Manchesters reached these positions ahead of time, but on the way up they had had to pass through a German artillery barrage and the punishing fire of a well-concealed machine gun. Their losses had been considerable; all the commanders of the leading companies had been killed or severely wounded. There was some hesitation whether an immediate further advance on Montauban should be risked. It would mean that the assault columns had to go forward with their left flank exposed, for the right wing of 18th Division was hanging back. On the other hand, it was realised that the quick fall of Montauban would greatly benefit the operations

of the 18th Division, and as soon as the covering barrage had lifted, the brigade charged up the slope. It was in some disarray owing to the heavy casualties it had suffered, but it was effectively screened from enemy observation by a smoke barrage launched from Glatz Redoubt. The task turned out to be much easier than expected, since the Germans had by that time recognised the hopelessness of their position. The attackers found the trench along the southern edge of Montauban and the ruins of the village deserted; and a few hundred German soldiers left in the trench on the ridge 200 yards north of Montauban—it was the eastern stretch of the defence line called Montauban Alley—surrendered without a fight. Nord Alley had been secured in the meantime, and the successful operations of the 30th Division were rounded off with the capture of an important German observation post at La Briqueterie, to the east of Montauban. Fighting had ceased before 1300 hours; during the rest of the day the troops were hard at work digging new trenches and building supporting strongholds in anticipation of a German counterattack on Montauban.

The 18th Division, under the command of Major-General Maxse, had been in the area around the village of Carnoy since March 1916 and was therefore well acquainted with the terrain and the nature of the German defences. Its first objective, corresponding to that of the 30th Division, was the Train Alley/Pommiers Trench line, which was the continuation of Dublin Trench westwards from Glatz Redoubt, to be reached by 0830 hours. The Germans had abandoned their first trench line on this front and withdrawn to the support line, Breslau Trench; but in No-Man's Land they had fortified and manned a large crater field, which had come into being as a result of extensive mine fighting during May. It was a formidable obstacle and its existence was one of the reasons why the three brigades of the division made progress at very different speeds.

The 54th Brigade, forming the left wing, advanced between two mines which men of the Royal Engineers had set off a few minutes before zero. The destructive and demoralising effect of these mines had been considerable, so that the brigade had little difficulty in overrunning the German front and support lines. The 11th Royal Fusiliers on the left then moved on so quickly that they arrived at Pommiers Trench, the first objective, when the trench was still under the fire of the British artillery. The advance of the other leading battalion, the 7th Bedfordshire, was al-

most as quick, although it had severe losses before the German machine guns in the third trench could be rushed. Both battalions entered Pommiers Trench at 0750 hours. At the same time the 53rd Brigade also arrived there, having overcome resistance from the western edge of the crater field in No-Man's Land with the aid of a flame-thrower, and crushed some stiff German opposition at several points behind Breslau Trench. The brigade did not, however, succeed in capturing the strongpoint The Loop at the eastern end of Pommiers Trench, and one of its battalions, the 6th Royal Berkshire, lost 12 officers and 339 other ranks in the attempt. The two leading battalions of the 54th and 10th Essex of the 53rd Brigade then advanced on Pommiers Redoubt, which was situated about 300 yards behind Pommiers Trench. A frontal assault failed, but by means of outflanking movements the attackers managed to penetrate through the barbed wire on the western and eastern sides of the redoubt, and after savage hand-to-hand fighting the last few survivors of the garrison surrendered at 0930 hours.

The hardest fighting of the morning fell to the lot of the 55th Brigade on the right. The advance of 7th Queen's across No-Man's Land was slowed down by heavy machine gun fire from the eastern part of the crater area, into which a party of the 7th Buffs had vainly tried to force an entry. By the time the 7th Queen's approached what had been the German support line, but was now, in fact, their front line, their strength had been greatly reduced, the British barrage had already moved on, and the Germans had rushed reinforcements to the trench and the strongpoints behind it. In consequence, the advance of the battalion came to a halt before Breslau Trench. This check also affected the 8th East Surrey on the right, for their left flank was exposed to enfilades while they were struggling to overcome enemy resistance in the already-mentioned maze of trenches, The Warren. Only when the Germans in The Warren began to fear for their line of retreat after the fall of Glatz Redoubt, and gradually withdrew, did the 8th East Surreys, now supported by two companies of the 7th Buffs, succeed in getting near their first objective, Train Alley, which, however, they had no longer the strength to attack immediately.

Two and a half hours after zero it looked as if the 18th Division, despite its successes on the left wing, might not be able to attain the objectives of the day; but with the fall of Montauban and Pommiers Redoubt German resistance in the whole area weakened considerably. Shortly after 1000 hours the

While their comrades in the foreground take cover, men of the 34th Division press their attack on La Boiselle

French infantry, more successful than the British, advance across trenches captured from the Germans. The photograph was taken from a French aeroplane

7th Queen's finally cleared Breslau Trench and moved up to Train Alley, and a little later The Loop surrendered to the 6th Royal Berkshires. Only in one stronghold, about midway between Breslau Trench and Train Alley, did the Germans maintain themselves, but this could not stop the general British advance. The Germans were forced to withdraw from Montauban Alley at one point after another into the Caterpillar Valley, which lay beyond the ridge. Finally, the seizure of two advanced lines immediately overlooking the valley was accomplished without difficulty, and the success of the XIII Corps was complete.

The famous 'Iron Corps'

The French XXII Corps—the famous 'Iron Corps', which had distinguished itself in the Battle of Verdun—found it even easier than the British 30th Division did to overrun the whole of the German first position. The objective of the corps was a line running about 1,000 yards behind the German front; Hardecourt was just outside, Curlu inside that line. The French troops crossed No-Man's Land under the useful cover of a thick morning mist. They found the German trenches, and even many of the dugouts, completely destroyed and the greatly outnumbered enemy unable to put up more than sporadic resistance. An exception were the detachments of the *63rd* and *6th Bavarian Reserve Regiments* that garrisoned Curlu. The first attack on that village was repulsed by a counterattack of the

Bavarians, and the French had to form a provisional front facing Curlu. Everywhere else the objectives had been reached by mid-day, and when the 30th Division, with which the French had linked up at Glatz Redoubt, captured Montauban, the commander of the French 39th Division suggested a joint attack on Hardecourt with, possibly, a further advance upon the German second position. It was a tempting suggestion, but as at that time the situation in part of the area of the 18th Division was precarious and the 30th Division might be ordered to lend a helping hand, the French proposal had to be rejected. In fact, a golden opportunity was missed in this way. We know now that the Germans expected and feared an attack on Hardecourt, for they had hardly any forces left to defend it. In the afternoon the French renewed their operations against Curlu, and after a fierce bombardment lasting over an hour the village was stormed at 1830 hours.

In the sector of Lieutenant-General Horne's XV Corps, adjoining the XIII Corps on the left, the front described a sharp curve around the village of Fricourt, so that the right wing of the XV Corps was facing north, the left wing east. The German defences, held by six battalions of the *28th Reserve Division,* were particularly strong in this area. Fricourt and the village of Mametz, east of Fricourt, were veritable fortresses, and a tight network of trenches extended over an area of 1,200 yards in depth. From the apex of the

triangle formed by Fricourt and the wood behind it started the Willow Stream Valley, the stream itself forming the demarcation line between the areas allotted to the 7th Division and the 21st Division respectively. The German second position was here three miles behind the front line, and there were two strong intermediary lines: Fritz Trench—Railway Alley—Crucifix Trench and White Trench—Wood Trench—Quadrangle Trench; this second intermediary line was the final objective that the corps was to reach on the first day. Fricourt was considered too strong for an immediate frontal assault: part of the right brigade of the 21st Division and the left brigade of the 7th Division therefore remained in their front trenches for the time being, waiting for the other battalions to isolate Fricourt village and Fricourt Wood by their advance. It was also hoped that successful operations in the adjoining sectors —that of the XIII Corps on the right and of the III Corps on the left—would threaten the safety of the whole German position in the Fricourt sector and so lead to a collapse of German resistance.

The advance of the 7th Division, south of the Willow Stream Valley, had two immediate objects: to capture Mametz and to form a defensive flank facing Fricourt. On the front of the outer brigade, the 91st, No-Man's Land was only 150 to 200 yards wide, and German opposition in the front trenches was exceptionally weak; but machine gun and rifle fire from Mametz and from Danzig Alley, a deep trench running through the village from the south and continuing eastwards, inflicted heavy losses on the leading battalions. Despite this they advanced steadily uphill, and shortly after 0800 hours the 1st South Staffordshires, having rushed Cemetery Trench close to the southern edge of Mametz, were beginning to penetrate into the village, while at the same time the 22nd Manchesters were occupying Bucket Trench, less than 200 yards away from the first intermediary line. From then on, however, German resistance stiffened. The bulk of the South Staffordshires were forced to fall back on Cemetery Trench, and the advance of the 22nd Manchesters was halted. Reinforcements from the supporting battalions failed at first to improve the situation. It was only after two heavy re-bombardments of Danzig Alley and Fritz Trench beyond it that the tide turned again. More reinforcements were brought up, and before 1400 hours Danzig Alley and a section of Fritz Trench were in British possession. By that time the 1st South Staffordshires had resumed the attack on Mametz, this time with success.

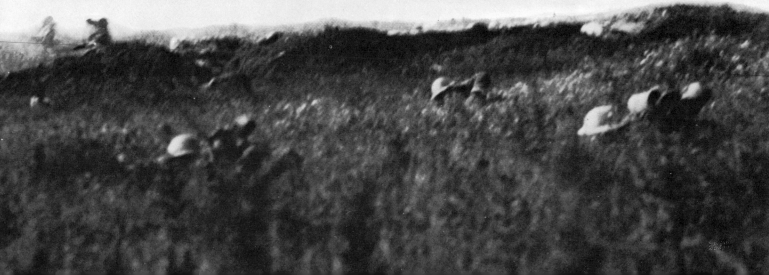

Only the northern quarter of the village was still in German hands.

Whilst the operations against Mametz, though more difficult and time-consuming than expected, thus proceeded satisfactorily, the 20th Brigade struggled in vain to establish the defensive line towards Fricourt, a line which was to run from a point east of Bois Français near the front trenches of the 22nd Brigade to the north-western edge of Mametz. The 2nd Border Regiment on the left got past the German front line fairly easily, and in spite of heavy casualties during their further advance reached their objective, Apple Alley, shortly after 1000 hours. On the right wing of the brigade, the 2nd Gordon Highlanders rushed the German defenders in the front trench before these could throw the bombs with which they were preparing to meet the attack; only the left company suffered severely when it was held up by a stretch of uncut wire. Subsequently, however, the battalion was exposed to heavy fire from The Shrine, a strongpoint in front of Cemetery Trench, and stubborn resistance had to be overcome before it could occupy Shrine Alley, about 300 yards behind the

so heavily that they were forced to stop their advance when they had taken the front trench. This check had not been expected; the supporting battalions had been ordered to pass through the lines of the leading battalions to the second objective of the day between 0830 hours and 0900 hours, by which time it had been hoped the first objective would be in British hands, but instead of this they had to be sent up as reinforcements in order to carry the advance beyond the German front trench. Eventually the brigade reached the Sunken Road and detachments moved into Crucifix Trench. A counterattack by strong German bombing parties was repulsed. The 64th Brigade captured the German front and support trenches within ten minutes, although the two leading battalions had lost most of their officers and more than half of their effectives in No-Man's Land. There was again some hard fighting before the brigade reached Sunken Road and could send parties forward to occupy Crucifix Trench. Any advance on the second objective, however, had to be postponed because of the machine gun and rifle fire which came from the woods lying ahead.

in the III Corps area to the north matters were developing as satisfactorily as they were in fact in the sector of the XIII Corps. Even so, he could make such a decision only by almost wilfully ignoring the known facts of the situation. The 50th Brigade HQ pointed out that the 7th Green Howards, on the left of the intended attack, were facing the strongest German defences in the whole area and would have practically no chance after the elimination of the 10th West Yorkshires, who had been meant to provide the necessary protection on the Green Howards' left flank. The protest was in vain, and the results were foreseeable. The battalion ran into a devastating machine gun barrage as soon as they left their trenches; within minutes it lost 15 officers and 336 other ranks. The survivors held on in shell holes in No-Man's Land until darkness allowed them to return to their starting positions. The 7th East Yorkshires, trying to come up in support of the Green Howards, suffered a similar fate. The 22nd Brigade of the 7th Division, attacking with two companies of the 20th Manchesters and a company of the 1st Royal Fusiliers, also failed, if less catas-

▽ Tractors bringing up British 8-inch howitzers at Death Valley, near Mametz. The men are sheltering from shell bursts straddling the road
▷ French and British progress on the first day

front line and still far short of the objective, Orchard Alley; and for the time being no further progress could be achieved. In the centre of the 20th Brigade's front the 9th Devonshires were unable to penetrate beyond the German support trench, and it took death-defying courage to get even this far. From their first steps into No-Man's Land, here 400 yards wide, they came under punishing fire from high ground behind the German front trench, from Fricourt Wood, and from the trenches south of Mametz. By the time the battalion had reached and cleared the German support trench it had suffered crippling losses, most of them in No-Man's Land.

A strong counterattack

The 21st Division, attacking in an easterly direction, disposed of four brigades, the 50th Brigade having been attached from the 17th Division. The 62nd Brigade was in reserve. The 63rd and 64th Brigades had as their first objective the occupation of Crucifix Trench, but in order to reach it they had to clear a sunken road running about 700 yards behind the German front line. The left battalion of the 50th Brigade, the 10th West Yorkshires, was to form the defensive line towards Fricourt.

The two leading battalions of the 63rd Brigade crept into No-Man's Land five minutes before zero hour, but were detected by the German machine gunners and lost

Just as the 20th Brigade did not succeed, as we have seen, in forming a front towards Fricourt in the area south of the Willow Stream Valley, the 10th West Yorkshires of the 50th Brigade failed to do so on their side, and here the failure was much more calamitous. The leading companies passed through No-Man's Land without much difficulty and reached Red Cottage at the northern fringe of Fricourt. But before the third and fourth companies could reach the German front trench, the defenders had brought out their machine guns from the dugouts. Exposed to murderous fire from several directions, both companies were practically annihilated in No-Man's Land; only a few survivors got as far as the front trench, where they held out until nightfall. All the regimental staff, including the Lieutenant-Colonel in command, were killed. The companies at Red Cottage were now completely isolated and succumbed to German counterattacks later in the morning.

The direct attack on Fricourt, to be carried out by the centre of the XIII Corps, was scheduled for 1430 hours, and the corps commander persisted in this plan although neither of the wings had achieved the measure of success which had been considered an essential precondition. He was motivated by an overoptimistic view of the general situation, partly engendered by the totally misleading information that

trophically. The leading companies crossed No-Man's Land without serious loss and occupied the trenches immediately behind the German front line, but the support units sustained crippling losses, so that the assault lost its initial momentum. After a series of fierce attacks and counterattacks the brigade was able to hold on in the German positions which they had captured, including the second support trench and stronghold known as 'The Rectangle', but a further advance on Fricourt could not even be attempted.

During the afternoon, nothing of importance happened in the area of the 21st Division, but the 7th Division managed to reach the whole of its first objective against gradually diminishing German resistance. The northern part of Mametz was captured, after a last desperate stand by a small German party, at 1600 hours; the bulk of the garrison and the staff of the *109th Reserve Regiment* had withdrawn earlier. By evening the entire Fritz Trench had been cleared, junction had been made with the left wing of the XIII Corps, and the flank facing Fricourt had been established.

If the successes of the XV Corps in the Fricourt Salient were much less complete than those of the XIII Corps in the Montauban sector they were still quite satisfactory. Fricourt itself was still in German hands, but it was abundantly clear that the Germans would not be able to hold the

THIRD ARMY

37   Front   2nd   3rd

46   91 Res Div

Fonquevillers   Ablainzevelle   Ervillers

VII
Corps   Gommecourt   Bucquoy   15 Res Div
                55 Res Div
        56   Achiet
Hebuterne   170 Div   le Grand
        48 Div   Achiet
FOURTH   52 Div   le Petit
ARMY   66 Div
        31 Div   Puisieux   Grevillers   Bapaume
                    au Mont   SECOND ARMY
VIII   169 Div   Irles   XIV Res Corps
Corps   4 Div   121 Div   Miraumont   Pys   Beaulencourt
        Beaumont   26 Res Div
Mailly   Hamel   119 Res Div   Grandcourt   le Sars   le Transloy
Maillet
        29 Div   10 Bav Div
        Hamel   Courcelette
X Corps   36   99 Res   Thiepval   Martinpuich   Flers
        49   Div
        32 Div   180 Div   Pozieres
III Corps   8 Div   Ovillers   28 Res Div
Aveluy   la Boiselle   185 Div
                Contalmaison   Longueval
        19 Div   Guillemont
        34 Div   110 Res Div   62 Div   12 Res
        21 Div   111 Res   109   Div   Combles
        Albert   17 Div   Div   Fricourt   Montauban
                    Mametz   7   18   30   12 Div
Ancre   (VI Corps)   Hardecourt
        XV Corps   XIII   Maurepas
                        Corps   Maricourt
BRITISH & FRENCH   XX
FRONT LINE AT ZERO   Corps
OBJECTIVES FOR JULY 1
SUCCESSFUL ATTACKS
UNSUCCESSFUL ATTACKS
POSITIONS GAINED & HELD AT NIGHT
Morlancourt   GERMAN
FRONT 2nd 3rd LINES
LOST TRENCHES
RAILWAYS   Hem   Clery
ROADS
0 MILES   3
Somme
0 KMS   4

HEIGHT IN FEET   SIXTH
OVER 140   ARMY   56
100 - 140
UNDER 100   12I Div   XVII
Herbecourt   Corps

Within the first twelve hours 60% of the officers and 40% of the men had become casualties

◁ A working party of men from various regiments in a sunken road near La Boiselle on the British lines of communication. On the left is a stretcher party, and behind them are German prisoners
▽ Bringing in the wounded at Beaumont Hamel. Total British casualties on the first day were 57,470. French losses were comparatively light

position for very long. In the areas north and south of the Willow Stream the British forces had penetrated the strong German defences in a depth of over 2,000 yards, and the capture of Mametz was an important achievement by itself. The cost, however, had been heavy: the casualties of the day numbered over 8,000 – about 2,000 more than the casualties of the XIII Corps.

In dealing with the southern part of the front we have described the movements of the units engaged in the attack in some detail. This was possible and appropriate because conditions in the front zone of the German defences were, on the whole, as the general staff had assumed them to be, even if German resistance was rather stiffer, and British losses were consequently higher, than had been hoped. With one or two exceptions, the assault forces managed to accomplish the first task of clearing the enemy's front positions, and that being done, an orderly advance on planned objectives could begin. There were delays and setbacks, but only within a margin that must be allowed for in the planning of any large-scale operation; and where unexpected situations arose in individual cases, officers and men usually showed themselves adaptable enough to deal with them.

Unsurpassable courage
However, when we turn to the sectors north of the Fricourt Salient we are confronted with an entirely different picture. Along that whole front the effect of the preparatory bombardment had been miscalculated, and the aims of the attack were thwarted before the troops could come to grips with the enemy. It would be misleading to describe these events as if we were concerned with properly conducted military operations. There would be no sense in trying to assess success or failure in different parts of the front with reference to tactical objectives when, in fact, plans broke down almost everywhere from the start, and none of the day's objectives was approached, let alone reached. The British attack presents a story of unsurpassable courage and discipline; but if we consider that warfare, for all its horror, can still have an element of reason and purpose, then military history reached one of its lowest points on that day in 1916.

Shortly before zero hour, the Middlesex and Devons left their assembly positions and began to crawl across No-Man's Land, towards the German front line trenches. A storm of bullets from machine guns and rifles met this advance, much of the fire being in enfilade from the direction of La Boisselle and Orvillers. The space to be crossed was anything between 500 and 700 yards, a terribly long distance when the advance had to be made through a perfect hail of bullets. Moreover the enemy began to speed up his barrage and soon four shells a minute were falling in No-Man's Land and the British trenches beyond. At 0730 hours the barrage lifted and the Middlesex and Devons rushed towards the enemy's trenches. The first three waves of both battalions were shot to pieces. Of the first wave only a few gallant survivors reached the German front line, some men of the Middlesex crossing the enemy's front line and getting actually as far as his second line; they were never seen again.

At 0800 hours a message reached battalion headquarters from the brigade that the enemy's front line had not been forced and C Company was ordered to delay its advance. But at about 0823 hours, as the nerve-racking 'rat-tat-tat' of the enemy's machine guns, from across No-Man's Land, seemed to have died down, C Company was ordered to advance. On reaching the front line trenches, however, the reason hostile machine gun fire had died down was at once apparent: all movement in No-Man's Land had ceased. The intervening space – that dread space of dead land – was littered with motionless forms. The head of B Company had apparently penetrated the enemy's trenches; their helmets could be seen on the parapet and still and inert bodies hung over the enemy's wire. All was comparatively silent and the survivors of the company lay close in shell holes in front of the battered entanglements. On the parapet of the enemy's trenches could be seen the bodies of West Yorkshiremen, intermingled with those of men of the Middlesex and Devon Regiments. All were still, dead and living alike, for any movement instantly brought down a hail of machine gun and rifle bullets.

These quotations from the diary of a battalion refer to incidents that happened in the sector of the III Corps, but with different names of places and units they might describe the situation at almost any point between Gommecourt and La Boisselle. In many places the assault was completely stopped in No-Man's Land; in others small groups persevered and overran the nearest German trenches, but since the strength of the German dugouts had been underrated, not enough emphasis had been laid in the instructions on the need of 'mopping up': when the attackers had passed and were advancing under fire from the defences in front of them, the Germans climbed out of their dugouts and opened fire from the rear. Even in the few cases when larger columns, already crippled by their losses in No-Man's Land, managed to penetrate to some point in the depth of the German first position they found themselves isolated and were lucky if they could fight their way back to the trenches from which they had started. Such actions were gallant forays, but they were not, as they were meant to be, part of a general advance, and they brought no tactical advantage. Inevitably, communication between battalion and brigade headquarters, brigade and division headquarters, and division and corps headquarters broke down to a large extent in such conditions, and there was another factor which contributed to the general lack of direction: the commanders of divisions were expressly forbidden to make personal inspections of the combat zones. The nature of the fighting has been summed up by a German eyewitness: *The special mark of the battle of the Somme was this: wherever the attackers met some resistance they split apart. Thrust was followed by counterthrust, and in each narrow space there was utter destruction without any larger purpose. Like two beasts of prey, each of which has sunk its fangs so deeply into the other's flesh that it cannot let go, so the two armies were tearing one another to pieces, and soon the leaders on either side were but impotent bystanders; all they could do was to send fresh forces forward, but they could not bring about any change in the monotony of the battle.* The confusion, as the quotation indicates, was as great on the German as on the British side, though, of course, the Germans had an essentially more straightforward task, namely, to prevent a British breakthrough at any threatened point.

Sheer madness

The disasters of July 1, 1916, were failures of generalship—there can hardly be any argument about that. Especially the methods adopted for the first assault appear in retrospect as an act of sheer madness, which turned the potential asset of numerical superiority into a decisive disadvantage. It is reported that on some occasions German soldiers left their trenches and stood on the parapet to fire with greater ease at the crowded formations of the approaching British. If that was, as an English writer called it, a display of idiotic bravery, it was also a clear demonstration of the fact that even in the open a machine gun can be used with deadly effect against an enemy advancing 'at a steady pace' and 'in successive waves of extended lines'.

As we have seen, the tactical planning of the British High Command was based on an over-sanguine belief in the efficacy of the bombardment and the theory that only rigid, detailed instructions were suitable for an army in which most officers and men had little or no combat experience. But it should not be assumed that these decisions were taken quite casually and without serious argument. Thus General Rawlinson, with the approval of Sir Douglas Haig, had emphatically advocated an attack before sunrise, so that the assault troops could approach the German front trenches under cover of semi-darkness, but the French generals had insisted that good light for the artillery was the more important consideration; and as far as their own sector was concerned they may have been right.

Haig had also been in favour of infiltration rather than a massed assault, that is to say, an advance of small detachments, probing the weaknesses of the enemy positions, instead of waves. In this case it was the opposition of his own army commanders that persuaded him to abandon the idea, and it is, of course, true that such infiltration methods would have required, besides a more flexible system of artillery cover, a greater measure of independent decision on the part of officers of lower rank and NCOs, and for this it would certainly have been better if more veterans had been available. But rigid planning and instructions to the effect that 'officers and men in action will usually do what they have been practised to do, or have been told to do in certain situations' did not help matters when plans went completely awry; on the contrary, they merely inhibited, at least in the all-important first stages, the great native talent for shrewd improvisation. The verdict of a commentator in the Official History seems justified: 'That greater success was not gained was as much due to faulty tactical direction from the General Staff, and to lack of experience in the higher ranks, as to rawness in the lower ranks.'

That things might have turned out very differently if more suitable tactics had been employed is shown by the single permanent (if limited) success achieved in the sector of the X Corps, the area around the village of Thiepval. This was a particularly well fortified zone, containing four major strongpoints, one of which was the Leipzig Redoubt at the tip of the salient formed by the German front line. The attack on the Leipzig Salient was carried out by the 97th Brigade of the 32nd Division; the 16th and 17th Highland Light Infantry formed the leading battalions. Commanding officer of the brigade was Brigadier-General Jardine, who had been attached to the Japanese army in the Manchurian War of 1904-1905, and had absorbed the Japanese tactics in dealing with the entrenched machine gun positions of the Russians. On his orders, the leading companies left their trenches seven minutes before zero hour and crept forward in small groups to within 40 yards of the German front trench, and when the barrage lifted at 0730 hours, they surprised the enemy with a sudden, determined rush. The method worked: before more than a handful of the defenders could leave their dugouts, the German front trenches were overrun and the redoubt was firmly in British possession. An immediate advance by the 17th Highland Light Infantry on the Hindenburg Trench about 150 yards farther on soon came under fire from another redoubt, and it would have been futile to press it, in view of the fact that the British assault forces on the left and right of the brigade had not been able to force the German front positions. Brigadier Jardine was informed that both flanks of the detachment were exposed, and that the barrage was moving on without any troops following it. Under these circumstances he again disregarded the General Staff instructions, in two respects: he gave orders that the Highlanders should be withdrawn before they were faced with almost certain annihilation, and that two batteries should be taken out of the barrage in order to cover the retreat to Leipzig Redoubt, which was carried out without much loss.

This is not to say that different tactical planning would have achieved the breakthrough which (despite later denials) was certainly the concrete aim of the Allied leaders. As conditions were, such a result was probably altogether out of reach. All that can be asserted with confidence is that more could have been gained with much less sacrifice, and this is why the first day of the Somme battle is so often remembered with great bitterness. With the wisdom that comes after the event we know that the planners banked far too

The disasters of July 1 were failures of generalship

much on the hoped-for efficacy of the preliminary bombardment; but we must remember that a 'battle of material' on that scale was then without a precedent from which lessons could have been learned. Nor would it be fair to blame the British leaders too heavily for underrating the strength and quite novel sophistication of the German defence works. More difficult to understand is the obstinacy with which the generals persisted when it had become very obvious that the planned methods of attack would not work. Faulty judgment is frequent and pardonable in all human affairs, but in a military leader the unwillingness to face facts is a cardinal sin. We have seen that ominous reports brought back by patrols in the last two days before zero were taken rather lightly; in one instance such a report was dismissed with the comment that the men were scared.

There was also blind obstinacy at work in connection with the frontal assault on Fricourt, but the best example is provided by the operations of the VII Corps of the Third Army in the Gommecourt sector at the northern end of the front. The attack in that region had been planned as a subsidiary action, designed to bind enemy forces which might otherwise be used elsewhere against the British Fourth Army. Neither Gommecourt itself nor any particular German line in the area were designated as tactical objectives. It was not without misgivings that this sector had been chosen for a purpose of this sort. The German defences there were even stronger than at any other point. No-Man's Land was very wide, the hilly terrain was a factor in favour of the defenders, and the front was too narrow to be suitable for a massed attack. But then, a massed attack was hardly required. Since Falkenhayn had refused to provide the reinforcements which his army commander, General Fritz von Below, had urgently demanded, the Germans found themselves in the difficulty that they were holding positions of great strength, but had barely enough men and artillery to defend them. They could not without the grave risk of a local enemy breakthrough greatly reduce their forces in any front section. All that was necessary to prevent them from doing so was to keep the threat of an impending attack alive by limited offensive action whenever there was a sign of weakening resistance. But the British corps commander, General Snow, and the General Officers under him were not men of half measures, as one historian has phrased it rather euphemistically. What should have been a feinting operation was turned into a full-scale battle—or, rather, a series of ferocious engagements—which lasted well into the evening.

The attack on Gommecourt was pressed as relentlessly as if the outcome of the war depended on the capture of the village. Wave after wave was thrown into this hopeless battle, and individual advances were attempted again and again. At the end of the day not a square inch of ground had been gained. The VII Corps may have achieved its object: 'to divert against itself forces which otherwise might be directed against the main attack near Serre', but at the appalling cost of nearly 7,000 casualties. The operations in the Serre area had failed nonetheless, as had all the other attacks north of the Fricourt Salient; and there was not even the consolation that the Germans had had an equally high price to pay for their successful defence. German losses in that sector amounted to a little over 1,200.

From the rest of the operations in the northern and central sectors we may single out the action of the 36th (Ulster) Division in the area of the X Corps, because that action started with great promise and demonstrates all the more effectively how useless it is to persevere with an isolated advance when its success cannot be exploited owing to the failure of connected operations. In the northern half of the sector two fortified villages, St Pierre Divion and Thiepval, were situated at a short distance behind the German front-line. North-east of Thiepval lay Schwaben Redoubt, a large strongpoint with a front

and smoked with every sign that it was to be attacked in the afternoon and at 1600 hours, with all the German defensive fire falling north of the Albert road, the 6th Wiltshires and the 9th Royal Welsh Fusiliers slipped across into La Boiselle to the south. The two battalions bombed their way forward into the centre of the village, supported by the 9th Cheshires. Before dark they had connected up their line with their comrades in the Schwaben Höhe. General von Stein did not, however, declare this loss to Army headquarters. As on the previous night, when he had concealed his withdrawal from Fricourt by making it appear that the village had fallen during the assault on July 1, so now he simply stated that 'the main positions of La Boiselle have been held despite a second (enemy) attempt to storm them'.

Grünert dismissed

The next day, Monday, July 3, Falkenhayn came to Below's headquarters at St. Quentin. With him was Tappen, Chief of the Operations Staff at Supreme Command. Though it is almost certain that he had known of Pannewitz' plan to withdraw from the Flaucourt plateau — and made no attempt to prevent it — he demanded to know how such a voluntary abandonment of ground could have been permitted, reminding Below and Grünert that 'the first principle of position warfare must be to yield not one foot of ground; and if it be lost to retake it immediately by counterattack, even to the last man'. Consistent with the principles and discipline of the general staff corps, Grünert was dismissed. His replacement was Colonel von Lossberg.

Happily for Below, Falkenhayn brought him other and better news. As promised, three divisions and three flights of aircraft were *en route* for *Second Army* from the general reserve. Two more were being withdrawn for him from Crown Prince Rupprecht's army, two from Verdun. Notwithstanding the reservations he had expressed to Below, Falkenhayn had curtailed operations against the fortress zone as soon as he heard of the Somme bombardment on June 24. On July 1, he ordered 16 heavy batteries to be sent to *Second Army*, 15 from Verdun, all of which should be in position by the 3rd. A further 22 were being assembled.

Such time as Rawlinson had had to exploit his enemy's weakness was passing swiftly. During the day, scouts of the Royal Flying Corps saw columns of men, guns and wagons entering Bapaume. The bombers attempting to pass through to strike these and other targets reported persistent attacks by a number of German aircraft.

Haig's anxiety had grown during the 2nd. After visiting Gough, he cancelled the attack by VIII Corps on the 3rd and limited that by X Corps to the assault on Thiepval spur. He pressed again for the combined movement forward of XV and XIII Corps. Congreve's corps was not, however, moving that day. The Army plan was to assault the Thiepval spur, Ovillers and the remainder of the defences at La Boiselle at 1515 hours. At 2100 hours, Horne hoped to capture Shelter and Bottom Woods.

At 0255 hours, while the artillery was firing the preliminary bombardment, Gough telephoned to say that the two brigades of X Corps could not be ready

Above: British prisoners help the Germans to bring in their wounded across the jungle of twisted wire and broken posts. Many British units lost almost all their numbers during the fighting

before 1400 hours. The attacks on Ovillers and La Boiselle began without them, therefore, the infantry leaving their assembly trenches promptly at 1515 hours. Opposite Ovillers, the five battalions of the 12th Division — West Kents, Queen's, Buffs, Berkshires and Suffolks — with their detachments of gunners and sappers — crossed No-Man's Land and passed quickly through the gaps in the enemy wire. Then, in a dawn delayed by extensive clouds, they were lost in shadows and the smoke of bursting shells and bombs. Even before they reached the almost deserted front German trench, red rockets were shooting up from the fortified observation posts covering Ovillers, instructing the batteries back along the road to Bapaume to fire on the British assault. Understandably anxious not to hang about in the open under the enemy shrapnel, the assault pressed on without clearing completely the deep dugouts in the support trenches. Soon from these and trenches outside the circumference of the advance emerged three or four groups large enough to attack piecemeal the five battalions. Caught in the fire of the machine guns, the driving power of the British infantry fell away. Still, through the early part of the morning, one or another company drew in on Ovillers, capturing outlying houses. Attempts were made to reinforce them from the trenches of the 12th Division but No-Man's Land was rent by shrapnel and high explosive, despatched precisely to deny such a move. What finally defeated the assault force was the shortage of grenades and small arms ammunition. At about 1000 hours, a few small parties struggled home to their own line. By noon, the count disclosed that 2,400 officers and men had been lost.

At about 0700 hours that morning, one attempt to reinforce the assault on Ovillers had been made by 9th Essex Division. In the smoke and blast which broke up the battalion's movement over No-Man's Land, one rifle company lost direction to veer southeast across the Albert road. It thus came in through the left flank of the assault on La Boiselle, evading the observation of the enemy whose eye at this point was on the village. Piecemeal it

gathered in 220 Germans. Meanwhile, the two foremost brigades of the 19th Division were fighting through the eastern half of La Boiselle, capturing prisoners from the many weak units among the strong points and interconnecting tunnels. But relief was already on its way for the German garrison. A regiment reconstituted and reinforced on the 2nd was marching towards Pozières, from which it delivered in the afternoon a strong counterattack at a time when the British, having taken the whole of La Boiselle, had lost many men and were short of ammunition.

The German *190th Regiment* drove them almost out of the ruins. Two of the British battalion commanders had been killed and another wounded. The leader of those remaining was an extraordinary cavalryman, Adrian Carton de Wiart, commanding the 8th Glosters; the more remarkable because he had lost an arm already at the Second Battle of Ypres and wore a black patch over the eye socket which had been emptied in Somaliland. The soldiers called him 'Nelson', and somewhat like the great sailor, he declined to be rebuffed by the enemy's fire. Often leading a storming party, he brought his force back into La Boiselle. Grenades were collected from the dead and wounded they passed; Carton de Wiart, lacking a hand, used his teeth as a mean of removing split pins from the Mills bombs, thus originating one of the most pronounced features of war fiction. When it was dark, they had recaptured over half the village and were able to link up with the 12th Division by a trench dug alongside the Albert road.

To the north of III Corps, the attempt by two brigades to fight their way forward at 0600 hours from the Leipzig Redoubt and the other shallow enclaves on the Thiepval spur was a brief and costly failure. The lesson plainly to be learnt from Thiepval to La Boiselle was that the frontal attack into strong enemy defences was the most expensive way of operating and the least promising. It was not a new lesson. To the east of Fricourt, however, the defences were still weak. Although snipers and a number of isolated machine guns hindered the advance of the bat-

Above: Playing with fire? British soldiers take time off from fusing Stokes mortars for a game of cards. Their newspaper would have reported recent Allied successes

talions of 21st and 17th Divisions on Shelter and Bottom Woods, they could not stem it. At 1130 hours it appeared that a counterattack was developing: a contact aeroplane reported a column approaching from Contalmaison. Without waiting for artillery support, the left hand brigade commander, Brigadier-General Rawling, moved up his reserve battalion and directed them to attack the German column from the flank under the covering fire of his Stokes mortars. It was quickly done, and a surprise to the Germans who yielded 800 officers and men to the Allies as prisoners.

Major decisions

By 1500 hours, all objectives had been taken. Six hours of daylight remained. XV Corps' headquarters had already been informed by an air observer that its troops had occupied the woods and connecting trenches: and the report included the priceless news that both Mametz Wood and the quadrilateral of trenches connecting the wood with Contalmaison had been evacuated by the enemy. Soon there came a request from 17th Division to patrol forward with a view to occupation of these empty defences. General Horne replied that he could not 'engage in patrol action which might bring on an engagement before he was prepared to accept it'. His corps was to pay dearly for this decision. Relenting after a second request, he allowed the 7th Division to occupy the southern strip of Mametz Wood after dark. General Congreve similarly gave way to the entreaties of his infantry, permitting the occupation of Bernafay Wood after a bombardment of 20 minutes and a set-piece assault. Inside were 17 men of the 12th Reserve Division, three abandoned field pieces, three machine guns. Each corps commander found it necessary to ask Rawlinson's permission before taking these major tactical decisions.

It had not been an easy day for Rawlinson. His interview with Foch that morning had been inconclusive; the French would not co-operate in any movement while Rawlinson kept XIII Corps inactive. In the afternoon, he was present at an unpleasant meeting between Haig and Joffre.

The object of the visit (to me), Haig wrote in his diary, *was to discuss future arrangements. Joffre began by pointing out the importance of our getting Thiepval Spur. To this I said that, in view of the progress made on my right near Montauban, and the demoralised nature of the enemy's troops in that area, I was considering the desirability of pressing my attack on Longueval. I was therefore anxious to know whether, in that event, the French would attack at Guillemont. At this, General Joffre exploded in a fit of rage. 'He could not approve of it.' He ordered me to. attack Thiepval and Pozières. If I attacked Longueval, I would be beaten! I waited calmly till he had finished. His breast heaved and his face flushed! The truth is the poor man cannot argue, nor can he easily read a map. But today I had a raised model of the ground before us. I quietly explained what my position is relatively to him as the 'Generalissimo'. I am solely responsible to the British Government for the action of the British Army; and I had approved the plan, and must modify it to suit the changing situation as the fight progresses. I was most polite. Joffre saw he had made a mistake, and next tried to cajole me. . . . I had gained an advantage through keeping calm. My views have been accepted by the French Staffs and Davidson (chief of the operations section at GHQ) is to go to lunch with Foch tomorrow, to discuss how they (the French) can co-operate in our operations (that is the capture of Longueval).*

Haig thus succeeded in securing French co-operation where Rawlinson had failed; but Rawlinson's procrastination had reduced the advantage of agreement. For the tide had turned—at least for the time being—against the Allies. The two divisions from the German general reserve were deploying into the line; a third was approaching, the fourth close behind. All heavy batteries lost in the bombardment had now been replaced with an addition of 14 to the total Below had arrayed before July 1. By July 6, the regimental machine gun companies were completely reconstituted and within a week these were supplemented by independent companies.

Stein's front was contracted to the sector Gommecourt-Albert Road. A new *VI Corps* headquarters took command under Lieutenant-General von Gosler from the road to the north bank of the Somme. South of the river, the discredited Pannewitz was replaced by Lieutenant-General von Quast. These organisational arrangements simplified the control of the defence.

Even the weather turned, culminating in a thunderstorm on the afternoon of July 4. The trenches were filled with water; the dirt tracks in the forward areas, the broken shell-torn ground became heavy with clinging mud. 'Walking, let alone fighting, became hellish.'

Haig made his own changes in organisation. Gough's position had been regularised on July 3: VIII and X Corps became under him the 'Reserve' Army. As army commander, Gough now answered directly to the Commander-in-Chief. The next day, his right boundary was brought down to the Albert-Bapaume road so as to permit Rawlinson's army to concentrate for a renewal of the offensive. No longer willing to stay aloof, the Commander-in-Chief urged on Fourth Army the need to secure Contalmaison, Mametz Wood and Trônes Wood as a preliminary position from which to launch the assault. Gough was ordered to capture Pozières to secure the left flank. The programme of relief, planned several weeks before, was activated so as to bring in a succession of troops from quieter areas to take their turn at the arduous work ahead.

Horne began with an attempt to take Mametz Wood, but despite a series of ruthless orders to 'attack', 'attack again', 'repeat the attack', his obedient infantry could not triumph over the cross-fire of emplaced machine guns, the intensified shellfire and the rain. Eventually, by a combination of III and XV Corps, Contalmaison and Mametz Wood were taken on Thursday, July 13. In the meantime, Gough had struck for Pozières with five battalions but succeeded only in squeezing round the south-eastern outskirts of Ovillers. Much of his remaining strength was absorbed in holding the German counterattacks round Thiepval. The Ulster lodgement was lost; Leipzig Redoubt was just held after four intense local actions. On the extreme right, Congreve was still struggling on July 13 to take possession of the once empty Trônes Wood.

The prizes so dearly won by Pulteney's and Horne's corps were not asked for lightly. At some stage—it is not precisely clear when—Rawlinson and his chief of staff had come to the idea of renewing the offensive by a large-scale night attack. Given possession of Contalmaison, Mametz Wood and the northern portion of Trônes Wood—all on the far bank of the Willow Stream—there was everything to be said for the use of darkness in which to form' up in No-Man's Land for a rush forward into the enemy trenches just before dawn. It was an unusual concept and hence likely to be a surprise. If it could be organised and kept secret, so many of the dreadful features of the deliberate assault in daylight would be obviated.

But the French were not enthusiastic. They could not believe that an assault by several divisions in this manner could be kept secret from beginning to end, and they did not accept that the organisational problems of leading out such a mass of men in darkness to the many precise forming-up places could be overcome. There were, besides, such matters as artillery control, maintenance of direction by the troops, the phasing-in of support battalions. Foch would have nothing to do with such an operation, and his staff derisively stated that it was 'an attack organised for amateurs by amateurs'. On his own initiative, the kindly Fayolle offered Rawlinson a barrage, to be fired on his behalf across the common flank with Balfourier's static corps.

Haig, himself, was also unconvinced at the outset. He enquired acidly among his staff how Rawlinson expected XIII Corps' headquarters, which took five days to reorganise its troopers after the victory at Montauban, to cope with a night operation of this magnitude. But he was won round by Rawlinson's advocacy. His only proviso was that they must secure Trônes Wood beforehand.

From July 8 to 12, the 30th Division struggled daily in good and bad weather to capture the long wood pointing due north to Longueval. Balfourier's XX Corps helped by pushing forward to recapture Hardécourt and the knoll of Maltz Horn

Above: Dogs were sometimes used to take messages to and from the front. Special attachments were strapped to them to carry the notes. *Below:* Wearing the trophies of the day's fighting, soldiers of the 13th Royal Fusiliers take a brief rest after the attack on La Boiselle on July 7

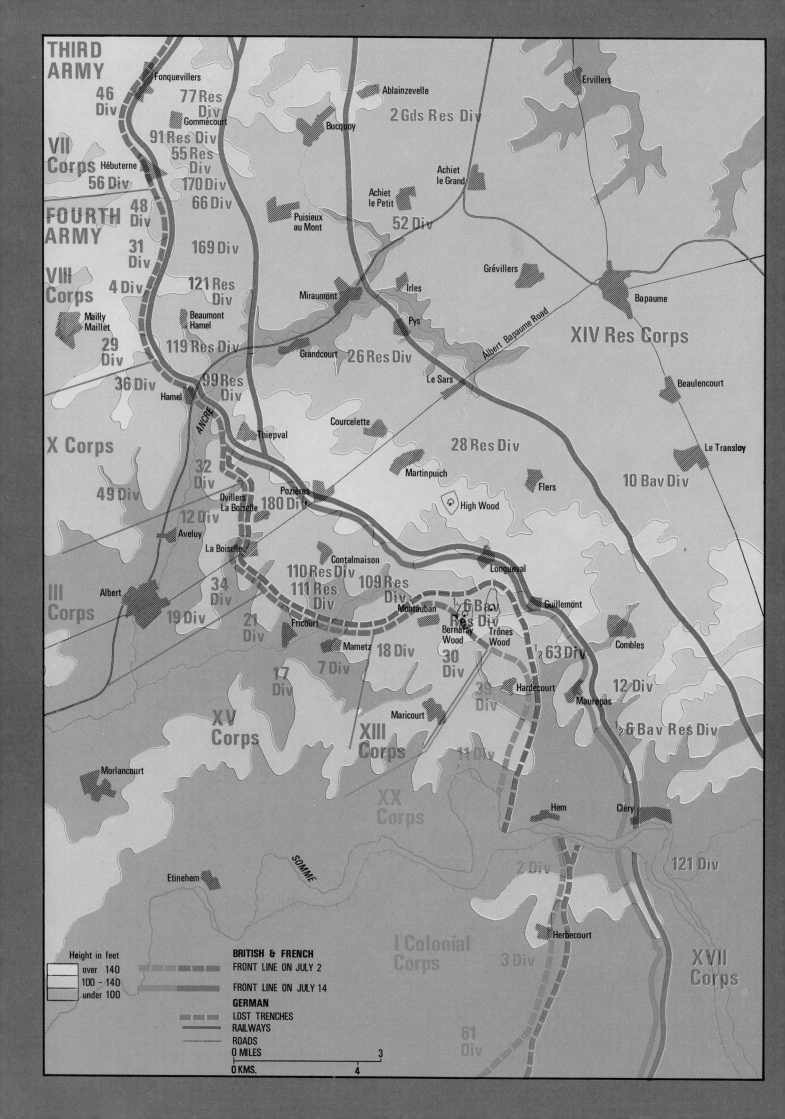

THIRD ARMY

46 Div

77 Res Div

Fonquevillers

Gommécourt

91 Res Div

55 Res Div

VII Corps

Hébuterne

56 Div

170 Div

66 Div

FOURTH ARMY

48 Div

31 Div

VIII Corps

4 Div

121 Res Div

Mailly Maillet

29 Div

119 Res Div

36 Div

99 Res Div

Hamel

ANCRE

X Corps

32 Div

49 Div

Ovillers La Boiselle

12 Div

180 Div

Aveluy

La Boiselle

III Corps

Albert

34 Div

19 Div

21 Div

Fricourt

110 Res Div

111 Res Div

Contalmaison

109 Res Div

Mametz

18 Div

7 Div

17 Div

XV Corps

Morlancourt

XIII Corps

Maricourt

Montauban

Bernafay Wood

30 Div

Trônes Wood

½ 6 Bav Res Div

39 Div

Hardecourt

11 Div

XX Corps

SOMME

Etinehem

Ablainzevelle

2 Gds Res Div

Bucquoy

Achiet le Grand

Achiet le Petit

Puisieux au Mont

52 Div

Grévillers

Miraumont

Irles

Pys

Grandcourt

26 Res Div

Le Sars

Albert Bapaume Road

XIV Res Corps

Bapaume

Beaulencourt

Le Transloy

Courcelette

28 Res Div

Martinpuich

Flers

10 Bav Div

High Wood

Longueval

Guillemont

½ 6 Bav Res Div

½ 63 Div

Combles

12 Div

Maurepas

½ 6 Bav Res Div

Hem

Cléry

2 Div

121 Div

I Colonial Corps

3 Div

Herbecourt

XVII Corps

61 Div

Farm. The Germans were not prepared to lose the wood. Twice, when the British infantry had occupied the greater part of the tangled interior, they counterattacked successfully. On July 12 a fresh division, the 18th, commanded by Major-General Maxse, was brought in to relieve the 30th, which had lost the equivalent of five of its nine battalions in the struggle.

Already postponed by two days, the Fourth Army's offensive was due to begin at 1525 hours on the 14th. The entire wood, Maxse was told by Congreve, was to be captured 'at all costs' by midnight on the 13th. As Maxse's battalions only completed their occupation of the trenches at 1700 hours on that same day, it was an order almost impossible to obey. Reconnaissances, assault and artillery plans were made in haste throughout the morning and orders issued in the afternoon. At 1900 hours, the 7th Queen's, 280 strong, bolstered by a company of 7th Buffs, set out from Bernafay Wood to seize the northern tip of Trônes. Their task was to cut off any enemy driven north. The remainder of the Buffs and 7th Royal West Kents advanced from the south to clear through the trees.

As the British bombardment ended, a German barrage burst on them. The Buffs and West Kents persevered, leaving their wounded to be brought in by brigade stretcher parties. Soon brigade headquarters heard the sound of heavy small arms fire from different portions of the wood. For almost three hours there was no news of any of the infantry; then, at 1030 hours, a message came back with a large number of wounded Buffs. They had captured their first objective—a strong point commanding an important ride—but were now so weak in numbers that their second advance had been thrown back. At 1100 hours, what remained of the 7th Queen's came in—80 strong. The West Kents did not return at all; they had been virtually destroyed as a unit.

General Maxse passed this unhappy news to XIII Corps headquarters at midnight. Congreve's question as to what they intended to do about it was met with the reply that the 54th Brigade were ready to go in in place of the 55th.

Fear versus optimism

Preliminary moves for the main assault were already being made. Partially screened by an outpost line pushed forward immediately after darkness to within a few hundred yards of the German front trenches, six brigades of Fourth Army—on the left, two from XV Corps; on the right, four from XIII—were being led out by guides under a full moon to form up in areas carefully marked. It was comparatively quiet. The bombardment fired intermittently over the preceding four days was now replaced by the customary night harassing. The principal aim of this plan was to give the enemy no hint of an immediately impending attack. But there was an important secondary advantage to be gained: the stocks of shells were not abundant. There had been strict rationing for some days of all natures of ammunition above 4.5-inch. Both Haig and Rawlinson

Left: British and French gains during the second phase of the fighting around the Somme. 'Daring' had become the password of the new Allied offensive and it brought some success

were thus particularly grateful to Fayolle for the support of the French flank batteries.

Otherwise, French fears of catastrophe persisted. That evening, the eve of Bastille Day, the British liaison officer with Sixth Army came to Querrieu to beg Rawlinson on behalf of Balfourier to postpone the assault until full daylight.

'Tell General Balfourier with my compliments,' said General Montgomery, Fourth Army Chief-of-Staff, 'that if we're not on Longueval Ridge by 8 o'clock tomorrow morning, I'll eat my hat.'

The outcome of this proposition now depended upon the 22,000 men moving in a series of columns in single file out from the trenches under the bright moon. By 0300 hours on the morning of July 14, all were in place, trench mortars and medium machine guns immediately on the flanks or in the rear. To many, the remaining minutes of waiting, while a chill morning mist rose about them, seemed endless. Others, exhausted after a day of carrying ammunition and stores for the assault force, were delighted to rest. Between foremost infantry and supports, the engineer field companies, at hand to fortify the defences to be seized on the Longueval Ridge, waited with their own assorted loads. For a brief time, the front fell silent except for the distant sound of the barrage being fired north of the Ancre on the front of Hunter-Weston's VIII Corps.

The Germans opposite were not aware of their immediate danger but expected 'an attack at some point within the next few days'. IV Corps, under General Sixt von Armin, was coming in to the line in relief. Its 7th Division was taking over the sector from Pozières to Bazentin-le-Petit wood on the night July 13. Standing patrols, a hundred metres or so in front of the trenches, saw and heard nothing. Opposite Longueval, a battalion of the 16th Bavarian Regiment, aware of operations against Trônes Wood, sent out two fighting patrols. One disappeared, never to be seen again; the other encountered briefly a British party—perhaps a part of the screen established by XIII Corps. When it returned to report contact, two other parties went forward to investigate but each came back to say that they could find nothing. Sentries remained above ground, looking forward into the moonlight.

At 0320 hours that morning, those watching were dazzled and deafened by a sudden blaze of light on the southern and western horizon. The Allied howitzers and trench mortars began on the instant to rain shells and bombs on the German positions. To the east the sun was rising. From the patches of ground mist, the leading battalions rose to come forward when, precisely five minutes after its beginning, the artillery barrage lifted. Such a brief period of bombardment misled the Germans. With the exception of one Bavarian unit, they remained below in their deep shelters. In a final rush, the British battalions carried the first line. Even where the wire remained uncut, the storming parties which had broken in won adequate time for their comrades to cut the barriers by hand. The Allied barrage lifted again at 1535 and 1625 hours, the faithful infantry following it each time. Those of the enemy emerging from their deep dugouts to catch the assault battalions in the rear—as on July 1 and immediately afterwards—were taken by the support battalions pressing in deliberately to defeat them. Despite brave German counterattacks, XV and XIII Corps were established on the ridge by 1000 hours, with almost every objective in their hands. When the news reached Fourth Army headquarters, the French liaison officer, Captain Serot, passed it to Balfourier's staff. 'They dared to do it,' he said, 'and they have succeeded.' 'Well,' came the reply, 'General Montgomery won't have to eat his hat!'

Attack and counterattack

Sixt von Armin took command of the embattled front at 0900 hours in the morning. Already, he had learnt that a British sweep—under the dynamic direction of Colonel Maxwell of the Middlesex—was driving the German garrison from Trônes Wood; two German regiments on Longueval Ridge had been completely overwhelmed; three battalions, at one point or another, had withdrawn behind detachments shortly to be destroyed, and once again the artillery had suffered severely. Once again, the sector under attack was reinforced piecemeal and for some hours it proved impossible to say accurately which portions of it were manned and which portions were open.

The noise of battle around the village of Longueval and, on its eastern edge, Delville Wood, correctly indicated that a fierce struggle continued there. Apprised of this situation in XIII Corps on his right, Lieutenant-General Horne declined to allow his 3rd Division commander, Major-General Haldane, to exploit his front now open and empty. To this and several other suggestions that morning that the infantry in the centre should press on to the almost deserted High Wood 1,000 yards ahead, he sent a reminder that the cavalry were coming through. But soon the news that Longueval had been counterattacked caused the cavalry to be held back by XIII Corps. In fact, the South Africans who had joined the exhausted Highland and Lowland Scots were helping not only to beat off the German counterattacks but to recover lost ground.

High Wood remained open through the afternoon. Overhead, the Royal Flying Corps sent message after message reiterating the absence of a formed defence on and around it. At last, in the late afternoon, the 7th Division was sent forward; and in the evening a few squadrons of cavalry came up, so that by the time night fell at least some sort of a British line had been formed across the southern half of this high point on the Longueval Ridge.

At last, too, the German reinforcements were flocking in. The sector opposite Hunter-Weston was clearly too well defended to be attacked. At Ovillers a daylight assault had been driven back. Below gave Sixt von Armin almost every reserve available to plug the gap on the crest through which it was believed that the British had broken through between Longueval and Pozières.

These reports reckoned without that excessive caution which characterised Congreve and Horne and, once again, it robbed the assault forces of the full fruits of their victory. By midnight, the northern half of High Wood was occupied by a strong force of Germans behind whom were four battalions furiously digging new trenches and dugouts. High Wood had become highwater mark.

THE SOMME BLOODY AND FUTILE ATTRITION

On July 15 the Battle of the Somme entered its third phase. Thousands had already died, now thousands more would follow them to hastily dug graves in the shell-pitted ground. *Below:* In action at last — Kitchener's 'new men'

There had been no breakthrough. Nor the least sign that one was imminent. After all the rumours, after all the hopes and all the gallant idealism, the 'Big Push', the Somme offensive, had proved a macabre anticlimax.

A fortnight's butchery had brought advances on less than half the original 16 mile assault front. The Allied armies had won themselves a mere sliver of land, nowhere more than two and a half miles deep. The French, north and south of the River Somme, in their more modest attacks, had, it was true, done better.

But the disaster that befell the British was so great that it was difficult at first to grasp its scope. The greater its magnitude, the more impossible was it for those responsible to accept it. Neither Haig nor his fellow officers gave any hint that they acknowledged the numbing truth. On the contrary, in Britain people read in their daily papers, side by side with the endless casualty lists, official descriptions of the 'methodical capture of the whole of the enemy's first system of defence'. Such reporting was not merely an attempt to keep up spirits on the home front: even in communications to the other commanders GHQ was writing of the 'good prospects' for the Fourth Army on the Somme.

In the German High Command, despite heavy casualties and the constant bombardment that was beginning to tell on the troops, confidence was returning and plans were being laid for a counterattack. The offensive had produced no more than localised crises; and it was now certain, Falkenhayn wrote, that the 'enemy would fail to reach his objective in the nibbling

tactics to which he was compelled to resort'.

The counterstroke planned to recover the lost ground was doomed to failure, however. General Sixtus von Armin, brought from the north to command the German *IV Corps* whose sector stretched from Pozières to Ginchy, proposed to strike the British line from Longueval village to Bazentin-le-Petit. The attack was to be launched from his second position, the so-called 'Switch Line', a trench running east—west south of Flers and Martinpuich, and later to become notorious as it was contended for yard by yard. The men were tired from long marches and British air reconnaissance allowed movement only at night, but they got as far as they could. Then, harassed by British aircraft and artillery, and unable to move their own guns in time, the task proved too much.

The British generals, meanwhile, issued their own orders for 'the next phase of the battle'. General Sir Henry Rawlinson, 'Rawly', the executive officer in charge of the British part of the offensive, demanded full exploitation of their gains and complete capture of earlier objectives, taking advantage of the 'confusion and demoralisation of the enemy'.

The British orders apparently ignored the fact that those very objectives were to have been taken by the initial waves in the first day's fighting; that Bapaume, the first stride in the advance to the Rhine, still lay many kilometres away. German plans ignored, in their turn, the fact that insistence on holding every inch of ground and recapturing all losses by suicidal counterattack would double and treble their casualties.

So for a third week, in Caterpillar Valley where the batteries stood, a few miles behind the fighting line, the British gunners laboured and sweated. They worked with their crude and only partially effective gas masks pinned to their shirts, ready to be pulled on whenever the hooters croaked or the shell-case alarms clanged.

The roads to the valley were lined with traffic, every rail siding had its howitzer, well camouflaged under nets. On one corner, where the road to the valley turned, the Germans had a gun registering. From time to time one of the slow moving limbers or the steam traction engines which drew the guns would be hit. For a moment or two everything behind would stop as vehicle, dead or wounded driver and disembowelled horses were dragged aside. Then the procession went on.

Thousands of tons of metal rained down upon that sliver of earth round the Ancre and the Somme. It turned the men into querulous, irritable cynics, restless even when body and soul were exhausted, fighting like automata.

The ground shook as from an earthquake. Dugouts crumbled again and again, burying their occupants. Crushed bodies of suffocated soldiers were later found among the wood splinters. Even the rats panicked and took refuge with the men who killed them with their trenching tools. The Somme was not another place, 'somewhere in France', it was another world, where men lived amid the reek of putrefaction and the sickly sweet smell of gas, a muddy, dusty and shellpitted land, thick with the detritus of war.

And into this world round the Ancre and

Below: German machine gunners. Now they fought in a landscape of stunted trees and dead bodies. *Inset:* Germans bring up a trench gun

Somme now marched the new men, the fresh divisions coming to relieve those who had been in the battle from its beginning. They were cheerful, confident men who believed what they had been told – that July 1 had been a turning point and that the battle of trench and dugout was soon to give place to a war of movement. They were the reservists of 'Kitchener's Army', or the draftees from the Fatherland, or from the villages and fields of France, bank clerks, bricklayers, farm labourers, businessmen, poets, teachers, and they were undeterred even by the sight of the unshaven, gaunt-eyed, mud-caked men whose places they were taking. Among them were also the men of the British Empire: South Africans, Australians and New Zealanders.

For the South Africans a task was quickly found. At the very tip of the British advance and, according to GHQ, forming an obstacle to the advance, was the village of Longueval and the adjoining Delville Wood. The South Africans were ordered to take it 'at all costs', and the south part of the wood fell in less than two hours. All but the northern quarter was taken in their second assault; then they dug in under heavy shellfire. They repulsed counterattacks – by rifle fire alone when all their machine guns had been knocked out.

The Germans had assembled over 180 field guns, howitzers and medium and heavy guns for Armin's counterattack. After the frontal assault failed they turned their frustrated rage upon the South Africans and the whole wood was set ablaze.

For five days the South Africans held on.

When at last the relieving troops reached them they found, amid the broken charred stumps of trees, the few survivors surrounded by their own and the German dead. In some trenches there were as few as six men.

The South African Brigade which had gone into battle with 121 officers and 3,032 other ranks was found at roll-call on July 21 to be down to 27 officers and 751 other ranks. On the German side the *26th Regiment* which had been at full strength on July 13 was down to ten officers and 250 other ranks.

GHQ now believed that the Germans were demoralised and near retreat. The British generals had so bewitched themselves with their idea of imminent victory that they urged the Commanders of the First and Second Armies further north to help it along. Action elsewhere would also, they believed, teach the Germans not to fill gaps at the Somme by milking quieter parts of the front.

Dummy figures
It was decided to focus the attack north of Loos, site of the previous year's disasters. The objective was to be Aubers Ridge, including the village of Fromelles. The attack was to be on a front only 4,000 yards wide, but the preliminary bombardment was to give the appearance that a big offensive was coming. To deceive the Germans further during barrage lifts the infantry would show dummy figures and bayonets at their parapets. The basic fallacy behind the whole plan was, as Captain Sir Basil Liddell Hart pointed out, that 'while simulated preparations for a large-scale attack

would cause the enemy natural apprehension, the actual delivery of a narrow fronted local attack would merely disclose the bluff.' Furthermore, the location itself was unpromising. The terrain was flat and waterlogged. The attackers would have to advance under the eyes of the Germans on Aubers Ridge, who would, besides, observe the assembling forces.

Plans went ahead, nonetheless, and the recently arrived 5th Australian Division with their guns were assigned to the Second Army. By mid-July all was ready. The Germans, as they watched the preparations, mounted a series of raids which flared into fierce encounters. These, as well as heavy rain and fatigue among the assault forces, caused two postponements and it was finally decided that the attack should go forward on July 19.

The day broke clear and fine with good visibility and at 1100 hours the barrage began. It was very heavy, but it could be seen that it was not destroying the German parapets, a disheartening failure for the intended attackers, who had already been told that in many places the German wire was uncut.

An hour later the Germans began to retaliate and not only killed many of the British gunners but, in several cases, hit the improvised ammunition dumps. Furthermore, the Germans were not deceived by the dummies.

At 1730 hours the 61st Division began the infantry attack. Because of the water-logged ground the lines were not trenches but breast-high 'defence works' and the only exits were 'sally ports'. The German machine gunners, in well emplaced, con-

Below: French troops in reserve take a much needed rest before going up the line. *Inset:* French artillerymen moving a gun into position

crete positions, sighted their guns on the British infantry and many units were destroyed before the advance started.

The Australian Division began advancing in high spirits, only to be checked like their comrades by uncut wire and machine guns.

As day turned to night the situation became critical. The 8th Australian Brigade, which had had one of the few successes of the day and had managed to secure a lodgement in the German lines, asked for support. There was none to be given. Despite this, they held their position until the next afternoon, repulsing a counterattack and fighting their way out of the rapidly closing net.

In March, after inspecting the newly arrived Australians, Haig had written of them in the highest terms. Less than 12 hours later the 5th Australian Division lay shattered in the marshes of Fromelles. They had lost 5,500 men. Many wounded lay out in No-Man's Land and, had it not been for an informal truce arranged between an officers' batman and a Bavarian officer, would have died there.

Late on the night of July 19, when the attack was some hours old, Falkenhayn telephoned the German *Sixth Army* to ask about the situation. He was quickly reassured. On the afternoon of July 20 he telephoned again. The attack had been delivered and repulsed, he was told. Captured British orders proved it to be merely a holding action.

At the same time Falkenhayn ordered the *183rd Division,* relieved after fighting on the Somme, to go to the *Sixth Army,* while the *Guard Reserve Corps* of the *Sixth Army* was sent to Cambrai. In this way, *Sixth Army* contributed yet another fighting unit for the Somme. It was the final sneer at the Fromelles attacks.

In due course GHQ reported the Fromelles attacks back to London, describing them as 'some important raids'. With a few ill-chosen words in a despatch the cynicism of the Somme was spread even to those keenest of soldiers, the Australians. Never again did they believe a British communiqué.

With the collapse of the attacks at Fromelles, the 'nibbling' at the Somme continued, always with heavy loss of life and massive expenditure of *materiel.* Even GHQ expected little of them but insisted they were essential prerequisites of any further 'general attack'. So day in and day out they continued. Sometimes unremitting courage and determination brought rewards and an attack would be successful. More often it encountered equal courage and determination on the other side and failed.

New horrors

To the Germans, once an attack had been repulsed, was left the task of disposing of the dead. Often all that could be done was to throw the corpses into disused communication trenches and seal them off with a few sandbags.

But there were minor victories, sometimes unlooked for. On July 17 the fortress of Ovillers on the Albert-Bapaume road, enveloped by the British advance, surrendered. As the staring-eyed, starving, louse-ridden, German defenders—some units containing as few as 30 men—stumbled out, their British captors, in one of those vain gestures of war, presented arms

British machine gunners wearing their gas masks. They worked with the masks pinned to their shirts, ready to be pulled on when the gas bells clanged

in tribute to their brave defence. The fall of this besieged fortress did, however, free an area round Ovillers as far as the western approaches to Pozières.

It was here that the next pressure on the Germans was to be applied. On July 21 a conference of corps commanders and their artillery officers had taken place at General Gough's Fourth Army Headquarters. They decided on a further general attack all along the line next day. On the right it would be carried out in combination with the French; on the left it would include Pozières. This was a village of red-roofed houses, tiered up the hillside, lying along the Albert-Bapaume Road like a reversed letter L. The Picardy countryside scene was completed by an old-fashioned windmill on the crest of the hill about 100 yards behind it. The village stood at the junction point of the Fourth and Reserve Armies. Against it the Fourth Army was to launch men of the 1st Division, largely Territorials, while the Reserve Army would put in the newly arrived men of the I Anzac Corps.

Things began badly. The French were not ready. Foch tried to make up for this by ordering XX Corps, next to the British left, to display activity to convince the Germans that an attack was coming soon. At about the same time, two attempts on High Wood and the Switch Line which ran through it failed, the first with a loss of 1,000 officers and men. Companies of the 19th Battalion, the Manchester Regiment, who had attacked Guillemont, a mile south east of Longueval, entered the village despite uncut German wire. There they besieged the commander of the German *Second Battalion* of the *104th Regiment* in his headquarters and set up four machine gun posts to forestall reinforcements. However, they could be given no support because No-Man's Land was under heavy bombardment. To make things worse the 2nd Battalion, Green Howards, who were also to have attacked the village lost their way in the smoke and dust of battle.

The Manchesters were ordered to withdraw, but some of them, unable to get out, held out against the German units and were overwhelmed only when, with almost

all their number wounded, they ran out of ammunition.

On the left, however, it was a different story. Here the English Territorials and the Australians had launched their two-pronged attack on Pozières from the left and right of the Bapaume road. The Territorials, on the left, had captured most of their objectives. Then, before first light on July 23, the Australians—who faced the battle with such eagerness that, according to Haig's Diary, one regiment began with 900 men and finished with 1,300 after men resting had joined the fray—crept forward under artillery cover. When the barrage lifted, they rushed forward by the light of German flares and took the trench fronting Pozières. The German *77th Regiment,* holding it, fled. By early morning they reached their final objective: the right side of the Albert-Bapaume road.

For the next seven hours the men, on their own initiative, methodically flushed out the remaining machine gun nests in cellars and under ruins. Throughout they were heavily shelled.

Fresh attempts were made the following morning to capture the rest of Pozières. After one attack failed they went through the village and, with heavy casualties, occupied the cemetery on the left and a line of outposts on its northern edge. To all intents and purposes Pozières was in British hands.

But Pozières gave observation of a wide area and accordingly the German forces were told it must 'at any price' be recaptured. On July 24, General von Böhn, commander of *IX Reserve Corps,* took command and delegated Major General Wellman's *18th Reserve Division* to retake the village. A heavy bombardment fell upon the Australians, who waited to see the field grey uniforms advancing. The attack failed to arrive.

The commander of the *157th Regiment,* urged to attack from his position behind the village, pleaded that his men were not ready. Wellman threatened him with court martial and he hurriedly began preparations for an attack, only to be dogged with misfortune at each step. Orders to one regiment were misunderstood. Flamethrower and pioneer detachments were spotted and destroyed as they moved forward. A serious shortage of artillery ammunition was discovered. The attack was cancelled.

A little glory
Later that day, however, and on the next, counterattacks were launched, only to be repelled by artillery and rifle fire.

Thus, for the Allies there was some reason to hope that July might end with a little glory. On July 30 the combined Franco-British attacks which had been agreed by General Rawlinson and General Fayolle, the commander of the French Sixth Army, were launched. The village of Guillemont was entered, without loss, by the 2nd Battalion Royal Scots Fusiliers, who pushed forward and held out against a counterattack, only to be overwhelmed in the afternoon when a support company, believing itself surrounded, withdrew. In the meanwhile the 2nd Battalion Oxfordshire and Buckinghamshire Light Infantry, also advancing on Guillemont, overran the German front positions and got close to the railway station, only to be destroyed by well hidden German machine guns.

The only gain through a day of heavy casualties was a small area to the left of the French positions. For the French themselves gains made at the beginning had had to be abandoned because of failure in support.

The offensive moved into its second month. It was, in the words of the Official History, 'A period of fighting when hardly any ground was gained and the struggle became more than ever a grim test of endurance.'

At the beginning of August a matter which had been vexing commanders for some time was brought to light. This was the growing friction between the British and the French on the boundary of the two national armies. The British felt they were being weakened as one French division next to them was withdrawn and orders were issued for the withdrawal of XX Corps, the 'Iron Corps', as they were called. In fact XX Corps had been fighting since the beginning and had been reconstituted four times. Despite their high reputation they had been criticised by the French Supreme Command for lack of progress and had, in turn, blamed the failure on the British on their left. Diplomacy and good liaison work on both sides managed, however, to plaster over this crack in the Entente and the battle went on.

On the British right the Australian 2nd Division, which had replaced the 1st, was planning an attack round Pozières for August 2, but before it could take place assembly trenches had to be dug. Under constant artillery bombardment the task became a major military operation with losses as great as in an attack. One pioneer unit lost 230 officers and men in ten days and even then the trenches were not ready in time and the attack had to be postponed.

When, finally, it did take place, the area had been under such constant bombardment from both sides that all that remained of the village on the hilltop was a powdery debris of bricks and earth, six feet thick. Maps became useless as landmarks were obliterated and troops overran the flattened enemy trenches, to become targets for the German machine guns set up in

every concealed shellhole or piece of ruin. Artillery spotters found it impossible to direct guns with accuracy and on several occasions British bombardments came down on their own troops. All the same the trenches between Pozières village and the windmill fell, and by evening the Australians dug in round what had once been the mill itself.

From their new vantage point the Australians could see little sign of German infantry or trenches, but the RFC spotters warned of signs of an impending attack. The first assault on August 6 was dispersed with small arms fire, but that night after heavy shellfire the Germans succeeded in breaking the Australian line.

It occasionally happens that the tide of battle is turned by a single man. This was the case here. Lieutenant Albert Jacka of the 14th (Victoria) Battalion, who, as a private at Gallipoli, had been the first Anzac to win the VC, was responsible for what the Australian official history called the 'most dramatic and effective act of individual audacity in the history of the AIF'. With a party of his men he got out of the dugout, attacked the Germans in the rear and routed them.

This latest German defeat, small in itself, meant that after a fortnight's battle General Wellman's *18th Reserve Division* was brought almost to its end as a coherent fighting force. Its losses, returned on August 9, were over 8,000 officers and men.

Haig had told the Anzac Corps Commander, Lieutenant-General Sir William Birdwood, when his troops were on their way to the line: 'You're not fighting Bashi-Bazouks now—this is serious, scientific war.' Now he had to congratulate what he called the 'Colonials' on taking Pozières. More practically gratifying, however, was the vista over the slopes which opened to them. There, below, they could see the Germans taking away their guns and destroying their dumps.

Chaos and destruction
In spite of Australian successes at Pozières, Rawlinson was still worried at the continuing resistance in Longueval and Delville Wood. Haig had also been concerned, for some time past, about the consequent vulnerability of the guns in Caterpillar Valley.

On July 27 Longueval and Delville were bombarded with every available gun and patrols reported a 'horrible scene of chaos and destruction'. Even so it was impossible to hold the wood, for though the British troops had established a line roughly through the middle, the mandatory counterattacks which followed penetrated their line.

However, almost as soon as the British pre-attack bombardment began, a company of German *8th Grenadiers (Leib Grenadiers)* surrendered. These surrenders were now becoming more commonplace and they were the direct consequence of the conditions under which the defenders were now existing. Allied artillery superiority was making reliefs impossible and German troops were forced to remain in the line long after they had ceased to be viable fighting units. Furthermore, the difficulty of supplying men in the line meant that they had to take with them personal supplies of food and seltzer water (ordinary water was not available). The Germans were desperately short of artillery because

efficient Allied counterbattery activity was destroying their batteries while the overworked remainder were bursting on their emplacements. The shortage of trained troops was such that in August the *II Bavarian Corps* was sent men of the *Landsturm*, home defence territorials normally reckoned too old for front line service. They had to be sent back as 'merely a danger'.

Haig, who had previously opposed Joffre's theory of attrition, the 'wearing out battle' as he called it, on the ground that it was not always clear who was wearing out whom, now officially embraced the idea. He realised, however, the importance of maintaining pressure on the Germans in France to stop any mass movement to the Russian front.

On show
However, Haig's attention was temporarily distracted from the serious side of the war by a visit to the front on August 12 by King George V. There followed the customary round of official luncheons and banquets, award presenting and handshaking; guests included the French President, Raymond Poincaré, and the Commander-in-Chief, General Joffre. The King was even shown, as earnest of the success of the offensive, captured German trenches.

Joffre, as the original apostle of attrition, was, like Haig, preoccupied with the political and military need to support the Russians, and had come round to the view that the best way of doing so was by a combined attack on a broad front. At a meeting of the two Commanders-in-Chief it was agreed by the British, who in Joffre's view were never as active as they should have been, that they would launch attacks from the Somme to High Wood on August 18 on condition the French also attacked the whole of their narrower front north of the Somme at the same time. It was planned that the British would try to take Guillemont by the evening of the 18th, and the French would go for Maurepas and Angle Wood, to cover the British right.

The day of the attack was dull and showery and on the left of the line against High Wood there was no success. On their right, however, the British pushed forward round Guillemont. There was a setback to the French from a German counterattack, but by morning the Germans had withdrawn and the area was reoccupied.

On other parts of the front, too, there were signs of minor successes in the next few days. In yet another bloody encounter at Delville Wood the line was pushed forward, and by August 19 there were indications that the German defences in front of *III Corps*, on the left, were weakening. Part of the Switch Line was occupied west of High Wood by patrols of 1st Battalion, Northamptonshire Regiment from the 1st Division, with little resistance, and reconnaissance showed that a considerable length was now empty. Angle Wood fell to the French and on the 24th they completed the capture of Maurepas.

On the other hand, the Germans were still strong elsewhere. They recaptured a stretch of trench, threatening the left of the Australian forward position, while German aircraft, quiescent for weeks because of Allied air superiority, suddenly became active and spotted Australian attack preparations.

Four days later the British commanders

decided that the thorn of Delville Wood had troubled them enough and it should be finally extracted. A fierce encounter followed with the 10th Battalion of the Durham Light Infantry, from the 14th Division, in a surprise attack, driving the Germans from their last hold, only for another part to be retaken two days later. The Germans also made other gains in the wood, though at such cost that one German unit had almost all its officers killed.

By this time changes had taken place in the German High Command and Falkenhayn was replaced by Hindenburg, with Ludendorff as his Quartermaster-General. The immediate effect at the front was that the strategy of holding rigidly every yard ceased to be practised.

Combined attack
Meanwhile, Joffre and Haig had once again conferred and produced their customary agreement for a combined attack. It was to take place on August 30 and to be pushed deep enough into the enemy's lines to cause serious disorganisation. However, the weather had now broken and it was necessary to postpone the operations of the French Sixth Army and the British until September 3, and that of the French Tenth Army to September 4.

Once more the start was unpropitious. The French 127th Regiment was pinned down by German machine gun fire and the French 75-mm guns which were to have covered the British left had been moved at short notice, and without warning, to meet a counterattack. The 2nd Battalion of the Kings Own Scottish Borderers attacked just the same and some observers thought they had prevailed as they saw no withdrawal. The truth was there was no one left to withdraw, as all the first waves lay dead or wounded.

At the same time the Australians launched an attack on Mouquet Farm, 'Moo-Cow' Farm as they called it. It proved to be a highly defended fortress with a system of strongholds built deep beneath it, some holding as many as 200 men. The Germans were able to emerge from the numerous exits among the debris and surprise the Australians, so that the attack—first of many on the fortress—failed.

The same day, at noon, the 95th Brigade of the 5th Division advanced to attack the German trenches at Guillemont. The German front line was carried and the advance continued to the German second position with enemy resistance being overcome by

Above: German front line troops advancing. A moment's hesitation in the face of death could mean more certain death in front of a firing squad. *Below:* British supporting troops moving up—'just one more of those bloody and futile rushes at the fence'

rifle fire in one of the few battles of the Somme campaign in which musketry was used.

After their own shaky start the French were now having some success. They took the better part of Clery and most of the German defences on the Clery-le-Forêt road as well as the village of le Forêt itself; high ground south of Combles was also taken and Bois Douage entered, and the following day the French further improved their position round Clery.

The next stage in the battle from the British point of view was the capture of Guillemont. The 59th Brigade advancing under cover of a rolling or 'creeping' barrage, which had now become established practice, pushed forward with such dash they suffered casualties from the British guns, but surprised the Germans. By the end of the day, Guillemont was in British hands.

Darkness brought rain, but the line was linked to the south-western outskirts of Ginchy, north-east of Guillemont, though an attack on the village itself was halted by machine gun and sniper fire from the Germans still in Delville Wood.

The weather of the next two days was windy and showery, but the Allied attacks were pressed home. Falfemont Farm was cleared, enabling the French left to advance once more, patrols pushed forward and captured ground round Combles and the French VII Corps entered Clery.

South of the Somme the French Tenth Army attacked and in three days fighting Soyécourt was captured and Chilly surrounded when bad weather brought operations to a halt.

Then, on September 9, the 1st Battalion Royal Munster Fusiliers, checked in their intended assault, wheeled and routed the nearest Germans, then pressed on and in a short time were streaming into Ginchy. By the late afternoon the 8th Battalion Royal Dublin Fusiliers had carried the attack through the village while other Irish units were clearing the western part of Ginchy. The Germans surrendered in large numbers while many others fled.

Delville freed

With the fall of Ginchy the Germans finally relinquished their grip on Delville Wood. Thus the terrain on which so many lives had been expended fell, as it were, to a side blow.

On the left, attempts were made early in September to extend the advantage gained at Pozières by attacks to envelop Thiepval. The most important part of this attack was astride the Ancre, where the 39th and 49th Divisions were engaged. The 49th, south-east of the river, advanced after an excellent barrage, crossed No-Man's Land, with few casualties, and managed to capture sections of the German trench. However, one of its constituent units, the 1st Battalion 5th Duke of Wellington's, was held up by the German wire and failed to capture its objectives. Mist prevented signalling and, as it cleared, the drift of troops back to their own lines portended failure.

Beyond the river, where the 39th Division was attacking, the story was much the same. Some footings were gained in the German lines, but the withdrawal of the 49th meant the Germans were able to enfilade their own captured trenches from the east and at the same time they shelled the British troops heavily. No withdrawals were started until the supply of ammunition failed and some units were engaged throughout the night.

Summer was past and the battle dragged on, still undecided, into the shortening and cooling of the autumn days. The I Anzac Corps, men who were used to fighting in warmer climates, cleared more German trenches, took more prisoners and were, in their turn, relieved. Their place was taken by another colonial unit, the Canadian Corps.

The pressure on the Germans still did not relent, but at GHQ at Amiens new ideas were taking shape. A strict policy of economy of men was ordered to conserve the 'Final Reserves' — in Haig's phrase — and individual commanders were not allowed to use more than two battalions in any single attack. Even with this restriction, two companies of the 8th Battalion Duke of Wellington's and two of the 9th Battalion, West Yorkshires, on September 14, gained ground at Thiepval Spur, taking the German front line and its associated trenches.

Two days earlier the French had reported further good progress. Bois d'Anderlu had fallen, and the village of Bouchavesnes. The French had penetrated the German defences north-west of Merrieres Wood and VII Corps had repulsed strong counterattacks.

But GHQ and Haig, busy planning, conferring, meeting their French counterparts, had little time for minor encounters or their losses.

Those in command rarely had time to consider the lives and deaths of the tired men who fought on day after day in the front line. Little was said of them except criticism: 'Units of that division did not really attack, and some men did not follow their officers', Haig, describing one of the many minor attacks, dismissed it as 'just one more of those bloody and futile rushes at the fence' and GHQ threatened to introduce 'battle police' with orders to shoot down loiterers. As it was, a moment's hesitation in the face of death could — and did — mean a more certain death standing, gas mask reversed over head, before a firing squad, the punishment for 'cowardice in the face of the enemy'.

Not surprisingly, the men fighting on the Somme responded to what they saw as hostile apathy with equally hostile apathy. The soldiers knew that whatever plans GHQ might now be fashioning would in the end, only bring about their death. For many of those taking part, the Somme excursion was summed up by two soldiers found in Delville Wood. One was South African, one German; they had killed each other at precisely the same instant with their bayonets. And that, they said, was how the battle would end: when the last two soldiers, the 'Final Reserves', confronted and killed one another.

The riderless horses of a French cavalry regiment forage among the mud and debris for patches of grass

Further Reading
Aitken, Alexander, *Gallipoli to the Somme* (Melbourne)
Bean, C. E. W., *Anzac to Amiens* (Canberra 1946)
Bean, C. E. W., *The Australian Imperial Force in France 1916* (Sydney 1929)
Blake, Robert (ed.), *The Private Papers of Douglas Haig 1914-1919* (London 1952)
Falls, Cyril, *The First World War* (London 1960)
Girard, General Georges, *La Bataille de la Somme en 1916* (Paris)
Gristwood, A. D., *The Somme* (London 1927)
Haig, Douglas (ed.) J. H. Boraston, *Despatches 1914-1918* (London 1919)
Hankey, Lord, *The Supreme Command 1914-1918* (London 1961)
Joffre, Marshal, *Memoirs* (London 1932)
Kabisch, E., *Somme 1916* (Berlin 1937)
Lawson, J. A., *Memoirs of Delville Wood* (Cape Town 1918)
Masefield, John, *Battle of the Somme* (London 1917)
Monash, Lieutenant-General Sir John, *The Australian Victories in France* (London)
Terraine, John, *Douglas Haig: The Educated Soldier* (London 1963)
Westman, Stephen, *Surgeon with the Kaiser's Army* (London 1968)

THE SOMME
The Last Phase

From September 25 to November 18, 1916, the French and British on the Somme laboured for a victory that was never to be realised. Individual actions gained them a few thousand yards of ground: in four months, the Allied line crept forward a few miles. In daunting conditions of rain and sleet and the first snowfalls of a hard winter, both sides manifested a sobering courage and determination, constantly unmatched by the scope of their achievements.

To a reader, the last phase of the Somme battles from September 25 to November 18 1916 makes a confused and rather tedious story. To the men who fought through these two autumn months it was remembered as one of the most exhausting and dismal periods of the whole of the First World War. The mud of the Somme during the wet weather of October 1916 was never to be forgotten by those who struggled and suffered through it.

Under the general title of the Battle of the Ancre, the final phase of fighting on the Somme is broken down in the official British record of the war into five separate battles:

● September 25 to 28: Battle of Morval.
● September 26 to 28: Battle of Thiepval Ridge.
● October 1 to 18: Battle of the Transloy Ridges.
● October 1 to November 11: Battle of the Ancre Heights.
● November 13 to 18: Battle of the Ancre.

The distinction between one battle and another is necessary to enable the course of events to be clearly followed, but it should not be imagined that those who actually fought in them were aware of such a neat pattern.

To understand the Battle of Morval it is important to look briefly at the operation which had preceded it, known as the Battle of Flers-Courcelette, and which took place from September 15 to 22 in the southern sector of the British front.

September 15 was a fine autumn day, but the ground was muddy after recent rains. After a small preliminary operation to clear out some Germans near Delville Wood, the assault was made at 0620 hours. In the end a belt of ground some 2,500 yards deep was gained on the whole front, the greatest penetration of over 3,500 yards being made, with the help of tanks, at Flers in the centre. The British infantry did not follow up quickly enough, and the crisis for the Germans was overcome by

the effective use of their reinforcements, with six more divisions arriving during the battle. The Germans fought very well on the first day, in spite of temporary local panic caused by the tanks, and the British suffered heavy casualties. This was the first occasion in which tanks were used in the war, and there has been much controversy since as to whether they were wisely employed or not.

Fighting continued on September 16 and 17, and small areas of ground were gained. September 18 and 19 were very wet days, and on September 19 General Fayolle stated at a conference that owing to bad weather the French Sixth Army, which was to co-operate in further attacks, would not be ready until September 22. Due to heavy rain, the date was postponed until the 23rd, but the bad weather persisted, and no action took place on that day or on the 24th. At a conference held at Chantilly, Joffre and Robertson agreed that the offensive must go on, but the French were very short of ammunition, so D-Day had to be postponed until September 25. The aim of the planned attacks was to capture objectives on the front of the Fourth Army from around Gueudecourt to Morval, and for the Reserve Army to take Thiepval Ridge. In the case of the Fourth Army, the renewed effort was largely required to secure ground

which had not been taken during the Battle of Flers-Courcelette, and was planned as an advance of 1,200 to 1,500 yards in three stages. First came the capture of Gueudecourt and ground either side of it; then the Combles-Gueudecourt road; and third, ground to the east of Morval and Lesboeufs.

At the request of the French Sixth Army, zero hour was fixed at 1235 hours on September 25, though the bombardment was begun at 0700 hours on the previous day. The French, however, did not assault until 1600 hours on September 26, and then achieved very little. The fighting on September 25 on the British front took much the same course as on September 15: success came mostly in the early stages. The advance of XIV Corps to take Morval and Lesboeufs went smoothly, and by 1800 hours troops were dug in to the east of both villages, having penetrated the enemy front to about 2,000 yards on a front 3,000 yards wide. XV Corps, however, did not capture Gueudecourt, and to the north-east of Martinpuich III Corps were unable to advance against strong opposition. To the south of the British sector, the French were making extremely slow progress, and Foch

Up and over: Canadian troops with fixed bayonets move in to make a raid on German trenches. Despite conditions which made 'mere existence a severe trial of body and spirit', the Canadians were able to preserve their traditional *élan*

called on Haig at 1000 hours on September 25 to ask if he could pass some French troops through Morval to attack one of his main objectives, the village of Sailly-Saillisel, from the west. His request was readily met, and it was agreed that the French should extend their left flank and take over some of the ground then held by the British.

On September 26 the Germans retired from Combles, which was taken over by the British and the French. A German withdrawal from Gueudecourt also took place, allowing members of XV Corps to move in. On September 27 and 28 the main activity involved handing over part of XIV Corps' sector to the French, which was carried out smoothly. The Battle of Morval died down on September 28. It had been moderately successful for the Allies: tanks had not been used much, though one was employed in a successful small action early on September 26 just south of Gueudecourt during the capture of the 'Gird' trenches.

At 1235 hours on September 26, exactly 24 hours after the previous day's barrage had opened to the south, fire was brought down on the German trenches opposite the Canadians. During the afternoon and evening they advanced up to 1,000 yards, and at 1800 hours the Canadian Corps Commander told General Gough that 'on the whole' the situation was good, since the crest of the ridge had almost been reached. On II Corps' front, the main achievement was the seizing of Thiepval village, a mess of rubble and ruins, but strongly held by the Germans, who had made good use of the cellars which remained intact and which provided excellent cover. Mainly responsible for the success at Thiepval were the 12th Middlesex and 11th Royal Fusiliers of the 54th Infantry Brigade, supported by two tanks.

During the next four days—September 27 to 30—the Canadian Corps extended its territory to a depth of nearly 1,000 yards to the north-east of Courcelette, but made little progress west of the village. Troops of II Corps progressed several hundred yards north of Thiepval village, but on neither Corps' front was the main objective, the top of the Thiepval Ridge, reached. The Germans fought with great skill and determination, and although the British gained the top of the ridge in many places, they did not succeed in taking it.

Troops from Verdun

September was a difficult month for the Germans, but in one area they had a relatively easy time: against the French, their *Second Army* was never severely pressed. As a result, most of the reinforcing divisions which were made available to the Germans at the end of the battle at Verdun were sent to their *First Army,* who were opposite the British.

One effect of the Somme attacks during July and August had been to shake German confidence in their military leadership in the west, and thus to bring about the departure of Falkenhayn. The well-known team of Hindenburg and Ludendorff then took over direction of the German war effort, and they made their first visit to the Western Front on September 8, when all army commanders and their chiefs-of-staff were assembled at Cambrai to meet them. These commanders made it clear to Ludendorff that they felt their position to be most precarious, and stressed the heavi-

ness of their casualties since July 1, 1916. He in his turn questioned some of their tactics, in particular their tendency to hold ground very closely without clear reasons for retaining it.

The new measures taken by Hindenburg and Ludendorff were threefold. First, they gave orders for preparation of a rear defensive line on the Western Front, which was soon to become known as the 'Hindenburg Line'; they then ordered the formation in Germany of 11 supplementary divisions to reinforce the Western Front, and thirdly the 'Hindenburg Programme' was put forward for doubling ammunition output in German factories, as well as trebling that of artillery and machine guns. Ammunition demands were becoming enormous: on the Somme in September 1916, 5,725,440 rounds of field artillery ammunition, and

Above: A railway wagon carries food for the trenches. Its cargo of shells destroyed, British soldiers pose in its bullet-riddled hulk a few miles from the front lines. The battle for the Somme decided little; for a total of more than a million casualties, a belt of ground 30 miles long had been won by the Allies

1,302,000 rounds of heavy artillery ammunition, were consumed.

The German difficulties were not unknown to their opponents. With Thiepval secure, and the assurance of his Intelligence staff that the Germans had already committed 70 divisions to battle since the start of the Somme offensive and had lost at least 370,000 men, Haig now felt that no relaxation of pressure was acceptable, and decided to increase the frontage of his offensive by bringing back part of the Third Army. He therefore ordered that preparation should be made for another great attack on October 12, and sent out instructions by letter to the commanders of the three armies under his control on September 29 1916, in which their objectives were given as follows:

Fourth Army: Le Transloy, Beaulencourt,

the ridge beyond the Thilloy-Warlencourt Valley, and Loupart Wood, which lay between Thilloy and Irles.

Reserve Army—southern sector. From Loupart Wood westward through Irles to Miraumont. This attack was to be launched northwards from Thiepval Ridge.

Reserve Army—northern sector. The direction of Puisieux, with the troops on the right joining the other half of the Army at Miraumont, cutting off enemy forces in the Ancre Valley. This attack was to be launched eastwards from the line Beaumont Hamel to Hébutène.

Third Army: The spur south-east of Gommecourt to secure the left flank of the Reserve Army.

Haig believed that these tasks were within the capabilities of the three armies concerned; but they were never achieved. Again and again attacks failed and operations were postponed or curtailed. The main cause of this lack of success was the terrible weather, which broke on October 2, and turned the ground into a sea of mud.

A 'severe trial'

To fully understand the difficulties which the weather imposed on the Allied advance, it is necessary to grasp the nature of the 50 square miles of ground which three months' fighting had given them, across which lay the communications between the front line and the rear. From a position such as the north end of High Wood, almost the whole British battleground was visible to the eye on a clear day. To reach this place from the old Allied front line of July 1, some four miles of bad roads had to be traversed. At the best they were mere country tracks, roughly made with no solid foundation. And they had to support traffic such as could never have been imagined by those who had made them. Ten or 12 horses were sometimes required to move an 18-pounder field gun; ammunition had to be sent up by pack mule, and it was said that men died from the effort of trying to walk through the battlefield carrying verbal messages. The Somme mud could cling to the feet of a man to the size of a football. The Official History records that: *By the middle of October conditions on and behind the battle front were so bad as to make mere existence a severe trial of body and spirit. Little could be seen from the air through the rain and mist, so counterbattery work suffered and it was often impossible to locate with accuracy the new German trenches and shell-hole positions. Objectives could not always be identified from ground level, so that it is no matter for surprise or censure that the British artillery sometimes fired short or placed its barrages too far ahead. The infantry, sometimes wet to the skin and almost exhausted before zero hour, were often condemned to struggle painfully forward through the mud under heavy fire against objectives vaguely defined and difficult of recognition.*

Had they been able to see more of the area it would have been of great military value, but it would hardly have given cause for pleasure. John Buchan, who was a war correspondent at the front, wrote this description of the battle area: *Let us assume that early in October we have taken our stand at the northern angle of High Wood. It is only a spectre of a wood, a horrible place of matted tree trunks, crumbling trench lines, full of mementoes of the dead and all the dreadful débris of*

Above: An ammunition wagon bogs down in the mud. In the prevailing conditions, 10 or 12 horses were often required to move even light loads; men actually died from the effort of walking

battle. To reach it we have walked across two miles of what once must have been breezy downland, patched with little fields of roots and grain. It is now like a waste brickfield in a decaying suburb, pockmarked with shell holes, littered with cartridge clips, equipment, fragments of wire, and every kind of tin can. Over all the area hangs the curious, bitter, unwholesome smell of burning — an odour which will always recall to every soldier the immediate front of battle. Our own front is some thousands of yards off, close under that hillock which is the famous Butte de Warlencourt. Far on our left is the lift of the Thiepval Ridge, and nearer us, hidden by the slope, are the ruins of Martinpuich.

Le Sars and Eaucourt-l'Abbaye are before us, Flers a little to the right, and beyond it Gueudecourt. On our extreme right rise the slopes of Sailly-Saillisel — one can see the shattered trees lining the Bapaume-Péronne road — and, hidden by the fall of the ground, are Lesboeufs and Morval. Behind us are things like scarred patches on the hillsides. They are the remains of the Bazentin woods and the ominous wood of Delville. The whole confines of the British battleground lie open to the eye, from the Thiepval Ridge in the north to the downs which ring the site of Combles. Look west, and beyond the dreary country we have crossed, rise green downs set with woods untouched by shell — the normal, pleasant

land of Picardy. Look east, beyond our front line and the smoke puffs, across the Warlencourt and Gueudecourt Ridges, and on the sky-line there also appear unbroken woods, and here and there a church spire and the smoke of villages. The German retirement in September was rapid, and we have reached the fringes of a land as yet little scarred by combat. We are looking at the boundaries of the battlefield. We have pushed the enemy right up to the edge of habitable and undevastated country, but we pay for our success in having behind us a strip of sheer desolation.

General Rawlinson's plan for the battle of the Transloy Ridges was to start with an operation on October 1 1916 to straighten out his line in the area of Le Sars and Eaucourt l'Abbaye, before undertaking the major advance ordered by Haig. This first part of the plan went well, and by the evening of October 3 nearly all objectives had been taken. A slight dip in the line remained in the middle opposite the 47th Division, but after dark on October 5 it was able to extend its outposts to include the ruined mill north-west of Eaucourt-l'Abbaye. The stage was now set for the next phase, due to start two days later.

Water-logged

The comparatively successful beginning was not to be followed up during the operations which followed. Between October 7 and 12, in appalling conditions, numerous assaults were made by III, XV, and XIV Corps. The only places where a little ground was gained were at Le Sars, by III Corps, and north of Gueudecourt, by XIV Corps. On the evening of October 12 Rawlinson was, as the Official History puts it, 'conscious that most of what he had planned to accomplish on October 5 still remained to do'. He decided to renew

Above: Congestion on a road to the front. Staff cars, mule limbers and ambulances mingle with marching infantry. *Below:* A shell bursts beyond the barbed wire entanglements near Flers

his attack on October 18, and obtained the approval of Haig, who hoped to obtain the co-operation of the French. Orders went out to Fourth Army on October 13, and the importance of preparing adequate assembly trenches, as well as improving communications to the front, was emphasised, as well they might be, since the plan was to assault in the darkness at 0340 hours, nearly two hours before sunrise. Under certain circumstances this would have been an excellent plan, but in the conditions which actually prevailed at that time on October 18 it was not a great success. The Official History describes what happened:

In almost every brigade, forming-up positions had been taped out in front, and careful compass bearings taken of the direction of the advance. When the moment of assault arrived the British front positions and the approaches to them were a maze of water-logged shell holes and flooded trenches. As the troops struggled forward through the darkness, officers and men stumbled and fell in the slippery ooze; rifles and Lewis guns became clogged with it so that bomb and bayonet were soon the only weapons.

On XV Corps' front, two tanks were kept ready in Flers, to be used at dawn if the assault in darkness failed. One of them crossed the front-line at 0800 hours. For 20 minutes it fired at German positions,

with considerable success. The tank commander eventually got out and signalled for the nearby British infantry to take advantage of this breakthrough, but they were so exhausted, and there were so few surviving officers in the area, that nothing happened. Pushing the enemy before it, the tank went forward some distance towards Le Barque before turning and retreating the way it had come. This was the last chance: by the end of the following day all Allied efforts in the Fourth Army area had petered out.

The tasks given to the Reserve Army for October had been to attack northwards from the Thiepval Ridge towards Irles and Miraumont, and eastwards towards Puisieux from the Beaumont Hamel-Hébutène line. In the northward attack, involving the Canadian Corps and II Corps, a continuous line of German trenches running from the notorious Schwaben Redoubt, north of Thiepval, was the target for capture. It ran for some 5,500 yards and for its first 1,500 yards was known as Stuff trench, and thereafter became Regina trench. In the early days of October great efforts were made, mainly by the Canadian Corps, to reach Regina trench from positions north of Courcelette. The heaviest fighting took place between October 7 and 10. At the end of this very costly and particularly gruelling period of fighting a belt of ground approximately 2,000 yards wide, and varying in depth between 200 and 500 yards had been taken, but this was only half way to Regina trench. At the other end of the sector, in the area of Stuff trench, men of II Corps fought some fierce actions from October 11 to 14, eventually driving the Germans from their last hold on the redoubt.

II Corps renewed the attack on October 21, and this time advanced to and captured some 5,000 yards of German trenches. The last section of Regina trench was eventually taken by the 4th Canadian Division at midnight November 10. Using moonlight to see their way, and the cover of light mist, two battalions advanced as close as possible to the German line before zero hour. After an eight-minute barrage the Canadians stormed the trench before the enemy were ready: four machine guns and 87 prisoners were taken for a total of 200 Canadian casualties. Thus, after some six weeks the objectives given to the northward attack of the Reserve Army had been achieved, though the cost was heavy.

The proposed eastward advance did not take place during October. On V and XIII Corps' fronts there were many trench raids, and patrolling was constant, but the major battle was constantly postponed. Eventually, it turned into the final phase of the Somme offensive, the Battle of the Ancre. It was fought by the British Fifth Army, the former Reserve Army, under the command of General Gough.

No transport problems

The Germans north of the Ancre valley were confident in their ability to hold a strong position. However, General Gough believed that his prepared attack against the Beaumont Hamel salient might just succeed. The slow progress of the Fourth Army during October had led the Germans to the conclusion that the British offensive had ceased for the winter. Because of the state of the ground, the Ger-

mans felt that an attack on a large scale was physically impossible, especially an attack on a fortress which had so successfully repulsed British efforts when they had advanced with fresh troops and full impetus at the height of summer. But they did not realise that the area from Thiepval northward did not suffer from transport difficulties to the same degree as the ground on the southern Somme front. The British advance in the north sector would be launched from trenches that had been occupied at the beginning of the Somme battles in July. Here, the problem of crossing five or six miles of shell-torn roads, as in the areas where the greater gains had been made, did not exist.

The topographical features of the new battleground should be understood. North of the Schwaben Redoubt the British

Above: The road to captivity: a German prisoner, helmet askew, seems to be content with his lot

front curved sharply to the north-west, crossing the Ancre 500 yards south of the hamlet of Saint Pierre Divion, and extending northwards along the foot of the slopes on which lay the villages of Beaumont Hamel and Serre. From the high ground north-west of the Ancre several clearly marked spurs descended to the upper valley of the stream. The main spur was a long ridge with Serre at its western extremity, and the village of Puisieux on the north. Beaucourt-sur-Ancre was on the south and Miraumont at the eastern end. South of this there was another feature running from a point 1,000 yards north of Beaumont Hamel to the village of Beaucourt. On the south-west side of the spur was a shallow depression up which ran the Beaucourt-Beaumont Hamel road, and it was defined on the north-east by the Beaucourt-Serre road. The northern bank of the Ancre was thus marked by slopes and pockets. On the south bank there was a stretch of flattish ground under the Thiepval Ridge extending up the valley past Saint Pierre Divion to Grandcourt.

On the night of Friday, November 10,

there was still some doubt as to whether the ground had dried out enough to justify an attack, though there had been no rain since the 8th, and colder weather had set in. Gough discussed the situation with his corps commanders, and decided to launch his attack at 0545 hours on November 13.

By now Gough had positioned 282 heavy guns in support of his Fifth Army—one gun for every 35 yards of front, and a 30,000-pound mine to be fired at zero hour under a stronghold near the tip of the salient. At Beaumont Hamel itself gas was to be used, and in order to secure surprise as to the date and hour of the attack, the sector had been shelled for an hour on successive mornings. At the last minute, on November 12, Haig arrived to assess the operation's chances of success. He was not prepared to risk an unsuccessful attempt, but he went away satisfied that the prospects were good.

Both Fifth Army's corps were involved in the Battle of the Ancre. V Corps now had four divisions in the line—2nd, 3rd, 51st (Highland) and 63rd (Naval) Divisions, and one—the 37th Division—in reserve. II Corps comprised 18th, 19th, 39th, and 4th Canadian Divisions, with 32nd Division in reserve. The main attack was naturally to be undertaken by V Corps, not only because of the better state of the ground behind its lines, but because it had been much less used during the previous months, and was therefore readier for action than II Corps.

The planned operation on V Corps' front was divided into three stages. The first required an advance of about half a mile from Beaucourt station up the Beaumont Hamel valley and round the eastern end of that village, then across Redan Ridge and the slopes in front of Serre. Three lines of German trenches had to be taken, and in places a fourth line as well. The second objective, 600 to 1,000 yards further on, ran from the western edge of Beaucourt, along the eastern slope of Redan Ridge, then south of Serre, and finally round the eastern edge of that village. The final objective on the right was Beaucourt, down on the Ancre, while the left of the corps' front was to be positioned along the western slope of the valley.

South of the Ancre, II Corps was to attempt to drive the Germans from the remains of their trench system between the Schwaben Redoubt and Saint Pierre Divion, then to clear the south bank of the river, and establish a line, facing roughly north-east, opposite Beaucourt. They were also given the task of securing the two principal bridges across the Ancre, the only points at which the river could be crossed.

All objectives achieved

At 0545 hours on November 13, in a wet fog with visibility down to 30 yards, the attack took place as planned. The final barrage came down, the great mine was fired, and the elements of the Fifth Army committed to the first stage of the battle moved into action. The results on II Corps' front were successful. By 0815 hours troops of the 19th Division had achieved their objectives at a cost of less than 200 casualties, while enemy losses were obviously heavy in killed and wounded and 150 prisoners had been captured. The 39th Division had been given three tanks

The front now
had the aura of a
decaying suburb . . .

Fortified ruins

German front line

No-Mans Land

British front line

**Forward Observation
Officers Post**
with telephone line
(partly buried
to battery), containing
FOO and signallers
to observe enemy
movements

Average range
2000-5000 yards
depending on
ground

Gunlayer to put
on range and angles
and sight aiming
post.

Man to open and
close breech after
shell and charge
are loaded and
fired.

Three men to set
fuses and handle
shells and charges
as required

Guns camouflaged
in dip in ground

NCO in charge of
gun. He received and
acknowledged orders
by holding out his
right arm.

Signallers and Officer
in charge of guns.
Orders given vocally
as to range, angles,
and rate of fire.

Telephone line
to wagon and horse
lines, store,
ammunition, limbers etc.
Average distance from
guns 1000 to 1500
yards according to
roads available.

Line to Brigade HQ

Top: Resourcefulness in adversity. Royal Engineers build a makeshift bridge over the Ancre
swamps near Aveluy. Rain had been falling for
several weeks, breaking up the ground, and
the infantrymen were often wet to the skin even
before they went into battle. *Left:* The chart
shows the layout and establishment of an 18-
pounder battery. *Above:* Exhaustion sets in:
British troops sleep in their trenches near
Thiepval Ridge. This area was not as badly
damaged as that south of the Somme, but rain
and cold had seriously debilitated the troops

to help it, but none of them was of much use: two never reached the front line, and the third crashed and turned on its side on reaching the German lines. However, by 0832 hours a message reached divisional headquarters that all objectives had been achieved; within three hours II Corps had done all it set out to do with relatively light losses.

On V Corps' front immediately north of the Ancre was the 63rd Naval Division. A composite force under Lieutenant-Colonel Bernard Freyberg eventually got right up to the edge of Beaucourt, though on November 13 they could get no further. Six tanks had been allotted to the Naval Division and were brought forward during the afternoon, but could not be brought into action until the following day.

On the left of the Naval Division, the 51st Highland Division was faced by what was known as the Y Ravine salient, and by the fortified village of Beaumont Hamel. Both the two brigades committed to the initial assault began well, despite heavy fighting. Early in the afternoon, the left hand brigade entered Beaumont Hamel, but although German resistance began to weaken, it took most of the afternoon to get through the ruins of the village and establish a line on its eastern edge, which had been the preliminary objective.

The 2nd Division made limited advances towards Redan Ridge on a front of some 1,000 yards but in the north the 3rd Division was totally unsuccessful in its advance towards Serre. The Official History explains why: *Serre, on its little knoll, commands the whole of the slope to the west, and the fog was not so thick as to hide the British advance from the enemy. There was no question of a swift assault, for the heavy loam that had crumbled under the incessant bombardments dried more slowly than the chalk surface further south, and the troops of the 3rd Division lost the battle in the mud.*

Finally, mention must be made of attacks by troops of XIII Corps, made on the left of the 3rd Division to assist its extension of its defensive flank. After a relatively successful start, the British were heavily counterattacked. At 1630 hours on November 13 Gough decided not to renew his efforts, after the failure of the 3rd Division's attempts to advance. XIII Corps decided to withdraw its men as well, and by 2130 hours the same night the 92nd Brigade was back where it started, but had suffered 800 casualties.

Overall, the fighting on November 13 was a partial success for the Allies. II Corps had done all that was required; V Corps seemed to be in a position to make further advances at Beaucourt and Beaumont Hamel, though not yet at Serre. Therefore the Naval, Highland and 2nd Divisions were sent orders that night to push ahead on November 14.

Heavy blow
The Germans had been shaken by the extent of the British attack on November 13, as there had been a general feeling that the weather had brought an end to such operations for the year. The success of the British troops fighting astride the Ancre was described by Ludendorff as 'a particularly heavy blow'. German losses on the whole of the Somme front from November 1 to 18 are given as 45,000 in all: nearly one quarter of these must have been suffered on November 13th.

German records contain evidence of the utter misery of life on the Somme front at the end of 1916. They were not so well equipped nor so well fed as the British, and individuals spent longer stretches in the line without relief. The weight of shelling and gas attacks which they endured was also heavier, but the devastation behind the front on their side was not comparable to that suffered by the British: when they were relieved in the line they could get away more quickly and had easier access to dry billets in villages.

After an intense spell of artillery fire starting at 0600 hours on November 14, the infantry renewed their advance on the V Corps' front at 0620 hours. It was another cold and misty morning, but the weather cleared later, and allowed air reconnaissance to start again. The first

... pockmarked with shell holes and littered with rubbish

success of the day was marked up with the capture of Beaucourt by the Naval Division, which was reported at 1030 hours. For his part in the activities leading to this achievement Colonel Freyberg was awarded the Victoria Cross. Twice wounded on November 13, he remained at his post, but was eventually severely wounded by a shell on November 14 and had to be evacuated from the front line.

The attacks by the 51st Highland Division further north were less successful. Slight advances were made early on, but much ground had to be given up later when members of the 7th Argyll and Sutherland Highlanders and 9th Royal Scots were shelled at 1100 hours by a British heavy battery, and were forced to withdraw from the enemy trenches which they had just occupied.

At mid-day General Gough visited V Corps' headquarters, where he found the Corps Commander in an optimistic mood, no doubt largely due to the capture of Beaucourt. Plans were quickly made for a combined attack by V and II Corps the following day; orders went out on the evening of November 14 from Gough, and a copy was sent to Haig in Paris. But a prompt telephone call from Haig followed, during which he stated that he did not wish Fifth Army to undertake any further operations on a large scale before his return. The next day's plans were accordingly reduced in scope to a small attack on the boundary between 51st and 2nd Divisions. Only a few troops were involved but they suffered heavy casualties and gained nothing.

Haig's Chief-of-Staff visited Fifth Army at 0900 hours on November 15, and explained the Commander-in-Chief's objections to a further offensive. After he had left, Gough spoke to his corps commanders, and they all agreed that they should try one more attack. Accordingly the Chief-of-Staff was contacted and asked to obtain Haig's permission for this final effort. In the evening he saw Haig in Paris, and reluctantly permission was granted.

On November 16 and 17 the weather was cold, but clear. Aerial reconnaissance

late on November 17 showed that the Germans had abandoned some trenches near Grandcourt, and orders were given for them to be occupied that night. But on the whole, activity over the two days was limited to 'tidying-up' operations, and to preparations for the attack on November 18. Both II Corps and V Corps were to be involved in this last attack, the aim of which was not entirely clear, though it was best described as an attempt to 'tidy up the line', using Grandcourt as a pivot. But not only was the aim unclear, the instructions were inadequate, containing 'hurried amendments to the orders of corps and lower formations, and eleventh-hour preparations which, as previous experience had shown over and over again, were fatal to success.'

The results of the attack on November 18, which continued until November 19 in places, were more successful than might have been expected. South of the Ancre the 4th Canadian Division achieved all its objectives, and in doing so took a belt of ground 2,500 yards wide and about 1,000 deep. The 19th Division averaged an advance of 500 yards towards Grandcourt, but failed to reach it. North of the Ancre, the 37th Division, which had relieved the 63rd, and 51st Highland Division pushed on up to 1,000 yards beyond Beaucourt and Beaumont Hamel, encountering only weak opposition and being able to take trenches already vacated by the enemy. The Official History gives us an idea of the conditions endured by those taking part in these attacks, and of the reasons for their success: *During the night the first snow of the winter had fallen, and at 0610 hours on November 18 the assault was delivered in whirling sleet which afterwards changed to rain. More abominable conditions for active warfare are hardly to be imagined: the infantry, dark figures only visible for a short distance against the white ground, groped their way forward as best they could through half-frozen mud that was soon to dissolve into chalky slime. Little wonder that direction was often lost and with it the precious barrage, while the objectives, mantled in snow, were hard indeed to identify. Observation from the air was impossible; ground observers could see little or nothing, so that the batteries, in almost as bad a plight as the infantry, were, for the most part, reduced to firing their prearranged programme, regardless of the fortunes of the advance. To the sheer determination, self-sacrifice and physical endurance of the troops must be attributed such measure of success as was won.*

So at last on November 19, 1916, the Somme battles came to an end. During the four and a half months since July 1 the German casualties had been 660,000, and the British and French about 630,000. For more than a million casualties a belt of ground a few miles deep and little more than 30 miles wide had changed hands.

Further Reading
Buchan, John, *A History of the Great War* (Nelson 1933)
Churchill, W. S., *The World Crisis 1916-1918* (Butterworth 1927)
Farrar-Hockley, A., *The Battle of the Somme* (Batsford)
Military Operations, France and Belgium 1916 (Macmillan 1938)

BREAKTHROUGH AT ARRAS

The General

'Good-morning; good-morning!' the General said
When we met him last week on our way to the line.
Now the soldiers he smiled at are most of 'em dead,
And we're cursing his staff for incompetent swine.
'He's a cheery old card,' grunted Harry to Jack
As they slogged up to Arras with rifle and pack.

· · · · · · · ·

But he did for them both by his plan of attack

Siegfried Sassoon

It would not have been surprising if there had been occasions when Sir Douglas Haig asked himself who was trying hardest, the Germans or the French, to hinder his efforts to launch the combined offensives by First and Third Armies in the Vimy-Arras sector, timed for April 8, 1917. The original Arras plan had been concocted in co-operation with Joffre, but had been heavily modified after Nivelle had become the French C-in-C. Now the British contribution was to be strictly subordinated to the main effort, to be delivered by the French across the Chemin des Dames. Yet the British offensive was to be an immense affair for all that, taking in the capture of Vimy Ridge, the German defence of which had for so long held the French at bay, and the thrusting of a thick wedge out towards Cambrai—and even beyond, it

was hoped—the northern anvil upon which Nivelle, with his French hammer, would smash the German armies he hoped to pursue after his victory in the south.

But as the British prepared their detailed plans, the Germans suddenly began to withdraw into the Hindenburg Line. At once, supplementary contingency schemes had to be formulated, in case a wholesale German withdrawal along the entire front completely nullified what had already been planned. So little was known of the new German line that it was not even clear whether it was the sector immediately opposite the Arras front or the Switch Line between Drocourt and Quéant which was intended for permanent occupation.

The new German defensive zone to the south-east of Arras was sited on a reverse slope which denied the Allies any chance of observation. Outposts covered three lines of defence, of which the rearmost defended the artillery positions. A feature of each line was the system of mutually supporting, prefabricated machine gun strongpoints. But overshadowing everything else were the deep belts of newly-laid barbed wire, which shone with 'a sinister blue sheen' in the sunlight, leaving a lasting impression on all who saw them. Here was a formidable obstacle—anything up to 8,000 yards in depth, based on the principle of a lightly occupied front line reinforced by a strong reserve in rear. The function of the latter was to counter penetrations after they had occurred, for it was by now accepted that although the front line trenches would

At Feuchy Chapel, the limit of the first day's surprisingly rapid breakthrough—a battery of 18-pounders in the open, British infantry going down and a tank going up

almost inevitably be lost after a serious bombardment, the position as a whole could be retained by the reserves making a counterattack to restore the situation. The German position to the east and north of Arras, however, contained features unlike those of the new line to the south. There the front line was more often than not on a forward slope and easily scanned by observers on the British side, and nowhere was this more apparent than on Vimy Ridge where, in places, the German trenches were as good as held up to view.

Prior to the offensive, seven German divisions were positioned opposite the sector held by the British, with six in reserve. There were strange anomalies in their deployment, however. If penetrations of the front line were to be accepted, then the reserves ought to be kept fairly close to the front, ready to intervene at speed. In fact, to afford them complete rest from long-range bombardment, they were anything up to 30 miles in rear and, at the earliest, could not hope to enter battle until 36 hours after the British attack had started. Moreover, the commander of *Sixth Army*, General von Falkenhausen, did not embrace the new defensive doctrine wholeheartedly. He had told his infantry to hold the front line at all costs, even though the defences were laid out for a defence in depth. Thus the main reserve was not only too far away, but the local reserve was also to a great extent within range of the British bombardment and could thus be consumed along with the front line troops. Fully aware that a storm was coming, the Germans were nevertheless late in strengthening their foremost defences and the mountains of shells at Douai were too far from the guns they were meant to supply. For all their withdrawal to a position of strength, the Germans were by no means invulnerable.

Right: Soldiers of the 51st (Highland) Division attack through German barbed wire. Held back after it had crossed the first belt of German trenches, confusion began in the 51st Division when one battalion lost its way and turned 90 degrees right. Only one of the division's platoons reached its objective
Below: A British reconnaissance patrol returns from a front which now lay open to an advance

To the north of Arras the offensive was to advance over ground dominated to the east by the long slope, climbing smoothly to the crest of the Vimy escarpment, from which it plunged steeply to the plain of Douai beyond. The closer it came to the canalised River Scarpe, where it drove eastward through marshes, cutting the battlefield in two, the shallower the drop became. South of the Scarpe, too, where the ground was more complex and rolling, the configuration of the escarpment persisted and here, almost due east of Arras, the village of Monchy-le-Preux dominated the surrounding countryside almost as completely as did the highest point of the escarpment above Vimy.

This sector was made unique by one strange feature. Not only was Vimy Ridge honeycombed with tunnels and caves, but so also were the environs of Arras. The stone which had been used in the building of the city had been quarried from caves to the south-east, beneath St Sauveur and Ronville, and this contributed to the natural tunnels. In addition, there was an underworld of sewers conforming to the course of the stream named Crinchon round the eastern suburbs of the town, and leading the effluence of the area into the Scarpe. The existence of the caves had been discovered, much to their surprise, by the British shortly after they had taken over. They had quickly seen it as a comparatively simple but profitable task to link the sewers to the caves and thus provide a safe covered approach right into the fighting line. Throughout the winter of 1916/17, in the greatest secrecy, this work had gone on and, by March, it was all but finished. The project gave access into the middle of No-Man's Land near the Cambrai and Bapaume roads. In the caves there was accommodation for nearly 30,000 men, lighting, ventilation, proper drainage, a power plant, administrative centres and a hospital. A new town lay beneath Arras—the springboard for the attack to relieve the old city above.

On January 2 Haig's orders for an offensive, to begin on April 8 (later changed to April 9), were received by his army commanders. Allenby's Third Army was to throw the biggest punch eastward from Arras: Horne's First Army was to take Vimy Ridge on the northern flank, while Gough's Fifth Army was to operate against the southern flank, though Gough's orders, quite naturally, had to be severely modified when the Germans withdrew in February and March.

'The Bull'

The personalities of the commanders had a great and not altogether fair effect on the plans. Horne and Gough were articulate and persuasive men in conference: Allenby, though, had a robust physique but a shy and reticent personality, and was unimpressive in debate, being inclined to angry, frustrated outbursts when he was thwarted. He was extremely courageous under fire but in his frequent visits to the front he had failed to achieve an understanding with his men: he found it hard to converse easily with them. He was nicknamed 'the Bull', but he was no blockhead. He was one of the most resourceful of the British generals, the first to use every modern aid and the last to charge headlong and thoughtlessly. Throughout, Allenby endeavoured to surprise his opponents, even at risk to other aspects of the enterprise, but his remote inability to communicate his wishes to those above and below him was a constant threat to the execution of his superbly conceived plans.

The core of Allenby's offensive at Arras was to be a dynamic blow delivered by eight infantry divisions followed up by three cavalry divisions, erupting eastwards on either side of the Scarpe. Punching the hole for the infantry would be some 2,000 guns, of which about a third were to be heavy ones. The frontage of the main assault was to be about 7,000 yards, to be widened further as other infantry divisions joined in with flank attacks on either side of the central thrust. Of these flank attacks, the one on the left, against Vimy Ridge, was the more important: the right flank attack, never very ambitious, was gradually reduced in scale by the march of events.

There were facilities enough for both flank attacks to deploy, and the task of Horne's First Army, on Vimy Ridge, was made easier by the presence of the under-

Imperial War Museum

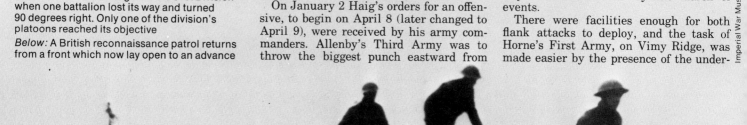

ground passages leading to that part of the front. But Allenby's main force had to attack through Arras, which lay at the tip of a narrow salient, and had then to exploit this initial penetration of the German front with a violent pursuit in depth. Therefore his follow-up force would have to pass through, or close by, Arras city and could easily be delayed by German shell fire playing on the few possible routes. As a result, the vital, rapid exploitation was liable to be delayed by a stifling traffic jam in which the predominant cavalry element could become inextricably mixed. It became essential to widen the frontage of the attack, to use the tunnels as jumping off places and somehow to prevent the Germans from bombarding Arras itself.

Artillery firepower would dominate the efforts of both sides as never before, but morale and training would still be the most critical factors. The British army, now a keener instrument than it had been in 1916, was still suffering from many limitations. The process of turning citizens into soldiers was incomplete and training at all levels both rigid and inadequate. So many of the best regular officers and men had been killed in the first few months of the war that there were insufficient survivors to pass on the basic organisational skills. With the increasing complexity of the war, staffs multiplied by swarms to deal with the myriad problems in rear of the battle. But these officers were inexperienced and unfamiliar with their work, and so the wheels of the various new organisations creaked. In the infantry, knowhow grew from experience in battle, of which there had been no shortage, but casualties had been so high that very often it was the most experienced who had been wiped out, and this hampered the dissemination of their hard-won knowledge to others. There was a gulf in communications between officers and men. As a result there were repeated instances in which the loss of officers paralysed subsequent actions because the men were not aware of the plan.

The steady decline of the German army has already been described, but certain points about it are worth emphasising. Though it was well supplied with muni-

tions, its reliability was becoming suspect: the troops gave up too readily for Ludendorff's peace of mind. Some officers felt they would be 'no longer capable of carrying out major attacks'. They could not win without attacking. Overall, though, expectations for the future were pessimistic.

In *matériel* the British were taking the lead. True the tanks—and the British could muster only 70 of the older type of machine for use in April—were not an important factor and would be spread thinly across the front at Arras. But in artillery they were considerably stronger than the Germans: moreover, though the artillery had been strengthened by the arrival of many new heavy batteries, it seemed that it would also be more efficient, as new, but as yet unproved, techniques of considerable tactical importance had been developed. These Major-General Holland, Allenby's Chief of Royal Artillery (CRA), wanted to put into practice at once. Since Allenby wanted surprise, Holland proposed reducing the five-day bombardment, prescribed by GHQ, to 48 hours, though he intended to deliver the same weight of metal. A careful system of reliefs to rest the men and mitigate barrel wear was worked out: but when this offering was sent to GHQ the gunners there persuaded Haig to reject it. The high priests of bombardment took sides in an argument which split the gunners down the middle and was resolved by making Holland a corps commander and giving Allenby a new CRA who was amenable to GHQ thinking. Allenby was baffled. It must be added, however, that Allenby's attempt to carry out what was common practice a few months later came at a difficult moment in development. The new methods had not yet been tried out even in minor actions: it would have been a gamble to attempt them on a large scale when so much was at stake. In the event, the appalling carnage wreaked by the artillery when it began serious work on April 4 seemed to justify the shorter bombardment, although when the date of the attack was postponed by 24 hours and the shooting was thus prolonged, there were gunners in Third Army who heaved a sigh of relief since persistent falls of snow had obscured observation and they were unsure

how much wire remained uncut. Yet by then the Germans at the front were either dead or marooned in a sea of shell holes. Some companies had been isolated for 48 hours; rations were not getting through, the trenches had been ploughed in and the wire was in ribbons—and this despite numerous examples of inaccurate ranging and malfunctioning fuses. To this had to be added the effect of gas shells fired into the German battery positions. A new type of shell made for a much more intense concentration of gas was used and this hampered, and in cases almost prevented the German crews from working their weapons.

False faith in cavalry

After the guns had done their work it would be the turn of the infantry to breach the line but, as usual, faith in enduring success was placed upon the cavalry: first the horsemen would pass through the bottleneck at Arras, then across ground which had been churned into a wilderness by shellfire, surging on across deep and wide trenches and over grasping strands of wire against an opponent who might or might not be terrified by their appearance. They were easy targets once they hove in sight—one machine gun was usually enough to stop a regiment. The troopers did not possess very high morale —they remembered the previous failures. Moreover, the severe winter of 1917 had taken its toll of their mounts' health—a weakness which was still more pronounced among the transport animals. As a result of the latter's failure the movement of guns and supplies in the battle area, forward of the railways, became enfeebled: it is a fact that the ditches beside the roads around Arras were full of dead horses and mules before the offensive started. The hopes of supporting a deep penetration through the German lines were thus threatened from the outset.

Easter Monday, April 9, was a day of sleet and snow, after a winter of most atrocious weather. The average infantryman, trudging into battle with a pack half his own weight on his back, might have doubted if he was meant actually to fight as well as support this weight on his back: moisture now added to his load and soon

each man was chilled to the bone. The ground he was to cross was quite open to the weather—only the Germans had the slightest cover, and that had mostly been turned into a ruin by the British artillery.

Looked at from Third Army's centre line, where it followed the line of the Scarpe, the frontage of attack was one, but operationally it divided neatly into three sectors—the most important being the one in the centre, where the main punch was to emerge from the suburbs of Arras, supported by the two shoulder operations, to left and right.

The left shoulder was the assault on Vimy Ridge, and here the great Canadian assault went almost according to plan—soon there were Allied troops looking far across the plain of Douai for the first time in 30 months. On the immediate right of the Canadian assault matters were not so conclusive. Here the 51st (Highland) Division, the left flank of XVII Corps, was meant to forge the link between the Canadians and the rest of the corps, moving to seize the crest of Vimy Ridge where it overlooked the village of Bailleul. This division was commanded by Major-General G. M. (Uncle) Harper, a stubborn and old-fashioned soldier, who had been among those to resist the introduction of machine guns, and who now insisted upon implementing a plan of attack which ran contrary to his corps' commander's wishes. He had no tanks (which was probably as well since he was also anti-tank), and reallocated battalions to the two leading brigades, thereby upsetting normal command arrangements, besides decreasing the size of his follow-up force. But he sent his Highlanders into action with the feeling that they were supreme—unstoppable and irrefutably right in all they did. Unfortunately for them the men of *1st Bavarian Reserve Division* held similar beliefs and fought back with great ferocity. Nearly everywhere the 51st Division was held back after it had crossed the first belt of German trenches and confusion set in when one battalion lost its way and turned 90 degrees right to face due south on what it took to be the objective. In fact, it held a communication trench, and was well short of the objective, therefore exposing

those who were trying to advance in the south to all the defensive vigour of the unshaken Germans. Every attempt to persuade Harper of the why and wherefore of his men being in the wrong place was met with a loyal and point blank denial. The only Highland platoon to reach the objective—adjacent to the successful Canadian right—came back when it discovered Canadians on one side but no other Scots on the other. The 51st Division worked as if it were an independent unit.

The main punch

In centre, things went better. The failure on the part of the 51st Division, while severely embarrassing its neighbour on the right, in no way prevented XVII Corps from executing its main task of driving deep into the German lines along the north bank of the Scarpe. In a great swathe from Roclincourt, on the left, to St Laurent on the right, the men of 34th and 9th Divisions rose from their trenches and cellars to finish what the artillery had all but accomplished on its own. Their final objectives were on the Point du Jour Ridge—the line Bailleul to Athies—and having got that far the 4th Division passed through and seized Fampoux by nightfall—thus breaching the last recognisable defences, to the west of the DQ Switch, to make a large breach in the German line—the cavalry's great opportunity.

To begin with, the 34th Division enjoyed a steady advance across its front—except on the extreme left where the tardiness of the 51st Division had brought confusion. The right-hand brigade of the 51st, on being repelled, fell back through the advancing left-hand brigade of the 34th until, in the end, all that brigade could do was conform with the 51st while giving intermittent flank support to the rest of the 34th Division. It might have been a lot worse but for the action of one man—Private Bryan of the 25th Northumberland Fusiliers. Already wounded by the fire from a machine gun sweeping the front, he nevertheless spotted the gun and made for it on his own, charging into the pit and wiping out the crew. Victoria Crosses are given for acts of great courage: Bryan's was all that and, more unusual, vital in

deciding the course of an action along a large stretch of front, for if the failure of the 51st had shunted down the line, the whole attack might have foundered.

Northumberland pluck had saved the day, and the 34th Division reached nearly all its objectives on the Point du Jour Ridge. Here the *14th Bavarian Division* fled in such disorder that it received a 'mention' from Ludendorff: 'One of our divisions failed.' Saturated by the worst of the gas attack, which forced its gunners to work for hours on end in gas masks, this division was deprived of both artillery support and reserves. The gas did not kill many men; providing they had their masks to hand they were safe. But wearing the things reduced efficiency and this, together with the suffocation of so many horses drawing ammunition carts, starved the guns of shells—for though there were mountains of shells in Douai, very few had been dumped by the gun pits.

Only in front of the 34th Division did the wire hold firm. But once the men reached their objective, they pleaded for permission to go further. It was just the same on their right with the 9th (Scottish) Division. This had been in the line before Arras, on and off, since December and knew the ground over which it was to attack well. The troops simply had to reach the objective quickly, so that the 4th Division could be given an uninterrupted passage beyond. But its nagging concern was of a failure south of the river, exposing its right flank to fire from Observation Ridge, north of Tillois, which held them up before they could even reach their objective, the southernmost extension of the Point du Jour spur. Habitually each platoon, each company, each battalion and so on looked left and right at its fellows—and in rear to see they were being followed—and only then to the front to tackle the Germans.

In the 9th Division, the most sanguine hopes and the worst fears were realised. Almost to schedule the Scots, with their comrades of the South African Brigade, cleared the Germans from before them. The

Too late to hinder seriously the massive British barrage, German shelling explodes an ammunition dump in Arras on the second day

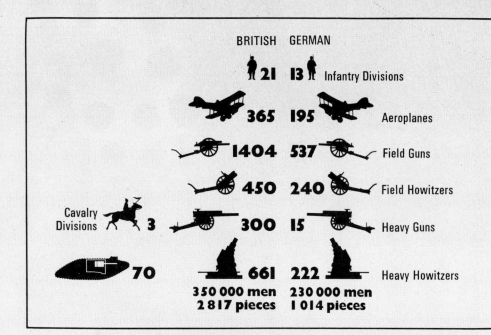

	BRITISH	GERMAN	
	21	13	Infantry Divisions
	365	195	Aeroplanes
	1404	537	Field Guns
	450	240	Field Howitzers
Cavalry Divisions 3	300	15	Heavy Guns
70	661	222	Heavy Howitzers
	350 000 men 2 817 pieces	230 000 men 1 014 pieces	

11th Royal Scots, part of 27th Brigade, was commanded by Lieutenant-Colonel W. D. Croft. He recorded:

When our turn came to cross No-Man's Land we found the most appalling mix-up of the division. Even at that early hour there were Highlanders who had wandered on my left, and also South Africans. Most of my people were too much to the right and it was all one could do to get them back into their proper places in time for the advance on our second objective, the railway line.

Losses had been heavy, and we were getting it in the neck from machine guns on the railway. Then down the slope went that throng of lads, and up they climbed to the railway close under our barrage.

Nothing could stop them that day, though there were Boche machine guns everywhere, and skilfully placed too. In some cases they were placed in tunnels under the embankment. It took us some time—we were on the left flank of the division—to clear the railway cutting, which was stiff with dug-outs and contained many Boches.

In the middle of our long halt at the second objective—we stayed there about

four hours—we suddenly saw heavy columns of our infantry wending their way across the ridge to their assembly positions near the railway cutting. The Boche observers must have seen them too, for as one of the battalions crossed the ridge a 5.9-inch opened on them.

But we cast many an anxious look to the right during the first half of the battle, for we could see with half an eye that they were not going quickly across the river.

But as we advanced the Boche fire slackened appreciably, and as we approached that formidable belt of wire it died down

Top left: The balance of forces before Arras.
Top centre: In the cage—some of the 7,000 German prisoners taken between April 9/14.
Top right: Although parts of the German army were affected by low morale which caused some formations to surrender too readily, resistance at Arras was often bitter in the extreme.
Right: Victorious and exultant, men of the 37th Division embus at Arras after having been relieved from Monchy-le-Preux on the third day; they had torn an enormous gap in the German front and an unprecedented breakthrough seemed possible. *Below:* A German counterattack over badly-churned-up ground

altogether. Even the pill-boxes seemed to show no sign of life. What could it mean? Some trap, no doubt, and we set our teeth and went for the wire. It was a tough job getting through the wire, even with little or no opposition, and then we saw an in-spiring sight – a mob of Boches haring away out of the trenches. It was too much for the Borderers who raced us for the Point du Jour. What a sight it was when we got there! One could see half the world and everywhere one looked were fleeing Boches. Even far-away Monchy seemed covered with fugitives.

The telephone spoke to Frank Maxwell: 'Are the Boches on the run?' 'Is cavalry good business?' 'Yes, 10,000 times yes, but it must be done now. Too late tomorrow . . . Why can't we go on? . . .' And so forth.

Then the 4th Division came through us. They had been marching all day without the excitement of battle to buoy them up. On they went and disappeared into the blue.

A yawning gap such as had never been before known had opened in the front of XVII Corps. If the Germans were surprised, so were the British – they were quite in-capable of adjusting themselves to open

warfare, it was so unexpected. The 9th Division was ready to continue independ-ently but the plan stipulated the 4th Division and, in any case, it was almost impossible to halt the artillery barrage even if this had been desired – which it was not. In fact the 4th Division had not begun to move out of Arras when the 9th reached its objective, and it did not pass through the latter until seven hours after this. Moreover, the nearest cavalry was still six and a half miles north-west of Arras in GHQ Reserve and could not hope to enter the gap until the next morning.

Nevertheless, for seven hours after that first break the gap was still there, with the 4th Division marching almost unopposed into German-held territory. Prisoners, in-cluding a general, poured in, and there was absolutely no sign of strong German counteraction. By nightfall most of the day's tasks had been completed, the rear-most German line had been penetrated and only the eastern fringe of Fampoux con-tinued to hold out, and then largely be-cause its defence was bolstered by opposi-tion from the south bank of the river.

South of the Scarpe, VI Corps all but

Mortars firing —
a painting by the German war artist Frost

kept pace with the XVII. Making full use of the Arras underways, its units were able to launch the assault straight into the forefront of the battle with troops who were dry and almost unscathed. The paralysing effect on the German guns of the bombardment and the gas had made a fact of General Holland's boast, when he was still Allenby's chief artillerist, that 'he would stand on a chair in the Grande Place of Arras during the opening attack with a noose round his neck, the chair to be kicked away when the first enemy shell fell there'.

Allenby's attention, as the reports of progress began to trickle in, was focused on the southern bank of the Scarpe, his hopes reaching out to the capture of Monchy-le-Preux on the second day.

Across the line of advance lay a dense web of trenches linked by numerous communication trenches. North of the Arras-Cambrai road there were no less than six lines of trenches within 2,000 yards of each other, made all the more difficult to cross by the bits of wire entanglement which had survived the bombardment. South of the road, in and around Tilloy and thence south to the Harp, the earth-

works were slightly less complex, yet stronger because each line of trenches was either anchored to a group of buildings or sited to conform to some outstanding topographical feature. The left sector rested on Tilloy and terminated at Blangy on the banks of the Scarpe. Beyond this the ground slopes gently up to Observation Ridge, which juts out from Tilloy northwards towards the river and dips sharply down to it. But in addition, commanding the flat, tree-studded bottom of the Scarpe valley, was a man-made ridge—the embankment carrying the Arras-Douai and Arras-Lens railway. Three railway tracks converged on embankments standing 20 feet above the surrounding land, and here the Germans had dug many machine gun posts. Thus Railway Triangle was a fortress in its own right. It was this feature which had worried the 9th (Scottish) Division as it made for the Point du Jour: its continued occupation by the Germans could stop the whole of the northern flank of VI Corps because it could fire at short range and had an unimpeded view of the western approaches to Observation Ridge. After crossing Observation Ridge

Above: The *Lusitania,* a British Mark II (male), on the outskirts of Arras. It played a pivotal rôle in spearheading the capture of Monchy. *Below:* The German reserves, like these with their transport and field cookers, were caught napping by the suddenness of the breakthrough

there is a sharp drop into a narrow gully, which burrows towards the Scarpe to the west of the village of Feuchy, blocked at its northern end by the railway, high on its embankment. This was Battery Valley, an ideal position for the German guns since the sides of the valley gave protection in a well-advanced position: its vulnerability could only be exposed if the top of Observation Ridge fell into hostile hands.

The central axis of the British advance climbed a long undulating slope along the Arras-Cambrai road. First came Chapel Hill, and to its left, midway to the river, Orange Hill. Connecting Chapel Hill and Orange Hill, which are virtually one feature, was a well-wired and dug line called the Wancourt-Feuchy Line, and this was the last line of defence covering Monchy, which comes fully into view after these two hills have been crossed. The distance between any of these features

Below: The remains of a British cavalry attack on the outskirts of Monchy; once again their performance had been disappointing, for they had waited too far in the rear because they were an easy target. *Inset. Left:* Canadian troops rest in the ruins of Arras before going up to the front. *Centre:* German prisoners keep flooding in, much to Ludendorff's alarm — he convened a Court of Enquiry to fix the blame on anybody but himself, even though it was his Hindenburg Line which had failed. *Right:* Fixing scaling ladders in the nine-foot trenches

is between 1,000 and 8,000 yards, and observation from one to the next quite unimpeded in clear weather. Hence no one feature could be seized without the simultaneous engagement of the others.

Railway Triangle at once proved the main centre of German resistance, the men of *10th Grenadiers* in the *11th Division* hanging on grimly and so severely cutting down the men of 15th (Scottish) Division that the entire attack came to a halt. Once again it took a single man to correct matters — and this time it was the divisional commander of the 15th, coolly observing the check, passing orders to the men to reorganise for a fresh attempt and demanding that the artillery programme — against the gunners' wishes — should be brought back and restarted, even if uncertain communications made such a course risky. But a single tank saved the day — one called *Lusitania* which, between breakdowns and spells of overheating, took on each German machine gun in turn and 'shot' the Scots onto their objective.

The advances to Observation Ridge by the right hand brigade of the 15th (Scottish) Division and both leading brigades of the 12th Division were of similar pattern. The German front line gave way easily enough, but resistance hardened on the approaches to the ridge. Here the wildest type of bomb and bayonet fighting broke out as the British infantry charged home. For a while there was a hold up and the schedule began to fall behind until, again, a few individuals decided the issue.

Stalemate set in until the renewed barrage crashed down — drumming across the men of the 12th Highland Light Infantry, incidentally, since they had already advanced beyond the point at which the artillery shoot was restarted.

Scraping and cringing in the cold mud, the Scots prepared to receive the dose of medicine meant for the Germans. By a miracle they escaped with few casualties, but the chilling experience distilled a confidence which prompted them to despise their own shells and follow so close behind the barrage that they were on the objective before the Germans could get their heads above ground.

The reserve brigades of both the 15th and 12th Divisions arrived almost simultaneously on Observation Ridge and now the German guns in Battery Valley stood exposed to vengeance.

An exultant charge

After years of subjugation to shell fire, pumped at them by men and weapons they never saw, here at last was the hidden enemy exposed to their mercy. A wild charge into the very muzzles of the guns, the rarest of events, followed, swept along by the courage of exultant triumph as the Scots dashed in among the flying Germans and their abandoned guns. Here and there resolute Germans stood by their guns and fired point-blank at the charge, until they were chopped down as they worked. A few gun teams managed to get away, but they left no less than 60 pieces behind, some of which were quickly swung round

and discharged at their late owners in the near distance.

But the hurly-burly in the valley consumed more valuable time: the infantry were falling further behind the barrage.

The difficulties of infantry/artillery co-operation were being exposed by contrast. The 15th (Scottish) Division had tampered with its artillery programme and as a result had brought its own men under fire, yet the 46th Brigade could now move close behind its barrage and in the end become the only formation to reach its objective, the Wancourt-Feuchy Line, and advance beyond it. The 12th Division, however, allowed its barrage to proceed without waiting for the infantry and so its men went unsupported and were soon brought to a halt by uncut wire and the machine guns.

The 12th Division could expect no help from the right. The 3rd Division had taken Tilloy after a stiff struggle, and the Harp had fallen after good work by the tanks, but now there were no tanks left and the

8th Brigade found itself on its own, without barrage or tanks, confronted by uncut wire. Nevertheless, the 12th and 3rd Divisions had accomplished what would have been miraculous had it been accomplished on the first day of the Somme. They had not reached all their ambitious objectives but they had seized the entire German front line and put the Germans to flight. Comparison was bound to be made, however, with the exciting events close by the Scarpe where the 15th Division, moving easily along the southern bank—by reason of good control and a little bit of luck—had ripped a hole in the Wancourt-Feuchy Line (with the aid of a tank). The way for the follow-up division, the 37th, was clear and, in fact, the divisional cavalry regiment, the Northamptonshire Yeomanry, had already, at 1700 hours ridden through and was on the outskirts of Fampoux, having chased German infantry, captured some guns and collaborated with the 4th Division on the north bank. Monchy at that moment lay practically undefended.

Then the 37th Division was denied its great opportunity as conventional generalship took over. Instead of sticking ruthlessly to plan and following the 15th Division through, this division allowed its brigades to go separate ways and to become committed to action in aid of 12th Division's failure, when the way to success was open at Monchy. When at last the divisional commander had got control of matters again, it was almost dark and Monchy was but 2,000 yards away, but it was felt that nothing further could be done that day. The British army had not yet broken itself of the habit of shutting shop at dusk: only raids and long-prepared attacks were ever launched in the dark; impromptu assaults never.

What was nearly impossible for infantry was quite out of the question for cavalry. Throughout the night of April 9/10 the cavalry waited in miserable, wet bivouacs in the outskirts of Arras, with no hope of joining in the battle until next day—by which time German resistance was likely to have been re-established—and principally concerned with their endeavours to feed their already weakened mounts. Because horses had only a limited resistance to the elements, they could not stay long without shelter. During the winter they had become 'soft' in billets and now they were not 'hard' enough to spend a night in the front line ready to plunge ahead at crack of dawn to exploit an infantry and artillery victory. They always had to be brought so far back from the front to feed, that their intervention next day was bound to be critically postponed by the time it took to ride to the front again.

We now turn to the right shoulder. The southern flank of Third Army's attack was intended to give VI Corps more room and was to be delivered by VII Corps. Unlike the rest of the Third Army it did not jump off at 0530 hours but moved later, and then in succession of divisions from the left. Thus, while the 14th Division was due to attack at 0734 hours on the left of the corps, the 21st Division (on the extreme right) would not go over the top until 1615 hours. Only here did Allenby sacrifice the advantages of surprise and expose his men to the agony of suspense as they waited

Imperial War Museum

Imperial War Museum

to attack an opponent who was fully forewarned as well as being snugly ensconced in the strongest and least damaged part of the Hindenburg Line. The echeloned attack was arranged to take advantage of leverage with an expanding succession from the left: but there were those, including the corps' commander, General Snow, who felt its success would be in inverse proportion the further it went to the right.

At first the 14th Division did well on the right of the 3rd Division, profiting as it did by close proximity to the main punch and from having some tanks supporting it. Yet the tanks only put the finishing touches to a job already well done by the artillery, and on this front the elements of the German *17th Reserve Division* surrendered most willingly as the British arrived at the entrances to their dug-outs. Here and there, German machine guns hit back, artillery pounded assembly areas and the tanks finally received some attention. But Telegraph Hill fell and with it the Harp—the tanks rolling down wire, coming under fire, a few suffering hits, while most of the rest bogged down in the churned-up ground. By nightfall, however, the 14th Division

had advanced over 4,000 yards, taken many prisoners and guns and done precisely what Allenby desired of it by shielding the right flank of the main punch; but its indirect leverage would take longer to have widespread effect.

With the 56th Division, the assault went in with a rush on a 350-yard front, behind the barrage, only a few minutes after the 14th. The 56th had hoped to achieve a deep penetration by pouring waves of reserves across its narrow front, but heavy fighting broke out in and around the village of Neuville Vitasse, which acted as a breakwater. Three German companies belonging to the *17th Reserve Division* were wiped out, but so too were a great number of the British infantry caught on uncut wire. The arrival of a solitary tank to crush the wire got things moving again, but the momentum of the attack had been lost and the final objectives remained untaken.

With this first set-back on the left of the corps, subsequent failures were inevitable as there was a total lack of leverage and distraction. The unshaken *18th Reserve Division,* dug deeply into its new, strong shelters, made safer by uncut wire—wire

which had remained uncut because, after the strategic withdrawal, the British had less time in which to destroy it—held firm. In places it looked like a repetition of the first day of the Somme. On the 56th Division's right, the 30th Division, which was pushing in German outposts, came up against untouched wire, a rising storm of artillery and machine gun fire, and was stopped short of the front line. This was shortly after 1200 hours and so the 21st Division (on its right) when it went over in the late afternoon can have been in no doubt as to its coming fate. A few units penetrated into the German front line but could not hold their gains. To all intents and purposes the right flank's attack had failed and the Hindenburg Line had proved its strength.

Even so, a vast gap had been pushed through the German defensive system in front of Arras. And to the Germans, who were aware that it would be at least another 24 hours before their divisions destroyed at the front could be replaced by those rushing up from deep in rear, the outlook was grim. Even where the shattered line looked like coalescing, as

on Chapel Hill, it was only wafer thin: the slightest nudge and it would disintegrate again. Ludendorff showed characteristic signs of acute disturbance while Rupprecht, the Army Group Commander, cursed Falkenhausen, the *Sixth Army's* commander, for holding his reserves so far in rear.

In effect there was a gap in the German line at least two miles wide opposite the Canadians, with a veneer of defence beginning to gather itself in the plain below Vimy Ridge. In front of the 51st Division, had its men but known it, there was nothing except stragglers, and so from here to Fampoux, a distance of nearly 7,000 yards, only a few knots of resistance were to be found. South of the river a neat puncture had been drilled by the 15th Division and the Northamptonshire Yeomanry. Beyond this, things were not quite so fluid, but the defenders of the Hindenburg Line were already starting to vacate their positions as the pressure to their right threatened to overspill and overwhelm them from flank and rear.

On the night of the 9/10th it was so cold that several infantrymen died from exposure: indeed the weather was one cause of

the hiatus on the 10th after the dramatic success of the 9th. There should have been a fierce drive past Monchy, splitting the German front in two, perhaps reaching the Drocourt-Quéant Line before it could be occupied by the German reserves: there was little enough to stop it, the Germans continuing to fall back whenever they were brought under the slightest pressure.

Yet instead of a strong drive there was merely a fastidious tidying up of confusion: the 51st Division at last admitted its errors of navigation and struggled back on course towards the objective it might have taken on the first day, with the 34th Division conforming on its right. Allenby's orders, strongly reflected in the corps' orders, demanded a ruthless advance, but the artillery could not get forward to give support. An artillery officer described the trouble

Above left: Crossing the railway line between Arras and Feuchy, a wiring party takes up corkscrew supports to secure the British gains. *Above right:* German prisoners go down the line and (in the background) British troops go up. *Below:* A British Mark I bogged down in mud which had been lashed by sleet and churned by heavy shellfire

which progressively affected the entire front: 'Continual storms of snow, hail and rain do not make it any easier to move guns across country which has undergone a five days' intense bombardment. Albeit, we got 'em up somehow by relays, with 12 to 14 horses in the guns, and the gunners harnessed to the waggons'—but not soon enough to be of maximum use.

A golden opportunity lost
The front was coalescing again, inevitably, as the Germans had remained undisturbed, even for just a few hours. When, at 1630 hours, the leading regiment of the 1st Cavalry Brigade (from the 1st Cavalry Division) at last arrived, it was 24 hours too late. Some time before, the 4th Division had been told to push on beyond Fampoux but the start time had been delayed until 1500 hours. In fact, at 1325 hours, the division's commander had heard that he was to support the 1st Cavalry Brigade in an advance past the Gavrelle-Roeux road and so he cancelled the attack scheduled

for 1500 hours although it was the very thing required to get the cavalry on to its objective, Greenland Hill.

At last the cavalry arrived. Snow was falling. The commanders conferred and, in the middle of the discussion, a report came in that the Germans were attacking, although they were doing no such thing. Tamely, possibly prudently now that the Germans seemed really prepared, but without a whimper, this golden chance was allowed to slip.

Earlier that day things had looked promising around Orange Hill and Monchy also. Though at no point south of the Scarpe had the attack reached its final objective on the first day, the first lunge towards Monchy brought resounding success; at 1200 hours, the 3rd and 12th Divisions swept through the German line which had held them up the previous evening, flowed smoothly forward to the right of

Orange Hill and crossed the valley to the long slope on top of which sat Monchy. The gap had opened wide again opposite the critical Monchy Spur, and all the situation needed was exploitation; to help matters, a junior German staff officer, without the knowledge of his commander, had given orders to evacuate the Wancourt-Feuchy Line.

After a miserable, confused night, the two leading brigades of the 37th Division had at last been disentangled from the 12th Division and were also ready to enter the gap. On their left, the 63rd Brigade started trickling parties across the valley in a disjointed sort of way. This irregular method of advance, visible in part to the watchers on Orange Hill, gave an indistinct picture of what was actually happening: in fact, it was being pecked at all the way by machine gun and rifle fire, casualties were mounting and there was no way to get to grips with the defenders, because the field artillery, as elsewhere, had yet to drag its guns into range of the Germans.

Exhausted after a rapid advance, a British soldier sleeps on a German arms dump

Imperial War Museum

Monchy was now disintegrating under a steady downpour of heavy shells from the British long-range guns. The Germans were shelling the British advance from positions on Greenland Hill north of the river, but the British artillery was not allowed to reply because they had been told that the 1st Cavalry Brigade might soon be on Greenland Hill—the Cavalry Brigade had, in fact, called off the attempt.

Still the advance crept along and still it seemed that the cavalry might find an opening that day. All morning it waited patiently just behind the front, the units on the right coming under fire from an un-cleared German position near Wancourt. At one time, the 8th Cavalry Brigade, from north-west of Monchy, thought it saw a chance to slip through with a couple of squadrons, but like the other watchers in the 37th Division it was wrong, and the horsemen came under the lash of machine gun fire. For one wild moment they tried to come into action at a gallop, but the fire was too much and horses and riders began to fall. Only a sudden blinding snowstorm, as thick as any smoke screen, gave them the cover under which to withdraw.

On the afternoon of the 10th, German infantry from the reserve formations at last began to put in an appearance, filing over the ridge beyond Monchy. Ever fearful of a continued British advance, the Germans at last began to take heart at the sight of some of their fresh gun batteries galloping forward to unlimber and come into action. 'There was a great arc of our batteries on a wide front behind our en-dangered positions. It was a most memor-able and magnificent battle picture, lit by the evening sun.'

On the early morning of April 11 the airmen of both sides were out in clearer weather to see if Monchy had fallen. North of the Scarpe the Germans remained em-placed just as they had been the previous day, firing steadily into the flank of the village and its approaches. Allenby still appeared confident of victory south of the river and gave orders which called for a general advance. He spoke of 'pursuing a defeated enemy' and 'masking and passing-by isolated enemy detachments'.

At Monchy, 'C' Battalion of the Tank Corps persuaded three of its surviving tanks to crawl to the front line during the night of the 10th in readiness for an attack at dawn on the 11th in support of the 111th Brigade, from the 37th Division. The ground was now carpeted with snow, and tanks and men became sharply silhouetted against the white background. Keeping on the move, particularly for the tanks, was essential for evading the German fire, which now could be aimed more easily than usual.

But the order to the supporting gunners had not arrived in time, zero hour was put back two hours and the tank commanders, realising that they would be sitting ducks if they stayed waiting in the open, went ahead on their own without artillery sup-port. After a wary, stealthy approach they staged a lonely battle in and around the ruins of Monchy.

For nearly two hours the machines, fully closed down and therefore half blind, tried to subdue several hundred Germans. The crews suffered badly as a hail of machine gun bullets criss-crossed the armour. Soon, one was in flames and a second had fallen silent to armour-piercing bullets. At last,

when all seemed lost, the British barrage fell on the village and almost immediately hit the surviving tank. Only then did there arrive a mixed bag of infantry, Scots from the 15th Division, feeling their way in from the north-west, and men of the 111th Brigade, up the slope from the west.

For one exciting moment it seemed as if the triumphs of the 9th were to be con-tinued. The newly arrived *17th Bavarian Regiment* broke at once. Into Monchy from the east rode two regiments of cavalry at full gallop—such a sight had not been seen for years. But it could not last. German shells fell like rain, sweeping men and horses aside and driving the survivors to dismount, dive for cover and join in the fight like ordinary infantry mortals as the first serious German counterattack in 48 hours began to take shape. One of those Germans put his thoughts in a letter shortly before being killed: *We went into the line on April 10. The whole night of the 10/11th we were digging ourselves in, in order to get cover from the fire. Then came the morning of April 11. Never shall I forget April 11! The English had been firing in the front line all night and in the morning they attacked, and our troops went streaming to the rear. Our company it was which swarmed out into the open, and, under the shell, shrapnel, machine gun and rifle fire, dug itself in again, and in spite of heavy casualties, brought the English advance to a standstill. That was at 0500 hours. From then till 1500 hours we lay only six yards from the British. Then fresh troops arrived, counterattacked, and won back all the ground that had been lost in the morning. We were again masters of the situation.*

The German position was cemented by a miscellany of units, flung into the line as they arrived, along the best part of the Oppy-Méricourt Line to just south of Gavrelle, thence bent back in front of Fampoux with a nest of resistance sur-rounding Greenland Hill. From there fire could be directed across the river in front of a new line hastily being dug from Pelves through Bois du Sart, Bois du Vert and across the main road to Wancourt Tower.

There was no breakthrough, and Nivelle's offensive on the Chemin des Dames was all of four days off. Haig had to keep the Germans busy and, as so often before, could only return to attrition in the short term, since a major attack was only a long term business. Now began a battle of rags and tatters to keep the Germans busy, to seize jumping off places for a subsequent offensive timed (later) to start on April 23 and to gain shelter from the inevitable German retribution.

On the 14th there was a last fling at Monchy—a half-cocked battle conceived as part of a major plan to seize the Bois du Sart, Bois du Vert and the hilltop wind-mill known as Wancourt Tower. Although not all the troops could be got ready in time, the 88th Brigade was allowed to attack due east out of Monchy with two battalions, leaving the village unguarded. These two battalions, well supported by artillery, in fact almost achieved the im-possible, breaking the *23rd Bavarian Regi-ment* and charging up the opposite slope. But they charged into a sack the neck of which was tied shut by German counter-attacks rushing in from the flanks. And those German attacks did not stop just there, but turned west and made for Monchy, where Lieutenant-Colonel Forbes

Robertson of the Royal Newfoundland Regiment and nine others found them-selves the sole defenders. For five hours, until help at last came, this tiny party successfully held the village while a bar-rage of artillery fire sealed off the eastern approaches. Nevertheless it was a com-mentary not only on British persistence but also on fading German prowess that the Germans had first been broken by the initial attack and second been defeated by such light odds—the plea that artillery ammunition had run out was no more than an excuse.

The offensive muttered on in the old and costly routine of attrition on ground which was new to the British. Possession of Vimy Ridge and Monchy relieved the communi-cation centre at Arras from direct German observation and fire. The Third Army's casualties amounted to 8,238 in the three days' fighting from April 9 to 11—extremely light by comparison with several previous offensives. In return, the British had cap-tured 7,000 prisoners, 112 guns and a great German fortress position, and dis-rupted some six German divisions, whose total casualties were about 21,000. The Germans called it a *débacle* and Ludendorff convened a Court of Inquiry to fix the blame on anybody but himself. Yet it was his Hindenburg Line which had failed.

In success the British had also failed— failed to recognise a gap about 10,000 yards wide and to pass men through it. Infantry had halted from exhaustion of themselves and their reserves; artillery could not extend non-stop help to the infantry because it could not drag its guns or its ammunition through mud at the same pace as the infantry could advance; and the cavalry had waited far in rear because it was too easy a target and you cannot dig a trench to take a horse.

The existing tanks had again shown their possibilities and made important local contributions, but they were neither in shape nor present in sufficient numbers to be decisive, although their heavy losses suggested to Ludendorff that this was one technical threat he could dismiss as a possible future danger. The fundamental failure on the British side was the system of attack and the communications for com-mand and control. There was no quick and reliable way of passing information from front to rear or converting data into up-to-date orders which could maintain a con-tinuous and expanding flow of troops in the forefront of the battle. Quite the reverse would happen as units inclined inwards to a single point, contracting from the flanks, until but one easily arrestable axis of advance was being followed.

The break-in at Arras was among the most resounding successes achieved by the British army on the Western Front—and certainly greater than anything prior to 1917. Yet it achieved nothing enduring— only a list of faults to be overcome and of new lessons to be learned.

Further Reading
Croft, W. D., *Three Years with the 9th Division*
Die Osterschlacht bei Arras (Reichsarchiv)
Liddell Hart, Sir Basil, *The Tanks* (Cassell 1959)
Ludendorff, Gen. E., *My War Memories* (Hutchinson)
Military Operations: France and Belgium 1917 (Macmillan 1940)

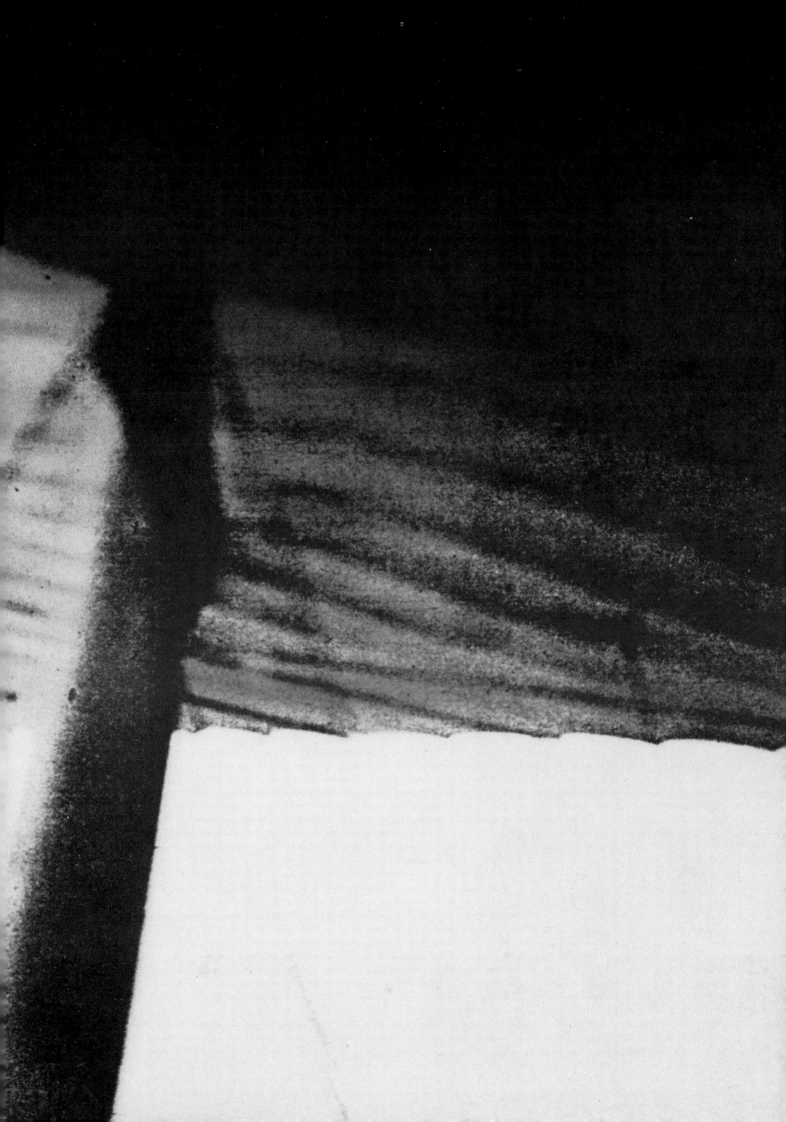

BLOODY APRIL

'Bloody April' 1917 marked both the high and low water points of the Allied struggle for mastery of the air-over the Western Front. The Germans, though inferior in numbers, were introducing superior machines, and the Allies' pilots had to exert all their courage and tenacity to match and then beat the Germans
Above: Allied fighters, such as this Nieuport, were still handicapped by inadequate armament. *Below:* Shepherd and charge: a Nieuport seen from the Farman it is escorting

The four months which culminated in 'Bloody April', 1917, taught one very important lesson: numerical superiority in the air cannot make up for technical inferiority. The preparations for the Battle of Arras and the battle itself came at a time when the Royal Flying Corps was suffering from a preponderance of obsolete aeroplanes, inadequate training for pilots and slow delivery of new types. The German air force, on the other hand, had recently been reorganised, new fighter aircraft were in production and, most important of all, morale, thanks largely to the inspiration of Oswald Boelcke, recently killed in an accident on the Somme, was higher than it had ever been. It is significant that when General Nivelle was discussing his proposed big push at a London conference in January, Sir Douglas Haig expressed the view that the Royal Flying Corps would not be ready for an offensive by April 1. At the same time Nivelle's plans greatly extended the front for which the British armies were responsible – they were to relieve the French as far south as the Roye-Amiens road, so that the French C-in-C could concentrate his forces and deal the Germans a tremendous blow on the Aisne, a blow which was supposed to rupture their line 'within 24 or at most 48 hours'.

However, in February Allied grand strategy was neatly upset by the German High Command. Instead of waiting for the pincer movement which was to have nipped off the salient created by the Somme fighting, the German armies moved back to the Hindenburg Line defences they had been building throughout the winter. After much bad weather had hindered flying, a patrol of RFC Sopwith Pup single-seaters returned from offensive patrol to report large dumps burning and villages in flames: the salient was being evacuated and the country between the old and the new front lines laid waste in a 'scorched earth' policy. Complete plans for the German withdrawal were captured on March 14 and a British advance accordingly planned for March 17. For the first time since 1914 there would be something approaching open warfare as the British Fourth and Fifth Armies moved steadily forward for the next two weeks. There was little air opposition because on March 3 the Germans in their turn had captured General Nivelle's strategic plans for the great thrust on the Aisne and were massing their air forces to the north and south of the fighting around the Hindenburg Line, knowing that no important offensive could be launched from the now fluid British front line. The Aisne/Champagne sector was the affair of the French, and the main RFC concentration, supported by RNAS fighter squadrons, was on the Third Army front near Arras, and opposite the German fighter station at Douai, once the home of Immelmann and Boelcke, now HQ of Manfred von Richthofen's new *Jagdstaffel 11*, with V-strutter Albatros D IIIs (160/175-hp Mercedes D IIIa in-line water-cooled 'six').

During the British advance to the Hindenburg Line, 'Contact Patrol' techniques learned on the Somme were put into effect, Aeroplanes co-operated closely with infantry and cavalry, carrying messages (dropped in message-bags), and sending out W/T 'zone calls', identifying tactical targets for the gunners and discovering (usually by drawing infantry fire) the German strongpoints. In practice aircraft were little needed, since opposition was slight and ground communications (cavalry and field telephone) reasonably effective. For long-distance reconnaissance of and behind the Hindenburg Line the army wings of the Fourth and Fifth Brigades, RFC, made some use of single-seater fighters – a return to the original idea of 'scouts'. Photographic maps of the line were made by FE 2bs of No 22 Squadron escorted by No 54's Sopwith Pups (80-hp Le Rhône rotary).

The Battle of Arras began for the ground forces on Easter Monday, April 9, for the airmen five days before that. Their job was to clear the air of German machines so that corps aircraft of the First Army (holding a line roughly from the Béthune-La Bassée road south to the village of Angres, opposite Loos) and the Third Army (concentrated opposite Vimy Ridge and down to the Scarpe) could get on with their work of trench-mapping, artillery ranging and counterbattery work.

The German air force, well equipped with tractor single-seaters – Halberstadt and Albatros scouts, each armed with a pair of LMG 08/15 machine guns synchronised to fire through the propeller, in contrast with Allied machines' one gun, had profited by the lull between the Battle of the Somme and the Battle of Arras to train the hand-picked pilots of which the new *Jagdstaffeln* (fighter squadrons) were composed. A steady procession of sitting targets was provided by the BEs of the RFC on corps work or long-range reconnaissance, when head-winds often, reduced cruising speed to a snail's pace.

The RFC now learned the dangers of standardising and keeping in service an obsolete machine. A formation of six BE bombers, each virtually unarmed, required an escort of six FE 2b fighter-reconnaissance aircraft plus an 'umbrella' of six Sopwith Pups – an expensive way indeed of delivering six 112-pound bombs or a shower of 20-pound Cooper bombs from 6,000 feet with primitive bomb-sights. But Major-General Trenchard, commanding the RFC in France, and his French opposite number, *Commandant* du Peuty, in charge of the *Groupement de combat* on the Aisne, believed firmly that an offensive policy must be maintained whatever the cost. The aeroplane, they held, could not be used defensively because the sky was too vast. 'Victory in the air,' de Peuty announced in a note from GQG on April 9, 'must *precede* victory on land.' Again, 'Your task is to seek out, fight and destroy *l'aviation boche.'* The constant presence of Allied aircraft far behind the German lines not only worried the civilian population but pinned down quantities of fighters and AA gunners who could otherwise have been employed against 'corps aircraft' engaged in vital mapping, artillery spotting and counterbattery work above the trenches. Furthermore, reasoned Trenchard, if his airmen managed to retain the initiative when poorly equipped, there would be absolutely no holding them when equipment improved. Events were to prove him right.

April 1917 started early upon its 'Bloody' reputation. In the five days before the infantry attack, in a snow-storm, on April 9, 75 British aeroplanes were shot down with a loss of 105 crew (19 killed, 13 wounded and 73 missing). Wastage too was very high: 56 aeroplanes crashed and written off. Pilots were being posted to squadrons with as little as 10 hours solo to their credit and often with no experience whatever of the type they were to fly in combat. The average expectation of life for a British airman on the Western Front during the month of April 1917 was 23 days. The 25 squadrons, one third of which were single-seater units, lost 316 airmen killed in action from an establishment of 730 aircrew, a casualty rate of over 40% not counting those wounded, missing and grounded.

A magnificent exploit on the credit side, however, was a raid on Douai aerodrome by FE 2ds of 100 Squadron during the night of April 5/6. Two days later the FE 2ds made another raid on Douai, bombing the aerodrome and railway station twice. Meanwhile the squadron's two FE 2bs, whose armament of Vickers one-pounder pom-pom guns had arrived only that day, attacked trains and other ground targets.

The worst piece of news reaching RFC HQ during the opening week concerned the Bristol Fighters, of which so much had been expected. Six F2As led by Captain W. Leefe Robinson, VC, of Zeppelin fame, had been 'jumped' by Manfred *Freiherr* von Richthofen and four of his *Staffel* in Albatros D III single-seaters from Douai. Richthofen shot down two, and two more fell to his comrades; the remaining two reached home, one badly damaged. From the wreckage the Germans could learn only that the unidentifiable engine was a V-12 of considerable power. The lesson drawn belatedly by the RFC was that the Bristol should be flown like a scout, using the synchronised Vickers as main armament, the observer's Lewis being a heaven-sent bonus to protect the tail. Flown thus, the Bristol was a most formidable fighting machine, and was to make a great name for itself later in the war.

In the opening days of the Battle of Arras air fighting ran through the gamut of aerial tasks: unsuccessful attacks on kite balloons, artillery shoots to flatten German wire, photography, bombing and fighting. As infantry moved forward through unseasonable Easter snow, contact patrol aeroplanes, using Klaxon horn and Verey pistols, kept track of the advance. Zone calls were sent out to indicate special targets, and the gunners' response proved so prompt and accurate in counterbattery work that aircraft were able to turn upon infantry targets – the 'trench-strafing' which was to become a permanent and hazardous feature of squadron life. On the 10th, Nieuports of 60 Squadron went on tactical photographic reconnaissance, an unusual job for single-seaters. On the 11th Richthofen equalled Boelcke's score of 40 by shooting down a BE 2c of No 13 Squadron which lost a wing as it dived. Miraculously the crew escaped with bruises.

Unwilling to leave the front for a spell of celebration – and propaganda – leave, the *Jasta* commander insisted upon adding one more to his score. In fact he added two: on April 13, the first fine day of the battle, an RE 8 shortly after 0830 hours and an FE 2b at mid-morning. The former was one of six RE 8s, in which four were escorting the other two. All six were shot down, because the slow and cumbersome biplane was no match for a single-seater and by a series of misfortunes the OPs of three Spads, six FE 2ds and a flight of Bristol Fighters which were supposed to escort them past Douai failed to appear. Richthofen was allowed to remain at the front. British 'Offensive Patrols' met few HA (Hostile Aeroplanes), which were all joining in the battle, but RFC bombers were active all day, and that evening's mission against

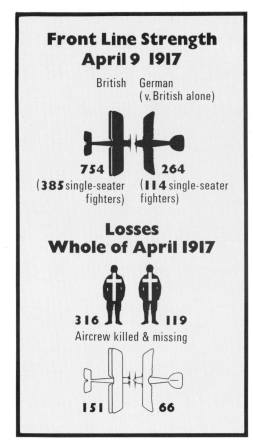

Front Line Strength
April 9 1917

British   German
(v. British alone)

754   **264**

(**385** single-seater fighters)   (**114** single-seater fighters)

Losses
Whole of April 1917

316   **119**

Aircrew killed & missing

151   **66**

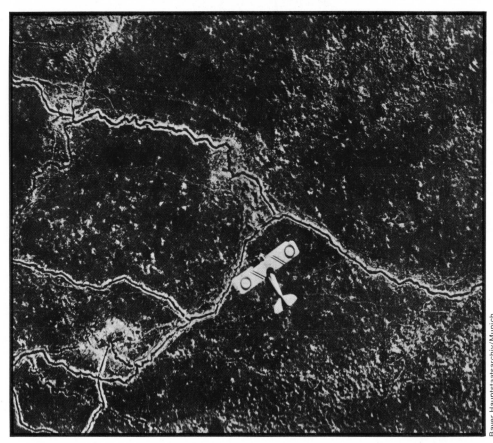

Bayer Hauptstaatsarchiv/Munich

Left: The credit and debit of 'Bloody April', in which the RFC suffered air crew losses totalling 40%. *Right:* A Spad VII over the Hindenburg Line

Henin-Liétard railway station shows the scope and complication of such missions. Six 230-pound bombs and seven 112-pounders were dropped, the force comprising 12 Martinsyde G 102 'Elephants' escorted by five Spads and six Sopwith Pups, plus nine FE 2d pusher bombers with an escort of six Nieuports. Only one Martinsyde was lost, but on the way home the FE leader mistook a patrol of V-strutter Albatros for friendly Nieuports, and *Jasta 11* claimed three more victims.

It was a high time for the great individualists, the *as* (aces) as the French called them. The activities of the great fighter pilots are too numerous to mention in detail, but it may be noted here that Boelcke's record score of 40 was being challenged not only by his pupil, Richthofen, but also by the Frenchmen Georges Guynemer and René Fonck, and the young Englishman Alfred Ball. Guynemer and Ball, particularly, believed in hunting alone and attacking unseen from extremely close range, although they took part also in Flight and Squadron patrols.

Thanks largely to Boelcke, whose *Jagdstaffel* had practised full squadron take-offs and patrols as early as September 1916, much had been learned about fighter tactics. Acting at first in pairs as Boelcke and Immelmann had done in the Fokker *Eindekker* days, single-seater pilots had learned to operate in flights of three, or, preferably, four (two pairs), under a flight commander. After trying line-ahead, line abreast and echelon formations, both sides hit upon the Vee ('vic') and diamond, with the leader in front where his view was clear and his Verey light or 'wing waggling' signals could be seen. Pilots picked their own targets when the signal to attack was given, and reformed afterwards at a prearranged rendezvous. Four machines were regarded as the maximum for one leader to control, and when larger formations were used these were built up from several groups each under its own flight commander.

Into the battle the High Command of the *Luftstreitkräfte* moved reinforcements comprising two *Jagdstaffeln* (fighter squadrons), four *Abteilungen* of corps aircraft, and two *Schutzstaffeln* of armoured close-support biplanes with downward-firing guns, the new AEG J I two-seaters (200-hp Benz water-cooled six-cylinder engine). Their appearance coincided with the withdrawal of No 3 (Naval) Wing from Luxeuil, the base from which Sopwith 1½-Strutters had been engaged in strategic bombing of Germany. This enterprise, very much to the taste of RNAS pilots, was not relished politically by the French, who feared damage to the property of loyalists in Alsace-Lorraine and lived in dread of reprisals against French towns including Paris, which lay alarmingly close to the front.

The second phase of the Battle of Arras opened on April 16,

when General Nivelle launched his widely publicised offensive on the Aisne. The fighters were commanded by *Commandant* du Peuty, the able ex-cavalryman whose 'offensive thinking' had early influenced Trenchard. Du Peuty was still under 40, a fact which did not endear him to certain senior officers. Under his command came *Groupes de combat* 11, 12 and 14, plus three *escadrilles* of Nieuport and Caudron machines—on paper four *groupes,* or 200 aeroplanes. In fact he had 131 machines on April 16, and only 153 by April 21, his maximum, to which could be added 30 machines from the Paris defences. Staff arrangements were woefully, and it seems almost wilfully, muddled. Pilots were sent to Le Bourget on ferry duty who should have been in action, and the front of the *Groupe des Armées de Reserve* was divided geographically, not according to commands. The staff had also decreed, on April 1, that each army must file its expected air requirements by 2000 hours the previous day.

German supremacy

There were to be six standing patrols along the whole front, three for each sector comprising:

● two patrols (one offensive, one defensive) at 6,000-8,000 feet (corps aircraft height); and
● one high patrol.

There was no zone call system, and often fighter *escadrilles* were not warned of local attacks or changes of plan.

German fighter supremacy was such that on April 13 it was requested that zero hour for the offensive on the 16th should be advanced to first light, as German dawn patrols would otherwise discover all. German fighters did, in fact, harry the front line during the attack, driving away French artillery and contact patrols. There was a continual cry for close, that is defensive, fighter support, notably from General Mangin, and in fact during the Verdun attack low patrols did operate at 2,000-3,000 feet between 0500 and 0615 hours to drive off marauding HA and to attack balloons. Bad weather limited du Peuty's long-range offensive patrols ('fortunately', said his detractors), and when these did go out, in patrols of six, 'never less than five', the Germans avoided combat, thus giving unconscious support to du Peuty's opponents on the French staff, who were quick to speak of 'wasting petrol', 'shadow-boxing' and the like. Theirs was to be the last word. *Commandant* du Peuty eventually resigned, and despite his cavalry background joined an infantry unit in the trenches, where he was killed.

In machines, too, France was weak. The Spad S VII (150-hp Hispano-Suiza) was a good fighter, as witness the scores of Guynemer and other aces, but the pusher Voisins and Farmans were

hopelessly outclassed. Only slightly better able to defend itself was the Caudron 4, a twin-engined three-seater (two 130-hp Hispano-Suizas) which lasted until replaced by the Letord I (two Hispano-Suiza V-8s). The *Aviation Militaire* also possessed for some reason the Paul Schmitt 7, an extraordinary biplane of great span, minimal performance and no fewer than 12 sets of interplane struts. The PS 7 (265-hp Renault) was unique in that the angle of incidence of the entire biplane cellule could be varied to give either maximum speed or maximum lift, but the drag was so great that neither speed nor lift was sufficient. The Paul Schmitt was armed with two machine guns and proved extremely unhandy in the air. Strangely, all documents relating to its adoption are missing from the French archives. The French also used Sopwith 1½-Strutters in two-seater and single-seat bomber form. Criticising it, with some justification, as more of a touring machine than a combat aeroplane, they applauded its *'exploits sportifs'* with the 240-pound bomb. French aviation, so brilliant during the early war years, was far from happy in spring 1917, despite the gallantry of individual airmen.

The new German tactics of ignoring offensive patrols the better to concentrate above the trenches were employed also on the Arras front, where the Germans, said General Trenchard, were 'undoubtedly slipping underneath our high patrols without being seen by them'. Even when a force of Bristol Fighters and RNAS Sopwith Triplanes trailed their coats above Douai itself *Jasta 11* failed to rise. Richthofen preferred to meet Nieuports in the air, which he did on April 16. Six Nieuports met four Albatros and four Nieuports went down.

Economical of aeroplanes, the Germans made few fighter sweeps behind the British lines, and because in their 1914 retreat they had prudently dug in on high ground affording a view over the plains, they had less need of aerial reconnaissance than had the RFC. Strangely, they made no sustained bombing attack on Calais, Boulogne and Dieppe, where disembarkation could have been severely hindered.

As the ground forces prepared for a new assault in the Arras sector to take some of the sting out of Nivelle's failure further south, bad weather kept most machines on the ground. The four days from the 16th to the 20th were virtually 'washed out'. On the 21st a preliminary bombardment flattened German wire and sorties were made against the balloons directing counterbattery fire. Two were shot down on the Third Army front and one on that of the Second Army. Three others were damaged but hauled down in time because the Germans had discovered a method far quicker than the winch: the cable was passed under a pulley and hitched to a lorry which then drove away, towing the balloon rapidly to the ground. The counter to this, invented by Major L. Tilney, CO of No 40 Squadron (Nieuports), was a hedge-hopping fighter attack at ground level. The Nieuport 17 sesquiplane was still the favourite mount of Captain Ball, the RFC's top-scoring pilot. He preferred it to his new SE 5, which was now operational after No 56 Squadron's CO had improved upon the Royal Aircraft Factory's design of the cockpit. W. A. Bishop, another future VC, also cherished his Nieuport 17 although clearly it was outperformed,

Could the agility of the Triplane match the heavier armament of the Albatros?

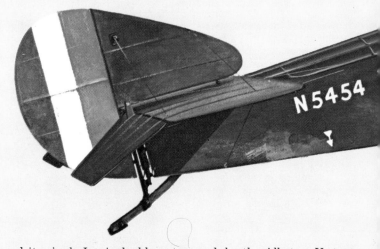

and its single Lewis doubly outgunned, by the Albatros V-strutters it had inspired. A further four Nieuports were lost to *Jasta 11* pilots on April 21, but the RFC was past its bad time. The factory strikes at home which had halted production had now largely been settled and supplies of vital new aircraft were reaching the front. The SE 5 was in action, Sopwith Pups and Triplanes were more than a match for the German fighters, and the Sopwith Camel was on its way. Admittedly the SE was in trouble with its Hispano engine and with a new and secret gun-synchronising device for its Vickers but there was a Lewis on the centre-section and these teething troubles would soon be overcome.

The new synchronising gear had the great advantage that it could be fitted quickly to any type of engine. Invented by George Constantinesco, a Rumanian mining-engineer and developed by him with Major C. Colley, Royal Artillery, the device was known in the RFC as the CC gear, and must count as one of the simplest and most useful inventions of the war. It worked on the same principle as a modern car's hydraulic brakes, and may be described diagrammatically as a column of liquid in a pipe sealed by a plunger at each end. Pressure exerted at one end, by an engine cam, could not fail to reach the other and exert a similar and simultaneous pressure on, for example, the trigger of a gun. Tested on a BE 2c in August 1916, the design was adopted forthwith. The first squadron so equipped, No 55 (DH 4s), landed in France on March 6, 1917. Meanwhile obsolete machines like the BE 2c, FE 2b, 'Strutter' and the early marks of Spad continued to suffer, and occasionally to mistake Albatros for the friendly though outmoded Nieuport.

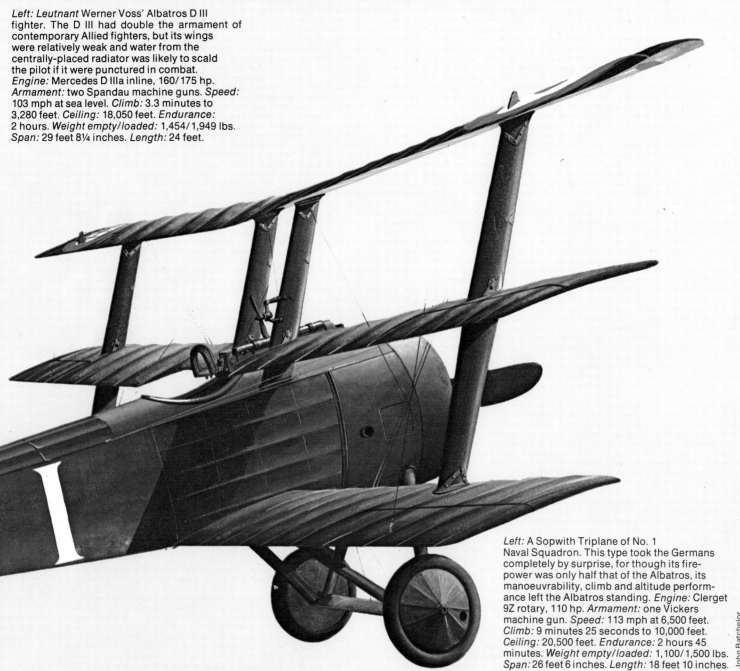

Left: Leutnant Werner Voss' Albatros D III fighter. The D III had double the armament of contemporary Allied fighters, but its wings were relatively weak and water from the centrally-placed radiator was likely to scald the pilot if it were punctured in combat. *Engine:* Mercedes D IIIa inline, 160/175 hp. *Armament:* two Spandau machine guns. *Speed:* 103 mph at sea level. *Climb:* 3.3 minutes to 3,280 feet. *Ceiling:* 18,050 feet. *Endurance:* 2 hours. *Weight empty/loaded:* 1,454/1,949 lbs. *Span:* 29 feet 8¼ inches. *Length:* 24 feet.

Left: A Sopwith Triplane of No. 1 Naval Squadron. This type took the Germans completely by surprise, for though its fire-power was only half that of the Albatros, its manoeuvrability, climb and altitude performance left the Albatros standing. *Engine:* Clerget 9Z rotary, 110 hp. *Armament:* one Vickers machine gun. *Speed:* 113 mph at 6,500 feet. *Climb:* 9 minutes 25 seconds to 10,000 feet. *Ceiling:* 20,500 feet. *Endurance:* 2 hours 45 minutes. *Weight empty/loaded:* 1,100/1,500 lbs. *Span:* 26 feet 6 inches. *Length:* 18 feet 10 inches.

John Batchelor

Haig's second offensive opened on April 23, St George's Day, on a 9-mile front, Croisilles-Gavrelle. Fortunately two Triplanes of Naval 1 had, two days before, dispersed an unusually powerful German reconnaissance formation of 14 DFW C Vs and escorting Albatros, disappointing them of vital information. Tiny, compact and with the masses of engine, pilot and tanks closely concentrated, the 'Tripehound' was immensely manoeuvrable and in its element at 16,000 feet, where this engagement took place.

Over the lines on St George's Day, German fighters from a variety of units harried the unfortunate corps aircraft as they wheeled in figures of eight spotting for the guns, while army squadrons gave what support they could. In an area bounded by Lens, Henin-Liétard, Bullecourt, Sains and the battle line itself 48 British scouts and Bristol Fighters plus 20 two-seater fighter-reconnaissance machines were on Offensive Patrol, while the number of famous names figuring in the day's engagements read like 'Who's Who': Ball, Bishop, Hermann Göring, Lothar von Richthofen (brother of Manfred) and of course Richthofen himself. That evening a bombing raid on Epinoy by six FEs of 18 Squadron escorted by five Pups was attacked by two formations of Albatros and Halberstadt fighters and there developed one of the first big 'dog-fights' of the war, as British Fighters, Triplanes and Nieuports hastened to join in a fight, which lasted for an hour. Later FE 2d night bombers of 100 Squadron overflew Douai to bomb Pont à Vendin station, also machine gunning troop trains whereby desperately needed German reinforcements arrived late and almost too tired to relieve their comrades in the trenches.

During daylight fighter opposition was intense. New German two-seaters were also in service, including the Albatros C V (220-hp Mercedes D IV straight-eight) and C VII (200-hp Benz IV six) which would outperform an SE 5 at 10,000 feet. Whatever motives had led the *Jagdstaffeln* to avoid combat earlier in the month, they were now deployed in full force and full of spirit. On the morning of April 29, picturesquely, the Richthofen brothers each shot down a Spad before entertaining their father, Major Albrecht *Freiherr* von Richthofen, to lunch in the mess. At 1600 hours Manfred destroyed an FE after a stiff fight over Inchy, while on yet another sortie the two brothers scored again, against a pair of BE 2ds. In a final combat of the day, when *Jasta 11* was involved with 11 Triplanes of Naval 8 and one Nieuport of 60 Squadron, Manfred secured his 52nd victim, but only after Captain F. L. Barwell's Nieuport, absurdly underpowered and under-armed in comparison with the Albatros, had defended itself magnificently for almost half an hour. Not all Manfred von Richthofen's victims were easy ones, though it must be pointed out that although without so many defenceless BEs and antiquated pushers in the sky his score would undoubtedly have been smaller.

The Red Baron

Quantity production of factory-designed BE 2, FE 2 and RE 8 biplanes made up to some extent for the Allies' lack of high ground. It was therefore essential for the Germans to shoot them down. With so many targets the German rate of scoring was high—four times (and on some sectors even five times) the RFC rate; but the RFC fighters were usually matched against fighters, either on offensive patrol or while driving the predatory Albatros from its

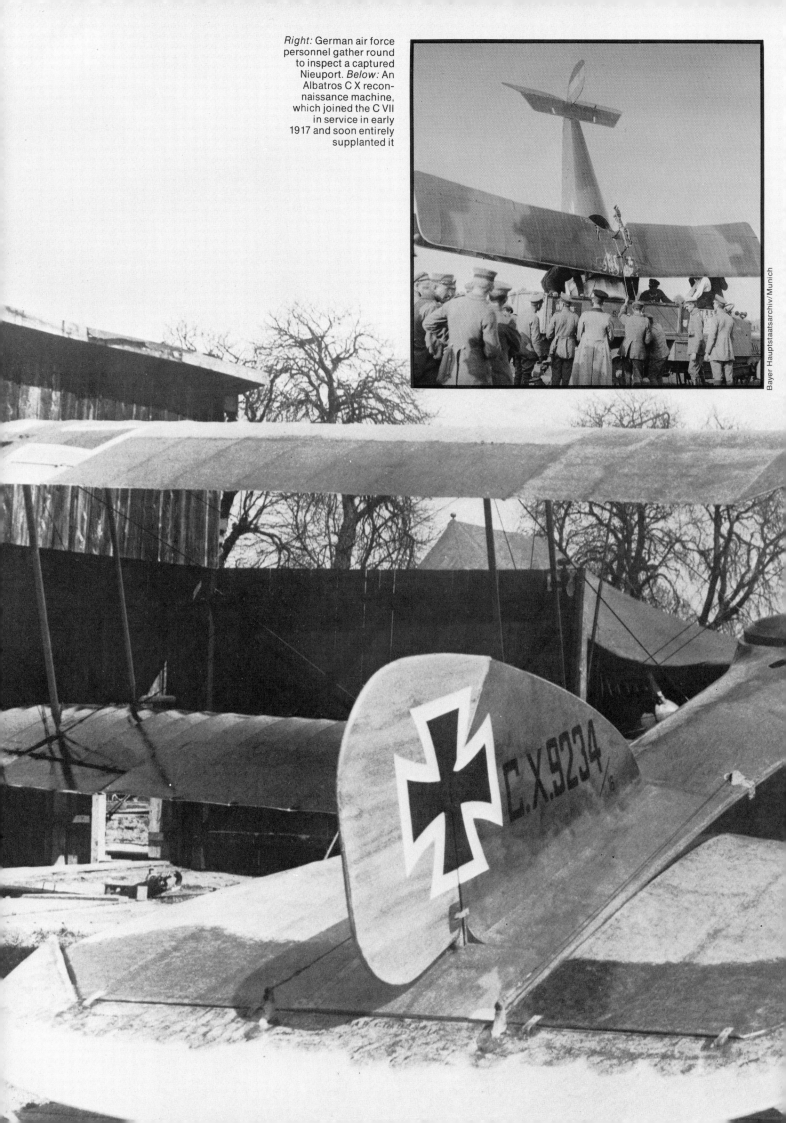

Right: German air force personnel gather round to inspect a captured Nieuport. *Below:* An Albatros C X reconnaissance machine, which joined the C VII in service in early 1917 and soon entirely supplanted it

Bayer Hauptstaatsarchiv/Munich

C.X.9234

prey. Their antagonists, the *Jagdstaffeln* invented by Boelcke in 1916 and efficiently developed by Richthofen, had done well, thanks to good equipment, good training – and plentiful targets. There was also the *panache* that characterised the elder Richthofen. It was a master stroke to paint the aeroplanes of his squadron in brilliant colours – quite against German army regulations – while reserving the only almost totally red machine for himself, a return to the personal style of the mediaeval knight, with his crest and coat of arms. No better publicity device has ever been invented than the blood red aircraft of 'the Red Knight'.

Further to raise the rate of scoring it was now decided to increase the local striking power of the *Jagdstaffeln* by banding together four of them into a larger group. *Jasta 11* was combined with numbers *3, 4* and *33* into an independent fighter wing called *Jagdgruppe 1* which first went into action, rather clumsily, on April 30, the day on which *Rittmeister* Manfred von Richthofen went on leave to celebrate his 52 victories. Reorganised on his return, and now comprising *Jagdstaffeln* numbers *11, 10, 6* and *4*, this unit became the true 'Richthofen Circus', a private army of mobile trouble-shooters known after July as *Jagdgeschwader 1*.

'Bloody April' was over. The supply of new machines from England improved and new types came into service capable of outfighting the Albatros D III and Halberstadt scouts which had taken such toll during the worst month in the history of British air fighting overseas. French airmen too had taken a terrible beating during the ill-fated 'push' of General Nivelle, now fortunately superseded.

In the RFC casualties would have been lighter if those responsible for supply had been more flexible in outlook. It would have been perfectly possible to update the Royal Aircraft Factory's series of helpless BE two-seaters so that pilot and passenger changed places, giving the observer a clear field of fire. Frederick Koolhoven of Armstrong-Whitworth had refused to build BEs and the result was the FK 8, the 'Big Ack', a far more robust and effective machine. The lack of British engines, a result of blind trust in the French aviation industry, led to many casualties, for a rotary Le Rhône or Clerget of 110-hp or 130-hp, although marginally sufficient for a single-seater fighter, was woefully inadequate in two-seaters like the Sopwith 1½-Strutter. The Factory's air-cooled stationary engines, based on Renault designs, lacked smoothness, power and reliability, while the cooling scoops devised by Factory designers had a disastrous effect on the performance of BE and RE aeroplanes.

Technical inferiority must always mean a high casualty rate. Machines already proved obsolete against the Fokker monoplane in 1915 could not be expected to hold off an Albatros D III, and it is not surprising that some squadrons during Bloody April lost more aircrew than there were chairs in the Mess. Perhaps Trenchard's policy of 'offensive at all costs' was unduly robust for the machines under his command. But the Royal Flying Corps did all he required of it during both periods of German air supremacy, and the fact that RFC pilots never lost their offensive spirit was to prove decisive during the coming struggles with the 'Circus', and the tremendous ground-strafing days of 1918.

PASSCHENDAELE

The very name Passchendaele (the soldiers' name for the Third Battle of Ypres) evokes the horror of the fighting there in August, 1917. Although casualties were fewer than on the Somme, weather and ground conditions were the worst that British soldiers have ever been expected to endure. The British barrage had churned the waterlogged ground of Flanders into a morass in which movement was scarcely possible, and the August rains made the situation even worse.

Moving off behind their barrage at 0350 hours on July 31, the assaulting battalions of Second Army, which was to play a supporting rôle to Fifth Army, found the wire well cut everywhere in front of them and the defenders of the outpost zone either disabled, ready to surrender or already in flight. The advance was not unopposed but such opposition as the British and Australians of II ANZAC, IX and X Corps met was quickly overcome. By noon the whole of the German outpost zone, on the army's northern front, where it touched Fifth Army's front, had been occupied, in places to a depth of 1,000 yards.

But this success was a subsidiary one. It was Fifth Army's effort which counted. And its success on July 31 was mixed. Gough's left hand corps, which included the Guards, who had touch with the French First Army to the north, did well—almost

as well, indeed, as the French who, as at the Somme, managed to get further on this the opening day of their ally's offensive than any British unit. The neighbouring corps, XVIII, also achieved the German second line without too much difficulty and in places secured bridgeheads across the little river which ran parallel with the front and 2,000 yards from the British line. There were many tales of gallantry reported that morning, altogether 12 soldiers were to win the Victoria Cross on July 31, in almost every case for total disregard for personal safety in manoeuvring to outflank and destroy one of the countless German pill-boxes or shell-crater machine gun nests which dotted the front of attack.

It was these machine gun nests which II Corps' divisions found such an obstacle, when they moved off behind their barrage towards the dawning sun on July 31. Their

objectives were the crucial ones: the 'high' ground between Klein Zillebeke and the Ypres-Roulers railway, none of it more than 200 feet high but all of it providing the observation posts from which the Germans detected every trace of movement within the salient and the cover behind which they concentrated in safety their own reserves and artillery. It was known that the greater proportion of the German guns was located on and behind the Gheluvelt plateau, the approach to which lay across the neck of land between the little re-entrant valleys of the Bassevillebeek and the Hanebeek and was covered by the ruins of a number of woods, first Shrewsbury Forest, Sanctuary Wood and Château Wood, then Nun's, Glencorse, and the 'beer' woods, Bass, Stout and Bitter. None any longer bore any resemblance to a stand of living timber. The

Above: A distant shell bursts on Pilckem Ridge, August. *Below:* During the battle for Langemarck British troops move forward over shell-torn ground near Pilckem, captured from the Germans in the first day of the offensive. *Opposite:* The first month's fighting in the Flanders campaign.

trees were broken down to shattered stumps and the trunks lay about on a bed of slimy bare earth and shell holes. Much of the debris the Germans had wired together, manufacturing thereby a nearly impassable barrier.

It was through this wilderness, defended by the front battalions of four German regiments, that the leading brigades of the 24th, 30th and 8th Divisions had to find their way, assisted in the centre (30th Division's sector) by 52 tanks of 2nd Tank Brigade. On the right the 24th Division, detailed to form a defensive flank towards Second Army, advanced easily enough on the right, getting to its second objective without severe loss, but the centre brigade was held up on the far edge of Shrewsbury Forest by a collection of pill-boxes at a point called Lower Star Post (after a feature around which thousands of officer cadets had manoeuvred in Sandhurst days before the war). Unable to get forward, it could not provide flank protection to the right hand brigade, which was forced to withdraw, while the left hand brigade, itself taken in flank by enfilade fire from Dumbarton Wood, failed to hold its first objective. This division's success had therefore to be regarded as very partial.

Its neighbour, 30th, had even less success to report at the end of the day, and heavier casualties. Its commander did not start hopefully, since he knew that GHQ would have preferred to substitute another division for his. One of the 'Pals' divisions, recruited by Lord Derby in Manchester and Liverpool, it had suffered dreadfully on the

Somme, from which its spirit had never really recovered. The misgivings of GHQ were borne out at the very beginning of the advance, when a sudden German bombardment drove one of the brigades back into its dug-outs, thereby delaying the men's start and depriving them of the protection of the barrage. It was to their credit that this brigade nevertheless recovered itself and pressed on without artillery cover through Sanctuary Wood to the crest line and captured the ruins known as Stirling Castle. But they were late in doing so, had had to be reinforced by the battalions detailed for the next phase in order to get as far as this, and were quite unable to press any further forward. The line secured was generally that of the first objective. This news did not penetrate to divisional, let alone corps headquarters. The preparatory bombardment and the creeping barrage was accordingly laid down for the advance to the third and fourth objectives and it was not until the battalions ordered to take them advanced into the rear of the first phase battalions that anyone else in the division discovered how ill they had fared during the day's fighting.

Costly and unsuccessful

The third assaulting division of II Corps, 8th, had also had a costly and unsuccessful day. Early and comparatively cheaply, reaching their first objectives, the leading battalions were able to consolidate on the far side of Bellewaarde Lake by the time the supporting battalions moved through,

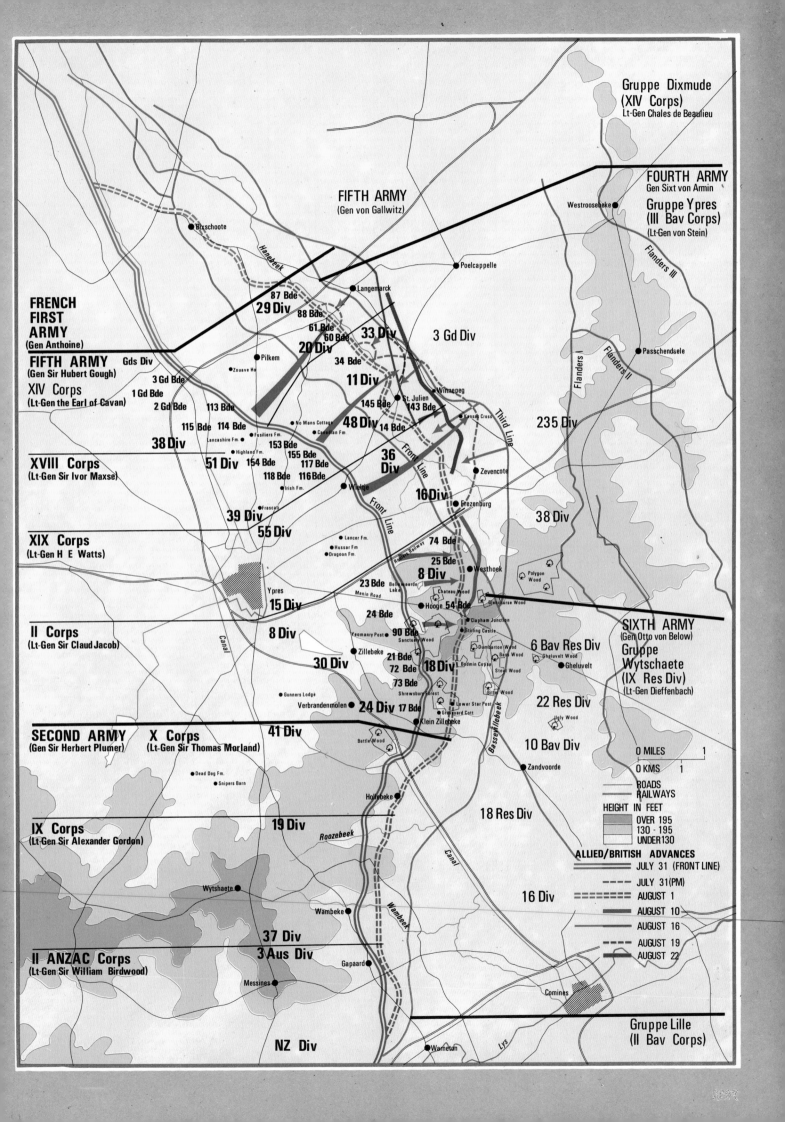

Gruppe Dixmude
(XIV Corps)
Lt-Gen Chales de Beaulieu

FOURTH ARMY
Gen Sixt von Armin

Gruppe Ypres
(III Bav Corps)
(Lt-Gen von Stein)

Westroosebeke

FIFTH ARMY
(Gen von Gallwitz)

Flanders III

Brxschoote

Poelcappelle

Hanebeek

87 Bde
29 Div
88 Bde
61 Bde
60 Bde
20 Div
34 Bde

Langemarck

33 Div

3 Gd Div

Flanders I

Flanders II

Passchendaele

FRENCH
FIRST
ARMY
(Gen Anthoine)

FIFTH ARMY
(Gen Sir Hubert Gough)   Gds Div

Pilkem

11 Div

St. Julien
Winnepeg

235 Div

XIV Corps
(Lt-Gen the Earl of Cavan)

3 Gd Bde
1 Gd Bde
2 Gd Bde   113 Bde

Zouave Ho

145 Bde   143 Bde

Kansas Cross

Third Line

115 Bde   114 Bde

No Mans Cottage

48 Div   14 Bde

38 Div

Fusiliers Fm.
Lancashire Fm.
Highland Fm.

Canadian Fm

36
Div

Zevencote

38 Div

Front Line

XVIII Corps
(Lt-Gen Sir Ivor Maxse)

51 Div

153 Bde
154 Bde   155 Bde 117 Bde
118 Bde 116 Bde

Irish Fm.

Wieltje

16 Div

Frezenburg

39 Div
55 Div

Frascati

Front Line

XIX Corps
(Lt-Gen H E Watts)

Lancer Fm.
Hussar Fm.
Dragoon Fm.

Roulers Railway

74 Bde
25 Bde

Polygon
Wood

8 Div

Westhoek

23 Bde

Bellewaarde
Lake

Chateau Wood

Glencourse Wood

15 Div

Ypres

Menin Road

Hooge   54 Bde

SIXTH ARMY
(Gen Otto von Below)

II Corps
(Lt-Gen Sir Claud Jacob)

24 Bde

8 Div

Yeomanry Post

90 Bde
Sanctuary Wood

Clapham Junction
Stirling Castle

Dumbarton Wood

Bass Wood
Gheluvelt Wood

6 Bav Res Div

Gruppe
Wytschaete
(IX Res Div)
(Lt-Gen Dieffenbach)

Zillebeke

30 Div

21 Bde
72 Bde
73 Bde

18 Div

Bodmin Copse

Stout Wood
Bitter Wood

Gheluvelt

Shrewsbury Forest

Verbrandenmolen

24 Div   17 Bde

Lower Star Post
Graveyard Cott

Ugly Wood

22 Res Div

Gunners Lodge

Klein Zillebeke

10 Bav Div

0 MILES   1

0 KMS   1

SECOND ARMY
(Gen Sir Herbert Plumer)

X Corps
(Lt-Gen Sir Thomas Morland)

41 Div

Battle Wood

Zandvoorde

ROADS
RAILWAYS

HEIGHT IN FEET

Dead Dog Fm.
Snipers Barn

OVER 195
130 - 195
UNDER 130

IX Corps
(Lt-Gen Sir Alexander Gordon)

19 Div

Roozebeek

Hollebeke

18 Res Div

ALLIED/BRITISH ADVANCES

JULY 31 (FRONT LINE)

JULY 31 (PM)

AUGUST 1

Wytschaete

16 Div

AUGUST 10

Wambeke

Wambeek

AUGUST 16

37 Div
3 Aus Div

AUGUST 19

II ANZAC Corps
(Lt-Gen Sir William Birdwood)

Gapaard

AUGUST 22

Messines

Comines

Gruppe Lille
(II Bav Corps)

NZ Div

Warneton

Lys

behind a new barrage, to go on to the second objective. That was reached soon after 0600 hours but, lying as it did on a reverse slope (to the British front line) it was under direct view of the Germans, themselves still ensconced on high ground at Westhoek opposite, who called or put down heavy artillery and machine gun fire on it. The position had to be abandoned.

Many of these obstructions and delays might have been overcome had the tanks of 2nd Tank Brigade been able to keep up with the infantry. As Tank Corps headquarters had warned, however, the ground was quite unsuitable for the employment of tanks and, confined as they were by the ground to movement in the gaps between the woods, they were easily spotted and hit by German shell fire. Nineteen in all were knocked out, 17 in front of a monster pill-box at 'Clapham Junction' on the Menin Road which all efforts by British artillery to destroy had quite failed. Twenty-two others broke down or were ditched in the bad going.

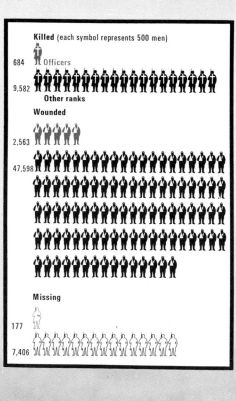

Killed (each symbol represents 500 men)

684 Officers

9,582 Other ranks

Wounded

2,563

47,598

Missing

177

7,406

Left: British and Dominion casualties, July 31 to August 25. *Below:* Stuck in the mud—jacking and hauling a field gun, Pilckem Ridge

German defensive doctrine emphasised the necessity for counterattack, immediately by the front units affected, as quickly as possible thereafter by the *Eingreif* divisions if their help should prove essential. Since the British had almost nowhere occupied more than the German outpost zone, there was no reason to call the *Eingreif* divisions into play. On XIX Corps' sector, however, footholds had been secured in or beyond the German third line. The integrity of his defensive system was threatened and serious counterattack therefore expected. At 1100 hours a severe barrage, emanating from behind the Gheluvelt plateau, fell on the sector between the Ypres-Roulers railway and St. Julien, shortly followed by the appearance of German infantry en masse (since identified as belonging to the *50th Reserve Division*, northern *Eingreif* division of *Gruppe Ypres*). Under their assault, the 39th Division gave way, carrying with it successively the formations on its right, each of which found itself with a flank in the air. By 1630

almost all of XIX Corps' most advanced positions had been regained by the Germans and the weary British infantry had been thrust back to the line of their second objectives. Elsewhere XIV Corps held their line against counterattacks, and the French, rebounding vigorously, chased their assailants beyond the point from which they had started, thus adding to their gains for the day. During that day and into the afternoon of August 2, the Germans launched haphazard raids and assaults of this nature but failed to alter the geographical outcome at all significantly. Their first and most of their second trench lines had passed to the British.

It was not a particularly brilliant result in view of all the effort expended on preparation and plans and the lives lost in the attempt (3,700 in all, with over 20,000 wounded and missing, some of the latter category properly belonging to the 'killed'). Most of these losses had been suffered, not in the assault, but during the period of consolidation, when all communication

had as usual been lost with the artillery, and during the German counterattacks. No cure for this loss of communication was known nor was one expected.

Nevertheless it was Haig's considered decision, after visiting Gough on July 31, that the offensive should be pressed home, and that as quickly as possible. On August 1 his view was somewhat changed, however, by his Operations Branch, which pointed out that no advance was likely to succeed until Fifth Army, and in particular II Corps, had been reinforced by fresh divisions and until a further bombardment had been completed. Operations Branch laid particular stress on the importance of the Gheluvelt plateau, an appreciation they believed shared by the Germans, and urged that the next stage of the offensive take the plateau as its primary aim.

So it was decided. But in the meantime rain had begun to fall, heavily and uninterruptedly. It had begun to fall, in fact, on the afternoon of July 31, just as the first of the German counterattacks came

in, so that by the end of the first stage of the battle on August 2, the battlefield was already beginning to take on the appearance by which it would ever afterwards be remembered. The innumerable shell holes had begun to fill to the brim with water (the water table hereabouts was only three feet below the surface), the paths to liquefy, the trenches to collect a foot of slop at the bottom, even the pill boxes (of which a number were now in British hands) to become slimy and mud-choked at doors and embrasures. Under the weight of bombardment, some pill boxes were eventually to settle in the semi-liquid soil until door lintels were flush with the ground, barring all access.

The bombardment had been resumed immediately after the lull in the infantry fighting on August 2. Despite the fact, however, that the British had chosen the Gheluvelt plateau as their next main objective, they did not and could not bring the total weight of their artillery to bear on the German batteries on and behind it. So superior were German observation facilities that it would have been to invite even higher casualties than those actually suffered had the British massed any more of their guns on the exposed plain due east of Ypres.

Disappointment and intense hatred

It was for resulting reasons, the inaccuracy of the preparatory bombardment and the weakness of the accompanying barrage, that the attack of II Corps on August 10, planned to secure the Gheluvelt plateau and overwhelm the German artillery positions, achieved very much less than expected. As on July 31, the infantry advanced easily enough onto their objectives, actually securing all those assigned, but as soon as German counterattacks began, they were unable to summon accurate or prompt help from their own guns and fell victim to the well-rehearsed German tactical scheme. The German counterattack barrage was so organised as to cut the forward British troops off from contact with their rear, thus denying them reinforcement, resupply or casualty evacuation. By the afternoon, the three assaulting battalions of the two right hand brigades, 7th Queens, 11th Royal Fusiliers and 7th Bedfordshire, had all been much reduced in numbers, were without food or water and were short of ammunition. But since the troops who should have reinforced them were judged not fit for the task in the circumstances, and since the commander of 18th Division wished to keep his reserve brigade intact against eventualities, it was decided to let the exposed battalions fall back further to positions in which they could be supplied more easily. Thus the brunt of the August 10 attack resulted, admittedly in the gain of a little ground on the left at Westhoek, but also in a second failure to clear up the Gheluvelt problem.

Despite this disabling factor, Gough decided to press on with the extension of his gains, meagre as they were, attacking in conjunction with the French. The attack, by all four corps, was scheduled for August 14, but the onset of particularly heavy rain twice caused its postponement for 24 hours so that it did not begin until August 16. Its outcome might have been foreseen.

On the right, the battered divisions of II Corps once more set out across the muddy wilderness of the Gheluvelt plateau.

The 56th Division was reasonably fresh, but that did not save it from disaster on its start line, where several of its leading companies were caught by a sudden German bombardment and broken up. Others of its battalions did better but only isolated parties reached their objectives in and around Polygon Wood. The 8th Division, which had suffered over 3,000 casualties in the first two days of the offensive and had had only a fortnight's rest, did surprisingly well in view of this treatment, arriving promptly on its first objective. But the failure of 56th Division meant that its flank hung in the air and of this the Germans soon became aware. Bold parties of infiltrators quickly took up positions behind the foremost battalions of 8th Division and, as the situation became more and more difficult, they were ordered to withdraw as night drew in more or less to their start lines.

The two divisions of XIX Corps, attacking to the left of II, 16th Irish and 36th Ulster, were neither fit for the task. Both had been continuously in the line since August 4 and their battalions had been reduced, by what was known engagingly as 'trench wastage', to two-thirds or even half their strength. In consequence, an observer noted, the attacking waves they sent forward were like those for a raid rather than a major offensive. Despite that and despite heavy casualties suffered from the outset, the leading battalions pressed on magnificently. Their task, however, was hopeless. So few were the mopping-up parties available to 16th Division that their waves of infantry were shot down from behind by Germans emerging unscathed from dugouts and positions already 'captured'. The 36th Division was held up by wire and strongpoints which it had not the men to outflank. And at 0900 both divisions were suddenly subjected to devastating counterattack by the *5th Bavarian* and *12th Divisions,* supported by an intense bombardment. The foremost companies of the 16th Division, 7th Royal Irish Rifles and 9th Royal Dublin Fusiliers, were at that moment almost onto their objectives and went down fighting beneath the overwhelming mass of German infantry. The rest of both divisions fell back under this pressure to their start lines, onto which the corps commander decided to bring back the barrage as a precaution against the Germans pressing their attack further still.

On the northern flank, beyond the gaze of the German observers on the high ground, XVIII and XIV Corps again did better on August 16 than their less fortunately placed neighbours. They had also been better able to prepare their attacks, largely untroubled by bombardment, and had made such careful arrangements as siting armourers' shops far forward in order that rifles choked with mud could quickly be cleaned, and passed forward again during the course of the battle. As a result both corps gained ground, 20th and 29th Divisions advancing almost 2,000 yards to take Langemarck, scene of the *Kindermord* in 1914.

Gough seemed not the least discouraged by the progress of the battle when visited by his corps commanders on the day following this, the third round of the battle, on August 17. He warned them to be ready for another resumption on August 25 and meanwhile ordered them to undertake preparatory operations with the object of securing jumping-off positions. Some of these attacks, as on August 20, when seven tanks were employed, were profitable and cheap. On August 22, however, a succession of small operations all along the front resulted in heavy casualties for very little result. Both XVIII and XIX Corps took a little more ground to the south of Langemarck, certainly not worth the 3,000 casualties. On the same day, at a slightly later hour, II Corps made yet another attempt to establish a firm hold on the Gheluvelt plateau. The two light infantry battalions assigned, 6th Somerset and 6th Cornwall, upheld the traditions of their regiments in the most splendid manner. After a spirited advance, during which they took numerous prisoners and secured possession of Glencorse Wood, they were prevented from advancing further but settled down determinedly to defend what they had taken. Under steady shelling and frequent counterattack, they were to remain out, unsupported and unsupplied, for over two days, until August 24.

The outcome was a bitter disappointment to GHQ and at a conference between Haig and Plumer on August 25 it was decided that the responsibility for carrying on the battle should be transferred from Fifth to Second Army. Haig, long Gough's protector, had wearied of his overoptimistic forecasts and of his slapdash planning—though by no means before Gough's own soldiers, many of whom would long feel an intense hatred for the staff of Fifth Army. Plumer's methods, proved at Messines, did not promise to achieve a quick breakthrough. His 'step by step', siegecraft tactics would, on the contrary, win results only slowly. But they were sure. And as Haig had at last grasped that nothing could be done at Ypres until the Gheluvelt plateau had been captured, he now turned to the one man who, he could be certain, would win it for him. Later on the same day he conveyed to Gough the news that Plumer was to be given command of II Corps, with which in three weeks he would launch a major offensive. In the meantime, Fifth Army was to press its offensive.

During the morning and afternoon of August 27, therefore, the infantry groped their way forward through driving rain, scarcely able to keep their footing in the sea of mud to which the weather and the bombardment had reduced the surface of the battlefield. Nowhere was any ground gained, though in XVIII Corps' sector 'the Germans at first showed every inclination to surrender; but on seeing the slow progress of the infantry struggling over the slippery ground, they opened rapid fire at close range'. It was an episode which aptly summarised the character which the battle had now taken on.

Further Reading
Edmonds, Brig. J. E., *Operations in France & Belgium 1917,* Vols 1-2, Official History of the War (Macmillan)
Gibbs, P., *From Bapaume to Passchendaele* (Heinemann 1918)
Gladden, E. N., *Ypres, 1917* (Kimber 1967)
Gough, Sir Hubert, *The Fifth Army* (Hodder & Stoughton 1931)
Richards, F., *Old Soldiers Never Die* (Faber & Faber)

Passschendaele
THE SECOND PHASE

The first twenty-six days of the Third Battle of Ypres had
cost the Allies 70,000 casualties for very limited gains.
Command of the crucial sector of the battle now passed from
Gough to the more cautious Plumer, who could be relied upon
only to commit men to an attack aimed at limited objectives
and with overwhelming artillery cover. Fine weather began to
dry out the marsh in which the battle was being fought. Could
Plumer's tactics save Haig's still cherished plan for a grand
strategic breakthrough and reduce the appalling Allied losses?
Above: Ypres cathedral, September 1917

The battle of Passchendaele was now Plumer's. But it was with heavy reluctance that he had taken over its direction (from the slapdash Gough), a reluctance which Haig had overcome only by insistent and urgent prompting. His reluctance, moreover, was understandable. The battle, which by the beginning of September had been in progress—progress being understood in a very relative sense—for just over a month, had resulted so far in gains of ground nowhere more than 4,000 yards deep, less at the essential points, and had cost nearly 70,000 casualties, 15,000 of them fatal. During August much of the battlefield had become waterlogged, due in part to the early onset of the autumn rains but also to the disruption of the man-made drainage system by prolonged artillery fire.

Much of this fire, moreover, had come from the German artillery, the British Fifth Army having failed to achieve superiority in gunpower—the vital factor in trench offensives. Since it had also failed to drive the Germans from the slight but decisively important heights which com-

manded the battlefield (and which gave them observation of the whole plain of Flanders) their gunners were able, as the British never had been, to pick off targets of opportunity deep within the attackers' rear area. Reinforcement, re-supply and the relief of troops in the line thus remained a risky and costly affair for the British, undertaken as far as possible only at night. Even so, a blind German bombardment of any of the well known traffic bottlenecks was more likely than not to find victims: the passage of the Menin Road, artery of the offensive, was reckoned, by the transport drivers who nightly made it, an increasingly risky gamble.

But besides these purely objective factors, Plumer had a particular reason for resisting Haig's request that he take over command of the crucial II Corps sector from Gough. For his skill lay in a special sort of operation, demonstrated in his brisk and cheap capture of the Messines Ridge in June. His method demanded lengthy preparation and was tailored to the achievement of strictly limited objectives.

The Passchendaele battle, however, had extended objectives, or had been endowed with them at its inception, and had recently become a race against time, in particular against the coming of the even heavier rain which late autumn would bring.

Haig, who no doubt foresaw Plumer's objections, disarmed him by offering to grant him time for preparation, and agreed to settle for a limited gain: the Gheluvelt plateau, behind which sheltered the principal concentration of German artillery. If he did not speak to Plumer of 'breakthrough' or of such lesser but related designs as 'clearing the Belgian coast' it was not because he had surrendered belief in such notions himself, but probably because he judged it unproductive to try them on that hardheaded old warhorse. In any case, he judged the battle realistically enough to grasp that nothing would come of it until the German guns had been beaten into silence.

There were those, however, and they were becoming numerous, who doubted whether anything would now come of the

Imperial War Museum

Bundesarchiv

Above: The battle of the Menin Road Ridge, September 20—shells bursting on the main road to Zonnebeke. The first of the three battles in the second phase of Third Ypres, the battle achieved its final objectives by midday. 'Another terrible assault was made on our lines,' Ludendorff recorded, '. . . the enemy's onslaught was successful, which proved the superiority of the attack over the defence.'
Left: A forward German reconnaissance unit with dog

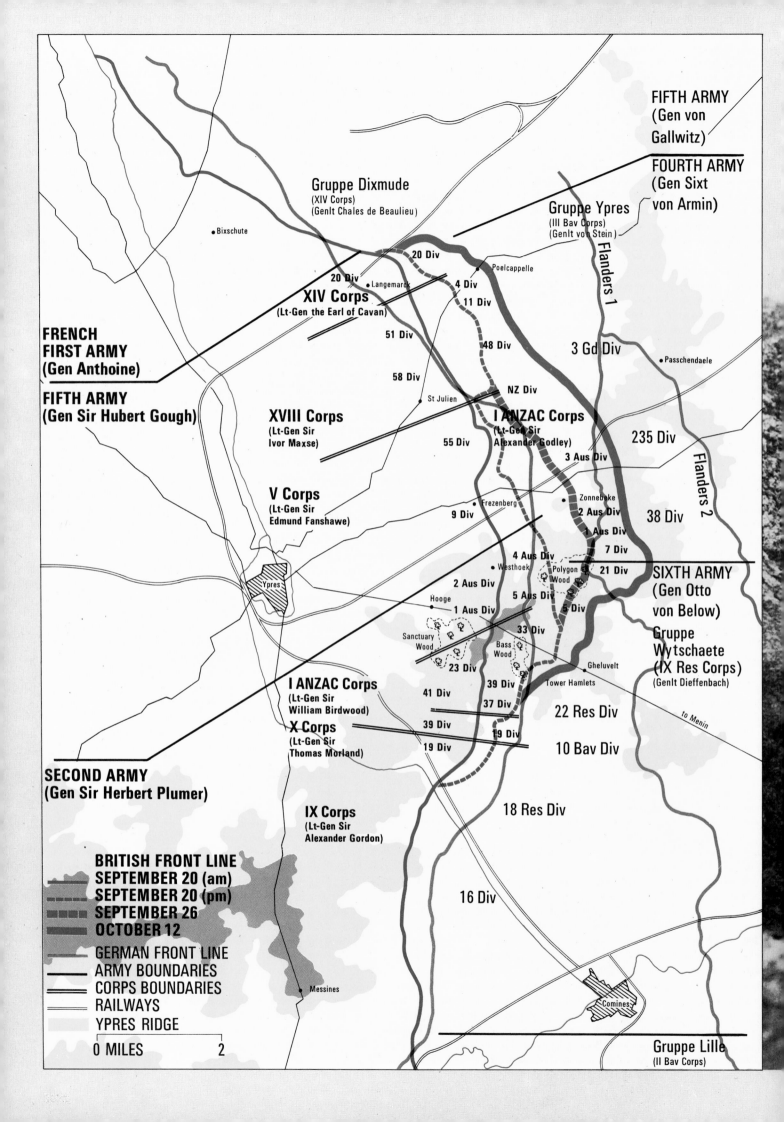

FIFTH ARMY
(Gen von Gallwitz)

FOURTH ARMY
(Gen Sixt von Armin)

Gruppe Dixmude
(XIV Corps)
(Genlt Chales de Beaulieu)

Gruppe Ypres
(III Bav Corps)
(Genlt von Stein)

• Bixschute

Flanders 1

20 Div

• Poelcappelle

20 Div

• Langemarck

4 Div

XIV Corps
(Lt-Gen the Earl of Cavan)

11 Div

• Passchendaele

51 Div

48 Div

3 Gd Div

FRENCH
FIRST ARMY
(Gen Anthoine)

58 Div

St Julien

NZ Div

235 Div

FIFTH ARMY
(Gen Sir Hubert Gough)

XVIII Corps
(Lt-Gen Sir
Ivor Maxse)

I ANZAC Corps
(Lt-Gen Sir
Alexander Godley)

3 Aus Div

Flanders 2

55 Div

2 Aus Div

38 Div

V Corps
(Lt-Gen Sir
Edmund Fanshawe)

• Frezenberg

9 Div

1 Aus Div

7 Div

4 Aus Div

• Westhoek

Polygon Wood

21 Div

SIXTH ARMY
(Gen Otto
von Below)

Ypres

2 Aus Div

5 Aus Div

5 Div

Hooge

1 Aus Div

33 Div

Gruppe
Wytschaete
(IX Res Corps)
(Genlt Dieffenbach)

Sanctuary
Wood

Bass
Wood

• Gheluvelt

23 Div

39 Div

Tower Hamlets

I ANZAC Corps
(Lt-Gen Sir
William Birdwood)

41 Div

37 Div

22 Res Div

to Menin

X Corps
(Lt-Gen Sir
Thomas Morland)

39 Div

19 Div

10 Bav Div

SECOND ARMY
(Gen Sir Herbert Plumer)

19 Div

18 Res Div

IX Corps
(Lt-Gen Sir
Alexander Gordon)

16 Div

BRITISH FRONT LINE
SEPTEMBER 20 (am)
SEPTEMBER 20 (pm)
SEPTEMBER 26
OCTOBER 12
GERMAN FRONT LINE
ARMY BOUNDARIES
CORPS BOUNDARIES
RAILWAYS
YPRES RIDGE

• Messines

Comines

0 MILES   2

Gruppe Lille
(II Bav Corps)

'Blood and mud, blood and mud. They can think of nothing better!'

Far left: The fighting in the Ypres sector, August 25—October 6, 1917. *Left:* 4th Division cooks in the Westhoek sector, October

battle at all. Foremost among them was the Prime Minister, David Lloyd George, who had disliked the project from the outset and saw all his worst forebodings realised. 'Blood and mud, blood and mud,' he was heard continually to mutter during this period, 'they can think of nothing better.' The litany was provoked in part by Haig's disingenuous despatch to the War Cabinet of September 2, in which he admitted that the offensive had fallen behind schedule, but blamed the delay on the bad weather and a shortage of heavy shells, and insisted that the weakness of the French made continuation essential and promised a speedy resumption. It was not surprising therefore that the Prime Minister should have displayed more than usual interest in a French request to the British to match their own transfer of heavy artillery from France to Italy in support of a forthcoming Italian offensive; or that, on hearing of it, Robertson, Haig's faithful acolyte in the War Office, should have sensed another attempt by Lloyd George to reduce Haig's striking power; or that Robertson's warning should have brought Haig hotfoot to London.

When the two soldiers met the Cabinet Committee next day, it was to listen to a distinctly chilly strategic summary by the Prime Minister. The Russians were incapable of further effort, a judgement which the recent failure of the Kerensky Offensive and present disintegration of their armies rendered irrefutable; the Germans would therefore shortly be able to reinforce the Western from the Eastern Front; the French were recuperating; the Americans would not arrive in any numbers until the following year; the British had ceased to make progress in Flanders; the Italians had begun a major offensive on the River Isonzo. Lloyd George's conclusion was that operations on the Western Front should be shut down temporarily and heavy artillery lent to the Italians, whose offensive promised to achieve much.

'I've 'eard different' was Robertson's retort, his aitches giving way as always under strain. He and Haig, arguing that it was unlikely the Italians would make anything more of the eleventh Isonzo offensive than they had of the previous ten, and aided by the silence or indecision of the rest of the Cabinet Committee, were eventually able to elude the fetters which the Prime Minister had hoped to cast round their strategic freedom of action. Haig left the meeting with permission given, or at least not refused, to proceed with the next

round and having given no promise to divert guns to the Italians. But his enemy, Wilson, temporarily isolated from the world of power in Eastern Command, commented in his diary: *Haig is not going to do anything really serious at Ypres this year. . . . [He], Robertson and Kiggell [Haig's Chief-of-Staff] are running the maxim of superior forces at the decisive point, etc, into the ground. I believe that Lloyd George, knowing that Haig will not do any good, has allowed him to keep all his guns, etc, so that he can, later on, say: 'Well, I gave you everything. I even allowed you to spoil the Italian offensive. And now, owing to gross miscalculation and incapacity, you have entirely failed to do anything serious except lose a lot of men.' And in this indictment he will include Robertson and then get rid of both of them.*

It was a forecast of results, if not an analysis of motives, of uncanny accuracy. But Lloyd George was already taking steps to limit the scope of Haig's strategy by reducing the flow of men from Britain to France. Manpower in any case was running

short, the main untapped supply being the new class of 18-year-olds, supplemented by returned wounded, 'comb-outs' of non-combatant corps and reserved occupations, unhorsed Yeomen and unsaddled Cyclists. Even before Lloyd George had embarked on his policy of retaining as many men of these categories as possible in England, the divisions at the front had begun to report increasing deficiencies of infantry soldiers. Most divisions were nearly 2,000 short by early September. Since they were all still organised on a 12 battalion basis (13 including the divisional Pioneer Battalion) their 'trench strengths' remained higher than those of the German divisions, which had been on a 9 battalion establishment for over a year. But it would increasingly become a question how much longer the British could afford their ampler style; more important, Lloyd George seemed to hope that these shortages would raise fundamental questions about BEF strategy.

One important question about that strategy had not been raised in London on September 4, and that concerned the neces-

sity of 'taking the pressure off the French'. The French had undoubtedly been in straits since the spring mutinies, and Pétain had certainly asked Haig to distract the Germans' attention from his front meanwhile. But Haig had not made Pétain's request the justification for his offensive plans when he first mooted them. By September, however, his ally's predicament had become a frequent refrain of Haig's, and he was subsequently to make it the whole explanation for his Flanders strategy of 1917. The evidence was growing, however, that the French recovery, for which Haig claimed to be winning time, was already well under way. On August 26, at Verdun, Pétain had launched a limited offensive on a front of 11 miles, in which all objectives had been secured, including the heights known as Côte 304 and the Mort'Homme, captured by the Germans at such heavy cost in February 1916. This success made it reasonable to ask whether the French any longer needed protecting from the Germans as energetically as Haig insisted. Since Pétain pressed his requests

for assistance, a weighty appeal arriving on September 19, Haig was able to avoid having to answer the question.

He was thus free to concentrate his attention, from September 5 onwards, almost exclusively on Plumer's plans and preparations for the assault on the Gheluvelt Plateau. Plumer had submitted his proposals on August 29; as expected, they were for a battle divided into four clearly limited stages, each of short duration, fairly widely separated in time and aimed at limited objectives. The operation order for the first step, 1,500 yards deep, was issued on September 10. It prescribed a weight and concentration of both infantry and artillery power as yet unmatched on the Western Front. The principal blow was to be struck by I Australian and New Zealand Corps and X Corps, on the front taken over from Fifth Army between the line of the Ypres-Roulers railway and Shrewsbury Forest. IX Corps, on the right, was to make a subsidiary attack; Fifth Army, on the left, was to launch a diversionary assault along its whole front. The success of the operation would lie, however, with the four first line divisions of 1 ANZAC and X Corps: these were 2nd and 1st Australian Divisions and 23rd and 41st Divisions. After some bargaining over boundaries with Gough, Plumer had been able to reduce the front of attack of each to 1,000 yards. The divisions were to attack on a two brigade front, each brigade with a battalion leading and three in close support. Each division was to have its third brigade in reserve and behind each division another was to be held close by.

This was a normal, if rather dense, deployment. The weight and complexity of the supporting barrage, or more accurately barrage system, was unprecedented. There were to be five belts of fire in all, drenching a swathe of territory 1,000 yards deep with metal and explosive. The first belt was to be a shrapnel barrage fired by 170 18-pounders; the second a high-explosive belt fired by 166 18-pounders and 114 4.5 inch howitzers; the third a belt of bullets fired by 240 Vickers machine guns; the fourth a high-explosive belt fired by 120 6-inch howitzers; and the fifth similar, fired by 168 heavy pieces, from 60-pounders to 9.2 howitzers. The density of guns along the front was higher than ever before recorded, one gun to 5.2 yards.

The barrage was to move over the first 200 yards in eight minutes, lifting 50 yards every two minutes, and was then to slow to a rate of 100 yards every six minutes. As always the infantry was enjoined to follow as close behind the barrage as possible. This injunction made sense, for the curtain of shells forced the defence into shelter and the quicker the infantry could arrive on its positions after the barrage had lifted, the less likely was it that the defence could man its firing positions, and the lower were the attackers' casualties likely to be. But to follow a barrage closely, even one fired by gunners in whom confidence was felt, was a tense experience, the boiling curtain of smoke and dust, and the unrelenting noise, urging every nerve in a man's body to retreat or hide from it, rather than keep pace with its slow advance. Even the most skilful gunners, moreover, could not guarantee 100% avoidance of 'shorts', shells which because of faults in material or the gun-laying drop among friendly instead of enemy troops.

Above: A party of men crosses a muddy pool in Château Wood, once a stand of living timber, October. *Right above:* Searching the body of a dead comrade for identification papers, Château Wood. *Right below:* German anti-aircraft unit. Aircraft played an important part in Plumer's battle preparations, reporting objectives to the artillery

127

Nevertheless, experience had proved beyond question that safety overall lay in hugging the rear edge of the barrage. The chance of 'shorts' causing casualties on this occasion would be reduced by the formation prescribed for the attack; instead of moving in dense waves, the infantry were to advance in loose lines, composed of small groups each charged with a specific task of penetration or 'mopping up'.

Two of the assaulting divisions, 1st and 2nd Australian, could be counted on to make the best use of the creeping barrage. Now highly skilled and battle-hardened and still well up to strength, these contingents of fit and pugnacious colonials had acquired a reputation equalled by only a small élite of British divisions. The great mass, to which the other two attacking divisions, 23rd and 41st, both belonged, were of noticeably lower quality; weaker in numbers, particularly of fighting infantry (a scarcity heightened by Lloyd George's recently initiated policy of retaining troops at home as a brake on Haig's offensive inclinations), they were also obviously less 'for it'. In the trenches these Kitchener battalions displayed a splendid stoicism, and in the attack a decent obedience to orders and to their officers, but the heroic spirit displayed by the original Kitchener volunteers, and squandered on the Somme, animated few of the conscripts of 1917.

Fortunately during the three weeks preceding Plumer's offensive, a sudden improvement in the weather did much to raise the army's heart, besides making the plan look a good deal more feasible than it had in August and greatly facilitating the tasks of preparation. These were herculean. Several thousand yards of plank road had to be built across the face of the battlefield in order to make 'jump-off' possible; 3,200 yards of it were needed in I ANZAC Corps' area alone, demanding a daily delivery at Corps railhead of 250 tons of cut beech. Laid lengthways, with another transverse layer above, these planks provided a firm (though initially floating) path four or five feet wide, sufficient to let mules, carrying parties and columns of limbers get forward to battalion and battery positions. The labour gangs, 13,500 strong, also had to lay extensive networks of duckboards across the crater fields, essential if the infantry were not to drown on the way to the front line. As the ground dried out, however, which it did with surprising suddenness under the mid-September sun, cross country movement again became possible, though it could only be tried by larger groups at night.

Faulty defence
The plight of the German infantry was not much more enviable at this moment of the battle than that of the British. Current German defensive doctrine, as laid down by the tactical expert, Lossberg, who had been sent to *Army Group Rupprecht* in order to conduct the defence, prescribed a very deep position held thinly in the 'outpost zone', with the 'main line of resistance' some 2,000 yards behind. Since the British had now captured the outpost zone, the 'main line of defence' was the first line of defence and its concrete pillboxes were no longer available as shelter for the German garrison battalions. They were condemned, like their enemies, to find what cover they could in shell hole positions further to the rear, which afforded

little protection either from the elements or from bombardment. Behind them stood the *Eingreif* (counterattack) divisions ready to 'lock in' to the battle wherever the British penetrated.

But penetration was not Plumer's object for September 20, hence, in part, the failure of German defensive tactics that day. For fail they did. At the outset, a German barrage caught the 1st Australian Division as it was forming up in the morning mist and caused casualties and some confusion, but the infantry recovered from it quickly and pressed forward. They, together with 2nd Australian and the two British divisions, were to share an exhilarating experience that morning. Beginning at 0540 hours they were to follow a barrage which had almost everywhere killed, disabled or dazed the German defenders, even inside the pill-boxes which dotted the front of attack. Some of the pillbox garrisons showed fight but often a 'fatal confusion' ran through them, 'the weaker spirits being ready to surrender while some brave men continued to fire'. At a pillbox, where one German had fired between the legs of another attempting to surrender, and hit an Australian sergeant, a Lewis gunner, shouting

'I'll see to the bastards', fired three or four bursts into the entrance killing or wounding most of the crowd inside (the pillboxes were crowded because nearby German infantry had almost everywhere taken shelter within from the barrage). At another pillbox, the garrison of which made signals of surrender but subsequently killed a much loved Australian officer, the attackers were with difficulty prevented from carrying out a wholesale extermination. At a third, where the Germans tried to surrender rather late, some Australians 'went mad' in the words of their commanding officer, and threw bombs into a crowd of them until only an officer and 40 men were left. But these were cases of exceptional behaviour on both sides; generally the Australians had little to do but follow the barrage and accept the surrender of the Germans, who in many cases came out to meet their captors, waving white handkerchiefs or bandages.

At about 1345 hours the infantry had secured all its objectives, with the exception of a section of Gheluvelt Plateau

Top: After the September 20 attack – disabled British tanks at Clapham Junction – picture taken from the Menin Road looking across the wastes of Flemish mud towards the stumps of Sanctuary Wood. *Above:* Ypres after three years as a front line town.

known as Tower Hamlets Spur, and the barrage stopped; it had lasted for eight hours and eight minutes. The gunners remained on the 'qui vive' for counterattacks; the infantry began to dig in.

Towards 1500 hours German infantry, now known to be from the *236th Division* of the counterattack reserve, were seen 'dribbling across' from the Butte (the butts of a pre-war Belgian rifle range, one of the most commanding spots on this billiard table battlefield) to the eastern edge of Polygon Wood in which, an artillery observer reported, 'our men are souvenir hunting'. At this the SOS rockets were fired and the barrage crashed down again. No Germans emerged through it and no organised movement was observed after it lifted.

September 20, the 'battle of the Menin Road Ridge', could therefore be counted a

FIELD-MARSHAL SIR DOUGLAS HAIG

Imperial War Museum

Top: Field-Marshal Sir Douglas Haig. Haig commanded the army from 1914-15, and was commander-in-chief of the expeditionary forces in France. *Bottom:* General Sir Hubert Gough (left). Sir Hubert was in command of the 3rd cavalry brigade in 1914.

success. X Corps had just failed to take all of Tower Hamlets Spur and some of Fifth Army's objectives on the left remained beyond the final line reached. But on a front of eight miles between Zillebeke and Langemarck, Plumer had achieved gains of at least 1,500 yards and secured the base for his next advance. He had also dislocated the German defensive system and inflicted heavy losses. Unfortunately, his men had also suffered much: including the casualties suffered on the 21st-23rd in attempts to capture the rest of Tower Hamlets, the total was over 20,000, of which about 15% were fatal.

Second Army remained in good heart nevertheless, and by September 26, despite a German spoiling attack the previous day, it was ready to undertake the second of Plumer's 'steps'. This was designed to capture the whole of Polygon Wood, an Australian operation, with X Corps covering the right and Fifth Army advancing in conformity on the left: the extreme depth of advance was to be about 1,200 yards. The artillery necessary to support the push had been brought forward some 2,000 yards in the preceding week, and at 0550 hours on September 26 its by now well rehearsed barrage crashed down on the German half of the crater field. The surface was a jumbled patchwork of powdery, bare ground and wet shell holes, but conditions at first were generally dry enough for a dense curtain of dust to mingle with the

smoke of bursting shells which the infantry followed gratefully. As a week before, they found the German defenders dazed and ready to surrender and by 1200 hours had achieved almost all their objectives. A company commander of the *3rd Battalion 34th Fusiliers* in defence at Zonnebeke opposite the British V Corps has left an impression of the overwhelming impact of the Plumer offensive method. *About 0600 hours a sergeant near the entrance shouted out that he thought the English were coming. I hurried out. The air was filled with smoke and this together with a ground mist made it difficult to see more than twenty yards or so . . . Then the shelling slackened only to move on and become stronger than ever behind us. Suddenly I heard shouts of 'the English' from in front. I called the men out and we took up a position in the mass of shell holes on either side. Almost at once figures appeared moving towards us through the fog. They were coming on at a steady pace bunched together in groups between the water-logged shell holes. We opened fire and threw hand grenades into the midst of them. For a moment the attack was held, but looking round I could see more English advancing past us to right and left, and realised that our only hope was to run for it. With the few men near me I started back towards Zonnebeke but, after a few yards, saw it was hopeless as the enemy had already closed in ahead of us in their advance. The noise of machine gun fire from the village made us hope that a counterattack would soon be made to regain the position and four of us ran back. We had scarcely time to slam the door of thick oak planks when it was ripped away by a hand grenade.*

In fact, the German sector commander at Zonnebeke *had* been preparing a counterattack, as were all the others along the assaulted front. Three *Eingreif* divisions, *17th, 236th* and *4th Bavarian*, began to advance through the positions held by *50th, 3rd,* and *23rd Reserve Divisions* from about 1300 hours onwards and came under British fire soon after 1500. Everywhere their thrusts were broken up by intense barrages and they were forced to fall back or at best dig in close to the new British line. As on September 20, Plumer's limited method had disrupted the Germans' defensive system by ensuring that their counterattack divisions would have to deliver battle within range of supporting artillery. In consequence these divisions took up to two hours to advance 1,000 yards and lost an eighth of their fighting strength in the process. Again, however, the British had lost 15,000 casualties, of which about 10% were fatal, for a gain of about 1,000 yards on an 8,000 yard front; and there were still ridges to their eastward, Passchendaele ridge among them.

Haig, nevertheless, declared himself extremely satisfied with the progress of operations, and in conference with Gough and Plumer on September 28 revealed that he intended after the completion of Plumer's third 'step' to institute a breakthrough attempt again. His intelligence staff assured him, he said, that the Germans could not for very much longer sustain the losses now being inflicted on their front divisions and that the Belgian railway bottleneck made it impossible to reinforce the Ypres sector at the speed necessary to make good this erosion of their strength. In the face of his army com-

manders' barely disguised disbelief, he explained that he did not count upon breakthrough in early October, but merely wished to be ready for it; so had ordered two divisions of cavalry to concentrate immediately in rear of the attacking armies and the other three to remain within call and he was shelving offensive plans for other sectors of the front, notably a plan for a tank attack at Cambrai. Six infantry divisions were in consequence to be brought to Ypres from elsewhere.

Plumer's preparations for the third 'step' proceeded meanwhile as before. The plan now was to make the sector north of Polygon Wood around Broodseinde the centre of effort, using all four Australian divisions, with Fifth Army and the British divisions of Second Army attacking on the right and left respectively. The only element of novelty was the absence of a preparatory bombardment — it had been decided to unleash the barrage simultaneously with the infantry assault.

At 0600 hours on the morning of October 4, against a misty dawn with a light drizzle falling, the barrage crashed down and the infantry, chasing it hard to get clear of their own positions before they were caught by the German counter-bombardment, advanced into the crater field.

Lossberg, the German defensive expert, had issued new instructions following the failure of his tactics on September 20 and 26 when the *Eingreif* divisions had arrived too late. On this day the divisions in line were crowded into the front of the defended zone and the leading regiments of the *Eingreif* divisions were installed ready in the rear area of the battle zone. As a result, the unheralded barrage caused immense casualties among the densely packed Germans caught within its 1,000-yard spread and nullified all efforts made by local commanders to get counterattacks going. This was the first of the 'Black Days' which Ludendorff was to record in his diary. It left the German army in Flanders nearly 30,000 men weaker and their positions again dented in the most sensitive sector.

Yet the wastage of British and Australian divisions had continued at a consistent rate and the depth of ground won on October 4 averaged only 700 yards. Worse still, the weather had now taken a turn for the worse. The drizzle which had begun on the morning of October 4 continued for the two following days, interspersed with heavy rain which became steady on October 7. It was enough to transform the Ypres battlefield, where the water table lay nearly everywhere only three feet below the surface and which was kept passable only by the careful maintenance of an extensive drainage system, into a soupy marsh. On the evening of October 7, Plumer and Gough again obeyed a summons to GHQ at Montreuil. Their views were solicited. Both declared that they would welcome an order to close down the Ypres offensive. Haig declined to give it. He explained, as he had done so frequently during the last six months, that he could not risk taking the pressure off the Germans with the French still so weak, and even if a breakthrough should not now materialise, he preferred that his troops should winter on higher ground than that they now occupied. He therefore expected to receive early news of their plans to re-open the offensive on October 9.

Passchendaele
THE FINAL PHASE

On October 9, 1917, it began to rain once more on Passchendaele Ridge, and on the 26th when the Canadians launched a third major assault it was still raining and the ground was drowned in mud.

When the Canadian Corps was ordered by Sir Douglas Haig to capture Passchendaele Ridge, the battle in the Ypres salient had been going on since the beginning of August 1917. Slowly and painfully, British, Australian, New Zealand and French soldiers had pushed forward against the higher ground that dominated the flat battlefield surrounding what was left of the city of Ypres. More than 400,000 casualties (British and German) had been suffered since that day in August when British tanks had moved hopefully along the Menin Road, and then slithered off into the mud. Whatever may be said about the need for these attacks, or about the early optimistic strategic estimates that caused the fighting to commence near Ypres in 1917, it is clear that attrition-slogging for land and killing Germans had come to dominate the minds of the men at GHQ by the time October arrived. At that point in time, kindly weather and the sacrifices of thousands of men had brought the thrusting point of the attack to within about 2,000 yards of Passchendaele village.

Although this article will deal with the purely Canadian effort, before going on to sum up the whole campaign, it must be stated that to separate the British-Anzac effort on October 12 from the Canadian push that followed is an unsatisfactory way of proceeding—for two reasons. First there is the fact that the Anzacs who had been in action in the salient for some time were not in any sense defeated troops. The Australians still had their heads up. When they handed over to the Canadians, after October 20, they explained meticulously the dangers and opportunities to their fellow colonials. On all sides comments were made about the mutual respect these soldiers showed for each other. Perhaps it was the fact that they were both proud homogeneous groups—but the fact is that when they looked on one another they liked what they saw. Furthermore it must be borne in mind that a party of Australians had actually arrived at Passchendaele village at one stage only to withdraw because of a series of unfortunate misunderstandings.

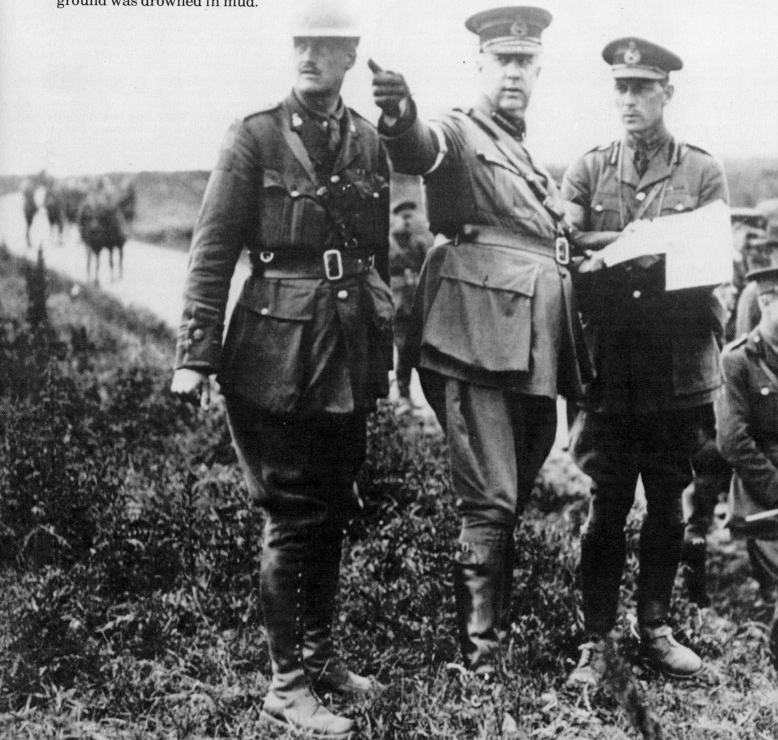

A second reason lies in the fact that Haig had decided to take Passchendaele on October 7 before the French made their push towards the Houthulst Forest on the northwest of the battleground on October 9, and before the Anzacs and British were so badly smashed up on October 12. Also the rains had not come by October 7. It is true that there had been much rain in August, but September was not rainy and not all ground around Ypres was impassable. The rains that came in October, beginning on the 9th, broke the drainage system on the heights. Haig should perhaps have foreseen what barrage and rain might do to the ground. The fact is that when he ordered, on October 7, the attack to go in, against the advice of his army commanders, Plumer and Gough, he had made his commitment—a commitment that involved the Anzac and the Canadian Corps.

The geographical/military situation that had long existed on the Ypres salient was that to the northeast of the town the ground was low and traversed by streams that generally ran in a northwest/southeasterly direction, such as the Steenbeke. This flat land with its intricate drainage system was dominated by a crescent of high ground extending in a slow curve from Westroosebeke. Passchendaele, some six miles on the west of Ypres, trailed southwards towards the Messines Ridge about four miles southeast of the town. When Messines was taken in June, the southern extremity of the strongpoint that the Germans held then lay across the Menin Road—known at its eastern end as the Gheluvelt plateau. Everything west and east of this crescent was visible to German gunners and their artillery range extended well to the north of Ypres. For the Germans it was an extremely pleasant position. For the Britons and French under their observation and open to sniper fire it was hell; cover, except that which they dug, was almost non-existent. By October 7, however, nearly all the Gheluvelt plateau, and the ridge up through Polygon Wood to Zonnebeke-Broodseinde was won from the Germans. All that was wanted to complete the capture of the high crescent was an attack on Passchendaele Ridge, bounded on one side, roughly by Broodseinde, and on the other along the Goudberg Spur. Unfortunately the fact that Haig did not include the capture of Westroosebeke (north of Passchendaele) in these final plans makes it less than likely that he was thinking as seriously of capturing strategic ground as he was of simply taking Passchendaele, killing 'Germans and claiming a victory.

Looking more closely at the battleground that Haig had determined to capture, one sees a ridge with three spurs running off it in a southwesterly direction. The most northerly and shortest of these was the Goudberg Spur, the approaches to which were over low ground of almost quicksand variety. The middle spur, about one mile in

Left: General Sir Arthur Currie directing a practice attack. He was convinced that the task the Canadians had been set was not so much impossible as irrelevant. In its assessment of Passchendaele, the British Official History distorts the record on two important counts—it minimises the extent of the mud, claiming that it was no worse than on the Somme in 1916, and doubles the German casualty figures and nearly halves the British

length, known as the Bellevue Spur was about ¼ mile wide and was divided from the main ridge by the Ravebeek stream, ordinarily about five feet wide but now surrounded by low, inundated ground. It was planned that the Allied attacks would follow these pieces of relatively high ground. It can be readily appreciated that the combination of concentrated German artillery in a narrow area, spurs protected and intersected by very difficult ground, carefully disposed pillbox positions and approach terrain that had been cut up by months of artillery fire and had been hideously fought over did not make for an ideal battleground.

This, quite naturally, was the immediate opinion of Sir Arthur Currie, the commander of the Canadian Corps. When given his orders, he objected to the task before him. He could see clearly that he had been set a task that was not so much impossible as irrelevant. The rains had come by October 13 when Currie was dragged into Haig's web. Could the Canadian Corps take Passchendaele? It was probable that they could but Currie, according to John Sweetenham, estimated the cost at 16,000 casualties. Nevertheless, he was ordered to attack.

Currie, however, was not overawed by the red tape at GHQ. Haig knew that but he wanted the agony over swiftly. Currie, however, was certain that careful preparations were necessary, and that the operation had to be done in careful stages. He got his way. He liked and co-operated well with the Army Commander, General Plumer. The preparations, although they may not always have appeared so to the troops who attacked, were thorough and as good as they could be in that hellish area. Currie had set himself to do what he could to reduce the agony of his men's coming ordeal. He was omnipresent on the field—and in the Ypres salient that feat is worth noting in itself. He was offered paper returns of the whereabouts of Anzac guns that had disappeared in the mud. He refused to proceed unless the paper was replaced by gun metal and made sure that he got it. Indeed some 300 field pieces were moved up within range and operated at heavy cost to the Germans. They were a prime factor in final success. Currie preferred to lose shells rather than men.

Moment of respite

General Currie set out to satisfy himself about three things. The first, as has been seen, was that the artillery support should be as formidable as supply and placement in difficult terrain could make it. The second was that the troops who were to make the attack should have some acclimatisation time between their arrival at the forward positions and the moment when the actual attack went in. In the past it had often been the case that troops would arrive at their jumping-off places only a few hours before they attacked, having marched up the line throughout the preceding night. These arrangements were not by any means perfect in the event, but most of the assaulting troops in the first wave had a day or two to look about them before being asked to fight. Also, in the same manner as the retiring Anzacs briefed the first stage Canadians, so did the 3rd and 4th Divisions instruct their eventual relief force—the 1st and 2nd Divisions—when their turn came. Any

soldier who has had experiences of a panicky takeover will appreciate the value of this mode of proceeding. Finally, Currie visited each of his brigades in turn and, with the aid of models, set out the nature of the task that the officers and men faced. His briefings expressed confidence concerning the result, but made little effort to hide the formidable nature of the undertaking. The mood engendered seems to have been one of grim determination.

The support that the Canadians got from the Anzacs on their right when the attack went in on October 26 gave them a secure flank. To the left of the Goudberg Spur the anchor was less firm. However, French elements attached to the Fifth Army had put in a spirited attack some days before the Canadians went in, and on the 26th itself they marched forward about one-tenth of a mile towards the Houthulst Forest at the very north of the salient. The Canadians on the 26th, however, moved off at 0530 hours in the rain. On the right, following the barrage, and after a see-saw fight south of the Ravebeek, against very heavy German artillery and despite three counterattacks, the 4th Division was securely in its assigned objectives by 1000 hours. The 3rd Division, on the left, had a rough time as well. Cleverly sited pillboxes, especially at Laamkeek on the south edge of Bellevue Spur, plus a magnificent defence by the Germans, made movement difficult. But continual pressure directed in front of Bellevue Spur, plus the piecemeal destruction of pillboxes, enabled the troops on the far left to outflank these obstacles from higher and firmer ground. By 1530 hours the Canadians were on Bellevue Spur—just; but there they were to stay. Meanwhile, south at 'Gheluvelt, X Corps put in a 'forlorn' against the Tower Hamlets. It failed with the loss of about 3,500 casualties. Feverishly the Canadians worked towards the next step. Special mule and manpower lines were traversed with supplies, ammunition, and the fresh regiments coming up to relieve those who had done the work since October 26.

The morning of October 30 was cold. It did not begin to rain until about 1100 hours, but the ground was very damp. At 1730 hours another barrage rechurned the muck and the advance resumed. Success was swift. On the far right, by 2030 hours, all of the 4th Division's objectives were taken. The cost was as terrible as the advance was swift; one battalion lost half its strength. For the 3rd Division the Bellevue Spur had to be fought for foot by foot, and the great success on its left by which the Goudberg Spur was approached closely was endangered by the fact that firm contact with the 18th Division on the left was not always easy to maintain. It was still touch and go in the late afternoon, but the Canadians had decided not to go back. For his energetic, intelligent and determined action amid Vapour Farm, the key position on the edge of Goudberg Spur, George Pearkes won a VC. Strong, but not carefully concerted attempts at counterattack on the part of the Germans were held.

On November 2 the 4th Canadian Division left Passchendaele for good. They were relieved by the 2nd Canadian Division, and the 1st Canadian Division replaced the 3rd Division on November 4.

At 0600 hours on November 6 Currie

let his men go for the third time. They wasted no time. Following the swiftly moving barrage they were into Passchendaele village by 0710 hours. Over the whole salient they had reached their objectives by 0900 hours. A final push across the Passchendaele-Westroosebeke road on November 10 that took one hour finished Currie's job. The Canadians were on all their objectives. The victors were relieved on November 14; they had suffered 15,654 battle casualties.

What trench, where?

The description of the fighting in this action has been linked to the name of General Arthur Currie, and has assiduously avoided any attempt to isolate Canadian units for praise or blame for three reasons. In a short space it is not possible to be satisfactorily detailed and judicious. Secondly, Currie had both planned intelligently and catered to morale carefully. Thirdly, any attempt to describe the fighting at Passchendaele is bound to be based on isolated scraps of evidence. Even those who were there are unsatisfactory witnesses in the larger view.

It is not quite sufficient, in delineating the main outlines of the Passchendaele battle, to simply refer to low, higher ground, spurs, defiles and distances. The approaches to Passchendaele Ridge, after the drainage system had been broken by artillery, and the rains poured down steadily in October, were not all exactly the same but they were similar. Everyone knows the story of General Kiggell, who, when he saw the approaches to the battlefield for the first time, burst into tears and said, 'My God, did we really send men to fight in that?' Upon which he received the cool reply, 'It gets worse further up.' Similarly most have heard stories of men and animals who, moving on the duckboards laid down near the mud, were sometimes drowned if they slipped off into the mud or crater holes filled with filth and water on either side. This was true of all the approaches and made the supply problem especially difficult, for in a small salient the Germans swiftly had the range of the ribboned routes. Consequently, casualties amongst support and communication troops were disproportionately high – over 1,500.

To describe in detail the forward positions is an impertinence for one who must rely upon hearsay, photographs, and the words of some few keen observers. On one occasion a writer incautiously used the expression 'front line trench' to one who was there. The reply was a scornful, crushing question 'What trench – where?' To understand, just a little, one has to attempt to grasp three things. Firstly, there was no proper front line 'position', but only a series of craters filled with water in which men existed. The lines between these craters occupied by Canadians were maintained by human beings who made connections with other groups by exposing themselves – by making lateral quick dashes over exposed ground. Secondly, the problem of what was in front of them was difficult to determine for infantrymen, both Canadians and Germans. Shelling was constant, and to find out where a machine gun or a sniper was required considerable exposure and risk, for the lips of craters are not natural observation points; indeed they generally bar the field of vision ahead. Scouting under these conditions was vital – but it

was no fun. Thirdly, German aeroplanes were in movement overhead as frequently as the weather allowed. They made it difficult to move Lewis machine guns about because they were specifically sent up to discover and destroy them. Consequently, when an attack went in the machine guns had to be manhandled about swiftly: they were vital to the prevention or holding of counterattacks, and it was difficult to know in advance where they could be sited once the rolling barrage ahead of the attack had torn up and re-cratered the ground ahead. Another fact that makes an understanding of this ghastly place difficult is the use of the word Passchendaele 'Ridge'. Strictly speaking, the expression is geographically accurate, but to Canadian eyes the slope was so imperceptible that the advancing troops almost doubted its existence, until they were on top and looked back over the slowly undulating sea of mud towards Ypres. To make the point clearer one need only think of Vimy—where the 'ridge' is a high promontory. But it is not the height of a rise of land that confers advantages on a defender as any visitor to, say, Gettysburg can see. The

slope towards Cemetery Ridge is easy—but a deadly artillery killing ground. The German front line troops were inhibited from view-finding, like the Canadians, by the rims of craters. But their gunners could view their target areas more expertly. General Currie's gunners could roll a barrage, but to select and pinpoint targets was not so easy.

German morale begins to crack
One of the most ironical factors concerning this fight was that it was the mud, so terrible in many ways, that minimised casualties to a certain extent. Muck absorbs the blast of high explosive and this undoubtedly cut down on the value of German artillery fire—except for direct hits, which are not so easy to obtain. Indeed, it is likely that the 'Ridge' could not have been taken early in October when the ground was a little harder, and the execution by shell bursts must have been consequently intensified.

Another interesting feature of 'Canada's Fortnight' at Passchendaele was the fact that counterattacks were not more heavily put in by the Germans. Many who

were there would no doubt dispute this, but at Passchendaele the Germans displayed more of a brave reluctance to yield ground rather than a co-ordinated determined desire to retake what they had lost. One reason for this was undoubtedly the fact that Currie did not let his rushes overextend themselves: that is, the infantryman was not asked to take more than he could be reasonably expected to hold. Another is the fact that Canadian machine gunners got up fast and took on counterattack formations at deadly close range, despite German sniping and good German aircraft work. The Lewis guns were very well handled from both a mechanical and a tactical viewpoint, and they undoubtedly saved many badly smashed up companies from the results of those horde attacks at which the Germans were so formidable. Another reason was the terribly effective Canadian rolling barrage and the swift savagery of its closely followed infantry advance. Finally, it may be that there was something to be said for Haig's view that German morale in front of the Ypres salient was on the verge of cracking—or had cracked.

◁ Cleaning up the mess. Canadian pioneers 'clean up' Passchendaele, looking (among other things) for artillery pieces which had disappeared in the sea of mud ▷ On a drier part of the battlefield, six German prisoners carry a British casualty

Caporetto

Indescribable confusion reigned among the
Italian defenders as the Austro-German infantry
advanced through the driving snow and rain along
the Isonzo front on the morning of October 24. It soon
became apparent that a rout was in progress. The
invasion of war-weary Italy had begun.
Below: The big push begins — a small party waits to
follow up a flame thrower attack

The enormous losses which the Italian armies had suffered since 1915 in 11 offensives on the Isonzo—during the Eleventh Battle of the Isonzo alone, between August 24 and September 10, 1917, the Italians had lost about 150,000 men dead, wounded, missing and captured—were the mainspring for the feverish antiwar propaganda pursued by the Italian Socialist and Communist Parties. If during summer 1917 their catchphrase—'Next winter not another man in the trenches'—had been sheer fantasy, by early autumn it had grown to be a threatening spectre haunting the Italian Chiefs-of-Staff. And yet General Cadorna believed it possible to take up the offensive once again, immediately after the Eleventh Battle of the Isonzo had died away, even though it would be possible only with substantial material help from the Allies.

On September 11, 1917 the British Minister of War, Lord Derby, paid a visit to the *Commando Supremo* in Udine during a tour of Italy. In his company were the Adjutant-General Sir Nevil Macredy and Major-General F. B. Maurice, the Director of Military Operations. At a meeting with Cadorna and his deputy, General Porro, Cadorna renewed his promises to continue attacking, promises he had made during the Chantilly consultations in the spring, so long as the Allies would maintain the pressure on the Western Front. But now he felt himself forced to press Lord Derby for urgently needed heavy, mountain and field artillery. He would then be in a position to set up the new divisions which would be urgently needed not only for a new offensive, but also in the event of a total Russian collapse, which was to be expected and which would release 70 or 80

Austrian and German divisions for the Italian Front.

Lord Derby declared, probably from personal judgement, that the British expected to be able to send 40 heavy batteries (160 guns) to the Italians, and in addition Cadorna could count on receiving six heavy howitzer batteries from the beginning of October. However, while he could not promise any heavy field artillery, he was convinced that the French would help there.

In fact, a week after these talks 200 British and French guns were on their way to the Italians, but they were still *en route* when Cadorna suddenly, on September 20, sent a written communiqué to the British and French Military Mission, at GHQ, to the effect that he no longer intended an autumn offensive. He would have to adopt defensive measures because an

Austrian counteroffensive had to be reckoned with. In their annoyance, and without first checking Cadorna's arguments, the British and French governments immediately gave the order to withdraw the guns. Cadorna was accused of having attempted to extract the guns under false pretences, so the French batteries and two of the three British artillery groups were stopped during transportation and returned to France. This exhibition of deep mistrust of the Italians seems to have been caused by a clever piece of deception on the part of German secret agents in Switzerland who had broadcast the rumour that a large scale Austrian offensive on the Isonzo could be reckoned with during spring 1918.

The withdrawal of the promises made by the British Minister of War severely weakened the Italian army, and in view of its poor morale and of the Allies' refusal to help, Cadorna was filled with a deep sense of gloom. When pressed by the Allies, Cadorna later justified his decision for assuming the defensive on the grounds that he had expected a joint Austro-German offensive, for on September 14 the Austro-Swiss border was closed, the Austrian Emperor and the German Attorney met in Bolzano, and simultaneously six German divisions arrived. Furthermore, it was ascertained that about 60 Austrian battalions had been transferred from Carso northwards to the Bainsizza. The danger of a double offensive by the Austrians and Germans, from the Trentino and the Isonzo, seemed obvious.

The Italians wait with confidence
In fact this had been nothing more than Austrian deception, and in any event towards the end of September the Italian High Command came to realise that the offensive was to take place only on the Isonzo. On October 6 Italian reconnaissance had identified 43 Austrian and German divisions on the whole Italian Front. Of these, 18 stood opposite the Italian Second Army on the upper Isonzo, and 11½ divisions opposite the Italian Third Army on the middle Isonzo. Furthermore, it had been established that the German Alpine Corps and the German 12th Division, together with two Austrian divisions, were approaching the Isonzo. During the next few days still more reports arrived that strong German forces were grouping in the Save valley east of Caporetto (Karfreit). Large concentrations of troops near Tolmein (Tolmino) were identified; and on October 9 Intelligence confirmed 'The last week of October might be accepted as the most probable date for the beginning of the enemy offensive.' Then the information became even stronger. On the afternoon of October 20 a defected Austrian officer, born in Bohemia, revealed that the start of the offensive had been postponed to October 26 on account of bad weather, and that German troops would attack in the area of Tolmein: the next day Austrian deserters of Hungarian nationality divulged that the offensive would take place along the whole Isonzo front, from the Adriatic to Flitsch (Bovec), with the centre of gravity in the area south of Tolmein. The chief objective was to be the Kolovrat ridge. Four hours of heavy artillery fire accompanied by gas shelling were to begin the offensive. This barrage was then to be followed by one-and-

a-half hours of mortar fire against infantry positions. The attack was to be made on October 25 or 26.

All this corresponded exactly with what was to happen. Cadorna and his staff, however, considered the Austrian counteroffensive over difficult mountain terrain totally impossible. 'The attack is coming, but I am confident of being able to meet it', Cadorna telegraphed on October 21 to Major-General Maurice: 'Owing to the very difficult country on the Tolmein sector, I am of the opinion that an attack there can be checked without difficulty and I am consequently holding that sector lightly.' And so they waited events with some confidence. On October 22 they gathered from a tapped telephone conversation that Austrian artillery were to open fire on October 24 at 0200 hours.

On the other hand, Austrian and German staff officers had already realised that it was precisely this sector of the Italian Isonzo front which was the most vulnerable point. If they succeeded here in breaking through the Italian mountain position, then the whole Isonzo front could probably be rolled up from above and from the rear and laid open. Conrad von Hötzendorff had already given this advice during consultations with the Germans on January 23, 1917, and suggested a joint offensive. But, as in 1916, this had not been greeted with any enthusiasm by the Germans because the German High Command was preoccupied with events on their own Western Front. But they held out the prospect of returning to his suggestion after the expected Nivelle offensive. A month later, however, Conrad had been dismissed as Chief of the General Staff of the Austro-Hungarian army and posted as commander of the Austrian Trentino front.

Following the Italian success in the Eleventh Battle of the Isonzo, and fearing that Cadorna would begin his new offensive immediately, the Austrian High Command remembered Conrad's plan of offensive of January 1917 and the German interest in it. Ludendorff, who was engaged on other plans and did not favour a reduction in forces on the Western Front, at first declined. But Hindenburg agreed in principle after the Emperor Karl had intervened with Kaiser Wilhelm. Lieutenant-General Krafft von Dellmensingen, highly experienced in mountain warfare, was delegated to reconnoitre the situation on the Isonzo front. There he realised that the plan suggested by Austria could lead to success, whereupon the German High Command agreed to support a counteroffensive on the Isonzo. On September 10 the final plans for the offensive were drawn up between the two HQs. There they decided, as Archduke Eugen, Commander of the Austrian front between the Carnic Alps and the Adriatic, later reported, that this offensive would have to throw back 'the Italians across their state boundary, and, if possible, right across the Tagliamento'.

For this purpose the German Fourteenth Army, composed of two Austrian and two German corps, was assembled under the command of the German General Otto von Below. They also put at its disposal some Jäger and storm battalions, well equipped with artillery. The offensive was nominally under the command of Archduke Eugen, but the Germans had reserved command to themselves for all operations, as

was usual for any joint enterprise. Thus the Austrians had little influence on the actual course of operations.

The attack was to be led by four Gruppen. The Gruppe under the Austrian General Alfred Krauss, comprising the Austrian I Corps HQ, the 3rd (Edelweissdivision) Infantry Division, the 22nd Rifle Division, the 55th Infantry Division, and the German Jäger Division, was to attack in the Flitsch valley in the direction of Saga and the Stol, and break across the basin of Caporetto. In the north this Gruppe was to be supported by the left inner wing of the Austrian Tenth Army with an attack across the Neveasettel into the valley of the Fella of Pontebba as far as Gemona. The Gruppe under the Bavarian General Freiherr von Stein, with HQ Bavarian III Corps, the Austrian 50th Infantry Division, the German 12th Infantry Division, the German Alpine Corps, and the German 117th Infantry Division, was first of all to take the Monte Matajur by storm, and then to advance with Gruppe Krauss. The Gruppe under General von Berrer, with German II Corps HQ, the German 26th (Württemberg I) Infantry Division, and the German 200th Infantry Division, was to secure the left flank of Gruppe Stein and at the same time advance on Globacêk. The Gruppe under Austrian Feldmarschalleutnant Scotti, with Austrian XV Corps HQ, the Austrian 1st and German 5th Infantry Divisions, had to support Gruppe Kosak during the crossing of the Isonzo in the Selo-Kal area. This Gruppe, drawn up on the north wing of the Austrian Second Army, under the Austrian Feldmarschalleutnant Kosak (with the Austrian 60th and 25th Infantry Divisions) was to deflect the Italians from the combat area of the German Fourteenth Army by an advance on the Heights of Vrh. The remaining Austrian units on the Isonzo had to take part only in the artillery barrage and to make local skirmishes.

Misunderstandings and indolence
The jumping off positions occupied by the Austrians and Germans were excellent, and their forces were numerically superior. In the Flitsch basin both the Austrian élite divisions (Edelweiss and 22nd Rifle Division) faced half the Italian 50th Division on a frontage of only three-and-a-half miles. Both divisions had the German Jäger Division as a reserve. South of Flitsch the 50th and 55th Infantry Divisions faced the other half of the Italian 50th, 43rd and 46th Infantry Divisions on a front of about 11 miles wide. Strongest of all were the massed combat units at the bridgehead of Tolmein. On a breadth of about three miles, opposite the Italian 19th and 65th Infantry Divisions, stood one Austrian and three German divisions in the front line, with three German reserve divisions in the immediate vicinity. And about 12 miles to the east of Caporetto were three additional Austrian reserve divisions. Opposing the whole front of Fourteenth Army were only three Italian infantry divisions and one Alpini group, of which one division was in the third line from the Kolovrat to the Monte Matajur. The Italian 50th Division in the Flitsch basin had practically nothing behind it. The actual Italian reserves lay in the sector between Cividale and Cervignano, to the south.

The Austrians' artillery superiority was

also immense. *Fourteenth Army* had 1,845 guns, of which 492 were heavy German 24-cm mortars. Furthermore, at Flitsch a German gas battery was placed in position, whose task it was to gas a corridor about 65 feet deep behind the Italian first line in Flitsch, through which the road from Flitsch to Saga leads. The majority of the German and Austrian batteries used gas shells which contained a gas against which the Italians' gas masks afforded very little protection.

Bad terrain, bad weather

The battle terrain was difficult. In the sector of *Gruppe Krauss* attacks had to be made mostly across hills between 3,000 and 6,000 feet, with heavily wooded slopes. The terrain was more favourable for attack in the sector Caporetto-Tolmein-Cividale-Plava, on the Isonzo. The Isonzo has a mountain ridge on its right bank from Saga as far as Tolmein, but which is broken by the Caporetto basin running from east to west. At this time of year the snow line lay at about 3,000 feet. As it had been raining continuously since October 10, the date for the attack (originally set for October 20) was repeatedly postponed, until it was eventually agreed on as October 24, despite bad weather. In fact, it eventually began in bad weather—it rained in the valleys, snowstorms raged on the hills, while both mountain slopes and valleys were draped in mist.

On the Italian side Cadorna had meanwhile taken several countermeasures which either were accompanied by misunderstandings or were met with the indolence of the Italian corps commanders. That the Austrian counteroffensive was to

The uniform of the American Red Cross, with whom Ernest Hemingway served during Caporetto

Malcolm McGregor

▽ Caporetto—the rout of the Italian army on the Isonzo. '400,000 soldiers were going home with the determination that for them at least the war was ended.'

take place on Second Army's front was, from the very beginning, a source of differences of opinion between Cadorna and the commander of Second Army, Lieutenant-General Capello. Second Army occupied a front between the Vipacco stream south of Gorizia (Görz) and the Monte Rombon north of Flitsch. Cadorna advocated defence with small local counterattacks. Capello, on the other hand, believed it possible to remain elastically on both the offensive and the defensive, and so make a series of separate attacks into the left flank of the Austrians and Germans in the valley of the Vrh and from the Bainsizza. Therefore he concentrated his three reserve corps in the area between Plava-Monte Kuk, south of Caporetto, but without regard for his exposed wing in the Flitsch basin, which was now seriously weakened. Too late had Cadorna taken into consideration the danger of exposing the reserves behind Second Army's left wing. On October 20 he ordered Second Army to counterattack. Meanwhile Capello became ill and his deputy, General Montouri, did not obey Cadorna's order. He merely demanded minor troop adjustments which in their turn were not carried out by the corps commanders. Not until Cadorna himself went to the most seriously threatened IV and XXVII Corps on Second Army's left wing did he succeed in reinforcing IV Corps at Caporetto with 34th Infantry Division (VII Corps). This division, however, was still moving towards the front when, on October 24 at 0200 hours, the Austrian and German attack began with powerful artillery fire along the whole Isonzo front, from the Adriatic to the Monte Rombon.

In the Flitsch-Tolmein district the guns

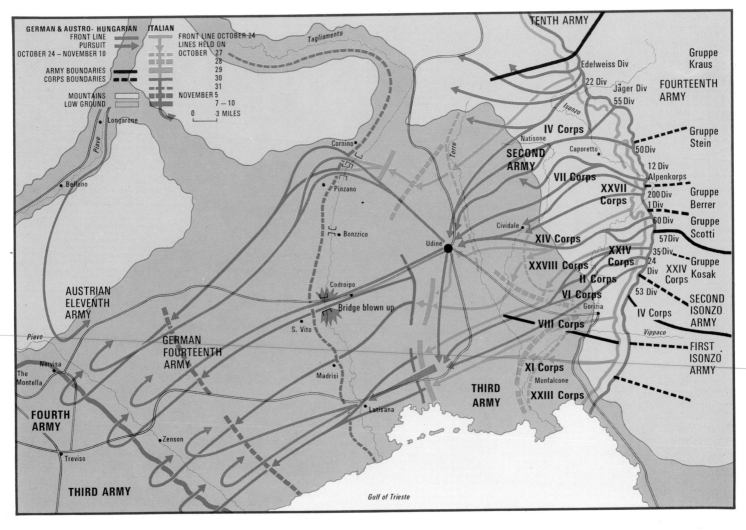

fired gas shells for two-and-a-half hours. 'Enemy artillery replied at once', according to the records of the Austrian General Staff, 'and their powerful and numerous searchlights nervously sought out our batteries and front lines. Soon the Italian fire lessened and searchlight activity diminished. The gas had obviously done its work and prevented the Italian artillery from directing their fire against our closely-packed storm lines.' After a pause lasting two-and-a-half hours the whole Isonzo front came under fire from high explosive shells from more than 3,500 guns, which were joined at 0700 hours by mortars. It was aimed at the Italian infantry lines, the HQ, ammunition dumps, approach roads and the Italian guns. At 0700 hours the infantry stormed forward from their lines. The first phase of the Austro-German counteroffensive had begun.

The gas shells had had appalling effects on the Italian lines. In one blow all communication links between the command posts and the front lines were destroyed. Panic spread rapidly among the Italian IV Corps, and also among 19th Infantry Division of XXVII Corps which lay west of Tolmein, while turmoil set in at HQ. Chaos was complete when at 0800 hours two powerful mines exploded in the Italian lines at Monte Rosso and at Monte Mrzli, followed immediately by the attack of the German and Austrian infantry.

After only one-and-a-half hours, during which the attackers met with hardly any resistance in Flitsch itself, Gruppe Krauss had routed the Italians and had to halt their race forward until their own artillery could catch up. General Krauss had given the order, before the offensive, to attack not only the Italian mountain positions — as Below had insisted — but also the valleys. Simultaneously with the advance of Gruppe Krauss, Lieutenant-General Stein had broken through where the two Italian corps joined up.

On the Italian side it soon became apparent that Cadorna's instructions had not been heeded and that therefore the bulk of XXVII Corps still lay on the Bainsizza, and that the Italian first lines in the Caporetto sector were only thinly occupied. Here the German 12th Infantry Division quickly broke through the Napoli Brigade, transferred by Badoglio at the very last minute to the extreme left wing of his corps, of whom only a section so far had moved into position. Stein's units crossed the Isonzo and immediately pushed on north and west in the direction of Monte Matajur and along the foot of the Kolvrat ridge. At 1100 hours they broke through the Italian lines on the left bank of the Isonzo. At 1600 hours the Germans occupied the town of Caporetto and swung into the line Starjiski-Staroselo-Matajur.

During the late afternoon of October 24

it became apparent that a 15-mile-wide penetration had been made in the Italian lines between Flitsch and Tolmein. Surprised by the impetus of the offensive, but above all shocked by the fact that suddenly they faced German instead of Austrian soldiers, the panic which had developed among IV Corps after the barrage degenerated into a flight which the officers could no longer control. Badoglio's 19th Division was swept along by this flight. By the evening Gruppe Stein had got a footing on the left bank of the Isonzo and had already advanced along the foot of the Kolovrat as far as Creda and towards the Monte Matajur.

The attacks by Gruppen Berrer and Scotti in the Tolmein-Selo sector had turned out to be not so successful, for here Badoglio had carried out Cadorna's order of October 20 more faithfully. The attackers encountered obstinate resistance. Nevertheless, by evening they had reached the eastern spur of Monte Jessu (Jěza) — Berrer dominating the Kolovrat, and Scotti the

bottom of the Globaček valley.

It was only at about 1900 hours that Cadorna was able to make a partial analysis of events on Second Army's front. Two reserve divisions were sent to the Monte Globaček area. The commander of Third Army, the Duke of Aosta, was ordered to despatch two divisions, as also was the commander of First Army in Trentino, Conte Pecori-Giraldi, who was to send off two divisions to the Isonzo as fast as possible. At 2100 hours Cadorna received the first news of the catastrophe which had befallen IV Corps. He reacted promptly and correctly by ordering XXIV and II Corps to withdraw from the Bainsizza during the night, to turn toward the north, and to join up with VII Corps in the Natisone valley and on the southern slopes of the Kolovrat.

Meanwhile Lieutenant-General Capello had gone to his HQ in Cormons, despite his severe bout of influenza, having already received garbled and unconnected reports on events at IV Corps. He was not

This page. Top: The Italians were shocked when they realised that they faced German instead of Austrian soldiers. Shock became panic, which in turn rapidly degenerated into flight. *Bottom:* The Italian sign reads – 'POW Camp'. Built by the Italians for Austrian prisoners, the camp at Cividale was soon filled with some of the 50,000/60,000 Italian prisoners captured in the first three days of the offensive. *Opposite page. Top:* Under shellfire, German machine gun sections pursue the Italians across the Isonzo. *Bottom:* The Italians' 'systematic withdrawal' to the Tagliamento

Kriegsarchiv/Vienna

Staatsbibliothek/Berlin

particularly disturbed by them, but arranged for three of his reserve divisions to be despatched to the upper Natisone valley, in order to establish a block there. Then he moved his HQ to Cividale.

By this time Cadorna had already ordered the commander of the Carnian Zone, Lieutenant-General Tassoni, to occupy the summit of the Monte Maggiore which commanded the Uccea valley west of Saga, and to hold it at all costs. This summit was to be the pivot of the Italian defence if the Isonzo position had to be given up. Around midnight Cadorna ordered the Duke of Aosta and Lieutenant-General Capello to prepare the Tagliamento for defence, discreetly and under greatest secrecy.

'400,000 soldiers were going home'
The catastrophe on the left wing of the Italian Second Army did not become fully clear until October 25 when Capello had to inform Cadorna, during the morning, that every position on his front east of the Isonzo had been lost, and that the Austrians and Germans were already advancing on the Monte Stol and pressing forward to Luico. The news arrived at about midday that the Monte Stol had been lost: it had been defended to the last round of ammunition by Alpini troops until they had had to retreat. It was now that the first thoughts of a large scale withdrawal emerged in the mind of the *Commando Supremo* in Udine.

Cadorna himself had been working on the idea when he ordered the Duke of Aosta, during the early hours of October 25, to withdraw Third Army's heavy and medium artillery behind the River Piave. At midday he received the very sick Capello, who implored him 'to give up contact with the aggressors and to withdraw at once to the Torre, or better still, behind the Tagliamento'. Cadorna agreed and Capello proceeded to his HQ at Cividale.

The catastrophe which was developing around the Italian armies could probably have been reduced if Capello had not suddenly become so weak during the early afternoon while he was working on the orders for withdrawal that he had to hand over his command to General Montouri. Even Cadorna had become uncertain and consulted Montouri on the retreat. He, in turn, insisted on consultation with his corps commanders and then informed Cadorna at 2100 hours that he considered the continued defence of the present positions held the promise of success.

How General Montouri reached this conclusion, which was wildly divorced from reality, is uncertain. Ronald Seth writes: 'How the corps commanders and Montouri ever reached this opinion is one of the great mysteries of the whole battle. The only possible solution seems to be that the corps commanders were so out of touch with what was happening that they were ignorant of the true facts; and yet this seems incredible.' Anyway, the fact was that on the evening of October 25 two Italian corps were already fleeing from the mountains to the Friuli-Venetian Plain, and the Austro-German troops began to reap a

success not hitherto experienced on the Italian Front. General Emilio Faldella remarked in his *History of the First World War* that it was a question of a grave error of leadership on the part of the *Commando Supremo* and the command of Second Army: 'On the subject of the reserves, the principal mistake was that they were held too far back from the Plezzo (Flitsch) valley. If there had been only one division at Bergogna ready to occupy the Stol and the valley of the Uccea, which leads up to the Saga, there could have been better resistance during the day of October 25.'

However it may be, the Austro-German High Command had analysed correctly the vulnerable point of the Italian Isonzo front and there crushed the Italian troops by surprise tactics, though it must be said that the troops in the front line fought valiantly, with the exception of those at Caporetto. The German *12th Division* had already gained the upper reaches of the Natisone valley at Creda by nightfall on October 24. During the next day they encountered strong resistance which was broken only when the German *Alpine Corps* succeeded in forcing a way across the Monte S Martino and between Luico and the Monte Matajur, right across the mountain range towards the south.

Thus when the first German troops reached the Friuli-Venetian Plain in the Cividale area, units of *Gruppe Krauss* in the north had reached S Giorgio in the Resia valley from the direction of Saga, captured the Monte Rombon and crossed the Nevea saddle in the direction of the Racolan valley towards Chiusaforte and towards Resiutta in the Fella valley. That meant that the Austrian *Kaiser Light Infantry Regiment 3* had captured, on October 26, the Monte Maggiore—the pivot of the Italian defence, as envisaged by Cadorna. In the south *Gruppen Berrer* and *Scotti* occupied the Globacëk and advanced on the Italian third line of defence at Monte Corado. The Austrian *Second Army* routed the Italians, who were already in the process of abandoning their positions, from the Bainsizza and on the Isonzo. Only the Austrian *First Army* was kept in reserve. With the advance on October 27 by the German *Alpine Corps* and the German *200th* and *26th Divisions* beyond Cividale and on to the River Torre only a few thousand yards from the Udine, the rout of the Italian army was complete. The Austrian Press did not exaggerate unduly in its reports of the capture of 60,000 Italian soldiers, while the reports by the German *Fourteenth Army* on Italian positions suggested the wholesale flight of Italian units from the mountains into the Venetian Plain.

At midnight, October 27, Cadorna received a report that the Austrians had penetrated the Porta di Montemaggiore. With the Italian Isonzo army in complete rout, he had no alternative but to order a 'systematic withdrawal' to the Tagliamento, and to reiterate his pleas for assistance from his French and British allies.

John Batchelor

'Soon the Italian fire lessened and searchlight activity diminished. The gas had obviously done its work. . . .'

△ Austrian 15-cm heavy field howitzer M 99.
Range: 6,780 yards. *Weight in action:* Two
tons 8.5 cwt. *Weight limbered:* Two tons 14.6
cwt. *Weight of shell:* 1.56 lbs. *Muzzle velocity:*
960 feet-per-second. *Elevation:* −2 degrees/
+45 degrees. *Crew:* Eight. *Rate of fire:* Two
rounds-per-minute
◁ Austrian 15-cm heavy field howitzer M 14.
Range: 8,858 yards. *Weight in action:* Two
tons nine cwt. *Weight of shell:* 2.8 lbs.
Muzzle velocity: 1,120 feet-per-second.
Elevation: −5 degrees/+70 degrees. *Crew:*
Eight. Motor transport was frequently employed
▽ Austrian 10.4-cm field gun. *Range:* 13,670
yards. *Weight in action:* Two tons five cwt.
Muzzle velocity: 2,230 feet-per-second.
Elevation: −10 degrees/+30 degrees. The gun
was made of nickel steel, and the shrapnel
shell had 70 bullets

▽ The *feld grau* uniform of the Austrian
infantry, introduced in late 1915. Shown is the
Austrian-style steel helmet with a ventilation
hole in the top, although usually a cap rather
than a steel helmet was worn. He is carrying a
tornister (calf-hide full pack), a bread bag on
his hip, and the M 1895 Mannlicher 8-mm rifle

Special Order No 6.

1. To-morrow the Tank Corps will have the chance for which it has been waiting for many months,—to operate on good going in the van of the battle.

2. All that hard work & ingenuity can achieve has been done in the way of preparation

3. It remains for unit commanders and for tank crews to complete the work by judgment & pluck in the battle itself.

4. In the light of past experience I leave the good name of the Corps with great confidence in their hands

5. I propose leading the attack of the centre division

Hugh Elles.
B.G.

19th Nov. 1917.   Commanding. Tank Corps.

Distribution to Tank Commanders.

At 0620 hours on November 20 1917, 381 tanks moved forward from their last assembly points, led by their commander General Elles flying his flag in one of the leading machines in the true style of a 'land admiral'. The wire was easily crushed, German troops in the front lines fled in terror, and a huge hole almost six miles wide and up to 4,000 yards deep was torn in the formidable Hindenburg Line. This was the dramatic birth of large scale tank warfare. Had Haig's armies at last discovered the real answer to barbed wire and machine-guns? *Above:* Brigadier-General Hugh Elles, Commander of the Tank Corps at Cambrai, painted by Sir William Orpen. *Above right:* Elles's Special Order, issued on the day before his Tank Corps went into action

CAMBRAI
THE BRITISH
ONSLAUGHT

The dramatic events in the vicinity of Cambrai in November 1917 occupy a special place in the history of the First World War in general and in that of the Royal Tank Regiment (formerly the Tank Corps) in particular. November 20 saw the birth of large scale tank warfare, and for a brief but glorious moment it seemed that a decisive breakthrough had at last been achieved, and that an element of strategic mobility was about to return to the Western Front after three years of trench warfare. In fact the success was to prove more illusory than real, and the ringing of church bells throughout Great Britain on November 23 (the sole time this was authorised before the Armistice) was decidedly premature, for the well-known conditions of stalemate and positional warfare were to reassert themselves within three days of the offensive's opening. Nevertheless, as John Terraine has written: 'After Cambrai there could be no further argument; the decisive weapon of land warfare in the mid-twentieth century had now definitely arrived. A new dimension of war was established. Haig's armies had at last discovered what the real answer to wire and machine guns was.'

Haig had been considering 'an attack of surprise in the centre with tanks, and without artillery bombardment' as early as February 1917. As the autumn of a year more dismal than any of its predecessors set in, the idea hardened into a firm resolve. Haig noted in his diary for September 16: 'I discussed with Byng some operations which he proposed. I told him I would give him all the help I could.' This laconic entry marks the practical genesis of the Cambrai offensive. General Sir Julian Byng, Commander of Third Army, was told that his command would be reinforced to a total strength of 19 divisions, and that the entire Tank Corps would be placed at his disposal. With these forces he was to launch a surprise attack on the German lines near Cambrai on a date—still to be confirmed—in November.

The choice of both place and time was carefully considered. The rolling chalk-based downlands of the Somme region promised far better going than the morass of the Flanders front. It had also been a relatively quiet sector of the front for some time, and the ground was comparatively free of shell holes. Furthermore, the main line of the Hindenburg defences (to which the Germans had retired earlier in 1917) swung away to the northwestward and then north in a vast sweeping curve, and the capture of the ridge near the village of Bourlon would provide a superb view over the Germans' rear areas almost as far as Valenciennes. A quick surprise attack here might yield useful results. The Cambrai plain had been suggested as a suitable site for a large scale tank raid by Lieutenant-Colonel J. F. C. Fuller, GSO 1 to Brigadier-General Hugh Elles, commanding the Tank Corps, in June 1917. Apart from being well drained, the area was bounded by two canals to west and east, the Canal du Nord, and the St Quentin respectively, and the Allied front included thick woods, more particularly near Havrincourt, and these would help conceal the final preparations. Intelligence reported only two German divisions in the line, with no more than five, and 150 guns, in support. A refined version of Fuller's plan earned Elles' full approval, and was forthwith forwarded to both GHQ and General Byng. Simultaneously, a second plan calling for a similar combined tank and infantry onslaught without a preliminary bombardment over the very same ground was being prepared by Brigadier-General H. H. Tudor, CRA to 9th (Scottish) Division. This scheme reached Third Army headquarters on August 23 via IV Corps. It was a plan based on these two schemes which won Haig's approval at a conference with Byng on September 16.

The timing of the offensive was of the greatest importance to the British Commander-in-Chief. At first it seems he envisaged Cambrai as a purely diversionary attack, intended to ease pressure from the embattled divisions still locked (in September) in the agony of Third Ypres. In fact, however, that terrible offensive was to come to an unmourned conclusion two weeks before the opening of Cambrai. Nevertheless, Haig well understood the need to strive for a success somewhere on the Western Front to set against the dismal tale of failures at Ypres, mutinies in the French army, the catastrophic situation developing on the Russian Front, and, more recently, the massive Italian disaster at Caporetto. There was no idea in Haig's mind of delivering a war-winning blow at Cambrai—he knew his resources would never permit a massive exploitation even if the attack proved a success—but he was aware of the vital need to give the Allied governments and peoples some evidence of at least one tangible success to compensate in some measure for the horrific casualty lists incurred in earlier failures. His object, then to quote the Cambrai Despatch, was 'a local success'.

Sir Julian Byng, not surprisingly, was more ambitious. Briefing his corps commanders at Albert on October 26, he painted a picture of a three-stage battle opening the way to greater things. In the first phase, some 409 tanks followed by infantry were to smash a five-mile breach through the Hindenburg Line in the sector bounded by the two canals; their initial advance would coincide with the laying down of an unregistered bombardment by 1,003 guns which would provide the Germans with no warning of what was afoot. Next, a 'cavalry gap' would be carved towards the River Sensée, involving the capture of the key communication centre of Cambrai, the domination of Bourlon ridge, and the establishment of bridgeheads over the Sensée itself. Thirdly, the victorious Third Army would sweep north and west up the German line towards Valenciennes.

Haig, as we have seen, was not so optimistic as his subordinate, and insisted on modifications to the plan. First, he laid down a 48-hour deadline for the initial breakthrough; if that was not achieved by the time limit, the offensive would be closed down. Secondly, he insisted that Cambrai should be masked, but not actually captured, in phase two; far more important, in his view, was the physical occupation of Bourlon ridge—and the wood and village of the same name—which would afford a superb view over the German rear areas for artillery observation posts at the earliest moment possible. Thirdly, Haig knew that the exploitation envisaged by Byng was beyond his means. The French, eager to share in such a promising operation, had placed five divisions at his disposal near Peronne, intending to roll up the German line southwards in the exploitation phase, but the British Staff were not too keen to accept this aid. As for Third Army, no less than 14 of its 19

Left: A British Mark IV, destroyed by German shell fire

Right: Mark IVs wait to move forward again across terrain (rolling chalk-based downland, comparatively free of shell holes) which promised good going for Fuller's standard tank drill

Far right: General Sir Julian Byng, Third Army. He was more ambitious than Haig in his estimate of the breakthrough possible at Cambrai. Haig had laid a 48-hour deadline for the initial onslaught — if the major objectives were not achieved the offensive was to end

divisions had been bled white at Third Ypres, and both men and resources were almost at exhaustion point. As Brigadier-General John Charteris, Haig's Chief of Intelligence, wrote: 'We shall have no reserves. We shall be alright at first; afterwards is in the lap of the God of battle.' At GHQ there was therefore little hope of a runaway success.

The Hindenburg Line

A word must here be devoted to the Hindenburg Line. The position comprised three lines of double trenches. The front line consisted of advanced posts, then a wide fire trench, with a support trench some 200 yards to the rear. A mile back was the official Hindenburg Support Line, once again two trenches deep, and two miles behind that was a third position, almost completed, known to the Germans as *Siegfried II.* Six belts of wire, the main one 100 yards deep, protected the main positions, and all support and rearward positions were similarly provided for. Holding the Cambrai sector of this strong position were the *20th Landwehr Division,* the *54th Division,* and part of the *9th Reserve Division,* which, together with the *183rd* further south, formed the *Gruppe Caudry* (or *XIII Korps*); this formation formed part of General von der Marwitz's *Second Army* (HQ at Le Cateau), which in turn was under Crown Prince Rupprecht of Bavaria's headquarters. The front line forces were not particularly strong, as Ludendorff subsequently admitted, for the German forces had also suffered considerably at Third Ypres. By a stroke of good fortune, however, the leading elements of the *107th Division,* being transferred from the Eastern Front, began to detrain at Cambrai on November 19, and were placed under temporary command of *54th Division* for use in any (as yet unforeseen) emergency.

General Byng entrusted the brunt of the initial phase of 'Operation G Y' to his III and IV Corps, with the Tank Corps to the fore. Lieutenant-General Sir William Pulteney (III Corps), had four divisions (6th, 12th, 20th and 29th), a cavalry detachment, and the 2nd and 3rd Tank Brigades at his disposal. His task was to engage three divisions in the assault phase, and with them secure the offensive's right flank (aided by VII Corps on

its right). First his divisions would be expected to breach the Hindenburg defences from Crèvecoeur to Bonavis, secure the line of the St Quentin Canal, and then force crossings at Marcoing and Masnières to form a bridgehead, through which the 2nd and 5th Cavalry Divisions of Lieutenant-General Sir C. T. McM. Kavanagh's Cavalry Corps would then advance to bypass Cambrai, sever its railway links, and pour on towards Cauroir, and Iway, to seize crossings over the Sensée. On Z+1 they would be followed by the 3rd and 4th Cavalry Divisions, whilst III Corps infantry formed a defensive flank from Gonnelieu to La Belle Etoile.

Meanwhile, Lieutenant-General Sir Charles Woollcombe (IV Corps), would initially have committed two divisions — the 62nd (West Riding) and the 51st (Highland) — to the battle, supported by the advance of a third — the 36th — on the left or northern flank of the offensive zone. They would be led into battle by the tanks of the 1st Tank Brigade, and it was ultimately decided that the corps would have 1st Cavalry Division under command. The IV Corps' task was to breach the German lines along its sector, capture Havrincourt, Flesquières, Graincourt and Cantaing in the process, and then pass through its reserve divisions and the cavalry for the all important attack on the Bourlon complex (ridge, wood and village) — Sir Douglas Haig's prime objective for the first stage of the battle. It was envisaged that the 1st Cavalry Division would aid in the isolation of Cambrai by establishing contact with the main Cavalry Corps to its right, before wheeling left to attack Bourlon village from the northeast.

Once these objectives had been achieved, Byng would commit his reserve (V Corps — the Guards, 40th and 59th Divisions) to secure the Sensée crossings, and create a bridgehead to the heights beyond. These troops would advance over IV Corps communications. All these associated operations would be supported by some 300 Allied aircraft, four squadrons being earmarked for close tactical support of the assault itself. Finally, on November 17, HQ Third Army notified all senior commanders that the offensive was to open at 0620 hours on Tuesday, November 20.

Meanwhile, feverish but well-concealed preparations were being undertaken at all

levels. One thousand guns were moved up and placed in camouflaged emplacements, and their crews instructed in the means of opening the bombardment without prior registration or ranging. Thirty-six special trains were steadily moving up the 476 tanks, first to the corps mounting area at Bray-sur-Somme, then towards their individual battalion 'lying-up' areas immediately behind the front. One by one, battalions were taken out of the line to train in tank/infantry tactics. The form of these followed the proposals of Fuller: tanks were to operate in groups of three, each vehicle carrying a heavy fascine of wood (weighing $1\frac{3}{4}$ tons), in association with four platoons of infantry, following in file at prescribed distances in two waves. The 'Tank Battle Drill' would be followed by every assault formation except the 51st (Highland) Division, whose commander, Major-General G. M. Harper, a soldier 'of extremely strong views' (according to Woollcombe) imposed a variation which was to have important repercussions on his sector.

Stage by stage the broad intention (but not the date) was revealed to lower formations. The final moves took place from November 17. The tanks (each battalion having a fighting strength of 36 machines supported by a further six) moved forward

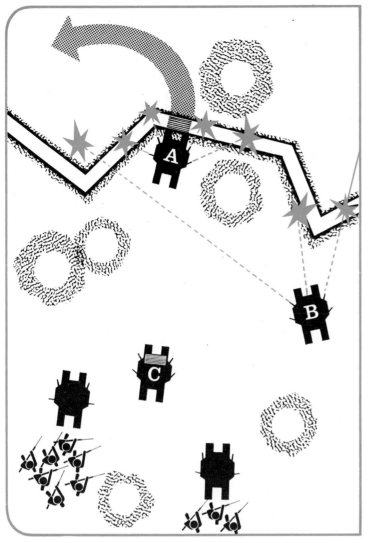

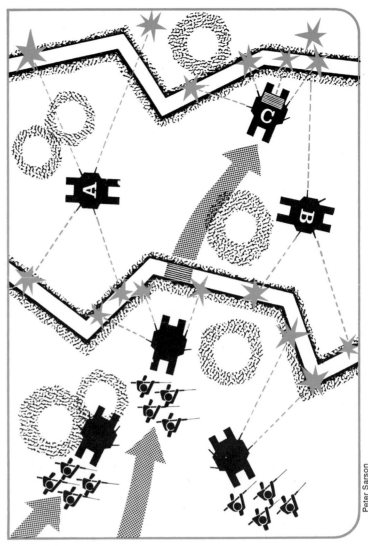

Peter Sarson

Opposite page. Top left: A fascine-laying Mark IV. The fascines, carried on the unditching rail and released from inside, were 4½ feet in diameter, 10 feet long and 1½ tons in weight. *Top right:* The rôle of the 32 special grapnel-tanks. *This page. Above and Above right:* A closer view of Fuller's tanks' battle drill, showing in more detail the relationship between infantry and fascine-laying tanks

the German line to relieve its battered neighbour of all distractions.

The struggle for Bourlon reached its peak on November 23, when Major-General Sir John Ponsonby's 40th Division reached the crest of Bourlon Wood, but failed to penetrate the village beyond. In the space of 72 hours this single division was to lose 4,000 casualties. The Germans were suffering too, but Moser (commanding *Gruppe Arras*) noted that 'our artillery and aeroplanes are gaining the ascendancy more and more'.

Haig and Byng called for new efforts, but tempers were becoming brittle. 'If you don't take Fontaine, General Harper,' Sir Charles Woollcombe declared to the commander of 51st Division, charged with a new objective on the right of 40th Division, 'God help you!' Despite this admonition, little progress was ultimately made, and 40th Division's flank remained dangerously exposed. Shortages of manpower were being experienced, and Byng authorised IV Corps to use 1st Cavalry Division in infantry rôles. He also brought in the Guards Division to relieve the 51st.

A further major effort was ordered for midday on November 24; the gallant 40th

Division and the dismounted 9th Cavalry Brigade were to be thrown against Bourlon at noon; the Guards were to attack the Fontaine sector, and the 36th and 56th Divisions were to clear German positions between Moeuvres and Inchy.

The battle was ferocious; at first it seemed that 40th Division might take the village, but by 1100 hours they had been repulsed save for one small party under Colonel Wade which clung to a segment of the village for two days. By this time the whole of the Cavalry Division was involved, but by last light the Germans had regained the northern edge of the Wood. Sir Douglas Haig might still publicly talk about a breakthrough by three cavalry divisions, and had managed to detain two divisions earmarked for transfer to Italy. Brigadier-General Charteris (his Intelligence chief) was aware of the true situation: 'Things have not gone well. Our troops are tired, and the Germans are getting up large reinforcements; we have none available.'

Byng continued to fling his weary and depleted divisions against Bourlon, but to no avail. He switched his divisions to and fro, set new deadlines, tried to inspire his commanders and men to new exertions, but it was by now beyond the power of Third Army. Colonel Wade was rescued on November 26, and heavy bombardments were hurled at the Germans, who by now had seven divisions in the line, four of them in the key sector, and their artillery strength was 500.

The last effort, as it proved, was made on November 27. The 62nd and Guards Divi-

sions, accompanied by 30 tanks, advanced yet again against the Bourlon and Fontaine sectors. Casualties were heavy. Fontaine was partly overrun, but a German counterattack, ten battalions strong, proved too heavy, and the Guards Division was driven back to its start line. By this time the 2nd Guards Brigade had been reduced to 500 men. At the day's end, the British line in Bourlon Wood had been driven back to the crest amongst the trees.

After this failure the Commander-in-Chief was prepared to concede failure, and Third Army was ordered to close down its offensive. On November 28, IV Corps headquarters issued a significant order: 'Wire should be got up at all costs today, and wiring on the Bourlon perimeter systematically carried out by pioneers and R.E.' This signalled the end of the British adventure of Cambrai: the old conditions of stalemate had reasserted themselves.

But the history of the Battle of Cambrai still had another, final, act to run. German artillery were now hurling shells against the newly-extemporised British positions in Bourlon Wood. On other sectors, both November 28 and 29 were relatively quiet days — but to some this seemed more menacing than reassuring. These fears were proved correct when, at 0830 hours on November 30, an intense German bombardment rained down on the British lines. Soon alarm signals were being received from many sectors. As one sergeant of the 1st Royal Berkshires reported to his officer: 'SOS gone up in 27 different places, and the Bosche coming over the 'ill in thousands.' The German counteroffensive had begun.

CAMBRAI
THE GERMAN

Ten days after the tank surprise at Cambrai the Germans repaid the compliment with one which was similar in principle but different in method. Without a long artillery preparation, a short hurricane gas and smoke bombardment cleared the way for an infantry attack using new infiltration tactics. This was a foretaste of the offensives which were to smash through the British and French armies in spring 191

David Chandler

COUNTERATTACK

Below: A German war artist's impression of the first day of the stunning counterattack

A battery of 77-mm's in action.
Shell fire was the greatest single cause of tank casualty at Cambrai,
accounting for over one third of all losses on the first day (65 out of 179 tanks)

Following the eventual stabilisation of the front after the exhaustion of General Sir Julian Byng's dramatic but brief offensive, it was not long before the German High Command was planning a counteroffensive. On November 27, while the battle of Bourlon Wood still raged, Ludendorff conferred with Crown Prince Rupprecht at Le Cateau. Meantime 20 divisions were being massed in the Cambrai area. Ludendorff was convinced that 'there has never been such an opportunity' for a successful blow, and insisted that all should be in readiness by November 30.

The plan envisaged a short, intense bombardment followed by a rapid attack by *Gruppe Caudry* and *Gruppe Busigny* in the general direction of Metz, the village immediately to the south of Havrincourt Wood. If successful, the German generals hoped that this would compromise the whole British salient and compel its evacuation. Meanwhile, *Gruppe Arras* (some seven divisions and 130,000 men strong) would fire heavy barrages and conduct demonstrations designed to distract the British IV Corps (Lieutenant-General Sir Charles Woollcombe), and once the eastern attacks had become well established, Lieutent-General Otto von Moser was to launch an attack with three divisions to the west of Bourlon Wood and drive southwards. Reserve divisions would be held in readiness to consolidate and exploit the gains on both sectors of the German attack. The minimum to be achieved was the recapture of the Hindenburg position, but some officers spoke hopefully of a major breakthrough.

November 28 saw the opening of a heavy bombardment against Bourlon Wood, 16,000 rounds of gas and high explosive shells being pumped into the ravaged area. The violence of this shelling served to convince the British High Command that the major German blow, if and when it came, would almost certainly be launched against the northern part of the salient. Not that warnings of other possibilities were lacking. Major-General J. S. Jeudwine, GOC 55th Division (VII Corps), whose troops were holding a six-mile front facing *Gruppe Busigny*, reported ominous German concentrations in the vicinity of Banteux and Twenty-Two Ravines. Indications of a coming attack included German artillery registration on hitherto unshelled areas, a marked increase in German air activity over the front line, and the measures taken to prevent Allied aircraft reconnoitring in the Banteux area. Yet there was little sense of urgency at either GHQ or Third Army Headquarters, and Byng authorised no preliminary movement by the slender reserves.

The British generals later denied vehemently that they were taken by surprise by both the scale and direction of the German onslaught unleashed on November 30, and attempted to blame junior commanders for lack of proper vigilance. Be that as it may (and subsequent research has not borne out the conclusions reached by the Cambrai Enquiry), in the words of the late Sir Basil Liddell Hart, the Germans 'repaid the tank surprise by one that was similar in principle if different in method'. When the German guns abruptly crashed out shortly after dawn on November 29, there was no immediate indication of the line of the coming attack. All too soon, however, SOS signals were hurtling skywards and reports of attacks flooding into HQ VII Corps, as wave after wave of German troops (some 12 in all, the rearward lines being led by mounted officers) emerged one after another from the Banteux Ravine at the precise time (0700 hours) that Jeudwine had asked for the heavy bombardment. The focal point of the German attack was the boundary between III and VII Corps, and the brunt of the onslaught was borne by Major-General W. D. Smith's 20th Division and Major-General A. B. Scott's 12th Division—occupying the right of Pulteney's sector—and Jeudwine's over-extended 55th on the extreme left of VII Corps. The southernmost limit of *Gruppe Busigny's* attack was opposite Vendhuille, but the northern extension rapidly grew as, at about 0800 hours, the Germans committed *Gruppe Caudry* to the attack from Bantouzelle to Rumilly, and drove forwards towards Marcoing. Thus III Corps suddenly found three of its four front line divisions heavily, and then critically, involved.

The form of attack was novel on the Western Front. Behind the intense and short bombardment, the German infantry came forward in groups, employing infiltration tactics. Centres of strong opposition were deliberately bypassed by the leading formations, which pressed on towards the rear exploiting the line of least resistance. Low-flying aircraft, strafing and bombing, gave close support, and num-

bers of artillery batteries advanced immediately behind the infantry. Similar methods had been employed with success in both Russia (notably at Riga) and Italy. They worked well enough in France on this bleak late-November morning, and would be re-employed on a huge scale the following spring with even more telling effect. The speed of the German penetration took many formations completely by surprise. Major-General Sir B. de Lisle (GOC 29th Division) was almost captured at Quentin Mill. Headquarters of 35th Brigade (12th Division) was surrounded, but Brigadier-General B. Vincent rallied his staff and fought his way out back to Revelon Ridge, where he began to form 'Vincent Force' from men of many units in an effort to stem the tide of the German advance, which was overrunning the gun-line, capturing many pieces before they could be withdrawn.

The British line is torn open

Soon the rear area of III Corps was jammed with retreating transport and guns, and here and there the flood was joined by units of administrative troops. Numbers of front line battalions found themselves cut off, and communications were plunged into chaos. Generals desperately tried to find reserves to bolster the collapsing front. But the German advance swept remorselessly forward, and by 1030 hours an eight-mile sector of the British line from Les Rues Vertes to Vendhuille had been driven

in, the maximum penetration bringing the Germans to within two and a half miles of Metz after their capture, in succession, of Gauche Wood, Gonnelieu and Gouzeaucourt. The significance of Metz to the German plan lay in the fact that through it ran the most important route up the Grand Ravine to Flesquières and distant Bourlon Wood.

On the northern sector, meanwhile, another heavy engagement had flared up at about 0930 hours as Moser's *Gruppe Arras* began the secondary attack against IV and VI Corps. The German *49th Reserve, 214th* and *221st Divisions* advanced along a three-mile front running from Tadpole Copse in the west to the approaches to Bourlon Wood, supported by the fire of 500 guns. However, the Germans found themselves facing a maelstrom of artillery fire. In anticipation of just such an attack, Third Army had allocated IV Corps no less than eight division's worth of supporting artillery, together with corps and army heavy batteries, and these now made their weight of fire felt. Thus, when the German *3rd Guards Division* (east of Bourlon) attempted to probe towards Cantaing, the attack was disintegrated by gunfire, and by midday it had made no progress. On Moser's main sector of attack, however, the greatest pressure was felt by 56th Division (VI Corps), 2nd and part of 47th Divisions (both parts of IVth Corps). Despite heavy casualties, the German attacks kept coming forward. One group of eight British machine guns, part of 2nd Division, fired all of 70,000 rounds into the flank of successive attacks at close range

with dire effect. Nevertheless, so well pressed-home were the German attacks, that at 1030 hours IV Corps warned its artillery to be ready to fall back at short notice and took preliminary measures to garrison the Hindenburg Support Line in case it should prove necessary to abandon the front. For a time it seemed impossible that Major-General F. A. Davidson's 56th Division could remain in line, but it did hold despite relentless pressure and a growing shortage of ammunition. The Germans made some ground near Tadpole Copse, but nothing vital was lost. On the right of the 56th, the brigades of 2nd Division (IV Corps) also came in for a difficult time. For a period they found themselves out of contact with Major-General C. E. Pereira's headquarters, but 'A' Squadron of King Edward's Horse provided the GOC with 15 gallopers, who maintained a tenuous link with the embattled front line. Many units sacrificed themselves during these desperate hours, and many deeds of great gallantry were performed. The net result was that *Gruppe Arras's* attack proved abortive on November 30. The *Official History* justly describes this as 'an outstanding British achievement in the war on the Western Front'.

It must be recognised, however, that this local success was made possible only at the cost of absorbing a very high proportion of Third Army's resources in terms of both men and guns. Haig urged Byng 'to use his reserves energetically' as GHQ took steps to move four divisions from other sectors towards Bapaume and Peronne as a safeguard against a German breakthrough.

But Byng had soon played almost all his cards; as we shall see, the whole of the Cavalry Corps was eventually committed in support of VII and III Corps, as well as 61st Division to man the Hindenburg Support Line. By 1100 hours it had also proved necessary to transfer the Guards Division from IV to III Corps command.

The major area of crisis remained on the eastern sector, where confusion was threatening to convert defeat into disaster. A series of circumstances staved off this danger. Brigadier-General Vincent's intrepid force on Revelon Ridge was first joined by 20th Hussars, who at once entered the fight in a dismounted rôle. Next to appear was 1st Guards Brigade from Metz, the first echelon of Major-General G. P. T. Fielding's division to be sent up from a rest area to patch the staggering line. The 1st Guards Brigade did more: extemporising a counterattack towards Gouzeaucourt, by 1130 hours it had succeeded in clearing the village, while to the south large numbers of British cavalry extended the *ad hoc* line. The recapture of Gouzeaucourt was consolidated by the arrival of 36 tanks of 'A' and 'B' Battalions, switched to the south after the abrupt cancellation of their movement order to the Somme. Then 5th Cavalry Division, after a considerable approach march from Peronne, passed through the Guards towards Villers Guislain, only to be halted by severe German fire. Snow was of the opinion that it would have been far better to unleash the cavalry against the overextended southern flank of the narrow and still disorganised German corridor extending from the east of Gouzeaucourt, but Byng insisted on committing the cavalry to frontal operations. This decision may have sacrificed a chance of a telling riposte to the German breakthrough, and the Germans were afforded an opportunity to consolidate their gains. Be that as it may, by dusk some sort of a British line had been cobbled together, linking the shattered right wing of III Corps with the left of VII. By last light, 3rd Guards Brigade had come up, with 2nd in support in Gouzeaucourt Wood. The 20th Division was rallying on Welsh Ridge, and on its left 29th Division was still in firm possession of Marcoing after a day of heavy fighting. Administrative confusion had still to be sorted out, and many men went hungry. Others were more fortunate. 'Our rations captured', noted Lieutenant-G. E. Chandler of 11th Essex (2nd Division), who had spent an exhausting day digging extemporised positions, 'but another division shared with us'.

On December 1 much of the drama of the day's fighting again centred around the events on the southern flank. With the intention of forestalling a renewed German attack, at 0630 hours 3rd Guards Brigade launched an attack towards Gonnelieu. It did not fare too successfully, but the appearance of a single tank at a critical moment near Green Switch Trench caused many Germans to surrender. Better fortune blessed 1st Guards Brigade which, aided by 16 tanks of 'H' Battalion, succeeded in retaking much of Gauche Wood and Quintin Mill. Mounted action by 4th and 5th Cavalry Divisions on the left of the Guards achieved little of positive value, but there were now 74 tanks available in support of III and VII Corps flank.

In the centre matters did not go well, both Masnières and Les Rues Vertes were lost, but the German impetus was by now nearly exhausted. The same was true of the northern side of the salient, where the immediate crisis was deemed to have passed by the end of December 1. Lieutenant-General Sir E. A. Fanshawe and HQ V Corps was able to relieve Lieutenant-General Woollcombe and HQ IV Corps—the original hand-over planned for the 30th having been postponed.

The Germans had not yet quite shot their bolt, however. After a reasonably quiet day on the 2nd, they advanced once again on December 3 and took possession of La Vacquerie from 61st Division, which had relieved parts of the exhausted 12th and 20th Divisions only the previous day. The same day, it was deemed necessary to withdraw from the British bridgehead on the east bank of the St Quentin Canal and reconcentrate 29th Division around Marcoing. Meanwhile, the German line assumed its final shape, running from south of Quentin Ridge to Welsh Ridge and thence to Marcoing.

Ludendorff stridently claimed 'an offensive victory on the Western Front' but admitted that matters had not developed 'quite as well as I had hoped'. High British staff circles were far from happy with the overall situation. On December 2, Haig visited the front and told Byng 'to select a good winter line' but not to issue any orders on the subject at that point. The problem was to find a truly secure position. Anxiety centred around the continued German possession of Bonavis Ridge; unless it could be recovered, Haig considered that Third Army's position would remain precariously unbalanced, and the whole Marcoing/Bourlon salient would be compromised. Yet there were no fresh troops whatsoever with which to attempt its recapture, and the thought of becoming involved in a battle of attrition through the winter was unattractive to say the least, and, as Haig pointed out to the CIGS, there would be no question of sending further aid to Italy under the prevailing circumstances. A hard decision had to be taken. On December 3 it was decided that the Bourlon salient must be evacuated; the orders were issued next day. On the night of the 4th/5th the evacuation began, the troops falling back to the 'Yellow Line', some 2,000 yards ahead of the chosen final position. Thus blood-stained Bourlon Wood, the Marcoing area, and long stretches of the Hindenburg Line, were all abandoned to the Germans. The operation was completed by the early hours of December 7. To the west of the Canal du Nord, the British line was almost back where it had been on November 19. In the centre, Havrincourt, Flesquières and Ribécourt remained in British hands, the new line here running along parts of the Hindenburg Support Line, but from Welsh Ridge it swung sharply away to the southwest, and the Germans were left with considerable areas of former British territory in their possession. Losses and gains more or less cancelled each other out.

Not unnaturally, the Germans were astounded by these unforeseen developments. 'We are jubilant,' wrote Moser; 'since 1914 the first withdrawal of the proud Briton'. Ludendorff later described it as 'a good ending to the extremely heavy fighting of 1917. Our action has given us valuable hints for an offensive battle in the west if we wished to undertake one in 1918.'

For the immediate future, however, the Germans needed rest and recuperation as much as their opponents. So ended the famous battle of Cambrai. For the British it had proved 'a sombre sunset after a brilliant sunrise' (Liddell Hart).

The cost of the 17 days of triumph and tragedy had not been light. From November 20 to December 8, the 19 divisions of Third Army had lost 44,207 men. Over 6,000 of these casualties, together with the loss of 103 field and 55 heavy guns, had been the cost of November 30. The German *Second Army* (ultimately 20 divisions strong) confessed to 41,000 casualties, and the loss of 145 guns, but probably excluded considerable numbers of lightly wounded. Of their total admitted loss, 14,000 were suffered during the counteroffensive. What had been gained by either side from these exertions? In terms of the Western Front, precious little ground or overall advantage. It is true that two German divisions from the Eastern Front, intended for Italy, had been diverted to Flanders, but the British programme for reinforcing their Italian allies had also been at least partially disrupted. On the other hand, both sides had learnt much of tactical value: on the British side the employment of tanks; on the German the value of infiltration tactics.

As might be expected, there was much criticism in London about the reasons why 'a resounding victory' had been allowed to degenerate into 'a disastrous rout' (Lloyd George). Characteristically, Haig did not flinch from accepting the ultimate responsibility. On December 3 he had written '. . . whatever happens, the responsibility is mine'. At the Cambrai Enquiry, several senior officers, including Byng, tried to blame negligence on the part of the fighting soldier. 'I attribute the reason for the local success on the part of the enemy to one cause and one alone', testified the commander of Third Army, 'namely—lack of training on the part of junior officers and NCOs and men.' Although General J. C. Smuts, consulted by the War Cabinet as an independent assessor, substantially agreed with this assertion, the verdict has been much modified with the passage of time. In the words of a recent historian of Cambrai, Robert Woollcombe, 'the High Command was responsible for the confusion, and the troops for the valour'. Perhaps the ultimate reason for the bitter disappointments of the period between November 30 and December 7 has been most aptly summarised by John Terraine: 'Two years of offensive strategy had diverted the British army's attention from defensive problems.' This was demonstrably true at Cambrai. This shortcoming, together with the weariness of the troops, the shortage of adequate reserves, and the failure of British military intelligence to estimate correctly the strength and intentions of the Germans, accounts in large measure for the final outcome of this celebrated engagement which brought the bitter year of 1917 to an unmourned conclusion.

Further Reading
Liddell Hart, Sir Basil, *The Tanks,* Vol 1 (Cassell 1959)
Terraine, J., *Douglas Haig* (Hutchinson 1963)
Woollcombe, R., *The First Tank Battle: Cambrai 1917* (Barker 1967)

THE ARGONNE

It is often thought that because the end of the war was near the battles of late 1918 must have been easy by comparison with the earlier bloodbaths. This assumption is unfair both to the Allies who won those battles and to the doggedness of the German resistance. Another natural assumption is that the Allies would have learnt

Below: Small FT17 tanks, heavily camouflaged against German aircraft, await the offensive. In fact tanks were useless in the ravines and dense forests of the Argonne

Following America's successful sally into the war at St Mihiel Pershing's First Army moved up through Verdun against the impregnable natural and man-made defences of the Argonne. To everyone's surprise, not least their own, the Americans continued their resolute advance.

major lessons from previous mistakes, and would not continue to invite heavy casualties; unfortunately, even in the final stages, the mass assaults which had proved so costly earlier were still the only tactic used by the Allies. The final blows at German resistance were planned for September 26 and the days following. The great attack was to begin with strong thrusts from the French Fourth Army and the American First Army in the Champagne-Argonne sector. The following day the British First and Third Armies would launch an attack through the line of the Canal du Nord, the

Left: An American Balloon Company moves up to the front. Aerial observation was not, however, very helpful, for the German defences were easily concealed in the dense undergrowth

Bottom: Renault 37-mm tank. *Weight:* 14,300 lbs. *Armament:* 37-mm gun, with 237 rounds of ammunition. *Dimensions:* Length 16 ft 5 ins; width 5 ft 7½ ins; height 7 ft. *Engine:* 35 bhp. *Speed:* Cross-country 2.2 mph; on roads 4.8 mph. *Range:* 22 miles. *Armour:* Front 16-mm; sides 8-mm; top 8-mm; belly 6-mm. *Turret:* Either round (22-mm) or panelled (16-mm). *Crew:* 2 men. *Below:* A column of Renaults at Suvigney

next day the Belgian army and the British Second Army would set off with the object of liberating Bruges and Brussels, and on September 29 the British Fourth and the French First Armies would be committed in the centre. Allied morale was higher than it had been for years. This was not so much due to the possibility that the end of the war was in sight—for some had been anticipating that since 1914—but to the fact that the wave of major offensives launched by the Germans earlier in the year had been checked and countered. In contrast, German morale should have been low but, as experience has often shown, the troops were driven back to feel that they were defending their homeland and as a result they fought with quite unexpected doggedness and determination. Undoubtedly German spirit had been dampened by the inadequacy of reinforcements, and the gloomy news from home and other fronts, but balancing this was the greater expertise they had developed in defensive technique. This was highly sophisticated, and varied according to the nature of the ground. Sometimes the assault would be contained by elastic yielding, with appropriate counterattacks; at other times there would be hard resistance at selected points so that the attack could slide by and be enfiladed. In the Argonne sector the Germans had had four years to prepare a defence with meticulous care. This was the area assigned to the American First Army, whose objective was to reach what was known as the Buzancy line. Once accomplished, the Germans would be prevented from outflanking the French Fourth Army. On the face of it this task seems relatively simple: in fact it was of great importance as it would stop the Germans from splitting the Allied offensive, and of enormous difficulty because of the nature of the ground. Immediately behind the Americans were the battlefields of Verdun, which can have been little help to morale. The devastation of this and other areas made the provision of supplies extremely difficult, for roads, villages and drainage had been systematically destroyed in the bombardments of the past. Furthermore, the Argonne forest is spread over the ridges which lie between the Aire and the upper Aisne: it would be difficult to find less inviting country for an invader. Even without shell fire the area would have been difficult enough but when the forest was subjected to preliminary bombardment it became almost impenetrable. The effect of bombing and shelling ahead of advancing infantry is intended to soften up the opposition, but on numerous occasions, when applied at random, it will hinder the advance more than help it. This is what happened on the Argonne. The Germans laid down further obstacles by filling the forest with wire and netting, which could not be removed by shelling, or pushed aside by tanks. The latter were of limited use in this region—although the Americans had 189 of them—for the forest was full of deep ravines.

'Scorched earth' policy
There were other hazards, inside and outside the forest. The bulk of the American forces were, in fact, east of the Argonne forest, and the Germans had made every effort to make them as unwelcome in that area as in the forest itself. They did this by following a normal routine of the type which later became known as the 'scorched earth' policy. Towns and villages were set on fire, all road and railway bridges demolished, embankments and cuttings were destroyed by explosives, and crossroads were blown up. Wells and water supplies were polluted. There was also an elaborate array of booby traps. These measures were designed to be much more than merely vindictive; they had the considerable military value of delaying the allied advance. The troops had to proceed so cautiously, treating the most innocent-looking installations—such as an abandoned dugout or sniper's platform—with such extreme care, that progress was much slower than commanders had expected. The front assigned to the American army was 22 miles wide. The First Army, which was commanded by General Pershing, incorporated 15 infantry divisions and one cavalry division. Nine of these were in the front line, three were in immediate reserve and the remainder were in Army reserve. Each American division was nearly twice the size of a British or French division but this was not, in the event, an unqualified advantage. There were only two usable roads in the area of the advance, one on each flank, and both were exposed to constant German artillery fire. Constructing roads and repairing bridges for the advance of a large army is difficult enough at the best of times but the nature of the countryside—not forgetting the attentions of the Germans—made it particularly difficult.

But a drive forward in this area was absolutely essential if the war was to be over by the end of the year; if it could not be made, the whole programme would be put back six months. Whatever the casualties of an all-out attack in the autumn they could hardly fail to be surpassed by the continual drain caused by bombardment and illness, followed by a spring offensive against positions which would have had months to perfect their defences. Nevertheless Pershing must have had considerable doubts about committing inexperienced American troops. In reaching his decision he had to weigh very carefully whether the advantage of using fresh keen troops who would acquire heavy casualties through inexperience was justified when six months later they would be vastly more sophisticated militarily, but lack some of the drive they had earlier possessed.

Top: Rudimentary communications. Information is recorded and orders retailed through a loud hailer. Gas masks were obligatory

Above: An American Field Hospital at Neuvilly, improvised in the ruins of a church. Casualties among the 'doughboys' were high

The first stage went very well. The main body of the First Army, to the east of the forest, advanced seven miles in the first two days, but in the following eleven days it gained no more than two miles. This slow progress was partly due to dogged German resistance but probably owed more to supply problems. Approximately 300,000 troops were engaged in the battle from 0530 hours onwards on the opening day, September 26. Some had been in position for several days, others had only come into the line during the night to the somewhat awesome sound, for new troops, of 2,700 guns delivering a preliminary three-hour barrage. During the First World War large scale attacks were usually preceded by barrages which sometimes went on for days on end. These were intended to destroy all strong points, and morale as well, although in practice this was not always the case. Nevertheless, on this occasion they were essential, because of the enormous care with which the German positions were protected by lines of barbed wire, machine gun nests, concrete bunkers, and enfilading trench systems. At this stage in the war miracles could not be expected—in any sector. British, Commonwealth, French, and Belgian troops had all fought long and exhausting campaigns, had been decimated and had been rebuilt, were highly skilled and professional, but could not be expected to produce the wild dash of the earlier years. By contrast the Americans lacked the professionalism which comes from battle experience, although full enough of energy and verve. Yet in these last bitter months there were many surprises. The Allied armies which had fought through three and a half years of the most gruelling campaigns the world has ever known, suddenly produced a speed, dash, and alacrity which no one—least of all themselves—could ever have dreamed of. The Americans who already had the *St Mihiel* offensive on their hands could not reasonably be expected to move half a million men and their equipment in secret by night into a new sector—and then fight like demons in one of the most disheartening areas of the war. Yet they did. Right in the middle of their area was the strongly-fortified town of Montfaucon which Foch had not thought they would capture until early 1919; instead they bypassed it on the first day and occupied it on the morning of the second. Montfaucon, which was on a hill, was considered to be impregnable to an infantry attack. The cost of its capture was high—even after it had been bypassed—for the Germans had established numerous camouflaged machine gun posts on platforms in the trees. Remains of similar platforms may still be seen in the woods of northern France, and some may well contain booby-traps—much rusted but still lethal. The only surviving building at the time of its capture was a château which Crown Prince Rupprecht had used as an observatory in 1916. From the basement 30 feet below ground he watched the attacks on Verdun through a periscope which, in turn, was protected by a concrete cylinder. The periscope was captured by the US Signal Corps and is now in the museum at West Point. The weather throughout the attack was particularly bad. The Americans were in action for 47 days between the opening of the Argonne attack and the end of the war and it rained on 40 days out of that 47. Not only did men have to shuffle along from one hold-up to another on the inadequate roads but conditions were at times so bad that rations could not reach them at all. Continuous rain beating steadily on a steel helmet produces an irritation peculiarly its own even without the nagging headache which it invariably leads to. To the men moving in the battle area the whole panorama of men, machines and horses must have seemed one of unrelieved chaos. In parts indeed it was—and took days to sort out—but that overall it was an operational success was largely due to the skill of Colonel G. C. Marshall, Assistant Chief of Staff (Operations) First Army. Another name which was becoming prominent was that of George S. Patton. At this stage he was a Colonel and was wounded in the early stages of the Argonne fighting, for which he was awarded the Distinguished Service Cross. His views about war were aptly summarised by his remark that 'no one ever won a war by dying for his country but only by making some poor bastard die for his,' but his appeal as a leader probably lay in the fact that in the armies he subsequently commanded, the life he valued least was his own.

Ludendorff: under pressure

The Argonne campaign not only upset calculations by the results it achieved, but by the rapidity with which they were accomplished. Foch—Commander-in-Chief of the Allied armies by this time—had expected very small gains and did not anticipate a successful end to the war until well into the following year. The initial successes on all fronts—especially on that of the Americans—made him rapidly revise his timetable. Ludendorff, while realising that pressure was mounting against him, had by no means decided the war was lost. On the contrary, in spite of being jolted back on several fronts he still believed he could regroup his forces into a tight defensive perimeter of which the various sectors had such daunting names as the Siegfried, Hundung, Brunhilde, Kriemhilde and Michel positions. On some of them he was prepared to give way—if necessary—and retire to equally strong positions behind, but the cumulative effective would be to hold the Allies off German territory till the following spring. By that time the Allies would be as anxious for peace as the Germans, and the terms should be correspondingly more favourable. The Argonne, however, was not one of the areas in which Ludendorff was prepared to give ground; he was as surprised as Foch at the events which took place there. Although the Kriemhilde position lay behind the Argonne, and the incomplete Freya position (second-line defence with the Hagen and Hermann positions) lay between the Kriemhilde and Sedan, this was too vulnerable an area for any loss of territory to be accepted without misgiving. Although the Americans gained three miles in the first two days they soon found the going tougher, partly because Ludendorff now began switching other divisions to this vital sector. Ultimately 40 German divisions were in the field against some 630,000 American troops.

The initial American gains were by no means even. The thrust that had penetrated three miles into the German position within the first two days barely managed to advance two miles in the next ten, because of the supply problem. The ingenuity of German delaying tactics now increased. One road had a vast crater in it. Railways were liable to produce surprises, for when the broken track had been repaired, and the first train ran, mines under apparently intact stretches would send not only the track but also the trains skywards. Troops advancing on the left of the American sector came under flanking fire from the forest; and it became obvious that the forest could not be bypassed, as had been hoped, but would have to be cleared. The best way of accomplishing that was thought to be by penetrating from the sides. But in places it turned out to be a matter of fighting from tree to tree. There were three main problems: the area was so full of precipitous unclimbable slopes that an orderly advance was impossible, the nature of the terrain, combined with rain and occasional fog, made it impossible for units to keep in proper communication with each other, and the wire, some of it laid much earlier in the war, was concealed in the dense undergrowth.

The 'Lost Battalion'

One of the most remarkable episodes of the campaign was that of the 'Lost Battalion'. The battalion was never in fact lost—as its approximate position was known—but it was completely surrounded by Germans in the forest, and was fortunate to survive at all. The battalion, which belonged to the 77th Division, consisted of nine companies and was commanded by Major Charles W. Whittlesey. Its total strength was 550 men. On October 2 General Pershing had decided there was nothing to be gained by units trying to maintain communications in the forest, and that the best policy was to drive straight ahead. Positions which were captured would be held. By this process the Americans would establish a strategic network of strongpoints throughout the forest, and so fully occupy its German inhabitants that they would be distracted from their attacks on the flank of the advancing American main force. When the order to push ahead to indicated points was given, Whittlesey had already experienced its possible effects. The battalion had already been cut off from September 28 to October 1, although on that occasion some contact had been maintained. On October 2 it set off again towards the Charlevaux valley. Opposition was lighter than expected and they reached their objective and dug in. As they had been hampered very little by the Germans they had soon lost touch with flanking units, which presumably had found the going harder. Whittlesey had some misgivings about the battalion's isolation despite his orders. However, any suspicions he had about the vulnerability of his position changed to certainties when one of his pickets reported hearing German voices behind them. With limited ammunition, no rations, and very little chance of making contact with the rest of the division the battalion's position began to look dangerous. The most important question was how serious the German opposition was likely to be. This uncertainty was soon resolved. Patrols soon discovered there were Germans on all sides, and that those behind had run up a barbed wire screen dotted with machine guns. As Whittlesey took stock of his position the Germans began to straddle the area with artillery and mortar-fire; with no means of digging adequate trenches the battalion was fully exposed to the barrage. It took the Germans a little time to realise what a splendid prize had fallen into their hands—no less than a complete battalion. At first they assumed that a detachment, perhaps of company strength, had ranged too far ahead, which could be mortared into submission without serious fighting, from lack of food and ammunition. When they realised that a full battalion had fallen into their potential grasp they saw no need to change their tactics; all they did was to increase the volume of their mortar and artillery fire. In case Whittlesey should decide to break out to the rear of the position they put up some more barbed wire and sited a few more guns. They need not have troubled. Whittlesey's orders had been to capture ground and hold it; there was no question in his mind of not obeying them to the letter.

Whittlesey had not, up to this point, had much chance of showing his worth. He was a lawyer, not a professional soldier; he was not over-communicative, and he was short-sighted. His troops, thinking he looked like a crane, nicknamed him 'Bird legs'; later this nickname was used with that affection and respect only given to commanders who have been through the mill along with their men. Whittlesey's battalion had markers to indicate his position to friendly aircraft but these were of little value in the thick forest. In any case the rest of the division knew where he was—the problem was how to reach him. Supplies were dropped from the air but fell outside the battalion's narrow perimeter. Nine men ventured out—without permission—to recover the supplies, but all were killed or captured. One was blindfolded and sent back with a note demanding the battalion's surrender. Whittlesey, a man of few words, wasted none on this occasion; he ignored the demand. At first he had tried to get runners through the German lines to let headquarters know exactly where he was, but these were all killed. It was essential that the division should know not only exactly where he was, but also the straits he was in. Having set out with iron rations a week before the battalion was now living on dew, grass, and leaves. The wounded were dying and all ranks were suffering from exposure. But he could not be sure that the rest of the division was aware of this. For all they knew he might have captured a cache of supplies.

'Cher Ami': pigeon hero

Whittlesey had four carrier pigeons, and with these he tried to send back details of his exact position. Unfortunately for him —and them—three were shot down by observant German marksmen. The fourth was carrying the most serious news of all: because the division did not know the exact position of the unit, the 'Lost Battalion' was coming under its own artillery fire. This last pigeon was called 'Cher Ami'. In spite of its name it was a British pigeon which had been one of a consignment of 600 sent by British pigeon fanciers to the American army. When the United States came into the war it was impossible for them to provide all necessary equipment from their own resources immediately. Apart from tanks and guns and aircraft there were other, less military but equally essential, supplies. Among them were

pigeons, which could often get a message through when all other communication aids had failed. There were already 20,000 carrier pigeons in service with the American army, of which 5,000 were overseas.

'Cher Ami' set off with the last message. The watching Americans saw it rise in the air, then set off in purposeful flight to its loft 25 miles away. But the German marksmen were watching too. As it crossed their positions it met a storm of fire. One bullet broke its leg—the leg which held the vital message capsule—another damaged its wing, and a third broke its breastbone. It stopped as if jerked by a wire and then, to the dismay of the battalion, it began to spiral downwards. Just before it reached the trees it made a last effort and, to the joy of the almost incredulous watchers, came back into flight and set off on its long journey home. The barrage was lifted. 'Cher Ami' became something of a national hero. He was taken back to the United States and given full VIP treatment, but only survived a year. After his death he was stuffed and put on display in the Smithsonian Institute in Washington, DC.

But the lifting of the barrage was not the end of the battalion's troubles. The Germans, finding that siege tactics would take too long, now turned to infantry assaults.

Below: In the Argonne—a forbidding prospect for any attacker and quite impassable for tanks

Some of the most pressing occurred on the right flank, which was held by Captain Holderman with one company. Holderman had already been wounded twice but was still in command. At one point he crawled out and helped to bring in some wounded; at another he sallied out and shot a German carrying a flame-thrower. But there were many others who also deserved commendation, among them Captain McMurtry, who was twice wounded, and two pilots, Goettler and Bleckley, who were shot down in a vain attempt to locate the battalion position by flying at tree-top height. The difficulty of pinpointing the exact position of the battalion stemmed from the nature of the terrain. The Argonne ridges are up to 750 feet high; one looks very much like another, and there are no reliable landmarks. Although the approximate position of the battalion was known, it had already been shown that a more accurate reference was needed if artillery fire was not to wipe out friend and foe alike. Furthermore, the Germans had not failed to provide against relief by infantry attack. In the circumstances a detailed map of the battalion's position was essential to headquarters if it was to rescue Whittlesey's men before they were exterminated by American or German fire. The battalion

was determined not to accept the German offer of surrender. A number of runners had already been sent out to contact Division, but all had been killed and it seemed suicidal to send another. Nevertheless, when Whittlesey asked for a volunteer he got one immediately; Private Abraham Krotoshinsky. Krotoshinsky was, of course, in no shape to set off on a difficult and dangerous mission through the German lines. He was weak from exposure and lack of sleep, and he had had no proper food for a week. At one point he was so close to being discovered that he was actually trodden on under a covering of leaves. However, he slipped through, and after a hurried meal led the first relief party back. When the rescue had been accomplished, and the attack was rolling forward again, Whittlesey was much embarrassed by the attentions of the Press. He disavowed making any defiant remarks; he had merely ignored the invitation to surrender, and he insisted that any credit was due to his men and not himself. He was believed on the first two points but not on the third.

But the relief of one small battalion did not mean that the forest was cleared. There was much heavy fighting still to do. The 327th regiment of 28th Division swam the Aire in early morning fog and similar

Left: Gunners search out pockets of German defence, meticulously prepared over four years

Below: The ORBAT of an American division, showing its organisation and establishments

Südd-Verlag

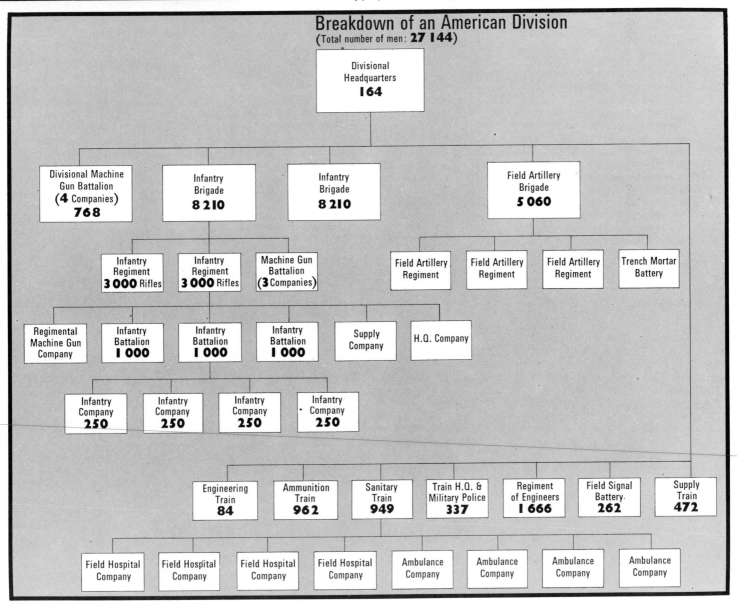

Breakdown of an American Division
(Total number of men: **27 144**)

- Divisional Headquarters **164**
  - Divisional Machine Gun Battalion (**4** Companies) **768**
  - Infantry Brigade **8 210**
  - Infantry Brigade **8 210**
  - Field Artillery Brigade **5 060**
    - Infantry Regiment **3 000** Rifles
    - Infantry Regiment **3 000** Rifles
    - Machine Gun Battalion (**3** Companies)
    - Field Artillery Regiment
    - Field Artillery Regiment
    - Field Artillery Regiment
    - Trench Mortar Battery
      - Regimental Machine Gun Company
      - Infantry Battalion **1 000**
      - Infantry Battalion **1 000**
      - Infantry Battalion **1 000**
      - Supply Company
      - H.Q. Company
        - Infantry Company **250**
        - Infantry Company **250**
        - Infantry Company **250**
        - Infantry Company **250**
- Engineering Train **84**
- Ammunition Train **962**
- Sanitary Train **949**
- Train H.Q. & Military Police **337**
- Regiment of Engineers **1 666**
- Field Signal Battery **262**
- Supply Train **472**
  - Field Hospital Company
  - Field Hospital Company
  - Field Hospital Company
  - Field Hospital Company
  - Ambulance Company
  - Ambulance Company
  - Ambulance Company
  - Ambulance Company

determination was shown by other units. But casualties were high.

Two other remarkable individual feats took place at this time. The first was that of Corporal Alvin C. York, of the 328th Regiment of 82nd Division. York was not a professional soldier; in fact he belonged to a religious group which strongly emphasised the commandment 'Thou shalt not kill'. When he was called up by the army it required the joint efforts of the chaplain and the commanding officer to dissuade him from being a conscientious objector: a discussion consisted largely of lengthy quotations from the scriptures. However, once his doubts were resolved York soon showed he had all the attributes of a first-class soldier; as he had been brought up in Wolf River Valley, Tennessee he had little to learn about marksmanship or fieldcraft.

On October 8, 1918, when York's platoon was advancing towards the Decauville railway, they were checked by heavy machine gun fire from all sides. Sixteen men, including York, were at once detached to work around to the left and to try to outflank the posts. Stealthily, the detachment moved round, sometimes crawling, to the rear of the German positions. There, to their considerable pleasure, they captured the German battalion HQ with one volley only. However, the noise was sufficient to alert the machine gun posts and the guns were quickly trained on to the Americans; six were killed and three seriously wounded; of those left York was the most senior.

York's idea of command was to detail the surviving members of the platoon to guard the prisoners while he himself went out hunting round the battalion's forward positions. For a man of his upbringing and skill it was not too difficult; every time a German raised his head to take aim he received a bullet. Eventually, the Germans, goaded into desperation by losing man after man to this imperturbable frontiersman who found it 'easier'n shooting turkeys', tried a charge, led by a lieutenant; York dropped them one by one with shots from his Service revolver. A German major, not realising that all the shots were coming from one man, decided there was no alternative to surrender, which he offered for all the detachments in his area. York accepted. The major, with York's pistol in his back, took him round the positions. Occasionally York had to fire a round to encourage the stubborn but had soon amassed what turned out to be a total of 132 men: members of a Prussian Guards regiment. When he returned to his own lines an astonished officer asked how many there were: 'Sorry, lieutenant,' he said, 'I ain't counted them properly yet.' York proved a great disappointment to those who tried to lionise him. He refused to appear in a film, he refused to make speeches, and he refused a lecture tour, for all of which he was offered enormous fees. He merely said: 'It's over; let's forget it.'

Another notable feat at this time was that of Sergeant Woodfill, of the 60th Infantry, during the attack on Cunel. Like York, he was an expert marksman, and had killed so many German machine gunners while pressing home the attack that he was described by General Pershing as 'the greatest of all the American heroes of the war'. In fairness to other men in other theatres of the war it must be recognized—as York and Woodfill would have been quick to acknowledge—that the

Opposite page: The progress of the Argonne offensive from September 26 to the Armistice. *Above:* One of several unwilling heroes to emerge from the Argonne fighting, Corporal Alvin C. York. Finding himself the senior survivor of an ambushed detachment he set out to fight the German army single-handed and his marksmanship, learnt in the Tennessee backwoods, deceived part of a Prussian Guards regiment into surrendering. With unsophisticated naïvety he shrugged off attempts to exploit the incident—'It's over; let's forget it,' he protested

nature of the country helped them considerably.

The first week of the Meuse-Argonne campaign—tough though it was—was fast and successful compared with the days which followed. By this time Ludendorff was fully alert to the dangers of the situation on this front and was pouring in reinforcements. Apart from the frontal opposition there was the constant menace of flanking fire, on the left from the Argonne forest, and on the right from the Meuse heights. By October 10 there were over a million Americans in the battle area, nearly all of whom were actively engaged. On that day, precisely two months after the formation of First Army, the American

Second Army was constituted, with headquarters at Toul. Command of First Army was given to Lieutenant-General Hunter Liggett, and command of Second Army to Major-General Robert Bullard. The Americans, although making numerous mistakes and often incurring unnecessary casualties, continued to push forward, to their own surprise and gratification as much as that of their allies. The Germans, even more surprised, nevertheless took a heavy toll. On October 14 the Kriemhilde line was attacked; three days later, after bitter fighting, it was breached. But even the penetration of this formidable position did not bring a respite to the now battle-weary Americans. There were yet more trenches to be taken, more guns to be silenced, and more strongpoints to be captured. Romagne and St Juvin were succeeded by Barricourt, Bois Consenvoye, Etrayes, and Haumont. The Germans were beaten but not broken; it was necessary to keep the attack rolling forward in order to prevent the Germans from regrouping and stabilising their position. The final thrust was launched on November 1 after a brief but heavy bombardment. On November 3 the Lille-Metz railway was severed and three days later the Americans were closing in on Sedan. For diplomatic reasons it was decided that the relief of Sedan should be left to the French (although in the event there was some confusion over this). First Army set off in the direction of Longwy and Second Army towards Briey, but the Armistice was declared before they reached them.

The Americans, although arriving late on the scene, had done more and better than anyone had expected. Compared with other nations their time in action was short, but it was not for that reason unimportant. In fact, it probably shortened the war by at least six months. The cost in lives was proportionally high: their total casualties were 264,092. The Americans had a greater variety of weapons than any other army for in the early stages they had to rely heavily on their allies. They had French 75's, 155 howitzers and cannons, Chauchat automatic rifles, and Hotchkiss machine guns, and they had British Stokes 3-inch mortars, Newton 6-inch mortars, 8-inch howitzers and Enfield rifles. Eventually they produced excellent weapons of their own in the shape of Browning machine guns and automatic rifles, and Springfields. However, many of the foreign weapons they used had been built under licence in American factories. In the best traditions of a nation which had produced such notable weapons as Gatlings, Maxims, and Colt revolvers, the best light machine gun of the war was the invention of an American—Colonel I. N. Lewis. Up above the battlefields Americans were flying French, British, and Italian aircraft; twelve of their 48 squadrons were equipped with American built De Havillands. Nowadays, when so many of the armies, navies and air forces of the world are using American equipment it is interesting to recall these figures.

Further Reading
Pitt, Barrie, *1918: The Last Act* (Cassell 1962)
Farrow, Edward S., *American Guns in the War with Germany* (Dulton 1920)
Liggett, Major-General Hunter, *A.E.F.* (Dodd Mead 1928)

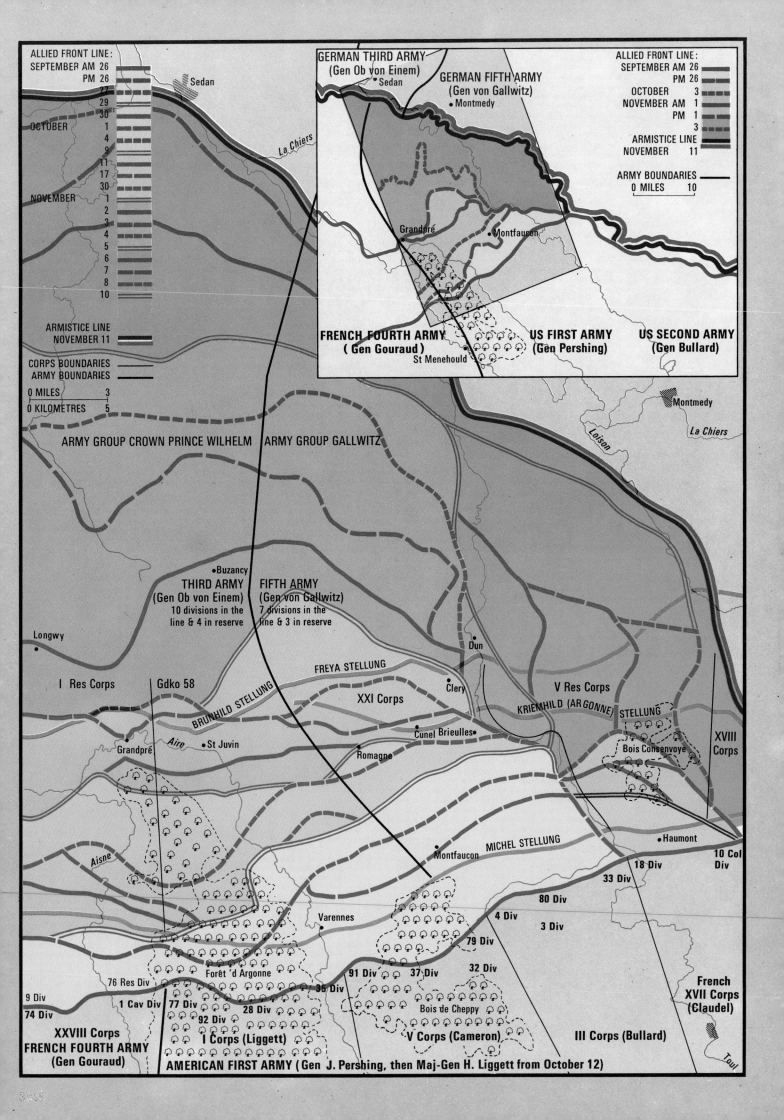

ALLIED FRONT LINE:
SEPTEMBER AM 26
PM 26
27
29
30
OCTOBER 1
4
9
11
17
30
NOVEMBER 1
2
3
4
5
6
7
8
10

ARMISTICE LINE
NOVEMBER 11

CORPS BOUNDARIES
ARMY BOUNDARIES

0 MILES 3
0 KILOMETRES 5

ALLIED FRONT LINE:
SEPTEMBER AM 26
PM 26
OCTOBER 3
NOVEMBER AM 1
PM 1
3
ARMISTICE LINE
NOVEMBER 11

ARMY BOUNDARIES
0 MILES 10

GERMAN THIRD ARMY
(Gen Ob von Einem)
• Sedan
GERMAN FIFTH ARMY
(Gen von Gallwitz)
• Montmedy
• Grandpré
• Montfaucon

FRENCH FOURTH ARMY
(Gen Gouraud)
• St Menehould
US FIRST ARMY
(Gen Pershing)
US SECOND ARMY
(Gen Bullard)

• Sedan
La Chiers

ARMY GROUP CROWN PRINCE WILHELM | ARMY GROUP GALLWITZ

Loison
• Montmedy
La Chiers

• Buzancy
THIRD ARMY
(Gen Ob von Einem)
10 divisions in the
line & 4 in reserve
FIFTH ARMY
(Gen von Gallwitz)
7 divisions in the
line & 3 in reserve

• Longwy

• Dun

I Res Corps | Gdko 58
FREYA STELLUNG
• Clery
V Res Corps
KRIEMHILD (ARGONNE) STELLUNG
XVIII Corps

BRUNHILD STELLUNG
XXI Corps
• Cunel Brieulles
• Bois Consenvoye

Aire • St Juvin
• Grandpré
• Romagne

Aisne
MICHEL STELLUNG
• Montfaucon
• Haumont
10 Col Div
18 Div
33 Div
80 Div
4 Div
3 Div
79 Div

• Varennes
French XVII Corps
(Claudel)

Forêt d'Argonne
91 Div 37 Div 32 Div
35 Div
9 Div
1 Cav Div 77 Div 28 Div
Bois de Cheppy
74 Div
92 Div

XXVIII Corps
FRENCH FOURTH ARMY
(Gen Gouraud)
I Corps (Liggett)
V Corps (Cameron)
III Corps (Bullard)
AMERICAN FIRST ARMY (Gen J. Pershing, then Maj-Gen H. Liggett from October 12)

Toul

BATTLE OF JUTLAND

Here at last was the 20th-century Trafalgar: the long-awaited clash of the mighty dreadnoughts. As the two fleets collided in the North Sea and turned the full fury of their huge guns upon each other, the unexpected happened, suddenly, in many quarters. The story of this most controversial battle is told both by a British and a German Naval historian

British View

With the arrival of spring 1916, the First World War was eighteen months old. On land a decision had eluded the opposing armies; they had settled into a war of attrition bleeding both sides white. At sea the two most powerful fleets the world had ever seen faced each other across the North Sea, each eager to engage the other, but neither able to bring about an encounter on terms favourable to itself.

The British Grand Fleet, under Admiral Sir John Jellicoe, was concentrated at Scapa Flow, in the Orkneys, whence, it was calculated, the northern exit from the North Sea could be closed to the enemy, while the German fleet could still be intercepted and brought to battle should it threaten the British coasts. The British ability to read German coded radio messages enabled them to obtain warning of any impending moves.

The German High Seas Fleet, numerically much inferior to its opponent, could contemplate battle with only a portion of the British Grand Fleet. From almost the beginning of the war its strategy had been aimed at forcing the British to divide their strength so that this might be brought about. Raids by the German battle-cruiser force, commanded by Rear-Admiral Hipper, on English east coast towns had been mounted. The failure of the Grand Fleet to intercept these had resulted in the Grand Fleet's battle-cruiser force, under Vice-

Admiral Sir David Beatty, being based at Rosyth; and when Hipper again sortied in January 1915 he had been intercepted. In the battle of Dogger Bank which had followed, the German armoured cruiser *Blücher* had been sunk and the battle-cruiser *Seydlitz* had narrowly escaped destruction when a shell penetrated her after turret, starting a conflagration among the ammunition. Only flooding the magazine had saved her.

Further adventures by the High Seas Fleet had been forbidden by the Kaiser and the Germans had launched their first unrestricted U-boat campaign against Allied merchant shipping. For the rest of 1915 the High Seas Fleet had languished in port, chafing against its inaction.

But in January 1916, its command had been taken over by Admiral Reinhard Scheer who had at once set about reanimating it. Raids on the English coast were resumed. As before, the Grand Fleet, in spite of the warnings received through radio interception, had been unable to reach the scene from Scapa Flow in time to interfere. Jellicoe was forced to agree to his 5th Battle Squadron—the fast and powerful Queen Elizabeth-class ships—joining Beatty's Battle-cruiser Fleet at Rosyth.

When in May 1916, the U-boat campaign was called off at the threat of American intervention on the Allied side and the submarines recalled, Scheer had the conditions necessary for his ambition to bring

about a fleet action on favourable terms by bringing the three arms of the fleet simultaneously into play. His surface forces were to sortie for a bombardment of Sunderland and lure the enemy to sea where his U-boats could ambush them, while his Zeppelin airships would scout far afield and so enable him to avoid any confrontation with a superior enemy concentration.

Plans were drawn up for the latter part of May; the actual date, to be decided at the last moment, would depend upon when the fleet was brought up to full strength by the return of the battle-cruiser *Seydlitz* from repairs caused by mine damage during a previous sortie, and upon suitable weather for the airships to reconnoitre efficiently. Meanwhile the U-boats, sixteen in number, sailed on 17th May for their stations off Scapa, Cromarty, and the Firth of Forth. Their endurance made the 30th the latest possible date. The *Seydlitz* did not rejoin until the 28th, however, and then a period of hazy weather set in, unsuitable for air reconnaissance.

Against such a development, an alternative plan had been prepared. Hipper's battle-cruiser force was to go north from the Heligoland Bight and 'trail its shirt' off the Norwegian coast where it would be duly reported to the British. Beatty's battle-cruiser fleet from Rosyth would come racing eastwards to fall into the trap of the High Seas Fleet battle squadrons, waiting some forty miles to the southward of

Imperial War Museum

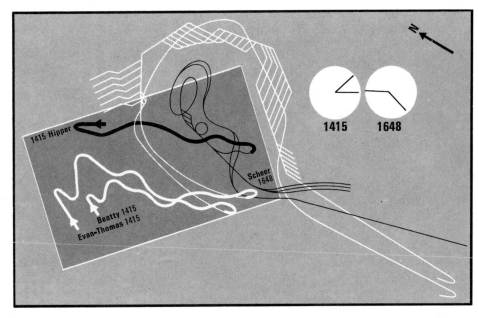

Right: The context of the first phase of the battle: the battle-cruisers' run to the south. Realising that he cannot hope to deal with Beatty on his own, Hipper decides to turn and lure Beatty's battle-cruisers down onto Scheer's main part of the High Seas Fleet to the south.
As a result of signalling faults, the most powerful element of Beatty's force, the 5th Battle Squadron, is left behind at first, giving Hipper a slight superiority of numbers. Combined with their initial better shooting, and the poor protection for the vitals of the British ships, this enables the German battle-cruisers to despatch two of their opponents. And then over the horizon appears Scheer.
Above: Phase One of the engagement in detail

Hipper, before the Grand Fleet from Scapa could intervene.

The trap is set

Such a plan—assuming an unlikely credulity on the part of the British—was naïve, to say the least, even allowing for the fact that the British ability to read German wireless signals was not realized. Nevertheless, when the thick weather persisted throughout the 28th and 29th, it was decided to employ it. On the afternoon of 30th May, the brief signal went out to the High Seas Fleet assembled in the Schillig Roads— 31GG2490, which signified 'Carry out Secret Instruction 2490 on 31st May'.

This was duly picked up by the Admiralty's monitoring stations and though its meaning was not known, it was clear from various indications that some major operation by the German fleet was impending. At once the organization for getting the Grand Fleet to sea swung into action; the main body under the commander-in-chief, with his flag in the *Iron Duke*, including the three battle-cruisers of the 3rd Battle-Cruiser Squadron, who had been detached there from Rosyth for gunnery practice, sailed from Scapa Flow; from the Cromarty Firth sailed the 2nd Battle Squadron, the 1st Cruiser Squadron, and a flotilla of destroyers. These two forces were to rendezvous the following morning (31st) in a position some ninety miles west of Norway's southerly point. When joined,

they would comprise a force of no less than 24 dreadnought battleships, 3 battle-cruisers, 8 armoured cruisers, 12 light cruisers, and 51 destroyers. Beatty's Battle-Cruiser Fleet—6 battle-cruisers, the four 15-inch-gun, fast Queen Elizabeth-class battleships, 12 light cruisers, 28 destroyers, and a seaplane carrier—was to steer from the Firth of Forth directly to reach a position some 120 miles west of the Jutland Bank at 1400 on the 31st, which would place him sixty-nine miles ahead of the Grand Fleet as it steered towards the Heligoland Bight. If Beatty's fleet had sighted no enemy by that time, it was to turn north to meet Jellicoe.

Thus, long before the first moves of Scheer's plan to lure Beatty out had been made, the whole vast strength of the British fleet was at sea. The schemer was liable to have the tables turned on him. The first aim of Scheer's project had already been missed. His U-boats had failed to deliver any successful attacks on the British

squadrons as they sortied; furthermore their reports of what they had seen added up only to various isolated squadrons at sea and gave no warning that the Grand Fleet was at sea in strength.

At 0100 on 31st May, therefore, the first ships of Hipper's force—five battle-cruisers of the 1st Scouting Group (*Lützow* (flagship), *Derfflinger, Seydlitz, Moltke, Von der Tann*), four light cruisers of the 2nd Scouting Group, and 33 destroyers led by another light cruiser—weighed anchor and steered north past Heligoland and through the swept channels, leaving the Horn Reef light vessel to the eastward of them. They were followed, fifty miles astern, by Scheer, his flag in the *Friedrich der Grosse*, leading 16 dreadnought battleships, 6 predreadnoughts, and accompanied by 5 light cruisers of the 4th Scouting Group and 39 destroyers led by a light cruiser.

By 1400 Hipper was abreast the Jutland Bank off the Danish coast—his scouting light cruisers spread on an arc extending

HMS *Agincourt* (foreground) with HMS *Erin* beyond her. The *Agincourt* carried the largest number of heavy guns mounted on any one capital ship: 14 12-inch guns in seven centreline turrets. The *Erin* was armed with ten 13.5-inch guns in five turrets. Both ships were originally ordered by foreign buyers (the *Erin* by Turkey and the *Agincourt* by Brazil) but taken over by Britain at the beginning of the war

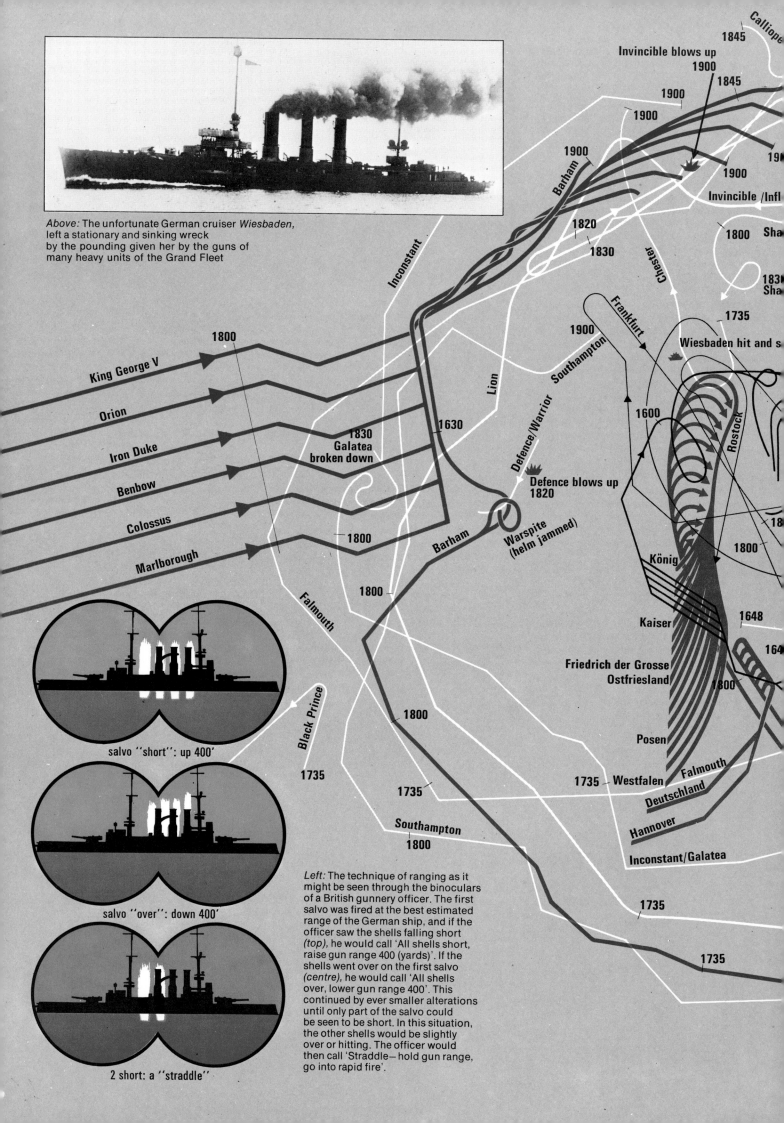

Above: The unfortunate German cruiser *Wiesbaden*, left a stationary and sinking wreck by the pounding given her by the guns of many heavy units of the Grand Fleet

Calliope

Invincible blows up
1900

1845

1845

1900

1900

1900

1900

Barham

1900

Invincible /Infl

1820

1800

Sha

1830

Chester

183
Sha

1800

1735

Frankfurt

1900

Southampton

Wiesbaden hit and s

King George V

Orion

Iron Duke

Benbow

Colossus

Marlborough

1800

Inconstant

1600

Rostock

1830
Galatea
broken down

1630

Lion

Defence/Warrior

1800

1648

König

Kaiser

1800

164

1800

Defence blows up
1820

Warspite
(helm jammed)

Barham

Falmouth

1800

Friedrich der Grosse
Ostfriesland

1800

salvo "short": up 400'

Black Prince

1735

1800

Posen

1735

1735 — Westfalen

Falmouth

salvo "over": down 400'

1735

Deutschland

Southampton
1800

Hannover

Inconstant/Galatea

Left: The technique of ranging as it might be seen through the binoculars of a British gunnery officer. The first salvo was fired at the best estimated range of the German ship, and if the officer saw the shells falling short *(top)*, he would call 'All shells short, raise gun range 400 (yards)'. If the shells went over on the first salvo *(centre)*, he would call 'All shells over, lower gun range 400'. This continued by ever smaller alterations until only part of the salvo could be seen to be short. In this situation, the other shells would be slightly over or hitting. The officer would then call 'Straddle—hold gun range, go into rapid fire'.

1735

1735

2 short: a "straddle"

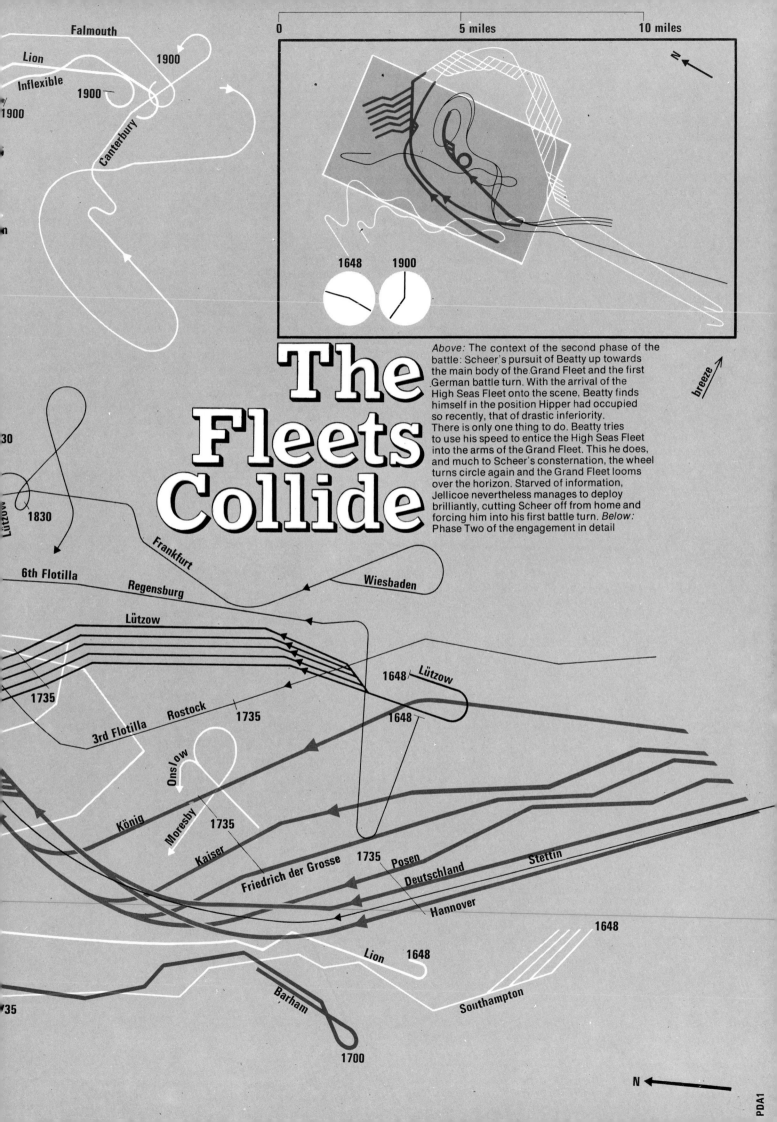

Falmouth
Lion
Inflexible
1900
1900
1900
Canterbury

0   5 miles   10 miles

N

1648   1900

breeze

The Fleets Collide

Above: The context of the second phase of the battle: Scheer's pursuit of Beatty up towards the main body of the Grand Fleet and the first German battle turn. With the arrival of the High Seas Fleet onto the scene, Beatty finds himself in the position Hipper had occupied so recently, that of drastic inferiority. There is only one thing to do. Beatty tries to use his speed to entice the High Seas Fleet into the arms of the Grand Fleet. This he does, and much to Scheer's consternation, the wheel turns circle again and the Grand Fleet looms over the horizon. Starved of information, Jellicoe nevertheless manages to deploy brilliantly, cutting Scheer off from home and forcing him into his first battle turn. *Below:* Phase Two of the engagement in detail

30

Lützow

1830

6th Flotilla

Frankfurt

Regensburg

Wiesbaden

Lützow

1735

3rd Flotilla   Rostock   1735

1648   Lützow

1648

Onslow

König

Moresby

Kaiser

1735

Friedrich der Grosse

1735   Posen   Deutschland   Stettin

Hannover

1648

Lion   1648

Barham

Southampton

35

1700

N

PDA1

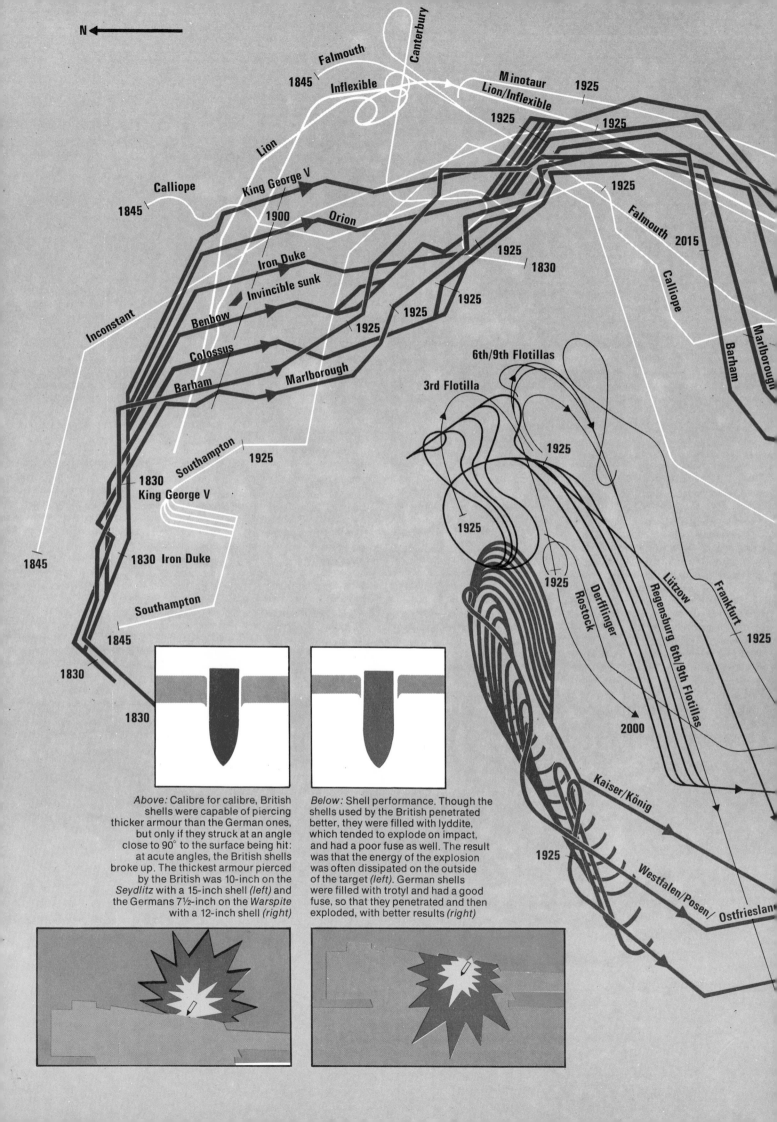

N ←

1845
Falmouth
Inflexible
Canterbury
Minotaur
Lion/Inflexible
1925
1925
1925
1925
1925
Lion
Calliope
1845
King George V
1900
Orion
Falmouth
2015
Iron Duke
1925
1830
Calliope
Invincible sunk
1925
Inconstant
Benbow
1925
Barham
Colossus
Marlborough
Marlborough
Barham
6th/9th Flotillas
3rd Flotilla
1925
Southampton
1925
1925
1830
King George V
1925
Derfflinger
Rostock
Lützow
Regensburg 6th/9th Flotillas
Frankfurt
1830 Iron Duke
1925
Southampton
1845
2000
1830
Kaiser/König
1830
1925
Westfalen/Posen/
Ostfriesland

Above: Calibre for calibre, British shells were capable of piercing thicker armour than the German ones, but only if they struck at an angle close to 90° to the surface being hit: at acute angles, the British shells broke up. The thickest armour pierced by the British was 10-inch on the *Seydlitz* with a 15-inch shell *(left)* and the Germans 7½-inch on the *Warspite* with a 12-inch shell *(right)*

Below: Shell performance. Though the shells used by the British penetrated better, they were filled with lyddite, which tended to explode on impact, and had a poor fuse as well. The result was that the energy of the explosion was often dissipated on the outside of the target *(left)*. German shells were filled with trotyl and had a good fuse, so that they penetrated and then exploded, with better results *(right)*

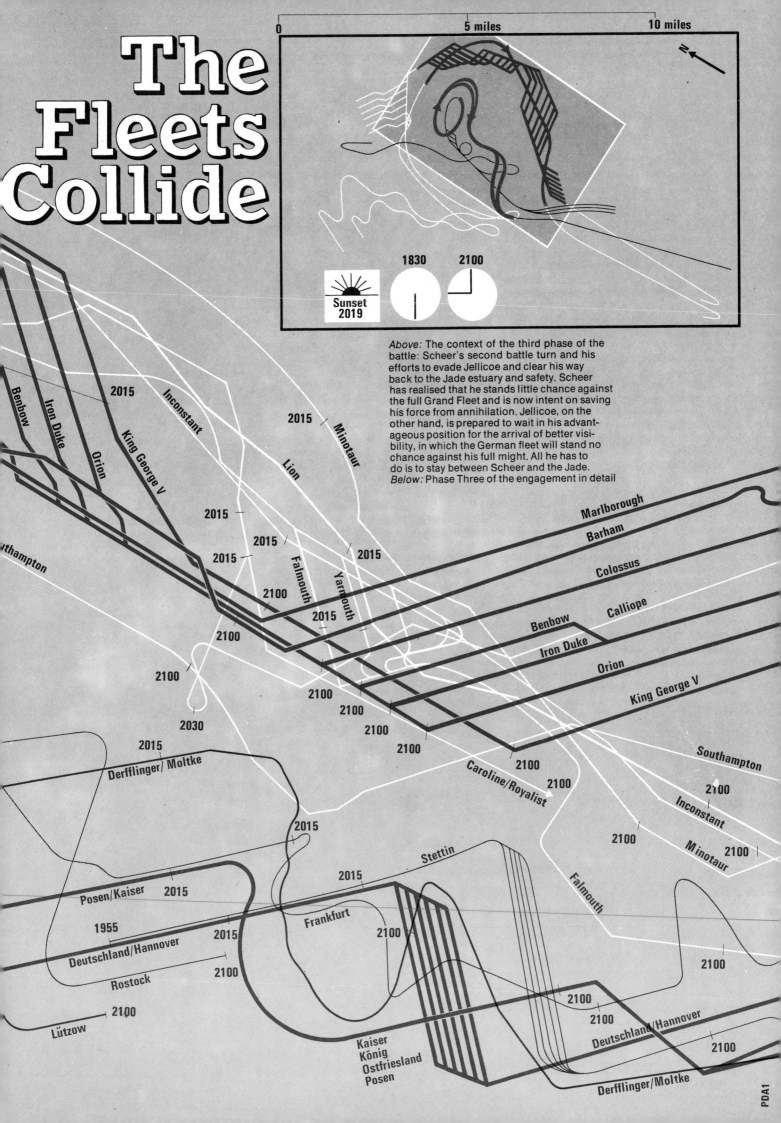

The Fleets Collide

0   5 miles   10 miles

1830   2100

Sunset 2019

Above: The context of the third phase of the
battle: Scheer's second battle turn and his
efforts to evade Jellicoe and clear his way
back to the Jade estuary and safety. Scheer
has realised that he stands little chance against
the full Grand Fleet and is now intent on saving
his force from annihilation. Jellicoe, on the
other hand, is prepared to wait in his advantageous position for the arrival of better visibility, in which the German fleet will stand no
chance against his full might. All he has to
do is to stay between Scheer and the Jade.
Below: Phase Three of the engagement in detail

Benbow
Iron Duke
Orion
King George V
Inconstant
2015
2015
Lion
Minotaur
Southampton
2015
2015
Falmouth
2015
Yarmouth
2015
2100
2015
2100
2100
2100
2030
2015
Derfflinger/Moltke
2015
2100
2100
2100
2100

Marlborough
Barham
Colossus
Calliope
Benbow
Iron Duke
Orion
King George V
Southampton
Inconstant
2100
2100
Minotaur
2100
Caroline/Royalist
2100
Falmouth
2100

2015
Posen/Kaiser   2015
1955
Deutschland/Hannover   2015
Rostock   2100
2100
Lützow

Stettin
2015
Frankfurt
2100

Kaiser
König
Ostfriesland
Posen

2100
2100
Deutschland/Hannover
2100
Derfflinger/Moltke

PDA1

from ahead to either beam, some seven to ten miles from the battle-cruisers. It was a clear, calm, summer day with visibility extreme but likely to become hazy as the afternoon wore on. Unknown to Hipper and equally ignorant of his presence, Beatty was fifty miles to the north-westward, zig-zagging at 19 knots on a mean course of east and approaching the eastward limit set for his advance, with his light cruisers scouting ahead in pairs. The signal to turn north was made at 1415 and was obeyed by all except the light cruiser *Galatea* which held on to investigate smoke on the eastern horizon. This came from a Danish merchantman and was simultaneously being investigated by the western-most of Hipper's light cruisers, the *Elbing*. The two warships thus came in sight of one another, reported, and fired the opening shots of the battle of Jutland.

The two battle-cruiser admirals turned at once towards the sound of the guns which soon brought them in sight of one another on opposite courses, when Hipper altered course to the southward to lead his opponents towards the advancing German battle squadrons. That these were at sea was still unknown to either Beatty or Jellicoe. The British radio monitoring stations had been led to believe that the High Seas Fleet was still in harbour, misled by an arrangement on the part of

Beatty's flagship, HMS *Lion,* in action at Jutland after her 'Q' turret had been destroyed by cordite flash after a hit by a heavy shell fired by the *Lutzow*

Scheer's staff which transferred the flag-ship's call-sign to a shore station so that the commander-in-chief would not be distracted by administrative matters.

The battle-cruisers open fire

The *Lion,* leading *Princess Royal, Queen Mary, Tiger, New Zealand* and *Indefatigable* (in that order), turned on a parallel course and at 1548 each side opened fire. Hipper was outnumbered, six ships to five. He would have been even more, perhaps disastrously, inferior, but for Beatty's impetuosity in racing at full speed into action without waiting for the 5th Battle Squadron, which was not only initially six miles farther from the enemy but, owing to signal confusion, failed to conform at once to Beatty's movements. By the time it did so, it was ten miles astern, and it was not until twenty-seven minutes after action had been joined that the 15-inch guns of the British battleships could open fire.

In the interval much had happened. Hipper's ships had quickly displayed a gunnery superiority over their opponents who were very slow to find the range. The *Lion, Princess Royal,* and *Tiger* had all been heavily hit before a single German ship had suffered; though the *Seydlitz, Derfflinger,* and *Lützow* were then each hit hard, the advantage had continued to lie with Hipper's ships and at 1600 Beatty's rear ship, *Indefatigable,* had blown up and sunk as shells plunged through into her magazines. Almost simultaneously the *Lion* had been only saved from a similar fate by flooding the magazine of her mid-ship

turret when it was penetrated by a shell from the *Lützow.*

But now, at last, the 5th Battle Squadron (*Barham, Valiant, Warspite, Malaya,* lying in that order) was able to get into action. Their gunnery was magnificent. The two rear ships of Hipper's line were quickly hit. Disaster must have overwhelmed him but for a defect of the British shells, some of which broke up on impact instead of penetrating the armour. Nevertheless, it seemed impossible Hipper could survive long enough for Scheer's battle-squadrons, still over the horizon, to come to his rescue. In spite of this the German battle-cruisers continued to shoot with deadly accuracy and at 1626 the *Queen Mary,* betrayed, like the *Indefatigable,* by her inadequate armour, blew up.

Meanwhile, a destroyer battle had been raging between the lines, the flotillas on each side moving out to attack with torpedoes and meeting to fight it out with guns. Of all the torpedoes fired, one only, from the British *Petard,* found a billet in the *Seydlitz,* but did not damage her enough to put her out of action. Two British destroyers were sunk.

The fast-moving battle had left the majority of Beatty's scouting cruisers behind, except for Commodore Goodenough's 2nd Light Cruiser Squadron which by 1633 had succeeded in getting two miles ahead of the *Lion.* At that moment to Goodenough's astonished gaze the top masts of a long line of battleships hove in sight. In the radio rooms of the ships of the British fleet, the message, which all had

almost despaired of ever hearing, was taken in: 'Have sighted enemy battle fleet, bearing SE. Enemy's course North.'

Hipper had been saved in the nick of time, and his task of luring Beatty brilliantly achieved. Goodenough's timely warning, however, enabled the latter to escape the trap. Before the enemy battle fleet came within range, Beatty reversed course to the northward. The 5th Battle Squadron held on for a while to cover the damaged battle-cruisers' retreat. By the time they turned back themselves they came under heavy fire from the German battle squadrons and *Malaya*, in particular, received damaging hits. In reply they did heavy damage to the *Lützow, Derfflinger,* and *Seydlitz,* as well as hitting the leading German battleships.

The situation had now been reversed, with Beatty drawing the enemy after him towards a superior force the latter knew nothing of — the Grand Fleet, pressing southwards at its best speed of 20 knots. Jellicoe's twenty-four battleships were in the compact cruising formation of six columns abeam of each other, with the fleet flagship leading the more easterly of the two centre columns. Before encountering the enemy they would have to be deployed into a single battle line to allow all ships to bring their guns to bear. If deployment was delayed too long, the consequences could be disastrous. To make a deployment by the right method, it was essential that the admiral should know the bearing on which the approaching enemy would appear.

For various reasons — discrepancy between the calculated positions of the two portions of the fleet and communication failures — this was just what Jellicoe did not know. And, meanwhile, the two fleets were racing towards each other at a combined speed of nearly 40 knots. Even though Beatty's light cruisers had made visual contact with Jellicoe's advanced screen of armoured cruisers at 1630, though the thunder of distant gun-fire had been audible for some time before the *Marlborough*, leading the starboard column of the Grand Fleet battleships, sighted gun-flashes through the gathering haze and funnel smoke ahead at 1750, and six minutes later Beatty's battle-cruisers were sighted from the *Iron Duke* racing across the line of Jellicoe's advance — and incidentally spreading a further pall of black smoke — it was not until nearly 1815 that at last, in the nick of time, the vital piece of information reached the commander-in-chief from the *Lion:* 'Enemy battle fleet bearing south-west.'

Jellicoe's vital decision

During the next minute or so, through the mind of Jellicoe as he stood gazing at the compass in its binnacle on the bridge of the *Iron Duke,* sped the many considerations on the accurate interpretation of which, at this moment of supreme crisis, the correct deployment and all chances of victory depended. The decision Jellicoe made — to deploy on his port wing column on a course south-east by east — has been damned and lauded by opposing critics in

the controversy that was later to develop.

To the appalled Scheer, as out of the smoke and haze ahead of him, between him and retreat to his base, loomed an interminable line of dim grey shapes from which rippled the flash of heavy gunfire, and a storm of shell splashes began to fall round the leading ships of his line, there was no doubt. His 'T' had been crossed — the worst situation possible in a fleet action. Fortunately for him a counter to such a calamity, a simultaneous 'about turn' by every ship of the battle columns — a manoeuvre not lightly undertaken by a mass of the unwieldy battleships of the day — had been practised and perfected by the High Seas Fleet. He ordered it now, and so, behind a smoke screen laid by his destroyers extricated himself from the trap so brilliantly sprung by Jellicoe.

His escape was only temporary, nevertheless. Between him and his base was a force whose full strength he had been unable as yet to determine, which he must either fight or somehow evade.

While the trap was thus being sprung on Scheer, some final spectacular successes had been achieved by the Germans. Of the 5th Battle Squadron, the *Warspite,* with her helm jammed, had charged towards Scheer's battle line and before she could be got under control again, had been severely damaged and forced out of action. Jellicoe's advanced screen of armoured cruisers had been caught at short range by Hipper's battle-cruisers and the leading German battleships as they emerged from the smoke haze. The *Defence* had been

overwhelmed and blown up, the *Warrior* so heavily damaged that she staggered out of action to sink on her way back to harbour. Then the German battle-cruisers had encountered the three battle-cruisers attached to the Grand Fleet. In a brief gun duel at short range, the Germans had suffered many hits and further damage; but in reply had sunk the *Invincible* whose magazine was penetrated in the same way as in the *Indefatigable* and *Queen Mary*.

This was the last major success for the Germans, however. They had fought magnificently and, with the aid of superior ship design and ammunition, had had much the better of the exchanges, though the *Lützow* was by now fatally crippled, limping painfully off the scene, and only the stout construction and well-designed compartmentation of the other battle-cruisers was saving them from a similar state. But Scheer was now desperately on the defensive, though he had not yet realized that it was the whole Grand Fleet he had encountered. As soon as his initial retreat brought relief from the concentration of fire on his van, he reversed course once again in the hope of being able to cut through astern of the enemy to gain a clear escape route to the Horn Reef lightship and safety behind his own minefields. Once again he ran up against the immense line of dreadnoughts of which all he could see in the poor visibility to the eastward was the flickering orange light of their broadsides. Once again he had hastily to retire or be annihilated.

While he was extricating himself he launched his much-tried battle-cruisers on a rearguard thrust and his destroyer flotillas to deliver a massed torpedo attack. The former miraculously survived a further hammering before being recalled. The latter launched a total of twenty-eight torpedoes at the British line. More than any

SMS *König*, one of the German dreadnoughts, opens fire. Her broad beam, which all the newer German ships possessed, gave her a much steadier firing platform than the narrower British ships

other single factor they were to save the High Seas Fleet from disaster, robbing Jellicoe of the fruits of the strategic masterpiece he had brought about.

The counter to the massed torpedo attack by destroyers, which could be backed by long-range torpedo fire from retreating battleships, had been carefully studied. There were several alternatives; the only one sufficiently effective in Jellicoe's opinion, was a simultaneous turn away by his own battle line. This was promptly carried out – a turn of 45 degrees.

Contact lost

The two battle fleets were now on widely diverging courses and rapidly ran out of range and sight of one another. By the time the twenty-eight torpedoes had been avoided – not one scored a hit – and the British battle line turned back to regain contact, more than fifteen miles separated Jellicoe and Scheer. Sunset was barely half an hour away. Yet there was time in the long summer twilight ahead for the battle to be renewed on greatly advantageous terms for Jellicoe if he turned at once to an interception course. That he did not do so until too late for various reasons, not the least of which was the failure of his scouting forces to keep him informed of the enemy's position and movements, was to be the central feature of much criticism.

The van of the German battle fleet came, in fact, briefly into view from the nearest British battleship division at the moment that Jellicoe, who was not willing to accept the uncertain fortunes of a night action, ordered a turn away and the adoption of a compact night cruising disposition. The opportunity was let slip, never to return.

Nevertheless, at this stage, as night settled down over a calm sea, the outlook for Scheer was bleak, indeed. Between him and his base was an overwhelming enemy force. Unless he could get past it during the night, the battle must be resumed at daybreak and, with a long summer day ahead, it could only spell annihilation for him. He decided his only hope was to try

to bludgeon his way through, regardless of consequences. To his fleet he signalled the course for the Horn Reef Light at a speed of 16 knots, adding the instruction that this course was to be maintained at all costs.

Jellicoe, having formed his night disposition and ordered his flotillas (many of whom had not yet been in action) to the rear, was steering a course slightly converging with that of Scheer but at a knot faster. From Jellicoe's point of view, Scheer had the choice of two routes – to the entrance of the channels which began at the Horn Reef Light or southward into the German Bight before turning eastward round the mined areas. The extra knot would keep the Grand Fleet between Scheer and the latter. If he chose the former he must pass astern of Jellicoe's battle squadrons, where he would encounter the massed British flotillas which could be counted on to inflict severe losses and to keep Jellicoe informed.

In the event the British flotillas failed to do either of these things. The pre-dreadnought battleship *Pommern* and a light cruiser were their sole victims in a series of night encounters, and they passed no information of the position and course of the enemy. On the other hand Scheer's message to his fleet was intercepted by the Admiralty and was passed to Jellicoe, though a further message in which Scheer asked for airship reconnaissance of the Horn Reef area at dawn which would have clinched the matter, was withheld.

In the absence of certain knowledge of the enemy's movements, Jellicoe held on through the night. Scheer crossed astern of him and by daylight was safe, a development which seemed little short of miraculous to the German admiral.

The battle of Jutland was over. Controversy as to its outcome was to rage for decades. The bald facts, of which German publicity made the most in claiming a great victory, while the British Admiralty's communiqué did nothing to explain or qualify them, showed that a superior British force had lost three capital ships,

three cruisers, and a number of destroyers against one battle-cruiser, a pre-dreadnought battleship, four cruisers, and some destroyers sunk on the German side.

Even to-day more than fifty years since the battle, it is not easy to strike a balance sheet of victory and defeat. British losses were largely the result of inferior armour protection in their battle-cruisers, which had been accepted in favour of mounting bigger guns, the advantage of which had been lost through faulty design of armour-piercing shells. Even so, one of the surviving German battle-cruisers only reached harbour in a sinking condition, another was a hideous shambles with 200 casualties, bearing witness to the pounding they had received even from defective shells.

The High Seas Fleet was no longer fit for battle on the morning of the 1st June 1916 and could only make for harbour and repairs, fortunately close at hand. The Grand Fleet was largely intact and ready to renew the fight. Jellicoe may be said, perhaps, to have lost the battle of Jutland. Scheer can hardly be judged to have won anything but an escape from annihilation.

So much for the immediate results of the encounter. They do not add up to a victory for either side. In the larger context of the war at sea as a whole, it is no easier to weigh the results. When Scheer led the High Seas Fleet out once again in August 1916 (except for *Seydlitz* and *Derfflinger*, still under repair), he narrowly escaped being caught in a second Jutland trap, with no safe base under his lee this time, in spite of Zeppelin reconnaissance aloft. Both Scheer and the Kaiser's general headquarters were finally convinced that the risks to be faced in attempting to bring about a sea fight were unacceptable. The High Seas Fleet, built at such cost to challenge Great Britain's seapower, was ordered back on to the defensive. The fatal decision was taken to revert to the unrestricted submarine warfare which was to bring America into the war.

It is true, of course, that the High Seas Fleet kept 'in being', forced the continued maintenance of the huge Grand Fleet, absorbing many thousands of trained seamen and a hundred destroyers which could have been more profitably employed combating the U-boats. On the other hand, that same High Seas Fleet, its ships lying idle in harbour, the morale of its crews sinking, degenerated into a centre of discontent and revolution. In August 1917 Scheer had to quell an open mutiny. A year later, when ordered to sea by its new commander, Hipper, it flared into revolt and led the disintegration of the Kaiser's Germany. This, too, can be accounted one of the consequences of Jutland—perhaps the most important when reviewing the whole war.

German View

Jutland was the last of many naval battles fought by long lines of closely spaced big ships with heavy guns. Its tactical details are well-known, for each ship kept a log. Its results were inconclusive. It was the climax of the Anglo-German naval rivalry, with the scuttling of the German fleet at Scapa Flow three years later as the anticlimax.

This rivalry, which cost both nations dearly, was at least partly caused by the fact that the Germans did not fully realize the implications of seapower. In their difficult position in central Europe they needed a navy of some strength to balance the fleets of the Franco-Russian alliance. But from their inferior strategic position in the south-eastern corner of the North Sea they could neither protect their overseas trade nor attack the sea routes vital to Great Britain. When war broke out in 1914 the Royal Navy was not compelled to attack the German bases but could content itself on the whole with a distant blockade from Scapa Flow.

In the first two years of the war there were a number of operations and clashes in the North Sea which did not change the situation, since neither side wanted to give battle too far from their own bases. In 1916 this changed to some extent. Admiral Reinhard Scheer, the new commander-in-chief of the German High Seas Fleet, was more aggressive than his predecessors. On the Allied side, the Russians felt the blockade heavily and clamoured for the British to force the Baltic so that they might receive ammunition and raw materials which they needed desperately. An operation of that kind had no prospects of success, however, as long as the High Seas Fleet was intact. Therefore it was decided that stronger efforts should be made to bring it to battle. The Grand Fleet under Admiral Sir John Jellicoe had been considerably reinforced by new ships. In spring 1916 it was almost twice as strong as the German fleet.

Early in March, the German fleet made a sortie into the southern North Sea and came within sixty miles of Lowestoft. On 25th March British light forces operated south of Horn Reef, and aircraft from a seaplane-carrier tried to bombard airship sheds. Bad weather prevented contact of the heavy ships. On 25th April German battle-cruisers bombarded Lowestoft. Early in May the British repeated the attempt to attack airship sheds. Both fleets were at sea, but no contact was established.

For the second half of May, Admiral Scheer planned an operation with all his forces. The battle-cruisers were to bombard Sunderland, and twelve submarines were stationed off the British bases to attack the squadrons of the Grand Fleet when they put to sea. Scouting by airships was necessary for the German fleet to avoid being cut off by superior forces. When the time ran out for his submarines after two weeks at sea and the weather remained unfavourable, Scheer compromised on a sweep of his light forces through the Skagerrak backed up by the battle fleet. Shortly after midnight of 30th to 31st May 1916 the German scouting forces (5 battle-cruisers, 5 light cruisers, and 30 destroyers under Rear-Admiral Hipper) left Schillig Roads near Wilhelmshaven, soon followed by the battle fleet (16 new and 6 old battleships, 6 light cruisers, and 33 destroyers).

The Grand Fleet at sea
At that time the Grand Fleet was already at sea, course set for the Skagerrak, too. The bombardment of Lowestoft had roused

public opinion, the situation of the Russians had deteriorated, and Jellicoe now planned to set a trap for the German fleet. Light cruisers were to sweep through the Skagerrak deep into the Kattegat; in the meantime the main forces would take up position near Horn Reef to meet the Germans who were sure to come out in order to intercept the British cruisers operating in the Kattegat.

In the early afternoon of 31st May occurred the first of the incidents which greatly changed the course of the events. The British battle-cruiser fleet, under Vice-Admiral Sir David Beatty in *Lion*, changed course from east to west to rendezvous with the battle fleet under Admiral Jellicoe in *Iron Duke*. At 1430 *Lützow*, flying Admiral Hipper's flag, was only forty-five miles east of *Lion* steering a slightly converging course. Contact would have been made considerably later but for a small Danish steamer plodding along between the two forces. Two German destroyers and a British light cruiser were dispatched to examine her. Soon the first salvoes were fired; the first hit (a dud) was made by *Elbing* on *Galatea*.

Within minutes wireless messages informed the admirals of the situation. Signals went up, Hipper swung his force round, and Beatty soon followed suit. The crews were alerted by bugles sounding action stations, guns and powder rooms were manned, steam was raised in reserve boilers, and damage parties assembled deep down in the ships. The gunnery officers climbed to their elevated positions, received ready reports from turrets, range-finders, and fire-control-stations, and then reported their batteries ready for action to their captains. Now a hush of expectancy fell over the great ships while the distance decreased by nearly a mile a minute.

At first, sight was obscured by the smoke of the cruisers. Then these fell back on their battle-cruisers, and the huge shapes of the adversaries came into each other's sight, but only for the few men whose duty was to watch the enemy. Almost all the technical personnel and most of the sailors fought without seeing an enemy ship.

Hipper faced heavy odds, ten ships with heavier guns against his five. His plan was simple: to draw the enemy to Scheer's battle fleet, which was following at a distance of fifty miles. His smaller calibres (11- and 12-inch as against 12-, 13-, and 15-inch in the British ships) made it imperative for him to get comparatively close before opening fire. He offered battle on a north-westerly course, reversed course when Beatty tried to cut his force off, and with a few terse signals coolly manoeuvred his fine ships through the danger zone. At 1548 they were at the right distance (16,500 yards) and in perfect order. The *Lützow* opened fire.

Beatty's ships started answering quickly but they were not yet in formation to use all their guns. Because of delays in signalling, the four powerful and fast battleships of the Queen Elizabeth-class had fallen astern and were out of range. Conditions for a gunnery duel were perfect: visibility was good, especially to the west, and there was hardly any seaway.

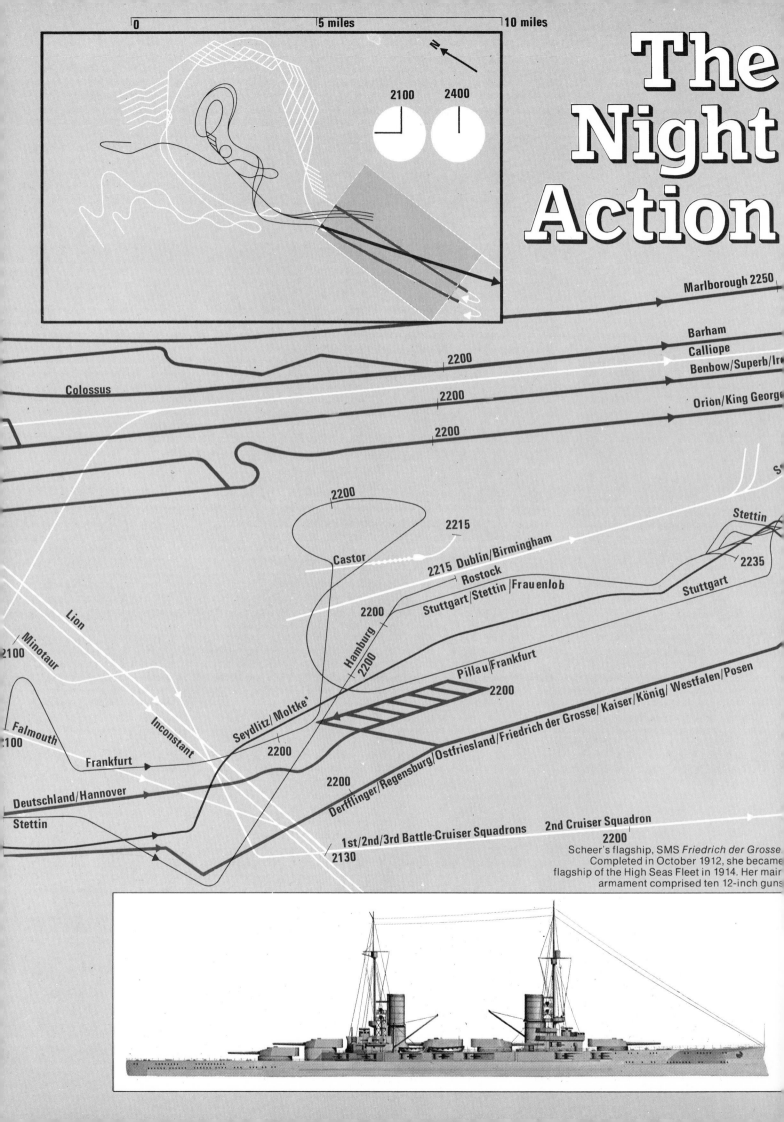

0   5 miles   10 miles

2100   2400

The Night Action

Marlborough 2250

Barham
Calliope
Benbow/Superb/Ir

Colossus

2200

2200

Orion/King George

2200

S

2200

2215

Stettin

Castor   2215 Dublin/Birmingham

2235

Rostock

Stuttgart/Stettin/Frauenlob   Stuttgart

Lion

2200

Minotaur

Hamburg

2100

2200

Pillau/Frankfurt

2200

Seydlitz/Moltke'

Falmouth

2100

Inconstant

2200

Frankfurt

Derfflinger/Regensburg/Ostfriesland/Friedrich der Grosse/Kaiser/König/Westfalen/Posen

Deutschland/Hannover

2200

Stettin

1st/2nd/3rd Battle-Cruiser Squadrons   2nd Cruiser Squadron

2130

2200

Scheer's flagship, SMS *Friedrich der Grosse*.
Completed in October 1912, she became
flagship of the High Seas Fleet in 1914. Her main
armament comprised ten 12-inch guns

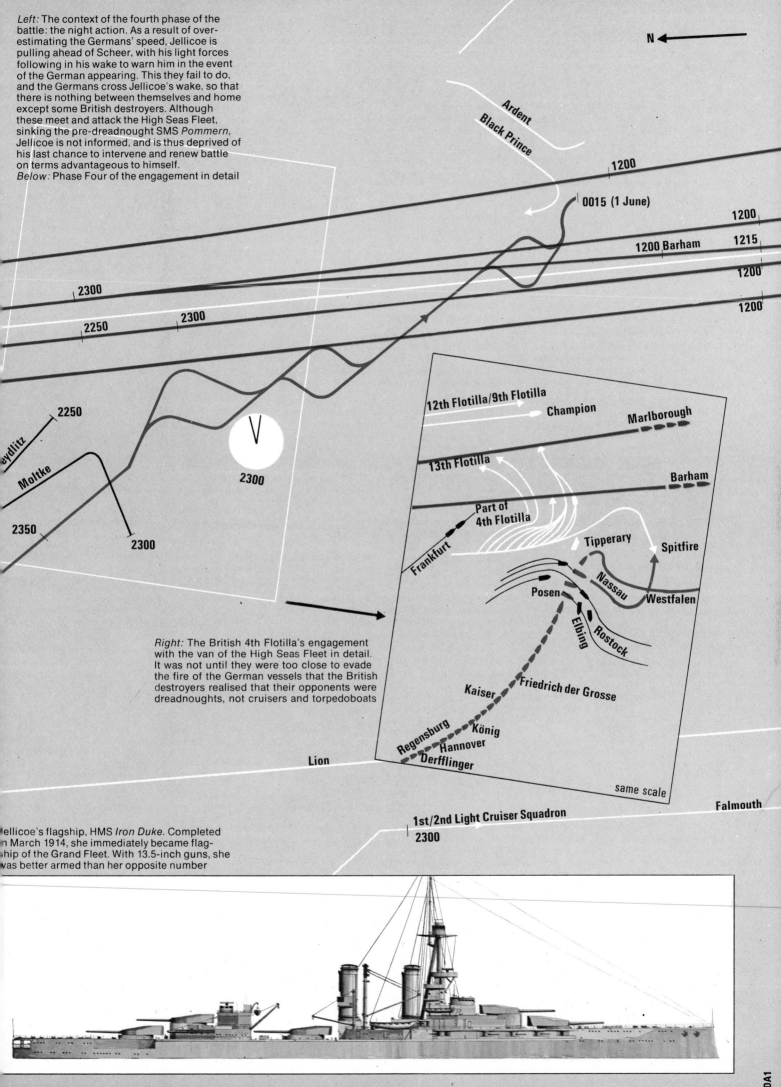

Left: The context of the fourth phase of the battle: the night action. As a result of over-estimating the Germans' speed, Jellicoe is pulling ahead of Scheer, with his light forces following in his wake to warn him in the event of the German appearing. This they fail to do, and the Germans cross Jellicoe's wake, so that there is nothing between themselves and home except some British destroyers. Although these meet and attack the High Seas Fleet, sinking the pre-dreadnought SMS *Pommern*, Jellicoe is not informed, and is thus deprived of his last chance to intervene and renew battle on terms advantageous to himself.
Below: Phase Four of the engagement in detail

N

Ardent

Black Prince

1200

0015 (1 June)

1200

1200 Barham   1215

1200

2300

1200

2250   2300

eydlitz   2250

Moltke

2300

2350

2300

V

2300

12th Flotilla/9th Flotilla   Champion   Marlborough

13th Flotilla   Barham

Part of
4th Flotilla   Tipperary   Spitfire

Frankfurt   Nassau

Posen   Westfalen

Elbing   Rostock

Right: The British 4th Flotilla's engagement with the van of the High Seas Fleet in detail. It was not until they were too close to evade the fire of the German vessels that the British destroyers realised that their opponents were dreadnoughts, not cruisers and torpedoboats

Friedrich der Grosse

Kaiser

Regensburg   König

Hannover

Derfflinger

same scale

Lion

Falmouth

Jellicoe's flagship, HMS *Iron Duke.* Completed in March 1914, she immediately became flag-ship of the Grand Fleet. With 13.5-inch guns, she was better armed than her opposite number

1st/2nd Light Cruiser Squadron

2300

First blood to the Germans

The first salvoes all appear to have fallen wide, perhaps because the range-takers were more interested in the details of their foes than in measuring the distance exactly. After three minutes the Germans obtained hits on *Lion*, *Princess Royal*, and *Tiger*. Because the first target in sight had been light cruisers, the gunnery officer of *Lützow* had given orders to load shells detonating on impact. For reasons of ballistics he did not change over to armour-piercing shells. *Lion* was hit twelve times and suffered heavy casualties, but minor injuries only, except for one shell which penetrated the roof of a turret, killed the gun crews, and ignited powder-bags. The turret-commander, Major Harvey of the Royal Marines, was fatally wounded but before he died he ordered the magazines to be flooded and thus saved the ship.

Now disaster struck the rear of the British line. Here *Indefatigable* and *Von der Tann* fought an even match. At 1604, *Indefatigable,* hit by two salvoes in quick succession, erupted in a violent explosion, turned over to port and disappeared in the waves. *Von der Tann* had fired fifty-two 11-inch shells in all. Twenty minutes later a similar fate overtook *Queen Mary* who had come under the concentrated fire of *Derfflinger* and *Seydlitz*. After vehement detonations she capsized and went down with her propellers still turning. *Tiger,* the next astern, barely avoided crashing into the wreck.

In spite of these losses the situation now eased for the British. The magnificent 5th Battle Squadron, ably handled by Rear-Admiral Evan-Thomas, came up and took the rear ships of the German line under fire. When one of the projectiles, weighing almost a ton, struck *Von der Tann* far aft, the whole ship vibrated like a gigantic tuning-fork. Hipper increased speed and distance and sent his destroyers to the attack. They were met by British destroyers, and in the ensuing mêlée

Nomad and two Germans were sunk. At the same time 1630 the 2nd Light Cruiser Squadron under Commodore Goodenough sighted smoke to the south-east and, soon after, a seemingly endless column of heavy ships surrounded by light cruisers and destroyers.

Now the tables were turned. Under heavy fire Beatty reversed course and steered to the north to draw the High Seas Fleet to the British Battle Fleet. *Barham* and *Malaya* received several hits which did not, however, impair their speed, but, *Nestor,* attacking the German van with some other destroyers, was sunk. When her boatswain was rescued with other survivors he was mainly disgusted at the smallness and squalor of the coal-burning torpedo-boat which had picked him up.

All through these events the British Battle Fleet had been steadily drawing nearer, in cruising formation with its twenty-four battleships in six divisions, these in line abreast, screened by armoured and light cruisers and destroyers. The 3rd Battle-Cruiser Squadron, under Rear-Admiral Hood in *Invincible*, was twenty-five miles ahead and far to the east of its calculated position. Jellicoe, 'the only man who could lose the war in an afternoon', was now faced with the decision on which course to form his divisions into single line ahead. In all war games and exercises the rule had been 'towards Heligoland'. Yet the reports he received were incomplete and contradictory, it was impossible to get a clear picture of the situation. At the last moment, when Beatty's battle-cruisers came in sight, Jellicoe ordered his division to turn together to port to the north-east. In this way he gained a favourable position for crossing the enemy's T. He was unintentionally assisted by the 3rd Battle-Cruiser Squadron, which almost missed the Germans, but now closed in from the east and brought the German van between two fires. The light cruiser *Wiesbaden* soon lay dead in the water. For

hours the battle raged around her, she was fired upon by many British ships, but did not sink until 0200 on 1st June. Only one survivor was picked up.

The delay in forming the line of battle put part of the screen and the 5th Battle Squadron in a difficult situation at what was later called 'Windy Corner'. Making room for Beatty's battle-cruisers to go to the van of the line, some armoured cruisers came into range of the German battleships. *Defence* blew up in view of both fleets; *Warrior* was saved a similar fate by the chance intervention of *Warspite*. The 5th Battle Squadron was forced to countermarch and came under the fire of several battleships. After a hit *Warspite*'s rudder jammed; she turned towards the German line, thus masking *Warrior,* who was able to creep away, but sank on the next morning. *Warspite* almost collided with *Valiant* and made two full circles at high speed before her rudder was in working order again. Heavily damaged she was ordered home and reached Rosyth after evading the attack of a German submarine.

Visibility was now generally decreasing and greatly varying as a result of masses of funnel and artificial smoke. For the commanders-in-chief it was most difficult to gain a reliable picture of the actual situation from their own limited observations (radar was not yet invented) and the reports of their subordinates. For a few moments Scheer toyed with the idea of splitting his line to take Windy Corner under two fires. However, there was no battle signal for this promising but unusual procedure, his van was evidently hard pressed, and so he continued with his battleships in line ahead. With the loss of the destroyer *Shark* the 3rd Battle-Cruiser Squadron had inflicted heavy damage on the Germans and now took up station at the head of the British line followed by Beatty's battle-cruisers.

For more than half an hour the German ships could see no more than the flashes of

The might of the Royal Navy concentrated in the North Sea: seemingly interminable lines of dreadnoughts and super-dreadnoughts

the enemy guns. Then at 1830 visibility suddenly improved, *Lützow* and *Derfflinger* sighted *Invincible*, the leading ship, at a distance of 9,500 yards and sank her in a few minutes. There were only six survivors, among them the gunnery officer who, as he said, 'merely stepped from the foretop into the water'.

At that time Scheer ordered a battle turn reversing course to get his ships out of the overwhelming enemy fire. Beginning from the rear the heavy ships had to turn to starboard in quick succession until single line ahead was formed on the opposite course. Light cruiser squadrons and destroyer flotillas had to conform. This manoeuvre was all the more difficult because the fleet was now disposed almost in a semi-circle, but it was successful, supported by a destroyer attack on the centre of the British line. The fleets drew apart, and the fire slackened and then ceased altogether. A German destroyer was crippled and sank later, and the battleship *Marlborough* received a torpedo-hit which reduced her speed.

The German fleet now steamed to the west south-west, and the British fleet slowly hauled round to the south. With its higher speed it had a good chance of cutting off the Germans from their bases. Scheer sensed this even though contact had been lost completely. Therefore he ordered another battle turn to the old course with the express intention to deal the enemy a heavy blow, to surprise and confuse him, to bring the destroyers to the attack, to facilitate disengaging for the night, and, if possible, to rescue the crew of the *Wiesbaden*. The execution of this plan has been criticized but there is no doubt that Scheer succeeded in getting his fleet out of a difficult situation although his van suffered heavily.

The German thrust was directed against the British centre. The attacking ships soon came under heavy fire without being able to reply effectively because visibility was better to the west and favoured the British gunnery. Scheer saw his fleet rush into a wide arc of gun flashes and decided to support the destroyer attack by the battle-cruisers while the battle fleet executed its third battle turn. To the battle-cruisers he made the well-known signal, 'Ran' ('At them'), which meant charging regardless of consequences. *Lützow* could not take part because after twenty-three hits she was far down by the bow and could steam no more than 15 knots. So *Derfflinger* led that death ride. Her captain transmitted Scheer's signal to all battle stations and was answered by a thundering roar, gun crews shouting, stokers banging their shovels against bulkheads. The destroyers went in, fired torpedoes, and retreated, the battle-cruisers then turned after receiving numerous hits. Not a single torpedo reached a target, for Jellicoe turned away. Contact ceased again and a lull in the battle followed. Both fleets hauled round to the south until their courses converged. The Germans proceeded in inversed order and in several columns, the British in single line ahead, sixteen miles long.

At sunset (2020) the terribly mauled battle-cruisers again came under the fire of the leading British battleships, the old ships of the II Battle Squadron under that of the British battle-cruisers. The Germans were silhouetted against the western horizon, their opponents were hardly visible to them. As a British officer later wrote: 'I sighted an obsolete German battleship firing in a desultory way at apparently nothing.' All the German columns turned to the west; the British did not follow but took up night-cruising order, the battleships in divisions abreast, destroyer flotillas following in their wake, course south-east, speed 17 knots. Jellicoe intended to put himself between the Germans and their bases and to renew the battle at daylight. Scheer collected his units practically on the same course which took some time, and at 2300 headed south-east for Horn Reef, speed 16 knots. Because of the heavy odds against him, he wanted to fight a renewed battle nearer to his bases. It was another whim of fate that, as a consequence, the German main body crashed through the British flotillas which were not looking for the enemy but were waiting for the day battle. In contrast the German destroyers searched in vain for the heavy ships of the enemy.

The night actions

During the short northern summer night there were numerous clashes. They started with a furious fight between light cruisers at short distance. *Dublin* and *Southampton* suffered heavy damage and casualties; the obsolete *Frauenlob* was hit by a torpedo and sank with most of her crew. Next the 4th Destroyer Flotilla, led by *Tipperary*, converged upon the German van, came under the fire of half a dozen battleships, and turned away in disorder firing torpedoes and leaving *Tipperary*, burning fiercely, behind. When the battleships turned to starboard to avoid the torpedoes, the light cruiser *Elbing* was rammed and remained stopped with flooded engine-rooms. The battleship *Nassau* tried to ram the destroyer *Spitfire*: they collided on nearly opposite courses, and the destroyer bounced off the side armour of her robust opponent leaving part of her bridge behind. With her forecastle a shambles, *Spitfire* succeeded in limping home.

Both sides resumed course and soon met again. In the intense fire *Broke*, and immediately afterwards *Contest*, rammed *Sparrowhawk*, which kept afloat to the morning. This time a torpedo crippled the light cruiser *Rostock*. Half an hour later, shortly after midnight, the unlucky 4th Flotilla encountered the same ships for the third time and lost *Fortune* and *Ardent*. Most of the other destroyers were damaged, it was no more a fighting unit.

A short time later a large ship approached the centre of the German line from port. It was the armoured cruiser *Black Prince*. She had probably been damaged when *Defence* blew up, and had tried to follow the battle fleet. Too late she turned away, and in minutes was a blazing pyre. Without firing a single shot she disintegrated.

These clashes saved the 6th Battle Squadron from an encounter with German battleships. It lagged behind because torpedo damage prevented *Marlborough*, the flagship, from keeping up 17 knots. As it were the German van passed no more than three miles astern at around 0100. A little later it hit the rear of a line of thirteen destroyers belonging to four flotillas. *Turbulent* was sunk, others damaged, the Germans carried on. At early dawn, after a calm of an hour, they were sighted and attacked by the 12th Flotilla. The German ships succeeded in evading a great number of torpedoes but the old battleship *Pommern* was hit and broke in two after several detonations.

The great battle was over. At 0300 the Germans were approaching Horn Reef, the British battle fleet, thirty miles to the south-west, reversed course, neither commander-in-chief was inclined to renew the fight. Jellicoe went north to look for German stragglers. However, *Lützow*, *Elbing*, and *Rostock* had already been scuttled after German destroyers had taken their crews off. Both fleets steered for their bases. The *Ostfriesland* struck a mine in a field laid a few hours earlier by *Abdiel* but reached port without assistance.

The battle changed neither the ratio of strength between the two fleets nor the strategic situation. The British blockade continued, and Russia remained cut off from the supplies she needed urgently. The tactical advantage was with the Germans: they had inflicted about double their own losses on a greatly superior opponent. The fleet was proud of this achievement, and Scheer was willing to go on baiting the British. On 19th August 1916 both fleets were again in the North Sea but missed each other by thirty miles. However, it was evident – and Scheer said so in his reports – that the war could not be decided by this strategy. The situation on the fronts deteriorated after Allied offensives, and lack of food was painfully felt at home. Therefore the German government declared unrestricted submarine warfare two weeks before the Russian revolution broke out. The submarines did great havoc to Allied shipping, but brought the United States into the war.

As to the High Seas Fleet it did not

The losses in battle		
	British	German
Battle-cruisers	3	1
Armoured cruisers	3	-
Old battleships	-	1
Light cruisers	-	4
Destroyers	8	5
	tons 112,000	tons 61,000
Killed	6,000	2,500

remain inactive in port as has been alleged. In April 1918 it made its last sweep to the latitude of Bergen/Shetlands. But its main duty was now to support the submarine war by protecting the minesweepers and by giving its best young officers and ratings to the submarine arm. Other reasons for the sudden break-up of this efficient fighting force in November 1918 were psychological mistakes, malnutrition, and subversion, aggravated by the hopeless political and military situation of Germany.

BATTLE OF BRITAIN

Hitler's plan was to soften up Britain for the proposed invasion.
But he was not dealing with the same Britain that signed away
Czechoslovakia at Munich. Fortified and inspired by their war
leader, the British knew that the fate of the West could very well
hinge on their courage on land, and on their aggressive spirit
in the skies

BRITAIN AUGUST/SEPTEMBER 1940

In its element: the Spitfire, symbol of the battle

Keystone

◁ A Dornier in action: a stick of bombs streams from its bomb-bay

▷ Target and tracer-fire: camera-gun film from a British fighter records the end of a Me-110 fighter. The 110, at full throttle, streams smoke trails from its twin engines (top); tracer fire misses the starboard wing, then the first hit glows on the port engine which explodes (bottom)

◁ Two Dorniers fly over fires started by the first wave

▽ The Luftwaffe strikes at Fighter Command: on an RAF fighter base, a Spitfire in its bomb pen survives a low-level strafing run

Imperial War Museum

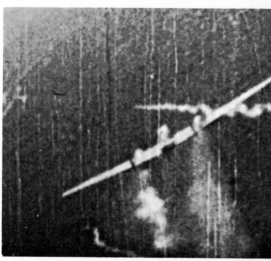

Ullstein

Imperial War Museum

R.A.F. Fighter Command
○ Command Headquarters
⊕ Group Headquarters
● Sector station
○ Fighter base
+ Low-level radar station
✠ High-level radar station
♨ Towns bombed

German bases
○ Fighter
● Twin-engined Me 110
+ Bomber
St (Stuka) Dive-bomber

0   50   100
Miles

Glasgow

NORTHUMBER-
LAND

Belfast

LUFTFLOTTE 5
from Norway and
Denmark

Newcastle
♨ Sunderland
**FIGHTER
COMMAND
GROUP 13**
♨ Middlesbrough

NORTH SEA

YORKSHIRE
Driffield
♨ Hull

Liverpool ♨
Merseyside
♨ Manchester
♨ Sheffield

Range of High-level Radar

FIGHTER COMMAND GROUP 12
⊕ ♨ Nottingham

Birmingham ♨   ♨ Coventry

♨ Norwich

Range of Low-level Radar

Amsterdam ■

NETHERLANDS
Rotterdam

Debden
Ipswich   Martlesham

London
Stanmore
FIGHTER Northolt North Weald
Uxbridge ⊕ Hornchurch
COMMAND Croydon Rochford
GROUP 11 Biggin Hill Rochester
Kenley Eastchurch
Andover West Malling Manston
Middle Wallop Detling Canterbury
♨ Worthy Down Hawkinge
Southampton ♨ Lympne
Portsmouth ♨ Ventnor
Tangmere
Portland
Ventnor

Swansea
Cardiff
Bristol ♨

**FIGHTER
COMMAND
GROUP 10**
Exeter ○

Plymouth ♨

Ghent
Calais
+ St
Antwerp
Lille
BELGIUM
LUFTFLOTTE 2

ENGLISH   CHANNEL

+ St
+ St
Amiens

Cherbourg
Le Havre

■ Paris

LUFTFLOTTE 3

+ St
Rennes

F R A N C E

182

The moment drew near for the Luftwaffe's great assault

From the very outset of the war a great German air assault had been expected in Britain. It was for fear of this that mothers and children had been evacuated from the big cities, the blackout enforced, gas masks and Anderson shelters distributed, thousands of beds held vacant in the hospitals. But no 'knock-out blow' from the air, or indeed any kind of blow at all—other than minelaying and raids on Scottish naval bases and east coast convoys—had disturbed the uncanny peace of the British Isles during the autumn and winter of 1939-40.

This quiet remained unbroken even when, in the spring of 1940, the war in the west came abruptly to the boil. Strange as it seemed at the time, there were in fact good reasons for Britain's unexpected immunity. Britain herself had not launched a strategic bombing offensive against Germany during the 'Phoney War' for fear of retaliation while the Allies were still the weaker side in the air. Germany had not launched any such offensive against Britain because she did not think she could achieve decisive results from German bases and because the Luftwaffe was largely cast for the role of military support. This support the Luftwaffe had given, with exemplary effectiveness, during the campaign in Poland; and now, as the Germans struck in the west, it operated in similar fashion in Norway, the Low Countries, and France. Meanwhile, it did not waste its strength in irrelevant activity against England.

This self-imposed restriction lasted until the German army entered the smoking ruins of Dunkirk. Within less than 48 hours, on the night of June 5/6, the Luftwaffe began to show a more lively interest in the British homeland. Some 30 German bombers—far more than on any previous occasion—crossed the east coast to attack airfields and other objectives; and the following night similar forces repeated the experiment. Then came a lull while the German armies in France struck southwards, again supported by the Luftwaffe. It lasted until the French sought an armistice, whereupon within a few hours German aircraft resumed night operations over Britain. From then on until the opening of their full daylight air offensive in August, the Germans repeatedly dispatched bombers—70 of them on the busiest night—against widely separated targets in England. Their intention was to give their crews experience in night operations and the use of radio navigational aids, to reconnoitre, and to maintain pressure inexpensively (their usual losses were one or two aircraft each night) until captured airfields in France and the Low Countries could be made ready for operations of a more intensive kind.

Meanwhile there was always the chance—or so it seemed to Hitler—that such operations might not be necessary. The Führer accordingly put out 'peace-feelers', at the same time encouraging preparations for the next stage of hostilities. This next stage, the invasion or occupation of Britain, was not one to which the Germans had already devoted long thought. The speed and completeness of the German victory in France had taken even the optimistic Hitler by surprise; and though his armed forces had given some casual attention in the autumn of 1939 to the general problems of invading Britain, it was not until German troops actually reached the Channel coast on May 20, 1940, that the project really came to life. From then on the German navy, anxious not to be caught out by Hitler, began serious planning; but the German army showed comparable interest only after the total defeat of France. On July 2 Hitler formally directed his services to proceed with this invasion planning, though on a purely provisional basis. On July 19 came his public peace offer; on the 22nd, its rejection.

If the Germans were to take advantage of the 'invasion season' in the Channel that year, their three services would now have to formulate and agree plans with extraordinary speed. This difficulty struck the German naval and military chiefs more forcibly than it did Hitler, who declared to his paladins that only the rapid elimination of Britain would enable him to complete his life's work by turning against Russia. On July 31 he accordingly disregarded the fast-waning enthusiasm of the German navy and army and ordered that an attempt must be made to prepare the invasion operation, to which the code-name 'Seelöwe' ('Sea Lion') was given, for September 15. The following day, August 1, he issued a directive concerning the only part of the venture on which all three German services were thus far agreed. It was for the preliminary stage, which must consist of the subjugation of the RAF. 'The German air force is to overcome the British air force with all means at its disposal, and as soon as possible.' With these words, Hitler finally decreed the Battle of Britain.

600 RAF sorties a day

While the plans for Sea Lion and the preliminary air battle were taking shape, the Luftwaffe was not of course idle. From its captured airfields it continued to harass Britain by night, and from July 10 onwards it waged increasing war by day against British shipping in the Channel. The German bombers were usually detected by the British radar stations, but since the attacks were delivered at the periphery of the British defensive system they set the Fighter Command a difficult problem. In such circumstances it was highly creditable to the command that the British fighters inflicted more casualties than they themselves suffered: between July 10 and August 10, as we now know, the Germans lost 217 aircraft, Fighter Command 96. On the other hand the German attacks, though sinking only a modest tonnage of British shipping, imposed a severe strain on Fighter Command, which was compelled to fly some 600 sorties a day at extended range at a time when it was trying to build up resources for the greater trials clearly soon to come. As Air Chief Marshal Sir Hugh Dowding, Air Officer C-in-C of the Fighter Command, pointed out to the Air Ministry and the Admiralty, if constant air protection was to be given to all British shipping in home waters, the entire British fighter force could be kept fully employed on that task alone.

These German attacks on shipping, however, were only a prelude to the air battle which the Luftwaffe had now to induce. The prerequisite of Sea Lion was that the Germans should gain air supremacy over the Channel and southern Britain. Only if the RAF were put out of business could the Germans hope to cross, land, and maintain communications without an unacceptable rate of casualties; for the destruction of the RAF would not only obviate British bombing attacks, but would also enable the Luftwaffe to deal, uninterrupted from the air, with the Royal Navy. And beyond this there was always the hope, ever present in the minds of Hitler and his service chiefs alike, that the Luftwaffe's success alone might be so great as to bring Britain to submission, or very near it. In that case, an invasion about which neither the German navy nor army was really happy could become something much more to their liking—a virtually unresisted occupation.

As the moment drew near for the Luftwaffe's great assault, the forces arrayed stood as follows. On the German side there were three *Luftflotten*, or air fleets. The main ones were Luftflotte II, under Field-Marshal Kesselring, in northern Germany, Holland, Belgium, and in north-eastern France; and Luftflotte III, under Field-Marshal Sperrle, in northern and western France. By day, these two air fleets threatened the entire southern half of England, up to and including the Midlands; and by night they could range still farther afield. In addition, to disperse the British defences and to threaten Scotland and north-eastern England there was also a smaller force, Luftflotte V, under General Stumpff, based in Denmark and Norway. Between them, the three air fleets on August 10 comprised over 3,000 aircraft, of which about three-quarters were normally serviceable at any one time. Roughly 1,100 of the 3,000 were fighters—for the most part Messerschmitt 109E's, virtually the equal of the opposing Spitfires of that date, but handicapped in a protective role by their limited range.

To escort bombers to the more distant targets, including those to be reached across the North Sea from Norway, there were some 300 Messerschmitt 110s; but these twin-engined fighters, though sturdy, could not compare in manoeuvrability with the single-engined Spitfire or Hurricane. The remaining 1,900 German aircraft were almost entirely bombers, mainly the well-tried if slow Heinkel 111, the slim, pencil-like Dornier 17, and the fast and more recent Junkers 88, but including also about 400 Junkers 87s—the Stukas, or dive-bombers. These had established a legendary reputation on the battlefields of Poland and France, but their range was very short and they had yet to face powerful and sustained opposition.

On the British side, the situation was a great deal better than it had been a few weeks earlier. On June 4, following the heavy losses of Hurricanes in France, Fighter Command had been able to muster only 446 modern single-engined fighters—Spitfires and Hurricanes—with another 36 ready in the Aircraft Storage Units (ASUs) as replacements. But on August 11, on the eve of the main air battle, Fighter Command had 704 of these aircraft in the squadrons and 289 in the ASUs. Its fighting strength had been virtually doubled during those ten critical weeks since Dunkirk, thanks to the fruition of earlier Air Ministry plans and the tremendous efforts of the air-

The Luftwaffe was able to use the entire coastline of occupied Europe: the British resources were to be strained to their furthest limits ◁

craft industry under the stimulus of the newly appointed Minister of Aircraft Production, Lord Beaverbrook.

Strengthening the shield

During those same ten weeks the British air defence system, built up against an enemy operating from Germany and possibly the Low Countries, had also been extended, thanks to schemes already worked out and in progress, to deal with forces operating from France and Norway. To the existing groups within Fighter Command – No. 11 Group, guarding the south-east, No. 12 Group, guarding the east and Midlands, and No. 13 Group, guarding the north-east up to the Forth – had been added another: No. 10 Group, guarding the south-west. The intermittent defences of the north-west, including Northern Ireland, had been thickened, as had those of Scotland.

This was not only a matter of providing more fighter aircraft and the pilots to fly them. It was also a matter of extending the main coastal radar chain, adding special radar stations to detect low-flying aircraft, extending Observer Corps posts for inland tracking over the south-western counties and western Wales, adapting more airfields for fighter operations, installing guns, searchlights, balloon barrages. All this was the concomitant, on the air defence side, of the gun-posts and the pill-boxes, the barbed wire and the dragon's teeth, that the inhabitant of southern England, enrolled perhaps in the newly formed Local Defence Volunteers and on watch at dawn and dusk for the arrival of German paratroops, saw springing up before his eyes along his familiar coasts and downlands.

The island's air defences had grown stronger and more extensive, but many grave deficiencies remained. Of the 120 fighter squadrons which the Director of Home Operations at the Air Ministry considered desirable in the new situation created by the German conquests, Dowding had less than 60 – and eight of these flew Blenheims or Defiants, no match for the Me-109s. Of the 4,000 anti-aircraft guns deemed necessary even before the German conquests, Anti-Aircraft Command still had less than 2,000. The early warning and inland tracking systems were still incomplete in the west and over parts of Scotland. There was a shortage of fighter pilots: new planes could be produced quicker than new skilled men to fly them. But whatever the deficiencies of the air defence system by day, they were as nothing compared with its alarming weaknesses by night, when ordinary fighters were useful only in the brightest moonlight, and when the men of the Observer Corps had to rely on ineffective acoustical detectors instead of their clear eyesight and a pair of binoculars.

Britain, however, had assets not yet mentioned. Among others, there was RAF Coastal Command, prepared both to carry out reconnaissance and to help in offensive operations; and there was RAF Bomber Command. Most of the latter's aircraft could operate safely only by night, and by night it was by no means certain that they could find and hit the more distant targets. The daylight bombers – about 100 Blenheims – were capable of much greater accuracy; but they needed fighter support, which could be supplied only at short range (assuming the Hurricanes or Spitfires could be spared). Against targets near at hand – airfields, ports, and shipping just across the Channel

– the British bombing force was capable of playing a vital part. Against distant objectives, its effectiveness at that date was more problematical.

In sum, the opposing forces, disregarding reconnaissance aircraft and units still stationed in Germany, consisted of about 1,900 bombers assisted by 1,100 fighters on the German side, and of about 700 fighters assisted to a limited extent by 350 bombers on the British side. The Germans had the advantage not only of numbers but of the tactical initiative – of the fact that they could strike anywhere within their range – while the British defences could react only to the German moves.

The British air defence system, however, though incomplete, was the most technically advanced in the world. The early warning supplied by the radar stations (which in the south-east could pick up enemy formations before they crossed the French coast), the inland tracking by the Observer Corps, the control of the British fighters from the ground in the light of this information and the continuous reporting of the fighters' own position – all this, designed to obviate the need for wasteful standing patrols, meant that the British fighters could be used with economy and could take off with a good chance of making interception.

One other factor, too, helped the British: the Luftwaffe's offensive against Britain was largely an improvised one; and Luftwaffe C-in-C Göring, though an able man, was also a vainglorious boaster who in technical proficiency was not in the same class as the opposing commander. The single-minded Dowding, in charge of Fighter Command since its formation in 1936 – the man whose obduracy had preserved Britain's fighter resources against the clamour to squander them in France – knew his job. Göring, as much politician as airman, scarcely knew his; while theoretically controlling and co-ordinating the entire offensive, in practice he was incapable of more than occasional acts of intervention. On the next level of command, Kesselring, in charge of the main attacking force – Luftflotte II – was for all his successes in Poland and France a novice in the forthcoming type of operation; while Air Vice-Marshal Keith Park, commanding the main defending force – Group 11 – had earlier been Dowding's right-hand man at Headquarters, Fighter Command. Unlike their opposite numbers, the two principal British commanders had lived with their problem for years. Their skill, experience, and devotion, like those of their pilots, offset some of the British inferiority in numbers.

Operation Eagle

By August 10 the three Luftflotten stood ready to launch the major assault – Operation Eagle ('Adler') – which would drive the RAF from the skies of southern Britain. Four days, in the opinion of the German Air Staff, would see the shattering of the fighter defences south of the line London-Gloucester, four weeks the elimination of the entire RAF. Allowing for the ten days' notice required by the German navy for minelaying and other final preparations before the actual D-Day, the date of the invasion could thus be set for mid-September.

August 11 was a very cloudy day, and the Germans confined their activity to bombing Portland and some east coast shipping. On the following day came what seemed to the British to be the beginning of the main attack: five or six major raids and many

minor ones, involving several hundred aircraft, including escorted Ju-87s, struck at airfields and radar stations along the south coast and at shipping in the Thames Estuary. Of the six radar stations they attacked, the raiders damaged five but knocked out only one – that at Ventnor on the Isle of Wight. It could not be replaced until August 23 – a sharp blow. Among the airfields, they hit Lympne, a forward landing ground, and Manston and Hawkinge, two important fighter stations in Kent, but all were back in action within 24 hours. Fighters from No. 11 Group challenged all the major raids, and frustrated completely one aimed at Manston. In the course of the fighting the Germans lost 31 aircraft, the British 22.

According to the German records, the next day, August 13, was Eagle Day itself – the opening of the Eagle offensive proper. The attack went off at half-cock in the morning, when a message postponing operations till later in the day failed to get through to some of the German squadrons. In the afternoon the main assault developed with a two-pronged thrust, Luftflotte II attacking over Kent and the Thames Estuary, while Luftflotte III, challenged by No. 10 Group, attacked over Hampshire, Dorset, and Wiltshire. The raiders hit three airfields severely – Eastchurch, Detling, and Andover – but none of these belonged to Fighter Command; their attacks on fighter stations such as Rochford were beaten off.

In the whole day's operations – which witnessed 1,485 German sorties and ended with a successful night attack on a Spitfire factory at Castle Bromwich, near Birmingham – the Germans lost 45 aircraft, Fighter Command only 13 (with six of the British pilots saved). This was a poor sort of Eagle Day for the Germans, but they were nevertheless well satisfied with their progress. They calculated that between August 8 and 14, in addition to successful attacks on some 30 airfields and aircraft factories, they had destroyed more than 300 British fighters in combat. In fact, they had destroyed less than 100.

After lesser activity on August 14 – a matter of some 500 German sorties, directed mainly against railways near the coast and against RAF stations – the Luftwaffe on August 15 attempted the great blow with which it had hoped to open the battle some days earlier. In clear skies the Germans sent over during the day no less than seven major raids, using all three Luftflotten in a series of co-ordinated attacks on widely separated areas. The first clash came at about 1130 hours, when some 40 escorted Ju-87s of Luftflotte II struck at Lympne and Hawkinge airfields in Kent. Then, about 1230 hours some 65 He-111s escorted by 35 Me-110s of Luftflotte V, operating from Stavanger in Norway, headed in to the Northumberland coast in an attempt to bomb airfields in the north-east. These formations were barely retiring when at 1315 hours another force of Luftflotte V, consisting of about 50 unescorted Ju-88s operating from Aalborg in Denmark, approached the Yorkshire coast on a similar mission. Little more than an hour later at 1430 hours, and once more at 1500, Luftflotte II struck again, on the first occasion north of the Thames Estuary against Martlesham airfield and on the second against Hawkinge and Eastchurch

▷ **Seen through German eyes: a British fighter pilot bales out of his stricken Hurricane; his parachute canopy is about to open (top)**

A seat in the sun—but both sides are at instant readiness for take-off. On RAF and Luftwaffe bases, the youth, the pipes, and the flying-kit were much the same. There is little to distinguish these pilots except the national markings on their aircraft

airfields and aircraft factories at Rochester.

Next it was the turn of Luftflotte III: at 1720 hours some 80 bombers, heavily escorted, came in to the south coast at Portland, bombed the harbour, and then attacked airfields at Middle Wallop and Worthy Down. Finally, at 1830 hours, 60 or 70 aircraft of Luftflotte II again penetrated over Kent, hitting West Malling airfields and the airfield and aircraft factories at Croydon. To round off the day's work, another 60 or 70 bombers made sporadic attacks during the hours of darkness.

All this German effort was fiercely challenged. Though the bombing had its successes, notably at Middle Wallop, Martlesham, and Driffield (Yorkshire) airfields and at Croydon, in no case did the British fighters allow the raiders to operate unmolested, and in many cases the primary objectives escaped unscathed. Especially significant was the fighting in the north-east, where No. 13 Group, involved for the first time in the battle, intercepted the formations from Norway well out to sea, and with the help of the anti-aircraft guns on Tyne and Tees destroyed eight He-111s and seven Me-110s, with no British losses. A little farther south, too, No. 12 Group and the local guns, tackling the formations from Denmark, brought down eight of the enemy with no loss on the British side. The Germans thus failed in their main hope—that Dowding, in his anxiety to protect the vital and heavily threatened south-east, would have left the north almost undefended. Instead, they discovered, to their cost, that their attacks across the North Sea were met before they reached the British coast, and that the Me-110s in a long-range escorting role were useless against Spitfires and Hurricanes. The lesson was sufficiently expensive to convince the Germans not to launch any further daylight attacks from this area.

The fighting on August 15 was the most extensive in the whole Battle of Britain. With 520 bomber and 1,270 fighter sorties, and attacks stretching from Northumberland to Dorset, the German effort was at its maximum. But so too was the German loss—75 aircraft as against 34 British fighters. This did not prevent an effort of almost equal magnitude on the following day, when the Germans sent across some 1,700 sorties, attacked a number of airfields (with particular success at Tangmere), and lost 45 aircraft in the process. With Fighter Command losing 21, the balance remained in the British favour.

The Luftwaffe switches strategy

The four days of intensive attack calculated to clear the skies of southern England were now over, and the Germans took stock. In the opinion of their Intelligence, Fighter Command, if not exhausted, was down to its last 300 aircraft. This appreciation was very wide of the mark, for Dowding still had nearly twice that number of Hurricanes and Spitfires in the front line, in addition to another 120 or so Blenheims, Defiants, and Gladiators. However, it encouraged the Germans to believe that another day or two of major effort might see the end of British opposition. On August 18 the Luftwaffe accordingly struck again in full force, chiefly against airfields in Kent, Surrey, and

Sussex; but in doing so they lost 71 aircraft while the British lost no more than 27. Clearly Fighter Command was still unsubdued. After a few days of minor activity owing to bad weather, the Germans therefore made their first great change of plan.

Up till then, the main German objectives had been airfields fairly near to the coast; after August 12 they had given up intensive attacks on radar stations—fortunately for Fighter Command—because they found them difficult to destroy. The airfields and other coastal targets they had continued to attack, partly to deny the airfields to the British during the proposed invasion period, but still more to force Fighter Command to join battle in their defence. The German theory was that by such attacks they might, without severe losses to themselves, inflict heavy losses on the RAF—for raids on coastal targets or those not far inland did not involve prolonged exposure to the British defences—while at the same time the Me-109s would be free from worries on the score of endurance and accordingly able to give maximum protection to the German bombers. Such was the German strategy when the battle began. It had not disposed of Fighter Command, so it was now changed in favour of attacks farther inland.

The first phase of the battle was thus over. So far, Fighter Command had more than held its own: 363 German aircraft had been destroyed between August 8 and 18, as against 181 British fighters lost in the air and another 30 on the ground. The period had also seen what proved to be the last daylight attack by Luftflotte V, and the last attempt by Luftflotte II to make regular use of its Ju-87s—both notable successes for the British defences.

At the same time, however, there was one aspect of the struggle which gave Dowding and the Air Ministry acute anxiety. During the same ten days, when Fighter Command had lost 211 Spitfires and Hurricanes, the number of replacements forthcoming from the aircraft industry had fallen short of this total by at least 40. In the same period, Fighter Command had lost 154 experienced fighter pilots: but the output of the training schools had been only 63—and those less skilled than the men they replaced. Fighter Command, while inflicting nearly twice as many casualties as it was suffering, was thus in fact being weakened—though not, as yet, at anything like the speed desired by the enemy.

It was to increase the rate of destruction of the British fighter force—which unchanged would have left Fighter Command still in existence in mid-September—that the Germans now switched to targets farther inland. They reckoned that by making their prime objective the fighter airfields, and in particular the sector airfields of No. 11 Group from which the British fighters in the south-east were controlled, they would not only strike at the heart of the British defences, but would also compel Fighter Command to meet their challenge with all its remaining forces. In the resulting air battles, they hoped to achieve a rate of attrition that would knock out Fighter Command within their scheduled time: though they also knew that in penetrating farther inland they were likely to suffer greater losses themselves. To guard against this, and to destroy as many Hurricanes and Spitfires as possible, they decided to send over a still higher proportion of fighters with their bombers.

The sector stations of No. 11 Group stood

in a ring guarding London. To the south-west, in a forward position near Chichester, lay Tangmere. Nearer the capital and south of it there were Kenley in Surrey and Biggin Hill in Kent, both on the North Downs. Close to London in the east lay Hornchurch, near the factories of Dagenham; and round to the north-east was North Weald, in metropolitan Essex. Farther out there was Debden, near Saffron Walden. The ring was completed to the west by Northolt, on the road to Uxbridge, where No. 11 Group itself had its headquarters—which in turn was only a few minutes' drive from that of Fighter Command at Stanmore. All the sector stations normally controlled three fighter squadrons, based either on the sector station itself or on satellite airfields.

Strikes at the source

The Germans had already severely damaged two of the sector stations—Kenley and Biggin Hill—on August 18. Now, on August 24, they struck hard at North Weald and Hornchurch. On August 26 they attempted to bomb Biggin Hill, Kenley, North Weald, and Hornchurch, were beaten off, but got through to Debden. On August 30 they hit Biggin Hill twice, doing great damage and killing 39 persons. The following day—the most expensive of the whole battle for Fighter Command, with 39 aircraft lost—they wrought great damage at Debden, Biggin Hill, and Hornchurch.

On September 1 Biggin Hill suffered its sixth raid in three days, only to be bombed again less than 24 hours later; and on September 3 the attack once more fell on North Weald. On the 5th the main raids again headed towards Biggin Hill and North Weald, only to be repelled, while on the 4th and 6th the attacks extended also to the Vickers and Hawker factories near Weybridge. The Hawker factory, which produced more than half the total output of Hurricanes, was a particularly vital target. Its selection showed that the Germans, perplexed by the continued resilience of Fighter Command, were also trying to cut off the British fighter supply at its source.

Between August 24 and September 6 the Germans made no less than 33 major raids, of which more than two-thirds were mainly against the sector and other stations of Fighter Command. This assault imposed on the command a still greater strain than the preceding one, against targets in the coastal belt. The fighting was more difficult for the British pilots, in that the proportion of German fighters to bombers became so high, and sections of the fighter escort so close; and over the whole fortnight a daily average of something like 1,000 German aircraft, of which 250 to 400 were bombers, operated over England. Twice, on August 30 and 31, the number of intruders was nearer 1,500.

In the course of the combats and the ensuing night operations the British defences destroyed 380 German aircraft, as against a Fighter Command loss of 286: but many other British fighters were seriously damaged, and no less than 103 fighter pilots were killed and 128 wounded out of a fighting strength of not much more than 1,000. In addition six of the seven sector stations of No. 11 Group sustained heavy damage: and though none was yet out of action, Biggin Hill could control only one squadron instead of its normal three.

So Fighter Command was being steadily worn down, and at a faster pace than in the opening phase. The wastage, both of fighters and of pilots, was far exceeding the output. In one sense the command was winning the battle; in another—if the Germans could maintain the pressure long enough—it was losing it.

The Germans, however, were not intending to fight a prolonged battle. They, too, could not afford heavy losses indefinitely—as may be seen from their decision after August 18 to hold back most of the vulnerable Ju-87s for the actual invasion, from their caution in employing Me-110s, and from their increasingly closer and more numerous fighter escort. Their attack, as we have seen, was meant to be a brief one, geared to Operation Sea Lion; and for Sea Lion they were now running short of time. This Hitler recognised at the end of August when he agreed that D-Day, provisionally set for September 15, should be postponed to September 21. For this date to be kept the German navy had to receive the executive order by September 11: and Göring's Luftwaffe had thus to administer the *coup de grâce* to the British fighter forces within the next few days. The attack on sector stations and other inland targets might be doing well, but in itself it was not proving decisive. On September 7 the Germans accordingly switched to another target, farther inland than most of the sector stations and, as they believed, still more vital—London.

Target London

The German decision to attack London was inspired by three beliefs. In the first place, operations against London could be expected to bring about still greater air battles and so—the Germans hoped—still higher wastage in Fighter Command. It was for this reason that Kesselring, though not Sperrle, strongly supported the change of plan. Second, an assault on the capital, if reinforced by attacks during the night against other main cities as well, might paralyse the British machinery of government in the final period before the invasion, or even terrorise the British people into submission. Third, an attack on the British capital would be, as the Germans saw it, an act of retribution. On the night of August 24/25, during the course of the Luftwaffe's usual scattered night operations, some badly aimed or jettisoned bombs had fallen on central London —the first of the war. Churchill and the War Cabinet had immediately ordered retaliation against Berlin; and during the following nights RAF bombers had found and hit the German capital—an occurrence which Göring had assured Hitler could never happen. The enraged Führer promptly vowed revenge and with Göring's eager concurrence unleashed the Luftwaffe against its supreme target.

On the night of September 4 German bombers laid flares over London; on the following two nights small numbers of aircraft dropped bombs on Rotherhithe and other places near the docks. These were the warming-up operations.

In the late afternoon of September 7 some 300 German bombers escorted by 600 fighters crossed the Kent and Sussex coasts or penetrated the Thames Estuary in a series of huge waves. A few bombed the oil installations at Thameshaven, still burning from earlier attacks; the rest, instead of bombing the sector stations, which the British fighters were alert to guard, held on until they reached the outskirts of the capital itself. Though nearly all the British squadrons ordered up eventually made contact, most of the raiders were able to put down their high explosive and incendiaries before they were molested. The attacks fell in full force on London's dockland east of the City. Huge fires sprang up among the dockside warehouses, especially at Silvertown, and these the Germans used as beacons to light their way to further attacks during the ensuing hours of darkness. That night, when 250 German bombers ranged over the capital in a prolonged assault from dusk to dawn, millions of Londoners had their first experience of what they imagined was Blitzkrieg, and what they were soon to call 'The Blitz'.

The climax of the battle was now approaching. Göring took personal charge of operations, and the bombers from Norway and Denmark joined Kesselring's forces for what were meant to be the final and deciding blows. Meanwhile, however, the German invasion preparations had not gone unobserved: since August 31 Spitfires and Hudsons of RAF Coastal Command had been returning with an impressive photographic record of the growing number of barges and other invasion craft in the ports and estuaries across the Channel. On August 31 in Ostend, for instance, there were 18 barges; by September 6 there were 205.

As the concentrations increased, Bomber Command began to attack them, using at first its daylight Blenheims. By September 6 the enemy preparations were sufficiently obvious for the British authorities to order Invasion Alert 2: 'Attack probable within three days.' The following day, when the German bombers turned against London, it seemed that the hour of supreme trial might be at hand. Alert 2 then gave place to Alert 1: 'Invasion imminent, and probable within twelve hours.'

That night, as the German bombs began to crash down on London, the code-word 'Cromwell' went out to the Southern and Eastern Commands of Britain's Home Forces, bringing them to immediate readiness. In the prevailing excitement a few commanders of Home Guard units rang church bells to call out their men, so spreading the impression that German paratroops had actually landed. Meanwhile, forces of the Royal Navy waited at immediate notice, and the Hampdens of Bomber Command— 'heavy' bombers of the time—joined Blenheims, Hudsons, and Battles in intensified attacks on French and Belgian ports.

It was with the British fully alert to what the next few hours or days might bring that the Luftwaffe now strove to repeat the hammer blows of September 7. On September 8 bad weather limited their daylight activity; but at night Luftflotte III was able to send 200 bombers against London in a lengthy procession lasting more than nine hours. The zone of attack now extended from dockland to the capital as a whole, with special attention to railways and power stations, and by the morning every railway line running south of London was for a brief time unserviceable.

On the next day, September 9, clouds again restricted activity in the morning, only for a further assault to develop in the late afternoon. More than 200 bombers with full escort headed for London; but such was the promptness and vigour of the interception that less than half reached even the outskirts of the capital, and the bombs fell widely over the south-eastern counties. No. 12 Group's Duxford wing of four squadrons, led by the legless pilot Squadron Leader Douglas Bader, enjoyed a notable success. All told, the British pilots shot down 28 German aircraft for the loss of 19 of their own.

Very different once more was the story at night. Again nearly 200 aircraft bombed the capital in attacks lasting over eight hours; this time some 400 Londoners were killed and 1,400 injured—all with negligible loss to the Luftwaffe.

Hitler again shifts D-Day

September 10 was a day of cloud, rain, and light German activity—though at night there was the usual raid on London, while other German bombers attacked South Wales and Merseyside. The next afternoon, while the Germans tried to jam some of the British radar stations, Luftflotte III attacked Southampton, and Luftflotte II sent three big raids against London. Many of the bombers got through to the City and the docks; and the balance of losses—25 German ones, against 29 by Fighter Command—for once tilted against the British. On their return, some German pilots reported that British fighter opposition was diminishing. But though the Luftwaffe still hoped to complete its task, the date was now September 11, and Fighter Command was still in existence. With the German navy requiring ten days' notice before D-Day, an invasion on September 21 thus became impossible. Accordingly Hitler now gave the Luftwaffe three more days' grace, till September 14, in the hope that a decision could then be taken to invade on September 24.

As it happened, September 12 and 13 were days of poor visibility, unsuitable for major attacks. Even the nightly efforts against London—which was now enjoying the heartening noise of greatly reinforced gun defences—were on a reduced scale. When September 14 came, Hitler could only postpone the decision for a further three days, till September 17. This set the provisional D-Day for September 27—about the last date on which the tides would be favourable until October 8. The Führer's order was contrary to the advice of his naval chiefs, who urged indefinite postponement—a tactful term for abandonment. Their worries had been sharply increased by the mounting intensity of the RAF's attacks on the invasion barges, large numbers of which had been destroyed the previous evening.

The Luftwaffe now strove to clinch the issue in the short time still at its disposal. Despite unfavourable weather, on the afternoon of September 14 several raids struck at London. Some of the German pilots reported ineffective opposition, and Fighter Command lost as many aircraft as the enemy. The night proved fine, but on this occasion no more than 50 German bombers droned their way towards London. The Luftwaffe was husbanding its efforts for the morrow.

Sunday September 15 was a day of mingled cloud and sunshine. By 11 am the British radar detected mass formations building up over the Pas-de-Calais region. Half an hour later the raiders, stepped up from 15,000 to 26,000 feet, were crossing the coast in waves bent for London. Park's fighters met them before Canterbury, and in successive groups—two, three, then four squadrons—challenged them all the way to the capital, over which No. 12 Group's Duxford wing, now five squadrons strong, joined the conflict. In the face of such opposition, the raiders dropped their bombs inaccurately or jettisoned them, mainly over south London.

Two hours later a further mass attack developed. Again British radar picked it up well in advance: and again – since they had had time to refuel and rearm – Park's fighters challenged the intruders all the way to, and over, the capital. Once more the Germans jettisoned their bombs or aimed them badly, this time mainly over east London, and, as before, further British formations harassed the raiders on their way back. Meanwhile a smaller German force attacked Portland. Later in the day other raiders – some 20 Me-110s carrying bombs – tried to bomb the Supermarine aircraft works near Southampton, only to meet spirited and effective opposition from local guns. When darkness fell, 180 German bombers continued the damaging but basically ineffectual night assault on London, while others attacked Bristol, Cardiff, Liverpool, and Manchester.

So closed a day on which Göring had hoped to give the death-blow to Fighter Command. In all, the Germans had sent over about 230 bombers and 700 fighters in the daylight raids. Their bombing had been scattered and ineffective, and they had lost the greatest number of aircraft in a single day since August 15 – no less than 60. Fighter Command had lost 26, from which the pilots of 13 had been saved.

This further German defeat on September 15 – combined with the attacks of British bombers against barge concentrations – settled the issue. When September 17 came, Hitler had no alternative but to postpone Sea Lion indefinitely. A few days later, he agreed to the dispersal of the invasion craft in order to avoid attack from the air. The invasion threat was over.

Göring orders more raids

Göring, however, was not yet prepared to admit failure: he still clung to the belief that given a short spell of good weather the Luftwaffe could crush Fighter Command and thereafter compel Britain to submit, even without invasion. Between September 17 and the end of the month his forces strove to attack London by day, whenever weather permitted, in addition to aircraft factories elsewhere. On only three days – September 18, 27, and 30 – was he able to mount a major assault on the capital, and on each occasion British fighters prevented intensive bombing and took a heavy toll of the raiders. The loss of 120 German aircraft during these three days (as against 60 by Fighter Command) was not one which afforded Göring much encouragement to continue.

Had the Luftwaffe's corpulent chief known them, he would not have derived any greater encouragement from the casualty figures during the whole three weeks his air force had been attacking London. Between September 7 and 30 Fighter Command had lost 242 aircraft, the Luftwaffe 433. Equally important, though Dowding was still gravely worried by the continuing loss of pilots (on September 7 his squadrons had only 16 each instead of their proper 26), his anxieties about aircraft were diminishing. From the time the Germans abandoned their attack on sector airfields in favour of an assault on London, the wastage of Hurricanes and Spitfires had been more than counterbalanced by the output of the factories.

The prize of victory had thus eluded Göring's grasp. On October 12 Hitler recognised this by formally postponing Sea Lion until the spring of 1941. In fact, this meant abandonment: Hitler's mind was now fixed on Russia. Until the German war machine could roll east, however, there was everything to be said, from the German point of view, for maintaining pressure on Britain, so long as it could be done inexpensively. During October the Luftwaffe, assisted by a few Italian aircraft, kept Fighter Command at stretch in daylight by sending over fighter and fighter-bombers, which did little damage but were difficult to intercept. At night the German bombers, operating with virtual impunity, continued to drop their loads on London.

The story of the 'Night Blitz' is one of civilian suffering and heroism, of widespread yet indecisive damage – and of slowly increasing success by the British defences. In the battle of wits against the intruders, perhaps the most vital developments were the discovery (and distortion) of the German navigational beams, the provision of dummy airfields and decoy fires, and the advances in radar which made possible accurate tracking overland.

Radar advances resulted in gun-laying radar that gave accurate readings of heights, and so permitted the engagement of the target 'unseen', and in ground-controlled interception (GCI) radar stations which brought night fighters close enough to the enemy for the fighters to use their own airborne radar (A1) for the final location and pursuit. It was only towards the end of the Blitz, however, that the GCI/A1 combination emerged as a real threat to the attackers, who began to lose three or four aircraft in every 100 sorties, instead of merely one.

Meanwhile, the Luftwaffe was able to lay waste the centres of a score or more of British cities. After the early raids in August, the weight of attack by night fell for a time almost entirely on London. Between September 7 and November 13 there was only one night on which London escaped bombing, and the number of German aircraft over the capital each night averaged 163. With the final postponement of Sea Lion, the attack then extended also to longer-term, strategic objectives – the industrial towns, and later mainly the ports, so linking up with the blockading actions of the German submarines.

On November 14 the devastation of Coventry marked the change of policy; thereafter Southampton, Birmingham, Liverpool, Bristol, Plymouth, Portsmouth, Cardiff, Swansea, Belfast, Glasgow, and many other towns felt the full fury of the Blitz. In the course of it all, until Luftflotte II moved east in May 1941 and the attacks died away, the Germans killed about 40,000 British civilians and injured another 46,000, and damaged more than 1,000,000 British homes, at a cost to themselves of some 600 aircraft. On the economic side, they seriously impeded British aircraft production for some months, but in other directions the damage they did was too diffuse to be significant.

Hitler's first setback

The 'Blitz' ceased not because of the increased success of the British defences, but because most of the German aircraft were needed elsewhere. Had Russia collapsed within the eight weeks of the German – and the British – estimate, they would doubtless have returned quickly enough, to clear the way for invasion or to attempt to pulverise Britain into submission. As it was, Russia held, and though the British people were subjected to further bombardments, they were not again called upon to face a serious threat of invasion.

Though the Night Blitz was inconclusive, the daylight Battle of Britain was thus one of the turning points of the war: it was the air fighting of August and September 1940, together with the existence of the Royal Navy and the English Channel, which first halted Hitler's career of conquest. The 1,000 or so pilots of Fighter Command who bore the brunt of that fighting – including the 400 or more who lost their lives – saved more than Britain by their exertions. By earning Britain a great breathing space in which the further progress of events was to bring her the mighty alliance of Russia and the United States, they made possible the final victory and the liberation of Europe from the Nazi terror.

Air Marshal Sir Hugh Dowding

1. Messerschmitt 109E
Known to Luftwaffe pilots as the 'Emil', the 109E was least as fast as the Spitfire but was found to be less manœuvrable, though more so than the Hurricane. Always handicapped by its short range, its performance as a fighter was further restricted by a bomb load later in the battle, when pressed into service in a fighter/bomber role.
Armament: Two 7·9-mm machine-guns and two 20-mm cannons.
Max speed: 357 mph

2. Messerschmitt 110
Göring's folly: the cream of the Luftwaffe fighter strength was deployed in 'destroyer' units, intended to smash through the fighter defences and provide long-range escort for the bombers. Against the Spitfire and Hurricane, however, the Me-110s had finally to be provided with escorts themselves, for the lack of manœuvrability meant that their powerful armament was all too often useless.
Armament: Two 20-mm cannons, four 7·9-mm machine-guns, one free-mounted 7·9-mm gun.
Max speed: 349 mph

8. Supermarine Spitfire

The Spitfire fighter was the most agile machine in the battle—it could out-manœuvre even the Me-109E. Another vital superiority was its fire-power: eight wing-mounted Brownings which, though out-ranged by the German cannon, held a decisive concentration of rounds per second. In the Battle of Britain the Spitfire also held the advantage of fighting on home ground, unfettered by the range handicap of the 109E.
Armament: Eight ·303-inch machine-guns.
Max speed: 361 mph

9. Hawker Hurricane

Britain's first monoplane fighter was the numerical mainstay of RAF Fighter Command in the Battle of Britain. The Hurricane's ideal role was that of bomber-interceptor; as a rule, only the Spitfire could tackle the Me-109 on level terms, though the Hurricane scored notable successes against the Me-110. During the battle the Hurricane was already being replaced by the Spitfire as the standard RAF fighter.
Armament: Eight ·303-inch machine-guns.
Max speed: 328 mph

8

9

3. Junkers 87

The famous gull-winged Stuka was the main weapon which Göring turned against the RAF fighter bases. But the easy victories of past campaigns had been won in the absence of adequate fighter opposition, and RAF pilots found the Stuka an easy prey. Severe losses in operations throughout August destroyed its reputation as the all-conquering weapon of the Luftwaffe, and the Ju-87 was withdrawn from the spearhead of the attack.
Bomb load: One 1,102-lb, four 110-lb bombs.
Max speed: 217 mph

4. Junkers 88

The Ju-88 was the most versatile aircraft in the Luftwaffe's armoury for the entire war, serving as level bomber, dive-bomber, and night-fighter, as well as carrying out valuable reconnaissance duties. It was used by the Luftwaffe as a medium bomber in the Battle of Britain; but neither speed nor its comparatively high number of defending machine-guns was adequate protection from the fire-power of Spitfires and Hurricanes.
Bomb load: 5,510 lb
Max speed: 292 mph

5. Heinkel 111

The standard level bomber of the Luftwaffe at the time of the Battle of Britain, the He-111 suffered from its design as a medium bomber ideal for Continental operations but handicapped —as were all German twin-engined bombers—by the distances to targets in the north of England. Göring was convinced that its use in mass would prove decisive; but the He-111, it was found, was unable to beat off determined RAF fighter attacks.
Bomb load: 5,510 lb
Max speed: 258 mph

6. Dornier 17

The Do-17 was the Luftwaffe's veteran bomber: the type first saw service in the Spanish Civil War. Despite subsequent modifications, it was very weak in defensive fire, especially to attacks from below and to the rear. Known as the 'Flying Pencil' from its slim fuselage, the Do-17 was often confused with the British Hampden bomber, many of which were fired at by their own anti-aircraft guns. Its slender lines dictated a light bomb load.
Bomb load: 2,210 lb
Max speed: 270 mph

7. Dornier 215

This variant was a development of the basic design of the Do-17 with the installation of more powerful Daimler-Benz engines. The Do-215 was faster than the Do-17—fast enough to tax the lower-rated British engines of the early Spitfires and Hurricanes in a chase. In its light bomb-load and weak defence armament, however, the Do-215 was as handicapped as the Do-17.
Bomb load: 2,215 lb
Max speed: 311 mph

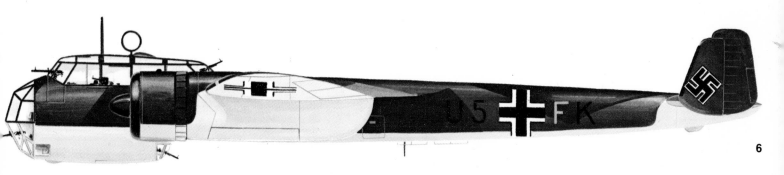

6

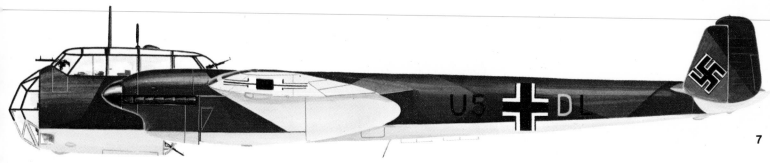

7

John Batchelor

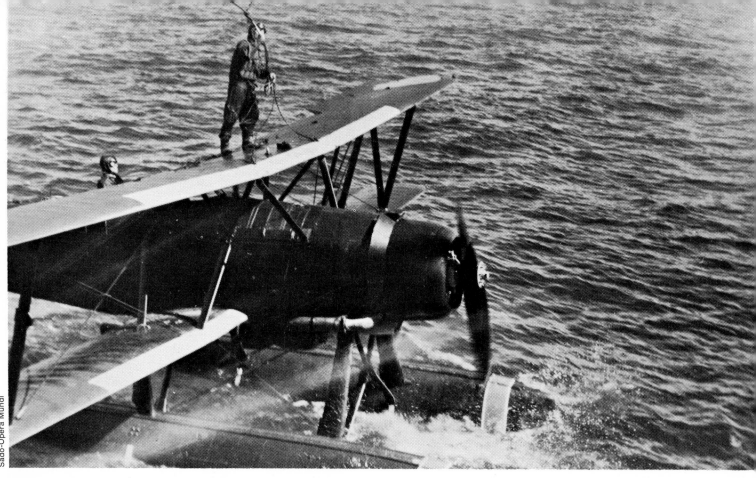

Sado-Opera Mundi

BATTLE OF THE CORAL SEA

Pacific May 1942

In the spring of 1942, following their rapid successes during the early months of the war, the Japanese were ready to extend their control over the Coral Sea by capturing Port Moresby in New Guinea—thus isolating Australia, and opening the way for further advances in the south-west. The battle which ensued was the first to be fought entirely by aircraft—no ship on either side made visual contact with the enemy—and when it ended, the Japanese had failed to achieve their objective, and their advance had been checked

△ Japanese air probe: a reconnaissance seaplane casts off from its parent warship. The Coral Sea battle was the first naval action to be entirely decided in the air
▷ *Lexington*'s 40-mm flak crews hit back at a Japanese air strike during the action in the Coral Sea

By the early spring of 1942, the very success which the Japanese had achieved in implementing their initial war plans had raised a fresh series of questions in the minds of those responsible for shaping Japanese naval strategy, and had caused a fierce and prolonged debate among the higher echelons of the Japanese naval command.

Up to May 1, 1942, the conquest of the Philippines, Burma, Malaya, and the Netherlands East Indies had cost the Japanese only 23 warships, none larger than a destroyer and 67 transport and merchant vessels. This amounted to less than 350,000 tons and fell far short of the anticipated 20 to 30% naval losses. Encouraged by this run of easy victories, the Japanese planners were thus encouraged to extend the ribbon defence perimeter they had originally conceived, without waiting for the proper consolidation of 'Greater East Asia'.

The subject of the debate was the direction which Japanese expansion should now take. The Naval General Staff, headed by Admiral Nagano, advocated either an advance westward against India and Ceylon, or a thrust southward towards Australia. Admiral Yamamoto and the staff of the Combined Fleet, on the other hand, argued that a prolonged struggle would be fatal to Japanese interests, and regarded the first priority as being the destruction of the United States aircraft-carriers in the Pacific, if Japanese security in the area was to be maintained. To this end, they urged early operations against Midway, Johnston, and Palmyra Islands, to the eastward, seeing these as necessary advanced bases for an attack on Hawaii. With the Combined Fleet in Hawaiian waters to support an invasion the United States fleet would certainly be drawn out into a decisive battle, and could be dealt with before the Allies brought their superior resources to bear against Japan.

The Japanese army, with its eyes on the Asian mainland and on Russia, objected to committing the large numbers of troops needed for the Naval General Staff's plans, and forced the latter to work out a more modest scheme for the isolation of Australia. This involved moving from Rabaul and Truk, where Japanese forces were already firmly entrenched, into Eastern New Guinea, and down the Solomons and New Hebrides to New Caledonia, the Fijis, and Samoa.

In theory, the formulation of Japanese strategy was the responsibility of the Army and Navy General Staffs, operating jointly as sections of Imperial General Headquarters. In practice, however, the ability of the Combined Fleet to influence naval strategy had been demonstrated by Yamamoto's insistence on the Pearl Harbor operation, despite the opposition of the Naval General Staff. Subsequent events had merely served to reinforce that influence.

While the debate on strategy went on, the first steps of the modified Naval General Staff plan were taken with the occupation of Lae and Salamaua in early March. Preparations for the capture of Port Moresby and Tulagi were under way by April. On the 18th of that month, the Doolittle raid on Tokyo, launched from the aircraft-carriers *Enterprise* and *Hornet,* inevitably strengthened Yamamoto's case for the Midway operation, and in the face of such failure to keep the capital itself immune from bombing attacks, the opposition of the Naval General Staff promptly vanished. By May 5, Admiral Nagano, Chief of the Naval General Staff, and acting in the name of the Emperor, issued Imperial General Headquarters Navy Order 18 which directed Yamamoto to 'carry out the occupation of Midway Island and key points in the Western Aleutians in co-operation with the army'—the operation to take place early in June.

Despite the fact that the Naval General Staff's plans had been thus undermined, the Port Moresby-Tulagi thrust had already proceeded too far to be called off, thereby forcing upon the Japanese two concurrent strategies which were destined to over-extend their forces. The occupation of Port Moresby had originally been scheduled for March, but the appearance of American carrier forces in the south-west Pacific had caused the Japanese to postpone the operation until early in May, so that the V Carrier Division of the Nagumo force, then returning to Japan after the Indian Ocean operations, could be used to reinforce the IV Fleet at Truk and Rabaul. The V Carrier Division, under Rear-Admiral Chuichi Hara, contained the powerful aircraft-carriers *Shokaku* and *Zuikaku.* A number of heavy cruisers which had seen service in the Indies were also spared for the invasion, together with the light aircraft-carrier *Shoho* from the Combined Fleet. The remainder would have to be furnished by the IV Fleet, under Vice-Admiral Shigeyoshi Inouye, who was given overall command of the operation.

The plan for Operation 'MO', as the impending attack was called, was based on simple premises, but was over-elaborate in the detailed machinery by which it was to be carried out. With the assistance of the South Seas Army Detachment and the navy, the Japanese were to invade Port Moresby—the key to Papua and the tail end of New Guinea—in order to safeguard their positions in New Guinea and in the Rabaul area, to provide a base which would bring northern Australia within range of their warships and bombers, and to secure the flank of their projected advance towards New Caledonia,

Fiji, and Samoa. Tulagi, which was also to be occupied, lay across the sound from Guadalcanal in the lower Solomons, and could be used as a seaplane base to cover both the Port Moresby operation and the subsequent advance to the south-east. Success in this venture would enable the Japanese to control the Coral Sea and to cut off and force Australia out of the war.

The organisation of Task Force MO, which was to execute the plan, comprised:
● The Port Moresby Invasion Group of 11 transports, carrying both army troops and a naval landing force, which, screened by destroyers, were to come down from Rabaul and around the tail of New Guinea through the Jomard Passage;
● A smaller Tulagi Invasion Group for setting up a seaplane base there;
● A Support Group, built around a seaplane-carrier, for the establishment of a base in the Louisiades;
● A Covering Group, under Rear-Admiral Goto, consisting of the *Shoho,* four heavy cruisers, and one destroyer, which was to cover the Tulagi landing, then turn back west to protect the Port Moresby Invasion Group;
● The Striking Force, commanded by Vice-Admiral Takagi, and containing the *Shokaku* and *Zuikaku,* which was to come down from Truk to deal with any United States forces that might attempt to interfere.

Naturally, Inouye expected opposition from the Allied forces in the south-west Pacific. He knew that about 200 land-based aircraft were operating from airfields in northern Australia, and that American air activity made the concealment of ship movements difficult. However, he estimated that Allied naval forces in the area were 'not large', and that only one aircraft-carrier, the *Saratoga,* would be available. He hoped that the prior occupation of Tulagi, due to be taken on May 3, and the establishment of a seaplane base there, would make it harder for the Allies to follow his movements from their nearest bases at Port Moresby and Noumea. The Support and Covering Groups and the Striking Force would cover the Port Moresby Invasion Group which would leave Rabaul on May 4, and land a sizeable force on the 7th.

Once the Allied task force entered the Coral Sea, Inouye thought he could destroy it by a pincer movement, with Goto on the west flank and Takagi on the east, while the Invasion Group slipped through the Jomard Passage to its destination. With the Allied force out of the way, he could then proceed with the bombing of bases in Queensland and the occupation of the Ocean and Nauru Islands, whose phosphorus resources were needed for Japanese agriculture.

In fact this plan was too complicated, revealing a typical weakness which was evident throughout the war. It demanded a level of tactical competence which the Japanese did not possess. The division of forces in the plan might well be fatal to its prospects of success, should the Japanese meet a determined enemy when they were not in a position to concentrate and co-ordinate the separate units effectively.

Nimitz anticipates the attack

To the Allies, Port Moresby was vital not only for the security of Australia, but also as a springboard for future offensives in the south-west Pacific. Admiral Chester W. Nimitz, Commander-in-Chief of the United States Pacific Fleet (CINCPAC), and General

Douglas MacArthur, Commander-in-Chief South-west Pacific Area, thus gave the threat the attention it merited. Since Pearl Harbor, the United States had succeeded in completely breaking the Japanese naval code, and therefore possessed accurate and fairly detailed intelligence concerning the Japanese plans. Before April 17, reports had reached CINCPAC headquarters that a group of transports, protected by the light aircraft-carrier *Shoho* and a striking force that included two large aircraft-carriers, would soon enter the Coral Sea. By the 20th Nimitz had concluded that Port Moresby was the objective, with the attack likely to develop on or after May 3.

It was one thing to know the nature of the task, but yet another to be able to summon up the resources to meet the situation. The *Saratoga* was in fact still in Puget Sound undergoing repairs for torpedo damage sustained in January. The aircraft-carriers *Enterprise* and *Hornet* did not return from the Tokyo raid until April 25, and were unlikely to reach the Coral Sea in time to participate in the coming battle, bearing in mind that they needed a minimum of five days for upkeep, and that Pearl Harbor was about 3,500 miles away.

A further complication was the rigid demarcation of command between Nimitz and MacArthur, according to the decision of the Combined Chiefs-of-Staff in March, whereby CINCPAC could exercise control over all naval operations in the Pacific, but could not usurp MacArthur's command of ground forces or land-based aircraft within the latter's area. Thus Nimitz could not readily call upon the 300-odd land-based aircraft of the USAAF and the RAAF for air searches in the area, even though the experience of these airmen in over-water work was limited. Inouye, on the contrary, had the XXV Air Flotilla at Rabaul, as well as all seaplanes, under his control.

Knowing, however, that he would have to rely mainly on air strike to frustrate Inouye's plans, Nimitz decided to utilise what remaining aircraft-carrier strength was available to him. For this task, he called upon the air groups of the *Yorktown* and *Lexington.* The *Yorktown* task force (No. 17) included the heavy cruisers *Astoria, Chester,* and *Portland*; the destroyers *Hammann, Anderson, Russell, Walke, Morris,* and *Sims*; and the tanker *Neosho.* This force had been operating out of Nouméa and was ordered to Tongatapu on April 14 for upkeep in preparation for a fight.

The *Lexington* task force (No. 11) was fresher, having left Pearl Harbor on April 16, after three weeks' upkeep. With the '*Lady Lex*', as she was affectionately known, were the heavy cruisers *Minneapolis* and *New Orleans,* and the destroyers *Phelps, Dewey, Farragut, Aylwin,* and *Monaghan.* Commanded by Captain Frederick C. Sherman, the *Lexington* could truly be called a happy ship; many of her crew had served with her since she was commissioned in 1927, while her air group included such notable naval aviators as 'Butch' O'Hare and John S. Thach. Rear-Admiral Aubrey W. Fitch, a distinguished carrier-tactician, had been on the flag bridge since April 3. Task Force 17, with the *Yorktown,* was commanded by Rear-Admiral Frank J. Fletcher, and had already been in the area for two months, having been involved in the Salamaua-Lae attack in March.

Even the combined strength of the air groups of these two aircraft-carriers amounted to less than 150 aircraft, but little else was available. Task Force 1, operating out of San Francisco, consisted mainly of pre-war battleships—these were simply not fast enough to keep up with the aircraft-carriers, nor could the oilers he spared to attend to their fuel requirements. All that remained were the ships of task Force 44, commanded by Rear-Admiral J. C. Crace, RN. Of these, the Australian heavy cruisers *Australia* and *Hobart,* then in Sydney, were ordered to rendezvous with Fletcher in the Coral Sea on May 4, while the heavy cruiser USS *Chicago* and the destroyer *Perkins,* at Nouméa, were ordered to join the same commander three days earlier, on May 1.

On April 29, Nimitz completed his plans. These simply detailed Fletcher to exercise tactical command of the whole force, designated Task Force 17, and ordered him to operate in the Coral Sea commencing May 1. The manner in which Inouye's threat was to be met was left almost entirely to Fletcher.

The opening moves

Fitch's *Lexington* force joined Fletcher as planned at 0630 hours on May 1, about 250 miles south-west of Espiritu Santo, and immediately came under Fletcher's tactical command. At 0700, Fletcher commenced re-fuelling from the *Neosho,* and directed Fitch to do the same from the *Tippecanoe,* a few miles to the south-west. Fitch had estimated that this task would not be completed until noon on the 4th, whereas Fletcher would finish 'topping up' by May 2.

Coral Sea—the first Japanese setback

The small map shows the Japanese strategy behind their outflanking move against New Guinea. Operations hinged on the vital bastion of Port Moresby; and Admiral Nimitz knew that the Japanese were planning yet another amphibious operation. The Japanese invasion-group, with the carrier *Shoho* and a cruiser force, was to head straight for Moresby around the tail of New Guinea. The carrier striking-force was to cruise into the Coral Sea past the Solomon Islands and ward off any US carrier opposition. The US Navy countermoves (large map) resulted in the first of the war's great carrier actions—one which lasted three days. In terms of enemy ships destroyed, the Japanese had the higher score; but they were forced to content themselves with occupying Tulagi and Florida islands in the Solomons. Their attempt to sieze Port Moresby had been a definite failure—their first major setback of the war

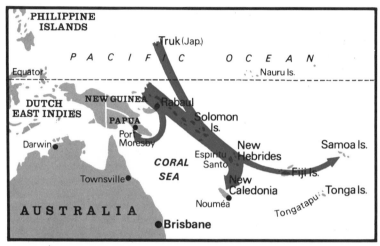

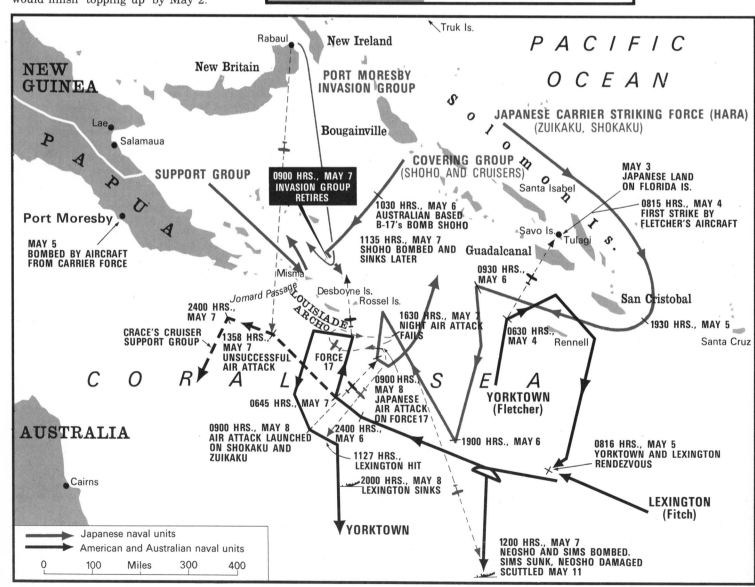

194

In the light of reports of the enemy's approach, Fletcher decided that he could not wait for Fitch and Crace, and steamed out into the middle of the Coral Sea to search for the Japanese. He headed west on the 2nd, leaving orders for Fitch to rejoin him by daylight on the 4th.

By 0800 hours on May 3, Fletcher and Fitch were over 100 miles apart, each ignorant of the enemy's detailed movements. In fact, the junior flag officer was to finish fuelling by 1310, but could not break radio silence to tell Fletcher of this fact, and instead headed towards the planned rendezvous. At 1900 the *Yorktown* force, now out on a limb, received the report which Fletcher 'had been waiting two months' to hear: the Japanese were landing at Tulagi and occupying Florida Island in the lower Solomons.

The news brought about an immediate change in Fletcher's plans. Ordering the *Neosho* and *Russell* to peel off and meet Fitch and Crace at the appointed rendezvous, then proceed with them in an easterly direction to rejoin *Yorktown* 300 miles south of Guadalcanal on May 5, Fletcher headed north at 24 knots, determined to strike Tulagi with the *Yorktown*'s available aircraft. Maintaining his course throughout the night, he arrived at a point about 100 miles south-west of Guadalcanal at 0700 on the 4th. By this time Fitch had received his new orders, while Crace, with *Australia* and *Hobart*, was nearing the rendezvous. Both were unable to help Fletcher in case of need, their south-easterly course actually increasing the distance between them and the *Yorktown*.

Fortunately for Fletcher, the Japanese had estimated that, once Tulagi was in their hands, it would remain unmolested. Goto's and Marushige's groups, which had supported the operation, had consequently retired at 1100 on May 3, after the island had been secured. Hara's carriers were still north of Bougainville, while the Port Moresby Invasion Group was only just leaving Rabaul. Furthermore, as Fletcher approached the launching position for his strike, he ran into the northern edge of a 100-mile cold front which screened his warships, and afforded a curtain for his planes until they came within 20 miles of Tulagi, where fair weather prevailed.

At 0630 hours on May 4, the first strike was launched from *Yorktown*, consisting of 12 Devastator torpedo-bombers and 28 Dauntless dive-bombers. With only 18 fighters available for patrol over the carrier, they were forced to rely on their own machine-guns for protection. According to the practice of the time, each squadron attacked independently. As so often happened during the war, the pilots overestimated what they saw, mistaking Admiral Shima's flagship, a minelayer, for a light cruiser, minesweepers for transports, and landing barges for gunboats. Beginning their attacks at 0815, aircraft of the two Dauntless squadrons and the Devastator squadron were back on *Yorktown* by 0931, having irreparably damaged the destroyer *Kikuzuki* and sunk three minesweepers, including the *Tama Maru*. A second strike later destroyed two seaplanes and damaged a patrol craft, at the cost of one torpedo-bomber; while a third attack of 21 Dauntlesses, launched at 1400, dropped 21 half-ton bombs, but sank only four landing barges.

By 1632 hours the last returning aircraft were safely landed on the *Yorktown*, and

the 'Battle' of Tulagi was over. Only three aircraft had been lost (the other two being Wildcat fighters which had lost their way returning to the aircraft-carrier and had crash-landed on Guadalcanal, the pilots being picked up that night by the *Hammann*). But, in the words of Nimitz: 'The Tulagi operation was certainly disappointing in terms of ammunition expended to results obtained.'

Nevertheless, a mood of considerable elation prevailed on the *Yorktown* that evening, the pilots believing that they had sunk two destroyers, one freighter, and four gunboats, and damaged a third destroyer, a second freighter, and a seaplane tender. At one stage Fletcher detailed *Astoria* and *Chester* 'to go into Savo Island and clean up the cripples the following dawn', but later cancelled the order, and headed the whole force south for his rendezvous with Fitch. Once again luck had been with him, for Takagi was by now making his best speed south-eastward from Bougainville, having received calls for help from Tulagi at noon that day. If Fletcher had not achieved complete surprise in his Tulagi strike, and Takagi had moved earlier, the *Yorktown* would have met the Japanese aircraft-carriers on her own, as Fitch was widening the gap between Fletcher and himself all through the daylight hours of the 4th.

The next day, the 5th, was a relatively uneventful one for both sides. Having rejoined Fitch and Crace at the scheduled point about 0816, Fletcher spent most of the day re-fuelling from *Neosho*, within visual signalling distance of the junior flag commanders on a south-easterly course. The ships were by now well out of the cold front and were to enjoy perfect tropic seas weather for the next two days.

The tension increases

Meanwhile, the various components of the Japanese force were entering the Coral Sea. Admiral Takagi's Striking Force was moving down along the outer coast of the Solomons, and at 1900 it rounded San Cristobal, turned west, and passed north of Rennell Island. By dawn on May 6 it was well into the Coral Sea. The Port Moresby Invasion Group and Marushige's Support Group were on a southerly course for the Jomard Passage, while Goto's Covering Group began re-fuelling south of Bougainville, completing this task by 0830 the next morning. One four-engined Japanese seaplane, operating from Rabaul, was shot down by a Wildcat from *Yorktown* but, as Inouye did not know where it had been lost, he used most of his aircraft on the 5th in a bombing attack on Port Moresby.

On the 6th, the tension grew, as both Fletcher and Inouye knew that the clash was bound to come soon. The American commander decided that it was now time to put into effect his operational order of May 1, and accordingly redeployed his force for battle. An attack group, under Rear-Admiral Kinkaid, was formed from the heavy cruisers *Minneapolis*, *New Orleans*, *Chester*, and *Portland*, the light cruiser *Astoria*, and the destroyers *Phelps*, *Dewey*, *Farragut*, *Aylwin*, and *Monaghan*. The heavy cruisers *Australia*, *Hobart*, and *Chicago*, with the destroyers *Perkins* and *Walke*, formed Crace's support group, while the air group, to be placed under the tactical command of Fitch during air operations, comprised the *Yorktown* and *Lexington*, and the destroyers *Morris*, *Anderson*, *Hammann*, and *Russell*.

The oiler *Neosho*, escorted by the destroyer *Sims*, was detached from Task Force 17 at 1755, and told to head south for the next fuelling rendezvous, which was reached next morning.

Throughout the 5th and 6th, Fletcher was receiving reports from Intelligence regarding the movements of Japanese ships of nearly every type; by the afternoon of the 6th, a pattern was becoming evident to him. It was now fairly obvious that the Japanese invasion force would come through the Jomard Passage on the 7th or 8th, and Fletcher accordingly cut short fuelling operations, heading north-westward at 1930 on May 6, to be within striking distance by daylight on the 7th.

Owing to the inadequacies of land-based air searches, he did not as yet have any clear picture of the movements of Takagi's aircraft-carriers, or of the Japanese plan to envelop him. His own air searches had in fact stopped just short of Takagi's force, which was hidden under an overcast, having turned due south at 0930 that morning – thus dropping down on Fletcher's line of advance. By midnight Task Force 17 was about 310 miles from Deboyne Island, off the tail of New Guinea, where the Japanese had established a seaplane base to cover their advance.

If the air searches of either side had been more successful, the main action of the Coral Sea might have taken place on May 6. Takagi, amazingly, ordered no long-range searches on 6th, thus missing the opportunity of catching Fletcher while the latter was re-fuelling in bright sunlight. A reconnaissance aircraft from Rabaul did report Fletcher's position correctly, but the report did not reach Takagi until the next day. At one point he was only 70 miles away from Task Force 17, but ignorant of its presence. Thus when he turned north in the early evening, to protect the Port Moresby Invasion Group, he once more drew away from the United States aircraft-carriers.

Some elements of the Japanese force had, however, been sighted on May 6. At 1030 hours, B-17s from Australia had located and bombed the *Shoho*, of Goto's Covering Group, south of Bougainville. The bombs had fallen wide, but Allied planes spotted Goto again around noon, then turned south to locate the Port Moresby Invasion force near the Jomard Passage. Estimating that Fletcher was about 500 miles to the south-west, and expecting him to attack the next day, Inouye ordered that all operations should continue according to schedule. At midnight the invasion transports were near Misima Island, ready to slip through the Jomard Passage. Marushige had dropped the seaplane-carrier *Kamikawa Maru* at Deboyne, and retired to the north-west; while Goto, protecting the left flank of the Port Moresby Invasion Group, was about 90 miles north-east of the latter island. The Japanese were in an optimistic mood, for everything was going to plan, and that very day they had heard the news of the fall of the Philippines and the surrender of General Wainwright's forces on Corregidor.

The next day the battle began in earnest. Accepting Hara's recommendation that a thorough search to the south should be made before he moved to provide cover for the Port Moresby Invasion Group, Takagi accordingly launched reconnaissance aircraft at 0600 hours. As Hara later admitted: 'It did not prove to be a fortunate decision.' At 0736 one of the aircraft reported sighting an aircraft-carrier and a cruiser at the eastern edge of the search sector, and Hara, accepting this evaluation, closed distance and ordered an all-out bombing and torpedo attack. In fact, the vessels which had been sighted were the luckless *Neosho* and *Sims*.

After a single Japanese aircraft had attacked at 0900 hours, 15 high-level bombers appeared half an hour later, but failed to hit their targets. At 1038 the *Sims,* by swinging hard to starboard, avoided nine bombs dropped simultaneously by ten aircraft attacking horizontally. However, about noon, a further attack by 36 dive-bombers sealed the fate of the destroyer. Three 500-pound bombs hit the *Sims,* of which two exploded in her engine room. The ship buckled and sank stern first within a few minutes, with the loss of 379 lives.

Meanwhile, 20 dive-bombers had turned their attention to *Neosho,* scoring seven direct hits and causing blazing gasoline to flow along her decks. Although some hands took the order to 'make preparations to abandon ship and stand by' as a signal to jump over the side, the *Neosho* was in fact to drift in a westerly direction until May 11, when 123 men were taken off by the destroyer *Henley* and the oiler was scuttled. But the sacrifice of these two ships was not in vain, for if Hara's planes had not been drawn off in this way, the Japanese might have found and attacked Fletcher on the 7th, while he was busy dealing with the *Shoho*.

Fortune indeed smiled on Fletcher that day. At 0645, when a little over 120 miles south of Rossel Island, he ordered Crace's support group to push ahead on a north-westerly course to attack the Port Moresby Invasion Group, while the rest of Task Force 17 turned north. Apparently Fletcher, who expected an air duel with Takagi's aircraft-carriers, wished to prevent the invasion regardless of his own fate but, by detaching Crace, was in fact weakening his own anti-aircraft screen while depriving part of his force of the protection of carrier air cover.

The consequences of this move might have been fatal but, instead, the Japanese were to make another vital error by concentrating their land-based air groups on Crace rather than Fletcher's aircraft-carriers. A Japanese seaplane spotted the support group at 0810, and at 1358, when the ships of Crace's force were south and a little west of Jomard Passage, 11 single-engined bombers launched an unsuccessful attack. Soon afterwards, 12 Sallys (land-based navy bombers) came in low, dropping eight torpedoes. These were avoided by violent manoeuvres, and five of the bombers were shot down. Then 19 high-flying bombers attacked from 15,000 to 20,000, the ships dodging the bombs as they had the torpedoes.

Before the day was out, Crace had survived another attack, this time from American B-26s which mistook his vessels for Japanese. By midnight he had reached a point 120 miles south of the New Guinea tail, later turning back south on hearing that the Port Moresby Invasion Group had retired.

While Takagi's aircraft were dealing with *Neosho* and *Sims,* the *Shoho,* of Goto's Covering Group, had turned south-east into the wind to launch four reconnaissance aircraft and to send up other aircraft to protect the invasion force 30 miles to the south-west. By 0830 Goto knew exactly where Fletcher was, and ordered *Shoho* to prepare for an attack. Other aircraft had meanwhile spotted Crace's ships to the west. The result of these reports was to make Inouye anxious for the security of the Invasion Group, and at

◁ The man who could have lost Port Moresby to the Japanese: Vice-Admiral Frank J. Fletcher, commander of the US carrier force in the Battle of the Coral Sea. He was to prove one of the best carrier admirals in any navy.
▽ A Japanese photograph of the Coral Sea action, showing the heavy cruisers of Fletcher's force taking action to evade a Japanese air attack

0900 he ordered it to turn away instead of entering Jomard Passage, thus keeping it out of harm's way until Fletcher and Crace had been dealt with. In fact, this was the nearest the transports got to their goal.

Major strike, minor target

Fletcher had also launched a search mission early on the 7th, and at 0815 one of *Yorktown's* reconnaissance aircraft reported 'two carriers and four heavy cruisers' about 225 miles to the north-west, on the other side of the Louisiades. Assuming that this was Takagi's Striking Force, Fletcher launched a total of 93 aircraft between 0926 and 1030, leaving 47 for combat patrol. By this time Task Force 17 had re-entered the cold front, while Goto's force lay in bright sunlight near the reported position of the 'two carriers'. However, no sooner had *Yorktown's* attack group become airborne than her scouts returned, and it immediately became obvious that the 'two carriers and four heavy cruisers' should have read 'two heavy cruisers and two destroyers' – the error being due to the improper arrangement of the pilot's coding pad. Actually the vessels seen were two light cruisers and two gunboats of Marushige's Support Group. Fletcher, now knowing that he had sent a major strike against a minor target, courageously allowed the strike to proceed, thinking that with the invasion force nearby there must be some profitable targets in the vicinity.

The attack group from *Lexington,* well ahead of the *Yorktown* aircraft, was nearing Misima Island in the Louisiades shortly after 1100, when Lieutenant-Commander Hamilton, leading one of *Lexington's* Dauntless squadrons, spotted an aircraft-carrier, two or three cruisers, and some destroyers, about 25 miles to the starboard. This was the *Shoho* with the rest of Goto's Covering Group. As the *Shoho* was only 35 miles south-east of the original target location, it was a simple matter to re-direct the attack groups over the carrier. The first attack, led by Commander W. B. Ault, succeeded only in blowing five aircraft over the *Shoho's* side, but he was closely followed by Hamilton's ten Dauntlesses at 1110, the *Lexington's* torpedo squadron at 1117, and the *Yorktown's* attack group at 1125. Under such a concentrated attack, the *Shoho* stood little chance: soon she was on fire and dead in the water – and, smothered by 13 bomb and seven torpedo hits, she sank soon after 1135.

Only six American aircraft were lost in the attack off Misima. Back on the American aircraft-carriers, listeners in the radio rooms heard the jubilant report from Lieutenant-Commander Dixon, leading *Lexington's* other Dauntless squadron: 'Scratch one flat-top! Dixon to carrier, scratch one flat-top!'

With the air groups safely landed again, Fletcher decided to call off any further strikes against Goto, as he now knew, from intercepted radio messages, that his own position was known to Takagi – although he had not yet located the other Japanese aircraft-carriers himself. The worsening weather dissuaded him from further searches, and he thus set a westerly course during the night of May 7/8, thinking that the Japanese invasion force would come through the Jomard Passage the next morning. He did not yet know of Inouye's timid decision to recall the transports.

May 7 had been a day of serious blunders from the Japanese viewpoint, but Takagi and Hara were determined to try once more to destroy the American aircraft-carriers before the next day. Selecting the 27 pilots best qualified in night operations, Hara launched a strike from the *Shokaku* and *Zuikaku* just before 1630, with orders to attack Fletcher if they managed to locate him.

In fact, the gamble came near to success. Although the Japanese aircraft passed close to Task Force 17, they failed to locate owing to the foul weather and poor visibility. The American combat air-patrol, vectored out by radar to intercept, shot down nine of Hara's precious aircraft. An hour later, some of the returning Japanese laid a course for home right over the American carriers, which they mistook for their own. At 1900 three Japanese aircraft were spotted on *Yorktown*'s starboard beam, blinking in Morse code on Aldis lamps. Though recognised, they managed to escape. Twenty minutes later, three more attempted to join the *Yorktown*'s landing circle, and one was shot down. Hara was to lose 11 more aircraft which 'splashed' when attempting night landings on his aircraft-carriers. Only six of the original 27 got back safely.

With the day's operations virtually at an end, the commanders on both sides now toyed with the idea of a surface night action. At 1930 the *Lexington*'s radar showed what appeared to be a Japanese landing circle 30 miles to the east, but Fletcher did not receive the report until 2200, by which time he knew it might be impossible to locate Takagi's new position (at that moment the Japanese carriers were actually 95 miles to the east of Task Force 17). Fletcher rejected the idea of detaching a cruiser/destroyer force for a night attack, as the last-quarter moon would not afford much light, and he urgently needed all the anti-aircraft protection he could get for the next day's operations. In his own words: 'The best plan seemed to be to keep our force concentrated and prepare for a battle with enemy carriers next morning.'

Inouye, meanwhile, had ordered Goto's cruisers to rendezvous east of Rossel Island and make an attack on the Allied force, though he did not specify whether the target was to be Fletcher or Crace. By midnight he had reconsidered the plan, ordered the invasion to be postponed for two days, and split Goto's cruisers up between the invasion

Brown Bros

Brown Bros

US Navy

US Navy

Top to bottom: Near misses burst alongside the *Shokaku* as she frantically zig-zags to avoid the bombs. Only two bombs hit the *Shokaku*, one damaged the flight deck well forward on the starboard bow, while the other destroyed a repair compartment aft. The *Shokaku* could still recover aircraft, but could no longer launch any. The lower photographs show the last US attacks on the light carrier *Shoho*; smothered by 13 bombs and seven torpedo hits, she sank soon after 1135 hours on May 7

Carrier duel in the Coral Sea

▷ **Top to bottom:** The loss of the *Lexington*. Listing and on fire from her leaking fuel, the *Lexington* is abandoned by her crew after several violent explosions. Then the *Lexington*'s crew is taken aboard the destroyer escort

US Navy

1942 May 1: Task Force 17 is formed under Rear-Admiral Fletcher to operate in the Coral Sea. *Japanese take Mandalay.*
May 2: Fletcher *(Yorktown)* leaves Rear-Admiral Fitch *(Lexington)* refuelling, and heads west to search for the Japanese.
May 3: 1100 hours: Following the successful Japanese attack on Tulagi, Rear-Admiral Goto *(Shoho)* moves to cover the Port Moresby Invasion Force.
1900 hours: Fletcher receives news of Tulagi landings and moves north. *Neosho, Russell* detached to rendezvous with Fitch.
May 4: Following an air-strike against Tulagi, Fletcher returns south.
May 5: Fletcher rejoins Fitch, and spends the day refuelling. The Japanese Striking Force under Vice-Admiral Takagi *(Shokaku* and *Zuikaku)* enters Coral Sea.
May 6: Fletcher re-forms his forces and sends *Neosho* and *Sims* south to the next refuelling rendezvous. *Corregidor surrenders: the whole of the Philippines is now in Japanese hands.*
May 7: 0600 hours: Japanese reconnaissance aircraft discover *Neosho* and *Sims*.
0645 hours: Fletcher detaches Cruiser Support Group under Rear-Admiral Crace (RN) to attack Japanese Port Moresby Invasion Group.
0810 hours: Crace sighted by Japanese aircraft.
0815 hours: American aircraft sight 'two carriers and four heavy cruisers'.
0830 hours: Fletcher sighted by *Shoho*.
0900 hours: Japanese attack *Sims* and *Neosho*. Inouye orders invasion fleet to turn away.
0926-1030 hours: Fletcher launches strike.
1100 hours: *Shoho* sighted.
1135 hours: *Shoho* sunk.
1358 hours: Crace attacked by land-based aircraft.
1630 hours: Hara launches air-strike which fails to locate the Americans.
2400 hours: Invasion of Port Moresby is postponed.
May 8: 0815 hours: American aircraft locate *Shokaku* and *Zuikaku*. Japanese locate *Lexington* and *Saratoga*.
0900-0925 hours: Both sides launch strikes.
1030 hours: *Shokaku* attacked and disabled.
1118 hours: *Yorktown* and *Lexington* attacked.
1120 hours: *Lexington* hit by torpedo, but continues to receive aircraft.
1247 hours: Major explosion on *Lexington*.
1300 hours: Takagi sends *Shokaku* to Truk.
1710 hours: *Lexington* abandoned.
1956 hours: *Lexington* sunk by torpedo.
2400 hours: Yamamoto orders Takagi to locate and destroy American forces, but these have withdrawn out of range.

Brown Bros

US Navy

412

US Navy

transports and Takagi's force. Takagi, too, on receiving his pilot's reports that the American carriers were 50-60 miles away, considered a night action, but his air crews were tired – and he was in any case forestalled by a call for protection from the transports, which it was his basic mission to protect, and which had now lost the cover of the *Shoho*. Thus the main action was delayed yet again, although both sides expected a decision on the 8th. Everything now depended on locating the enemy as early as possible in the morning.

The battle 'busts open'
In the event, the reconnaissance aircraft of both sides, launched a little before dawn, located the opposing aircraft-carrier force almost simultaneously, between 0815 and 0838. Fitch, now in tactical command of the American aircraft-carrier operations, had 121 aircraft available, while Hara, his opposite number, had 122. The Japanese had more combat experience and better torpedoes, while the Americans were stronger in bomber aircraft. Thus the two sides began the first ever 'carrier-versus-carrier' battle roughly on equal terms, although by moving south during the night, Fletcher had run out of the bad weather and lay under clear skies, while the Japanese remained under the shelter of clouds and squalls.

The first sighting of the Japanese carriers had been at 0815, by one of *Lexington*'s scouts, the pilot reporting that Takagi was 175 miles to the north-east of Fletcher's position. Later, at 0930, Lieutenant-Commander Dixon sighted the Japanese Striking Force steaming due south in a position 25 miles north-east of the original contact, but about 45 miles north of Takagi's expected position at 0900 as predicted on the strength of that contact.

The discrepancy was to cause trouble for *Lexington*'s attack group, which by this time was airborne. Fitch had begun launching his strike between 0900 and 0925, the *Yorktown* group of 24 bombers with two fighters, and nine torpedo-bombers with four fighters, departing ten minutes before the *Lexington* aircraft. The dive-bombers spotted the Japanese first, at 1030, and took cloud cover to await the arrival of the Devastators. While *Shokaku* was engaged in launching further combat patrols, *Zuikaku* disappeared into a rain squall. The attack, which began at 1057, thus fell only on the *Shokaku*. Although the *Yorktown* pilots co-ordinated their attack well, only moderate success was achieved. The slow American torpedoes were either avoided or failed to explode, and only two bomb hits were scored on the *Shokaku*, one damaging the flight-deck well forward on the starboard bow and setting fire to fuel, while the other destroyed a repair compartment aft. The *Shokaku*, now burning, could recover aircraft, but could no longer launch any.

Of the *Lexington* group, ten minutes behind, the 22 dive-bombers failed to locate the target, leaving only 11 Devastators and four reconnaissance-bombers for the attack. Once again the torpedoes were ineffective, but the bombers scored a third hit on the Japanese aircraft-carrier. Although 108 of the vessel's crew had been killed, she had not been holed below the waterline, and her fires were soon brought under control. Most of her aircraft were transferred to the *Zuikaku* before Takagi detached *Shokaku* at 1300, with orders to proceed to Truk. Although in poor shape, she was not 'settling

fast', as the American pilots had reported.

Captain Sherman, in the *Lexington*, had estimated that the Japanese attack on Task Force 17 would begin at about 1100, basing his deduction on Japanese radio traffic. In fact, the *Yorktown* and *Lexington* were to come under attack in the interval between the strikes of their respective air groups on the Japanese aircraft-carriers. The Japanese had begun launching at about the same time as the Americans, but their attack group of 18 torpedo-bombers, 33 bombers, and 18 fighters was larger, better balanced, and more accurately directed to the target. Although the American radar picked them up 70 miles away, Fitch had far too few fighters to intercept successfully, and was forced to rely mainly on his AA gunners for protection.

At 1118 hours the battle 'busted out', as one American sailor described it. The *Yorktown*, with a smaller turning circle than the *Lexington*, successfully avoided eight torpedoes launched on her port quarter. Five minutes later she came under dive-bomber attack but, skilfully handled by Captain Buckmaster, escaped unscathed until 1127, when she received her only hit – from an 800-pound bomb which penetrated to the fourth deck, but did not impair flight operations. During this time, the evasive manoeuvres gradually drew the American aircraft-carriers apart and, although the screening vessels divided fairly evenly between them, the breaking of their defensive circle contributed to Japanese success.

The *Lexington*, larger than the *Yorktown*, had a turning circle of 1,500 to 2,000 yards in diameter, compared with the 1,000-yard tactical diameter of her consort. Moreover, she had the misfortune to suffer an 'anvil' attack from the Japanese torpedo-bombers, which came in on both bows at 1118 to launch their missiles at altitudes of about 50 to 200 feet, and about half a mile from the '*Lady Lex*'. Despite valiant manoeuvres by Sherman, she received one torpedo hit on the port side forward at 1120, quickly followed by a second opposite the bridge. At the same time a dive-bombing attack commenced from 17,000 feet, the *Lexington* receiving two hits from small bombs. One exploded in a ready-ammunition box on the port side, while the other hit the smokestack structure. To add to the din of battle, the ship's siren jammed as a result of an explosion and shrieked weirdly throughout most of the attack.

Some 19 minutes later, the aircraft-carrier battle was, to all intents and purposes, at an end. At this point, honours were more or less equal – but for the Americans the real tragedy was still to come. At first it appeared that the doughty *Lexington* had survived to fight another day. A list of 7 degrees caused by the torpedo hits was corrected by shifting oil ballast, while her engines remained unharmed. To her returning pilots she did not appear to be seriously damaged, and the recovery of the air group went ahead. At about 1240 hours, Commander H. R. 'Pop' Healy, the damage control officer, reported to Captain Sherman: 'We've got the torpedo damage temporarily shored up, the fires out, and soon will have the ship back on an even keel. But I would suggest, sir, that if you have to take any more torpedoes, you take 'em on the starboard side.'

Minutes later, at 1247, a tremendous internal explosion, caused by the ignition of fuel vapours by a motor generator which had been left running, shook the whole ship. Although the *Lexington* continued landing her planes, a series of further violent ex-

plosions seriously disrupted internal communications. Yet another major detonation occurred at 1445, and the fires soon passed beyond control. Despite the fact that the destroyer *Morris* came alongside to help fight the blaze, while *Yorktown* recovered all aircraft still airborne, the need for evacuation became increasingly apparent.

At 1630 hours the *Lexington* had come to a dead stop, and all hands prepared to abandon ship. At 1710 Fitch called to Sherman to 'get the men off', the *Minneapolis*, *Hammann*, *Morris*, and *Anderson* assisting with the rescue operations. Evacuation was orderly – even the ship's dog being rescued – and Sherman was the last to leave the aircraft-carrier, sliding down a line over the stern. At 1956 the destroyer *Phelps* was ordered to deliver the 'coup de grace' with five torpedoes, and the *Lexington* sank at 2000, a final explosion occurring as she slipped beneath the waves.

The Battle of the Coral Sea was now over. The Japanese pilots had reported sinking both American aircraft-carriers, and Hara's acceptance of this evaluation influenced Takagi's decision to detach the *Shokaku* for repairs, as well as Inouye's order that the Striking Force should be withdrawn. Even though he thought that both American aircraft-carriers had been destroyed, the cautious Inouye still deemed it necessary to postpone the invasion, apparently because he felt unable to protect the landing units against Allied land-based aircraft. Yamamoto did not agree with this decision and, at 2400 hours, countermanded the order, detailing Takagi to locate and annihilate the remaining American ships. But, by the time Takagi made his search to the south and east, Fletcher was out of reach.

Tactically, the battle had been a victory for the Japanese. Although they had lost 43 aircraft on May 8 (as against 33 lost by the Americans), and Hara had been left with only nine operational aircraft after the *Zuikaku* had proved unable to take on all *Shokaku*'s aircraft, their air strikes had achieved greater results. The sinking of the *Lexington*, *Neosho*, and *Sims* far outweighed the loss of the *Shoho* and the various minor craft sunk at Tulagi.

Strategically, however, Coral Sea was an American victory: the whole object of the Japanese operation – the capture of Port Moresby – had been thwarted. Despite the occupation of Tulagi, later won back by the US Marines at a heavy price, the Japanese had gained very little of their initial objectives. Moreover, the damage to the *Shokaku*, and the need to re-form the battered air groups of the *Zuikaku*, was to keep both these carriers out of the Midway battle, where their presence might have been decisive.

Though the Coral Sea engagement was full of errors by the commanders on both sides, the Americans did take its lessons to heart. The ratio of fighters to bombers and torpedo-bombers was increased, and improvements were made in the organisation of attacks in the weeks that remained before the next great naval clash. But the really significant feature of the Coral Sea battle was that it opened a new chapter in the annals of naval warfare: it was the first ever 'carrier-against-carrier' action in which all losses were inflicted by air action, and no ship on either side made visual surface contact with the enemy.

The stage for Midway was now set.

BATTLE OF MIDWAY

Central Pacific, June 1942

The Battle of Midway must be accounted one of the truly decisive battles of history. In one cataclysmic blow, it wiped out the overwhelming Japanese superiority in naval air strength, the vital key to the successful prosecution of a war in the vast spaces of the Pacific. More than half the Japanese carrier strength—with the élite of their highly trained and experienced aircrews—were eliminated: they were to prove irreplaceable. From now onwards, the Japanese were on the defensive. The early run of victories which Yamamoto had promised had come to a premature end. Now a period of stalemate was to begin during which American production would rise to its overwhelming flood—which Yamamoto had also foreseen. The Rising Sun had passed its brilliant noon

USS *Yorktown* is struck by a Japanese torpedo

Pearl Harbor was a scene of intense activity during the last week of May 1942: a feeling of great impending events pervaded the atmosphere. On the 26th the aircraft-carriers *Enterprise* and *Hornet* of Task Force (TF) 16 had steamed in and moored, to set about in haste the various operations of refuelling and replenishing after a vain race across the Pacific to try to go to the aid of Rear-Admiral Frank Fletcher's Task Force 17 in the Battle of the Coral Sea. On the next day the surviving carriers of TF 17, the *Yorktown*'s blackened sides and twisted decks providing visible signs of the damage sustained in the battle, berthed in the dry dock of the naval base where an army of workmen swarmed aboard to begin repairs.

Under normal circumstances, weeks of work lay ahead of them, but now word had reached the dockyard that emergency repairs in the utmost haste were required. Work was to go on, night and day, without ceasing, until the ship was at least temporarily battle-worthy. For at the headquarters of the C-in-C Pacific, Admiral Chester Nimitz, it was known from patient analysis and deciphering of enemy signals that the Japanese fleet was moving out to throw down a challenge which, in spite of local American inferiority, had to be accepted.

So, on May 28, Task Force 16 sailed again, the *Enterprise* flying the flag of Rear-Admiral Raymond Spruance, and vanished into the wide wastes of the Pacific. Six cruisers and nine destroyers formed its screen; two replenishment tankers accompanied it. The following day the dockyard gave Nimitz the scarcely credible news that the *Yorktown* was once again battle-worthy. Early on the 30th she, too, left harbour and, having gathered in her air groups, headed north-westward to rendezvous with Task Force 16 at 'Point Luck', 350 miles northeast of the island of Midway. Forming the remainder of Task Force 17 were two cruisers and five destroyers.

The main objective of the Japanese was the assault and occupation of the little atoll of Midway, 1,100 miles west-north-west of Oahu, and forming the western extremity of the Hawaiian island chain. Together with the occupation of the Aleutian Islands, the capture of Midway would extend Japan's eastern sea frontier so that sufficient warning might be obtained of any threatened naval air attack on the homeland—Pearl Harbor in reverse. The plan had been given added impetus on April 18 by the raid on Tokyo mounted by Colonel Doolittle's army bombers taking off from the *Hornet*.

Doubts on the wisdom of the Japanese plan had been voiced in various quarters; but Yamamoto, the dynamic C-in-C of the Combined Fleet, had fiercely advocated it for reasons of his own. He had always been certain that only by destroying the American fleet could Japan gain the breathing space required to consolidate her conquests and negotiate satisfactory peace terms—a belief which had inspired the attack on Pearl Harbor. Yamamoto rightly believed that an attack on Midway was a challenge that Nimitz could not ignore. It would bring the US Pacific Fleet out where Yamamoto, in overwhelming strength, would be waiting to bring it to action.

The Japanese plan was an intricate one, as their naval strategic plans customarily were, calling for exact timing for a junction at the crucial moment of several disparate forces; and it involved—also typically—the offering of a decoy or diversion to lure the enemy into dividing his force or expending his strength on a minor objective.

Between May 25/27, Northern Force would sail from Ominato, at the northern tip of Honshu, for the attack on the Aleutians. The II Carrier Striking Force, under Rear-Admiral Kakuta—comprising the small aircraft-carriers *Ryujo* and *Junyo*, two cruisers, and three destroyers—would be the first to sail, its task being to deliver a surprise air attack on Dutch Harbor on June 3. This, it was expected, might induce Nimitz to send at least part of his fleet racing north, in which case it would find waiting to intercept it a Guard Force, of four battleships, two cruisers, and 12 destroyers.

Kakuta's force would be followed two days later by the remainder of the Aleutians force—two small transport units with cruiser and destroyer escorts for the invasion of Attu and Kiska on June 5. Meanwhile, from Hashirajima Anchorage in the Inland Sea, the four big aircraft-carriers of Vice-Admiral Nagumo's I Carrier Striking Force—*Akagi, Kaga, Hiryu,* and *Soryu*—would sail for the vicinity of Midway. There, at dawn on the 4th, their bombers and fighters would take off for the softening-up bombardment of the island prior to the assault landing two days later by troops carried in the Transport Group.

The original plan had called for the inclusion of the *Zuikaku* and *Shokaku* in Nagumo's force. But, like the *Yorktown*,

The moment of greatest danger in carrier warfare, when no retaliation against an enemy strike is possible—Dauntless dive-bombers ranged forward on USS *Enterprise* for refuelling and rearming

US Navy

the *Shokaku* had suffered damage in the Coral Sea battle and could not be repaired in time to take part in the Midway operation, while both carriers had lost so many experienced aircrews that replacements could not be trained in time.

Yamamoto's battle-squadron

In support of the Transport Group, four heavy cruisers under Vice-Admiral Kurita would also sail from Guam. Finally, three powerful forces would sail in company from the Inland Sea during May 28:

● The Main Body, comprising Yamamoto's splendid new flagship *Yamato,* the biggest battleship in the world, mounting nine 18-inch guns, the 16-inch battleships *Nagato* and *Mutsu*, with attendant destroyers;

● The Main Support Force for the Midway invasion force—two battleships, four heavy cruisers, and attendant destroyers—under Vice-Admiral Kondo;

● The Guard Force (mentioned above).

Parting company with Yamamoto's force after getting to sea, Kondo was to head for a supporting position to the south-west of Midway, while the Guard Force would proceed to station itself near the route from Pearl Harbor to the Aleutians. Yamamoto himself, with the Main Body, was to take up a central position from which he could proceed to annihilate whatever enemy force Nimitz sent out. To ensure that the dispatch of any such American force should not go undetected, Pearl Harbor was to be reconnoitred between May 31 and June 3 by two Japanese flying-boats via French Frigate Shoal (500 miles north-west of Hawaii), where a submarine was to deliver them petrol. As a further precaution, two cordons of submarines were to be stationed to the north-west and west of Hawaii by June 2, with a third cordon farther north towards the Aleutians.

Yamamoto's plan was ingenious, if over-intricate: but it had two fatal defects. For all his enthusiasm for naval aviation, he had not yet appreciated that the day of the monstrous capital ship as the queen of battles had passed in favour of the aircraft-carrier which could deliver its blows at a range 30 times greater than that of the biggest guns. The role of the battleship was now as close escort to the vulnerable aircraft-carriers, supplying the defensive anti-aircraft gunpower the latter lacked. Nagumo's force was supported only by two battleships and three cruisers. Had Yamamoto's Main Body kept company with it, the events that were to follow might have been different.

Far more fatal to Yamamoto's plan, however, was his assumption that it was shrouded from the enemy, and that only when news reached Nimitz that Midway was being assaulted would the Pacific Fleet leave Pearl Harbor. Thus long before the scheduled flying-boat reconnaissance—which in the event failed to take place because French Frigate Shoal was found to be in American hands—and before the scouting submarines had reached their stations, Spruance and Fletcher, all unknown to the Japanese, were beyond the patrol lines and poised waiting for the enemy's approach. Details of this approach as well as the broad lines of Yamamoto's plan were known to Nimitz. Beyond sending a small force of five cruisers and ten destroyers to the Aleutians to harass the invasion force, he concentrated all his available force—TF 16 and 17—in the area.

He had also a squadron of battleships under his command, to be sure; but he had no illusions that, with their insufficient speed to keep up with the aircraft-carriers, their great guns could play any useful part in the events to follow. They were therefore relegated to defensive duties on the American west coast.

For the next few days the Japanese Combined Fleet advanced eastwards according to schedule in its wide-spread, multi-pronged formation. Everywhere a buoyant feeling of confidence showed itself, generated by the memories of the unbroken succession of Japanese victories since the beginning of the war. In the I Carrier Striking Force, so recently returned home after its meteoric career of destruction—from Pearl Harbor, through the East Indies, and on to Ceylon without the loss of a ship—the 'Victory Disease' as it was subsequently to be called by the Japanese themselves, was particularly prevalent. Only the admiral—or so Nagumo was subsequently to say—felt doubts of the quality of the many replacements who had come to make up the wastage in experienced aircrews inevitable even in victorious operations.

Spruance and Fletcher had meanwhile made rendezvous during June 2, and Fletcher had assumed command of the two task forces, though they continued to manoeuvre as separate units. The sea was calm under a blue sky split up by towering cumulus clouds. The scouting aircraft, flown off during the following day in perfect visibility, sighted nothing, and Fletcher was able to feel confident that the approaching enemy was all unaware of his presence to the north-east of Midway. Indeed, neither Yamamoto nor Nagumo, pressing forward blindly through rain and fog, gave serious thought to such an apparently remote possibility.

Far to the north on June 3, dawn broke grey and misty over Kikuta's two aircraft-carriers from which, soon after 0300 hours, the first of two strike waves took off to wreak destruction among the installations and fuel tanks of Dutch Harbor. A further attack was delivered the following day, and during the next few days American and Japanese forces sought each other vainly among the swirling fogs, while the virtually unprotected Kiska and Attu were occupied by the Japanese. But as Nimitz refused to let any of his forces be drawn into the skirmish, this part of Yamamoto's plan failed to have much impact on the great drama being enacted farther south.

Setting the scene

The opening scenes of this drama were enacted early on June 3 when a scouting Catalina flying boat some 700 miles west of Midway sighted a large body of ships, steaming in two long lines with a numerous screen in arrowhead formation, which was taken to be the Japanese main fleet. The sighting report brought nine army B-17 bombers from Midway, which delivered three high-level bombing attacks and claimed to have hit two battleships or heavy cruisers and two transports. But the enemy was in reality the Midway Occupation Force of transports and tankers, and no hits were scored on them until four amphibious Catalinas from Midway discovered them again in bright moonlight in the early hours of June 4 and succeeded in torpedoing a tanker. Damage was slight, however, and the tanker remained in formation.

More than 800 miles away to the east, Fletcher intercepted the reports of these encounters but from his detailed knowledge of the enemy's plan was able to identify the Occupation Force. Nagumo's carriers, he knew, were much closer, some 400 miles to the west of him, approaching their flying-off position from the north-west. During the night, therefore, Task Forces 16 and 17 steamed south-west for a position 200 miles north of Midway which would place them at dawn within scouting range of the unsuspecting enemy. The scene was now set for what was to be one of the great decisive battles of history.

Deadly game of hide-and-seek

The last hour of darkness before sunrise on June 4 saw the familiar activity in both the carrier forces of ranging-up aircraft on the flight-deck for dawn operations. Aboard the *Yorktown,* whose turn it was to mount the first scouting flight of the day, there were Dauntless scout dive-bombers, ten of which were launched at 0430 hours for a search to a depth of 100 miles between west and east through north, a precaution against being taken by surprise while waiting for news from the scouting flying boats from Midway.

Reconnaissance aircraft were dispatched at the same moment from Nagumo's force. One each from the *Akagi* and *Kaga,* and two seaplanes each from the cruisers *Tone* and *Chikuma* were to search to a depth of 300 miles to the east and south. The seaplane carried in the battleship *Haruna,* being of an older type, was restricted to 150 miles. The main activity in Nagumo's carriers, however, was the preparation of the striking force to attack Midway—36 'Kate' torpedo-bombers each carrying a 1,770-pound bomb, 36 'Val' dive-bombers each with a single 550-pound bomb, and 36 Zero fighters as escort. Led by Lieutenant Joichi Tomonaga, this formidable force also took off at 0430.

By 0445 all these aircraft were on their way—with one notable exception. In the cruiser *Tone,* one of the catapults had given trouble, and it was not until 0500 that her second seaplane got away. This apparently minor dislocation of the schedule was to have vital consequences. Meanwhile, the carrier lifts were already hoisting up on deck an equally powerful second wave; but under the bellies of the 'Kates' were slung torpedoes, for these aircraft were to be ready to attack any enemy naval force which might be discovered by the scouts.

The lull in proceedings which followed the dawn fly-off from both carrier forces was broken with dramatic suddenness. At 0520, aboard Nagumo's flagship *Akagi,* the alarm was sounded. An enemy flying boat on reconnaissance had been sighted. Zeros roared off the deck in pursuit. A deadly game of hide-and-seek among the clouds developed, but the American naval fliers evaded their hunters. At 0534 Fletcher's radio office received the message 'Enemy carriers in sight', followed by another reporting many enemy aircraft heading for Midway; finally, at 0603, details were received of the position and composition of Nagumo's force, 200 miles west-south-west of the *Yorktown.* The time for action had arrived.

The *Yorktown*'s scouting aircraft were at once recalled and while she waited to gather them in, Fletcher ordered Spruance to proceed with his Task Force 16 'south-westerly and attack enemy carriers when definitely located'. *Enterprise* and *Hornet* with their screening cruisers and destroyers turned away, increasing to 25 knots, while hooters blared for 'General Quarters' and aircrews

The Cost of Victory

◁ Repair crews at work on the wooden flight-deck of the *Yorktown* after the first attack by Japanese dive-bombers. On this occasion she was struck by three bombs—one burst on the flight-deck and started a fire in the hangar, a second smashed three boiler uptakes, and put five of the six boilers out of action, and the third penetrated to the fourth deck and started another fire. Although the ship was temporarily halted, rapid repairs got her under way again before the second wave of torpedo-bombers arrived.

▽ Their attacks came from four directions, and in spite of violent evasive action, two torpedoes hit her port side, and she began to list heavily

◁ The *Yorktown*'s fuel tanks were torn open, and the flooding caused the 26-degree list; all power was lost, so it was not possible to right her by counter-flooding. Then the order was given to abandon ship.

▷ A salvage party moves along her steeply sloping deck. After the first abandonment, she continued to drift without sinking. So the following day, a salvage party went back on board, and she was taken in tow. But two days later a Japanese submarine, which had been sent to look for her, penetrated her escort screen, and torpedoed her twice. This time she sank— the major US loss at Midway

Imperial War Museum

203

manned their planes to warm-up ready for take-off. Meanwhile, 240 miles to the south, Midway was preparing to meet the impending attack.

Radar had picked up the approaching aerial swarm at 0553 and seven minutes later every available aircraft on the island had taken off. Bombers and flying-boats were ordered to keep clear, but Marine Corps fighters in two groups clawed their way upwards, and at 0616 swooped in to the attack. But of the 26 planes, all but six were obsolescent Brewster Buffaloes, hopelessly outclassed by the highly manoeuvrable Zeros. Though they took their toll of Japanese bombers, they were in turn overwhelmed, 17 being shot down and seven others damaged beyond repair. The survivors of the Japanese squadrons pressed on to drop their bombs on power-plants, seaplane hangars, and oil tanks.

At the same time as the Marine fighters, ten torpedo-bombers had also taken off from Midway—six of the new Grumman Avengers (which were soon to supersede the unsatisfactory Devastator torpedo-bombers in American aircraft-carriers) and four Army Marauders. At 0710 they located and attacked the Japanese carriers; but with no fighter protection against the many Zeros sent up against them, half of them were shot down before they could reach a launching position. Those which broke through, armed with the slow and unreliable torpedoes which had earned Japanese contempt in the Coral Sea battle, failed to score any hits; greeted with a storm of gunfire, only one Avenger and two Marauders escaped to crash-land on Midway.

Unsuccessful as these attacks were, they had important consequences. From over Midway, Lieutenant Tomonaga, surveying the results of his attack, at 0700 signalled that a further strike was necessary to knock out the island's defences. The torpedo attacks seemed to Nagumo to bear this out, and, as no inkling of any enemy surface forces in the vicinity had yet come to him, he made the first of a train of fatal decisions. At 0715 he ordered the second wave of aircraft to stand by to attack Midway. The 'Kate' bombers, concentrated in the *Akagi* and *Kaga,* had to be struck down into the hangars to have their torpedoes replaced by bombs. Ground crews swarmed round to move them one by one to the lifts which took them below where mechanics set feverishly to work to make the exchange. It could not be a quick operation, however, and it had not been half completed when, at 0728, came a message which threw Nagumo into an agony of indecision.

The reconnaissance seaplane from the *Tone*—the one which had been launched 30 minutes behind schedule—was fated to be the one in whose search sector the American fleet was to be found; and now it sent back the signal—'Have sighted ten ships, apparently enemy, bearing 010 degrees, 240 miles away from Midway: Course 150 degrees, speed more than 20 knots.' For the next quarter of an hour Nagumo waited with mounting impatience for a further signal giving the composition of the enemy force.

Only if it included carriers was it any immediate menace at its range of 200 miles—but in that case it was vital to get a strike launched against it at once. At 0745 Nagumo ordered the re-arming of the 'Kates' to be suspended and all aircraft to prepare for an attack on ships, and two minutes later he signalled to the search plane: 'Ascertain ship types and maintain contact.' The re-

sponse was a signal of 0758 reporting only a change of the enemy's course; but 12 minutes later came the report: 'Enemy ships are five cruisers and five destroyers.'

Nagumo's hopes crushed

This message was received with heartfelt relief by Nagumo and his staff; for at this moment his force came under attack first by 16 Marine Corps dive-bombers from Midway, followed by 15 Flying Fortresses, bombing from 20,000 feet, and finally 11 Marine Corps Vindicator scout-bombers. Every available Zero was sent aloft to deal with them, and not a single hit was scored by the bombers. But now, should Nagumo decide to launch an air strike, it would lack escort fighters until the Zeros had been recovered, refuelled, and re-armed. While the air attacks were in progress, further alarms occupied the attention of the battleship and cruiser screen when the US submarine *Nautilus*—one of 12 covering Midway—fired a torpedo at a battleship at 0825. But neither this nor the massive depth-charge attacks in retaliation were effective; and in the midst of the noise and confusion of the air attacks—at 0820—Nagumo received the message he dreaded to hear: 'Enemy force accompanied by what appears to be a carrier.'

The luckless Japanese admiral's dilemma, however, had been disastrously resolved for him by the return of the survivors of Tomonaga's Midway strike at 0830. With some damaged and all short of fuel, their recovery was urgent; and rejecting the advice of his subordinate carrier squadron commander—Rear-Admiral Yamaguchi, in the *Hiryu*—to launch his strike force, Nagumo issued the order to strike below all aircraft on deck and land the returning aircraft. By the time this was completed, it was 0918.

Refuelling, re-arming, and ranging-up a striking-force in all four carriers began at once, the force consisting of 36 'Val' dive-bombers and 54 'Kates', now again armed with torpedoes, with an escort of as many Zeros as could be spared from defensive patrol over the carriers. Thus it was at a carrier force's most vulnerable moment that—from his screening ships to the south—Nagumo received the report of an approaching swarm of aircraft. The earlier catapult defect in the *Tone*; the inefficient scouting of its aircraft's crew; Nagumo's own vacillation (perhaps induced by the confusion caused by the otherwise ineffective air attacks from Midway); but above all the fatal assumption that the Midway attack would be over long before any enemy aircraft-carriers could arrive in the area—all had combined to plunge Nagumo into a catastrophic situation. The pride and vainglory of the victorious carrier force had just one more hour to run.

When Task Force 16 had turned to the south-west, leaving the *Yorktown* to recover her reconnaissance aircraft, Nagumo's carriers were still too far away for Spruance's aircraft to reach him and return; and if the Japanese continued to steer towards Midway, it would be nearly 0900 before Spruance could launch his strike. When calculations showed that Nagumo would probably be occupied recovering his aircraft at about that time, however, Spruance decided to accept the consequences of an earlier launching in order to catch him off balance. Every serviceable aircraft in his two carriers, with the exception of the fighters required for defensive patrol, was to be included, involving a double launching,

taking a full hour to complete, during which the first aircraft off would have to orbit and wait, eating up precious fuel.

It was just 0702 when the first of the 67 Dauntless dive-bombers, 29 Devastator torpedo-bombers, and 20 Wildcat fighters, which formed Task Force 16's striking force, flew off. The torpedo squadrons had not yet taken the air when the sight of the *Tone's* float plane, circling warily on the horizon, told Spruance that he could not afford to wait for his striking force to form up before dispatching them. The *Enterprise's* dive-bombers led by Lieutenant-Commander Mc-Clusky, which had been the first to take off, were ordered to lead on without waiting for the torpedo-bombers or for the fighter escort whose primary task must be to protect the slow, lumbering Devastators. At 0752, McClusky took departure, steering to intercept Nagumo's force which was assumed to be steering south-east towards Midway. The remainder of the air groups followed at intervals, the dive-bombers and fighters up at 19,000 feet, the torpedo-bombers skimming low over the sea.

This distance between them, in which layers of broken cloud made maintenance of contact difficult, had calamitous consequences. The fighters from the *Enterprise*, led by Lieutenant Gray, took station above but did not make contact with Lieutenant-Commander Waldron's torpedo squadron from the *Hornet*, leaving the *Enterprise's* torpedo squadron, led by Lieutenant-Commander Lindsey, unescorted. *Hornet's* fighters never achieved contact with Waldron, and flew instead in company with their dive-bombers. Thus Task Force 16's air strike advanced in four separate, independent groups—McClusky's dive-bombers, the *Hornet's* dive-bombers and fighters, and the two torpedo squadrons.

All steered initially for the estimated position of Nagumo, assuming he had maintained his south-easterly course for Midway. In fact, at 0918, having recovered Tomonaga's Midway striking force, he had altered course to north-east to close the distance between him and the enemy while his projected strike was being ranged up on deck. When the four air groups from TF 16 found nothing at the expected point of interception, therefore, they had various courses of action to choose between. The *Hornet's* dive-bombers decided to search south-easterly where, of course, they found nothing. As fuel ran low, some of the bombers returned to the carrier, others made for Midway to refuel. The fighters were not so lucky: one by one they were forced to ditch as their engines spluttered and died.

The two torpedo squadrons, on the other hand, low down over the water, sighted smoke on the northern horizon and, turning towards it, were rewarded with the sight of the Japanese carriers shortly after 0930. Though bereft of fighter protection, both promptly headed in to the attack. Neither Waldron nor Lindsey had any doubts of the suicidal nature of the task ahead of them. The former, in his last message to his squadron, had written: 'My greatest hope is that we encounter a favourable tactical situation, but if we don't, and the worst comes to the worst, I want each of us to do his utmost to destroy our enemies. If there is only one plane left to make a final run in, I want that man to go in and get a hit. May God be with us all.'

His hopes for a favourable tactical situation were doomed. Fifty or even more Zeros concentrated on his formation long before they reached a launching position. High overhead, Lieutenant Gray, leading the *Enterprise*'s fighter squadron, waited for a call for help as arranged with Lindsey, thinking that Waldron's planes were the torpedo squadron from his own ship — a call which never came. From the cruisers and destroyers of the screen came a withering fire. One by one the torpedo-bombers were shot down. A few managed to get their torpedoes away before crashing, but none hit the enemy. Only one of the pilots, Ensign George H. Gay, survived the massacre, clinging to a rubber seat cushion which floated away from his smashed aircraft, until dusk when he could inflate his life-raft without attracting strafing Zeros.

Five minutes later it was the turn of Lindsey's 14 Devastators from the *Enterprise*. Purely by chance, as he was making his attack on the starboard side of the *Kaga*, the torpedo squadron from the *Yorktown* came sweeping in from the other side, aiming to attack the *Soryu*, and drawing off some of the fighter opposition.

The *Yorktown*'s strike group of 17 dive-bombers led by Lieutenant-Commander Maxwell F. Leslie, with 12 torpedo-bombers of Lieutenant-Commander Lance E. Massey's squadron and an escort of six Wildcats, had taken departure from their carrier an hour and a quarter after the strike groups of Task Force 16. A more accurate assessment of probabilities by Leslie, however, had brought the whole of this force simultaneously over the enemy to deliver the co-ordinated, massed attack which alone could hope to swamp and break through the defences. In addition, at this same moment, McClusky's dive-bombers also arrived overhead. McClusky, after reaching the expected point of interception, had continued for a time on his south-westerly course and had then made a cast to the north-west. There he had sighted a destroyer steering north-east at high speed. This was the *Arashi*, which had been left behind to depth-charge the *Nautilus*. Turning to follow her, McClusky was led straight to his objective.

The simultaneous attack by the two torpedo squadrons brought no result of itself. Scores of Zeros swarmed about them, brushing aside the puny force of six Wildcats. The massacre of the clumsy Devastators was re-enacted. Lindsey and ten others of his force were shot down. Of Massey's squadron, only two survived. The few torpedoes launched were easily evaded.

The sacrifice of the torpedo-bombers had not been in vain, nevertheless. For, while every Japanese fighter plane was milling about low over the water, enjoying the easy prey offered to them there, high overhead there were gathering, all unseen and unmolested, the dive-bombers — McClusky's 18, and Leslie's 17. And now, like hawks swooping to their prey, they came plummeting down out of the sky.

In the four Japanese carriers the refuelling and re-arming of the strike force had been almost completed. The decks were crowded with aircraft ranged for take-off. Nagumo had given the order to launch and ships were turning into wind. Aboard the *Akagi*, all eyes were directed downwards at the flight-deck.

Suddenly, over the rumbling roar of engines, the high-pitched rising scream of dive-bombers was heard. Even as faces swivelled upwards at the sound, the black dots which were 1,000-pound bombs were seen leaving three 'Hell-Divers' as they pulled out from their near-vertical dive. Fascinated eyes watched the bombs grow in size as they fell inexorably towards that most vulnerable of targets, a full deck load of armed and fuelled aircraft. One bomb struck the *Akagi* squarely amidships, opposite the bridge and just behind the aircraft lift, plunged down into the hangar and there exploded, detonating stored torpedoes, tearing up the flight deck, and destroying the lift. A second exploded in the midst of the 'Kates' on the after part of the deck, starting a tremendous conflagration to add to that in the hangar. In a matter of seconds Nagumo's proud flagship had been reduced to a blazing shambles. From time to time she was further shaken by internal explosions as the flames touched off petrol tanks, bombs, and torpedoes. Within a few minutes Captain Aoki knew that the damage and fires were beyond control. He persuaded the reluctant Nagumo that it was necessary to transfer his flag to a ship with radio communication intact.

Carnage in the Japanese carriers

Only three dive-bombers from the *Enterprise* had attacked the flagship. The remainder of the air group, 34 dive-bombers, all concentrated on the *Kaga*. Of four bombs which scored direct hits, the first burst just forward of the superstructure, blowing up a petrol truck which stood there, and the sheet of flame which swept the bridge killed everyone on it, including the captain. The other three bombs falling among the massed aircraft on the flight deck set the ship ablaze and started the same fatal train of fires and explosions as in the *Akagi*. Within a few minutes, the situation was so beyond control that the senior surviving officer ordered the transfer of the Emperor's portrait to an attendant destroyer — the custom obligatory when a ship was known to be doomed, and conducted with strict naval ceremony. The *Kaga* was to survive for several hours, nevertheless.

Simultaneously, with the *Akagi* and *Kaga*, the *Soryu* had also been reeling under a devastating attack. Leslie of the *Yorktown* was leading veterans of the Coral Sea battle, probably the most battle-experienced aviators in the American navy at that time. With deadly efficiency they dived in three waves in quick succession from the starboard bow, the starboard quarter, and the port quarter, released their bombs and climbed away without a single casualty. Out of the shower of 1,000-pound bombs, three hit. The first penetrated to the hangar deck and the explosion lifted the steel platform of the lift, folding it back against the bridge. The others landed among the massed aircraft, causing the whole ship to be engulfed in flames. It took Captain Ryusaku Yanaginoto only 20 minutes to decide to order 'Abandon Ship' to save his crew from being burnt alive, though the *Soryu*, like her sisters, was to survive for some hours yet.

Thus, in five brief, searing minutes, half of Japan's entire fleet carrier force, her naval *corps d'élite*, had been shattered. For the time being the *Hiryu*, some miles away, remained untouched.

On board the *Akagi*, though the bomb damage was confined at first to her flight and hangar decks and her machinery spaces remained intact, the fires fed by aviation petrol from aircraft and from fuel lines were beyond the capacity of the Japanese crew to master. They fought them for seven hours but by 1715 Captain Aoki had decided there was no hope of saving his ship. The Emperor's portrait was transferred to a destroyer and the ship was abandoned. Permission was asked of the C-in-C to hasten her end but it was not until nearly dawn on the following day — when Yamamoto at last fully understood the fullness of the Japanese defeat — that he gave his approval and the *Akagi* was sent to the bottom by torpedoes from a destroyer.

Petrol-fed fires similarly swept the *Kaga* and defeated all efforts to save her. Lying stopped and burning she became the target for three torpedoes from the *Nautilus* which, after her earlier adventure had surfaced and chased after the Japanese carriers. Even the stationary target, however, was too much for the unreliable torpedoes with which the Americans were at that time equipped. Of three fired, two missed, and the third struck but failed to explode. At 1640 orders were given to abandon the *Kaga*, and at 1925 two great explosions tore her asunder and sent her to the bottom.

The *Soryu*'s story was a similar one, of

The *Mikuma*, a heavy cruiser of the Support Force, was smothered with bombs and sunk, after her speed had been reduced by an engine-room explosion — petrol fumes from a crashed US dive-bomber had been sucked down into the starboard engine room, and exploded, killing the crew there

US Navy

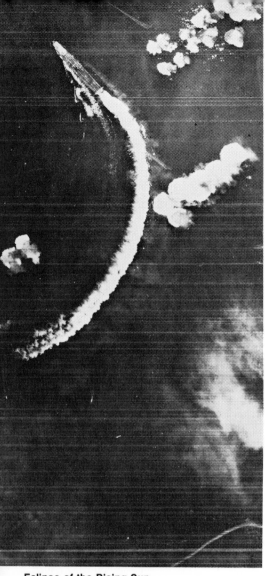

US Air Force

Brown Bros

It was not only the Japanese carrier force which suffered at Midway: while taking avoiding action after sighting a US submarine, two heavy cruisers—*Mikuma* and *Mogami*—of the Support Force collided, and became a tempting target for the US aircraft. **Right:** the *Mogami* survived their attentions, and in spite of severe damage was able to reach Truk.

Eclipse of the Rising Sun
△ In one terrible five minutes Japan's superiority in the Pacific was shattered for ever. While all the Japanese defences were concentrating upon massacring the slow US torpedo-bombers, 35 US dive-bombers arrived overhead, and *Soryu, Kaga,* and *Akagi* (seen here taking evasive action) were all reduced to blazing wrecks and had to be abandoned by their crews. Of the fleet carriers only *Hiryu,* cruising separately, was able to launch a counterattack. ▷ But she did not last long—about ten hours later, 24 US dive-bombers surprised her, and she was hit four times, one of the bombs blowing the forward lift bodily on to the bridge.

Top right: Admiral Nimitz, C-in-C US Pacific Fleet, foresaw the enemy moves.
Rear-Admiral Spruance (left), Task Force 17, evaded the Japanese trap. *Bottom left:* Admiral Yamamoto, C-in-C Japanese Combined Fleet; his plan was too complex. Admiral Kondo (right); his Midway support force never saw action

Imperial War Museum

intermittent internal explosions from within the great mass of flame and smoke which she had become. When Captain Yanaginoto gave the order 'Abandon Ship', he determined to immolate himself, dying in the flames or going down with her. A party of his men returning on board with the intention of persuading him or, if necessary, of forcing him to save himself, fell back abashed at the heroic, determined figure of their captain, standing sword in hand, facing forward, awaiting his end. They left him to his chosen fate. As they did so they heard him singing the Japanese national anthem. Yanaginoto's resolution held fast till 1913 hours when at last the Soryu and the bodies of 718 of her crew slid beneath the surface.

Much had taken place in the meantime before Nagumo's three aircraft-carriers suffered their death throes. The first survivors of the American strike groups to land back on their ships made it clear that one Japanese carrier had not yet been located. This was the Hiryu which, at the time of the attack, had become separated from the remainder. Admiral Fletcher therefore launched a ten-plane search from the Yorktown, and sent up a defensive patrol of a dozen Wildcats. It was none too soon. At a few minutes before noon, the Yorktown's radar gave the warning of enemy planes coming in from the west.

These were the Hiryu's attack group of 18 dive-bombers and six fighters, led by Lieutenant Michio Kobayashi, a veteran leader who had taken part in every operation of the Nagumo force. As soon as they had flown off, a further strike of ten torpedo-bombers and six Zeros, to be led by the redoubtable Tomonago, was ranged up. Kobayashi's force had followed some of the Yorktown's attack planes back and now concentrated on Fletcher's flagship. Wildcats—for once outnumbering the escorting Zeros—broke through to get at the 'Vals', shooting down ten of them, including the leader. Of the eight which remained, two were knocked down by anti-aircraft fire from the cruiser screen.

The six survivors, however, showed that they had lost none of their skill as they screamed down on the carrier. One 'Val' broke up under anti-aircraft fire, but its bomb sped on to burst on the flight-deck, killing many men, and starting a hangar fire below. A second bomb plunged through the side of the funnel and burst inside, starting more fires. With three boiler uptakes smashed and the furnaces of five or six boilers extinguished, the carrier's speed fell away until, 20 minutes later, she came to a stop. A third bomb penetrated to the fourth deck where for a time a fire threatened the forward petrol tanks and magazines.

His flagship immobilised, her radio and radar knocked out, Admiral Fletcher transferred his flag to the cruiser Astoria, and ordered the Portland to take the aircraft-carrier in tow. The damage-control organization worked wonders, however. Before the towline had been passed, the Yorktown was under way again and working up to 20 knots, and the refuelling of the fighters was in progress. Prospects seemed bright. Then a cruiser's radar picked up Tomonaga's air group, 40 miles away and coming in fast. There was just time to launch eight of the refuelling Wildcats to join the four already in the air, but they were unable to get through the screen of fighters to get at the 'Kates'—though they shot down three of the 'Zeros'. A tremendous screen of bursting

shells spread itself in front of the attackers, while the cruisers raised a barrage of splashes with their main armament, a wall of water columns through which it seemed impossible that the skimming 'Kates' could fly.

Yorktown fatally damaged

Five 'Kates' were shot down, but the remainder, coming in from four different angles, displayed all their deadly skill, boring doggedly in to drop their torpedoes at the point-blank range of 500 yards. It was impossible for the carrier to avoid them all. Two hit on her port side, tearing open the double-bottom fuel tanks and causing flooding which soon had her listing at 26 degrees. All power was lost, so that counter-flooding was impossible. It seemed that the Yorktown was about to capsize. At 1500, Captain Buckmaster ordered 'Abandon Ship'.

Meanwhile, however, the dive-bombers from Spruance's Task Force 16, operating some 60 miles to the north-east of the Yorktown, had wreaked vengeance on the Hiryu. Twenty-four Dauntlesses, of which ten had been transferred from the Yorktown, arrived overhead undetected soon after the few survivors of Hiryu's attack had been recovered. The aircraft-carrier circled and swerved to avoid the bombs from the plummeting dive-bombers, but in vain. Four of them hit, one of which blew the forward lift bodily on to the bridge. The others started the inevitable fires and explosions, and the same prolonged death agonies as the Hiryu's sisters were still suffering. By 2123 she had come to a stop. Desperate efforts to subdue the flames went on through the night; but at 0230 the following morning she was abandoned to be torpedoed by her attendant destroyers.

When the night of June 4 closed over the four smoking Japanese carriers and over the crippled Yorktown, the Battle of Midway was, in the main, over. Neither of the opposing commanders yet knew it, however, and manoeuvres and skirmishes were to continue for two more days. The Japanese commanders, except Nagumo, were slow to realise that the shattering of their four fleet carriers signified defeat and the end of the Midway operation. Admiral Kondo, with his two fast battleships, four heavy cruisers, and the light carrier Zuiho had set off to the help of Nagumo at midday on June 4, and soon afterwards Yamamoto was signalling to all his scattered forces to concentrate and attack the enemy. He himself, with the main body of his fleet, was coming up fast from the west bringing the 18-inch guns of the giant Yamato and the 16-inch ones of the Nagato and Mutsu to throw in their weight. Still underestimating his opponent, he was dreaming of a night encounter in which his immensely powerful fleet would overwhelm the American task force and avenge the losses of the previous day. The great fleet action with battleships in stately line hurling huge shells at each other was still his hope and aim.

Such a concept had been forcibly removed from American naval strategy by the shambles of Pearl Harbor. Raymond Spruance, one of the greatest admirals to come to the fore during the war, was not to be lured within range of Yamamoto's battleships, above all at night, when his carriers, at this time untrained for night-flying, would be at a tremendous disadvantage. At sunset he turned away eastwards, aiming to take up a

position on the following day from which he could either 'follow up retreating enemy forces or break up a landing attack on Midway'.

The Japanese C-in-C refused to credit the completeness of the disaster that had overtaken his fleet and the Midway plan until early on June 5 when, at 0255, he ordered a general retirement. Thus, when Spruance, after prudently steering eastwards to keep his distance from the still overwhelmingly superior Japanese surface fleet, and reversing course at midnight so as to be within supporting distance of Midway at daylight, sent a strike of 58 dive-bombers from his two ships during the afternoon of the 5th to seek out Yamamoto's Main Body, his airmen encountered nothing but a lone destroyer sent to search for the Hiryu.

Two final incidents remain to be briefly recounted. When Yamamoto ordered his general retirement, the squadron of four heavy cruisers of Admiral Kurita's Support Force, the Kumano, Suzuya, Mikuma, and Mogami, was to the westward of Midway, steering through the night to deliver a bombardment at dawn. They now swung round to reverse course in full view of the American submarine Tambor. As they steadied on their retirement course, from the flagship the Tambor was sighted in the moonlight ahead. The signal for an emergency turn to port was flashed down the line but was not taken in by the rear ship, Mogami. Failing to turn with the remainder she collided with the Mikuma, suffering serious damage which reduced her speed to 12 knots. Leaving the Mikuma and two destroyers to escort the cripple, Kurita hurried on with the remainder.

News of this attractive target soon reached Midway. Twelve army Flying Fortresses took off but were unable to locate it; but 12 Marine Corps dive-bombers sighted the long oil slick being trailed by the Mikuma, followed it up—and at 0805 dived to the attack. Their bombs failed to achieve direct hits, but the plane of Captain Richard E. Fleming crashed on the after turret of the Mikuma. Petrol fumes were sucked down into the cruiser's starboard engine-room and exploded, killing the whole engine-room crew.

The two cruisers nevertheless continued to limp slowly away, until the following day when Spruance, having abandoned hope of delivering another blow on Yamamoto's Main Fleet, was able to direct his dive-bombers on to them. The Mikuma was smothered with bombs and sunk, but the Mogami miraculously survived, heavily damaged, to reach the Japanese base at Truk.

While these events were taking place, far to the east the abandoned Yorktown had drifted crewless through the night of June 4/5. She was still afloat at noon the next day and it became clear she had been prematurely abandoned. A salvage party boarded her and she was taken in tow. Hopes of getting her to port were high until the Japanese submarine I-168, sent by Yamamoto for the purpose, found her, penetrated her anti-submarine screen, and put two torpedoes into her. At 0600 on June 7 the Yorktown sank at last. The major US loss at Midway.

At sundown on the previous day Spruance had turned his force back eastwards to meet his supply tankers. That the Battle of Midway, one of the most decisive battles in history, was over was finally clear to all.

△ Paulus directs the German bombardment
▷ Stalingrad in the first weeks of battle

Ullstein

Stalingrad, December/October 1942

The stubbornness of the Russian defence of Stalingrad baffled the Germans—and as they became tied down in the savage hand-to-hand fighting, they chose to regard it as a 'battle of attrition' in which the Red Army would be bled white. But it was the Wehrmacht which failed to understand tactical as well as strategic reality; it was the Wehrmacht which was being exhausted and forced to throw in all its reserves, while the Russians built up their strength, committing only enough troops to keep the Germans from breaking through

STALINGRAD: THE ONSLAUGHT

The fighting in the Eastern campaign reflects the whole spectrum of military experience. The cold steel and ferocity of the cavalry charge differ little from the Middle Ages; the misery and privation of interminable bombardment in a stinking dugout recall the First World War. Yet the dominant characteristic of the Russian front is a composite one. Open warfare and manoeuvre alternate with bouts of vicious infighting in a manner that evokes both the Western Desert and the subterranean grapplings in the Verdun tunnels.

Certainly the tremendous battle which was to be fought out in Stalingrad has its nearest parallel in the horrors of Falkenhayn's 'mincing machine' at Verdun. But there are significant differences. At Verdun the contestants rarely saw one another face to face: they were battered to death by high explosives or cut down at long range by machine-gun fire. At Stalingrad each separate battle resolved itself into a combat between individuals. Soldiers would jeer and curse at their enemy across the street; often they could hear his breathing in the next room while they reloaded; hand-to-hand duels were finished in the dark twilight of smoke and brick dust with knives and pickaxes, with clubs of rubble and twisted steel.

There was also a major strategic difference. The Germans—after their self-evident

failure to take the city by storm—were fond of drawing the Verdun parallel, of holding up the battle as a cleverly conceived attrition engagement designed to wear down the numerical superiority of the Red Army. But in fact this analogy was completely false, for the Soviet commitment was never (until the start of their counteroffensive in November) as massive as that of their enemy. The Red Army commanders might well have been glad of extra reinforcement, particularly during September, but the capacity of the Volga ferries simply did not permit it. While Paulus, in contrast, was given, and committed, everything he asked for.

At first, while the Germans were in the outskirts, it was still possible for them to draw advantage from their superiority in armour and aircraft. The buildings here had been of wood, and all had been burned down in the great air raid of August 23. Fighting took place in a giant petrified forest of blackened chimney stacks, where the defenders had little cover except the charred remains of the matchboard bungalows and workers' settlements that ringed the town. But as the Germans edged deeper into the region of sewers and brick and concrete, their old plan of operations lost its value. General Dörr has described how:

The time for conducting large-scale operations was gone for ever; from the wide expanses of steppe-land, the war moved into the jagged gullies of the Volga hil with their copses and ravines, into the facto area of Stalingrad, spread out over uneve pitted, rugged country, covered with iro concrete, and stone buildings. The mi as a measure of distance, was replaced by t yard. GHQ's map was the map of the city.

For every house, workshop, water-towe railway embankment, wall, cellar, and eve pile of ruins, a bitter battle was wage without equal even in the First World W with its vast expenditure of munitions. T distance between the enemy's army and ou was as small as it could possibly be. Despi the concentrated activity of aircraft an artillery, it was imposible to break out of t area of close fighting. The Russians su passed the Germans in their use of the terra and in camouflage and were more experience in barricade warfare for individual buil ings . . .

If the battle had a tactical pattern it w one which revolved around the fate of t Volga ferries, the lifeline of the garriso For although the Russians kept their heav and medium artillery on the east ban they were consuming small-arms ammun tion and mortar bombs at a prodigious rat and depended on the traffic across the Volg for many other services essential to th fighting spirit of the garrison, ranging fro the provision of vodka to the evacuation the wounded. The slight curve in the cour of the river and the numerous islets which obstructed the stream between Rynok and Krasnaya Sloboda made it very difficult to enfilade all the crossings even after guns had been installed on the right bank, and well-nigh impossible to do so at night, when the bulk of the traffic was on the move. The Germans were slow to realise this, and instead of putting all their energies into attacks at the extremities of the Russian position and working their way up and down the bank – a tactic which if successful would ultimately have left the garrison stranded on an island of rubble in the centre – they switched their effort to different points in the city, adopting the most extravagant method of simply battering away at one block after another. Each of the three major 'offensives' launched during the siege was aimed at cutting across the thin strip of ground the Russians held and reaching the Volga at as many points as possible. The result was that, even where they were successful in their aim, the attackers would find themselves stranded in a web of hostile emplacements, their access corridors too narrow to make the troops at their tip anything but a tactical liability.

If the Luftwaffe had been employed with single-minded persistence in an 'interdiction' role (in the sense, that is to say, in which the term came to be understood in the West), the Volga ferries might have been knocked out. Certainly Richthofen, had he been properly directed, could have done more about the Russian 76-mm batteries on the east bank, whose fire deterred VI Army from operating too close to the river. Yet the fact remains that while the Russians showed great skill and versatility in adapting their tactics as the battle wore on, Paulus mishandled it from the start. The Germans were baffled by a situation hitherto outside their military experience, and they reacted to it typically – by the application of brute force in heavier and heavier doses.

This bafflement extended from the senior commanders to the ordinary soldier. Hoffman (the diarist whose exultation at the August 23 terror raid has already been quoted) reflects this attitude in the epithets he attaches to the defenders, ranging progressively through incredulity and contempt to fear, and then to self-pity.

September 1: *'Are the Russians really going to fight on the very bank of the Volga? It's madness.'*
September 8: *' . . . insane stubbornness.'*
September 11: *' . . . Fanatics.'*
September 13: *' . . . wild beasts.'*
September 16: *'Barbarism . . . not men but devils.'*
September 26: *' . . . Barbarians, they use gangster methods.'*

There is no further comment for a month on the quality of the enemy, and during this time the entries are filled with gloom at the plight of the writer and his comrades in arms.

October 27: *' . . . The Russians are not men, but some kind of cast-iron creatures; they never get tired and are not afraid of fire.'*
October 28: *'Every soldier sees himself as a condemned man.'*

When Paulus returned to his headquarters after the conference with Hitler on September 12, H-Hour for his third offensive was imminent. This time VI Army was deploying 11 divisions, of which three were Panzer. The Russians had only three infantry divisions, parts of four others, and two tank brigades. This drastic reduction in the

defenders' strength was the result of Hoth's success in at last battering his way through to the Volga at Kuporosnoye, a suburb of Stalingrad proper, and thereby dividing the 62nd and 64th armies. Five days earlier, on September 4, Hoth's tanks had split the 64th Army for the first time by reaching the Volga at Krasnoarmeisk, and the bulk of the Russian force, which had spent itself in six weeks of continuous fighting against the élite Panzergruppe of the whole German army, was pinned down along a 12-mile strip of the Stalingrad-Rostov railway embankment.

The day after XIV Panzer Division took Kuporosnoye, Chuikov was appointed to the command of the isolated 62nd Army. That night he crossed by boat from Beketovka, and after a nightmare jeep journey up the left bank of the river to report to Khrushchev and Yeremenko at 'front' headquarters at Yamy, took the ferry at dawn from Krasnaya Sloboda across into the burning city.

Stalingrad had now been under continuous bombardment for 24 hours, as the whole of VI Army's artillery paved the way for Paulus's concentric assault. As their boat approached the landing stage, spent shrapnel and shell fragments were dropping in the inky water 'like trout', and they could feel the air temperature several degrees hotter from the flames. Chuikov reflected: 'Anyone without experience of war would think that in the blazing city there is no longer anywhere left to live, that everything has been destroyed and burnt out. . . . But I know that on the other side of the river a battle is being fought, a titanic struggle is taking place.'

Paulus had concentrated two 'shock forces' with the intention of converging against the southern half of the town and joining at the so-called 'central landing stage', opposite Krasnaya Sloboda. Three infantry divisions, the 71st, 76th, and 295th, were to move down from the Gumrak railway station, capturing the main hospital, to Matveyev Kurgan. An even stronger force, the 94th Infantry Division and the XXIX Motorised, was to strike north-east from the Yelshanka mining suburb, backed by XIV and XXIV Panzer.

Chuikov had only 40 tanks left in action, and many of these were no longer mobile, but had been dug in as armoured fire points. He also had a small tank reserve of 19 KVs, as yet uncommitted, but no infantry reserves whatever, for every man capable of carrying a gun had been sucked into the battle. Chuikov's predecessor, General Lopatin, had (allegedly) been convinced of the 'impossibility and pointlessness of defending the city', and this feeling of depression, wrote Chuikov, 'had undoubtedly communicated itself to his subordinates . . . on the pretext of illness three of my deputies [for artillery, tanks, and army engineering] had left for the opposite bank of the Volga!'

The defence problem was fourfold: first, it was essential to hold the flanks firmly anchored to the riverbank. Every yard of the steep Volga escarpment was precious to the Russians, who had tunnelled into it for depots, hospitals, ammunition dumps, fuel stores – even for garages for the 'Katyusha' trucks, which would reverse out of their caves, fire a salvo, and get back under cover in less than five minutes. The northern flank below Rynok was the stronger of the two, for here the vast concrete edifices of the Tractor Factory and the Barrikady and Krasny Oktyabr were virtually indestruc-

tible. But at the southern end the buildings were less substantial and the ground was relatively open, undulating mounds of rubble and occasional patches of scorched heath dominated by a few towering grain elevators. Here, too, lay the shortest route to the central landing stage, along the course of the Tsaritsa rivulet; and to the nerve centre of the Stalingrad defence system, Chuikov's own command post, which was in a dugout known as the 'Tsaritsyn bunker', sunk into the side of the river-bed at the Pushkin Street bridge.

The danger of concentrating his strength at the extremities was that Chuikov's very long west-facing front (it was over 15 miles from Rynok to Kuporosnoye as the crow flies, and double that length along the 'line') would be vulnerable to a concentrated assault on a narrow front, and in particular, that Matveyev-Kurgan, a grassy hillock of parkland that dominated the centre of the town, might be lost to the enemy before reinforcements could reach it.

Chuikov had sent urgent requests for infantry reinforcements to Yeremenko on September 13, when Paulus had started his attack, and he had learned during the night that the 13th Guards Infantry Division, a very strong unit under General Rodimtsev (who had started his experiences of street fighting in the Madrid University City, in 1936), would be sent over the river starting at dusk the following day. However, during the afternoon of September 14, Paulus's central attack broke through the Russian front behind the hospital and the Germans of the 76th Infantry Division began to pour into the rear areas of the town, obstructed only by a few snipers.

Lorry-loads of infantry and tanks tore through into the city. The Germans obviously thought that the fate of the town had been settled, and they all rushed to the centre and the Volga as soon as possible and grabbed souvenirs for themselves . . . we saw drunken Germans jumping down from their lorries, playing mouth organs, shouting like madmen and dancing on the pavements.

To deal with this breakthrough Chuikov used his last reserve of tanks, which meant bringing them up from the southern sector, itself under very heavy pressure, in daylight. His own staff officers and the bunker guard company were involved in the fighting, which raged all night. Infiltrating German soldiers got within 200 yards of the Tsaritsyn bunker, and some managed to get heavy machine-guns into position where they could fire on the central landing stage. Chuikov was now faced with the prospect of having his front once again broken into two pieces, yet to move any more troops from the southern end of the perimeter might lead to the collapse of the whole position there.

At this stage German tactics, though wasteful and unsophisticated, were highly abrasive against a defence stretched as thin as was that of the 62nd Army in the first days of Chuikov's command. They consisted of using tanks in packets of three or four at a time in support of each company of infantry. The Russians would never fire at tanks alone, but let them pass through into the field of fire of anti-tank guns and dug-in T-34s which were held farther back; so it was always necessary for the Germans to send infantry in first to draw the defender's fire. Once his position had been identified, the tanks would cover one another while they battered away at point-blank range until the building fell down. Where the houses were tall and substantial, this was a long and untidy business. Armour-piercing shot was useless—it would pass right through the walls, doing no more damage than a jagged hole about two feet across, yet to risk sending the tanks out with only high-explosive ammunition meant that they were at the mercy of any roaming T-34 that might come on the scene. Furthermore, although tank fire would gut the first two floors, the limited elevation of the turret often meant that unless the top storey was set alight the rest of the building went undamaged.

We would spend the whole day clearing a street, from one end to the other, establish blocks and fire-points at the western end, and prepare for another slice of the salami the next day. But at dawn the Russians would start up firing from their old positions at the far end! It took us some time to discover their trick; they had knocked communicating holes through between the garrets and attics and during the night they would run back like rats in the rafters, and set their machine-guns up behind some topmost window or broken chimney. . . .

The tank crews were understandably reluctant to take their machines into narrow streets, where their lightly armoured rear deck could be penetrated by anti-tank rifles or grenades thrown from above. It was necessary to accompany each attacking force with teams of flame throwers so that the buildings could be burned down, but this was an extremely hazardous occupation as a single bullet could turn the operator into a flaming torch. It was impossible to get sufficient volunteers without recourse to the punishment battalions, even though special rates of pay were introduced.

However, during the first days of their September offensive the Germans enjoyed a superiority of three-to-one in men and over six-to-one in tanks, and the Luftwaffe held complete dominion of the daylight air. From September 14 to 22, while VI Army was relatively fresh and the Russians were defending with the remains of units which had been badly battered in earlier fighting, was the period of Stalingrad's greatest peril.

'We beat off the next attack with stones'
During the night of September 14 the whole defence front was creaking so badly that Rodimtsev's division had to be sent into action by battalion, as soon as the men had formed up after disembarking from the ferries. The result was that it was dispersed over a wide area and many of the men were soon cut off in the strange wilderness of smoke and rubble in which they found themselves at daybreak. Yet even among these the stubborn refusal of the Russian to surrender while he still had ammunition played its part in dislocating the German advance. The account of a member of the 3rd Company of the 42nd Regiment, though its somewhat self-consciously heroic style may jar on Western ears, deserves to be quoted at length because of its relevance to the conditions of street fighting and the spirit of the defenders. At one point they found themselves cut off.

We moved back, occupying one building after another, turning them into strongholds. A soldier would crawl out of an occupied position only when the ground was on fire under him and his clothes were smouldering. During the day the Germans managed to occupy only two blocks.

At the crossroads of Krasnopiterskaya and Komsomolskaya Streets we occupied a

three-storey building on the corner. This was a good position from which to fire on all comers and it became our last defence. I ordered all entrances to be barricaded, and windows and embrasures to be adapted so that we could fire through them with all our remaining weapons.

At a narrow window of the semi-basement we placed the heavy machine-gun with our emergency supply of ammunition—the last belt of cartridges. I had decided to use it at the most critical moment.

Two groups, six in each, went up to the third floor and the garret. Their job was to break down walls, and prepare lumps of stone and beams to throw at the Germans when they came up close. A place for the seriously wounded was set aside in the basement. Our garrison consisted of forty men. Difficult days began. . . . The basement was full of wounded;

only twelve men were still able to fight. There was no water. All we had left in the way of food was a few pounds of scorched grain; the Germans decided to beat us with starvation. Their attacks stopped, but they kept up the fire from their heavy-calibre machine-guns all the time. . . . The Germans attacked again. I ran upstairs with my men and could see their thin, blackened and strained faces, the bandages on their wounds, dirty and clotted with blood, their guns held firmly in their hands. There was no fear in their eyes. Lyuba Nesterenko, a nurse, was dying, with blood flowing from a wound in her chest. She had a bandage in her hand. Before she died she wanted to help to bind someone's wound, but she failed. . . .

The German attack was beaten off. In the silence that gathered around us we could hear the bitter fighting going on for

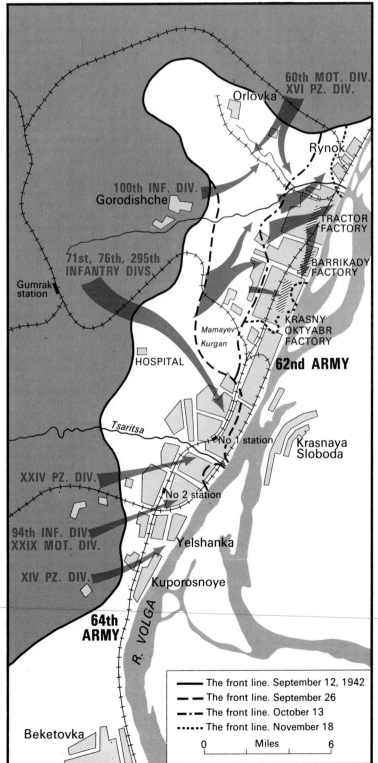

◁ Paulus' attempts to eliminate Stalingrad as a focus of Soviet resistance were unnecessarily extravagant: he mishandled the battle from the start, and made the fatal mistake of switching targets. Instead of trying to wipe out the Soviet supply ferries across the Volga, and cut off the garrison by concentrating on the wings of the Soviet position, Paulus tried to push through to the Volga on as broad a front as possible. In the three major 'offensives' of the battle, the Soviet defenders were quick to adapt to the changing tactics of the Germans, and they held their footholds on the west bank only by their mass of artillery on the east bank. Paulus' Luftwaffe strength was never concentrated against the Soviet artillery or supply ferries. He threw all the formidable resources of VI Army into battering Stalingrad into rubble, and achieved nothing but the attrition of his own forces

Maveyev-Kurgan and in the factory area.

How could we help the men defending the city? How could we divert from over there even a part of the enemy forces, which had stopped attacking our building?

We decided to raise a red flag over the building, so that the Nazis would not think we had given up. But we had no red material. Understanding what we wanted to do, one of the men who was severely wounded took off his bloody vest and, after wiping the blood off his wound with it, handed it over to me.

The Germans shouted through a megaphone: 'Russians! Surrender! You'll die just the same!'

At that moment a red flag rose over our building.

'Bark, you dogs! We've still got a long time to live!' shouted my orderly, Kozhushko.

We beat off the next attack with stones, firing occasionally and throwing our last grenades. Suddenly from behind a blank wall, from the rear, came the grind of a tank's caterpillar tracks. We had no anti-tank grenades. All we had left was one anti-tank rifle with three rounds. I handed this rifle to an anti-tank man, Berdyshev, and sent him out through the back to fire at the tank point-blank. But before he could get into position he was captured by German tommy-gunners. What Berdyshev told the Germans I don't know, but I can guess that he led them up the garden path, because an hour later they started to attack precisely that point where I had put my machine-gun with its emergency belt of cartridges.

This time, reckoning that we had run out of ammunition, they came impudently out of their shelter, standing up and shouting. They came down the street in a column.

I put the last belt in the heavy machine-gun at the semi-basement window and sent the whole of the 250 bullets into the yelling, dirty-grey Nazi mob. I was wounded in the hand but did not let go of the machine-gun. Heaps of bodies littered the ground. The Germans still alive ran for cover in panic. An hour later they led our anti-tank rifleman on to a heap of ruins and shot him in front of our eyes, for having shown them the way to my machine-gun.

There were no more attacks. An avalanche of shells fell on the building. The Germans stormed at us with every possible kind of weapon. We couldn't raise our heads.

Again we heard the ominous sound of tanks. From behind a neighbouring block stocky German tanks began to crawl out. This, clearly, was the end. The guardsmen said good-bye to one another. With a dagger my orderly scratched on a brick wall: 'Rodimtsev's guardsmen fought and died for their country here.'

On September 21 both sides were prostrate with exhaustion. The Germans had cleared the whole of the Tsaritsa river bed and established their guns a few yards from the central landing stage. They had also carved out a large section, about a mile and a half square, of the built-up area behind the Stalingrad No. 1 Station, lying between the Tsaritsa and the Krutoy gully. Chuikov had been forced to move his headquarters out of the Tsaritsyn bunker to Matveyev-Kurgan, and with the central landing stage area neutralised, the garrison was now dependent on the factory ferries at the northern end of the town.

At this stage the Germans were perilously close to gaining control of the whole southern half of the city, up to the Krutoy gully at least, as only one Russian unit, the 92nd

Infantry Brigade, was left fighting south of the Tsaritsa. But Hoth's forces were being seriously impeded by a number of isolated centres of resistance which had been left behind in the first armoured rush on September 13 and 14. These were mostly centred around the giant grain elevators, and in one case we have available the diaries of men who took part on either side in a particular engagement. First, the German:

September 16: *Our battalion, plus tanks, is attacking the elevator, from which smoke is pouring—the grain in it is burning, the Russians seem to have set light to it themselves. Barbarism. The battalion is suffering heavy losses. There are not more than sixty men left in each company. The elevator is occupied not by men but by devils that no flames or bullets can destroy.*

September 18: *Fighting is going on inside the elevator. The Russians inside are condemned men; the battalion commander says: 'The commissars have ordered those men to die in the elevator.'*

If all the buildings of Stalingrad are defended like this, then none of our soldiers will get back to Germany. I had a letter from Elsa today. She's expecting me home when victory's won.

September 20: *The battle for the elevator is still going on. The Russians are firing on all sides. We stay in our cellar; you can't go out into the street. Sergeant-Major Nuschke was killed today running across a street. Poor fellow, he's got three children.*

September 22: *Russian resistance in the elevator has been broken. Our troops are advancing towards the Volga. We found about forty Russians dead in the elevator building. Half of them were wearing naval uniform—sea devils. One prisoner was captured, seriously wounded, who can't speak, or is shamming.*

The 'seriously wounded' prisoner was Andrey Khozyaynov, of the Marine Infantry Brigade, and his version conveys a remarkable impression of the character of the Stalingrad street fighting, where the individual courage and tenacity of a few soldiers and junior NCOs, often out of touch and given up for lost by their own high command, could affect the whole development of the battle.

Our brigade was ferried over the Volga during the night of September 16 and at dawn on the 17th it was already in action.

I remember that on the night of the 17th, after fierce fighting, I was called to the battalion command post and given the order to take a platoon of machine-gunners to the grain elevator and, together with the men already in action there, to hold it come what may. We arrived that night and presented ourselves to the garrison commander. At that time the elevator was being defended by a battalion of not more than thirty to thirty-five guardsmen, together with the wounded, some slightly, some seriously, whom they had not yet been able to send back to the rear.

The guardsmen were very pleased to see us arrive, and immediately began pouring out jokes and witticisms. Eighteen well-armed men had arrived in our platoon. We had two medium machine-guns and one light machine-gun, two anti-tank rifles, three tommy-guns, and radio equipment.

At dawn a German tank carrying a white flag approached from the south. We wondered what could have happened. Two men emerged from the tank, a Nazi officer and an interpreter. Through the interpreter the officer tried to persuade us to surrender to

the 'heroic German army', as defence was useless and we would not be able to hold our position any longer. 'Better to surrender the elevator,' affirmed the German officer. 'If you refuse you will be dealt with without mercy. In an hour's time we will bomb you out of existence.'

'What impudence,' we thought, and gave the Nazi lieutenant a brief answer: 'Tell all your Nazis to go to hell! . . . You can go back, but only on foot.'

The German tank tried to beat a retreat, but a salvo from our two anti-tank rifles stopped it.

Enemy tanks and infantry, approximately ten times our numbers, soon launched an attack from south and west. After the first attack was beaten back, a second began, then a third, while a reconnaissance 'pilot' plane circled over us. It corrected the fire and reported our position. In all, ten attacks were beaten off on September 18.

We economised on ammunition, as it was a long way, and difficult, to bring up more.

In the elevator, the grain was on fire, the water in the machine-guns evaporated, the wounded were thirsty, but there was no water nearby. This was how we defended ourselves twenty-four hours a day for three days. Heat, smoke, thirst—all our lips were cracked. During the day many of us climbed up to the highest points in the elevator and from there fired on the Germans; at night we came down and made a defensive ring round the building. Our radio equipment had been put out of action on the very first day. We had no contact with our units.

September 20 arrived. At noon twelve enemy tanks came up from the south and west. We had already run out of ammunition for our anti-tank rifles, and we had no grenades left. The tanks approached the elevator from two sides and began to fire at our garrison at point-blank range. But no one flinched. Our machine-guns and tommy-guns continued to fire at the enemy's infantry, preventing them from entering the elevator. Then a Maxim, together with a gunner, was blown up by a shell, and the casing of the second Maxim was hit by shrapnel, bending the barrel. We were left with one light machine-gun.

The explosions were shattering the concrete; the grain was in flames. We could not see one another for dust and smoke, but we cheered one another with shouts.

German tommy-gunners appeared from behind the tanks. There were about 150-200 of them. They attacked very cautiously, throwing grenades in front of them. We were able to catch some of the grenades and throw them back.

On the west side of the elevator the Germans managed to enter the building, but we immediately turned our guns on the parts they had occupied.

Fighting flared up inside the building. We sensed and heard the enemy soldiers' breath and footsteps, but we could not see them in the smoke. We fired at sound.

At night, during a short lull, we counted our ammunition. There did not seem to be much left: one and a half drums for the machine-gun, twenty to twenty-five rounds for each tommy-gun, and eight to ten rounds for each rifle.

To defend ourselves with that amount of ammunition was impossible. We were surrounded. We decided to break out to the south, to the area of Beketovka, as there were enemy tanks to the north and east of the elevator.

During the night of the 20th, covered by

Rocket artillery—the BM-8 and BM-13 ('Katyusha') entered service with the Red Army soon after June 1941. Rapid production made it possible to increase the number of special artillery battalions every month; 3,237 Katyushas were produced in 1942, and in the opinion of all military specialists (Germans included) their performance and ballistic properties were formidable. The great force of fire from the Soviet field-rocket artillery was mainly due to its mass application. To achieve this, rocket-launcher brigades began to be formed in November 1942—and by the end of the year there were four rocket-launcher divisions. One salvo from such a division fired 3,840 missiles (weighing up to 230 tons) and had a devastating effect

John Batchelor

our one tommy-gun, we set off. To begin with all went well; the Germans were not expecting us here. We passed through the gully and crossed the railway line, then stumbled on an enemy mortar battery which had only just taken up position under cover of darkness.

We overturned the three mortars and a truck-load of bombs. The Germans scattered, leaving behind seven dead, abandoning not only their weapons, but their bread and water. And we were fainting with thirst. 'Something to drink! Something to drink!' was all we could think about. We drank our fill in the darkness. We then ate the bread we had captured from the Germans and went on. But alas, what then happened to my comrades I don't know, because the next thing I remember was opening my eyes on September 25 or 26. I was in a dark, damp cellar, feeling as though I were covered with some kind of oil. I had no tunic on and no shoe on my right foot. My hands and legs would not obey me at all.

A door opened, and in the bright sunlight I could see a tommy-gunner in a black uniform. On his left sleeve was a skull. I had fallen into the hands of the enemy.

The German offensive, which had opened so brilliantly, had reaffirmed in a few short weeks the Wehrmacht's power to make the whole world tremble, had carried the boundaries of the Reich to their farthest mark—was now, undeniably, stuck fast. For nearly two months the maps had remained unchanged.

The Propaganda Ministry affirmed that the 'greatest battle of attrition that the world has ever seen' was taking place, and daily published figures which showed how the Soviets were being bled white. But whether the Germans believed them or not,

the facts were very different. It was they, not the Red Army, who were being forced repeatedly to raise the ante. With the same coolness which stamped his refusal to commit the Siberian reserve until the battle of Moscow had already been decided, Zhukov was keeping the reinforcements of the 62nd Army to a bare minimum. In the two critical months from September 1 to November 1 only five infantry divisions were sent across the Volga—barely sufficient to cover 'wastage'. Yet in that period 27 fresh infantry divisions and nineteen armoured brigades were activated from drafts, new material, and cadre skeletons of seasoned officers and NCOs. All were concentrated in the area between Povorino and Saratov, where their training was completed, and whence some of them were sent in rotation to the central sector for brief periods of combat experience. The result was that while the Germans were slowly running all their divisions into the ground with fatigue and casualties the Red Army was building up a formidable reserve of men and armour.

The feeling of frustration at being halted so near (as it seemed) to complete victory was soon compounded by a sense of foreboding which heightened as the weeks followed one another with the army always in the same position.

The days were shortening again, you could definitely sense it. And in the mornings the air was quite cool. Were we really going to have to fight through another of those dreadful winters? I think that was behind our efforts. Many of us felt that it was worth anything, any price, if we could get it over before the winter.

While the spirits of the men alternated between frenzy and depression, recrimina-

tion and the clash of personalities enlivened the affairs of the army group at a higher level.

First to go were two tank generals, Wietersheim and Schwedler. The essence of their complaint was that the Panzer divisions were being worn out in operations to which they were completely unsuited, and that after a few more weeks of street fighting they would no longer have the ability to fulfil their primary task—that of engaging the enemy's armour in mobile battles. However, the dictates of military protocol do not permit corps commanders, however distinguished, to protest on broad strategic grounds, and each chose to complain on a narrower point of tactics.

General von Wietersheim commanded XV Panzer Corps, which had been the first unit of VI Army to break through to the Volga at Rynok in August. He certainly cannot be accused of timidity, for he had taken his corps across northern France in 1940 on Guderian's heels and been one of the very few officers in the German army who had recommended pressing on across the Meuse. Wietersheim suggested to Paulus that the attrition from Russian artillery fire on both sides of the Rynok corridor was having such effect on his Panzers that they should be withdrawn and the corridor held open by infantry. He was dismissed and sent back to Germany, to end his military career as a private in the Volkssturm in Pomerania, in 1945.

General von Schwedler was the commander of IV Panzer Corps, and had led the southern arm of the counterstroke against Timoshenko's drive on Kharkov in May. His case is an interesting one in that he was the first general to warn against the danger

THE STALINGRAD KATYUSHAS—A TRIBUTE FROM THE RANKS:

'We could certainly not have held Stalingrad had we not been supported by artillery and Katyushas on the other bank all the time. I can hardly describe the soldiers' love for them. . . . And as time went on, there were more and more of them, and we could feel it. It was hard to imagine at the time that there was *such* a concentration of guns firing their shells at the Germans, morning, noon, and night, over our heads!'

From *Russia at War*, 1941/45, by A. Werth, published by Pan Books Ltd.[1]

Novosti Press Agency

'Get close to the enemy's positions. Move on all fours, making use of craters and ruins. Carry your tommy-gun on your shoulder. Take 10 to 12 grenades. Timing and surprise will then be on your side . . . Into the building — a grenade! A turning — another grenade! Rake it with your tommy-gun! And get a move on!'

[General Chuikov sums up the fighting]

△ A German platoon forms up before plunging into the enemy-held ruins

of concentrating all the armour at the tip of a 'dead *Schwerpunkt*' and the vulnerability to a Russian attack from the flanks. (Practically every senior German commander in the southern theatre now likes to take the credit for this prescience. In fact, it seems to be due either to Schwedler or to Blumentritt. Blumentritt was sent out on a tour of inspection of the Don front between Voronezh and Kletskaya and submitted a report to the effect that '. . . it would not be safe to hold such a long defensive flank during the winter'. Görlitz places the time of this inspection in early August, but Blumentritt himself under interrogation put it in September.) But in the autumn of 1942 the concept of the Russians *attacking* was regarded as 'defeatist', and Schwedler, too, was dismissed.

The next head to fall was that of Colonel-General List, Commander-in-Chief of Army Group A. After the first rush across the Kuban, which had carried I Panzer Army to Mozdok by the end of August, the front of the German advance had solidified along the contour lines of the Caucasus range and the Terek river. Different factors accounted for this, notably the withdrawal of Richthofen's bombers to Stalingrad and a recovery by the defenders. Kleist has remarked:

In the early stages . . . I met little organised resistance. As soon as the Russian forces were by-passed, most of the troops seemed more intent to find their way back to their homes than to continue fighting. That was quite different to what had happened in 1941. But when we advanced into the Caucasus the forces we met there were local troops, who fought more stubbornly because they were fighting to defend their homes. Their obstinate resistance was all the more effective because the country was so difficult . . .

The result was that the first plan for the occupation of the oilfields was altered, and OKW directed List to force his way across the low Caucasus at their western end and capture Tuapse. Reinforcements, including three mountain divisions which would have been of great value to Kleist, were put into XVII Army instead. Had this been successful, the Germans would have broken across the Caucasus at their lowest point, and by capturing Batumi would have forced the Russian Black Sea fleet into internment and ensured the security of the Crimea and the compliant neutrality of Turkey. But in fact one difficulty after another supervened and, notwithstanding his reinforcement, List made little progress. In September, Jodl was sent as the OKW representative to List's headquarters to report 'the

Führer's impatience' and to try to get things moving.

But when Jodl returned he came with bad news: 'List had acted exactly in conformity with the Führer's orders, but the Russian resistance was equally strong everywhere, supported by a most difficult terrain.' Warlimont contends that Jodl answered Hitler's reproaches (and if he did, it was certainly for the first, and the last, time) by pointing 'to the fact that Hitler by his own orders had induced List to advance on a widely stretched front'.

The result was 'an outburst', and Jodl fell into disgrace: 'Further consequences were that Hitler completely changed his daily customs. From that time on he stayed away from the common meals which he had taken twice a day with his entourage. Henceforth he hardly left his hut in daytime, not even for the daily reports on the military situation, which from now on had to be delivered to him in his own hut in the presence of a narrowly restricted circle. He refused ostentatiously to shake hands with any general of the OKW, and gave orders that Jodl was to be replaced by another officer.'

Jodl's replacement was never in fact appointed, and the OKW Chief-of-Staff soon came back into favour, having learned his lesson, which, as he confided to Warlimont, was that: 'A dictator, as a matter of psychological necessity, must never be reminded of his own errors — in order to keep up his self-confidence, the ultimate source of his dictatorial force.'

However, before that particular trail of private ambition and intrigue is followed up, there is one more dismissal which must be recorded, together with its effect on the running of Führer headquarters. Relations between Hitler and Halder had deteriorated steadily since the removal of the pliant ObdH [Field-Marshal von Brauchitsch], who had acted as an absorbent pad between Hitler's violence and the Chief-of-Staff's dry acerbity. Manstein, who had seen them together in August while passing through headquarters to take up his command at Leningrad, was 'quite appalled' to see how bad their relations were. Hitler was abusive, Halder obstructive and pedantic. Hitler would taunt Halder with his lack of combat experience, in contrast to his own experiences in the front line in the First World War. Halder would mumble under his breath about the differences between professional and 'untutored' opinion.

Matters came to a head over a quite minor point, relating to the central front. Many of

-Opera Mundi

Sado-Opera Mundi

Ullstein

German tommy-gunners pick their way ough the wreckage of a gutted house

△ The infantry wait for a StuG-III Panzer assault-gun to smash a Soviet strongpoint

△ German machine-gunners push forwards into the tractor-works

Imperial War Museum

the German commanders, particularly Kluge (whose responsibility it was), believed that the counteroffensive the Russians were expected to launch in the winter would be directed against Army Group Centre. Paradoxically, this was in part due to the Russians' practice of giving their new divisions a baptism of fire in the quiet central sector before taking them back into strategic reserve. The new divisions would be identified, then seem to disappear. Kluge, and Halder himself, formed the erroneous opinion that they were being accumulated behind the front where they had been identified instead, as was the case, of being sent south. At all events, a rather childish quarrel blew up between Hitler and Halder concerning the date on which one of these units was identified, and around it larger issues were invoked, notably the need (as Halder saw it) to reinforce Kluge and thus, indirectly, the over-stretched condition of the Wehrmacht generally. On September 24, Halder was dismissed and Colonel-General Kurt Zeitzler brought from the West to take his place.

The occasion of Halder's dismissal is of particular interest to historians of the Second World War because of a change which was inaugurated at that time in the administration of the daily Führer conferences. These conferences had become the medium through which the war was being run and the directives promulgated. For the old OKH apparatus had been in decay since Brauchitsch's dismissal, and Halder's real fault, in Hitler's eyes, was his shuffling attempts to reserve to OKH (and thereby to himself) certain of the old prerogatives of the Generalstab and his tacit reluctance to accept Hitler's 'appointment' as Commander-in-Chief of the army as anything but temporary. With the advent of Zeitzler, who had no memories of the time when OKH ran the Eastern campaign with Hitler no more than a petulant voice at the end of a bad telephone line, the centralisation of tactical as of strategic administration would be complete. The final step in the consolidation of the daily conferences as the prime mover in the executive process was the introduction of stenographers who faithfully recorded every word spoken by every participant. To the extent to which these records have survived, they are of enormous importance in showing how the war was run by the Germans.

One of those who benefited from the reshuffle at Hitler's headquarters was a loyal, well-meaning Nazi, General Schmundt. Schmundt was promoted from the rather ill-defined post of Hitler's principal adjutant to that of head of the Army Personnel Office, where he enjoyed very considerable power in the field of posting and appointment. Paulus 'felt that he ought to send Schmundt his congratulations'.

Not long afterward Schmundt turned up at Paulus's headquarters, and the commander of VI Army launched straightaway into a long complaint about the condition of the troops, the shortages, the strength of the Russian resistance, the possible dangers if VI Army were to become too exhausted, and so forth. Perhaps he referred to the original text of Directive 41, which had limited his objective to bringing the Volga under gunfire—for he had certainly done *that*.

Schmundt, however, had the one answer which a reluctant commander can never resist. After some prefatory remarks about

the Führer's desire to see the Stalingrad operations 'brought to a successful conclusion', he broke the exciting news. The 'other officer' under consideration for the post of the Chief of the OKW staff was none other than Paulus himself! It was true that General Jodl's actual standing-down was hanging fire at the present time, but Paulus had been 'definitely ear-marked' for a more senior post, and General von Seydlitz would take his place as head of the VI Army.

Paulus may have been a good staff officer; as a commander in the field he was slow-witted and unimaginative to the point of stupidity. Equally certain, as can be seen from the course of his career up to and after capture, he had a keen awareness of the sources of power, or to put it bluntly, he knew what was good for him. With the news from Schmundt of what extra was at stake, he threw himself into preparations for a further offensive with a special enthusiasm.

This time Paulus had decided to strike head on at his adversary's strongest point—the three giant erections of the Tractor Factory, the Barrikady, and the Krasny Oktyabr, which lay in the northern half of the city, ranged one after another a few hundred feet from the Volga bank. This was to be the fiercest, and the longest, of the five battles which were fought in the ruined town. It started on October 4 and raged for nearly three weeks.

Paulus had been reinforced by a variety of different specialist troops, including police battalions and engineers skilled in street fighting and demolition work. But the Russians, though still heavily outnumbered, remained their masters in the technique of house-to-house fighting. They had perfected the use of 'storm groups', small bodies of mixed arms—light and heavy machine-guns, tommy-gunners, and grenadiers usually with anti-tank guns—who gave one another support in lightning counter-attacks. And they had developed the creation of 'killing zones', houses and squares, heavily mined, to which the defenders knew all the approach routes, where the German advance would be canalised. 'Experience taught us', Chuikov wrote:

Get close to the enemy's positions: move on all fours, making use of craters and ruins; dig your trenches by night, camouflage them by day; make your build-up for the attack stealthily, without any noise; carry your tommy-gun on your shoulder; take ten to twelve grenades. Timing and surprise will then be on your side....

Two of you get into the house together—you, and a grenade; both be lightly dressed—you without a knapsack, and the grenade bare; go in grenade first, you after; go through the whole house, again always with a grenade first and you after....

There is one strict rule now—give yourself elbow room! At every step danger lurks. No matter—a grenade in every corner of the room, then forward! A burst from your tommy-gun around what's left; a bit further—a grenade, then on again! Another room—a grenade! A turning—another grenade! Rake it with your tommy-gun! And get a move on!

Inside the object of attack the enemy may go over to a counterattack. Don't be afraid! You have already taken the initiative, it is in your hands. Act more ruthlessly with your grenade, your tommy-gun, your dagger and your spade! Fighting inside a building is

always frantic. So always be prepared for the unexpected. Look sharp! ...

Slowly and at a tremendous price the Germans inched their way into the great buildings, across factory floors; around and over the inert machinery, through the foundries, the assembly shops, the offices. 'My God, why have you forsaken us?' wrote a lieutenant of XXIV Panzer Division.

We have fought during fifteen days for a single house, with mortars, grenades, machine-guns, and bayonets. Already by the third day fifty-four German corpses are strewn in the cellars, on the landings, and the staircases. The front is a corridor between burnt-out rooms; it is the thin ceiling between two floors. Help comes from neighbouring houses by fire escapes and chimneys. There is a ceaseless struggle from noon to night. From storey to storey, faces black with sweat, we bombard each other with grenades in the middle of explosions, clouds of dust and smoke, heaps of mortar, floods of blood, fragments of furniture and human beings. Ask any soldier what half an hour of hand-to-hand struggle means in such a fight. And imagine Stalingrad; eighty days and eighty nights of hand-to-hand struggles. The street is no longer measured by metres but by corpses. ...

Stalingrad is no longer a town. By day it is an enormous cloud of burning, blinding smoke; it is a vast furnace lit by the reflection of the flames. And when night arrives, one of those scorching, howling, bleeding nights, the dogs plunge into the Volga and swim desperately to gain the other bank. The nights of Stalingrad are a terror for them. Animals flee this hell; the hardest stones cannot bear it for long; only men endure.

Stalemate at Stalingrad

1942 June 28: The German summer offensive begins with a breakthrough at Kursk.
July 5: Army Group B reaches the Don on either şide of Voronezh.
July 12: STAVKA sets up a new 'Stalingrad' Front.
July 23: Bock is dismissed. IV Panzer Army (Hoth) is ordered to swing away from Stalingrad, and assist I Panzer Army (Kleist) to cross the Don.
July 25: Kleist gets his light forces across the Don. VI Army continues its advance toward Stalingrad, but fails to liquidate Russian bridgeheads on the west bank.
July 29: Hoth's Panzers cross the Don at Tsimlyanskaya. Kleist captures Proletarskaya.
August 10: Paulus's troops reach the outskirts of Stalingrad, while Hoth moves up to rejoin them.
August 19: First German attempt to storm Stalingrad.
August 22: XIV Panzer Corps forces a narrow breach in the Russian perimeter at Vertyachi.
August 23: Germans reach the bank of the Volga.
August 23/24: Luftwaffe makes a terror raid on Stalingrad.
August 25: State of emergency declared in Stalingrad. Heavy fighting halts the German advance.
September 13: 'Final' German attack on Stalingrad begins. A breakthrough in the centre forces General Chuikov to commit his last reserves. But the German attack is halted.
September 24: Halder is dismissed.
October 4: The fourth German attack at Stalingrad, directed at the Tractor Factory, the Barrikady, and the Krasny Oktyabr, begins nearly three weeks of bitter fighting.

Soviet Russia, November 1942/February 1943 *Colonel Alexander M. Somorov*

Stalingrad was the watershed of the war. No other battle—possibly in history—has compelled the attention of the world to such a degree of fascination. The Soviet plan to trap and then crush the VI Army at Stalingrad was masterful and awesome: over 1,000,000 men were to swoop down on the German forces, cut them off, and then, unit by unit, annihilate them. And the plan's execution was no less imposing: when it was all over, the once-proud army of General Paulus, at its peak 330,000 men strong, had been utterly liquidated, and Stalingrad, scene of some of the war's most vicious combat, was once more in Russian hands. This account, by a leading Russian historian, assesses the course of the titanic struggle and weighs the effect of this catastrophe on German morale

STALINGRAD: THE RELIEF

German armour moves out to the edge of the
Stalingrad pocket after the Soviet encircling move

Hitler's Wehrmacht, recovering after its serious defeat before Moscow, developed its offensive in the summer of 1942 on the southern wing of the Eastern Front, and seized vast new areas of the Soviet Union, with an area of more than 150,000 square miles. And when German forces reached the neighbourhood of Voronezh, Stalingrad, and the foothills of the Main Caucasian Range, a very dangerous military situation faced the Soviet Union. But the aims set by the Nazis again remained unachieved. German Army Group B, consisting of 85 divisions and operating on the Voronezh and Stalingrad axes, was incapable of overcoming the resistance of the Soviet forces which opposed it, and its main strike force – IV Panzer and VI Armies – was drawn into prolonged and exhausting battles in the Stalingrad area. Army Group A – I Panzer and XVII Armies, comprising 25 divisions, was brought to a halt by the forces of Transcaucasus Front. The position of the German forces in the Caucasus and at Stalingrad was rendered more difficult still by the fact that almost all the German reserves had been expended.

In fulfilment of the Supreme Command's orders, the Red Army tied up enemy forces by active operations on other strategic axes of the Soviet-German front, thus depriving the German High Command of any possibility of redeploying its forces to the south from Army Groups North and Centre.

On October 14, 1942, Hitler ordered all forces to take up the defensive except for the Stalingrad area and some small sectors at Tuapse and Nalchik in the Caucasus, and the German troops were given the task of holding the line they had reached, whatever the cost. The German High Command believed that during the winter it could lay the foundations for a continuation of the Wehrmacht's Eastern Front offensive in 1943. In putting into effect measures to establish a stable defence for the winter, it paid particular attention to the central sector, where Army Group Centre was tied down by active Soviet operations, in the belief that it was here that a major Red Army offensive was being prepared. German Intelligence remarked, in mid-October 1942: 'It is evident that the enemy is preparing a major winter operation against Army Group Centre, and should be ready for it about the beginning of November.'

The Soviet Supreme Command had made a correct estimate both of the situation at the front in the autumn of 1942 and of the general balance of forces between Nazi Germany and the USSR. A sober analysis indicated that the prerequisites for a decisive turn in the course of the war had come into existence during the fighting. As for the strategic and operational situation, the greatest advantage lay in a decisive blow at the enemy's chief strike force, his most active and dangerous one – that on the southern wing of the front. And so the idea arose of surrounding and annihilating the enemy in the Stalingrad area, and then crushing the entire southern wing of the German army. The realisation of this concept had far-reaching consequences for world history, as events were to show.

The Soviet Supreme Command was already certain by the beginning of September that Germany's strategic plan for the summer of 1942 had been seriously disrupted. The Wehrmacht had done grievous harm to Soviet Russia, but its offensive capability had been sharply reduced, and its reserves exhausted. The German High Com-

mand could no longer rapidly transfer large strategic reserves from Germany or other theatres of war to the Eastern Front: there were no ready reserves left. There was no reason to expect a renewal of an important offensive, with introduction of major new forces, before the early summer of 1943. All these factors allowed attention to be concentrated on working out countermeasures in the Stalingrad area.

The Deputy Supreme Commander, Army General G. K. Zhukov, and the Chief of the General Staff, Colonel-General A. M. Vasilevsky, discussed these questions with STAVKA, and in the first fortnight of September they went to the combat areas on the Volga, to study the situation on the spot and then present their views and suggestions for a counteroffensive plan. Before they took off from Moscow, Stalin warned them to keep STAVKA's intentions completely secret.

Zhukov went to Stalingrad Front to familiarise himself with the state of the enemy's forces and to determine the requirements in men and resources for the counteroffensive. The bridgeheads occupied by Soviet forces on the right bank of the Don at Serafimovich and Kletskaya had also to be examined, and Vasilevsky flew to South-East Front to give particular attention to the troops and positions of 57th Army, the right wing of 51st Army, and the enemy facing them.

When Zhukov and Vasilevsky returned to Moscow, STAVKA held a conference, and several members of the Operations Directorate of the General Staff were invited to. In the course of the discussion the concept of the forthcoming strategic offensive was examined, as were the practical problems of carrying it out – the main strike axes, the forces and weapons needed, the areas and approximate schedules for concentration. It was decided to set up two autonomous fronts in the Stalingrad area (Don and Stalingrad Fronts) to replace the previous Stalingrad and South-East Fronts, which were under a single command, and to subordinate them directly to STAVKA. The decision to set up a new South-West Front, to the right of Don Front's sector, was also taken at this time, but in order to maintain secrecy, official promulgation of this decision was postponed to the end of October.

The main outlines of the counteroffensive plan, as approved by STAVKA at the end of September, were handed over to the appropriate members of the General Staff to be worked out in detail, and the commanders of the service arms were brought into the work. STAVKA put Zhukov in charge of preparing operations on the spot for South-West and Don Fronts, and Vasilevsky for Stalingrad Front.

Throughout October the General Staff and the Military Councils and staffs of the fronts concerned continued to work out the forthcoming operation, and the work was, in the main, completed during the second half of the month. STAVKA made some changes in the original plan, changes designed to increase the scope of the operation: the line of the main blow north-west of Stalingrad was moved to the area south-west of Serafimovich, and the numbers of men and weapons allotted to the counteroffensive were increased.

In its final form the plan for a counteroffensive (Plan 'Uranus') was notable for the purposefulness and boldness of its conception. The planned offensive operations were

vast in scale, comprising a unified strategic operation, on a front of 250 miles, by forces of South-West, Don, and Stalingrad Fronts. Their aim was, bluntly, to encircle and annihilate the enemy's main strike force. The forces executing the main manoeuvre for encirclement of the enemy were to fight their way forward up to 75-90 miles from the north and 60 miles from the south, and a special feature of the operation was that two fronts of encirclement, an inner and an outer, were to be created at the same time.

In the early days of November, the STAVKA representatives – General Zhukov, Colonel-General Vasilevsky, and the Commander of Artillery of the Red Army, Colonel-General N. N. Voronov – again arrived in the Stalingrad area to make the last round of preparations for Plan Uranus on the spot, together with the local front and army commanders.

Zhukov immediately called a summing-up conference on November 3 at 5th Tank Army of South-West Front, and in this conference the commanders of corps and divisions scheduled to attack on the main axis took part, as well as the front and army command personnel. A conference was then held at 21st Army of South-West Front, with the commander of Don Front taking part, and a few days later (on November 9 and 10), another was held at HQ Stalingrad Front.

In the rear, new armies, corps, divisions, brigades, and regiments were being created, and formations withdrawn from battles on the Volga and in the northern Caucasus were being brought up to strength and reconstituted. The Soviets possessed important reserves for the counteroffensive, and in the autumn of 1942 these were concentrating in the Stalingrad area.

Picking the right moment

It was crucially important to choose the right moment to open the counteroffensive. In the autumn it was gradually becoming clear – even to the High Command of the Wehrmacht – that the German offensive before Stalingrad was petering out, and that it had not succeeded in overcoming the Soviet resistance. Because of this it had become necessary to re-evaluate the strength of the Red Army and the Soviet state. As Lieutenant-General von Tippelskirch later wrote, all this caused 'serious apprehensions' in the German General Staff.

However, no real steps resulted from this, though former Wehrmacht generals have since the war constructed a treatment of historical fact convenient to themselves on this question, as on many others. As they put it, the whole tragedy for the German forces was that Hitler did not see – or, at any rate, did not understand in good time – the danger which threatened the flanks of the Stalingrad strike force, while the German General Staff, so they say, had correctly assessed the operational-strategic situation at Stalingrad.

Can one really believe that the German General Staff foresaw the counteroffensive which the Red Army was preparing?

In published material from Field-Marshal Paulus' personal archives an order from Zeitzler, the new Chief of General Staff of the Army, is cited, to the effect that 'the Russians already have no significant reserves, and are no longer capable of mounting a large-scale offensive. This basic view should be the starting point in any assessment of the enemy.'

The German command at Stalingrad view-

The Russians in Stalingrad had perfected the use of 'Storm Groups', small bodies of mixed arms—light and heavy machine-guns, tommy-gunners, and grenadiers usually with anti-tank guns—who gave one another support in lightning counter-attacks; and they had developed the creation of 'killing zones', houses and squares heavily mined and to which the defenders knew all the approach routes, where the German advance could be canalised, met with savage fire, and blunted

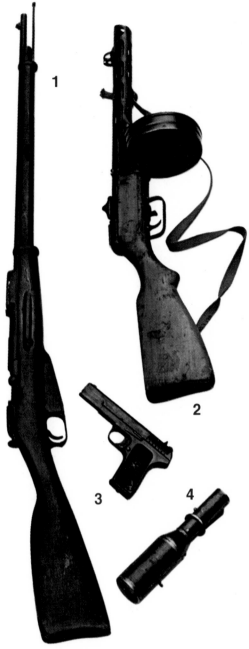

Even with the three firearms shown here, the impressive standardisation of the Red Army's equipment is strikingly obvious in their use of 7·62-mm calibre weapons

1. M-1930 7·62-mm rifle (5 rounds in magazine)
2. PPSH 7·62-mm submachine-gun (71 rounds in magazine)
3. Tokarev TT 7·62-mm automatic (8 rounds in magazine)
4. Standard hand-grenade

Deirdre Amsden

221

(South-West Front), and the troops of 65th Army (Don Front) developed their offensive south-eastwards and emerged on the left flank of the German VI Army.

Stalingrad Front took up the offensive on November 20, with 64th and 57th Armies on the right flank and 51st Army on the left. Because of the mist which hung over the Stalingrad steppe from morning onwards, the start of the offensive was postponed for two hours.

'Attack! It seemed that there was nothing more pleasing for those who had known the bitterness of retreat and the bloody labour of many months of defence,' wrote Marshal A. I. Yeremenko.

The artillery preparation was conducted in accordance with a carefully worked out plan. After a salvo of heavy M-30 Guards' mortars began a general bombardment by guns and mortars, lasting between 40 and 75 minutes.

Two divisions of 57th Army broke through between Lakes Sarpa and Tsatsa, striking south and south-west. The army then turned north-west, to encircle the enemy forces at Stalingrad. The main forces of 51st Army attacked from between Lakes Tsatsa and Barmantsak, making for Sovetsky. In the afternoon of November 20 mobile formations — 4th and 13th Mechanised and 4th Cavalry Corps — were introduced into the gaps which Stalingrad Front's shock groups had made on all three sectors, and they dashed into the depth of the Axis defence system.

'What if our Panzers are too weak?'

Stalingrad Front's offensive worried the enemy. Whereas HQ VI Army had to some extent foreseen the attack from the north, that in the south was completely unexpected. When he was told of it, Paulus said: 'The Soviet Supreme Command is closing a pincers. We are trying to prevent this with a counteroffensive by XIV and XLVIII Panzer Corps. But what if this attempt does not succeed? If our Panzer formations are too weak, what then? Then the enemy will tighten the noose and VI Army will be in the cauldron.'

The forces of South-West and Stalingrad Fronts, initially more than 125 miles apart, were moving irresistibly along their routes of encirclement. The 65th Army of Don Front, operating on the western flank, was also moving forward and overcoming the stubborn enemy opposition.

On November 21 the tank corps of South-West Front, with rifle and cavalry formations moving behind them, continued to develop their successful offensive. After 26th Tank Corps had refuelled, replenished its ammunition, and brought up lagging units, it renewed its attack at 1300 hours and by nightfall had fought its way to the vicinity of Ostrov and Plesistovsky farmstead, where it continued developing its offensive.

On the left flank of 21st Army, the 4th Tank Corps moved out from the Manoylino-Mayorovsky area with the task of reaching the Don on November 21 and seizing the crossings. On the same day it broke the resistance of the German XIV Panzer Corps and reached Golubinsky. The 21st Army went on crushing the enemy defence on the Verkhne-Fomikhinsky/Raspopinskaya sector, while the rifle divisions of its right flank fought to surround and annihilate the IV and V Rumanian Army Corps at Raspopinskaya.

The Soviet offensive radically changed the situation on the front at Stalingrad. Soviet tanks were in the immediate neighbourhood of German VI Army HQ. As General Mellenthin described it: 'HQ VI Army, on the bank of the Don, was directly in the way of the Russian tanks, and was forced to move for some time to the Chir river, west of the Don. However, after a few days it was moved by air to the Stalingrad area, and located itself around Gumrak.'

The senior adjutant of VI Army, Colonel W. Adam, was in charge of moving its HQ from Golubinsky to Nizhne-Chirskaya. This is how he describes the move:

In their feverish desire to save their own lives, people abandoned everything that hindered a hasty flight. They threw away weapons and equipment; vehicles fully loaded with ammunition, field kitchens, and baggage wagons stood motionless on the road, as men could move forward faster by un-harnessing the horses and riding them. Wild chaos ruled in Verkhne-Chirskaya. Soldiers and officers of the III Rumanian Army and the rear services of XI Army Corps, coming from the north, were added to those from IV Panzer Corps who were on the run ... Seized by panic and driven out of their minds, all looked the same. All were hurrying in the direction of Nizhne-Chirskaya.

On the morning of November 22 the last columns with the staff of VI Army arrived at Nizhne-Chirskaya. Paulus and his Chief-of Staff, General Schmidt, were already there. However, when Adam arrived to report, a radio message from Hitler had arrived, ordering Paulus to 'fly out at once from the cauldron which is forming and locate the army's command post near the [railway] station of Gumrak'.

If they were to achieve their mission of linking up with the forces of Stalingrad Front attacking from the south-east, the mobile formations of South-West Front had to force the Don off the march. The only road crossing of the Don in the offensive zone of 4th and 26th Tank Corps was at Berezovsky farmstead in the town area of Kalach. The enemy was fully aware of the importance of keeping this crossing in his own hands and of destroying it in good time if need be. To cover the bridge, VI Army had occupied a bridgehead on the high western bank of the Don, with its front turned rearwards, since it was considered that Kalach was the objective of the enemy forces which had broken through at Kletskaya. The bridge had been prepared for demolition.

Despite the steps which the enemy took, he was neither able to hold the bridge nor to blow it up. Its capture gave convincing proof of the growing skill in combat of Soviet soldiers and of their courage. On the night of November 21/22, when 26th Tank Corps had fought its way into the villages of Dobrinka and Ostrov, the corps commander (Maj-Gen A. I. Rodin) decided to exploit the dark of night for a surprise seizure of the bridge over the Don, and entrusted the task to a leading detachment, headed by the commander of 14th Motorised Rifle Brigade, Lieutenant-Colonel G. N. Filippov. The detachment comprised two companies of motorised infantry, five tanks, and an armoured car.

At 0300 hours on November 22, the column began to move at high speed down the Ostrov/Kalach road, Colonel Filippov in the lead vehicle and all lights switched on. His calculation was correct. The Germans took the approaching column for their own, and it passed through their defences without

Alfredo Zennaro

Novosti Press Agency

Top: Soviet BT tank smashed during the encircling movement. **Centre:** In Kotelnikovo, to the south-west of the trapped VI Army, Soviet soldiers examine captured German *Nebelwerfer* rocket mortars—one of the newest weapons in the Wehrmacht's armoury. **Right:** Out on the steppe, a Soviet AA battery forms part of the steel ring around VI Army

Novosti Press Agency

a shot being fired. It approached the bridge at 0600 and part of it crossed in its vehicles to the left bank of the Don, where it fired a rocket as a signal to the rest. After a short struggle the bridge guard, taken by surprise, was overcome. The detachment seized the bridge and then attempted to capture Kalach itself off the march. The Germans put up an organised resistance and tried to recapture the bridge. Colonel Filippov's detachment was surrounded, so it took up an all-round defence, repulsed all attacks by the superior German forces, and held the bridge until units of its parent corps arrived.

While mobile and rifle formations of South-West Front were moving south-eastwards, creating a front of encirclement around the enemy forces at Stalingrad, part of the infantry of the front was fighting to destroy the enemy forces which fought on in strongpoints. Within the ring formed by the infantry of 5th Tank and 21st Armies were the five infantry divisions which made up the Rumanian IV and V Corps. Towards the evening of November 23 these forces ('Raspopinskaya Group') sought to capitulate. Brigadier Stanescu, who commanded them, sent a party with a white flag to discuss conditions for the surrender of the entire force. They were told that all officers and men who surrendered would be guaranteed their lives, good treatment, and retention of their personal effects. All weapons, horses, carts, and other military material were to be handed over to the Red Army. These conditions were accepted, and 'Raspopinskaya Group' ceased to exist. Altogether 27,000 officers and men were taken prisoner, and a large quantity of arms and other booty captured.

While this was going on, South-West Front's main assault force was continuing to carry out its task of joining up with Stalingrad Front to surround the enemy forces. On November 23 the 19th Tank Brigade of 26th Tank Corps began its attack on the Germans in Kalach. By 1000 hours the Soviet tanks had burst into the town, but German resistance was fierce, and they succeeded by intense mortar and machine-gun fire in halting the Soviet infantry attacking on the north-western edge of the town. Some small units of 157th Tank Brigade, which had by now moved over to the right bank of the Don, came to the aid of the attacking infantry, and by 1400 hours Kalach had been liberated.

The strike force of Stalingrad Front also carried out its mission with brilliant success. After breaking through the front on the left flank of the IV Rumanian Army, rifle formations of 51st and 57th Armies advanced behind their mobile forces (4th and 13th Mechanised and 4th Cavalry Corps). By the end of the first day troops of 57th Army had advanced to the line Tsybenko/Novy Rogachik. In an attempt to stop the advance, the Germans threw in units from their XXIX Motorised Division and expelled the right-flank units of 422nd Rifle Division from the Nariman area, but their attempts to shore up their disintegrating front were repulsed: Nariman was liberated again on the morning of November 21.

In the offensive zone of 51st Army, General V. T. Volsky's 4th Mechanised Corps moved out ahead of the other attacking formations, and on November 20 seized Plodovitoye, the first village in the depth of the enemy defences. German resistance here was swiftly suppressed by a headlong attack made by a tank regiment of 36th Mechanised Brigade.

At dawn on November 21 Abganerovo railway station was seized in a surprise attack by a small tank unit of Corps HQ, and other units of General Volsky's corps fought their way into the railway station at Tingut at the same time.

The 4th Cavalry Corps was introduced into the gap behind Volsky's formations, and carried out a 40-mile march, aimed at cutting the enemy's retreat route to Abganerovo, passing through broken terrain with steep ravines, precipitous ascents and descents, and with ice slowing down the rate of movement. They moved without halts, pausing briefly now and then to allow the columns to close up. On November 21 the corps, pushing aside the weak enemy screening forces, approached the village of Abganerovo and occupied it.

The forces of Stalingrad Front continued to advance by day and night and to achieve the missions set them. During November 20/21 troops of 51st, 57th, and 64th Armies defeated three Rumanian infantry divisions and inflicted serious casualties upon another and upon the German XXIX Motorised Division. The result of two days of battle was that units of 57th Army reached a line from Nariman to the 'March 8' collective farm. The 13th Mechanised Corps continued to move towards the north-west, acting in concert with General Volsky's forces.

Units of 4th Mechanised Corps continued advancing to meet General Romanenko's 5th Tank Army moving down from the north-east. On November 22 they captured Krivomuzginskaya railway station and the Sovetsky farmstead. Other forces of Stalingrad Front—51st Army and 4th Cavalry Corps—attacking on the outer flank of the encirclement, advanced towards Kotelnikovo.

The distance between the forces of South-West and Stalingrad Fronts was now down to 6-10 miles. The Germans threw in the XVI and XXIV Panzer Divisions from Stalingrad to the Kalach and Sovetsky areas, in an attempt to prevent a link-up between the two Soviet fronts, but all the German counterattacks were repulsed.

22 German divisions trapped

At 1600 hours on November 23, units of the 4th Tank Corps of South-West Front, commanded by Major-General A. G. Kravchenko, and of the 4th Mechanised Corps of Stalingrad Front, commanded by Major-General V. T. Volsky, met near the Sovetsky farmstead. And so on the fifth day of the counteroffensive the forces of the two fronts, actively assisted by the right wing of Don Front, had closed the ring around the German strike force at Stalingrad. On the same day the forward elements of South-West Front's infantry divisions reinforced the success by reaching the Don near Kalach. The 13th Mechanised Corps and infantry of 57th and 64th Armies of Stalingrad Front held a firm defence on the Chervlenaya river, thus cutting off the retreat route to the south.

The three fronts had fulfilled the main task set them. In the ring was a large enemy force—the German VI Army and part of IV Panzer Army—comprising 22 divisions with a total of about 330,000 men. In addition to this the Soviet forces had defeated the III Rumanian Army, five divisions of which had been taken prisoner, and severely battered the IV Rumanian Army. An outer front of encirclement had also been created, more than 280 miles long, although only 160 miles of it were covered by the troops—100 miles by South-West Front and 60 by Stalingrad Front. Distance between the inner and outer fronts was a minimum of 9 to 12 miles on the most important axes, where the danger of a relieving blow by the enemy was greatest. The Germans had no solid defence line, and a breach more than 180 miles wide had been torn in their front, between Bokovskaya and Lake Sarpa.

The Soviet command took steps to ensure the safety of the encirclement operation from all angles. To this end it was important to move the outer front forward as quickly as possible, so as to isolate the surrounded enemy forces more firmly . . . and then liquidate them. Combat operations to liquidate the enemy forces at Stalingrad were begun by the three fronts as soon as the ring had been closed, and at the same time steps were taken to isolate the enemy forces in the small bend of the Don from the main body. The 21st Army of South-West Front renewed the offensive on the morning of November 24, heading eastwards, and by the 27th the bulk of its forces had crossed to the left bank of the Don. The 65th Army of Don Front also fought to encircle the enemy forces across the Don, resuming the offensive on the morning of the 24th and heading toward Vertyachi and Peskovatka.

The November counteroffensive had been successfully concluded, but liquidation of the encircled enemy forces would not be an easy matter—and the future course of the struggle against Nazi Germany largely depended on its success.

When the German High Command heard that Paulus' troops were surrounded it decided to restore the situation at Stalingrad whatever the cost, as the Volga front was the basis of its whole operational plan for the further course of the war. This decision cannot be viewed as just a chance or fatal mistake by Hitler: it flowed naturally from the strategic concept of the war in Russia, a concept to which not only the Führer but also the German generals were now pledged since the abandonment of Moscow as the prime aim.

The Germans were still convinced of their superiority over the Soviet Union and its armed forces. By great efforts they managed to stop further progress by Soviet forces south-west and south of Stalingrad, and the retreat of the shattered III Rumanian Army was stopped on the Chir river line. A defence line was organised in the Don bend between the mouth of the Chir and Vershenskaya railway station, consisting of IV Rumanian Army and hastily-assembled and transferred German combat groups, each of a strength up to a reinforced regiment.

The fresh XVII Army Corps later arrived in this area, and took up position along the Chir and Krivaya rivers, in the vicinity of Dubovskoye. The remnants of XLVIII Panzer Corps, which had been battered during the Soviet encirclement operation (it had been in reserve behind III Rumanian Army), occupied the gap between III Rumanian Army and XVII Army Corps. And so the Germans set up a new defensive front along the Chir, not far from Stalingrad. They also succeeded in stabilising the situation of the encircled troops to some extent.

When they had decided to relieve Paulus' forces, the German High Command set up a new Army Group Don, between Army Groups A and B, with Field-Marshal von Manstein as its Commander-in-Chief. It included Operational Group Hollidt (around Tormosin), the remnants of III Rumanian

Army, IV Panzer Army (formed from the staff of the old one and units arriving from reserve), and IV Rumanian Army (made up of VI and VII Corps). Divisions were brought hastily from the Caucasus, Voronezh, Orel, France, Germany, and Poland to reinforce Army Group Don, and the forces encircled at Stalingrad were also subordinated to Manstein. It now occupied a front from Veshenskaya railway station on the Don to the Manych river—more than 360 miles—and comprised about 30 divisions, six of which were Panzers and one motorised, not including the troops at Stalingrad. Seventeen of the divisions were facing South-West Front, and the remaining 13 (unified into the Hoth Group) were opposed by the 5th Shock and 51st Armies of Stalingrad Front.

The relieving operation was code-named 'Winter Storm'. Although the German forces dug in along the Chir were at Nizhne-Chirskaya, only 40 miles from Paulus' encircled troops, while the group commanded by Colonel-General Hoth was 75 miles away at Kotelnikovo, Manstein nevertheless decided to attack from the latter place, as it would not involve crossing the Don, and he believed the Soviet command would least expect an offensive from that quarter. The blow by XLVIII Panzer Corps of Operational Group Hollidt from the Nizhne-Chirskaya bridgehead was to be a secondary one.

The operation had to be postponed several times, while the forces were concentrating, but at last the order was given to begin the offensive on December 12. The LVII Panzer Corps of IV Panzer Army was to play the main part, and Paulus was ordered to strike out of the cauldron, but without giving up his positions at Stalingrad.

While the Germans had been taking urgent measures to restore the situation on the Volga, the Soviet forces had retained the initiative at Stalingrad itself. The Red Army's task was to put an end to the encircled forces and at the same time to conduct a headlong offensive on the outer front in the general direction of Rostov.

The Soviet Supreme Command had decided to proceed at once with the annihilation of the encircled enemy, and entrusted the task to Don Front and the main forces of Stalingrad Front (57th, 62nd, and 64th Armies). The offensive was launched on November 24, and fierce fighting developed, with the Germans resisting stubbornly and even counterattacking. By the evening of the 29th, the territory held by Paulus' troops had been almost halved, but Don and Stalingrad Fronts did not have enough troops available to carry out the basic mission of splitting up the enemy forces and defeating them in detail, as there were over 300,000 Germans present (not the 85-90,000 which the Soviet command initially assumed), and the Soviets had also underestimated the equipment and armaments at the Germans' disposal.

At the end of November preparation of a new Soviet offensive, code-named 'Saturn', began. In this operation South-West Front and the left wing of Voronezh Front were to defeat the main body of the Italian VIII Army, which was defending the middle Don between Novaya Kalitva and Vershenskaya, and the enemy forces on the Chir and around Tormosin, then to attack towards Millerovo and Rostov. South-West Front was reinforced by the new 1st Guards Army of Lieutenant-General V. I. Kuznetsov, deployed on its right flank, and by several new

formations assigned to South-West Front.

In the first ten days of December, the Soviet forces continued to operate on both the inner and outer fronts of the encirclement. Thus 5th Tank Army wore down the forces opposite it in stubborn fighting on the Chir line, so that they lost any ability they had to take part in Manstein's relief operation.

On December 8 STAVKA decided to make more careful preparations for destroying Paulus' forces: to regroup, reinforce from reserves, and make lavish provision of fuel and ammunition. In accordance with this decision the 5th Shock Army (Lt-Gen M. M. Popov) was set up on December 9, and deployed between the 51st Army of Stalingrad Front and the 5th Tank Army of South-West Front. Shortly afterwards the 2nd Guards Army (Lt-Gen R. Y. Malinovsky) arrived in the Stalingrad area. It was intended to complete preparations for the new offensive by December 18.

STAVKA initially intended to use 2nd Guards Army as part of South-West Front to develop the offensive in accordance with Plan Saturn from the Kalach area towards Rostov and Taganrog. But since the liquidation of Paulus' forces was taking longer than expected, and since the creation of Army Group Don showed that there was a danger of its relief being attempted, the original plans were re-examined, and as a result STAVKA decided to use 2nd Guards Army against the Hoth Group.

By December 12 the situation on the external front was that to the Hoth Group (13 divisions) the Soviet 5th Shock and 51st Armies opposed eight rifle divisions, some permanent fortifications, two mechanised and two cavalry corps, four tank brigades, eight artillery and mortar regiments from Supreme Command Reserve, and two regiments of rocket artillery.

Before beginning the relief operation, the Germans had a certain degree of superiority on the sector where they intended to strike, and the Soviet forces there were in a dangerous situation. But the general balance of forces on the southern wing of the Soviet-German front did not favour the Germans. The most they could hope for was to link up with VI Army and restore it to an active role. Had they achieved this, they would inevitably have made the military situation more difficult for the Soviets, and forced them to further efforts and sacrifices. But the Red Army foiled them yet again.

The attempt to save Paulus

General Hoth's attack began on the morning of December 12. The Germans operated out of Kotelnikovo towards the north-east, making their main effort on a narrow sector along the Kotelnikovo/Stalingrad railway. The VI and XXIII Panzer Divisions of LVII Panzer Corps attacked here, with cavalry and infantry on their flanks, the intention being that they should link up with Paulus' troops south-west of Tundutovo station. They were opposed by the 126th and 302nd Rifle Divisions of 51st Army.

After an artillery bombardment the enemy broke through the defences of 302nd Rifle Division at the railway halt of Kurmoyarsky. The Soviet units fought back fiercely, but the Germans exploited a large superiority in tanks and aircraft to develop their initial success, and by nightfall the forward units of VI Panzer Division had reached the southern bank of the Aksay river at some points, while XXIII Panzer Division had

Soviet troops capture one of the vital German airfields inside the Stalingrad pocket. Hitler was convinced that the Luftwaffe could supply VI Army from the air—but the distances were too great and the Russian offensive went from strength to strength. Pitomnik airfield fell on January 14, Gumrak airfield on the 21st; and the men of Hoth's relief force **(below)**, having battled to within 50 miles of the pocket, were hurled back by a well-executed Soviet counteroffensive. Now the isolated VI Army was doomed.

penetrated north of Nebykovo.

The attack was renewed at dawn on the 13th, with the main pressure still applied against 302nd Rifle Division. The Soviet 13th Mechanised Corps was brought in to stop the German advance, and during the day 30 *Sturmovik* ground-attack aircraft of 8th Air Army twice attacked the German tanks on this sector. The enemy again failed to outflank the 126th Rifle Division, but continued to press on units of 302nd, as they withdrew towards the Aksay. The second day of the offensive resulted in the seizure by VI Panzer Division of a bridgehead over the Aksay at Zalivskoye, from which a part of the force advanced to the Verkhne-Kumsky farmstead and seized it. The XXIII Panzer Division also reached the river and secured a bridgehead over the combined rail and road bridge at Kruglyakovo.

The arrival of Hoth's force at the Aksay created a real danger that they would break through the external front of encirclement. Until the Soviet 2nd Guards Army could arrive, the German offensive would have to be contained by 51st Army, and much depended on their steadfastness. It was decided to sever the German tanks from the motorised infantry and supply services, and then to destroy them separately along the Aksay line. A shock group of 51st Army, comprising 4th and 13th Mechanised Corps and some independent units, was set up for this purpose.

Both sides became active again on the morning of December 14. The Germans attempted to exploit their success at Verkhne-Kumsky. They had to: it was the junction of the most suitable north-south roads leading to Stalingrad. The 4th Mechanised Corps joined battle with the Germans there and at Vodyanskoye. The 13th Mechanised Corps got to close quarters with the enemy near the Biriukov railway siding, drawing part of XXIII Panzer Division into the battle. The 51st Army was heavily engaged all day, and as H. Scheibert, a German participant in the battle, later wrote: 'December 14, 1942, was an eventful day. It marked the start of the three-day tank battle in the Kalmyk Steppe, one of the greatest and fiercest tank battles of the Second World War.'

On the same day 5th Shock Army attacked the Germans in the Rychkovsky/Verkhne-Kumsky area, and after a stubborn fight Major-General P. A. Rotmistrov's 7th Tank Corps, with two infantry divisions, threw the Germans out of their bridgehead, thus easing the position of 51st Army on the Kotelnikovo axis.

On December 15, 4th Mechanised Corps, with reinforcements, succeeded in throwing the Germans out of the Verkhne-Kumsky farmstead and back to the Aksay river. Both sides spent the next day in minor engagements and preparations to continue the battle.

The dogged resistance of Stalingrad Front had prevented the Germans approaching the Myshkova river, thus making it possible for the 2nd Guards Army to approach and deploy. The army's orders were to complete the concentration north of the Myshkova of 2nd Guards Mechanised Corps by December 17 and to take up a defence line between Nizhne-Kumsky and Kapkinsky by the morning of December 18.

The Germans renewed their attack on Verkhne-Kumsky on the morning of December 17, with tanks and motorised infantry with air support trying to get from the Aksay to the Myshkova, north of which two infantry divisions and one mechanised corps of 2nd Guards Army were concentrating. From midnight the 87th Rifle Division, 4th Cavalry, and 4th Mechanised Corps were subordinated to this army.

The following day, December 18, the Germans threw XVII Panzer Division into the attack. It forced the lower Aksay near Generalovsky and reached the '8th of March' collective farm, 4 miles west of Verkhne-Kumsky, which VI Panzer Division was still trying to take.

General Volsky's 4th Mechanised Corps continued to hold off the enemy attacks, and on the evening of the 18th the general was notified that his corps had been awarded the title of 'Guards', becoming the 3rd Guards Mechanised. The corps continued to resist the attacks of the two Panzer divisions, but by the evening of the 19th had been forced

back from the Verkhne-Kumsky farmstead, and some units had to fight their way out of encirclement. Their resistance had played a very important role, for while they were fighting, 150 trainloads of troops and equipment of 2nd Guards Army were unloading in the Stalingrad area and taking up a defensive line along the Myshkova's north bank.

The German HQ could not reconcile itself to the obvious failure of its relief operation and continued until December 23 its vain efforts to break the Myshkova Line. Hoth's group was only 22 to 25 miles from the beleaguered Germans at Stalingrad, but its losses in men and equipment had been so great that its capacity for offensive operations had been shattered, and both Hoth and the commander of the 57th Panzer Corps, General Kirchner, acknowledged that 'unless fresh forces are brought up, the operation cannot continue'.

The general position of Manstein's forces was rendered even more difficult by the fact that while Hoth's offensive was still under way the Soviet South-West Front had dealt a crushing blow in operations to the north-west of Stalingrad. The shock groups of this front and of the left wing of Voronezh Front had opened an offensive on December 16 against VIII Italian Army, Operational Group Hollidt, and the remnants of III Rumanian Army, had smashed the enemy front after three days of battle, and were advancing south and south-east. The 17th Tank Corps (Maj-Gen P. P. Poluboyarov) captured Kantemirovka on December 19, and 24th Tank Corps (Maj-Gen V. M. Badanov) seized Tatsinskaya on the 24th.

The command of Army Group Don then learned that because of the defeat of the Italian and German forces on the middle Don, all formations on their way to the front

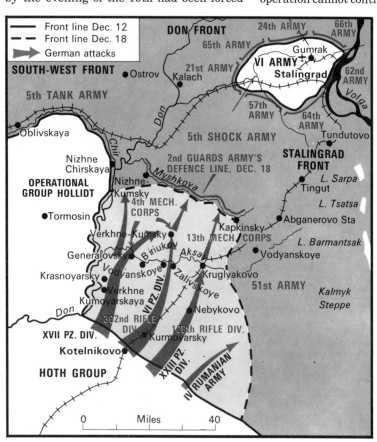

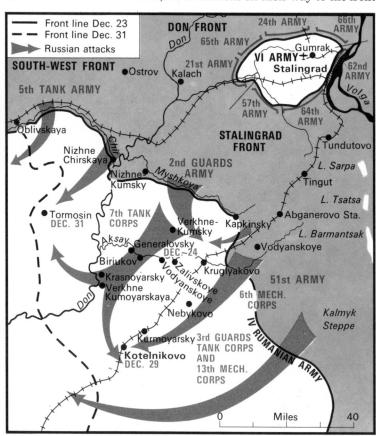

One last, desperate attempt at rescue

When the news of the Soviet encirclement of VI Army reached the German Army High Command, an immediate counteroffensive was prepared, to break through to the Stalingrad pocket and restore the Axis front. For this purpose, 'Army Group Don' had been set up under Manstein, who lost no time in issuing the orders for Operation 'Winter Storm'. Hoth, who led this relief attempt **(top left)** set off from Kotelnikovo on December 12 on a narrow front, and at first his 13 divisions had a marginal advantage. The operation started well—but the fierce resistance of 5th Shock Army took the momentum out of the German advance and allowed the Russians to reinforce the Myshkova river defence line. By December 23, the German attempts to break through at the Myshkova had failed completely: 'Winter Storm' had blown itself out, and there were no more Axis forces to throw into the relief attempt. Hoth fell back—and the Soviet Stalingrad Front took the offensive **(top right)**, widening the gap between the German front line and the trapped VI Army beyond hope of repair. During the first week of January, Soviet units moved into position on the outskirts of the VI Army pocket **(right)**, ready for the last act: the annihilation of VI Army, which began on January 9. By the end of the month, Paulus' men had been split into two isolated pockets in Stalingrad's ruins—and the last resistance ended on February 2

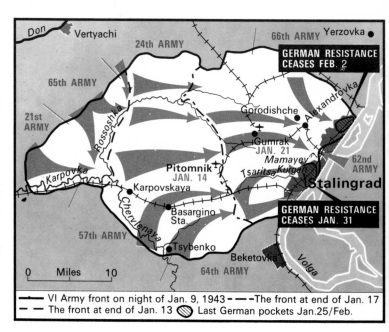

△ Soviet triumph: the Red Flag flies over the battered ruins of Stalingrad
▷ The end: among the 91,000 German POWs were 2,500 officers and 24 generals
▽ German humiliation: Field-Marshal Paulus, haggard and exhausted, is led into captivity after the surrender of January 31

Novosti Press Agency

were to be handed over to Army Group B. The XI Panzer Division, on its way to Kotelnikovo, returned to the lower Chir, and VI Panzer Division was also hastily ordered there. Manstein therefore decided to take up the defensive, pending the arrival of the SS 'Viking' Motorised Division from I Panzer Army in the Caucasus. Hoth's attack was for all practical purposes at an end.

Counterstrike against the relief force

By December 24, the Soviets had created favourable conditions for a *coup de grâce* on Hoth's force. Preparations for this had begun during the defensive battle, when

the balance of forces tipped in the Red Army's favour on the Kotelnikovo axis, through the transfer of 2nd Guards Army to Stalingrad Front and its reinforcement by the 6th and 7th Tank Corps. The Red Army had a superiority here of 2:1 in men and tanks, and 1.6:1 in artillery, though the Germans had a 1.7:1 superiority in aircraft.

The 2nd Guards and 51st Armies launched their offensive on the 24th, with 2nd Guards delivering the main blow. The Germans withdrew back to the Aksay, fighting stubborn rearguard actions as they went. General Rotmistrov's 7th Tank Corps crossed the river at night on December 25th, and by

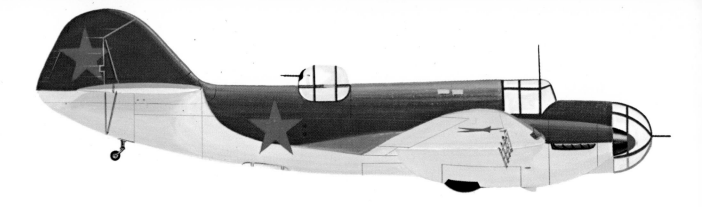

It is important to remember that the Soviet forces were not exclusively equipped with T-34 and KV tanks on the ground, and with Sturmoviks and Pe-2s in the air. These are some of the unsung mainstays of the Soviet armoury which—although eclipsed by more famous designs—nevertheless played a constant role in supporting the Red Army's 1942/43 winter offensives

△ **SB-RK Dive-Bomber.**
Crew: three or four.
Max speed: 279 mph.
Armament: three 7·62-mm machine-guns;
1,000 lb of bombs

▷ **BA-10 Armoured Car (1937).** *Crew:* three.
Speed: 50 mph.
Armament: one 45-mm cannon, one 7·62-mm machine-gun

dawn had seized Generalovsky. The offensive was also going well on the left and in the centre.

The 2nd Guards advanced on Kotelnikovo from the north, and 51st Army from the north-east. The 3rd Guards and 13th Mechanised Corps broke through IV Rumanian Army to begin a wide encirclement of the enemy forces at Kotelnikovo. At noon on December 27 the 7th Tank Corps attempted to break in to Kotelnikovo from the north, but failed, and a prolonged struggle began for the town, which the Germans were defending with picked troops.

While it continued, General Malinovsky began to clear the west bank of the Don, deciding on the 28th that a bridgehead be seized in the Krasnoyarsky/Verkhne-Kumoyarskaya sector, and the 2nd Guards Mechanised Corps put across the river. On the same day, 7th Tank Corps renewed its assault on Kotelnikovo, combining a frontal assault by two tank brigades with an outflanking movement by one brigade of tanks and one of motorised infantry. These moved round west of the Germans, struck their left flank, and had soon cut all the roads leading west and south-west from Kotelnikovo, as well as capturing the airfield with 15 aircraft, 800 cans of petrol, large numbers of heavy bombs, and some aircraft which landed later, unaware that the airfield was no longer in German hands. Both the town and the railway station had been entirely cleared of Germans by the morning of December 29.

The capture of Kotelnikovo was of help to General S. I. Bogdanov's 6th Mechanised Corps, units of which began moving towards Rotmistrov's force. The Germans, fearing encirclement, withdrew towards Rostov, leaving behind about 3,000 dead and

prisoners, 65 guns, much ammunition, and six wagons of food.

The way was now clear for disposing of the Germans at Tormosin, who were dangerously close to Paulus' force. But the attack on them by 5th Shock Army developed slowly, and STAVKA pointed out the necessity of liquidating the threat as quickly as possible to the command of Stalingrad Front and to General Malinovsky. Malinovsky therefore deployed his right-flank forces towards Tormosin, which was liberated on December 31, depriving the Germans of the road network and main stockpiles of Army Group Don, from which their forces in the Tormosin and Nizhne-Chirskaya areas were supplied.

By December 31 Stalingrad Front's forces had reached the line Verkhne-Rubezhny/Tormosin/Gluboky. During the Kotelnikovo operation the IV Rumanian Army had been finally defeated and IV Panzer Army thrown back with heavy losses to Zimovniki, 125 to 150 miles from Stalingrad. The remains of Army Group Don were withdrawing southward to the Manych river. Its offensive had ended in complete failure.

The Soviet offensive operations of December 1942 had caused great damage to the enemy. The VIII Italian Army had been destroyed, and the remnants of Rumanian III and IV Armies annihilated. Operational Group Hollidt and the new IV Panzer Army had been defeated. New possibilities for a strategic offensive in the whole southern sector were opening before the Red Army.

The last act
By the end of December the outer front was 125 to 150 miles away from the encircled German forces, which occupied an area of about 550 square miles, 33 miles across from

west to east and 22 miles from north to south. The choice before them was to surrender or be annihilated by the seven Soviet armies (21st, 24th, 57th, 62nd, 64th, 65th, and 66th) which surrounded them. Their commanders attempted to maintain their fighting spirit by inculcating faith that relief was near. Their delusion became stronger when they heard that the relief expedition of Army Group Don was on its way, but the failure of Manstein's offensive buried all their hopes.

Their situation became more and more hopeless. Almost all the territory held by them was being bombed or raked by Soviet artillery fire. Ammunition and fuel were running out, and the food position was especially bad. Air supply could not satisfy even their minimum needs, and hundreds of transport aircraft were shot down by Soviet aircraft and artillery during December. During the month 80,000 men were lost from wounds, hunger, and sickness, bringing the force down to 250,000.

Although their position was hopeless, they set up a dense network of fortifications and prepared for a long and stubborn defence. The German persistence with a lost battle could now be explained above all as a matter of Nazi Germany's political prestige.

Prestige was not, of course, the only explanation. The German High Command was endeavouring, by tying down Soviet forces at Stalingrad, to prevent a complete collapse of the southern wing of the Eastern Front. But after the failure of Manstein's offensive, and the loss of the airfield at Pitomnik in January, continued resistance by Paulus' troops ceased to have any strategic significance and became pointless.

The battle entered its final phase. Colonel-General of Artillery N. N. Voronov had arrived at Don Front HQ on December 19,

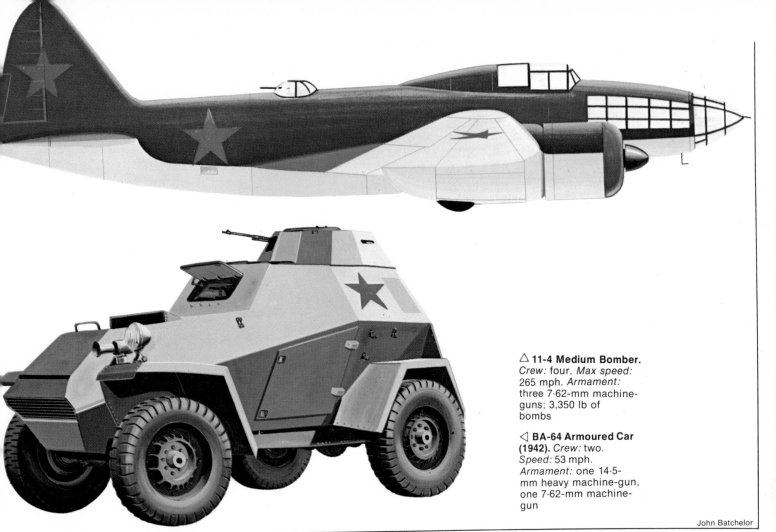

△ **11-4 Medium Bomber.**
Crew: four. *Max speed:* 265 mph. *Armament:* three 7·62-mm machine-guns; 3,350 lb of bombs

◁ **BA-64 Armoured Car (1942).** *Crew:* two. *Speed:* 53 mph. *Armament:* one 14·5-mm heavy machine-gun, one 7·62-mm machine-gun

John Batchelor

as STAVKA representative, with the task of helping to prepare the operation to destroy the encircled enemy. Don Front received reinforcements, and the three armies of Stalingrad Front operating on the inner front (57th, 62nd, and 64th) were subordinated to it from January 1, 1943. It was made responsible for all the operations to destroy the encircled force.

The liquidation plan (Operation 'Ring'), as finally approved by STAVKA on January 4, envisaged a methodical dissection of the German force and destruction of it by units. The Soviet forces regrouped, and 65th Army, which was to make the main attack, received large reinforcements.

The general balance of forces on January 10 did not give Don Front the 'overwhelming superiority' which German authors have since claimed. The Soviet forces did have superiority of 3:2 in guns and mortars, and 3:1 in aircraft, but the Germans were numerically superior in men and tanks by 6:5. But, naturally, Don Front's forces were in considerably better condition for fighting than Paulus' besieged army, and they did create superiority in men and material on the main axis, particularly in 65th Army's zone.

On January 8, in a desire to avoid useless bloodshed, the Soviet command proposed to Paulus that he capitulate. The proposal was signed by the STAVKA representative, Colonel-General of Artillery Voronov, and the commander of Don Front, Lieutenant-General Rokossovsky. It pointed out that the Germans had no real chance of breaking out, and proposed that they cease resistance; if they did so, they were guaranteed life and safety, and return to Germany or any other country they wished after the war. Immediate introduction of normal rations was

guaranteed, as was medical treatment for the wounded, sick, and frostbitten. The time limit for a reply was 1000 hours (Moscow time) on January 9, and the Soviet command warned that in the event of refusal combat operations aimed at destroying the encircled German forces would be initiated.

The German command rejected the ultimatum, thus costing the lives of tens of thousands more German officers and men. Don Front assembled on its start lines for the final blow that same night. The artillery bombardment by thousands of guns and mortars began at 0805 hours the next morning, and the bombers and ground-attack aircraft of 16th Air Army joined in.

At exactly 0900 hours Don Front took the offensive, its main blow being struck by 65th Army and the shock groups of 21st and 24th Armies, from the area south-east of Vertyachi eastwards towards the 'Red October' Factory, in an attempt to cut the enemy forces in two. Two secondary attacks were also arranged—from south of Tsybenko towards Basargino station by forces of 57th and 64th Armies, and from south-west of Yerzovka towards Gorodishche by forces of 62nd and 66th Armies.

The German resistance was stubborn, and three days of bloody fighting took place before the western salient of the defence was cut off. Forces of 65th and 21st Armies reached the western bank of the Rossoshka river by evening on January 13, and on the other sectors the Soviet troops continued to break down the enemy defences. The eastern bank of the Chervlenaya river was cleared of Germans, and on January 14 the main German airfield, at Pitomnik, was captured. The Rossoshka was crossed, and many villages were liberated, as well as the Basar-

gino, Karpovskaya, and Prudboy railway stations. In seven days of battle, over 300 square miles of the original 550 had been cleared of the enemy.

Don Front reached the immediate vicinity of Stalingrad itself by the evening of January 17 and the Germans, retreating eastwards, occupied their inner defensive perimeter. They were beginning to disintegrate but in submission to the will of their commander continued to fight.

The concluding stage of Operation Ring began. Voronov and Rokossovsky decided on a general assault along the entire front, with 21st Army taking the main load with an advance on Gumrak and the 'Red October' workers' settlement to cut the German force in two, and the right flank of 65th Army co-operating by attacking towards Alexandrovka and the northern edge of 'Red October'. STAVKA approved the plan.

The last German airfield—Gumrak—fell on January 21, and on the next day the offensive was renewed on the whole front, with infantry and artillery playing the main parts—on the 14-mile stretch of front occupied by 21st, 57th, and 64th Armies there were 4,100 guns and mortars. Between January 22/25 the Soviet forces advanced 6 to 9 miles, reaching the centre of Stalingrad and reducing the area occupied by the Germans to 36 square miles. In 16 days of fighting the Germans had lost more than 100,000 men killed, wounded, or captured.

At the 'Red October' settlement and on the Mamayev Kurgan the forces of Generals Chistyakov and Chuikov linked up. The tanks rolled in from the west to Stalingrad, its ruined factories and the great Russian river, the Volga, and with them the men of 21st Army's infantry moved in to meet the soldiers of 62nd Army, the legendary defenders of the fortress on the Volga.

The German force was now cut into two groups: the southern penned in the centre of the city and the northern squeezed into the area of the barricades and tractor factories, and the work of destroying these groups began on January 27. Despite the orders of their generals, German officers and men were now surrendering in large numbers. But there was still fierce resistance.

The 21st, 57th, and 64th Armies attacked the southern group and tightened the ring around it. Left-flank units of General Shumilov's 64th Army crossed the Tsaritsa river into the city centre. On the night of January 30/31, the 38th Motorised Rifle Brigade of Colonel N. D. Burmakov besieged the Central Department Store on the Square of Fallen Fighters. The Commander-in-Chief of the German VI Army had his HQ in its basement, and by noon he, his Chief-of-Staff (Lt-Gen Schmidt) and other generals and officers had been delivered to HQ 64th Army. The whole of the southern group laid down its arms that day, January 31, 1943.

As the commander of the northern group, General Schreck, refused to order capitulation, 62nd, 65th and 66th Armies completed the destruction of the enemy. A powerful artillery and air bombardment came down on him on February 1 and on the following day the northern group also surrendered. Fighting ceased on the banks of the Volga, and Stalingrad again became a rear-area city. Between January 10 and February 2, 1943, Don Front, under the command of General Rokossovsky, had destroyed 22 enemy divisions, more than 160 diverse units sent to reinforce VI Army, and their service units. Some 91,000 Germans, including over 2,500 officers and 24 generals, were taken prisoner, and about 120,000 killed.

The great Stalingrad battle ended in a historic Soviet victory. The counteroffensive on the Volga served as the start of a powerful offensive which developed over the immense front from Leningrad to the mountains of the Caucasus. It marked a great turning point in the entire war. The Red Army had recovered the strategic initiative, and was to retain it right up to the end.

Nazi Germany and its allies had suffered an irreparable defeat. Two German (VI and IV Panzer), two Rumanian (III and IV), and one Italian (VIII) Armies were destroyed, 32 divisions and three brigades annihilated, and 16 divisions heavily battered, losing more than half their personnel. Enemy casualties in killed, wounded, and captured were about 1,500,000, and huge quantities of equipment were lost, including about 3,500 tanks and self-propelled guns, more than 3,000 aircraft, over 12,000 guns and mortars, and 75,000 vehicles—enough to equip 75 to 80 divisions.

The destruction of the best part of the Wehrmacht at Stalingrad disrupted German military morale. The myth of invincibility was shattered once and for all. Hitler's war machine received a crushing blow which largely disrupted its ability to fight. The events on the Volga found an echo in the rear of Nazi Germany, shaking the foundations of Nazi power and strengthening the anti-Nazi movements in the countries of Hitler's bloc. The Red Army's victory caused an upsurge in the national liberation movement in the enslaved countries, and shook Germany's influence in the neutrals. Disagreements within the Nazi bloc intensified.

It would be difficult to overestimate the effect of these events in strengthening the forces of the anti-Nazi coalition. The impressive results of the Stalingrad battle created favourable conditions for operations by Anglo-American forces against Nazi Germany and its allies.

More equipment, greater skill
What were the reasons for the catastrophe which overtook Nazi Germany on the Volga?
● Without repeating what has already been said, it is worth emphasising that the course and outcome of the Stalingrad battle could not be separated from the general condition of the Soviet nation at that time. Thanks to the efforts of the Soviet people and Communist Party, the war industry achieved enormous successes in the second half of 1942, and in the course of the year gave to the Red Army over 25,000 aircraft, about 25,000 tanks, and almost 30,000 field guns of 76-mm calibre or above—considerably more than its German counterpart delivered in the same period. By autumn of that difficult war year many new tank and mechanised formations, air corps, and artillery regiments had been formed and sent to the front.
● The Red Army's fighting power had also grown by the time of the Volga battle through improved mastery of war and operational/tactical skill, as the enemy had cause to learn during the defensive battles and especially during the counteroffensive. The German generals and the troops they led had to acknowledge that developments on the Eastern Front were being determined not by the actions of the 'invincible' German army but by the will of the Red Army and the Soviet people. Soviet troops showed steadfastness and skill in defence, especially in close combat, and in attack were distinguished by bold manoeuvre, resoluteness, and high offensive élan. The Red Army's generals and officers exhibited in this battle mature skill in leading troops, courage and talent in accomplishing their missions. The Supreme Command, the General Staff, and the front commands gave convincing proof of how their skill in directing armed conflict had improved in the past 12 months.

The victory won by the Soviet people at Stalingrad testified that final disaster for Nazi Germany was inevitable. But the struggle was not yet over.

Stalingrad:

The Coup de Grâce

1942 October 14: Hitler orders all forces to take the defensive and stand fast, except for those in the Stalingrad area and some small sectors in the Caucasus.
Early November: The Red Army prepares a plan (Plan Uranus) for the relief of Stalingrad.
November 19: At exactly 0730 hours, some 3,500 Soviet guns and mortars open fire on the breakthrough sectors. The Soviet blow to free Stalingrad has begun.
November 20: Stalingrad Front takes up the offensive.
November 21: The onrush of Soviet armour forces General Paulus to move his HQ from Golubinsky to Nizhne-Chirskaya. Hitler then orders Paulus to relocate his HQ again, near Gumrak.
November 23: On the fifth day of the counterblow, South-West and Stalingrad Fronts link up, closing the ring around 22 German divisions.
November 24: The Red Army launches operations to annihilate the encircled German forces.
December 12: General Manstein launches Operation Winter Storm, a counterstrike with 13 divisions to relieve the trapped VI Army. Meanwhile, Soviet South-West Front has handed the Germans a crushing blow on the middle Don.
December 24: Soviet forces now attack Hoth's relief group. The Germans withdraw, and by December 31 it is clear that the Red Army has fresh opportunities for a strategic offensive in the southern sector.

1943 January 4: STAVKA approves the plan for Operation Ring
January 8: STAVKA proposes to Paulus that he capitulate: otherwise, his forces will be annihilated. Paulus rejects the ultimatum.
January 10: Operation Ring begins: at 0800 hours, the Red Army opens its final assault on Paulus' forces. At 0900 hours, Don Front takes the offensive.
January 31: General Paulus, trapped in Stalingrad, surrenders the southern group of his army. Two days later General Schreck surrenders the northern group. The VI Army is no more.

German prisoners of war after Stalingrad

Stalemate at Stalingrad: The Hand-to-Hand Battle

At Stalingrad each separate battle resolved itself into a combat between individuals. In the jumble of ruins—which the fighting widened daily—the tommy-gun and hand-grenade ruled supreme. Below are illustrated typical fighting men of both sides with their key weapons

1. KAR-98K 7·9-mm rifle (5 rounds in magazine)
2. MP-40 machine-pistol (32 rounds in magazine)
3. Walther P-38 9-mm automatic (8 rounds in magazine)
4. Standard hand-grenade

At Stalingrad the Germans were baffled by a situation hitherto outside their military experience, and they reacted to it characteristically—by the application of brute force in heavier and heavier doses. Paulus was reinforced by a variety of specialist troops, including police battalions and engineers skilled in street fighting and demolition work. But the Russians, although heavily outnumbered, remained their masters in the street-to-street, house-to-house, room-to-room, fighting

ALAMEIN: THE

Western Desert, October/November 1942

Major-General Sir Francis de Guingand describes what in British eyes has seemed the most important battle of the war – popularly known as the Battle of Alamein. This title ignores the First Battle of Alamein, fought over virtually the same ground 16 weeks before, at which Rommel's advance was halted and the Afrika Korps given the first inkling of its fate. For now the supply situation favoured the British. Between July and October many changes had been wrought in the 8th Army: the men were rested, conscious of their hard training, aware that for the first time their weapons and equipment were superior in both quality and quantity to the enemy's. And most important of all, they had seen the enemy beaten back at Alam Halfa and knew that he was no Superman. Now it would be demonstrated to the world

When the Axis armies in Africa rose to meet the onslaught of the 8th Army on October 23 they were at a disadvantage in almost every department. Not least of their deficiencies was the absence of their great leader, for Rommel was a sick man and had returned to Germany for rest and treatment on September 23. In his place General Stumme held command – disgruntled in the knowledge that, if an attack came, Rommel would return at once, convinced that he alone was capable of taking the right decisions in an emergency on the Alamein front against the British.

Yet even Rommel regarded a defence against an enemy as strong in material as the British as a 'Battle Without Hope' while, from his masters in Rome and Berlin, he had obtained many promises but little practical help. So, daily, his reserves of men, tanks, guns, ammunition, fuel, and supplies fell lower, making comparison with the British an even gloomier exercise. For instance, Rommel was aware of a British superiority of 2 to 1 in tanks when, in fact, it was nearer $2\frac{1}{2}$ to 1 overall (including 300 Italian tanks) and $5\frac{1}{2}$ to 1 counting Germans alone. And the Royal Air Force now dominated the air, making the Luftwaffe's despairing efforts appear puny by comparison. While in Rome, Rommel told Mussolini that unless the supply position was improved the Axis would have to get out of North Africa, but he sensed his failure to transmit the gravity of the situation and in Berlin he recoiled before a wall of blind optimism and false promises.

At the front, meanwhile, all Panzerarmee could do was prepare an even denser fortified area in the neck between the sea and the Qattara Depression, based on the prime con-

sideration that, if they were driven out into the open, they would be overwhelmed for lack of sufficient vehicles or fuel to withdraw or fight a mobile rearguard action. Thus they planned to hold each piece of ground at all costs, cleaning up each enemy penetration with an immediate counterattack.

The German system of defence which evolved was not unlike that to be found on the Western Front at the end of the First World War – a battle zone spread out in depth behind a screen of outposts, in an effort to acquire time for mobile reserves to assemble and counterattack. One technical feature, in particular, amplified the 1918 concept – anti-tank and anti-personnel mines. Some 500,000 of them, supplemented by buried British bombs and shells, were sown thickly around each defended locality, creating a deep belt along the length of the front.

In each sector Italian troops, well laced with Germans to give stability, waited the impact with mounting anxiety. The pattern they formed contained an invitation to a Battle of Attrition – it only needed the British commander to accept that invitation and a drawn-out battle would be in prospect.

Before the Battle of Alam Halfa was fought, Winston Churchill paid us a visit on his way back from Moscow (August 19) and stayed at our headquarters at Burgh-el-Arab.

General Montgomery took special care to see that the Prime Minister and his party would be comfortable. He gave up his own caravan and sited it within a few yards of the sea, so that our distinguished guest could bathe when he felt so inclined.

Imperial War Museum

Churchill gave us the most vivid description of his visit to Moscow and how he had to talk 'cold turkey' before it was accepted that Great Britain was doing something to win the war, but he had come away with a very deep impression of Stalin's leadership; and enthralled us with details of our gathering war effort, and what we were preparing for the enemy. I well remember him saying: 'Germany has asked for this bombing warfare, and she will rue the day she started it, for her country will be laid in ruins.'

Once Rommel had failed in his last desperate offensive, he was faced with two alternatives. Either to stay and await the attack which he knew would most surely be launched against him, increasing in the meantime the strength of his defences; or to withdraw to some favourable position before we were ready to follow him up in sufficient strength, thereby shortening his lines of communication and so rendering his supply position less precarious.

He chose the first of these courses, no doubt largely because he lacked the necessary transport and petrol for a withdrawal; but in any case a retreat would have been against his character and would certainly have proved very unpopular with the Axis High Command. His decision meant therefore that the longer we waited before launching our offensive, the more formidable his defences would become – particularly with regard to minefields, wire, and the construction of prepared positions.

It was therefore obvious that it was to our advantage to attack as soon as possible and this view was strongly held by Churchill, who started to press General Alexander – Commander-in-Chief Middle East – for an early offensive. He wanted this to take place in September. He had an additional important reason and that was the fact that Operation 'Torch', the Anglo/US landings in North Africa, was due to take place early in November, and therefore hard and prolonged fighting on our front would be of great benefit.

One day Alexander arrived at our headquarters, bringing with him a signal from Churchill saying that he more or less demanded that we should attack in September. After reading the document Montgomery said 'Hand me a pad, Freddie', and seizing it he wrote down these points:

● Rommel's attack had caused some delay in our preparations.
● Moon conditions restricted 'D' day to certain periods in September and October.
● If the September date was insisted upon the troops would be insufficiently equipped and trained, and failure would probably result. But if the attack took place in October then complete victory was assured.

Turning to Alexander, he handed over the pad and said: 'I should make these points in your reply; that should fix it.' A signal was subsequently dispatched on these lines and produced the required result; for what could any Prime Minister do with this clear-cut military opinion before him! Montgomery in his memoirs recalls that he told Alexander 'privately' that if the attack was ordered for September they would have to find someone else to do the job.

Taking all considerations into account, Montgomery decided that we should attack during the October full moon and the exact date fixed was the 23rd. It was essential that we should attack at night owing to the formidable minefield problem.

I now come to the plan itself. There was no way round the enemy positions; the sea and the Qattara Depression saw to that, so a hole had to be punched through their defences. Montgomery had decided to launch the main attack on the right flank with General Leese's 30th Corps, together with a secondary attack on the southern flank by General Horrocks' 13th Corps. The plan was to pass 10th Corps (General Lumsden) through the gap made by 30th Corps to sit astride the enemy's supply line, and so force him to deploy his armour against us, when it would be destroyed. This was in accordance with normal teaching. Having destroyed the enemy's armour, his troops could be dealt with more or less at leisure.

The Army Commander had laid down three basic fundamentals which would govern the preparatory period. These were: leadership – equipment – training. He soon put the first matter in order, and the re-equipment of the army was going well. But early in October he realised that the training of the army was still below what was required, and in view of this weakness made one of his rapid decisions. He would alter the conception of the plan so that instead of first going all out to destroy the enemy's armour, he would eat away the enemy's holding troops – who were for the most part unarmoured – and use our armour to stop the enemy from interfering. Without their infantry divisions to hold the line, providing firm bases for their mobile forces, the enemy's armour would be at a grave disadvantage and their supply routes would be constantly threatened. It was unlikely that they would stand idly by while this 'crumbling' process was going on, and so it was probable that we would force his armour to attack *us,* which, once we were in a position to receive it, would be to our advantage.

The final plan in outline as given out by the Army Commander on October 6 was as follows:

● Main attack by 30th Corps in the north on a front of four divisions [to secure a bridgehead – objective 'Oxalic' – beyond the enemy's main defended zone]. Two corridors were to be cleared through the minefields, and through these lanes 10th Corps was to pass.

● 13th Corps in the south was to stage two attacks. One directed on Himeimat and the Taqa feature. The other into the area of Gebel Kalakh and Qaret el Khadim. These attacks were to be made with the primary object of misleading the enemy and thereby containing forces that might otherwise be used against 30th Corps.

● Both the above corps were to destroy the enemy holding the forward positions.

● 10th Corps was to deploy itself [to a line 'Pierson', just west of 'Oxalic'] so as to prevent 30th Corps' operations from being interfered with. And its final object [by an advance to area 'Skinflint'] was the destruction of the enemy's armour.

● The attack was to start at night during the full moon.

The artillery plan was very carefully prepared. We would go into battle with great gun power and considerable supplies of ammunition. The battle was to open with a very heavy counter-battery bombardment, and then most of our artillery would concentrate on the enemy defences by barrage and concentrations.

The air plan was a good one. Before the battle Air Vice-Marshal Coningham's Desert Air Force had been wearing down the enemy's air effort. On one or two occasions he had shown brilliant leadership by taking advantage of fleeting opportunities when isolated rain storms had grounded portions of the enemy's air force. Low-flying attacks laid on with great rapidity had taken a very heavy toll of the enemy's aircraft and petrol.

During the first night our air forces were to undertake attacks against enemy gun positions, and so help our counter-battery plan. Later they were to switch to the areas where the enemy armoured divisions were located. Our available air strength on 'D' day was 500 fighters and 200 bombers – at that time a considerable force.

The 'going' was one of the matters which gave us a lot of anxiety, and we went to endless trouble to obtain information as to what the ground was like in the area over which we were making our thrusts. Air photos, interrogation of prisoners, questioning of our own troops who had at one time or another traversed the area – these were some of the means employed. We built six tracks leading up to 30th Corps' starting line, and this in itself was a tremendous task, constructed as they were through very soft sand.

Montgomery's dummy army

The deception arrangements were particularly interesting. We had decided quite rightly that strategic surprise was out of the question, for the enemy knew we were going to attack. On the other hand tactical surprise was quite possible. We considered we could delude the enemy as to the weight,

the date, the time, and the direction of our attack. Our plans were all made with this in view, and they proved most successful.

The first problem was to try to conceal our concentration as much as possible from the enemy. The staff worked out the complete layout on the day of the attack – the number of guns, tanks, vehicles, and troops. A very large 'operations' map was kept which showed this layout in various denominations. We then arranged to reach the eventual density as early as possible, and to maintain it up to the last moment, so that the enemy's air photography would show no particular change during the last two or three weeks. To achieve this we used spare transport and dummy transport. These were gradually replaced by those belonging to the assault units and formations as they came up to take over their allotted sectors. These changeovers took place at night, and we had special dummy vehicles made under which guns could be concealed. All moves forward were of course rigidly controlled, and slit trenches were dug and camouflaged at night in which the assault infantry could be concealed.

The next task was to make the enemy think that the main attack would be launched in the southern sector. This, I might add, was not very popular with 13th Corps, but they nobly accepted the plan for the common good. Besides various other methods adopted, we built large dummy dumps away to the south, and also a dummy pipe line and water installations. It was so arranged that the work would appear to the enemy to be aimed at completion a week or two *after* the actual date of our attack. Finally on the night of the attack itself the wireless traffic of the headquarters of an armoured division was so employed as to indicate that a large move of armoured forces was taking place in the southern sector.

On the night of the 23rd we arranged for a feint landing to take place behind the enemy's lines. About 4 pm a convoy sailed westwards out of Alexandria. After dark all but a few fast craft put back, but those remaining staged a dummy landing. Shelling of the coast, mortar and machine-gun fire, and light signals were used. It was timed to take place about three hours after our attack had started, and it was hoped that this would tie down enemy reserves. The loading of the ships was no doubt witnessed by enemy agents, who could see tanks being shipped and troops marching aboard. There is no doubt that all these measures helped materially to confuse the enemy and gained us tactical surprise.

On the administrative side there was a great deal to be done. The whole basis of administration had to be altered. Before, when we were on the defensive, the weight of resources was held back; now that we intended to attack they had to be placed as far forward as possible. The consequent carrying forward of supplies and the camouflaging of the dumps was no small task, and preparations were made to construct the railway forward as rapidly as possible. We also made preparations to open ports when they were captured and perfected our organisation for the recovery and repair of tanks and vehicles.

Montgomery's change in plan as regards the use of our armour nearly caused a crisis between himself and General Herbert Lumsden, who had been selected to command the 'Corps d'Elite' – the 10th Army Corps. Lumsden had fought with conspicuous gallantry when commanding an armoured division in the 'bad old days'. He was a cavalryman through and through and not unnaturally thought in terms of the mobile battle and yearned for the day when his armoured formations, equipped with modern tanks, would be launched through a gap made by the infantry, to roam far and wide. The Army Commander's new instructions were therefore not to his liking.

Shortly after this Lumsden held a corps conference at which he explained his plan and views to all the commanders in his corps. Montgomery was temporarily absent from the army on this occasion and I therefore decided to attend this conference myself.

It soon became clear to me that this new conception of the use of armour had not been fully accepted by the corps commander, and at the end of the meeting I had a talk with Lumsden pointing out the Army Commander's determination to fight the coming battle this way. But I could see that he was anything but happy and there appeared to be a recrudescence of the bad old habit of questioning orders.

On the Army Commander's return, I reported fully on what had taken place and he lost little time in making his views crystal clear to the commander of 10th Corps; and Lumsden, being a good soldier, accepted the position and made the necessary changes in his plans.

Large-scale rehearsals for the coming battle were carried out, and the lessons learned gone into very carefully by the various commanders. And by the end of the third week in October we realised that all these vast preparations were successfully reaching their conclusion. From the staff

Montgomery was determined not to begin his attack until the 8th Army had overwhelming superiority. Time was on his side, for the Allies now controlled the supply lines, and troops and new equipment – like this Sherman – could be delivered in unprecedented quantities. Meanwhile the Afrika Korps was not only starved of equipment but it would go into battle without Rommel, who was ill

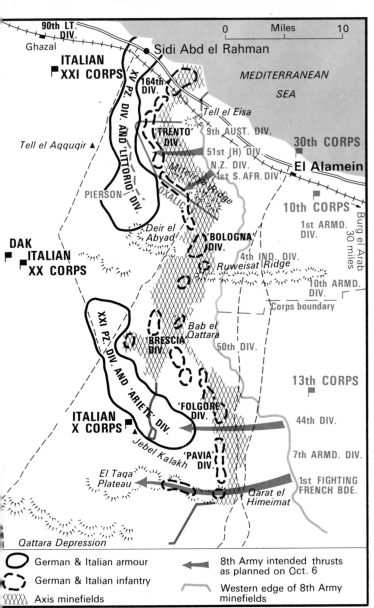

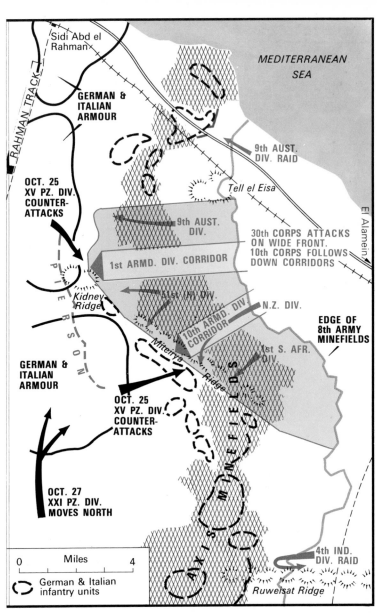

At Alamein in October the 8th Army was faced by an enemy position which could not be turned, but must be breached by direct attack. Montgomery at first intended to use 30th Corps to push two corridors into the enemy lines through which the tanks of 10th Corps would flood to force an armoured battle and cut the Axis supply lines. But weaknesses in his forces' training made him decide to alter this plan: 30th Corps was still to open two corridors through to 'Oxalic', but it was then to concentrate upon 'crumbling' the enemy's holding troops. The tanks were to go no further than 'Pierson', where they would cover the infantry and await the German armoured counter-attacks on ground of their own choosing. Further south, diversionary attacks by 4th Indian Division and 13th Corps would hold a large proportion of the Axis armour during the vital opening phase of the battle. On the Axis side, Stumme had split his armour (XV Panzer in the north, XXI Panzer in the south) to cover both possible lines of attack. This unprecedented step weakened his ability to mount a concentrated counterattack, but General Bayerlein believed that it had been approved by Rommel before he left Africa

After an extremely heavy artillery barrage, troops of 30th Corps, on a four-division front, advanced into the enemy minefields. By dawn on October 24 the infantry had reached most of the objectives of 'Oxalic', but stubborn enemy resistance and congestion in the corridors prevented the tanks from clearing the minefields. At first German reactions seemed hesitant and unsure—not only were Panzerarmee's commanders still uncertain as to where the real attack would come, but Stumme had died of heart failure on the first day, and for vital hours the Axis forces had no leader until General von Thoma was able to take over. It was not until the third day of the attack that a new Axis certainty about counterattacks showed that Rommel had returned. Throughout the 24th and 25th, 30th Corps inched forward, while 13th Corps successfully held XXI Panzer in the south. But Montgomery had realised that the impetus had gone out of the initial attacks, and, using attacks by 9th Australian Division in the north to cut off enemy forces in the salient and force Rommel to concentrate on their relief, he halted and began to redeploy 8th Army for a new breakout attempt

point of view there was a healthy slackening in the tempo of work, denoting that the stage was now set.

Montgomery had been indefatigable, and had satisfied himself that all was in readiness. He very rightly had decided that in order to get the best out of his troops it was necessary for them to know the whole plan so that they would realise how their particular contribution fitted in with the general scheme of things.

On October 19 and 20 he addressed all officers down to lieutenant-colonel level in 30th, 13th, and 10th Corps. It was a real tour de force. These talks were some of the best he had ever given, clear and full of confidence. He touched on the enemy situation, stressing their weaknesses, and

said he was certain a long 'dog-fight' or 'killing match' would take place for several days—'it might be ten'. He then gave details of our great strength, our tanks, our guns, and the enormous supplies of ammunition available. He drummed in the need never to lose the initiative, and how everyone—*everyone*—must be imbued with the burning desire to 'kill Germans'. 'Even the padres—one per weekday and two on Sundays!' This produced a roar. After explaining how the battle was to be fought, he said that he was entirely confident of the result.

The men were let into the secret on October 21 and 22, from which date no leave was granted, and by the 23rd a tremendous state of enthusiasm had been produced. Those soldiers just knew they would succeed.

On the morning of October 22, Montgomery held a press conference. He explained the plan, his intentions, and his firm conviction of success. Many of the war correspondents were rather shaken by the confidence—this bombastic confidence—which he displayed. They felt there must be a catch in it—how could he be so sure? Some, I think, thought the maze of minefields and deep defences that the enemy had constructed were too difficult a problem to justify such a sanguine attitude.

In the afternoon of the 23rd we drove up to our battle headquarters, tucked away on the coast within a few minutes of 30th and 10th Corps Headquarters. We had well protected buried cables running back to our main headquarters and to the various corps; vehicles

Line-Up for the Battle

Panzerarmee Afrika
Gen Stumme (until Oct 26) and Fld Mshl Rommel

Reserve
German 90th Light Division
Italian **Trieste** Motorised Division
Luftwaffe XIX Flak Division

North
German XV Panzer Division
German 164th Motorised Division
Italian **Littorio** Armoured Division
Italian XXI Infantry Corps—**Trento** Division

Centre
German XXI Panzer Division
Ramcke Parachute Brigade
Italian XX Infantry Corps—**Brescia**
and **Bologna** Divisions

South
Italian **Ariete** Armoured Division
Italian X Infantry Corps—**Pavia**
and **Folgore** Divisions

8th Army
Lieut-Gen Montgomery

30th Corps—Lieut-Gen Leese
51st (Highland) Division—Maj-Gen Wimberley
4th Indian Division—Maj-Gen Tuker
9th Australian Division
New Zealand Division—Lieut-Gen Freyberg
1st South African Division—Maj-Gen Pienaar
23rd Armoured Brigade Group
9th (UK) Armoured Brigade

13th Corps—Lieut-Gen Horrocks
7th Armoured Division—Maj-Gen Harding
50th Division—Maj-Gen Nichols
44th Division—Maj-Gen Hughes
1st Free French Brigade Group
2nd Free French Brigade Group
1st Greek Infantry Brigade Group

10th Corps—Lieut-Gen Lumsden
1st Armoured Division—Maj-Gen Briggs
10th Armoured Division—Maj-Gen Gatehouse
8th Armoured Division—Maj-Gen Gairdner

Rommel
Nehring
Thoma
Bayerlein

Montgomery
Leese
Horrocks
Lumsden

Allied leadership was new and backed by great material resources, but Axis command suffered from changes and resultant indecisiveness. When the offensive began, Panzerarmee was led by General Stumme, but after his death on the first day of the attack it was commanded by General von Thoma until Rommel, who had been ill, returned on October 26

50,000 German, 54,000 Italian　　　　　　　　**104,000**

195,000

211 German=85 Mark IIIs, 88 Mark III Specials,　　**489**
8 Mark IVs, 30 Mark IV Specials
278 Italian, mainly M13/40s

1,029　　170 Grants, 252 Shermans, 216 Crusader 2-pdrs,
78 Crusader 6-pdrs, 119 Stuarts, 194 Valentines

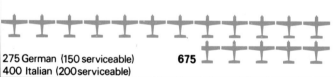

475 Field and Medium=200 German, 275 Italian
744 Anti-tank=444 German (86=8·8cm, 68=7·62cm,　**1,219**
290=5·0cm) 300 Italian

2,311　　908 Field and Medium
1,403 Anti-tank=554 2-pdrs, 849 6-pdrs

275 German (150 serviceable)　　**675**
400 Italian (200 serviceable)

750　　(530 serviceable)

---

were dug in as we were rather far forward and near the desert road, which would undoubtedly become—as it did—a target for enemy air attack. I decided to make this tactical headquarters my base, and it worked very well. My people could talk to me on direct lines and come up for conferences within the hour.

It was a lovely evening, and I drove out after dark to see by the light of the moon the move forward of some of the troops. All was going well, and everyone looked cheerful. This was the day for which so many of us had been preparing and waiting.

As the time drew near we got into our cars and drove to a good view-point to see the opening of the battle. We passed the never-ending stream of tanks and transport—all moving with clockwork precision. This was 10th Corps moving up to its starting line, with the moon providing sufficient light to drive by, but the night protecting them from

the prying eyes of enemy aircraft. We had some of our own machines flying over the enemy's forward positions making distracting noises; otherwise all seemed fairly quiet and normal. An occasional Very light and burst of machine-gun fire, a gun firing here and there, as would happen any night. We looked at our watches, 2130 hours—ten minutes to go. I could hardly wait.

A 1,000-gun barrage begins
The minutes ticked by, and then the whole sky was lit up, and a roar rent the air. Over 1,000 of our guns had opened up. It was a great and heartening sight. I tried to picture what the enemy must be thinking, did he know what was coming? He must do now. How ready was he? Up and down the desert, from north to south, the twinkling of the guns could be seen in an unceasing sequence. Within the enemy's lines we could see an occasional deep red glow

light up the western sky. Each time this happened Brigadier Dennis, the commander of 30th Corps artillery, let out a grunt of satisfaction. Another Axis gun position had been blown up. We checked each change in the artillery plan; the pause while the guns switched to new targets. It was gun drill at its best. Now the infantry started forward. We could see the periodic bursts of Bofors guns which, with their tracer shell, demarcated the direction of advance. Behind us great searchlight beams were directed towards the sky, to help the forward troops plot their positions, and so find out where they had reached their objectives, for few landmarks existed in this part of the desert.

About 2300 hours I crept away and drove back to our headquarters. I knew we could expect to hear little of interest for some time yet, and so I snatched an hour or two's rest before being wakened up to hear the first reports come in.

40-mm BOFORS ANTI-AIRCRAFT GUN. The Bofors, designed in Sweden, was one of the most widely used weapons of the war. It was not only an extremely effective anti-aircraft gun, but was also used during night attacks—such as Alamein—to fire tracer as a guide-line for advancing infantry. **Weight in action:** 2·4 tons. **Weight of shell:** 2 lb. **Rate of fire:** 120 rounds per minute. **Effective altitude:** 12,000 feet. **Crew:** Average of six.

As I closed my eyes I felt full of confidence and hope, but never did I think that this was the opening of a campaign that would bring us in so short a time to the very gates of Carthage.

Although the Battle of El Alamein was a comparatively small affair in relation to later battles fought during the war, for a number of reasons it must rank high in importance. To start with it meant the turn of the tide in Britain's fortunes. In fact the victory stood out as a priceless jewel after a series of depressing defeats. Then it provided a much-wanted stimulus to British morale, for it convinced our armed forces that, given the right leadership and weapons, they could beat the Germans, and it also inspired confidence among the British people in ultimate victory.

By previous standards in the Middle East, however, it was a great offensive and probably some of the bitterest fighting in the whole war took place over those sandy wastes. Our new commander never once lost his confidence or the initiative, while his troops were always convinced that they would win through in the end. I do not propose to give a very detailed description of the operations, but will confine myself to the broad framework of the battle and concentrate upon the highlights.

On that night of October 23/24, 30th Corps attacked with four divisions down two corridors cleared through the minefields. This attack was made on a fairly narrow front of 6 to 7 miles, with the northern flank tied to the Tell el Eisa feature, and the Miteiriya Ridge forming the southern limit.

The enemy's and our own dispositions at the outset of the battle are interesting for three reasons:

● The greater part of the enemy static defences was manned by Italians.
● The German infantry divisions, 164th Division and 90th Light Division, were echeloned in depth, protecting the vital coastal road sector.
● The German armour (Afrika Korps) was held in reserve and distributed equally between the northern and southern sectors.

Besides 30th Corps' main attack, a brigade of the 9th Australian Division carried out a feint between Tell el Eisa and the sea. This, together with the phoney seaborne operation, had a worrying effect on the enemy, while farther south the 4th Indian Division launched a strong raid from the area of the Ruweisat Ridge.

Then, at 0200 hours on October 24, the leading elements of the 1st and 10th Armoured Divisions crossed their start lines.

The Germans reel . . . and recover

Progress was good, and the task of clearing the lanes through the minefields went on well, but by the morning the armour had not managed to get out beyond them. Throughout the night, the Miteiriya Ridge was a very unpleasant place to be, and fierce fighting took place, for once the enemy had recovered from the initial shock, he concentrated his artillery and mortar fire on the corridors, and XV Panzer Division carried out a counterattack. The Army Commander examined the situation on the morning of the 24th, and decided that although a very good start had been made, it was important that there must be no slackening in the efforts to get the armour through, and that the 'crumbling' operations by the New Zealand Division must start at once.

In the south, 13th Corps had started on schedule. The French had successfully assaulted the high ground about Himeimat, but the soft sand had prevented their supporting weapons reaching them in time, and they were driven off again by a German counterattack. The other 13th Corps' attack, after making initial gains, was held up between the belts of minefields. The 24th was, therefore, spent in 'crumbling' operations in this area. These were, however, secondary to the main attack by 30th Corps, and in spite of these small set-backs their main object was achieved, for the XXI Panzer Division was still retained in the southern sector.

Now started a week of terrific fighting. By the evening of the 24th, the 1st Armoured Division had managed to get some elements out of the minefields in positions beyond, but 10th Armoured Division was not so fortunate, and was having a very difficult time. An attack they made at 2200 hours that night, supported by the corps artillery, made little progress.

The Army Commander went to bed in his caravan that night at his usual time—between 2130 and 2200 hours. As things appeared rather uncertain, I decided to stay up and keep in close touch with the corps. Towards 0200 hours on the 25th it was obvious that the situation in the southern corridor about the Miteiriya Ridge was not satisfactory. Congestion was considerable in the cleared lane through the minefields, and a lot of damage was being done by enemy shelling and mortar fire. General Freyberg, as usual in the thick of it, was personally directing operations from his tank in this critical zone.

Altogether I gained the impression that a feeling was developing in some quarters which favoured suspending the forward move, and pulling back under cover of the ridge. I decided, therefore, that this was an occasion when the Army Commander must intervene, and so I called a conference for 0330 hours at our Tactical Headquarters, asking Leese (30th Corps) and Lumsden (10th Corps) to attend. Then I went along to his caravan and woke him up. He appeared to be sleeping peacefully—in spite of a lot of attention from the enemy air force. He agreed with the action I had taken, and told me to bring the two corps commanders along to his map lorry when they arrived.

In due course I led the generals along the little path to the lorry. Montgomery was seated on a stool carefully examining a map fixed to the wall. He greeted us all most cheerfully, motioned us to sit down, and then asked each corps commander to tell his story. He listened very quietly, only occasionally interrupting with a question. There was a certain 'atmosphere' noticeable, careful handling was required, and Lumsden was obviously still not very happy about the role his armour had been given. After a while Montgomery spoke to the commander of the 10th Armoured Division on the telephone, and heard his version of the situation. He then made it quite clear that there would be no alteration to his orders. The armour could and must get through. He also ordered the headquarters of this division to be moved considerably farther forward.

The decision to make no change in the plan at that moment was a brave one, for it meant accepting considerable risks and casualties. But if it had not been made, I am firmly convinced that the attack might

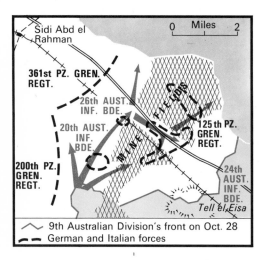

361st PZ. GREN. REGT.

26th AUST. INF. BDE.

20th AUST. INF. BDE.

200th PZ. GREN. REGT.

125th PZ. GREN. REGT.

24th AUST. INF. BDE.

Sidi Abd el Rahman

MINE FIELDS

Tell el Eisa

0 — Miles — 2

⌒ 9th Australian Division's front on Oct. 28
--- German and Italian forces

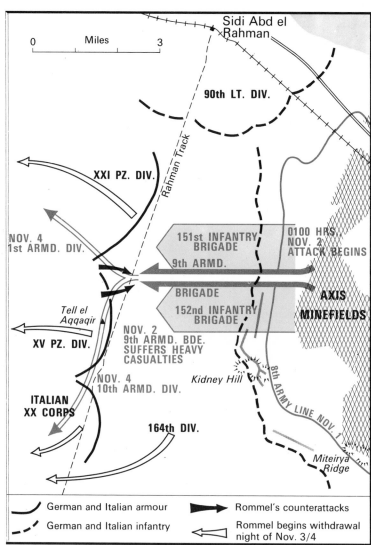

Sidi Abd el Rahman

90th LT. DIV.

XXI PZ. DIV.

NOV. 4
1st ARMD. DIV.

151st INFANTRY BRIGADE
9th ARMD.
BRIGADE
152nd INFANTRY BRIGADE

0100 HRS. NOV. 2 ATTACK BEGINS

AXIS MINEFIELDS

Tell el Aqqaqir

XV PZ. DIV.

NOV. 2
9th ARMD. BDE. SUFFERS HEAVY CASUALTIES

Kidney Hill

8th ARMY LINE NOV. 1

NOV. 4
10th ARMD. DIV.

ITALIAN XX CORPS

164th DIV.

Miteirya Ridge

Rahman Track

0 — Miles — 3

⌒ German and Italian armour   ◤ Rommel's counterattacks
--- German and Italian infantry   ⇐ Rommel begins withdrawal night of Nov. 3/4

Far left: The Australian thrust which cut off units of two German regiments and persuaded Rommel to concentrate his reserve in the far north. On the morning of November 2, after a heavy barrage, two infantry brigades began 'Supercharge' **(left)**, Montgomery's final thrust: the first armoured unit, 9th Armoured Brigade, was severely mauled, but when the 1st Armoured Division followed it and met XXI Panzer coming from the north, there was a confused tank battle in which the Germans lost much vital equipment. By the morning of the 3rd, Rommel had decided to retreat, only to receive a message from Hitler ordering him to hold the Alamein position at all costs. This order he prepared to obey until the news arrived that his defences in the south had been shattered by 14th Indian and 51st Highland Divisions (not shown on map), and General von Thoma had been captured. He was thus forced to fall back precipitately as the British armour threatened to surround his most precious force

well have fizzled out, and the full measure of success we achieved might never have been possible.

By 0800 hours on October 25 the leading armoured brigade of the 10th Armoured Division was reported to be 2,000 yards west of the minefield area, and in touch with the 1st Armoured Division to the north. In addition, we heard that the New Zealand Division and the 8th Armoured Brigade were clear of the main minefields, and were advancing south-westwards in accordance with the plan, drawing the XV Panzer Division into several counterattacks against us, which were all repulsed with heavy losses.

The attack switches to the north

By about mid-day Montgomery realised that the 'crumbling' operations by the New Zealand Division would prove very expensive and decided to switch the axis northwards, telling the 9th Australian Division to destroy the Germans in the salient. The 1st Armoured Division was ordered to fight its way westwards with the object of threatening the enemy's supply routes in the Rahman track area, where it would also threaten the rear of the enemy holding the coastal salient, but this attack made no appreciable progress until the night of October 26/27.

The Australian attack under General Moreshead went well – ground was gained and heavy casualties inflicted on the enemy. Here the enemy's defences were very strong (the garrison was mainly German) and I believe this area saw the most determined and savage fighting during the whole battle and made a major contribution to ultimate victory.

On the 26th the New Zealand and South African Divisions made slow progress, and the Army Commander decided to regroup. The 30th Corps required a pause to re-organise and, although we had forced our way through the main minefields, the enemy still had well organised anti-tank defences opposing us.

This regrouping produced the reserves required for the decisive phase of the battle. The New Zealand Division was pulled out of the line, their place being taken by moving the 1st South African and 4th Indian Divisions northward. The New Zealanders were given first priority for all tank replacements, and spent a day or so resting and bathing. We could see this cheerful body of men spread out along the beach from our headquarters, the horrors of the Miteiriya Ridge behind them, preparing themselves for the ordeal ahead.

During October 27 news came in that two enemy tankers and a merchantman had been sunk near the entrance to Tobruk harbour, and their loss may have had a considerable influence on the battle. At 1400 hours the Army Commander held a conference at which the regrouping plan was explained, and also plans for the continuance of the Australian attack. The 13th Corps was ordered to make final arrangements for moving the 7th Armoured Division and other troops to the northern sector, for during the night of October 26/27 the XXI Panzer Division had moved northwards, and so these forces could be spared. In the morning we had located, by wireless direction-finding, the headquarters of this German armoured division.

For most of the day, the two German Panzer divisions launched attacks against our positions. This suited us well, and the 1st Armoured Division excelled themselves, claiming 50 enemy tanks knocked out, as well as others damaged. In addition, the RAF was doing good work bombing the enemy as they formed up, so altogether it was an exciting and successful day – from our headquarters we could see the tell-tale pillars of black smoke towering up into the sky when tanks and vehicles were destroyed.

Now Montgomery decided that the 1st Armoured Division needed a rest, and withdrew it into reserve, turning their sector to defence, with infantry brigades, moved up from 13th Corps, and available for subsequent operations.

On the night of the 28/29 the Australian Division attacked again, and drove a wedge into the enemy positions which almost

reached the road between Sidi Abd el Rahman and Tell el Eisa, and although on the 29th the enemy did all in their power to destroy this wedge, these attacks made with both tanks and infantry completely failed.

October 29 was a very interesting day as plans and preparations went ahead for the launching of the break-out attack – given the code name of 'Supercharge'.

The Army Commander's intention was to launch this attack as far north as possible, but some of us felt that better results would be gained by adopting a more southerly axis; the farther north we went, the more Germans, mines, and prepared defences would be met.

During the morning we were paid a visit by Commander-in-Chief General Alexander, Minister of State Casey, and Alexander's Chief-of-Staff, Lieutenant-General McCreery. The Army Commander described the situation and his plans, and radiated confidence. He stressed that he had always predicted a ten-day 'dog-fight', and he was quite certain that he would win the battle. However, I soon realised that the Cabinet in London, if not some people in Cairo, were beginning to wonder whether Montgomery would after all fulfil his promise of 'Complete Victory'. It was inevitable therefore that interest was focused upon Supercharge and in discussions with McCreery I found that he also felt that it should be launched farther south.

After Alexander, Casey, and McCreery had departed, I felt more than ever worried about the sector chosen for Supercharge. It appeared to me that Rommel would do all in his power to protect his main supply dumps and his lines of communication which used the coastal road. He could not afford to take any risks on this portion of his front. So I went along to discuss the problem with Bill Williams (G-1 Intelligence) and found that he shared my views. Fortunately the latest intelligence reports showed that 90th Light Division had been moved to the northern sector, no doubt due to successes achieved by the 9th Australian Division. It became obvious therefore that the Axis front farther south had been weakened. I decided to take Williams along to see the Army Commander, and appraise him of the changing situation. Montgomery had previously been much impressed by Williams' explanation of how Rommel had distributed his German troops in order to 'corset' the Italian units, and he was quick to see that the present situation gave an excellent chance of attacking where the enemy was weakest — where most of the defenders were Italian or at least at the junction of the two Axis allies.

Montgomery was never slow in making up his mind — provided, of course, that he had the necessary facts — and in this case he immediately decided to change the axis of the forthcoming attack. I well remember leaving the map lorry in high spirits, and later on that day I rang up McCreery who was quite delighted at hearing the news. This decision was, I'm sure, a decisive contribution to victory.

The Australians continued their attack on the night of 30/31, crossed the coast road, and at one time it looked as if the bulk of the Germans inside the salient would be cut off and destroyed. They managed, however, to get away with the help of tank reinforcements, but this attack to the north had paid a big dividend, for it kept the enemy's attention focused on the coastal area, besides causing great damage among the Germans themselves.

On November 1 we heard that XXI Panzer Division had moved even farther north, and so everything was set for the final phase. After a delay of 24 hours [to rest the troops, and give more time for reorganisation] Supercharge was launched, helped by a creeping barrage at 0100 hours on the morning of November 2. Some 300 25-pounders and the corps medium artillery supported the attack.

The frontage of attack was 4,000 yards, and the depth of the advance 6,000 yards. The infantry (151st and 152nd Infantry Brigades) attacked, and everything went wonderfully well, so on reaching their objective the armour moved through and formed a bridgehead, through which it was proposed to pass the armoured divisions of 10th Corps. The objectives were reached, but the 9th Armoured Brigade suffered heavy casualties from enemy anti-tank weapons. Then the 1st Armoured Division came through to assist, and an armoured battle was fought.

On November 3 we knew that the enemy was beaten, as air reports came in showing that the retreat had started, and we knew that Rommel had insufficient transport or petrol to get back more than a portion of his force.

Yet November 3 still did not see us right out into the open country, for the enemy were still plugging the hole with anti-tank guns, but on the night of the 3/4 a clean break-through was made by the 51st and 4th Indian Divisions, after mounting a sudden attack with the greatest skill.

Bündesarchiv

An Italian machine-gun in action: Italian troops formed the main static element in the Axis line

The battle had been won in 11 days, which was just about the Army Commander's estimate of how long the heavy fighting would last. The enemy was defeated and in full retreat, and our armour and armoured cars were now operating in open country.

When on November 3 all information showed that the enemy was in full retreat, it was hoped that the Desert Air Force would cause havoc among his transport; for reports described a scene of vehicles, head to tail, four and sometimes eight deep, moving westwards either on or just off the road. Indeed we had visions of the retreat being turned into a complete rout, bearing in mind the fact that we enjoyed virtual air superiority. In the event, the results were very disappointing. When setting out along the road between the Alamein battlefield and Daba, I had expected to see a trail of devastation, but the visible signs of destroyed vehicles were few and far between. The fact is that at this period of the war we had not learned the technique of low strafing, for our fighter bombers had been employed in air fighting and bombing. I believe the attacks on the retreating columns were made mostly with bombs, and that the aircraft were not allowed to come down low; no doubt because our pilots had not been trained in low-flying attacks with cannon. I feel, however, that an opportunity was lost, and that it should have been possible to have produced a form of paralysis in the enemy's rearward movement.

It was also a great disappointment that we were unable to cut off completely Rommel's surviving forces and so save the long and arduous series of operations that took us to Tripoli and beyond. Montgomery, however, knew that it was only a matter of time, and in any case he was very unlucky, for the forces which he had ordered to cut off the enemy at the bottlenecks of Fuka and Matrûh were deprived of fulfilling their object through the interference caused by some most unusually heavy rain storms, which 'bogged' them down within a stone's throw of the retreating enemy.

MAJOR-GENERAL SIR FRANCIS de GUINGAND KBE, CB, DSO, was educated at Ampleforth and Sandhurst. He joined the West Yorks Regiment in 1920, and served in India, Ireland, Egypt, and the United Kingdom, before going to the Staff College, Camberley, in 1936. From 1939/40 he was Military Assistant to the Secretary of State for War, the Rt. Hon. Hore-Belisha, and became Director of Military Intelligence, Middle East, in 1942. He was Chief-of-Staff to Field Marshal Montgomery from 1942/45, at first with 8th Army and then with 21st Army Group, and Director of Military Intelligence at the War Office from 1945/46. Sir Francis retired in 1947 and emigrated to South Africa. He has written three books — *Operation Victory*, *African Assignment*, and *Generals at War* — and a number of articles on military and other subjects

The Hinge of Fate

1942 October 6: General Montgomery issues his final plan for 8th Army's offensive.
October 23: 2125 hours; artillery bombardment begins in the 13th Corps sector. 2140; 30th Corps bombardment begins. 2200 hours; 30th Corps with four divisions and 13th Corps launch two attacks — on Himeimat and Gebel Kalakh.
October 24: 0200 hours; leading elements of 1st and 10th Armoured Divisions begin to move through the corridors. By dawn most units of 30th Corps have reached their 'Oxalic' line objectives, but 10th Corps has been unable to clear the bridgehead and reach 'Pierson'. After a successful start, 13th Corps is held up between the minefields, but is successful in keeping XXI Panzer Division in its sector. By the evening, 1st Armoured Division has got some units out of the minefields, but 10th Armoured Division's attack at 2200 hours makes little progress.
October 25: 0200 hours; congestion in the southern corridor reaches a dangerous level, but after a conference at 0330 hours, Montgomery confirms that the attempt to break out must continue. 0800; the leading brigade moves clear. The New Zealand Division and 8th Armoured Brigade also clear the main minefield and turn to advance south-westward, fighting off counterattacks by XV Panzer. 1200 hours; Montgomery decides to switch the axis of the attack to the north — 9th Australian Division is to strike northward and 1st Armoured Division westward behind the coastal salient.
October 26: The 9th Australian Division gains ground, but all other attacks are held; Montgomery decides to regroup — the New Zealand Division moves back into reserve, and is replaced by the 1st South African and 4th Indian Divisions. Two German tankers — the *Proserpina* and the *Tergesta* — are sunk; Panzerarmee's fuel problem becomes acute.
October 27: XXI Panzer moves northward; the British redeployment continues with 7th Armoured Division being withdrawn from 13th Corps and brought north. A series of German attacks on 1st Armoured Division are thrown back with a loss of 50 tanks.
October 28/29: Further attacks by 9th Australian Division in the northern sector drive a wedge into the enemy position.
October 29: Montgomery decides to launch the break-out (Supercharge) as far north as possible, but revises his decision (on hearing that the German 90th Light Division has also moved north) in order to strike Italian not German troops.
October 30/31: The Australian attack continues in an attempt to cut off the enemy forces in the coastal salient.
November 2: 151st and 152nd Brigades launch Operation Supercharge, they reach their objectives successfully, and at 0615 9th Armoured Brigade advances, but is held up by heavy anti-tank fire. The 1st Armoured Division moves through to eliminate the opposition. At 2015 hours, after a conference with General von Thoma, Rommel decides to begin the retreat to the Fuka position.
November 3: Confused fighting, but during the night the break-through is achieved by the 51st and 4th Indian Divisions in the south.
November 4: After further fighting, Axis troops begin to retreat, followed by 1st, 7th and 10th Armoured Divisions.

Alamein: an Allied victory for all the world to see

During the slow and bitter 'crumbling' of the enemy defences, an Australian section approaches an enemy strongpoint through a smoke-screen

For much of the day during the 'dogfight' period the infantry would be pinned down by desperate enemy counterattacks

After four days of savage fighting the attacks had become bogged down, and Montgomery was forced to make a radical change of plan

For much of the battle the bulk of 8th Army's overwhelming armoured strength was held in the narrow corridors or kept waiting for the breakthrough

The initial attacks of the second phase of
the battle were again made by infantry
after a heavy artillery bombardment

Not until the eleventh day of the battle was
a real breakthrough achieved; then the 8th
Army was able to flood through the corridors

Imperial War Museum

Imperial War Museum

KURSK: THE CLASH OF ARMOUR

In the summer of 1943, one of the greatest clashes of the war took place on the Eastern Front: the Battle of Kursk. Like the Moscow and Stalingrad battles, it was vast in scale and terrible in intensity. Armies millions strong on each side were locked in a fierce and stubborn struggle which went on for 15 days —and the tank battles which took place were the largest in the war. The German attacks, aimed at regaining the strategic initiative in Russia and turning the course of the war, were utterly shattered

By the summer of 1943 there had been a radical strategic change on the Eastern Front—the decisive front of the war. After the offensive which followed the battle of Stalingrad, the Red Army had snatched the initiative from German hands, and had held it. The Soviet attacks had not only expelled the German invaders from the territory gained by them in 1942, but had liberated many of the towns and districts captured in 1941. Millions of Soviet citizens had been liberated from Nazi oppression, and the Red Army had begun the massive expulsion of the invaders from Soviet territory.

The defeats at Stalingrad and in the Soviet winter offensive at once raised for the German High Command the problem of how

the war in the East was to be carried on. Germany could forego an offensive and remain on the defensive. But what would the effect of this be on Germany and her allies? To forego an offensive would finally disclose to the whole world—and above all to the people of Germany herself—the dark prospect of losing the war. Only by an offensive could the Axis coalition be preserved from disintegration, faith in victory be maintained among the German people, the enslaved peoples of Europe be kept in fear, and the illusion of the might and invincibility of the German army be kept alive before the world.

That is why the German leaders decided to carry out a large summer offensive on the

Eastern Front, aimed at recapturing the strategic initiative and changing the course of the war in Germany's favour. They hoped thus to cement their bloc and revive Germany's fallen prestige. The Chief-of-Staff of OKW, Field-Marshal Keitel, expressed this view openly, when he said, at one of the conferences in the Reichschancellery: 'We must attack, on political grounds.'

Germany's military and political leaders also assumed that successes in the East would shake the foundations of the Allied coalition and cause it to disintegrate by increasing the dissatisfaction of the Soviet government and the whole of Soviet society at American and British delays in opening a second front in Europe. As the West

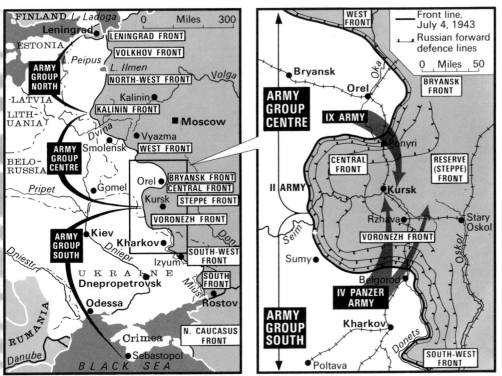

The Eastern Front in the summer of 1943 was dominated by the huge Kursk salient, bulging westwards between Orel and Kharkov. This the Germans were determined to eliminate in their third Russian offensive: huge Panzer concentrations under Model and Manstein were to pinch it out and exploit the breakthrough as far eastwards as possible. But the defences in the salient —in eight concentric belts—were the strongest yet tackled by the Wehrmacht in Russia

German historian Walter Görlitz writes, Hitler believed that 'the sooner a heavy new blow is struck at the Russians, the sooner the coalition between East and West will fall apart'.

In planning the summer offensive, the German leaders could not ignore their economic capabilities. Germany's economy, and above all its war industry, was growing unceasingly. Production of medium and heavy tanks, 5,700 in 1942, was 11,900 in 1943, and that of aircraft went up from 14,700 to 25,200. Twice as many guns and mortars were produced in 1943 as in 1942, and most of them were of new types. Ammunition production was almost three times as much in 1943 as it had been in 1940. And so the German High Command could not only replace its losses in arms and equipment, but also equip the new formations which were being established.

Great hopes were placed in the new equipment, particularly in the new tanks and assault guns whose production had greatly increased by summer 1943. The Pzkw-VI Tiger was a powerful machine, weighing 57 tons and carrying an 88-mm gun and two machine-guns. Its frontal armour was 4 inches thick, and that of the King Tiger was 6 inches. The new Pzkw-V Panther medium tank had also gone into mass production, and the new Ferdinand self-propelled gun, with frontal armour 8 inches thick, a quick-firing 88-mm gun, and one machine-gun, was also being produced.

The Germans had also paid much attention to re-equipping the Luftwaffe, which had already begun to receive new aircraft —the Focke-Wulf 190A fighter, with a maximum speed of over 375 mph, and the Henschel 129 for direct support of infantry on the battlefield. Both these aircraft were powerfully armed.

While they supplied their armed forces with new equipment, the German High Command was hastily replenishing its divisions which had been seriously thinned out in

their battles with the Red Army. By July 1943 the total manpower of the German armed forces was 10,300,000, almost exactly the same as in 1942. And so though the quality of the Wehrmacht had deteriorated considerably, it remained a powerful force with first-class equipment and capable of hard fighting.

Germany's situation was eased by the fact that no second front had yet been opened in Europe, and the High Command took advantage of this to transfer more and more formations and units to the Eastern Front. About 196 of the best German divisions (two-thirds of the German army) were fighting here, together with 32 divisions and eight brigades from Germany's allies, around 56,200 guns and mortars, 5,800 tanks and assault guns, and 3,000 aircraft.

The Soviet-German front remained as it had been, the chief and decisive front of the war, as at the time only seven German divisions and two brigades—2·7% of the German army—were in action against Anglo-American forces. The rest of that army—91 divisions and three brigades—was on duty in occupied territory.

The Germans decided to strike on a narrow sector in the area of the Kursk arc, to cut off the so-called 'Kursk salient' which had formed during the Soviet offensive in spring 1943. This idea was favoured by the shape of the front in that area. The German forces concentrated in the Orel and Belgorod regions hung over the flanks and rear of the Soviet troops in the salient. At the same time, this salient, which jutted deep into the German defences, was important for the Soviet forces as from it they too could strike at the flank and rear of the German forces at Orel and Belgorod (see map).

The Germans began their preparations at the end of the winter. After the plan had been considered from all angles at the highest level Hitler issued an order on April 15, 1943, for an offensive operation, code-named 'Citadel', in the area of the Kursk

salient. The order stated:

This offensive is of decisive importance. It must end in swift and decisive success . . . On the axis of the main blow the better formations, the best weapons, the better commanders, and a large amount of ammunition must be used. Every commander, every private soldier, must be indoctrinated with awareness of the decisive importance of this offensive. Victory at Kursk will be a beacon for the whole world.

According to the plan of Operation 'Citadel' the main blows at the Soviet forces were to be struck from south of Orel by IX Army of Army Group Centre, and from north of Kharkov by IV Panzer Army and Operational Group 'Kempff' from Army Group South. By striking in the general direction of Kursk, the German High Command reckoned to surround and destroy the forces of Central and Voronezh Fronts, defending the salient, to straighten the front line and, in the event of success, to develop their offensive into the rear of South-West Front (Plan 'Panther'). Nor did they exclude the possibility of a subsequent strike to the north-east, to outflank Moscow and come out behind the whole of the Soviet forces in the centre of the front.

In the zone facing Voronezh and Central Fronts the Germans concentrated a large force amounting to 50 divisions, 16 of which were Panzer or motorised, and totalling about 900,000 men, with around 10,000 guns and mortars, and 2,700 tanks. An additional 20 divisions on the flank of the strike force could be redeployed to support the assault troops. Therefore the Germans could use for the assigned mission about 70 divisions, more than one-third of all the German strength on the Eastern Front, and about a quarter of these were Panzer or motorised divisions. Air support was to be provided by a force of over 2,000 aircraft. Elite Luftwaffe units were transferred to the area—JG-51, the 'Mölders' fighter wing; the 'Condor Legion'; and others.

Since such special importance was attached to the forthcoming battle, OKH reviewed and revised the Citadel plan several times, and Hitler stated more than once 'there must be no failure'. Divisions which were to take part in the offensive were rested and made up to full strength in men and material. Particular attention was given to the terrain and the Soviet defensive system in the salient, and according to the German General Mellenthin, every square yard of it was photographed from the air. As he wrote in his book *Panzer Battles, 1939-45*: 'No offensive was ever prepared as carefully as this one.'

Training was made as realistic as possible, and practice firings and tactical exercises carried out regularly. In April General Guderian, at that time Inspector-General of the Armoured Forces, inspected the Panzer troops. As General Erfurth, a former member of the staff of OKW, later wrote: 'All the offensive power which Germany could assemble was thrown into Operation Citadel.' So everything possible was done to win the Kursk battle and turn the course of the war to the advantage of the Axis coalition.

After the winter battles of 1942-43, the Red Army had also begun to prepare a great summer offensive. But it soon became known that the German High Command was also preparing for a decisive offensive on the Soviet-German Front. Thanks to very good Intelligence, Russia's Supreme Command was able to find out not only the general concept and direction of the main strikes to be made by the German forces, but also how many of them there were, what resources they had, what possible reserves there were, when they were to arrive and, subsequently, when the offensive was to begin.

When they had analysed the German plans, the Soviets decided to go purposely on to the defensive in the Kursk salient, to wear out the enemy forces in defensive battles on previously prepared lines, and then to complete the destruction of the Axis shock groups by a counteroffensive in the Orel and Belgorod areas. If the counteroffensive developed successfully, it was to grow into a general Soviet offensive on a vast front, to crush the so-called 'Eastern rampart' of the Axis, and also to liquidate their Kuban bridgehead.

The actual defence of the Kursk salient was entrusted to Central Front (General K. K. Rokossovsky) and Voronezh Front (General N. F. Vatutin). Bearing in mind that the offensive which the enemy was preparing was large and had far-reaching aims, STAVKA concentrated large reserves in the area of the salient, and joined them into a Reserve Front (later renamed Steppe Front), under the command of Army General I. S. Koniev. The forces of this Front, which constituted a major STAVKA Reserve, were destined to reinforce Central and Voronezh Fronts on the sectors where a threat to them was being built up, to establish a solid defensive front east of Kursk, and later to take part in the counteroffensive, once the enemy had been exhausted and bled white. On-the-spot co-ordination of the fronts was conducted by the Deputy Supreme Commander, Marshal G. K. Zhukov, and the Chief of the General Staff, Marshal A. M. Vasilevsky.

Elaborate steps were taken to prevent an enemy breakthrough. The fronts were reinforced with large numbers of guns, tanks, and aircraft, the greatest concentration being made on the most likely axes of attack. For example, on the sector held by 13th Army, which was covering the most vulnerable axis, along the Orel-Kursk railway, almost half the artillery regiments of Supreme Command Reserve allotted to the Front were placed. The army was also given the 4th Breakthrough Artillery Corps, which had 484 guns, 216 mortars, and 432 field rocket-launchers. This made possible a hitherto unprecedented concentration of artillery in defence of about 155 guns and mortars of calibre exceeding 76 mm per mile of front—one and a half times the density established by the Germans for the coming offensive.

In the sectors held by 6th and 7th Guards Armies of Voronezh Front were 67% of the guns and mortars of the front, and about 70% of the artillery allocated from Supreme Command Reserve. The defensive system of the Soviet forces in the salient was deeply echelonned, saturated to the maximum with weapons, provided with a good system of trenches, and with many other engineer installations and obstacles.

Soviet 'hedgehog' defences

As the Germans hoped to attain their objectives by the massed use of tanks, the front commanders took special care over anti-tank defences, based on anti-tank strongpoints and areas and a system of minefields. Artillery reserves were allocated and trained in good time, as were mobile obstacle detachments. As a rule the strongpoints were allocated three to five guns each, up to five anti-tank rifles, two to five mortars, between a section and a platoon of sappers, and a section of submachine-gunners. On the most important axes, the anti-tank strongpoints had up to 12 guns each. Anti-tank and anti-personnel obstacles were widely used.

The depth of defence of Central and Voronezh Fronts on the axes of probable attack reached 95-110 miles. Adding the defence line of Steppe Front and the defence line along the Don river, it came to 160-180 miles, and comprised eight defence belts and lines. To picture the scale of the work done in the preparatory period, it is enough to mention that on Central Front's sector more than 3,100 miles of trenches and communication trenches were dug, approximately enough to reach from Moscow to Irkutsk. On the same front, the engineers laid about 400,000 mines and ground bombs, and the average density of minefields on Central and Voronezh Fronts reached 2,400 anti-tank and 2,700 anti-personnel mines per mile of front—six times that of the defence of Moscow, and four times that of Stalingrad.

Anti-aircraft defence of the forces was given great attention. Nine anti-aircraft artillery divisions, 40 regiments, 17 batteries, five troops, ten anti-aircraft armoured trains, two fighter aircraft divisions of the 'Air Defence of the Homeland' were concentrated in the salient. In addition more than a quarter of all heavy and light machine-guns and anti-tank rifles in the main defence belt, and up to half of them in the other belts, were allotted to air defence.

Responsible tasks were laid on the tactical air forces, which were to co-operate with the ground forces to repel the German attack and to seize air superiority. Even while the operation was being prepared the air armies made a series of attacks on Axis airfields, rail junctions, and concentration areas.

All personnel were trained for the forthcoming battles under an intensive programme in which priority was given to countering enemy tanks and aircraft and to skill in counterattacking enemy forces which had penetrated the defences. The Military Councils of the Fronts and Armies, commanders, political organs, party and Communist Youth organisations undertook an intensive effort to raise the political standard and morale of the troops. They organised discussions for them on various themes, including ways of countering the new German tanks.

The civilian population of those parts of the Kursk, Orel, Voronezh, and Kharkov regions adjacent to the front line gave active assistance to the Soviet forces in preparing for the coming battle. By April 1943 some 105,000 people from the Kursk area—collective farm workers, white-collar workers, housewives—were already building defence works, and by June there were 300,000 of them. Workers from the liberated areas gave invaluable aid in building a railway from Stary Oskol to Rzhava, which was most necessary for the supply of Voronezh Front's forces. In the three months of preparation the workers of the frontal areas dug thousands of miles of trenches throughout the salient, and with their help about 250 bridges and more than 1,800 miles of roads and tracks were repaired.

By the start of the defensive battle a large Soviet force was present in the salient. On a sector 345 miles long (13% of the Soviet-German Front), the Red Army had concentrated more than 20% of its manpower, nearly 20% of its artillery, about 36% of its tanks and self-propelled guns, and over 27% of its aircraft.

Unlike the Stalingrad and Moscow battles, the Soviet forces in the Kursk salient had a general superiority of 1·4 to 1 in men, almost 2 to 1 in guns and mortars, 1·3 to 1 in tanks and self-propelled guns, and almost 1·2 to 1 in aircraft. However, as the Germans were counting on a swift breakthrough, they had grouped most of their Panzer and motorised divisions in the first line, so that on the narrow breakthrough sectors in Central Front's zone they outnumbered the Soviets by more than 2 to 1 in tanks and almost 2 to 1 in men, and on that of 6th Guards Army (Voronezh Front) the German superiority was almost 2 to 1 in men and 6 to 1 in tanks. Consequently the German High Command expected to break the defences by a strong initial Panzer blow with strong air support.

The night before the offensive opened, an address by Hitler was read out to the troops. 'From tomorrow,' it said, 'you will be taking part in great offensive battles, whose outcome may decide the war. Your victory will convince the whole world more than ever that all resistance to the German army is, in the end, futile.'

But the offensive did not turn out as the Nazi war leaders would have liked. They had miscalculated, and failed to take the Soviet forces by surprise. As early as July 2, 1943, STAVKA, acting on Soviet Intelligence information, had warned the commanders of Voronezh and Central Fronts that the enemy offensive was likely to begin in the period July 3/6, and demanded increased vigilance and readiness to ward off the enemy strikes. And indeed, prisoners captured on July 4 stated that the offensive by the shock groups had been set for dawn on the 5th and that the units had already taken up their starting positions.

The Soviet command decided to undertake a powerful artillery and air counterpreparation against the Germans who were preparing to attack. Central Front's main artillery target was the enemy batteries. Voronezh Front also bombarded German batteries which were active, but in addition it directed its artillery counterpreparation against the Germans tanks and infantry.

At 0220 hours on July 5 hundreds of Soviet guns brought down a hurricane of fire upon the positions of the Germans as they prepared to attack. The calm before the July storm was ended.

The counterbombardment caused losses in men and equipment, and adversely affected German morale. It became clear to them that their plan had been uncovered, surprise had been lost, and the Russians were ready to meet them. The offensive had to be put off 1½ to 2 hours, to put the units in order. But the counterbombardment could not disrupt the offensive completely on either the north or the south face of the salient, and this is how events developed:

On the Orel-Kursk axis, the German IX Army (Colonel-General Model) began its artillery bombardment at 0430 hours—90 minutes behind schedule, and large bomber forces took off at 0510 hours. Under this artillery and air cover the tanks and infantry went into the attack on a 25-mile front at 0530 hours. The main blow was directed at the Soviet 13th Army (Lieutenant-General N. P. Pukhov) and the 48th and 70th Armies on either side of it. Three Panzer and five infantry divisions were thrown into the battle, and the main effort was concentrated

The deployment of German armour from the air. By July 5, nearly 2,700 tanks and assault-guns, spearheaded by the new Tigers and Ferdinands and stiffened by the medium Panthers, were moving up for the attack on the salient

Soviet Pakfronts smashed the Panzer attacks on Kursk
The basis of the Soviet anti-tank defence system lay in the artillery and tank concentrations which barred the way to Kursk. All other Soviet arms were secondary, merely supplementing their fire. As a rule, the anti-tank strongpoints contained 45-mm (above) and 57-mm anti-tank guns, seconded by 76·2-mm field-guns firing armour-piercing shot

against the left flank of 13th Army, on the Olkhovatka axis, where the defence was in the hands of 15th (Colonel V. N. Dzhangava) and 81st (Major-General A. B. Barinov) Rifle Divisions.

About 500 German tanks attacked on the main axis, Tigers and Ferdinands in groups of ten to 15 in the first echelon, medium tanks in groups of 50 to 100 in the second echelon, and the infantry following behind. About 300 bombers, operating in groups of 50 to 100, were thrown against 13th Army at the same time.

The Soviet Front Command directed the bulk of 16th Air Army (Lieutenant-General S. I. Rudenko) to the support of 13th Army, and fierce battle was joined on the ground and in the air. Four times the Germans tried and failed to break through in the course of the day. The Soviet troops beat them off stubbornly, holding on as long as possible to every piece of ground and putting in counter-attacks. The Germans were able to penetrate 13th Army's main defence belt only at the price of colossal efforts and casualties. During the battles of July 5/6, they moved forward up to 6 miles, losing in the process over 25,000 killed and wounded, about 200 tanks and self-propelled guns, more than 200 aircraft, and much of their artillery and other equipment. Furthermore, many of the German regiments lost a considerable part of their officers, the 195th Regiment of 78th

Infantry Division (XXIII Army Corps) losing all its company commanders in two days of fighting.

Five Germans attacks were repulsed
Since they had failed on the Olkhovatka axis, the Germans decided on July 7 to make Ponyri, a junction on the Orel-Kursk railway, their main objective, and fierce fighting broke out around it. The Soviet forces based there were able to strike at the enemy troops as they advanced, and a German infantry officer was later to describe the fighting here as one of the fiercest battles in the whole Eastern campaign. Five times during the day the Germans launched furious attacks, and five times they were hurled back by Major-General M. A. Yenshin's 307th Rifle Division, which defended Ponyri with a heroism matched by that of the tankmen, gunners, and sappers, who mined the routes along which the German tanks moved. On the morning of July 8, about 300 German tanks supported by submachine-gunners attacked positions held by Colonel V. N. Rukosuyev's 3rd Anti-Tank Brigade, the main weight of the onslaught falling on Captain G. I. Igishev's battery.

The Soviet gunners held their fire until the tanks were within 750-650 yards, and then destroyed 17 of them. But only one gun and three gunners were left, and the Ger-

mans pressed on again. Soon they lost two more tanks and were forced to withdraw. But the Soviet battery had been completely wiped out, the last survivors having been killed by a direct hit from a bomb. Three hours later, the Germans attacked again, and this time Senior Lieutenant V. P. Gerasimov's battery had to face the main assault.

The situation became so critical that the brigade commander radioed to the army commander: '1st and 7th Batteries have been wiped out, and I am committing my last reserve—2nd Battery—to action. Please assist with ammunition. We shall hold out or die here.' In this action against odds almost a whole regiment of the brigade was wiped out. But the German tanks did not get through.

By July 10, the Germans had committed almost the whole of their strike force, but had failed in their mission of rupturing the Soviet front and annihilating Red Army forces north of Kursk. The German tank and infantry formations were marking time, and suffering immense casualties while they did so. On their main strike sector they had penetrated no more than 6 miles, and IX Army, having already lost about two-thirds of its tanks, was forced to take up the defensive. Meanwhile the Soviet Central Front, now that it had disrupted the German plan to break through to Kursk

Even the mighty Tigers could not survive the Russian Pak guns
Hundreds of Tigers met the fate so emphatically described by the picture above. The Russian tanks fielded the 76·2-mm gun which was also serving very efficiently with the Pakfront artillery forces; and the T-34s and KVs eliminated hundreds of Tigers by getting close in and attacking from the sides, where the Tigers' armour was thinner

from the north began to prepare for the counterblow.

The Germans met with no more success on the south face of the salient. Here too they launched forces into the offensive on the first day – five infantry, eight Panzer, and one motorised divisions from Field-Marshal von Manstein's Army Group South. The main assault, against the sector held by the Soviet 6th Guards Army (Lieutenant-General I. M. Chistyakov), was carried out by strike forces of IV Panzer Army, under the command of Colonel-General Hoth, and was directed towards Oboyan, while III Panzer Corps of Operational Group 'Kempff' conducted a secondary attack in the general direction of Korocha, against the 7th Guards Army of Lieutenant-General M. S. Shumilov. About 700 tanks took part in the main assault on the first day of the offensive, and the divisions on the ground were heavily supported from the air, about 2,000 sorties being observed in Voronezh Front's sector on the first day.

The 52nd and 67th Guards Rifle Divisions of 6th Guards Army had to withstand a blow of particularly great force, and their resistance, as well as that of 7th Guards Army, was so stubborn that the Germans found it necessary to commit all the reserves of IV Panzer Army and Operational Group 'Kempff' in the course of the first day.

Voronezh Front Command decided that the Oboyan axis must be securely covered, so on the night of July 5/6 formations of 1st Tank Army (Lieutenant-General M. E. Katukov) and the 2nd and 5th Guards Tank Corps (from Front Reserve) moved into the second defensive belt, and 6th Guards Army was reinforced with anti-tank artillery.

A new German attack began on the morning of July 6, and fighting became especially fierce. Lieutenant-General Popel, the 'Member of Military Council' of 1st Guards Army wrote later in his memoirs: 'I suppose that neither I nor any of our other officers had ever seen so many enemy tanks at once. Colonel-General Hoth had staked everything on a knight's move. Against every one of our companies of ten tanks were 30 or 40 German tanks. Hoth well knew that if he could break through to Kursk, no losses would be too great and no sacrifices in vain.'

By the end of the second day the enemy attack towards Oboyan had penetrated the main defensive belt in the centre of 6th Guards Army and approached the second belt, to which the Soviet divisions withdrew. Here the Germans were halted by the tank corps. Most of the tanks had been dug in, and had become hundreds of armoured pillboxes, which the infantry and artillery used as the foundation of a strong barrier of fire. The German attack towards Korocha fared no better.

The Soviet air forces gave great assistance to the defenders, striking at the German tanks and infantry, and contesting the air fiercely with the Luftwaffe. Lieutenant A. K. Gorovets set up a world record by shooting down nine German aircraft in one dogfight, but was himself killed. It was in these battles that the Soviet fighter pilot, I. N. Kozhedub, who was to win the award of 'Hero of the Soviet Union' three times by the end of the war, opened his score.

After the failure to achieve success on the Oboyan sector, the German command decided to transfer its main efforts to Prokhorovka, so as to outflank Kursk from the south-east. Here were thrown in the best of the Waffen-SS Panzer forces, headed by the most experienced generals. The German view was that the attack on Prokhorovka should decide the battle in their favour. Altogether the Germans threw into the Prokhorovka area about 700 tanks and assault guns, about 100 of which were Tigers, and Operational Group 'Kempff' with about 300 tanks mounted a secondary attack on Prokhorovka from the south.

Voronezh Front command, in agreement with STAVKA, decided to mount a major counteroffensive against the wedged-in German force. The main role in this was entrusted to two armies which had arrived from STAVKA Reserve – 5th Guards (Lieutenant-General A. S. Zhadov) and 5th Guards Tank (Lieutenant-General P. A. Rotmistrov), supported by 2nd Air Army (Lieutenant-General S. A. Krasovsky), part of 17th Air Army (Lieutenant-General V. A. Sudets), and units of the Long Range Air Force.

The greatest tank battle in history

On July 12 the greatest tank battle in history took place in the Prokhorovka area. Here in the early July morning, on a relatively small area, in black clouds of dust and smoke, two mighty avalanches of tanks totalling some 1,500 machines moved to meet each other. General Rotmistrov, now Chief Marshal of Armoured Forces, in recalling this unprecedented battle, remarks that the first echelon of his 5th Guards Tank Army cut into the German line at full speed, and the diagonal attack was conducted so fast that the leading lines of tanks went through the entire German formation.

The lines became mixed up, with the Soviet tank gunners firing at the Tigers at point blank range, and an immense knotted mass of tanks formed. Over the battlefield swept the roar of motors, the clang of metal, and the flames from hundreds of burning tanks and self-propelled guns. The fierce fighting went on until late in the evening, and the Soviet tank men displayed great courage and skill. Here, too, the Germans failed to break through to Kursk.

In this one day the Germans lost here more than 350 tanks and over 10,000 officers and men, in making an advance of 20-25 miles. This day, July 12, was a turning point in the battle, for Bryansk and West Fronts now opened their offensive against the German forces in the Orel area. It was a day of crisis for the German offensive, for on it they were compelled to go on to the defensive on the southern face of the Kursk salient, and then to begin withdrawing to their start lines. On the 16th, the main German forces began retreating behind strong rearguards, and Voronezh Front launched its pursuit, followed on July 19 by Steppe Front; and by the 23rd the Germans had to all intents and purposes regained the lines which they had held on July 4. The third great German offensive in Russia had failed.

In sum, the offensive battle had resulted in brilliant fulfilment of the tasks set them by the Soviet troops. The Germans had been exhausted and bled white, and the strategic balance had changed even further in favour of the Red Army. The long and carefully prepared Citadel operation, by which the Germans had hoped to get back the strategic initiative, had suffered a total failure.

The question of timing the Soviet counter-offensive had already arisen during the defensive battle. The basis of the Soviet plan for the Orel operation was the idea of dissecting the enemy defence by a number of converging blows, and then destroying the isolated enemy forces unit by unit. Four strong blows were envisaged:
● by West Front (Colonel-General V. D. Sokolovsky) southwards to Bolkhov and Khotinets, so as to cut off the enemy in the Orel salient;
● by Central Front, in the direction of Kromy to meet Western Front;
● by Bryansk Front (Colonel-General M. M. Popov), two deep dissecting blows from the Novosil area, to outflank Orel from north and south.
German forces in the Orel bridgehead comprised 27 infantry, eight Panzer, and two motorised divisions of II and IX Armies of Army Group Centre, totalling some 600,000 officers and men, 6,000 guns and

mortars, and about 1,000 tanks and self-propelled guns. Over 1,000 German combat aircraft were available for their support. The area was well fortified, and only on the narrow sector where they had penetrated into the Soviet defences did the first-line forces lack positions prepared in advance. On the sector facing the left wing of West Front and the right and centre of Bryansk Front, as far as the Novosil area, construction of defence lines had begun over a year before in March 1942, and further south, in front of the left wing of Bryansk Front and facing Central Front, construction had begun at the end of March 1943.

Russian guns: 420 to the mile

In view of the importance which they attached to Orel, the Germans had set up a firm defence with a well-developed system of field fortifications protected by obstacles. In the depth of the defence were intermediate and rear belts, and cut-off positions, mostly along the rivers. Most of the villages had been prepared for an all-round defence. The defence lines, prepared in advance, and the large number of rivers in the depth of the defence, were a serious obstacle to the Soviet offensive, and it was the first time that Soviet troops had met with such a powerful defensive system. To break it required great skill, high morale, and offensive élan. The Soviet Command therefore decided to attack in depth, and provided its strike forces with large amounts of artillery. It is worth mentioning here that for the first time in the war a density of artillery of 420 guns and mortars to the mile was achieved, on the sector of West Front's 11th Guards Army (Lieutenant-General I. Kh. Bagramyan).

Preparation for the counterblow required special attention to be given to ammunition and fuel supply, and to training the troops in breaking through permanent defences. Commanders and political workers took care that every soldier knew his sub-unit's mission. Brief meetings and Party and Youth League assemblies took place in the companies and batteries in the front line. Many soldiers wished to go into battle as Communist Party members. Hundreds and thousands of them wrote in the hours before battle: 'I shall justify the party's trust in battle', or 'If I die, count me a Communist.'

By the beginning of the Orel operation, the Soviet superiority over the Germans was 2 to 1 in men, 3 to 1 in guns, 2·3 to 1 in tanks, and 2·7 to 1 in aircraft. By means of bold manoeuvre the superiority was even greater on the breakthrough sectors.

On July 12, after an intensive artillery and air bombardment, the left wing of West and the whole of Bryansk Fronts moved forward, while the German forces in the Belgorod-Kharkov area were still trying to break through the southern face of the salient, and IX Army was preparing to renew the offensive against Kursk from the north.

By the evening of the 13th, 11th Guards Army had broken through after intense fighting, on a front of 15 miles, and the assault force of Bryansk Front's 61st Army (Lieutenant-General P. A. Belov) on a front of 5 miles. The 3rd Army (Lieutenant-General A. V. Gorbatov) and 63rd Army (Lieutenant-General V. Y. Kolpakchi) had penetrated 9-10 miles. But the Soviet forces still faced an organised defence, and had to fight hard to destroy the large numbers of strongpoints in the depth of the defensive system.

The offensive mounted by 2nd Tank Army

During the dying offensive of IV Panzer Army: flame-throwers advance, backed by a camouflaged assault-gun and riflemen

was already on the first day causing hasty German redeployment of reserves to threatened sectors, and it was decided to unify the commands of II Panzer and IX Armies in the Orel salient under Colonel-General Model, who enjoyed the Führer's special confidence, and was known in the German army as 'The Lion of Defence'. On taking over command, he issued an order to II Panzer Army on July 14, in which he wrote: 'The Red Army has begun an offensive along the entire Orel salient. We face battles which could decide everything. In this hour, which demands great effort by all forces, I have taken under command your army, experienced in battle.' He issued a number of threatening orders, demanding that his troops stop the Soviet formations and stand to the last man, whatever happened.

But the Red Army's victorious offensive was no longer to be stopped by German orders, nor could the Third Reich any longer preserve its soldiers' faith in victory by the mere issuing of orders. They were haunted by the ghosts of their compatriots who had fallen at Moscow, Stalingrad, Ponyri, and Prokhorovka, and despite considerable reinforcement of the Orel salient at the expense of other sectors of the front, the Soviet counterblow continued to develop successfully.

By July 19, 11th Guards Army, which completely held the initiative, had broken through on its whole front to a depth of 45 miles, and its main forces were driving south towards Khotinets, while Bryansk Front had overcome the German resistance, broken through several intermediate defence lines, and by July 17 made a gap 22 miles wide and 15 miles deep. The Luftwaffe intensified its efforts to stop the Red Army, but the Soviet pilots replied in kind.

The French 'Normandie Niemen' squadron fought side by side with the Soviet airmen, and its volunteer pilots displayed courage, great skill, and determination in the struggle with the Luftwaffe.

By drawing much of the German Orel

With Citadel bogged down north and south of Kursk, Manstein is faced with an immediate Russian counteroffensive

force away from the Kursk direction, the offensive by West and Bryansk Fronts created favourable conditions for Central Front. It finished regrouping late on July 14, attacked on the 15th, and by the 18th its right wing had completely liquidated the German wedge into the Soviet defences on the Kursk axis, regained its former line, and begun to develop its attack towards Kromy.

The fighting grew fiercer and fiercer, and STAVKA decided to attain a further superiority of force over the Germans, so West Front was ordered to commit the 4th Tank Army (Lieutenant-General V. M. Badanov), the 11th Army (Lieutenant-General I. I. Fedyuninsky), and the 2nd Guards Cavalry Corps from reserve to the battle, while Bryansk Front was to commit the 3rd Guards Tank Army (Lieutenant-General P. S. Rybalko).

These reserves were deep in the rear, and to get them into battle proved very difficult, as torrential rains had begun and washed out the roads. The 61st Army of Bryansk Front, in co-operation with 11th Guards and 4th Tank Armies of West Front, liberated Bolkhov on July 29 and developed its advance towards Orel from the north, threatening the enemy's communications from Orel to Bryansk. At the same time Bryansk Front forces deeply outflanked the enemy force in the Mtsensk area and forced it to withdraw. Bryansk Front was simultaneously continuing to advance on Orel from the east. The German position was deteriorating further and further, and Colonel-General Model asked Hitler for permission to withdraw from the Orel bridgehead, warning the Führer uneasily of the danger of 'another Stalingrad'.

Because the general situation on the Eastern Front was serious, and that of the Orel force critical, the German High Command had already on July 26 resigned itself to abandoning the entire Orel area and withdrawing to the 'Hagen Line' (a defence line running east of Bryansk) by a well-planned retreat through several intermediate

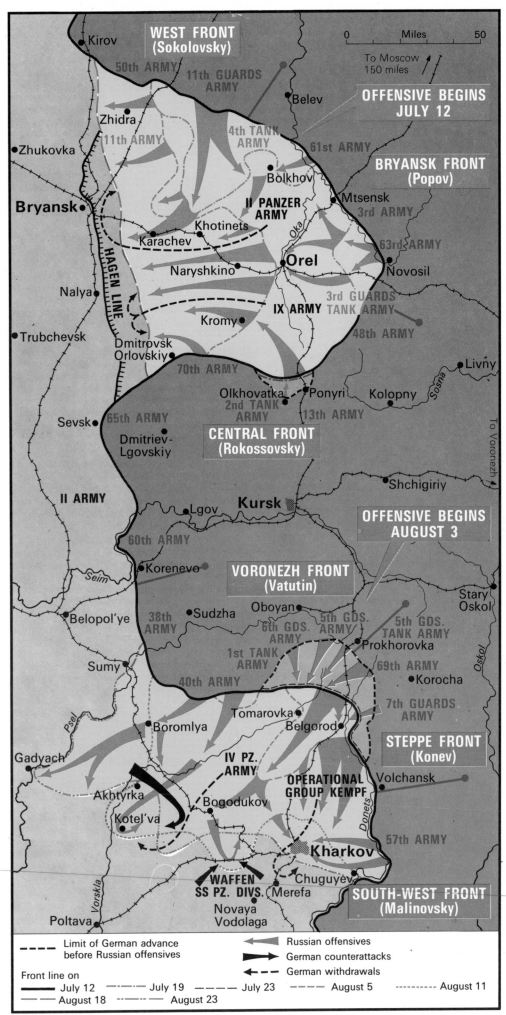

'Citadel' collapses – and the Russians recover Kharkov

A German 105-mm howitzer hammers back at the Soviet forces during the battle for the Orel salient

The Russians, too, had heavy tank losses: here a T-34 blazes   SS Grenadiers take shelter from a Russian bombardment

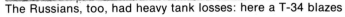

lines between July 31 and August 17. An area about 60 miles deep was to be cleared, to release more than 20 divisions by straightening the line, and to decimate the attacking Soviet forces by defensive battles on the new line.

'A question of getting out fast'

In an effort to secure an orderly withdrawal from the tip of the Orel salient, every effort was made to hold its flanks, but the plans were frustrated by Soviet ground and air attacks. Field-Marshal von Kluge, commanding Army Group Centre, wrote in his estimate of the state of his forces in the area: 'The staff of the army group is fully aware that its previous intention to strike the enemy as much as possible during the withdrawal is now impossible to fulfil, because of the over-exhaustion and reduced fighting capacity of the troops. It is now a question of getting out of the Orel salient as fast as possible.' On the night of August 3/4, advance units of the Soviet 3rd and 63rd Armies burst through to Orel, and by dawn on the 5th the town had been completely cleared of Germans.

The 5th, 129th, and 380th Rifle Divisions, the 17th Guards Tank Brigade, and a number of air force units especially distinguished themselves in the fighting for Orel, and were given the town's name as a battle honour. In Moscow on the evening of August 5, an artillery salute boomed out for the first time in honour of the forces which had liberated Orel and Belgorod, and it became customary from that date to mark Red Army victories by salutes in Moscow.

By August 5, Central Front's forces had reached the approaches to the important road junction and German supply base of Kromy, and by the 18th Bryansk Front and the right wing of Central Front had come up to the previously prepared defence line on which the Germans had dug themselves in. The Orel salient had been liquidated, and the German force there, which had been oriented to an offensive against Kursk, had received a shattering defeat.

Soviet partisan activity contributed to the success of the Orel operation. Between June 21 and August 3 alone, the partisans of Orel region blew up more than 10,000 rails, and as a result the rail junctions and stations filled up with German trains, which were then systematically bombed by the Soviet air force.

The Soviet counterblow lasted 37 days, during which time the Red Army advanced westwards about 95 miles, disrupting the German plan to attack Kursk from the north, throwing a strong German force back to Bryansk, destroying about 15 German divisions, and creating good conditions for further westward development of the offensive.

The forces of Voronezh and Steppe Fronts had had to begin the counterblow in difficult conditions. During the defensive battles and then in pursuit of the enemy they had lost heavily in men and equipment. And now they had to face a fight against an enemy in prepared defensive positions in the Belgorod and Kharkov areas.

The Germans were misled by the relative quiet which prevailed on the south face of the Kursk salient from July 24 to August 2. Since they remained in ignorance of the Soviet plans, and since their estimates of Soviet strength and deployment on the south face of the salient were wrong, they were not expecting a large Red Army offensive on that sector so soon. In addition they were short of forces in the Orel salient. Furthermore, South-West Front had begun an offensive out of the Izyum area on July 17 towards Barvenkovo, and South Front had launched one on the Mius river.

In the course of these operations South-West Front had crossed the northern Donets on several sectors, and was threatening to strike down behind all the German forces in the Donbass, while South Front had broken the strongly defended Mius river line and seized a bridgehead on its western bank. The German High Command therefore began transferring forces from the relatively quiet Belgorod-Kharkov area to improve its position in the Orel and Donbass regions, and thus the Soviet High Command's work in organising precise strategic co-operation on the whole front made the conditions favourable for a counterblow by Voronezh and Steppe Fronts aimed at Belgorod and Kharkov.

By now the main forces of the two fronts were concentrated north of Belgorod, well placed for a frontal assault at the junction between IV Panzer Army and Operational Group 'Kempff', against the enemy formations which had been most worn down and demoralised in the unsuccessful offensive against Kursk. Bearing all this in mind, and aiming to reduce the preparation time for the operation as much as possible, it was decided not to attempt any complicated regrouping but to strike hard with forces of both fronts in a south-westerly direction towards Bogodukhov, Balka, and Novaya Vodolaga, so as to cut off IV Panzer Army from Operational Group 'Kempff' and then destroy them.

In this phase Voronezh Front would operate against IV Panzer Army, attacking westwards towards Akhtyrka, while Steppe Front would turn south to Kharkov, simultaneously rolling up the German defence on the right bank of the northern Donets. While Steppe Front was approaching Kharkov the 57th Army of Army General Malinovsky's South-West Front was to strike westwards, so as to outflank Kharkov from the south. The operation was prepared extremely quickly, by great efforts on the part of the command, staffs, and political organs.

German forces in the area under attack comprised 18 divisions, four of them Panzers, totalling about 300,000 men, with over 3,500 guns and mortars and about 600 tanks, supported from the air by the 900 aircraft of Luftflotte IV. They were based on prepared positions with well-developed artificial defences. The tactical defence zone consisted of two belts totalling some 10-13 miles in depth. The main belt included two positions, each provided with strongpoints and focal points of resistance, joined by deep trenches, themselves linked by communication trenches. All villages had been made ready for a prolonged all-round defence, and the cities of Kharkov and Belgorod had been ringed with large numbers of weapons, well protected in wood and concrete emplacements.

By the start of the operation, the Soviet forces had a superiority of more than 3 to 1 in manpower, 4 to 1 in tanks and artillery, and 1·5 to 1 in aircraft. By skilful massing of men and weapons this superiority was even higher on the breakthrough sectors.

Voronezh Front's main striking force was to be made up of formations from 5th and 6th, 1st Tank, and 5th Guards Tank Armies. A high-density deployment of artillery and tanks was arranged, so that the breakthrough of the deeply-echelonned German defence would be rapid, and on the sector of 5th Guards Army, for example, there were about 370 guns and mortars, and up to 112 tanks, per mile of front. A special feature of the operation was Voronezh Front's plan to introduce the two tank armies into the gap made by the two infantry armies, to ensure a rapid and deep penetration.

The counterblow began on the morning of August 3, after a three-hour air and artillery bombardment. At 1300 hours, as soon as the infantry of 5th Guards Army had penetrated the enemy's main defence belt, the tank armies were sent into action. Their leading brigades completed the breaching of the German tactical defence zone and began to develop their success in the operational depth. Hard fighting went on in the whole breakthrough area throughout August 4, with the Soviet shock groups continuing to advance southwards, by-passing centres of resistance. They advanced up to 12 miles, and on August 5, Colonel M. P. Seryugin's 270th Regiment of the 89th Guards Rifle Division led them into Belgorod.

This powerful and unexpected Soviet blow worsened the situation of the Germans in the south. The Panzer divisions so recently moved away to Izyum, Barvenkovo, and the Mius river came hastily back, taking heavy punishment as they came from a series of Soviet air attacks.

The activities of Ukrainian partisans against railways behind the German lines were of great assistance to the Soviet forces, derailing more than 1,000 trainloads of German troops and equipment during the months of July and August.

A letter from the front

The breach made in their defences, and their losses during the first days of battle had a disintegrative effect on the German troops. In a letter to his brother a German NCO, Otto Richter, wrote:

Dear Kürtchen: You know me, I have never been one for losing my head or panicking. I have always believed firmly in our aims and in victory. But now I want to say goodbye to you. Don't be surprised, I really mean goodbye, and for ever. We attacked not long ago. If you only knew how disgusting and horrible it was. Our soldiers went forward bravely, but the Russian devils wouldn't go back for anything, and every metre cost us the lives of our comrades . . . And then those Russian devils came rushing down on us, we started to back off, a real ding-dong began. We abandoned Belgorod yesterday. There aren't many of us left . . . only 18 in our company. But that's not so bad, there are only nine in the 2nd . . . God, how will it all end . . . I know they'll kill me, goodbye, but I don't care, what's the point of living if the war's lost and the future black?

Richter was killed before he could post the letter.

Meanwhile the troops of Voronezh and Steppe Fronts were still pursuing the enemy. Elements of 1st Tank and 6th Guards Armies, after advancing over 60 miles in five days of continuous battle, seized one of the most important centres of enemy resistance, the town of Bogodukhov, on August 8, thus cutting the German Belgorod-Kharkov forces in two.

By the evening of August 11 Voronezh Front's troops had broadened their breakthrough considerably towards the west and south-west, and their right-wing forces had reached the enemy strongpoints of Boromlya, Akhtyrka, and Kotelva, while the left wing had cut the Kharkov-Poltava railway south of Bogodukhov and by-passed Kharkov from the west, thus creating a serious threat to the German forces still stubbornly defending the Kharkov area. Steppe Front's offensive also prospered between August 8/11, and they reached the outer defence perimeter of Kharkov.

The Soviet 57th Army (Lieutenant-General N. A. Gagen), which had crossed the northern Donets and taken the important enemy centre of Chuguyev, approached Kharkov from the east and south-east.

The Germans were now making desperate efforts to stop further Soviet progress and retain Kharkov, whose loss would open the door to a Red Army offensive into the Ukraine. The Soviet forces advancing south of Bogodukhov were especially dangerous, as they threatened to encircle the Germans at Kharkov from west and south. The German High Command therefore decided to use the main forces transferred from the Donbass against them, and on August 11 they assembled in the area three Panzer divisions of the Waffen-SS which had been made up to strength after heavy fighting—'Das Reich', 'Totenkopf', and 'Viking', and hurled them against 1st Tank Army and part of the left flank of 6th Guards Army.

Fierce fighting went on south of Bogodukhov from August 11/17. The Germans had managed to achieve superiority in tanks by introducing the Waffen-SS divisions, and were able to squeeze the Soviet forces away 12 miles to the north. However, the Soviet

Command moved formations of 5th Guards Tank Army in to assist, so the Germans failed in their plan to break through to the rear of Voronezh Front's strike force. By August 17, their losses forced them on to the defensive.

Following this failure, the German High Command began in mid-August to plan an offensive against Bogodukhov from the western (Akhtyrka) side. Their plan was to cut off the salient in the front south of Akhtryka, break through to Bogodukhov, and destroy the bulk of Voronezh Front's strike force. But the Soviet High Command foresaw this counterstrike and moved fresh forces into the Akhtyrka area to repel it. In three days of intense fighting, August 18/20, Voronezh Front shattered this enemy attempt too, first stopping the Germans and then throwing them back to their start line.

Steppe Front broke through the outer defensive perimeter of Kharkov on August 13, but the Germans continued to fight back doggedly from a broad system of defensive positions. They knew that if Kharkov fell, all their forces in the Donbass would be in danger, and had decided to stabilise the front and hang on to the Kharkov industrial region at whatever the cost. Manstein had received orders to this effect.

Between August 18/22 fighting was especially fierce on the flanks of Steppe Front, and the outcome was that by the evening of the 22nd the 5th Guards and 53rd Armies had by-passed Kharkov from west and south-west, while 7th Guards and 57th Armies had done so from east and south-east, thus threatening all the German forces there with complete encirclement. Only the road and railway from Kharkov to Merefa and Krasnograd remained open to them, and this narrow corridor was under constant air attack. The commander of Steppe Front, Marshal Koniev, wrote: 'The question was which solution to adopt. We could, of course, throw in all the forces needed to cut the corridor, surround the enemy in the city, and finish him off there . . . But destroying such a large force in a fortified town would take much time and mean many casualties. There could be another solution—to storm the city, drive the enemy out of it, and polish off what was left of him outside.'

On the afternoon of August 22, the Germans began to pull out. To prevent an orderly withdrawal, save looted property, and avert the destruction of the city, the commander of Steppe Front on the evening of the 22nd ordered a night assault. The task of capturing the city itself was entrusted to 69th Army (General V. D. Kryuchenkin) and 7th Guards Army. Fierce street fighting went on throughout the night of August 22/23. The Germans had' turned stone buildings into blockhouses, with medium artillery in the lower storeys and sub-machine-gunners and machine-gunners in the upper ones. All approaches to the city, roads entering it, and streets on its outskirts were thickly mined and barricaded.

But the Soviet troops by-passed the enemy fortified positions skilfully, filtered through his defences, and attacked his garrisons boldly from behind. By midday on the 23rd, after stubborn fighting, the city which the Germans had tormented was completely free of them. Most of the German forces were destroyed in the fighting and the remnants of them fled behind the Merefa and Mzha rivers, with the Red Army in hot pursuit, and leaving behind masses of abandoned equipment. The Soviet forces had destroyed

△ A German *Panzerkeil* (tank wedge) sweeps across open country towards the Russian lines

△ A German Pzkw-III Special advances through steppe grass set on fire by Russian shells. **Right:** The attack moves on

Rokossovsky

Vatutin

Koniev

Model

Manstein

Weichs

The generals who fought at Kursk

about 15 enemy divisions, and now they hung over the whole south wing of the German front, in an excellent position for a general offensive to liberate 'west bank' Ukraine and reach the Dniepr.

'Germany's last battle for victory'
The Battle of Kursk ended in a brilliant victory for the Red Army over a still strong and cunning enemy. It was one of the most important and decisive events of the whole war. It began during a changing balance of forces, when the Red Army was getting stronger and its command cadres growing in skill as organisers, and in the course of it the Red Army repulsed the last German attempt at a large summer offensive aimed at changing the course of the war in Germany's favour, preserving the Axis bloc from disintegration, and thus reducing the political consequences of its defeat at Stalingrad.

'Germany's last battle for victory', as the Germans themselves called it, was lost by them, and the dread spectre of catastrophe rose in its full height before the Nazi Reich and its Wehrmacht. The Chief-of-Staff of OKW, Keitel, later testified that after the defeat of the German forces in the summer of 1943 it became clear to the German High Command that the war could not be won by military means.

The prestige of German arms was irreparably damaged. Of the 70 German divisions operating in the area of the Kursk salient, 30 were destroyed, seven of them Panzer divisions. In 50 days' fighting the Germans, on their own figures, lost over 500,000 men killed, seriously wounded, or missing. The Red Army grasped the strategic initiative firmly, and retained it for the rest of the war. In essence, Kursk completed the radical turn-about in the war which had begun at Stalingrad.

The failure of the German offensive at Kursk buried once and for all the Nazi propaganda myth about the 'seasonal' nature of Soviet strategy, which alleged that the Red Army could attack only in winter. Reality showed that it could beat the Germans winter and summer. The German High Command had once again underestimated Red Army strength and overestimated its own strength and capabilities. Churchill wrote of the summer battles: 'The three immense battles of Kursk, Orel, and Kharkov, all in the space of two months, heralded the downfall of the German army on the Eastern Front.'

The failure of their offensive strategy in the East caused the Nazi ruling clique to look around for new ways of waging the war. They decided to assume the defensive on the whole Soviet-German front, to impose static warfare on the Red Army, and hence to gain time for an attempt at persuading the USA and Britain to settle for a 'draw', keeping Nazi Germany as a barrier against the 'Red Peril' in Europe. However, the incessant and constantly increasing hammer-blows of the Red Army put an end to this gamble. The Soviet government fought persistently to put into effect the decisions agreed by all the countries of the Allied coalition.

The brilliantly conducted third Soviet counterblow (after Moscow and Stalingrad) forced the Germans to throw all their main forces into the Soviet-German Front. Large fighter and bomber formations, and a number of units and groups from the other services, had to be transferred from the Mediterranean theatre. This made it considerably less difficult for the Allies to land in Italy, and made that country's defeat inevitable.

Germany's relations with the other countries of the Axis became considerably more difficult. When they saw the defeat at Kursk, the rulers of Finland, Hungary, and Rumania intensified the efforts which they had been making since Stalingrad to find a way out of their unpromising situation. The Red Army's victory gave increased impetus also to the struggle of the peoples suffering under the yoke of the Nazi 'New Order' in Europe.

In the countries of the anti-Axis coalition, the Kursk victory had a great influence on the people, enhancing their feelings of solidarity with the Soviet Union. After Orel's liberation, a friendly correspondence grew up between its citizens and those of the English borough of Hampstead, and a message of greeting sent by the 'Aid to Russia Committee' of a block of flats there said:
Citizens of Orel, we greet you. In the grim war both our great peoples are fighting, our friendship is cemented for ever by the blood of our sons, who are bringing death to Nazism. At last we see hopes of victory before us. We have shared the burdens of war—we shall share, too, the beautiful gifts of peace, proud of the fact that we both belong to the Invincible Army of Freedom.

And President Roosevelt, in a speech to the American people on July 28, said: 'The short-lived German offensive, which began in the first days of this month, was a desperate attempt to raise the morale of the German people. But the Russians did not allow themselves to be taken by surprise . . . The world has never yet seen greater devotion, determination or self-sacrifice than that shown by the Russian people and the Russian armies. . . .'

In Western historical writing, particularly in books by former Wehrmacht generals, the events at Kursk are wrongly described in many respects. Some of these authors deliberately keep quiet about the downfall of Citadel. Others write about it, but ascribe the defeat to mistakes by Hitler. By ignoring historical facts, they distort them. *The main point is not that Hitler made mistaken decisions which ruined the Wehrmacht's Russian campaigns. The mistake was in the idea of making war on the Soviet Union in the first place.*

The main cause of the failure of the Wehrmacht's offensive strategy was the steady rise during the war of the power of the Soviet state and its armed forces, and the Kursk battle was a new triumph for Soviet military skill. When they had uncovered the enemy's intentions the Soviet command decided to wear out the enemy strike forces by means of a carefully prepared defence, and only then to begin a counterblow. In the course of the battle it was shown that the Red Army had been more powerfully equipped, and that its officers had become more skilful in making use of all services and arms of service both in defence and in attack. In the air battles which took place here the Soviet air forces won superiority once and for all. The defeat of the Germans at Kursk began a great summer-autumn offensive by the Red Army over a front of 1,250 miles, from Velikiye Luki to the Taman peninsula.

Operation Citadel
1943 July 5: Operation Citadel, the Wehrmacht's attempt to cut off the Orel/Kursk salient, begins.

July 5/6: Germans push south 6 miles, losing over 25,000 killed and wounded, 200 tanks, 200 aircraft. The southern attack penetrates the first belt of the Soviet defence, then bogs down.

July 6/9: Determined Soviet resistance forces Model to commit the whole of his strike force, but the front holds. Central Front prepares a counteroffensive.

July 12: 'The greatest tank battle in history': the southern German attack struggles forward 20/25 miles for the loss of 10,000 men and 350 tanks. Bryansk and West Fronts take the offensive.

July 15: Central Front takes the offensive.

July 16: German withdrawal begins. Voronezh Front takes the offensive.

July 17: South-West Front takes the offensive.

July 19: Steppe Front takes the offensive.

July 23: German forces have withdrawn beyond their start-lines; Citadel has failed disastrously.

July 26: German High Command orders a planned withdrawal from Orel.

August 4/5: Soviet forces recover Orel and Belgorod.

August 6/11: Voronezh and Steppe Fronts close in on Kharkov.

August 22: Threatened with encirclement, German forces begin to withdraw from Kharkov.

August 23: Soviet forces recover Kharkov, threatening the whole south wing of the German front.

IMPHAL:CRISIS IN BURMA

Burma, March/July 1943

One of the most crucial battles of the war began when the Japanese swept round the British forces guarding the Chindwin, and probed into Manipur. There they found that the British, instead of collapsing into chaos as they had done on previous occasions, stood firm at Imphal, pinning down vital Japanese forces until relief could break through. General Evans, commander of 5th Indian Division during the latter stages of the battle, describes how the last Japanese offensive marked the beginning of the Allied reconquest of Burma. **Below:** a Lee-Grant leads a relief column towards Imphal

Some 400 miles north-east of Calcutta, as the crow flies, lies the state of Manipur on the borders of Assam, sandwiched between the wild Naga Hills to the north and the equally wild Chin Hills to the south. Its capital, Imphal, standing in an open fertile plain over 700 square miles in extent and 2,500 feet above sea level, is a matter of only 70 mountainous miles from the frontier with Burma (see map).

For inaccessibility, this out-of-the-way state might almost be compared with the country of Conan Doyle's imagination, for, instead of being isolated by unscaleable cliffs as was *The Lost World,* the plain is surrounded at all points of the compass by massive ranges of jungle-covered mountains, in places over 8,000 feet high. But, unlike *The Lost World,* in the days preceding the Second World War there were three entrances into the Imphal Plain, only one of which was capable of carrying motor transport—this being the narrow metalled road which began at Dimapur on the railway and, passing through Kohima, turned south to Imphal.

To travel along this 130-mile stretch of road had always been a somewhat hazardous experience since parts of it ran along a ledge with a precipice on one side overlooking a turbulent river and a sheer rock face on the other; hairpin bends were numerous; now and again the road passed through deep gorges or was hedged in by phalanxes of towering trees and thick jungle. But while creaking bullock carts, moving at snail's pace, were the main means of transportation, the road did not present the hair-raising conditions brought about when lorries began to be used: then the situation was very different and to overcome the probability of vehicles meeting head-on round a blind corner—and there was no room for two vehicles abreast—a control system had been imposed for up and down traffic at certain times of the day. But often, particularly in the rainy season, the road was out of action for days on end due to landslides or large sections being washed away by torrents pouring down the mountainside. From all aspects, as late as 1941, it was a dangerous, antediluvian, and unreliable line of communications.

The second entrance was by way of a track fit for pack animals which led eastwards from Silchar in Assam, winding its way through mountain passes and over swaying suspension bridges for more than 100 miles until reaching Bishenpur, a few miles south of Imphal.

The third and last was a 70-mile bridle path over the mountains from Tamu on the Indo-Burma frontier and on the edge of the steaming, disease-ridden Kabaw Valley beyond which flowed the 600-yard-wide, unbridged Chindwin river. At any time this path was used only by police and a few small traders, but during the monsoon it became wellnigh impassable. Such other tracks as existed in the mountains were those connecting the small villages inhabited by Naga or Kuki tribes and, being scarcely two or three feet wide, were passable only on foot.

For the most part, the Imphal Plain is a rice bowl, the paddy fields a luscious green in the monsoon (late May to early October) but turning to hard-baked mud for the six dry months of the year. Predominant is the sprawling, picturesque town of Imphal with the palace of the ruling Maharajah, golden domed temples, the bazaar and, in the days before independence, the bungalows and colourful gardens of European government officials. Otherwise, the plain is dotted with innumerable small villages sited near streams and generally enclosed with bamboo fences, within which stand dwellings of teak and thatch, at times barely visible in a forest of plantain and bamboo. Some of these villages have their own temples, their domes glistening in the sunlight amid the wisps of smoke from cooking fires, rising through the trees.

At the southern end of the plain, where it borders the wild, tangled mass of forest and mountains of the Chin Hills, is the vast Log Tag lake, for many years a favourite rendezvous for Christmas shooting parties, for here the duck rise in myriads to provide some of the best shooting in the world.

In all, even as late as the end of 1941, when standing in the evening light on the summit of one of the nearby hills and looking over the plain, one could not but feel that here was one of the most delightfully peaceful spots on earth and, seemingly, one never likely to be touched by the horrors of war. Yet, there were times when the surroundings presented a forbidding picture, for during the monsoon the rain, often accompanied by brilliant flashes of lightning and deafening thunder, poured down mercilessly—dark, lowering clouds covered the sky, sluggish streams became raging torrents, the mountains disappeared in cloud and mist. Then movement to all intents and purposes ceased except for essential business.

Sudden importance for Imphal

In January 1942, after the Japanese had invaded Burma from the south-east, catching the British entirely unprepared for such an eventuality, Imphal soon assumed an importance it had never known.

Thousands upon thousands of pitiful refugees, mostly in the last stages of exhaustion, starvation, and disease, streamed across the Chindwin and over the mountains to Imphal. So bad were the lines of communication from India to Manipur that only one division—the 23rd Indian—could be sent up to cover the withdrawal of the Burma Army and to repel any Japanese incursion into India. In May 1942, Burma Corps, led by General Slim, began to arrive after a long and exhausting withdrawal, the men mere skeletons of their former selves, but still carrying their personal arms.

With the monsoon about to break and the civil resources stretched far beyond their limits, the situation could hardly have been worse, though it could well have been made so had the Japanese advanced on Imphal. Fortunately they did not, for, having overrun Burma more quickly than they expected, they had overstretched themselves and needed time to reorganise and to put what they had conquered into a state of defence.

So, for the ensuing 18 months, the dividing line between the two forces virtually became the Chindwin river and, during the lull, all the British effort was put into improving the totally inadequate lines of communication from India, preparing Imphal as a base for future operations, and sending up more formations as and when sufficient progress had been made to supply and maintain them in the forward area.

By the late autumn of 1943, those who had known Imphal in the blissful days of peace would have been amazed at the extraordinary changes that had taken place. Although always liable to frustrating disruptions by

SHOWDOWN IN BURMA

By the end of 1943, the Japanese knew that British preparations for an invasion of Burma were reaching their climax. To forestall the attack, General Kawabe *(above)* commander of the Japanese Burma Area Army, decided that XV Army should launch a limited offensive to capture the forward supply base at Imphal, which would be vital for any British advance.
● While the XXXIII Division cut off the 17th Indian Division at Tiddim and forced the British to commit their reserves to rescue it, XXXI and XV Divisions would cross the Chindwin further north and fall on Kohima and Imphal. The success of the Japanese plan hinged on the rapid capture of the latter, for the jungle tracks made it impossible to supply the assault divisions adequately for a long period.
● The problem facing General Slim *(top),* commander of the British 14th Army, was simple but hazardous: to hold Imphal and pin down as many Japanese as possible, while the attack on Kohima was defeated and the road reopened.
● The two actions were interdependent: the Kohima battle could only be won if Imphal blocked the Japanese communications, preventing them from bringing forward all their troops, while the defenders at Imphal could not rely on air supply indefinitely if the road from Kohima were not reopened quickly.
● As the Japanese advanced, 4th Corps had to concentrate on Imphal—slowly enough to allow supplies to be moved back, but not so slowly that it was defeated piecemeal while retiring

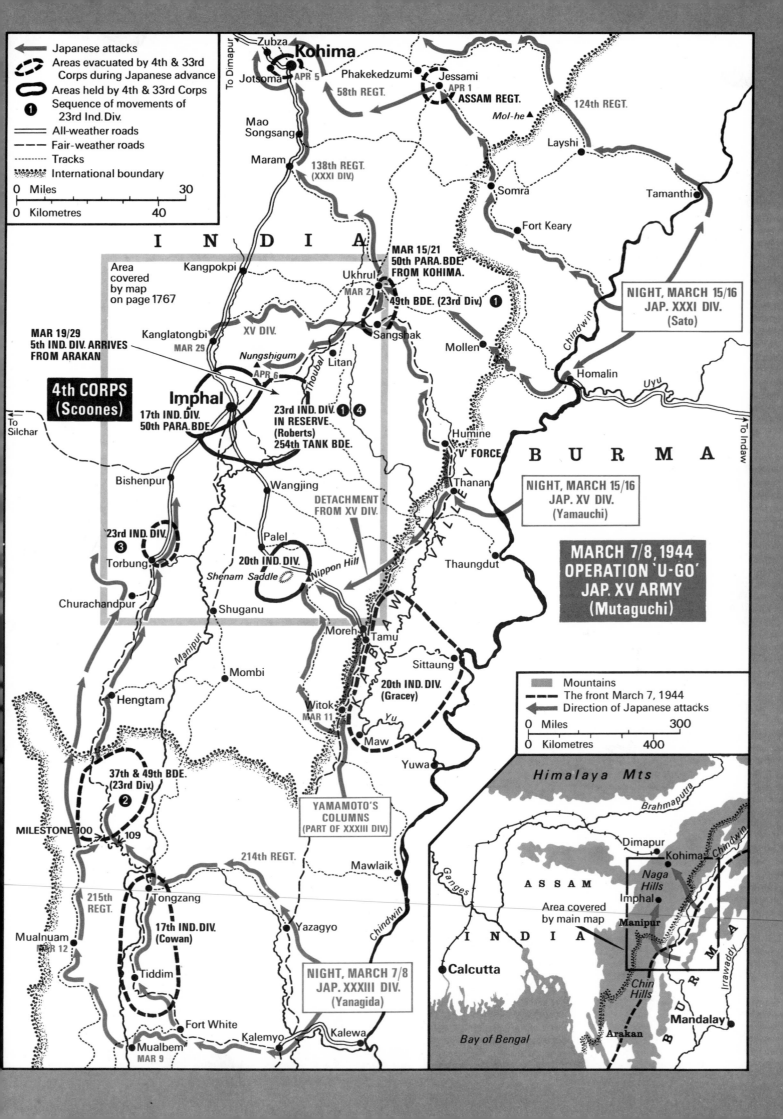

Japanese attacks
Areas evacuated by 4th & 33rd Corps during Japanese advance
Areas held by 4th & 33rd Corps
① Sequence of movements of 23rd Ind. Div.
All-weather roads
Fair-weather roads
Tracks
International boundary

Miles 0 — 30
Kilometres 0 — 40

I N D I A

To Dimapur
Zubza
Kohima APR 5
Jotsoma
Phakekedzumi
Jessami APR 1 **ASSAM REGT.**
58th REGT.
124th REGT.
Mol-he
Mao Songsang
Maram
138th REGT. (XXXI DIV.)
Layshi
Somra
Fort Keary
Tamanthi

NIGHT, MARCH 15/16 JAP. XXXI DIV. (Sato)

Area covered by map on page 1767

Kangpokpi
MAR 15/21 50th PARA. BDE. FROM KOHIMA.
Ukhrul MAR 21
49th BDE. (23rd Div.) ①
Sangshak
Mollen
Chindwin
Uyu

MAR 19/29 5th IND. DIV. ARRIVES FROM ARAKAN
Kanglatongbi MAR 29
XV DIV.
Nungshigum APR 6
Litan
Thoubal
Homalin
To Indaw

4th CORPS (Scoones)
To Silchar
Imphal
17th IND. DIV. 50th PARA. BDE.
23rd IND. DIV. IN RESERVE (Roberts) 254th TANK BDE. ① ④
Humine
'V' FORCE
B U R M A

Bishenpur
Wangjing
DETACHMENT FROM XV DIV.
Thanan
NIGHT, MARCH 15/16 JAP. XV DIV. (Yamauchi)

23rd IND. DIV. ③
Torbung
Palel
20th IND. DIV.
Shenam Saddle
Nippon Hill
Thaungdut
MARCH 7/8, 1944 OPERATION 'U-GO' JAP. XV ARMY (Mutaguchi)

Churachandpur
Shuganu
Moreh
Tamu
Sittaung
20th IND. DIV. (Gracey)

Manipur
Mombi
Witok MAR 11
Maw
Yu

Hengtam
Yuwa

Mountains
The front March 7, 1944
Direction of Japanese attacks
Miles 0 — 300
Kilometres 0 — 400

37th & 49th BDE. (23rd Div.) ②
MILESTONE 100
109
214th REGT.
Mawlaik

215th REGT.
Tongzang
17th IND. DIV. (Cowan)
Yazagyo
Chindwin

YAMAMOTO'S COLUMNS (PART OF XXXIII DIV.)

Mualnuam MAR 12
Tiddim

Himalaya Mts
Brahmaputra

Dimapur
Kohima
Chindwin
A S S A M
Naga Hills
Ganges
Area covered by main map
Imphal
Manipur
I N D I A
Chin Hills
B U R M A
Irrawaddy

Fort White
Kalemyo
Kalewa
NIGHT, MARCH 7/8 JAP. XXXIII DIV. (Yanagida)
Mualbem MAR 9

Calcutta
Bay of Bengal
Arakan
Mandalay

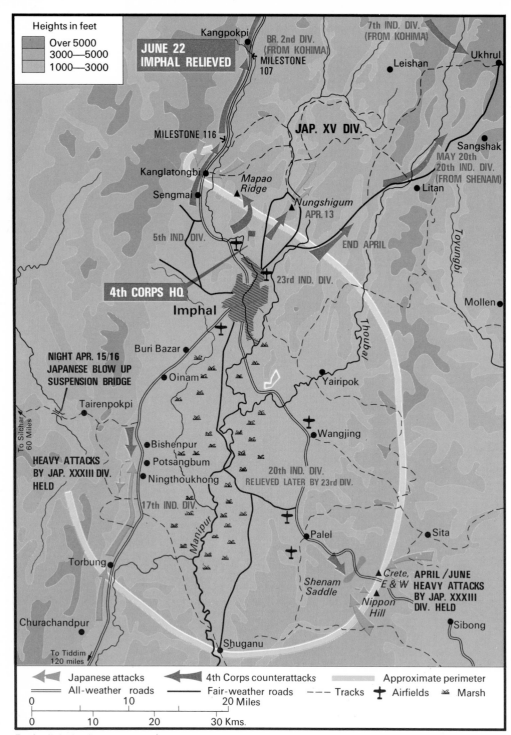

Heights in feet
- Over 5000
- 3000—5000
- 1000—3000

JUNE 22
IMPHAL RELIEVED

Kangpokpi

BR. 2nd DIV.
(FROM KOHIMA)
MILESTONE
107

7th IND. DIV.
(FROM KOHIMA)

Leishan

Ukhrul

MILESTONE 116

JAP. XV DIV.

Sangshak

Kanglatongbi

Mapao
Ridge

MAY 20th
20th IND. DIV.
(FROM SHENAM)

Sengmai

Nungshigum
APR. 13

Litan

Toyungbi

5th IND. DIV.

END APRIL

4th CORPS HQ.

23rd IND. DIV.

Mollen

Imphal

Buri Bazar

NIGHT APR. 15/16
JAPANESE BLOW UP
SUSPENSION BRIDGE

Oinam

Yairipok

Thoubal

Tairenpokpi

To Silchar
60 Miles

Wangjing

Bishenpur

HEAVY ATTACKS
BY JAP. XXXIII DIV.
HELD

Potsangbum

20th IND. DIV.
RELIEVED LATER BY 23rd DIV.

Ningthoukhong

17th IND. DIV.

Manipur

Palel

Sita

Torbung

Shenam
Saddle

Crete
E & W

APRIL/JUNE
HEAVY ATTACKS
BY JAP. XXXIII
DIV. HELD

Nippon
Hill

Churachandpur

Sibong

To Tiddim
120 miles

Shuganu

Japanese attacks — 4th Corps counterattacks — Approximate perimeter
All-weather roads — Fair-weather roads — — — Tracks † Airfields ⚓ Marsh

0   10   20 Miles
0 10 20 30 Kms.

By April 4, the first stage of the Imphal battle had ended: 4th Corps was concentrated at Imphal, and General Scoones could begin to hunt out and kill as many Japanese as possible, in thrusts up the road to Ukhrul against the Japanese XV Division. There was never any need or attempt to form an unbroken defence line, for much of the area was impenetrable jungle and mountain. Strong positions were held astride the main roads while patrols destroyed any Japanese infiltration

the forces of nature, the Dimapur-Imphal road was tarmacked and fit for two-way traffic; the bridle path from Imphal to Tamu, through the efforts of the Indian engineers, mechanical equipment, and thousands of Indian and local labourers, was rapidly becoming fit for the passage of the heavy Lee-Grant tanks; a road sufficient for light motor vehicles – described by one engineer as 'a series of boulders joined together by dust' – had been forced through the gigantic country of the Chin Hills to Tiddim, the capital, 160 miles south of Imphal: work was fast going ahead to complete the construction of six airfields, three of which were to be all-weather; dumps of supplies, ammunition, and petrol, together with hospitals, workshops, and other installations, were springing up everywhere on the plain and its surrounds. In fact, herculean measures were

being taken to make ready for offensive operations early in 1944.

General Scoones, the commander of 4th Corps – a shrewd man with an analytical approach to problems – was responsible for operations on this the Assam or Central Front of 200 miles from Homalin on the Chindwin to Tiddim in the Chin Hills. Under his command were the 17th, 20th, and 23rd Indian Divisions and 254th Tank Brigade, comprising 3rd Carabiniers (Lee-Grant tanks) and 7th Light Cavalry (Stuart tanks). Of the divisions, General Cowan's 17th Indian Division of two brigades was in and around Tiddim, occasionally in contact with the Japanese XXXIII Division, old opponents of the 1942 withdrawal, about Fort White on the track leading to Kalemyo. General Gracey's 20th Indian Division was centred on Tamu, its three brigades pushing out

towards the Chindwin and south down the Kabaw Valley. In the Imphal area, 23rd Indian Division under General Roberts was in reserve, as was 254th Tank Brigade. During early March of 1944, when 50th Parachute Brigade arrived from India, it was positioned at Kohima and given the task of preventing Japanese infiltration north of Ukhrul.

The layout of the corps was, therefore, not unlike two sledgehammers, 17th and 20th Divisions, on flimsy handles – the Tamu and Tiddim roads: between them stretched a 100-mile roadless tract of mountains and thick jungle so that to reinforce one division from the other meant a journey back to Imphal and out again. A parallel in this country, assuming London to be Imphal, would be one division based on Dover and the other on Taunton.

Unfortunate though this dispersion was, it was forced on Scoones for two reasons: first, he had to ensure that the whole front was under observation and the approaches from the Chindwin guarded, the gaps being filled in by 'V' Force (a combination of Assam Rifles and locally enlisted tribesmen); and second, because it was hoped to stage a limited offensive in the near future both across the Chindwin from Tamu and from Tiddim to Kalemyo at the southern end of the Kabaw Valley.

As for the Japanese, all information pointed to the fact that they had two divisions forward – XVIII and XXXIII; the former in the area of Homalin and the latter in the vicinity of Tiddim and the Kabaw Valley.

In the closing months of 1943 the situation was this: 4th Corps was planning for a limited offensive while, on the other hand, the Japanese had gone a long way towards preparing an offensive of a more far-reaching nature – the invasion of Manipur and the capture of Imphal.

The Japanese plan their attack

The development of Imphal as a base, the building of the various roads out of the plain, the extension and improvement of the airfields – these had not gone unnoticed by the Japanese. To them, these and certain other Intelligence factors pointed to one conclusion: an impending Allied offensive into Burma; and, following a series of conferences over a period of months, a decision was finally taken that the solution to the defence of Burma was to forestall Allied intentions by capturing their main base before operations could begin.

To this end, in September 1943, Lieutenant-General Mutaguchi, commander of the Japanese XV Army, a 56-year-old, fierce-tempered man of strong personality, whose opinions carried much weight, was instructed to prepare plans for Operation 'U-Go' – the capture of Imphal. To carry out his mission the troops allotted to him comprised XV, XXXI, and XXXIII Divisions, plus the greater part of I Indian National Army Division, a formation made up of civilians and Indian Army officers and men taken prisoner in Malaya and other theatres. Together with administrative troops, his total force amounted to just under 100,000 men.

Confident of success, Mutaguchi wasted no time in making his plan, but it was not until January 1944 that General Kawabe, commanding the Burma Area Army and responsible for operations in Burma, issued executive orders to him to put his plans into effect. The gist of Kawabe's instructions was that the assault on Imphal was to open at the end of the first week in March and would be preceded by an offensive, Operation 'Ha-Go', against 15th Indian Corps in Arakan, the object being to draw General Slim's attention and his reserves to that front and thereby ease the task of XV Army. The date fixed for the Arakan operation was one month before the main attack, in order that 14th Army reserves would be so committed that they could not be withdrawn in time to intervene effectively at Imphal.

A study of Mutaguchi's plan shows it to bear a strong resemblance to that of HQ Burma Area Army, since the opening moves were designed to attract Scoones' reserves away from Imphal before the main thrust was launched into Manipur.

On the night of March 7/8, General Yanagida's XXXIII Division was to spring a surprise attack on Cowan's 17th Division, not only by assaulting Tiddim itself, but also by moving to cut the road back to Imphal at Tongzang, 40 miles north of Tiddim, and again at Milestone 100 to prevent reinforcements arriving from Imphal. Simultaneously a strong detachment of infantry, tanks, and artillery under General Yamamoto, commanding the infantry of XXXIII Division, was to advance northwards up the Kabaw Valley on 20th Division and eventually establish itself on the Shenam Saddle, overlooking the plain from the east.

Mutaguchi, anticipating that Scoones would be compelled by these manoeuvres to send his reserves south to help extricate 17th Division and so allow his other two divisions a free run on Imphal and Kohima, ordered Generals Yamauchi and Sato, commanding XV and XXXI Divisions respectively, to cross the Chindwin on the night of March 15/16, a week later. The XV Division was to cut the road to Kohima north-west of Imphal and attack Imphal from the north, while XXXI Division was to capture Kohima and prevent any reinforcements from reaching the beleaguered Imphal. Having captured Kohima, Sato was to send troops to assist XV Division's attack. To complete the destruction of Scoones' Corps, XXXIII Division, having disposed of 17th Division, was to advance northwards and enter the Imphal Plain from the south. In estimating the timing of the operation Mutaguchi considered that it would be concluded in a month, after which he would go on to the defensive before the monsoon broke in May.

The whole success of the operation depended on this all-important calculation, since it was impossible adequately to supply XV and XXXI Divisions along the jungle tracks on which their advance was to be made. Instead, both divisions had to carry a month's supplies with them, supplementing them by foraging in the villages through which they passed. The early capture of Imphal and all it contained was therefore vital—otherwise the Japanese would find themselves in dire straits.

Ominous preparations

Although the preliminary moves of the Japanese XV Army were carried out with great secrecy, and were designed, if discovered, to give the impression that the Chindwin front was merely being strengthened for defence, with the coming of January 1944 certain events occurred and certain identifications were obtained which caused both Generals Slim and Scoones to believe a Japanese offensive was imminent and that a reappraisal of the situation was necessary.

In late December, XXXI Division was

Escape from the trap: troops of 4th Corps march on to the Imphal Plain as the epic siege begins

identified as having relieved XVIII Division, hitherto known to be in the Homalin district. Moreover, it was noticed by patrols that Japanese posts had moved close up to the Chindwin into places where they had not been seen before, and this was very shortly followed by reports from the RAF of a number of rafts concealed in a creek near Homalin, built to ferry troops across the river.

A few weeks later, as a result of a cleverly laid ambush by a patrol of 9/12th Frontier Force Rifles on the east bank of the Chindwin opposite Thaungdut, 35 miles south of Homalin, two Japanese bodies were recovered and brought back across the river. On them was the normal batch of papers and postcards which Japanese soldiers invariably carried and these, when translated, revealed that the men belonged to XV Division. An entirely new division had thus been identified, bringing the total up to three.

By lucky chance, a deep penetration patrol discovered that a new motor road had been built through the jungle between Indaw and Homalin and that it was being extensively used at night. A good line of communication now existed to XXXI Division, which had hitherto been dependent on jungle tracks.

As time went by, further evidence arrived to indicate that Japanese plans were well advanced, for the 213th Regiment of XXXIII Division, recently known to have been in Arakan, was identified in the Kabaw Valley, as also was a newly arrived heavy artillery regiment, while the first tanks to be seen in Burma were reported in the area of Yazagyo, 25 miles north of Kalemyo.

Finally, the RAF found that the Sittang bridge, blown up in the 1942 withdrawal, had been repaired to provide a direct land communication back to the notorious Siam railway and Bangkok: pilots also reported large numbers of bullocks collected in areas east of the Chindwin which could only be either for transport or rations on the hoof.

Then, on February 4, the Japanese attack

Gurkhas clean up Scraggy Hill during bitter fighting in the Shenam area

on 15th Corps opened in Arakan as planned, and within a few days General Slim's reserves were on the move to take part in that battle.

As early as February 3, Scoones had concluded that XV Army was in a position to launch an offensive which he considered would take the form of a cutting of the Dimapur road, somewhere near Kohima, by one regiment, and an all-out attack on 20th Division, while XXIII Division contained 17th Division. To meet such moves he proposed that 4th Corps should be reinforced by a further brigade to hold the area Kohima-Ukhrul, that 20th Division should take up a strong position around Tamu, while 17th Division continued offensive operations from Tiddim towards Kalemyo. He intended to use his reserve, 23rd Division and the tanks, to counterattack any advance on Kohima and also the flanks of those forces which attacked 20th Division.

But by February 29, as the Intelligence jig-saw puzzle built up, both Scoones and General Slim, who were in close and constant touch throughout, were of the opinion that the Japanese invasion would open on or about March 15 and that a firm plan was now necessary which could be put into operation at the press of a button.

Imphal – key to the situation

With its airfields, dumps of all commodities, hospitals, and workshops, the Imphal Plain was the key to the situation. Its loss would be catastrophic: organised resistance would come to an end and any thought of a reconquest of Burma could be dismissed for a very long time to come. Furthermore the Japanese would gain all they required.

The aim, therefore, stood out with unmistakable clarity – *to hold the Imphal Plain and destroy any enemy who entered it*. And to do this Scoones would have to fight the battle with 4th Corps concentrated. This would entail bringing the two outlying divisions back to Imphal; but this having been done, many benefits would accrue.

Although in infantry the two sides were approximately equal Scoones had a superiority in tanks, artillery, and in the air, but the Japanese, having the initiative, could concentrate superior forces at vital points. The open terrain of the plain would enable Scoones to put his advantages to the best use because not only could the tanks move with much greater freedom there than in the jungle, but the pilots of the RAF would be able to see their targets clearly. In other words, he would fight the battle on the ground of his own choosing.

Another great advantage in fighting concentrated would be that he would shorten his lines of communication to the divisions, while at the same time lengthening those of his enemy. However, whatever he did about communications, with the resources at his disposal he could never hope properly to safeguard the 130 miles back to Dimapur –

and this road was precisely the target which would appeal to the Japanese. If this vital link was cut – which was most likely – either the block would somehow have to be removed or other methods of supply introduced.

One major problem was what to do with the thousands of unarmed labourers employed on the roads and in the dumps. In the event of a battle, their presence would be a distinct embarrassment since they would have to be fed and protected: an early decision as to future policy was necessary so that plans could be made for the evacuation of these 'bouches inutiles' before the fighting began.

But by far the most difficult decision to be made was when to withdraw the outlying divisions. If they were withdrawn too soon and nothing happened, the loss of morale would be great, for much blood and sweat had been expended in getting them out to the Kabaw Valley and Tiddim. But if the order to withdraw was left until the Japan-

ese were in full cry, there was the possibility of 17th and 20th Divisions being defeated piecemeal.

So, after carefully weighing up the pros and cons, Scoones submitted to HQ 14th Army his conclusions and plan – conclusions which were similar to those General Slim had reached.

Scoones' aim remained unaltered: to hold the Imphal Plain and destroy any Japanese who entered it. The 17th Division, when ordered, was to make a clean break and return to the plain as quickly as possible, the necessary demolitions being made under Cowan's orders; on reaching the plain, one brigade was to guard the approach to Imphal by way of the Tiddim road, while the remainder of the division came into corps reserve.

The 20th Division was to remain in the Kabaw Valley until the enemy's intention became clear and then, on Scoones' order, Gracey was to concentrate his division

around Moreh, a few miles north-west of Tamu, in which a large dump of all commodities had been built up for the proposed limited offensive. There he was to wait until the considerable force of unarmed labour and machinery working on the road to Tamu had been evacuated, and the stores at Moreh either backloaded or destroyed, after which he was to withdraw to the Shenam Saddle and hold this crucial position to the last man.

The 23rd Division, minus one of its brigades – 49th Brigade, positioned in the area of Ukhrul, with the object of preventing a Japanese advance in this direction – together with 254th Tank Brigade and 50th Parachute Brigade, was given the task of wiping out any Japanese infiltration into the plain and protecting the road to Kohima.

In the vast administrative area of Imphal, a series of 'boxes' were formed with all-round defence, self-contained with food, water, and ammunition for ten days, and sited where possible to cover the airfields.

When approving the plan, General Slim left the all-important decision—when to withdraw 17th and 20th Divisions—to Scoones, the man on the spot, but made it clear that these orders were to be given only when Scoones was as sure as he ever could be that the Japanese assault had begun.

At the beginning of March, the stage was set for one of the greatest battles of the Second World War, the Japanese holding the advantage, as the initiative for beginning it lay with them.

'Sweep aside the opposition'

To the accompaniment of Mutaguchi's stirring order of the day in which he exhorted his troops 'to sweep aside the paltry opposition we encounter and add lustre to army traditions by achieving a victory of annihilation', the moves of XXXIII Division began on the night of March 7/8 as scheduled.

Yamamoto's column of infantry, artillery, and tanks advanced north up the Kabaw Valley towards 20th Division: the greater part of 214th Regiment marched stealthily along the track from Yazagyo to Tongzang and the hills overlooking the vital bridge over the fast-flowing Manipur river: some miles to the south-west of Tiddim, the bulk of 215th Regiment, using jungle tracks, moved to cut the road to Imphal at Milestone 100. This last move did not pass without notice, for, on March 9, a two-man Gurkha patrol near Mualbem, south of Tiddim, reported the crossing of the Manipur river at that place by some 2,000 Japanese with guns and animals, but since, by March 11, no confirmation was received from other troops in the vicinity, the accuracy of the report was doubted.

Events then began to move rapidly. On March 10, Tongzang was attacked and by March 12 the whole of 63rd Brigade of 17th Division was in action there: on March 12 further news of the enemy originally reported at Mualbem indicated that they had reached Mualnuam, north-west of Tiddim, and were continuing north: at the same time Japanese were seen near Milestone 108, threatening the Manipur bridge and the practically undefended and large administrative area at Milestone 109. The machine-gun battalion of 9th Jat Regiment, which Scoones had dispatched to guard the bridge over the Manipur river, reported the road cut both at Milestone 107 and 100. Furthermore, 100th Brigade of 20th Division at Witok, 30 miles south of Tamu, was attacked by Yamamoto's column on March 11.

It was now crystal clear that the Japanese offensive was under way, and that 17th Division's lifeline was in jeopardy at a number of places. Scoones, therefore, on the morning of March 13, gave Cowan permission to withdraw to the Imphal Plain and, at the same time, ordered Gracey to evacuate all the labour and machinery on the Tamu road. To meet the serious situation on the Tiddim road he ordered Roberts to send one of his brigades (37th Brigade), accompanied by a squadron of 7th Light Cavalry, to the assistance of 17th Division: but due to increased Japanese pressure, he was compelled on March 14 to commit a second brigade of 23rd Division (49th Brigade at Ukhrul) and to order its replacement by 50th Parachute Brigade from Kohima. Scoones was now left with only one brigade (1st Brigade) in corps reserve.

Although on March 13 he had been given permission to withdraw, it was not until 1300 hours on March 14 that Cowan issued

his orders for the move to begin at 1700 hours. That afternoon 16,000 marching troops, 2,500 vehicles, and 3,500 mules, collected from over a wide area, began the fighting march to Imphal, an operation which was to continue for 20 anxious days. At this moment, the picture on the Tiddim road resembled a Neapolitan ice of many layers, for, reading from south to north, there were first the Japanese following up the British 17th Division, then 17th Division, then Japanese at Tonzang, followed by the British garrison at Milestone 109, succeeded by a 10-mile Japanese road block from Milestone 109 to 100 and, finally, the two brigades of 23rd Division.

After much heavy fighting, 17th Division, supplied by air, crossed the Manipur bridge on March 17, blew it up, and began the breakthrough of the long roadblock from the south. Meanwhile, the dumps of supplies at Milestone 109 had been lost to the enemy.

Initial Japanese success

If Mutaguchi was at this stage fully aware that Scoones had been forced to commit two-thirds of his reserve, he must have felt well satisfied with the success of his plan; for XV and XXXI Divisions began their burst across the Chindwin between Homalin and Thaungdut on the night of March 15/16.

The method employed by the Japanese XV Division to cross its soldiers, guns, and animals was ingenious, and an excellent example of the improvisation called for on both sides throughout the Burma campaign by the lack of communications and dearth of equipment. Having collected and concealed a number of country boats on the east bank, these were lashed together and decking laid across them. Then, when darkness fell and the southern end was secured to the bank, the northern end was allowed to float downstream until it touched the opposite bank, where it too was secured and the troops hurried across. Just before dawn and the first Allied air reconnaissances, the further end of the boat bridge was dragged upstream by powered craft, the whole dismantled and concealed until required again the next evening.

But the ever-watchful 9/12th Frontier Force Rifles and V Force, although too weak to offer much opposition, gave due warning of this massed crossing before withdrawing westwards.

With nothing to stop them, XV and XXXI Divisions streamed along the mountain tracks towards their objectives in a series of columns, XV Division moving in two columns, the right passing through Sangshak to cut the Imphal-Kohima road at Kanglatongbi, the left travelling fast, again to Kanglatongbi, to attack Imphal from the north, while a detachment headed south towards Tamu to assist Yamamoto in his attack on 20th Division.

Near Homalin, XXXI Division crossed in three columns, and of these the two northern were directed to attack Kohima from the east, and the third, via Ukhrul, to cut the road about Mao, 20 miles south of Kohima and attack it from the south.

In the meantime the backloading or destruction of the huge dumps of supplies, ammunition, and petrol at Moreh had been in progress since the first contact with Yamamoto at Witok, and the labour force had been evacuated to Imphal. These operations had both gone according to plan and Yamamoto's advance had been slowed down considerably; but with the new threat to 20th

Division's left flank, Gracey was ordered to move back to the Shenam Saddle as arranged.

At this time, too, a decision was taken by the Supreme Commander, Admiral Mountbatten, at the request of General Slim, which was to cause an upset to the Japanese plan. It was to make aircraft available to fly in 5th Indian Division from Arakan beginning on March 19—a reinforcement which had originally been planned to take place by road and rail.

But so serious was the situation brought about by 17th Division's predicament and the necessity to expend so much of the corps reserve at the outset of the battle, that it was essential for more troops to arrive in Imphal with the least possible delay. The fact that the fly-in at such short notice of 5th Division's soldiers, guns, jeeps, and mules, less one brigade diverted to Dimapur, was completed without a hitch or casualty between March 19/29 speaks most highly for the army and air staffs responsible for its implementation and reflects great credit on the troops and pilots involved.

A masterpiece of improvisation

It was a real 'do-it-yourself' operation. Nobody knew how many aircraft would be available or of what type; the staff had had no previous experience of a move by air, while few of the troops, and certainly none of the mules, had ever travelled in an aircraft. Time was vital: the division was in action against the Japanese and had to be relieved before the move could begin: the nearest take-off airfield was the dusty earth strip at Dohazari and to reach it entailed a slow journey of 100 miles or more along a poor road with two waterways to be crossed, after which there would be a flight of over 250 miles, partly over enemy-held territory. This last demanded a complete revision, overnight, of load tables to enable the correct loads to be put into each aircraft.

An example of the speed with which units were moved is given in the timetable for an artillery regiment:
- *Monday, 1400 hours: Guns taken out of action.*
- *Tuesday: Unit moved to Dohazari, arriving at 1630 hours.*
- *Tuesday/Wednesday night: Guns dismantled for loading into aircraft.*
- *Wednesday: Flight to Imphal and guns reassembled on the airfield.*
- *Thursday: Guns in action on the Imphal front.*

Because this unprecedented operation had been ordered with no preparation, and there had been little time to brief the pilots, particularly those of the USAAF, some of the remarks overheard were distinctly unusual:

'Say, where do you want to go?' asked one pilot. *'Malum nahin Sahib'* ('I don't know') was the reply of the Indian officer in charge of the soldiers.

'Where are we off to and what is the name of the place we have just left?' enquired another when he was airborne. 'Never mind, we'll take a chance.' And they got there.

On arrival at Imphal, so critical was the situation with some Japanese only 30 miles away, that several units went into battle immediately on landing—one battalion commander finding two of his companies, which had preceded him, moving up to the front on different roads!

However, in a short time, all were collected again for the division to fight as a cohesive entity.

With the departure of 49th Brigade from

Ukhrul on March 15, less one battalion left behind, the first battalion of 50th Parachute Brigade arrived in the area on the same day, but due to transport difficulties it was not until March 21 that the whole brigade was able to concentrate. Almost coincidental with the arrival of the first battalion, strong enemy forces were reported approaching Ukhrul and a series of minor engagements followed until, on March 22, the brigade finally took up position at Sangshak covering the road back to Imphal. Meantime the left column of the Japanese XXXI Division had reached Ukhrul on March 21 and, hearing of this force which threatened its communications to the Chindwin, hurried south to eliminate it in conjunction with troops of XV Division.

The Sangshak position, held by three and a half battalions, was on a small hill 600 yards long and at its widest 300 yards. Within the perimeter were men, mules, guns, ammunition, and the field hospital, but the scanty water supply was just outside. So congested was this small area that every shell that landed could not fail but take toll of men, animals, and ammunition dumps. The fighting was desperate and round the clock; attacks were followed by counter-attacks to throw out the enemy who had penetrated; dead and wounded lay everywhere with no chance of burying the former or evacuating the latter. So bad did the situation become that on March 26, with casualties mounting minute by minute and the defenders, their supplies, and water almost exhausted (a large part of the air supply drops fell outside the perimeter), 50th Parachute Brigade was ordered to break out and find its way through the jungle to Imphal. Forced to abandon those wounded who were unable to walk and also much equipment, the brigade broke up into small parties and headed west through the jungle and mountains; most of them reached the newly arrived 123rd Brigade of 5th Division holding the entrance to Imphal from the north-east.

On the face of it, this action appeared to have been a disaster but, in fact, it had strong repercussions in favour of 4th Corps. The left column of the Japanese XXXI Division and the whole of XV Division had been held up, thereby throwing Mutaguchi's timetable out of gear; Japanese casualties had been heavy and these could not be afforded so early in the campaign; by the delay imposed by the parachute brigade, Scoones had gained a few precious days to reorganise the defences, to motor out numbers of unnecessary personnel and to motor urgent supplies into Imphal before the road was cut. The defenders of Sangshak had, in effect, made a valuable contribution to the outcome of the battle, and although the battalions suffered heavily, it was not long before they were ready for action again.

Elsewhere, the two outlying divisions were converging on the plain. By March 29, Gracey's 20th Division, having carried out an orderly withdrawal and having given Yamamoto yet another bloody nose while doing so, was firmly established on the Shenam Saddle. On the Tiddim road, the fighting had been violent and often hand to hand, the Japanese resisting stubbornly, but by March 28 patrols of 17th Division linked up with 37th Brigade at Milestone 102, after which the withdrawal to the plain was comparatively uneventful. Bringing 1,200 casualties with it, 17th Division marched into the plain on April 4, evacuated

its casualties by air, and went to rest and refit, while 23rd Division took up a position at Torbung, south of Bishenpur.

A week earlier, on March 29, the Japanese had cut the Imphal-Kohima road: the siege had begun and the only link with the outside world was by air.

Turning point of the battle

April 4, 1944: this was a red-letter day in the Imphal calendar and the turning point in this epic battle, since 4th Corps was at last concentrated and Scoones could turn his attention to the destruction of the Japanese.

The front was horse-shoe shaped and stretched for 90 miles from Kanglatongbi through Nungshigum, Shenam, and Shuganu to Torbung. General Briggs' 5th Division held off the Japanese to the north and north-east; 20th Division at Shenam covered the approach from Tamu and the east; 23rd Division kept the Japanese XXXIII Division at bay in the south, while 17th Division was recuperating in corps reserve.

Throughout, the Royal Air Force had given magnificent support to the operations, not only by attacking the Japanese forward troops and their lines of communication back into Burma, but also by working up an air supply which was to be the greatest operation of its kind in the history of modern warfare. By the time the battle was over their efforts had culminated in the delivery of, among other things, 14,000,000 pounds of rations, almost 1,000,000 gallons of petrol, 1,200 bags of mail, and 43,000,000 cigarettes, besides bringing in 12,000 reinforcements and evacuating 13,000 casualties and 43,000 non-combatants.

From captured documents and other sources the position of the Japanese forces was becoming clearer, and although that of XXXI Division was still obscure, all evidence pointed to the fact that the whole of it had gone to Kohima and not only one regiment as expected. The XV Division was strung out between Kanglatongbi and Litan, north-east of Imphal; and although XXXIII Division had taken a bad hammering on the Tiddim road, given reinforcements it could be expected to come on again at any time. Of importance were indications that the morale of some Japanese had already begun to wane and once the monsoon broke in a month's time, nature would assist Scoones to destroy the enemy who, with their flimsy supply arrangements, were bound to have great difficulty in maintaining their positions.

With all this information to hand, Scoones decided that 20th and 17th Divisions should hold the ring, from Shenam to the Tiddim road, while 5th and 23rd Divisions, beginning on April 16, hunted out and destroyed XV Division. But the unheralded appearance on April 6 of the best part of one Japanese regiment at Nungshigum, 4 miles from corps headquarters, caused an abrupt postponement of the latter operation.

From Nungshigum, a long high hill rising steeply to 1,000 feet above the plain and weakly held by 60 men of 3/9th Jat Regiment, one could see right in to the plain and overlook at least one of the airfields. Between it and the hub of 4th Corps there were no defences other than the 'boxes' manned chiefly by administrative troops. The threat was extremely serious and it was imperative that the Japanese be eliminated before they realised their advantageous position and advanced further.

Initially driven off, the Jats retook Nungshigum on April 7 and held it until the

Japanese, strongly reinforced, re-established themselves by the evening of April 11. It was only by an outstandingly gallant attack by 1/17th Dogra Regiment, supported by B Squadron of 3rd Carabiniers and all the artillery and aircraft that could be mustered, that Nungshigum was finally captured on April 13, the Japanese driven off for good, and this threat to the Imphal base removed. Japanese losses were extremely heavy, no less than 250 bodies being counted in one small area alone, but besides losing the British officers of the two Dogra companies and a number of men, five of the six tank commanders were killed when they raised their heads out of the turrets to guide their drivers, who were unable to see the ground in front, so steep was the slope. Except for isolated patrols, this was the nearest that any body of Japanese ever came to Imphal.

The action over, 23rd Division began successfully to harass the Japanese XV Division up the road to Ukhrul, even causing its commander to make some rapid midnight flits to avoid being captured. On its left, 5th Division made efforts to dislodge the Japanese, well dug-in on the Mapao ridge overlooking Imphal from the north-east, and to cut their communications north of Nungshigum.

Fanatical attacks

If the situation had been tense on the Ukhrul road, it was equally so at Shenam and on the road from Tiddim.

Nippon Hill, Sita, Crete East and West, Scraggy, Gibraltar, and Malta (names given to some of the features which made up the Shenam position)—these were the scenes of some of the most bitter fighting of the whole war and the casualties suffered by both sides were probably greater in proportion than in any other theatre.

For two and a half months, Yamamoto, in his attempt to reach the plain, hurled fanatical attacks at the British, Indian, and Gurkha troops of 20th Division and later of 23rd Division, who relieved the former in the middle of May. Hills which had been densely covered in jungle became completely bare; at times only a few yards separated the trenches, and in suicidal attacks Japanese climbed over the dead bodies of comrades hanging on the wire, or came to life to fight again after being buried in debris for days. Bad enough in dry weather, conditions became indescribable with the coming of the rain and mist of the monsoon. Yet the Indian divisions held firm while Yamamoto's attacks increased in ferocity—many were the individual and collective acts of heroism on both sides.

On the Tiddim road, around Bishenpur, Potsangbum, and Ningthoukhong, some of the obscure little villages which figured prominently in the battle, and along the Silchar track, XXXIII Division, like Yamamoto Force, made furious efforts to smash the defences of 17th Division reinforced by 32nd Brigade of 20th Division, and to break through to Imphal. On the night of April 15/16 three Japanese soldiers, with explosives, severed the Silchar track at Milestone 31 by blowing up the suspension bridge, one Japanese jumping to his death in the gorge. The other two went up with the bridge.

Day after day and night after night until some time after the siege was raised, the fighting went on incessantly. Counterattack followed attack, sometimes with and sometimes without tanks, each side trying to cut

'The fighting went on incessantly': troops of 1/17th Dogra Regiment prepare to attack Nungshigum

the other's communications by turning movements through the hills—one of which resulted in 17th Division HQ being closely overlooked from an adjacent hill and ten days elapsing before the enemy were killed or driven off. Of the five Victoria Crosses awarded during the battle, four were won on this particular part of the front.

The supply crisis
In early May, with the opening of the monsoon barely a fortnight away, Scoones' chief concern was the effect the weather would have on the air supply of the corps. Flying hours were bound to be reduced and already delivery was behind schedule: a shortfall in the next three months of some 15,000 tons was estimated and, consequently, it was probable that the ration scale, already reduced, would have to be cut still further unless the road was reopened by June 15.

The physical condition of the soldiers was also causing him anxiety as the monotonous dry ration was passing clean through them and giving little nourishment. Added to this, the deplorable conditions in which they lived and the continuous strain of fighting a cunning and ruthless enemy were having an effect on their physical endurance: care would have to be taken not to ask too much of them. On the other hand, the condition of the very few prisoners taken and the dead bodies lying around was clear evidence that the Japanese were in a much more parlous state.

On the credit side, too, was the fly-in of 89th Brigade of 7th Indian Division, to replace the brigade of 5th Division flown to Kohima in March.

In weighing up the situation, Scoones was determined to make the best use of the remaining days of fine weather to maintain the pressure on XV Division. The whole of 5th Division was, therefore, brought on to the Kohima road to break the Japanese block at Kanglatongbi and to force a way northwards while 20th Division, relieved from Shenam, moved on towards Ukhrul.

Mutaguchi, realising the desperate importance of speeding up the capture of Imphal, had ordered Sato, as early as the latter half of April, to send a regiment from Kohima to assist Yamauchi's attack on Imphal from the north. But a copy of those

orders had been captured near Kohima and, on General Slim's instructions, Stopford's 33rd Corps exerted all pressure to prevent this move taking place, so that Sato either could not or would not comply with the order.

Again, despite the reinforcements Mutaguchi had sent to General Tanaka's XXXIII Division (Yanagida had been relieved of his command in May), little or no progress was being made at Bishenpur, nor was Yamamoto any nearer his goal at Shenam. The picture indeed looked gloomy for the Japanese commander-in-chief, but it was to look a great deal more so by the end of May.

Crisis in the Japanese Command
By June 3, 1944, the battle of Kohima was over and 33rd Corps was preparing to advance south down the road to Imphal. Except for a staunch rearguard under General Miyazaki, the Japanese XXXI Division was in full retreat without food and ammunition and with no chance of receiving any, since the torrential rain had turned its lines of communication into seas of mud.

The Japanese XV Division, although no longer in a state to make any impression on the Imphal defences, was stubbornly resisting the advance of 5th Division, around Milestone 116, on the road from Kohima. Following Yanagida's dismissal, Mutaguchi was about to relieve both Yamauchi and Sato of their commands. With the exception of XXXIII Division, the Japanese XV Army was rapidly approaching disintegration.

The dismissal of all three divisional commanders did not help to maintain morale, for such an event was unparalleled in the annals of the Japanese army. From Japanese sources, Sato was described as a man of great courage, with an easy manner and open-hearted nature, and an inclination towards the unconventional. As the operation had gone on so his relations with Mutaguchi had become more and more strained until, in exasperation, he had dispatched a signal to HQ Burma Area Army which read: 'The tactical ability of the XV Army Staff lies below that of cadets', and had cut off wireless communication to his superior commander. His insubordination cost him his command.

Yanagida, of XXXIII Division, is recorded as a talented, intelligent man with a

tendency towards over-conscientiousness and overcautiousness, characteristics which were bound, at some time, to conflict with those of the driving, blustering Mutaguchi. His successor, Tanaka, who on first meeting gave an impression of toughness and brawn at the expense of brain, was in fact a resilient and sound commander, who kept his appointment up to the conclusion of the Burma campaign.

Finally, Yamauchi, who had studied at West Point and had later become the Japanese military attaché at Washington, was spoken of as a man of polished manners. It is said that from the outset he realised the immense potential strength of the Anglo-American forces and the danger of challenging it without proper preparation. Whether his handling of XV Division was in any way affected by this outlook it is impossible to say, but Mutaguchi felt that he had allowed General Scoones to seize the initiative from him and he, Mutaguchi, had lost confidence in Yamauchi.

Perhaps as a portent of things to come, June 22 broke fine and sunny, for early that morning the leading troops of General Grover's British 2nd Division and those of 5th Indian Division met at Milestone 107 on the Kohima road and the siege was raised. That night, with headlights blazing, a long convoy of lorries, with much-needed supplies, drove into Imphal.

But the battle was by no means over. The Japanese were still fighting viciously at Bishenpur and Shenam, and General Slim was determined to turn the defeat of XXXI and XV Divisions into a rout, despite the appalling weather and the weariness of his troops. He felt that he could call on them for one more big effort and they, in turn, showed him his confidence was not misplaced.

General Messervy's 7th Indian Division of Stopford's 33rd Corps, forcing its way south from Kohima through mist-covered mountains and jungle east of the Kohima-Imphal road, drove XXXI Division towards Ukhrul and the anvil provided by 89th Brigade and 20th Division moving east from Imphal. Still further east, 23rd Long Range Penetration Brigade hurried to cut Sato's lines of communication back to the Chindwin. Soaked to the skin, the British, Indian,

'The worst disaster of its kind in the annals of war': the Japanese army had over 53,000 killed or missing out of 85,000

and Gurkha soldiers dragged themselves and their mules up into the intense cold of the mountains or through steaming hot swampy valleys, while pilots of the RAF flew perilous sorties in cloud and mist to drop their supplies. Occasionally a few determined Japanese made a suicidal stand, but more frequently they were found dead or dying, half naked in the churned-up mud, with abandoned equipment lying everywhere; bombed-out transport columns, charred and black, littered the tracks or the hillside down which they had fallen; in the evil-smelling field hospitals, dead lay on the stretchers on which they had been brought, sometimes with a bullet hole in their foreheads, their comrades having put them out of their misery before leaving them. Such prisoners as were taken – and only a few more than 100 were captured throughout the four months, an indication of the tenacity of the Japanese soldier and his attitude to death on the battlefield – were in a ghastly condition of disease and starvation.

By July 18, when both Kawabe and Mutaguchi were agreed that further offensive action was out of the question, a general withdrawal was ordered to the line of the Chindwin. By then, besides losing most of its equipment, guns, tanks, and transport, the Japanese XV Army had sustained over 53,000 casualties, either dead or missing, out of an original strength of some 85,000. Of those that remained, the majority were suffering from minor wounds or malnutrition or both. Defeat had been utter and complete, but not without considerable cost to the British both at Imphal and Kohima – the casualties had amounted to 17,000, but of these, due to the admirable medical arrangements, many recovered to fight again another day. And they were to be needed, for even during this historic battle General Slim had been preparing plans for the advance into Burma and the capture of Mandalay.

A decisive victory
'Most of this force perished in battle or later of starvation. The disaster at Imphal was perhaps the worst of its kind yet chronicled in the annals of war.' That was how Kase Toshikazu, a Japanese Foreign Office official, summed up the battle in his book *The Eclipse of the Rising Sun,* published seven years later. Although his assessment of the enormity of the catastrophe may be an exaggeration, it does not alter the fact that at Imphal and Kohima the Japanese had suffered one of the greatest military defeats in their history.

But, besides being a victory as decisive as any of the Second World War, it had other far-reaching effects. The back of the Japanese army in Burma had been broken, the belief in its invincibility had gone for ever, and the possibility of the reconquest of Burma had become a reality. The initiative now lay with General Slim, who was to retain it until the conclusion of hostilities 12 months later, an advantage of which he was to make the best possible use.

The stakes had been high, since defeat to either side meant a débâcle of the first order. The four months' struggle had been a tense one with fortune favouring first one side and then the other. For the British it had been touch and go in the early stages, and how nearly did the Japanese succeed.

However strong one's feelings may be towards the Japanese military machine, there can be little doubt that XV Army achieved more than any other army could have in such difficult terrain and shocking weather conditions, with inadequate administrative arrangements, inferior armour and artillery, and sparse air support. This was in large part due to the amazing fighting qualities and endurance of the Japanese soldier, despite the failings of his superior commanders – qualities which made him the most formidable individual soldier in the world.

But in General Slim, Mutaguchi had a tough opponent and the most experienced in fighting the Japanese in this wild, inhospitable country. Far-sighted and quick to take advantage of any mistakes, possessed of great ability to inspire confidence in his subordinate commanders and troops, he imbued a determination in 14th Army which sustained it through adversity and steered it to success, while acknowledging in full the debt his army owed to the air forces.

Without the contributions made by the RAF, Indian air force, and the USAAF the result could have been very different. The demands made on them were many and varied: long-range disruption of the Japanese line of communications; close support of the fighting troops; transportation of reinforcements; quick evacuation of casualties; the entire supply of 4th Corps over a period of months and dropping of essentials to isolated positions – more often than not in the worst possible flying conditions. A truly magnificent effort.

But however brilliant the commander, his plans, and the arrangements to put them into effect, as always the final result must rest on the shoulders of the regimental officers and their men. Unless one has seen them – and a paper description is quite inadequate – it is difficult to realise the shocking conditions in which they lived and fought. Unless required to carry their arms, ammunition, and extra impedimenta up the mountains or through jungle, either on patrol or to attack an enemy position, they lived in soggy holes in the ground, frequently without relief for long periods. From these holes they beat off fanatical attacks by shrieking Japanese or took part in counterattacks to regain ground. Yet the morale and physical endurance of the British, Indian, and Gurkha soldiers stood up to the heavy and incessant strain, largely due to the high standard of leadership, the mutual confidence and friendship between all races and creeds in the Indian divisions, the magnificent work of the medical authorities – and, by no means least, to their innate sense of humour in the most adverse circumstances.

Needless to say, at the end of this crucial period of the Burma campaign many changes occurred in the Japanese High Command and, among them, Generals Kawabe and Mutaguchi were relieved of their appointments. The 4th Corps, 17th and 23rd Divisions, after two years in action, were sent back to India to rest and refit, and General Stopford's 33rd Corps, reinforced by 11th East Africa Division, took over the pursuit to the Chindwin by way of the Kabaw Valley and Tiddim road.

Had General Mutaguchi's plan succeeded, there is little doubt that the way to India would have lain open for the Japanese. But the Japanese army met its greatest defeat, and the reconquest of Burma was about to start.

THE GREAT
GAMBLE

Normandy, June 6, 1944

The day had dawned: the first Allied troops drifted down from the sky and struggled from the sea to begin the battle for Europe. For some it was to be an anti-climax to the months of waiting, training, thinking, wondering. For others it was to be chaos, confusion, and death. On one beach men walked ashore with next to no opposition, on its neighbour they were pinned down and massacred. There were moments of near disaster when a resolute German attack might have shattered the Allied beach-heads, but the Germans too were confused and bewildered by the weight of the massive attack. By evening the Allied foothold was secure: the great gamble had paid off

Below: Airborne Pathfinders, leaders of the paratroop drops which heralded the invasion, check their watches before take-off

By June 4, the weather was so bad that the invasion had to be delayed for one day. On the 5th, though conditions were still terrible, there was some slight hope of improvement. Appalled by the chaos which would ensue if there were more delay, Eisenhower decided that the risk must be taken: D-Day would be June 6

THE WAITING

Sunrise at two minutes to six on the morning of June 5, 1944, was an arbitrary statement rather than a visible fact marking the progress from dark stormy night to grey blustery day. The Channel heaved in a chaos of cruel pinnacles flecked white upon steel grey, and waves rose steeply to test the seamanship and try the stomachs of all those afloat in little ships. Clouds fled in tormented tattered shrouds over a cold sky. A gusty westerly, veering WSW to WNW at Force 5, whipped the spume into the faces of look-outs and helmsmen as scores of small craft reared and bucked towards their meeting place. By sunrise, 5,000 ships of half-a-hundred shapes and sizes had begun to move from their anchorages, and the wakes of many convoys already patterned the coastal waters of Britain from Fowey to the Nore. It was four years almost to the day since the remnants of an army had struggled back from Dunkirk, and the coastal waters of England had known any comparable activity. Admiral Ramsay had commanded then, and he commanded now, on this morning.

This fifth day of June is not one of those landmarks in history to be covered by easy generalisation. It was many things to many men. 287,000 men and a host of armoured fighting vehicles had been preloaded into ships, some of them since the first day of the month, some of them had been already shuttled and shunted, blind to sea and sky, daylight or darkness, sick, weary, wondering, aware that a moment would come when they would be spewed up like Jonahs upon an alien shore, bristling with devices of death and beaten with shot and shell.

The many thousands on deck, however sick and cold, could count themselves fortunate that they were not of the many thousands below, huddled in the great caverns of the LCTs (Landing Crafts, Tank), in the cramped quarters of the LSIs (Landing Ships, Infantry), in the dull yellow electric glow, and the stench of vomit.

While thousands waited in a grey limbo, thousands worked, manning the little ships and the great ships of war, alert in hundreds of gun turrets, crouched astride swivel seats behind a great array of weapons pointing to the sky, cloud ceiling 4,000 feet, and above that the sustained roar of 10,000 aircraft. Hundreds more wrestled with towing gear and hawsers, tugs grappling and towing strange ungainly shapes out of the estuaries in the wake of the Armada massing south of the Isle of Wight.

Towards evening there was a break in the weather, and in that brief hour a soldier wrote: 'It was a perfect summer's evening, the Isle of Wight lay green and friendly, and tantalisingly peaceful behind the tapestry of warships.' And in the dusk when the convoys began to move towards their date with destiny, men were answering cheer with cheer across the water, the pennants flew from the ships of war, and a British Admiral threw his cap in the air. Yet what a travesty of the truth this is to the thousands who seemed to inhabit a grey ante-chamber to a morgue, dull sickness upon them to eke out the miseries of the long blind ordeal of waiting.

Force U2a, part of Force U for Utah, had had the worst of it. 128 tank landing craft, crowded with men and armour, sailed out of the west through the hours of indecision, easted down Channel, turned about, plunged back into the teeth of the westerly to seek shelter in Weymouth Bay and in the lee of Portsmouth, easted again down Channel at last in the dusk of June 5 to set course for France.

Force O for Omaha had had also a long haul from the south-west, a turn and turn-about, an agonising drawing out of the hours of confinement. Already men on deck had kept watch upwards of 50 hours, and perhaps 50 more lay ahead before sleep. For these no cheers, no happy vision of the Isle of Wight, for their 'green and pleasant land' lay beyond the Atlantic.

Through the hours of darkness the immense convoys moved steadily, unmolested, on their courses in the buoyed channels cleared by the mine-sweeping flotillas, a wedge more than 50 miles wide, and with scores of small fighting ships ranging far out on the flanks probing for the enemy. There was nothing. The long lines of ships seemed to unwind on fabulous spools, drawing their component threads from a hundred havens of the English coast, to weave them into thick skeins to the Bay of Seine. The fierce turbulence of wind and sea failed to mask the strange 'unnatural' silence of the night. The sustained thunder of the fleets of bombers overhead, quenched for those below by the drenching sounds of sea, and the shuddering stresses of steel plates, seemed to accentuate the absence of the enemy. It seemed impossible that such an avalanche of ships and men could muster through the months, at last to fill the English Channel from shore to shore, and remain undetected. Surely no instrument more 'scientific' than the human ear would be needed to hear so vast a throb of power!

No signs of detection

Before the sun had set on the evening of the 5th, two flotillas of mine-sweepers stood off the coast of Normandy, well within sight, and easily able to distinguish houses on shore with the naked eye. The midget submarines of Lieutenant Honour's command were at their stations, close inshore marking the eastern flank and the dangerous rocks. There were no signs of detection. From 0200 hours on the 6th, the HQ ships of the assault moved into their transport areas, and prepared to put their assault craft into the water. The only interference came from the unfriendly sea, and the weather was not alone to thank, or blame, for this.

The sustained attacks from the air on the elaborate Early Warning System of the enemy had succeeded almost too well. In the entire Neptune Area from Cap d'Antifer to Barfleur, 74 radar stations were out of action, and the 18 still capable of working were silent. But it was not enough simply to blind the enemy, it was important also to mislead. For this purpose ten stations were deliberately left in working order north of the Seine, and on to these screens the Royal Navy contrived to produce a misleading web of shapes and echoes. It seems extravagant that such a claim is made, for it reveals a predominance over the enemy that reduces his forces to a stricken body, lacerated on all sides, unable to fly or float, but capable of inflicting grievous, even crippling, wounds upon those seeking to deliver the *coup de grâce*.

But there was no inclination on the part of the Allies to underestimate the powers of the German army in the west. Thus all through June 5 and the night, 105 aircraft of the RAF and 34 little ships of the Royal Navy contrived by means of weaving patterns over the sky and sea, and flying barrage balloons, to produce the 'echoes' in the enemy radar ears of a substantial fleet approaching the Pas de Calais. At the same time jamming operations and diversions were carried on against Cap d'Antifer and Barfleur. The silent approach of the great armada to spread out in a fan from 8 to 12 miles offshore enclosing the Bay of Seine is the measure of success.

Soon after 9 o'clock, the unusual length and content of the BBC broadcast warning to the French Resistance alarmed the Germans, and the XV Army in the Pas de Calais was alerted, while the VII Army in Normandy remained undisturbed. Nothing, it seemed, could prise von Rundstedt's mind away from its preconceived fixations, even the deadly facts of the elements of three airborne divisions dropping in the midst of his forces. Well before the first assault craft of the seaborne forces were in the water, the battle on land was joined.

AIR DROP IN THE WEST: 'CHAOS WILL REIGN'

Within half-an-hour of sunset on the night of June 5, while the leading ships of the seaborne assault moved into the buoyed channels to steer for France, the Pathfinders of the United States and British air forces took off from their English fields to light their beacons in the fields of Normandy. Soon after midnight these small vanguards of élite troops were moving silently in the midst of the enemy, the British to mark the dropping zones for the 6th Airborne Division to the north-east of Caen on the eastern flank, the Americans astride the Merderet river, and the road Carentan-Montebourg-Cherbourg in the area of Ste Mère-Église. Behind them more than 1,200 aircraft bore nearly 20,000 men into battle;

behind them the gliders for which the paratroops must clear the way.

The last warning of the brigadier commanding the British 3rd Parachute Brigade may well serve for all: 'Do not be daunted if chaos reigns: it undoubtedly will.'

The drop of the US 101st Airborne Division, as fully plotted as all subsequent information has made possible, spatters the map over an area 25 miles long by 15 miles broad, and with small isolated elements even further afield. Very few of these had even an outside chance of becoming part of the division. The men had been loosed, as it seems, recklessly upon the winds of Heaven, and thence to the flooded hinterlands, and maze of closed country, behind Utah Beach.

The US 82nd Airborne Division, largely due to the arrival of one regiment reasonably on its objectives, fared a little better, but of the remainder of the division only 4% were dropped in their zones west of the Merderet river. Thus the tasks of the division west of the Merderet, and the crossings of the Merderet and Douve rivers, could not be fulfilled. The division had become a regiment.

At dawn, when the seaborne landings were coming in on Utah Beach, the 101st Airborne Division mustered 1,100 men out of 6,600. By evening its strength had grown to 2,500 men. The 82nd Airborne Division, at least 4,000 men short on the day, was still only at one-third of its strength three days later. Both divisions had lost great quantities of equipment, and almost their entire glider-borne artillery, much of it in the floods of the Merderet and Douve rivers. Neither division was able to prepare adequately for the arrival of its glider-borne follow-up, the losses were severe and tragic.

Yet the remarkable fact is that so great a confusion was created in the enemy by this incoherent scattering of men in their midst that there was no possibility of reserves supporting the beach defenders. By the time the US 4th Infantry Division came in to land the battle of Utah Beach was virtually won.

No coherent pattern has ever emerged from the struggles of the isolated remnants of the airborne divisions on that day; nor will such a pattern ever emerge. The individual contributions of many men who fought bravely alone or in twos and threes will never be assessed. Even those who gave up without a fight added to rather than subtracted from enemy bewilderment. The Pathfinders of the airborne divisions did not do well. Many failed to find and to mark the dropping zones; some beacons were missing entirely, especially west of the Merderet in country infested by enemy; others were wrongly placed. Pilots under fire for the first time, many of them 'inadequately briefed', took wild evasive action, lost direction in the cloud banks, and overshot the dropping zones. Many came in too fast and too high, and spilled out their 'sticks' of men, adding greatly to the normal hazards of jumping.

Major-General Maxwell Taylor, commanding the 101st, dropped with a nucleus of his divisional HQ, and struggled all through the day to make contact and to bring some sort of order out of chaos. He felt 'alone on the Cotentin'. In the upshot the pattern may be seen dimly in the struggles of half-a-dozen colonels, each managing to group between 75 and 200 men round him, aided by the tell-tale click-clack of the toy 'crickets' with which every man was provided.

By a stroke of remarkable fortune a small band of men ambushed and killed the commander of the German 91st Division, returning from an 'exercise' conference to his headquarters. Thus the 91st Division, trained in the role of defence against airborne attack, and forming almost the sole available reserve behind the defenders of the Cotentin coast, was deprived of its commander and severely handicapped. There was no 'shape' or dimension to the airborne enemy, no focal point or points to counterattack, no time to think, no commander with the temerity to commit troops with the strength and purpose of knowledge.

While many German officers were sure that this must be the beginning of the main Allied assault – so long awaited and expected – and that the battlefield was Normandy, others, including Lieutenant-General Speidel, Rommel's Chief-of-Staff, and Lieutenant-General Blumentritt, Chief-of-Staff to Rundstedt, were doubtful. Thus the German military machine remained hesitant and palsied, its slender reserves uncommitted, its armour waiting, Rommel out of touch, Hitler sleeping. These things gave the airborne troops on the western flank an initial advantage of which, perforce, they were unaware, and saved them from the possibility of annihilation.

Throughout the whole day and night the 101st Airborne Division, reduced to much less than the effective strength of a single regiment, was not only isolated from its own widely scattered units, but also in complete ignorance of the fate of the 82nd Airborne Division. Ironically, it may have achieved at least as much in its confusion as it could have hoped for in coherence, for chaos bred chaos.

The one effective landing

The story of the 82nd Airborne Division is simple. Two of its regiments with the tasks of clearing the area west of the Merderet river and in the angle of the Douve, were not in the fight. It fell to one regiment to save the day, and to fight the one clear-cut battle fought by the US airborne forces on D-Day. While scores of men struggled in the swamps of the Merderet, dragging themselves towards the dry land of the railway embankment, concerned in the main with the problem of survival, the third regiment had dropped in a fairly tight group to the north-west of Ste Mere-Église. This was not due to chance, but to the determination of the pilots to find their targets. Long before the dawn, Lieutenant-Colonel Krause, finding himself on the outskirts of Ste Mère-Église with roughly a quarter of his battalion, bounced the town without waiting for more, and taking the enemy completely by surprise began to establish a solid base. By the afternoon the town was securely held, and four recognisable actions had developed, apart from a score or more of fragmentary encounters in the hopeless wilderness west of the Merderet.

The 82nd Airborne had dropped on the fringe of the assembly area of the German 91st Division, and its position from the outset was much more precarious than that of the 101st. All troops, however fragmentary, were at once in the midst of the enemy, and fighting for their lives within minutes of finding their feet. Some small groups up to 50 or 60 strong fought all day in the ditches and hedge-rows within 1,000 yards of others with whom it was impossible to make contact. Often they were unaware of their nearness.

The performance of the 101st and 82nd Airborne Divisions on D-Day may only be seen in fragmentary terms. At the end of the day the divisions had not made contact. Each believed it had lost some two-thirds of its troops. Neither one had cause for satisfaction, or the haziest idea of what was happening. All that they could do was to wait for the morning.

Fortunately, the enemy's confusion was equivalent to almost total breakdown. Hammered savagely and incessantly from the air, handicapped by the chance of a conference at Rennes of their senior commanders coinciding with the assault, their communications disrupted, and with, as it seems, a premonition of inevitable doom, their resistance was as fragmentary as that of the airborne troops infesting their imaginations as well as their fields. Many surrendered almost without a fight. Major von der Heydte, commanding the German VI Parachute Regiment, probably the finest enemy troops available in the Carentan area, has told of his difficulties in getting orders from his senior commanders. From the church steeple of St Come-du-Mont he had a personal view of the seaborne armada on the western flank. It seemed to him curiously detached from reality, almost peaceful. At noon the sun was shining, and the whole scene reminded him 'of a summer's day on the Wannsee'. The immense bustle of landing craft, and the warships fading into the horizon, lacked to his ears the orchestration of battle.

Von der Heydte sent his three battalions into battle, one to the north to attack Ste Mère-Église, another to the north-east to protect the seaward flank in the area Ste Marie-du-Mont, the third back on Carentan. Von der Heydte almost at once lost contact. Organised defence on the western flank had crumbled.

A host of men and vehicles had been loaded into ships . . . soon they would be spewed up like Jonahs upon an alien shore

287,000 men and a host of armoured fighting vehicles were pre-loaded into ships, some of them as early as the first of the month

△Grim-faced American troops file aboard a landing ship
▽British soldiers pass the time learning about their target

UTAH BEACH: 12 MEN KILLED

At 0200 hours on June 6, the leading ships of Force U, organised in 12 convoys comprising 865 vessels commanded by Rear-Admiral Moon, USN, moved into their assembly area 12 miles off the western coast of the Cotentin Peninsula, opposite the dunes of Varreville — Utah Beach. The assault upon Utah Beach on the extreme western flank was virtually an isolated operation. If all else failed it might have been reinforced to establish a bridgehead, to cut off the Cotentin Peninsula, gaining Cherbourg as a major port from which to mount some subsequent effort. In that event Overlord would be no more.

Field Order 1 states: '7th Corps assaults Utah Beach on D-Day at H-Hour and captures Cherbourg with minimum delay.'

Steadily in the hours before dawn the orders to 7th Corps reduced down to those few who would debouch into the shallows of the unfriendly sea. The 4th Infantry Division would establish the bridgehead; the 8th Infantry Regiment leading — the 1st Battalion on the right, 'Green beach'; the 2nd Battalion on the left, 'Red beach'; two companies of each battalion forward; 30 men to each landing craft; five landing craft to each company, 20 landing craft carrying 600 men in the van, with two companies of the 70th Tank Battalion in the first wave (see map on pages 274/275). Behind them, wave upon wave of their fellows and the waves of the sea, H+5, H+15, H+17, H+30, on and on through all the day and night, and beyond; infantry, armour, engineers, into the shallows, through the obstacles, the mine-fields, over the beaches, the sea wall, the causeways, the floods, inland to the villages and fields; 27 miles across the neck of the peninsula, Carentan to Lessay; north to Cherbourg.

H-Hour on the western flank was 0630 hours, but along the invasion beaches tidal-variations decreed four different H-Hours from right to left, from Utah Beach to Sword Beach, a span of one hour and 25 minutes. But the men on the right were in their own cocoons of loneliness. Now, in the bitter morning, they were being buffeted in the shallow draft vessels, the dark sky above them wild with the roar of aircraft, the crescendo rising, the blasting roar of the main armament, the scream of shells, and all around a turbulence of men and craft.

To the left, for nearly 50 miles, variations on the theme were unfolding over the waters, Omaha, Gold, Juno, Sword, and over the dark shore-line from end to end the dust was rising, blasted in towering columns by shells and bombs to hang, an opaque and ominous curtain, above the stage.

Enemy shells air-bursting over the water, the spasmodic explosions of mines, the shouts of men floundering, arms flung out, weighed down by equipment, created an uproar in the mind and senses in which the last cries of the lost, the total personal tragedies, were no more than the plaintive squeakings of mice in a cage of lions. The 60 men of Battery B, 29th Field Artillery Battalion, became a statistic on the debit side, dark shadows threshing in the water, under the water, part of the pattern at the bottom of the sea.

But the pattern advanced, untroubled by calamity, the second wave, the bulldozers on their craft, the special engineer units, all in position, the heavy armament of the bombarding squadron blasting the grey dawn to crimson shreds, 40 minutes to go. Some 276 aircraft of the US 9th Air Force roaring in over the beach defences, delivering their bombs, 4,404 bombs each of 250 pounds upon seven targets, 'according to the book'.

Seventeen of the 33 supporting craft seemed to tear the crackling scalp off the universe in an unbearable rasping agony as their mattresses of rockets shuddered inshore. Other craft were machine-gunning, perhaps in the hope of detonating mines, perhaps simply to boost morale, but all 'drenching the beaches with fire'.

About 700 yards to go, and on time, ten assault craft, 300 men on the left, ten assault craft, 300 men on the right; in their wakes 28 DD tanks, swimming, slopping the choppy water across their grey backs, the long muzzles of their guns like snouts, a seeming miracle thanks to the bold initiative and swift decision of their commander to launch close in at 3,000 yards, 'not according to the book'.

The beach was almost invisible behind the sand pall, blasted by

gunfire and bombs, joining it to the sky, and in it, under it, the enemy — if there could be an enemy!

Some 67 of the bombers had failed to release their bombs, one-third of the remainder had fallen between high and low water mark, the bulk of the rest on the fortifications of La Madeleine.

A swift, painless landing

Out of the leading wave of the assault craft smoke projectiles hurtled to the sky, demanding silence from the gunners of the bombarding force. About 300 yards to go, and the ramps down, 300 men of the 2nd Battalion, waist deep in water, floundering, finding their feet, wading in, rifles held high, to the dry sand, and the sudden upsurge of spirit. Normandy, the first men ashore, and not a shot out of the haze of battle, the grey shapes of the tanks crawling up out of the sea in their 'skirts', striking terror to the few who still lifted up their heads in the defences and dared to fire, a few wavering shots, 'desultory fire'.

These few men, and their comrades in the van, landing within minutes on their right, did not know that the south-easterly set of the tide had carried them more than a mile south of their target. It was a fortunate chance. Two hours later the leading troops were off the beach. The enemy strongpoints yielded to mopping-up operations in company strength, and the sea wall did not demand assault. Six battalions of infantry had begun to move off the beach by 1000 hours, and little more than an occasional air burst hampered the engineers at their toil, or reminded them of their extreme vulnerability as they placed their charges by hand. By noon the beach had been cleared at a cost of six men killed and 39 wounded out of the 400 involved in static roles, all of them sitting ducks without cover, and without armour.

Shortly after midday three battalions of the 22nd Infantry Regiment were moving north to open the northerly exit, the 3rd Battalion along the coast road to anchor a flank on Hamel-de-Cruttes, the 1st and 2nd Battalions wading diagonally, and miserably, waist deep, and often armpit and neck deep, across the floods all the way to St Germain-de-Varreville.

The 12th Infantry Regiment found the going worse, wading from the Grand Dune position immediately backing the beach, and crossing the line of march as they reached dry land, many of them soaked to the ears.

In all that day, the 8th and 22nd Infantry Regiments lost 12 men killed. Twenty times the number would have been counted fortunate; 100 times the number a misfortune to be looked for. A single resolute man armed with a flint lock could have accounted for more than 12 men on the beach in the first half-an-hour, including a brigadier-general and a colonel. The struggle of the 4th Infantry Division was mainly against the forces of nature, which were considerable. Eastwards it was different.

OMAHA BEACH: THE BLOODBATH

The beach of Omaha lies between the outcropping rocks of Pointe de la Percée in the west, and Port-en-Bessin in the east, a shallow arc of sand enclosed inland by bluffs rising in a gentle slope 150 feet to a plateau of tiny hedge-enclosed fields, deep lanes, and scattered hamlets built solidly of stone. It is a thinly populated region, the largest village, Trévières, 3 or 4 miles inland on the south side of the Aure river, counting not more than 800 inhabitants.

Three coastal villages, Vierville, St Laurent, and Colleville lie behind the beach at regular intervals a mile and a half apart, and linked by a narrow lane from 500 to 1,000 yards in from the shore line. A stretch of paved promenade along the 'front', and with a score or more of good houses between Vierville and St Laurent, backs a low sea wall of masonry and wood. Gullies opening from the beach give access up narrow lanes to the villages.

At low tide the sands slope gradually to the sea wall, and in places to a heavy shingle bank of stones 3 inches in diameter, a barrier 8 to 10 feet high between the beach and the reedy grasses of the bluffs.

War had become a battle of machines against machines

For months before D-Day, the crews of the specialised armour of British 79th Armoured Division had practised their techniques for breaching the German defences. On The Day they were highly successful, as British and Canadians rushed ashore. (1) The swimming Duplex Drive Sherman tanks were first ashore, taking up positions at water's edge from which they could engage and control enemy pillboxes. (2) They were followed by Crab flail tanks, which advanced up the beach in echelon, overlapping to ensure that *all* the mines in their path were cleared. (3) When the flails had reached the sea wall an AVRE with an SBG bridge would place its bridge; a DD tank would mount the sea wall to attack the pillboxes at closer range. This would be followed by an AVRE carrying a fascine to fill the anti-tank ditch. By now the infantry (red arrows) would be crossing the beach. (4) The flails continued to clear the minefields to open lanes through which the beach-head could be extended. Petard tanks would advance to destroy the last pillboxes by firing through the embrasures. At all times, reserves would be held to ensure that the loss of individual machines did not disrupt the whole landing

Seaward the stresses of the sea and the strong currents carve runnels in the wet ribbed sands.

The rocky shoulders of the bluffs of Omaha, flanking the crescent of the beach, provided concealed gun positions to enfilade the fore shore and the sea approaches, and behind the obstacle of the heavy shingle bank and the wall, the enemy defended entrenchments linking strongpoints, pillboxes, and concrete gun emplacements sited to bring devastating cross-fire to bear upon the beach. Theoretically, at least, light and heavy machine-guns, 75- and 88-mm artillery pieces, would make a beaten zone of the entire beach area from end to end. And behind the forward defensive positions the terraced slopes of the bluffs gave cover to further trench systems, machine-gun nests, and minefields.

The beach itself was moderately mined, especially in the areas between the gullies, and from low to high water mark an elaborate system of staggered lethal obstacles seemed to defy the passage of any craft larger than a matchbox. But all these things had been studied in some detail by small parties visiting the beaches by night, and from countless air photographs.

Omaha Beach held no mystery and no surprises. Even the bringing in of a new and vastly superior division – 352nd – had been observed by British Intelligence, and passed on to US 1st Army. Unhappily, this piece of information had seemed suspect to the 1st Army Command, and the assault troops were not informed. Yet it is inconceivable that they had been briefed to expect less than the worst the enemy could be expected to perform. To attack this superb defensive position General Bradley had rejected Hobart's magnificent array of assault armour, and had accepted DD tanks only with reluctance.

A terrible confusion

At 0300 hours on June 6, Force O, commanded by Rear-Admiral Hall, USN, and carrying 34,000 men and 3,300 vehicles and with a follow-up force, almost its equal, a few hours astern, began to put its assault craft into the water 12 miles off shore. There followed four hours of a macabre Dantesque confusion, through which men struggled blindly with the sea, a prey to despair, knowing the dregs of misery. While the larger vessels moved forward, finding difficulty in maintaining their stations in the heavy sea, the smaller craft were exposed to the full force of the north westerly, fighting seas up to 6 feet high, unstable and making water too fast for the pumps.

Some of the larger ships had put their assault craft into the water fully loaded, but others had put their men over the side into craft pitching and rolling wildly, an ordeal for men wracked with sea sickness. The sea, unfriendly through all the hours of the long passage, became in minutes a dark heaving formless jungle upon which men and boats wrestled like the damned in a labyrinthine maze of driven spume.

Almost at once ten small craft foundered, and upwards of 300 men struggled for their lives in a darkness which seemed to contain a kind of uproar in its relentless impersonal violence. Rudderless, foundering small craft and the sodden wreckage of equipment added to the menace, buffeting the men in their life jackets.

In nearly 200 assault craft, the crews and troops who must presently assault the enemy across open beaches in the face of withering fire, baled with their tin hats for their lives, in some boats 100% sea-sick, in all boats sodden, cramped, and cold. At last on the verge of nervous and physical exhaustion the assault troops neared the shore, and their craft strove to manoeuvre for the final run-in.

These men in the vanguard were more naked than they knew or greatly cared. Behind them the seas had stripped them steadily of guns and armour, and the teams of combat engineers had suffered no less than they. With a reckless irresponsibility the commander of the tank landing-craft carrying 32 DD tanks due to land at H−5 launched his massive vehicles into the steep seas 6,000 yards off shore. Even with well-trained crews there would have been small hopes for the tanks; as it was 27 were swamped within minutes and sank. Two, by brilliant seamanship and plenty of luck

'A foothold has been gained on the continent of Europe'

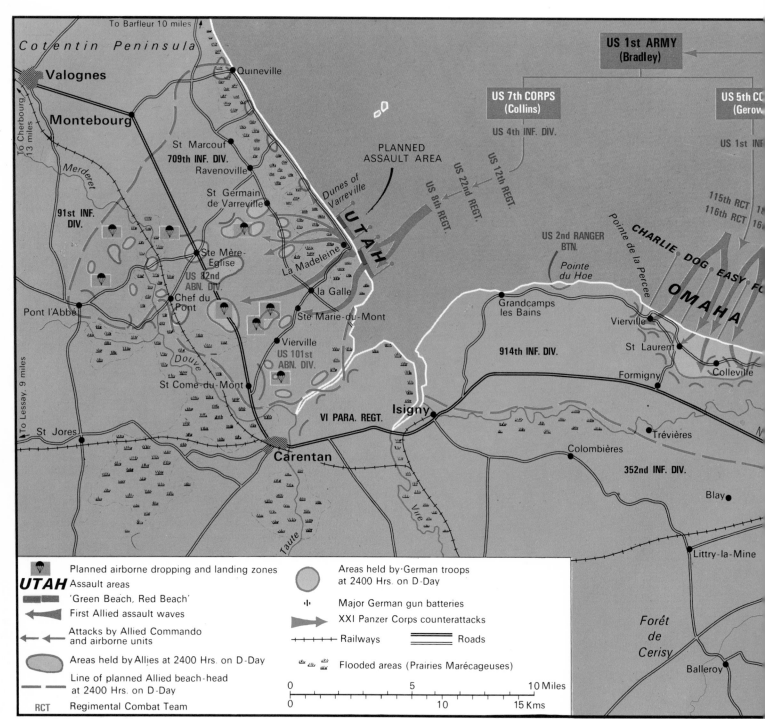

Planned airborne dropping and landing zones

UTAH Assault areas

'Green Beach, Red Beach'

First Allied assault waves

Attacks by Allied Commando and airborne units

Areas held by Allies at 2400 Hrs. on D-Day

Line of planned Allied beach-head at 2400 Hrs. on D-Day

RCT Regimental Combat Team

Areas held by German troops at 2400 Hrs. on D-Day

Major German gun batteries

XXI Panzer Corps counterattacks

Railways   Roads

Flooded areas (Prairies Marécageuses)

0   5   10 Miles

0   10   15 Kms

reached the shore. Three others were saved the ordeal by the jamming of the ramp of the landing craft, and were carried in. Thus the 96 tanks planned to provide vital close support for the 1,450 men of eight companies, and the first wave of the engineer teams, in the moment of assault had dwindled by almost a third of their number.

Disaster had also met the attempts to ferry the supporting artillery ashore in DUKWs. The small overloaded craft, almost unmanageable, quickly foundered. The 111th Field Artillery Battalion lost all its 105-mm howitzers save one. The 16th Infantry Cannon Company shared the same fate, and the 7th Field Artillery was very little better. The engineer teams, off-loading their heavy equipment from LCTs to LCMs, also had their troubles and losses. Nevertheless, in the last hour a great concourse of men, guns,

and armour approached the lethal regions of the shallows, their initial losses far less than must have been inflicted by an enemy capable of even a moderate challenge on the sea and in the air. But the sea and air belonged to the Allies. With 40 minutes still to go the powerful bombarding squadron opened fire on the coastal defences with a great armament from the 16-inch guns of the battleships to the 5-inch guns of the destroyers, deluging the line of the bluffs with fire and smoke. At the same time 329 out of the 446 Liberators sent to do the job attacked 13 targets on and about the beaches with more than 1,000 tons of bombs.

The leading assault craft were some 800 yards out when the barrage behind them lifted and the vast uproar muted to the violent staccato sounds of the guns in the close support craft in their wakes.

Overlord began with the paratroop drops: in the west to isolate the Cotentin peninsula by holding the Merderet/Douve line, in the east to shield the left flank by holding the line of the Orne. Despite scattered landings, both objectives were achieved: widely dispersed US paratroops prevented coherent German attacks on the Omaha sector, while the British destroyed the Orne bridges and pinned down the German armoured reserves in the Ranville area. Opposition to the landings varied considerably. On Utah Beach the troops went ashore at 0630 hours with negligible losses, and were off the beaches by 1200 hours. On Omaha, lack of specialised armour allowed very strong defences to hold the troops on the beach and slaughter them. By midnight the deepest penetration was hardly a mile. In the central sector, specialised armour brought

the British and Canadians swiftly over Gold and Juno Beaches and by the afternoon they were probing inland towards Bayeux and Caen. The Sword assault was equally rapid: by 1400 hours leading troops had reached Biéville and the Commandos were linking up with the paratroops. This proved a vital factor, for it was through the gap between Juno and Sword that the Germans made their one major counterattack — a battlegroup of XXI Panzer Division swept towards the coast, but turned back when British reinforcements were flown in to the airborne troops behind it. From the beginning, the main weight of German resistance was on the Allied left flank, and it was there that the German armour was pinned down, fortunately far from the precarious toe-hold at Omaha, which could have turned from a local disaster to a major crisis

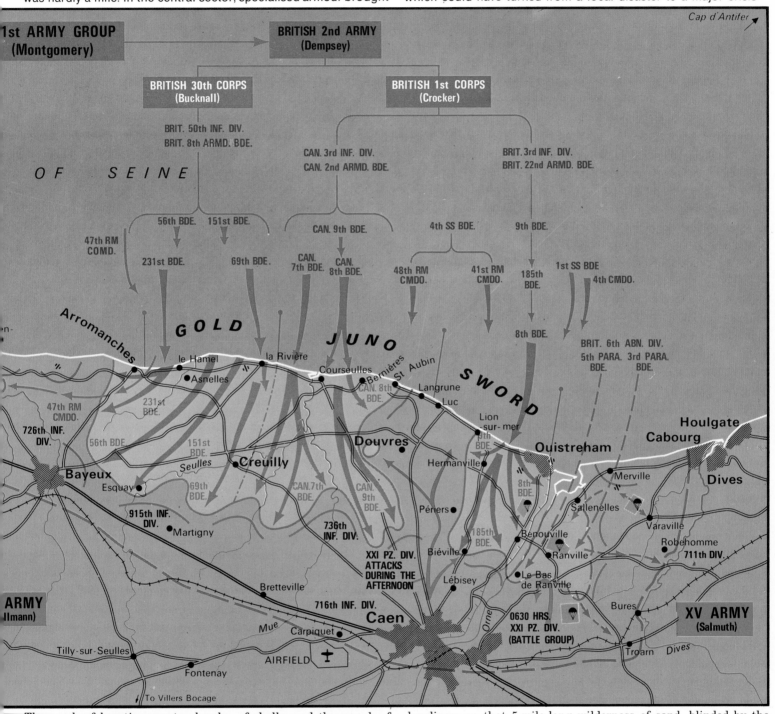

The crash of bursting mortar bombs, of shells, and the smash of machine-gun bullets against the ramps warned the assault troops that the enemy held them in his sights. The cries of men in the water, the sudden searing sheets of flame, the thunderous explosions as craft were hit by enemy shell and mortar fire, caught them up and splintered their isolation to fragments, and the ramps went down.

There is a devastating simplicity about disaster. There were no dry landings. The assault craft, and the larger LCVPs and LCMs grounded on the sandbanks, slewed in the sand runnels, and cast scores of men knee, waist, and neck deep into seas lashed not only by the wind, but by mortar bombs, shells, and machine-gun bullets. While isolated groups waded to the shore, dazed and bewildered by their

loneliness on that 5-mile-long wilderness of sand, blinded by the smoke of many fires raging on the bluffs, uncertain what to do, others, the great majority, were in the midst of infernos of exploding ammunition and engineer charges set off by direct hits. Here and there craft blew up in ferocious ovens of flame.

The LCTs of the 743rd Tank Battalion leading in the van on the right flank surged on with men diving from stricken craft on either side, seeking the shelter of the waves, while others fought for footholds, clawing their ways to the beach, weighed down with equipment, some on hands and knees, others dragging forward on their bellies, with their wounded and their wounds. But it was safer in the sea.

A direct hit on the leading LCT killed all the company officers,

'Do not be daunted
if chaos reigns.
It undoubtedly will'

save one, but eight of the DD tanks landed on the rim of the sea to open fire on the Vierville strongpoint: range 200 yards. The tanks of the 743rd were getting in further east, but the men without armour had little chance. When the ramps of the leading assault craft went down the enemy machine-guns tore through living flesh so that the front cavities of the vessels became in seconds raw wounds, thick with blood. Dozens leaped this way and that for their lives.

Within half-an-hour of H-Hour there were at least 1,000 assault infantry and engineers alive on the beach and in the shallows, but they were not fighting the enemy; they were fighting quite simply for survival, many exhausted, all too weary to drag their equipment across the beach, very few among them able to run, to assault, head-on, the enemy strongpoints.

Some went back to the water, and came in with the tide until at last it brought them, like flotsam, to the meagre shelter of the sea wall or the shingle bank. Very few of those scattered, almost at random, along the length of that beach, and all trained for the specific tasks with which, it was planned, they would be faced, knew where they were. Very few had come in on those 'stages' for which they had rehearsed. Boat teams, organised as fighting units, were miserably scrambled, and often alone, a detachment here, another 200, 300, even 1,000 yards away. For all many of them knew they were alone on the beach known as Omaha. The sea was behind them, and the blinding smoke, saving them from enemy fire in the lucky places, dazed them. The few officers were often slow to get their bearings, or to make up their minds what to do. Few found the leadership in that first hour which alone could have got them off the beach. Above all they were exhausted, and there was no refuge.

The engineer combat teams, coming in on the heels of the assault infantry, had suffered severely on the run-in, losing much of their vital equipment. Direct hits had blown some of their craft to pieces. Of 16 teams, each trained for its special role in its sector, only five came near to their assignments, and of these, three were utterly alone, unprotected by man or gun, naked to the enemy. Within minutes only three bulldozers out of 16 survived for the work of heaving aside the heavy barriers of angle iron and obstacles, and these lost their ability to manoeuvre as men took cover behind them.

Yet despite their crippling losses, and their exposure to the full force of enemy fire, the engineers salvaged what gear they could and strove to clear lanes through which the follow-up forces hoped to pass. Heavy mortar and shell fire detonated chains of fuses painfully laid by hand, and blew up whole detachments of engineers before they could get clear. The swiftly rising tide foamed round their feet, their waists, submerging the outer obstacles, and forcing the survivors to the sea wall and the shingle before their tasks were a tenth-part done. On the whole sector of the 116th RCT they had cleared two gaps. Far to the east, where scarcely a man had landed, they had cleared four gaps, but of them only one was marked. The effort had cost more than 40% of the engineer strength, most of it in the first half-hour.

But always behind the engineers, not only the rising tide, but the tremendous tide of men and vehicles pressed on, steadily wave upon wave, building up on the beaches, in the shallows, demanding an outlet. After three terrible hours the foreshore was a wilderness of wreckage, of burning vehicles, of shattered craft, and shattered men. Not one of the exits from the beach was open, not one of the defensive positions had been stormed, and a message went back to the sea to land no more vehicles, but only men.

Nevertheless, long before the destroyers of the naval force came close inshore to blaze away at the enemy strongpoints at little more than 1,000 yards, a desperate beginning of order was growing out of chaos, and men, tried to the limits of endurance, regained their feet, lifted up their heads, and began to fight for more than their lives. They had paid a terrible price for General Bradley's rejection of the specialised armoured fighting vehicles Montgomery had offered him, for these were the 'tin openers' to Normandy.

Only 100 tons out of 2,400 tons of essential supplies needed on D-Day went ashore. But at last men, reinforced by the waves of the follow-up battalions, were moving off the beaches. It did not look very hopeful to the generals in the command ships, but the hard outer crust of the defence had broken, and the enemy was without reserves. By night-fall the Germans had lost the battle of Omaha Beach, but the Americans did not know that they had won it.

On the eastern flank the British fought their different battles.

AIR DROP IN THE EAST: ALMOST OVERWHELMED

The task of the British 6th Airborne Division was to establish a bridgehead across the Orne river and the Caen Canal, midway between the city of Caen and the Normandy coast, and to protect the eastern flank of the seaborne landings. In its initial stages the task was both complex and of a desperate simplicity; complex because the pieces in the pattern were many, simple because there was no room for finesse, no time. A number of *coups de main* must succeed, and become one simple *tour de force*.

Two parachute brigades would land in the very midst of the enemy, on the boundary of the German VII and XV Armies, seize the vital objectives, and at all costs prevent reinforcements from reaching the main battlefields.

Powerful elements of the German 711th and 716th Divisions defended every village, strongpoint, and bridge; the XXI Panzer Division poised and ready to strike was on their right flank, and behind them the whole weight of the German armoured reserve lay within striking distance. Unless, therefore, the two leading brigades of paratroops could strike their blows like lightning out of the sky, and consolidate, unless they could clear landing places for the glider-borne brigade, and could have with them anti-tank guns, mortars, and the bulk of their heavy equipment, their task would be beyond hope. Whatever might be won by lightning strokes must inevitably be lost, even before the sun was up, and assuredly before the sun was down.

The 5th Parachute Brigade would seize the bridges across the Orne and the Caen Canal north of Ranville, clear and protect landing zones for their gliders, and establish a firm bridgehead.

The 3rd Parachute Brigade would demolish the bridges across the flooded Dives river at Troarn, Bures, Robehomme, and Varaville. They would block and hold all routes leading in from the south-east. They would destroy the powerful Merville battery of 155-mm guns and its garrison before it could enfilade the left flank of the seaborne attack with devastating fire. For this latter task there would be a maximum time of one hour.

It was 2330 hours on the night of the 5th when the first of six Albemarle aircraft of the Pathfinder force took off from their English field with 60 men who must light the beacons to lead the way. At the same hour, six gliders bore a small force of the 2nd Battalion, the Oxford and Bucks Light Infantry, and Royal Engineers to seize crossings of the Caen Canal and the Orne. It was a night of drizzling rain and gusty winds, and lit by tattered patches of moonlight; a night filled with the roar of aircraft, the bombers, the transports, the tugs and their gliders in their thousands teeming through the Channel sky from Le Havre to Cherbourg. Below them the wakes of 5,000 ships cleaving the gun-metal sea into greenish-white trails of foam.

At 0030 hours, the first of the Pathfinders touched down on the soil of France, two-thirds blown awry by the winds, beacons lost, equipment damaged, but enough on their targets to do the vital minimum as best they might. Within minutes the leading glider of the first of the *coup de main* parties crash-landed 47 yards from its objective, overwhelmed the enemy with the sleep still in their eyes, and seized intact the bridges over the Caen Canal and the Orne. Already the enemy tracer looped the sky, and the flak streaming up into the cloud-banks exacted a price in gliders and transports over the coast. A hot reception met the men of the 7th, 12th, and 13th Battalions of the 5th Brigade tumbling out of the cloud-banks. While many landed fighting, at once at grips with the enemy, others hung suspended in the trees, sitting ducks, few to survive.

A flare lighting up the medieval tower of Ranville Church pinpointed the position, and nearly half of the 7th Battalion was able to move swiftly to reinforce the bridgeheads. Civilians, possessed of an awful optimism, both hindered and inspired the British. By 0230 hours, the 7th Battalion was engaged desperately on both banks of the Orne against units of the German 716th Division and two battalions of Feuchtinger's XXI Panzer Division, which had been committed soon after 0100 hours. One company of the 7th, hard pressed at Bénouville, held on, fighting against time, knowing that relief could not reach them until early afternoon, but the colossal detonations of the naval bombardment preceding the seaborne landings brought inspiration.

The 12th Battalion, having seized Le Bas de Ranville, found itself in need of luck as well as inspiration. Its forward platoons, outnumbered twenty to one, faced 88-mm guns firing point blank at 70 yards, and with the breech block of their solitary 6-pounder smashed on landing, their only hope lay in the uncertainty of the enemy, and fortunately this was great. While Blumentritt strove to arouse an adequate sense of urgency in the German High Command, and obtain the release of the armoured reserve, Speidel was advising Rommel of the situation with equal urgency, and receiving orders for the employment of the XXI Panzer Division.

But Feuchtinger had committed a battle group of the XXI Panzer Division on his own initiative soon after 0600 hours. Had this battle group pressed its attack it must have overwhelmed the defenders of Le Bas de Ranville, and greatly restricted the bridgehead. As it was, the confusion in the enemy command, the widespread threats developing over the entire Normandy coast, was the luck the paratroops needed. At about mid-morning the German armour turned its back upon Le Bas de Ranville leaving the battered defenders in possession.

The effects of the struggle in the early hours on the extreme left flank were to have a vital significance in the crises developing on Omaha Beach, for when Feuchtinger was ordered to move his infantry battalions to counterattack the Americans, he was unable to extricate them from their fight with the 5th Parachute Brigade. His anti-tank battalion was also deeply committed in an attempt to save the 716th Infantry Division from the seaborne infantry and armour. Thus no reserves were available to move against 'Omaha' at the vital hour.

In the hours before dawn the enemy was unable to form a clear idea of the forces coming against him out of the sky from end to end of the Cherbourg Peninsula.

Meanwhile the third battalion of the 5th Parachute Brigade, the 13th, had landed well in a tight perimeter, and a strong force had advanced upon Ranville, leaving one company to clear stakes and mines against the coming of the glider-borne reinforcements. But the brigade was very thin on the ground, too many of its men lost in the trees, and many more engaged in a score of local savage encounters, which, in the end, could and did strengthen the position.

When the first of the Commandos fought through from the beach at Ouistreham, reaching the Orne bridgehead only two-and-a-half minutes behind schedule, the small force of the Oxford and Bucks Light Infantry, with the help of the 7th Battalion, had held for 12 hours against powerful counterattacks supported by artillery and mortars. One company, with all its officers killed or wounded, held on without relief for 17 hours. It was 1400 hours when No. 6 Commando crossed the Orne bridge on its way to reinforce the 9th Battalion of the 3rd Parachute Brigade. The Commando had then fought its way through enemy strongpoints, destroyed a battery in full blast against the beaches, and marched 9 miles.

Daring of a high order

It seemed impossible that a coherent pattern could emerge from the complex missions of the 3rd Parachute Brigade, or that seven major tasks, covering a 7-mile front from the town of Troarn, due east of Caen, to the coast at Merville, could be successfully fulfilled. Each demanded daring of a high order, meticulous planning, impeccable timing, and above all the ability to improvise if, as was almost certain, things went wrong.

The Albemarles carrying advance parties with the urgent role of clearing a way for a small glider-borne force with anti-tank guns, dropped their cargoes reasonably near their objective, but the brigadier, wounded and wallowing in the flooded Dives with his HQ, and elements of the 1st and 9th Battalions, did not regain the main body of the brigade before dusk. The 3rd Brigade had a bad drop. The smoke and dust from the heavy bombing of the Merville battery position obscured dropping zones on which many beacons were damaged, and failed to show up. Flak and the strong wind gusts played their parts; gliders parted from their tugs, many were hit, but above all, perhaps, 46 Group in particular had lacked the time for training. Now, on the day, on sea and land, the miserable and bitter battles waged by the Overlord planners for air and sea landing-craft, always denied until the last moment, were reaping a harvest in lives from end to end of the Peninsula.

On the left the Canadians of the 1st Battalion found sufficient strength to press home immediate attacks on their objectives at Varaville and Robehomme. While all kinds and conditions of civilian men, women, and children, including a boy of eleven and a Cockney woman of 55, a native of Camberwell, helped stragglers to rejoin their battalion, the solid nucleus of one company attacked Varaville, destroyed the bridge, and at once became too heavily engaged to extricate itself until late in the morning. Meanwhile a captain of Royal Engineers, with elements of the battalion, blew the Robehomme bridge.

These exploits, performed with satisfactory speed in spite of the chaos predicted by the brigadier, were outshone by a deed of a different order. This was the assault on the Merville Battery position.

The 150-mm guns of Merville were housed in concrete emplacements 6 feet 6 inches thick, reinforced by 12 feet of earthworks, and protected by steel doors. The perimeter fence, lined with a concertina barbed wire barrier 15 feet wide and 5 feet high, enclosed an area of some 400 square yards defended by a garrison of 130 men. At least 20 weapon pits and machine-gun positions were sited to protect every possible avenue of approach through surrounding minefields, and with no cover from fire for attackers over the open fields and orchards. At least one 20-mm dual-purpose gun completed the known armament of a battery which threatened the left flank of the seaborne assault at close range. It was imperative that the Merville guns should be destroyed. Direct hits by heavy bombs had failed to penetrate the casemates, and the naval gunfire, to be directed against the battery if all else failed, could only hope to put the guns out of action by direct hits through the embrasures or up the 'spouts'. Such hits occur by mere chance, and are not to be looked for.

A force of 1,000 Lancasters unloading a deluge of 4,000-pound bombs shortly after midnight failed to hit the target, but killed a number of cattle and provided some deep craters which might be useful cover for the attackers.

In the last four or five minutes of the flight from England, enemy flak forced pilots to take evasive action, and tumbled the battalion commander of the assault force into the garden of a German headquarters. The rest of the force lay scattered over an area ten times as large as it should have been. Yet at 0250 hours the battalion commander had assembled 150 men, one Vickers heavy machine-gun, a bare minimum of signals equipment, and 20 lengths of bangalore torpedo. Jeeps, 6-pounders, mortars, sappers, mine detectors, had all gone astray. With this force, organised in groups 30 strong, each with a special mission, the commander attacked. Within a minute or two of 0430 hours the assault went in. Half an hour later, after a hand to hand mêlée of a desperate and deadly intensity, the success signal blazed out. It had been a fight of gaunt shadow shapes against a spasmodic background of smoke, flame, and violent explosion. One of the battery guns had been destroyed by firing two shells simultaneously, and the other three by gammon bombs. A lieutenant, dying of his wounds, checked the destruction and was added to 66 British dead. Some 30 men were wounded, 20 of them

(Top) Landing ships close in on the
British beaches as fresh waves of tanks
and troops go ashore to consolidate the
beach-head which was already expanding
(Bottom) The scene ashore: burning tanks
of the first waves lie among the obstacles
they had so efficiently overcome

(Top) The bloodbath on Omaha: assault
troops shelter behind beach obstacles
and the few tanks which had managed
to get ashore through the heavy seas
(Bottom) The scene in the British sector:
men fall wounded while a few yards away
others move without any hurry

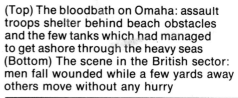

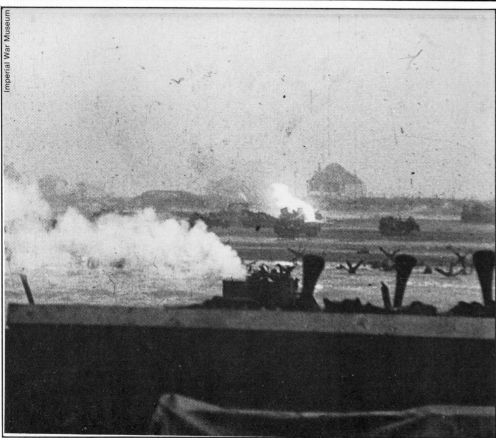

'A sense of chaos on the edge of the sea'

(Top) In some places the British assault troops had to fight their way ashore, in others they cleared the beach swiftly (Bottom) For many, the sea was more deadly than the enemy: survivors of a sunken US landing craft give artificial respiration to a friend

seriously. Not a man of the party was over twenty-one years of age, and few had fought before.

By early evening, the two brigades of the British 6th Airborne Division, anxiously awaiting their glider and seaborne reinforcements, had carried out their tasks, and established bridgeheads across the Caen Canal and the Orne. They had been strengthened by the arrival of the 1st Commando Brigade, and had blocked all roads from the east. Their future—if they were to have a future—must depend on the success or failure of the British 3rd Infantry Division, spearheading the left flank assault on the beaches.

By evening it had become clear that the advance out of the beachhead was too slow. Infantry had dug in too soon, when they should have pressed on. Traffic jams building up on the beach prevented the British from shaking loose until early afternoon, and Feuchtinger's armour, at last with its orders, was driving down, nearly 90 tanks strong, to the sea at Lion-sur-Mer. Nevertheless, the diversion of the German armour to meet the major threat of the British landing had saved the airborne from being overwhelmed.

SWORD BEACH: HITLER WAKES UP

The battle for the Orne bridgehead was already six hours old when Hobart's armour led the British and Canadian seaborne assaults to the rock-enclosed strips of beach fronting Ouistreham and Lion-sur-Mer, Langrune and Courseulles, la Rivière and le Hamel. Far away on the right, beyond the outcropping rocks of Port-en-Bessin, the Americans had suffered for a full hour under the guns of the enemy strongpoints on the long bare stretch of Omaha. The hopes of surprise in the east had seeped away, but it appeared to make no difference to an enemy hammered from the sea and sky.

A smoke screen veiled the whole British left flank from the powerful guns of the Le Havre batteries, which had withstood a hundred batterings from the air, and were a graver menace than the rough sea to the convoys assembling $7\frac{1}{2}$ miles offshore, and putting their hordes of small craft into the water. Enemy E-boats, choosing their moment to venture out of Le Havre, emerged momentarily from the smoke to discharge four torpedoes, one to sink a Norwegian destroyer, another to force the command ship, HMS *Largs,* full astern in evasive action, the remaining two to pass harmlessly between the warships.

Torrents of bombardment from the air soon after dawn were followed by greater bombardments from the sea, concentrating an enormous weight of metal and explosive upon the narrow coastal strips, the grey lines of buildings protruding like desolate crusts out of the mists of smoke and flame which tore the amphitheatres to shreds. The helmsman of an assault craft was seen to be hanging out over the stern acting as a human rudder. Men floundered to death by drowning; the assault and landing craft surged on, as if borne on the screaming, crashing ferocity of their own gun craft, which blazed away with 4·7s, rockets, Oerlikons, and machine-guns, while the armour and field artillery went into action from their carrying craft. Mines, mortar bombs, and shells erupted small craft out of the water to fill air and sea with falling wreckage; explosions tore the entrails out of larger vessels, and leapt into furnaces in which, miraculously, men survived.

The high wind was piling the rising tide above the outer belts of obstacles, and there was nothing for it but to ride in, attempting to navigate the lethal forest of angle iron, stakes, and steel, and crash down in the foam of waves breaking on the shore.

H-Hour was 0730 hours, with the armour leading in at H−5. Force S for Sword had put its DD tanks into the water 3 miles out, and it was clear that only fine seamanship on the part of their crews, the 13/18th Hussars, would bring them in on time, or at all. Low in the water, beaten by waves 4 feet high, the grey upper works were almost invisible, and a line of tank landing craft cutting across their bows sank two, and might have swamped a score but for a mattress of rockets falling short, and forcing the tank landing craft to alter course.

When the bombardment of the warships began to lift, the shore approaches were a turmoil of weaving craft and wreckage, and almost to the minute the flail tanks crawled on shore in the lead, eight assault teams, beating up towards the beach exits, engaging enemy guns point blank, followed by the whole strange 'menagerie' of armoured monsters, the bridging tanks, the bobbins, the petards, and 33 out of 40 DD tanks crawling up out of the water in time to shoot the infantry over the hazardous stretch of beach.

Within minutes, the wreckage of armour added a grotesque dimension to the inferno. A flail, losing its tracks, continued to engage an enemy 88, another brewed, a bridging tank lost its bridge, and somewhere a DD tank foundered in a bewildering mass of steel. Sappers leaving their armoured vehicles pressed on, clearing by hand. Men leapt from blazing craft in the shallows, and struggled

If the men could hurl themselves off the beaches they must win. There was no other place to stop them. . .

A tremendous tide
of men and vehicles pressing on,
steadily wave upon wave,
building up on the beaches,
in the shallows, demanding an outlet

towards the beach through the crumpled ruins of men and equipment.

On the right, the 1st Battalion of the South Lancashire Regiment, spearheading the 8th Infantry Brigade, quickly cleared the beach in the wake of the armour, and began to assault the strongpoints. The 2nd Battalion, the East Yorkshire Regiment, their brothers-in-arms on the left, fought their way more slowly to a foothold. Over all the beach, left and right, enemy mortar and small-arms fire was intense, thickened by the anti-tank guns sited on Périers Ridge, and the divisional artillery ranging on the barrage balloons.

Order out of chaos

Out of the seeming chaos and confusion, and the increasing wreckage on the beach, the threads of order began to emerge. By 0930 hours, Hobart's armour – manned by the 22nd Dragoons, the Westminster Dragoons, and two squadrons of the 5th Assault Regiment, Royal Engineers – had cleared seven out of the eight lanes through the exits. At La Riva Farm, the squadrons were rallying, some to aid Commando troops fighting for possession of the Ouistreham Locks, and for Lion-sur-Mer, others making ready to spearhead the infantry on the road to Caen.

The South Lancashires reached Hermanville in good time, one-and-a-half miles inland, confronting the vital Périers Ridge, bristling with Feuchtinger's anti-tank guns and defended by infantry of the 716th Division. But the 8th Infantry Brigade had lost its vital momentum. Enemy guns broke up armoured sorties, and the infantry dug in at Hermanville.

Meanwhile, by 1100, the 185th Brigade was assembling its three battalions in the orchards beyond Hermanville, and an immediate attack should have been pressed home against the Périers Ridge, not only to open the road to Caen, but for the urgent relief of the Orne bridgehead. Where Commando troops had marched boldly through, the infantry, dourly led, performed its slow set-piece gyrations.

A contributory cause of the slowness in front was, however, the growing mass of men and armour, striving to break loose from the beaches, and the impossible tangles of traffic in the narrow streets, the laterals, and leads out of the exits. The tanks of the Staffordshire Yeomanry, with the role of carrying the men of the King's Shropshire Light Infantry on the road to Caen, could not be prised loose from the mêlée. It was late when the guns of the Périers Ridge were silenced, and the Shropshires took the road alone.

The infantry of the line did all that its leaders demanded of it, but it was not enough. The East Yorkshires had taken a severe hammering, losing five officers and 60 men killed, and more than 140 wounded, in gaining their objectives. The Shropshires on the lonely road out of Hermanville were marching boldly into the midst of the enemy, their flanks bare. At 1600 hours, the battalion, joined by the self-propelled guns and armour of the Staffordshire Yeomanry, reached Biéville, barely 3½ miles short of Caen.

It was, in fact, a position of extreme difficulty, for at last Feuchtinger had his clear orders, Rommel was speeding on his way to his command, Hitler had awakened from the effects of his sleeping pills, and the German armour was on the move. At Biéville 24 tanks leading a powerful battle group of the XXI Panzer Division, probing for a crevice in the British assault, clashed head-on with the Shropshires and their armour. Self-propelled guns accounted for five enemy tanks, and the enemy withdrew. In spite of the armoured threats the Shropshires strove to press on, only to be halted by intense fire from the thickly wooded Lébisey Ridge. Casualties were growing steadily; a renewed armoured attack might develop at any moment, and the flanking battalions of the 185th Brigade were making very slow progress. Caen was a fading dream.

But Feuchtinger's armour was not coming that way again. The British, now in command of the Périers Ridge, had pushed the battle group further west, and the spearhead, bouncing off the Shropshires, and again off the British guns, was pounding northward down the wide gap between the British and Canadian landings, 90 tanks strong. There was nothing to stop them.

GOLD BEACH: HOBART'S SPEARHEAD WORKS

The main weight of the British seaborne assault fell on the right, on the beach code-named Gold, a shallow arc streaked with treacherous strands of soft clay, and behind that to the west the powerful strongpoints and fortified villages of Arromanches and le Hamel, and to the east, la Rivière.

It was 0725 hours when the leading flotillas carrying the flail tanks and armoured fighting vehicles of the Westminster Dragoons and the 81st and 82nd Assault Squadrons, Royal Engineers, closed the beaches of le Hamel and la Rivière. It was at once clear that the heavy air and naval bombardment had failed to silence the enemy guns, especially on the right. Only one of the flails serving the 231st Brigade's right flank succeeded in beating a lane up and off the beach, while in its wake others foundered, losing their tracks to mines and heavy machine-gun fire. On-coming craft, driven like surf boats by the strong wind and heavy seas, fouled obstacles and armour, creating a sense of chaos on the edge of the sea.

The squadron commander of the right flanking teams was killed at the outset in the turret of his AVRE, but many armoured vehicles, temporarily unable to crawl, engaged the enemy with their main armament, and were a valuable cover. But further to the east, beyond the immediate beaten zone of fire from the le Hamel strongpoints, the three assault teams serving the left flank of the brigade made good progress. While flails lashed the beach, lumbering on in the midst of eruptions of mines, mud, and sand, to gain the coast road, the bobbins laid mattresses over patches of soft blue clay, and fascine bridging tanks crawled over the beach with their huge unwieldy burdens, finally to fill craters, to make anti-tank barriers crossable, to pave the way for infantry, armour, and the great mass of vehicles bearing down, with a pressure impossible to deny, upon the beaches.

The DD tanks, finding the sea passage to the beach hopeless under their own power in the rough conditions, had been held back, later to beach dry shod, and add greatly to the early armoured firepower. Meanwhile, the spearhead role belonged to the flails and their supporting AVREs.

Well within the hour Hobart's armour had emerged from the turmoil of the water's edge and cleared four safe lanes out of six over the le Hamel beaches, and spearheaded the leading battalions of the 231st Brigade on to their objectives. Petard tanks all along the line were dealing out murderous treatment to fortified houses and strongpoints which would have tied up infantry platoons and companies, perhaps for hours, and taken a steady toll in dead.

On the 69th Brigade front facing la Rivière the flails and AVREs of the assault teams fought their way with infantry across the beaches in the face of intense mortar, anti-tank, and machine-gun fire directed from well-sited pillboxes, and houses linked together in systems of strongpoints. Three clear lanes were opened out of six from the edge of the sea to the edge of the marshland beyond the coast road. While petard tanks supporting the infantry blasted the coastal crust of strongpoints with their giant mortars, like ancient cannon, AVREs filled craters and anti-tank ditches with fascines, provided soft landings for armour behind walls, bridged culverts, and bulldozed tracks for the host of vehicles and men coming in fast on the rising tide. Within the hour armour and infantry were more than a mile inland, and the hard outer crust of the defence was broken.

Saved by the 'specials'

On the right flank of le Hamel there might have been a 'little Omaha' but for Hobart's armour. The 1st Battalion of the Hampshire Regiment, leading on the right flank, had had an uneasy passage. For them the sea-sick pills had not worked. They debouched from their assault craft 30 yards out into waves beating about their thighs and dragging at their feet as they struggled to dry sand. If they were grateful for anything it was simply that the movement of the sea had stilled, no longer to rack their guts with sickness. They had come in supported by self-propelled guns and field artillery firing from their carrying craft, aware of mortar and machine-gun fire from the enemy over the last half-mile. It had been uncomfortable rather than deadly. Smoke and flame obscured the beaches, but it seemed that the terrific bombing, followed by the naval bombardment, had failed to silence the enemy.

On the beach, in their first moments of comparative immunity before they came within the traverse of the le Hamel guns, they saw only the confusion of disabled armour, and swiftly discovered that for two-thirds of their numbers there were no safe lanes across the shambles of the beach. An immense weight of fire stopped them in their tracks as they strove to move up the beach, and no gunfire from the sea could bring them aid. With their battalion commander twice wounded and forced out of action, their second-in-command soon killed, there was nothing for it but to abandon the direct approach. Moving east the left flanking companies of the battalion gained les Roquettes, an objective of the 1st Dorsets on their left, and then swung right handed, seized Asnelles-sur-mer, and prepared to assault the le Hamel sanatorium. But it was afternoon before the sanatorium, resisting all infantry attacks, finally caved in to the devastating 'dustbins' of a petard, not the least of Hobart's 'specials'.

Meanwhile the 1st Dorsets, out of reach of the le Hamel guns, had stormed over the beach, covered by the guns of the 'specials', and swung right handed to gain the slight rise of Arromanches.

On the beach of la Rivière the 5th Battalion of the East Yorkshire Regiment and the 6th Battalion the Green Howards, leading the assault of the 69th Brigade, were in no doubt about the value of the armour. From the first, infantry and armour, greatly aided by close-support fire from gun craft, stormed the beach defences in complete co-ordination, and fought a tight battle through the streets, eliminating 88s and pillboxes, cutting out the enemy like a canker, and moving inland. Things had been bad, but not bad enough to curb their momentum on landing, and if men could hurl themselves over the first obstacle of the beach they must win. There was no other place to stop them but in the shallows and on the beaches.

By 1100 hours, seven lanes had been cleared on Gold Beach, the DD tanks were moving fast inland, and with them the 56th and 151st Brigades, carving out the centre, keeping the enemy off balance at all costs. Long before the le Hamel sanatorium had fallen the bridgehead was 3 miles in depth, the 56th Brigade was going well astride the la Rivière-Bayeux road, the 151st, on its left, racing for the high ground, and beyond into the Seulles valley, while left again the 69th pressed on for Creully. Even the right flank, delayed at le Hamel, had cut the Arromanches-Bayeux road, while the 47th Royal Marine Commando was working round to assault Port-en-Bessin.

The Commando had outstripped them all. Coming in to land west of le Hamel they had come under fire from the cliffs and lost four out of their 14 assault craft. Finally, forced eastward, they had run in east of the le Hamel position, hoping to find the way cleared ahead. It wasn't. They had had to fight their way through the coastal villages, each man humping 88 pounds of equipment, and covering 10 miles by early afternoon. By the time the 231st Brigade began to ease their sense of isolation they were occupying the high ground south of Port-en-Bessin. No men on their feet had done more.

JUNO BEACH: SOLID FOOTHOLD

By the time the Canadians stormed ashore with two brigades up astride the Seulles estuary, and raced for the sea walls, the rising tide had reduced the gauntlet of the beaches to as little as 100 yards at the narrowest point, and the battles of the beaches on the flanks were already from one to two hours old. The Canadians had no intention of being left behind.

The Canadian 7th Brigade, the Royal Winnipeg Regiment and the Regina Rifles leading, came in on the right, west of the Seulles river, beating the Canadian 8th Brigade to the beach by a minute or two. With them were eight, possibly ten, DD tanks manned by the Canadian 1st Hussars. The tanks had taken to the water 800 yards

out, threatened by the turbulent sea, in constant danger of swamping, threading their ways through a maze of scantlings jutting out of the water like the stumps of some petrified forest.

On the left, the Queen's Own Regiment of Canada and the North Shore Regiment led the Canadian 8th Brigade without armour, and raced for the sea wall, the heavy machine-guns of the enemy cutting swathes out of the Queen's Own in the 30 seconds or so it took them to reach the shelter of the wall. The landing craft carrying the assault armour of the engineers were still battling with the heavy seas and obstacles, and the DD tanks were coming in to land dry-shod when the spearhead infantry were well away, blasting the enemy out of Courselles and Bernières, and pressing on. When the Régiment de la Chaudière came in 15 minutes later there was scarcely a shot.

The Canadian battalions were borne in on a rough sea driven by the wind which flung them onto the beaches, and in one bound across them. The dangerous reefs and rocks of that narrow coast forced the assault craft to wait for the tide, and when at last they were clear of the reefs the larger craft had to charge the obstacles, hoping for the best, while the small craft strove to swerve and weave through tangles of angle iron and stakes. At one point 20 out of 24 assault craft blew up, and men struggled for the shore with the splinters of their landing craft falling from the skies about their ears. According to the record, 'chunks of débris rose a hundred feet in the air and troops, now hugging the shelter of a breakwater, were peppered with pieces of wood'.

Driven by the wind, the rapidly rising tide piling up the heavy surf, the helmsmen of the assault craft could only hang on and pray. The first three craft coming in on the Canadian left blew up, but their entire complement, save two killed, struggled out of the débris and water to make the beach and fight.

There were many brave men manning the landing craft all along the line from Sword to Utah, men fighting lone battles against outbreaks of fire and exploding ammunition, one man at least, a man named Jones, saving wounded from drowning in a flooded hold and amputating two horribly mangled legs. He was no doctor, merely a sick-berth attendant, but he did the job. And there were scores of 'Joneses' at sea that day off the beaches, but none had a struggle as grim as that of the men who carried the Canadians ashore on Juno.

The LCOCU (landing craft obstacle clearance units) of the naval demolition teams, and the beach units, striving to sort out the horrible muddle of mined obstacles, machines, and men, were under shell fire from enemy corps and divisional artillery long after the last mortar, machine-gun, and 88 of the beach defences, even the last sniper, had been silenced. Bulldozers not only bulldozed débris out of the way, but bulldozed beached craft back into the sea, giving them a start on the way back.

When the engineer assault armour of the 22nd Dragoons and the 26th Assault Squadron, Royal Engineers, reached the beach on the Canadian 7th Brigade front, the DD tanks which had landed with the infantry had settled the score with the worst of the enemy strong-points mounting the 75-mm guns and the heavy mortars and machine-guns, but there was plenty of mortar and automatic fire coming in from a bit further back. The flails were urgently needed to carve clear lanes through to the exits for the mass of armour and vehicles building up, and the petards and bridging tanks lumbered up behind them, to keep the infantry going at high pressure.

East of the Seulles the going was good, and on both sides of the river the flails had opened the exits before 0930 hours, the fascines and bridging tanks had bridged the worst of the craters and culverts, and opened the sluices of the Seulles to drain a crater as large as a village pond, and twice as deep.

On the left at Bernières, flails and petards had smashed exits through the 12-foot-high sea wall, and cleared lanes and laterals well in time to work in with the infantry against the pillboxes and strongpoints. Before noon on the right flank the flails were advancing inland under command of the Canadian 2nd Armoured Brigade.

Twelve lanes were cleared that day on the Juno beaches by

US troops begin to move off Utah Beach: by nightfall their beach-head was secure with 20,000 men ashore, and the leading units moving towards the areas held by the paratroops

On Omaha Beach there was no security: troops were still held on the beach—the deepest penetration was hardly a mile—and a determined counterattack could have swept them away

Hobart's armour, and the exits linked right through to join the brigade fronts. The DD tanks, beaching dry shod an hour behind the infantry, were swiftly off the beach, adding their firepower to the men storming on inland to keep the enemy off balance and not giving him a chance to form a second line. By late afternoon the Canadian 7th Brigade was challenging the 69th Brigade of '50 Div' for the lead, its armoured patrols probing for the main Bayeux-Caen road at Bretteville, while on the left, the Canadian 9th Brigade, breaking loose from the chaos and confusion on the beach, was through the 8th Brigade, and going well astride the Courselles road to Caen.

The centre bridgehead from Langrune to Arromanches was solid, 12 miles wide and growing deeper every hour. The bottleneck was behind, in the congestion of the narrow beach, the struggle of armour, vehicles, and men, to break loose from the appalling traffic jams. And on the right, there was the growing awareness of an ominous gap, the dangerous toe-hold of Omaha, the Americans inching slowly off the beach, their progress measured in yards.

Whatever happened the enemy reserves must be prevented from reaching Omaha, and it was this above all which made Dempsey pause, ready to reach out a helping hand, holding back his armour.

THE END OF THE DAY

It was late afternoon before the German High Command began to emerge from confusion. The lack of air reconnaissance, the blocking of radar, the dislocation of communications of every kind, had reduced observation almost to the eyes and ears of men. Reports could not be quickly confirmed, or information co-ordinated. Uncertainty inhibited the violent counterblows which alone could have driven the British and Americans back into the sea. And the instrument was lacking. The I Panzer Corps lay west of the Seine, immobilised, awaiting the decision of the Führer.

Field-Marshal Rommel had been right about the first 24 hours: they would be decisive. He had made repeated efforts to move the XII SS Panzer and the Panzer Lehr Divisions on a line St Lô-Carentan. Had these divisions been there, the Omaha beach-head must have been smashed; even had Rommel himself been there on the day, able perhaps to rouse Hitler out of his early morning dreams, it might not have been too late. It was too late when Hitler held his

afternoon conference, and released the XII SS Panzer Division.

All that could be done against the Allied air and seaborne assaults had been done by the forces immediately available. Feuchtinger, commanding the XXI Panzer Division, the only counterattacking force within reach, had reacted swiftly against the British airborne landings on the Orne, according to his standing orders. But at once there followed a long period of uncertainty, due partly to a breakdown in communications. When at last the division was put under command of the 84th Corps, General Marcks, the corps commander, was right in his appreciation that the British 3rd Division was the more potent threat, and that Caen must be at once powerfully screened. Nevertheless, too much time had been wasted, and he might have done better to commit the division against the airborne bridgehead. Had that been done the great glider-borne force might have arrived to a terrible reception.

As it was, Feuchtinger could not disengage his infantry battalions from the British, nor his anti-tank guns from the German 716th Division. He had been shot away from the Périers Ridge by British guns when he might have shot the British armour out of the way with his own guns—if he had had any.

But XXI Panzer Division did very well in view of its difficulties. Had they not taken fright at the impressive spectacle of 250 airtugs towing their gliders full of reinforcements for the airborne divisions on their flank, and at the evening sky black with the fighter escorts, the battle group, powerfully and swiftly reinforced, might have disrupted the British right flank on Sword Beach, and driven a dangerous wedge between the British and Canadians, down to the sea. Instead it withdrew to take up a position to the north of Caen. There was no second chance.

But it is unlikely that the XXI Panzer could have prevailed, even the first time. Air power had done its work for the Allies, sealing off the battlefield, holding the ring, denying mobility to the reserves, making of each day a hideous nightmare, and of each night a tortured crawling progress. Of the more than 11,000 sorties flown by the Allied air forces on June 6, not one single aircraft was lost to the Luftwaffe. Air superiority, it has been estimated by some staff authorities, multiplies superiority on the ground by three. On D-Day, Allied air power was overwhelming, and decisive.

The pattern of the Battle for Normandy was beginning to set

'Then, out of all the confusion, a certain desperate order began to emerge'

The British prepare to move off Sword Beach: by noon units were probing inland to Bénouville and Ranville, and during the afternoon the one serious German counterattack was neutralised

Bottlenecks in the coastal villages delayed the British advance out of Gold, and many units dug in too soon – but the German armoured reserve was pinned down far from vulnerable Omaha

United Press

by the end of the first day, with the British and Canadians thickening a stout shoulder on the left, holding off the entire enemy armoured reserve, while the Americans made ready to exploit the open right flank. If – if that right flank could have been smashed at the outset, vulnerable, almost defenceless, on the long beach of Omaha, then a terrible, nagging battle of attrition might have gone on and on, the British bridgehead virtually sealed off. But the 6th Airborne, and then the British 3rd Division, and then the Canadian 3rd Division, had made that 'if' impossible. General Bradley may have feared a German counterattack, but General Kraiss, commanding the German 352nd Division, knew that counterattack was impossible.

And the maintenance of an 'open right flank' was essential to Allied victory. That was the point and purpose of General Montgomery's strategy, and by the end of the day he knew that he would win; that he would impose his will on the shape of the Battle for Normandy. He didn't care much for 'phase lines' and estimates of progress. He was concerned with the end result.

Meanwhile, by taking a chance, Rundstedt had dared to move a powerful force of the XII SS Panzer Division to Lisieux, and as soon as the release order came through from the High Command, this group, under Kurt Meyer, was ordered at once to the battlefield. By midnight, constantly harassed and desperately short of fuel, it reached Evrecy, 9 miles south-west of Caen, to find its petrol dumps a burned-out ruin. When it was able to move it had to counter a powerful Canadian threat, for it was opposite the line of advance from Juno Beach. Thereafter, the British and Canadian 3rd Divisions absorbed its offensive power, and sapped its defensive strength.

The Panzer Lehr Division was nowhere near the battlefield on D-Day; or the day after.

'As a result of the D-Day operations a foothold has been gained on the continent of Europe,' General Montgomery was able to report.

For General Bradley, commanding the US 1st Army, it must have been a night of grave anxieties, even – but there is no evidence – of some self-questioning. For General Dempsey, commanding the British 2nd Army, there was cause for some satisfaction, but not for jubilation. Dempsey, of whom very little has ever been written, is a quiet, gentle man, a good strategist and a sound tactician. He confined himself absolutely, and with a remarkable devotion, to his work of soldiering. On that night of June 6, Dempsey knew that his

army had done enough. It was a good army, perhaps the last real 'army' Britain would ever produce. The dreams had faded; as they had been almost sure to fade. The vital momentum which might – might – have carried the Canadians and the British into the open country beyond Caen was never there. Beyond the Caen-Bayeux road there was no open country, only the bocage, the close-hedged, deep-ditched fields, the narrow lanes, the steep wooded valleys. The real open country had never been truly 'in the sights'. Perhaps it did not matter. The pattern of the struggle would have been different, but not necessarily more favourable to the Allies.

The bottlenecks, checking the forward troops, dragging at them, were the beaches, the coastal villages, the narrow exits and lateral roads choked with vehicles and armour, and behind the beaches the sea, rough, unpredictable.

The first of the landing craft, turning about, had reached the hards of England, the small ports, the estuaries, in the afternoon, swiftly replenishing ammunition, stores, men, cleaning and greasing the guns, setting forth a second time through the great maze of shipping. Through all the day and night the Mulberry tows were breaking loose, the tugs fighting scores of desperate battles with hawsers, winches, and chains, clawing at the huge unwieldy objects they sought to drag through the seas. Some 40% of the 'Whale' units broke away and were lost. But it would go on, and on.

It was a strange day and night on and off the beaches. Men clung marooned to obstacles and debris, on rocks, on the tops of drowned vehicles, while naval and small craft, DUKWS and outboard motors, buzzed and weaved about their business, impervious to croaking cries for help, and to the full-blooded curses of frustrated, angry, frightened men. Many of those picked up by craft on the 'turn-about' were carried straight back to England whether they liked it or not. There were a good many men wandering about for days in Normandy trying to find their units.

There was not much chance to rest in the bridgehead. The smoke rose from the burned-out houses lining the battered sea fronts from Ouistreham to Arromanches, and beyond to the desolation of Omaha and the isolation of Utah, the dunes of Varreville. In the midst of the monstrous chaos of the beaches, in the jungles of shattered craft, tank tracks, wheels, and twisted masses of iron and steel, the bodies of men lay under gas capes, awaiting burial.

Rommel had been right about the first 24 hours: they were indeed decisive. . . .

US Army

At Sallenelles on the left, in the 3-mile gap between Sword and Juno, and in the chasm between Gold and Omaha, there was no rest. The airborne and the Commandos were having a rugged time. Yet some lay in the meadows, and wrote home about 'butterflies' and 'bird song', which seemed the oddest things of all in the day.

Morale was high. To most of those not 'in contact', and not 'fighting' – and a minority is 'in contact' doing any 'fighting' – it seemed an anti-climax. One man called it 'a crashing anti-climax'. In a sense it was an anti-climax not to be dead, after so much waiting, training, thinking, and expecting 'God knew what'.

Some thought that the French were warm and friendly, others that they were suspicious and unfriendly, still others that they were indifferent. Many were startled by the extreme youth, or age, of the captured enemy and inclined to believe that it was going to be, what they called in those days, 'a piece of cake'. But the men who had charged the strongpoints, and gone into the cellars behind grenades, knew better. The German 716th Division had been cut to pieces, but its isolated 'bits' fought on.

The men, above all, who felt themselves to be 'out on a limb' that night were the US 82nd Airborne, holding on in Ste Mère-Église and with the 101st in scores of tiny 'pockets', wondering when their small seaborne 'attachment' was going to catch up. They didn't realise that many of their small bits and pieces would presently come together and give a much greater length and depth to the Utah bridgehead than it looked.

But the Utah bridgehead was sound. The entire 4th Division was on shore well before midnight, and much more besides, 20,000 men and 1,700 vehicles in round figures. The two leading regiments had lost twelve men killed between them. General Collins, the corps commander, was far more worried about the possible actions – or lack of actions – of Admiral Moon, than about the bridgehead. The General wanted to go on shore, but he dared not leave the *Bayfield*. The Admiral, worrying about his losses, wanted to suspend landing operations through the night.

General Gerow, commanding the US 5th Corps, with no such sea cares, but with plenty on shore, had set up his command post on the bluffs of that desolate stretch of coast. There were 'no rear areas on Omaha' that night, according to the record, no comfort, no feeling of security. Enemy were still firing from beach positions, sniping al night, and all through the next day. Barely 100 tons of supplies had come on shore, and the men were hungry, weary, hanging on grimly short of ammunition, sleep, short of most things. At the deepest poin the penetration on Omaha was not much more than 1,500 yards and there wasn't a line, not even the planned 'Beach Maintenance Line'. It was a miracle that they had gained a foothold, but they had Men without armour.

No one may ever know what General Bradley thought about it Why had he refused the flails, the petards, and all the rest of Hobart's armour? Chester Wilmot believed that it was Bradley's contempt for British 'under confidence and over-insurance'. Captain Sir Basi Liddell Hart summed up: 'Analysis makes it clear that the America troops paid dearly for their higher commander's hesitation to accep Montgomery's earlier offer to give them a share of Hobart's special ised armour.'

And the Supreme Commander's report states:
Apart from the factor of tactical surprise, the comparatively ligh casualties which we sustained on all beaches, except 'Omaha', were i large measure due to the success of the novel mechanical contri vances which we employed and to the staggering moral and materia effect of the mass of armour landed in the leading waves of the assault It is doubtful if the assault forces could have firmly established them selves without the assistance of these weapons.

The cost of the day in killed was not more than 2,500 men, 1,00(of them on Omaha Beach. At Towton Field, on 29th March, 1461 33,000 men perished by the sword and were buried there. Nearly 20,000 British troops were killed on the first day of the Battle o the Somme in 1916. War had become a battle of machines agains machines. Tens of thousands of tons of explosive, of copper, tungsten bronze, iron, steel, bombs, bricks, mortar, concrete, guns, tanks vehicles, ships, all 'blown to smithereens'. Bridges, railways, dumps factories and whole towns were flattened to rubble. It was a war for bulldozers.

And presently the men controlling the bombers sensed their power, making it almost impossible for men on their feet to get through. It will be an unhappy day for the world when men on their feet cannot get through.

BATTLE OF THE BULGE: THE ONSLAUGHT

**Ardennes, Belgium
December 16/19, 1944**

By early December 1944, Hitler had achieved a near-impossible: out of the armies which had fought, lost, and disintegrated in Normandy, France, Belgium, and the approaches to the German frontier, he had built up a new army group on the Western Front. What was more, this new force was intended not merely to hold the front, but to hurl itself on the weakest American sector, sweep westward to the Meuse as in 1940, and reach the Channel in one of the most daring armoured counteroffensives in history. The onslaught was the heaviest Panzer attack ever seen on the Western Front, and its success depended on the strictest adherence to a taut timetable of vital objectives. This is the story of how the disorganised and often panic-stricken American defenders met the full fury of what soon became known as the 'Battle of the Bulge'.

Right: German soldiers advance on the first day of the Ardennes offensive

As early as August 19, 1944, just after the successful Allied landings on the Mediterranean coast of France and on the actual day that almost the last of the German armour in the West was destroyed in the Falaise pocket, Hitler issued the following order: 'Prepare to take the offensive in November . . . some 25 divisions must be moved to the Western Front in the next one to two months.'

But how? Where, after the gigantic losses of men and material, could Germany find 25 divisions? The Führer's generals told him it would be a miracle if the Wehrmacht could replace half its losses; to create a whole new army group was impossible. Hitler replied that he would once again show them how to achieve the impossible.

For the first time Germany was put on a total war footing. Dr Goebbels was given dictatorial powers to increase war production and direct men into the army. The call-up age was lowered to 16, and no one escaped the scraping of the manpower barrel: non-essential workers, small shopkeepers, civil servants, university students, officer candidates in training, men formerly listed as unfit, prisoners from the jails—all were sucked into the great maw. Despite the heavy bombing, German war production actually increased to all-time records. After six to eight weeks' concentrated training, these new soldiers, *Volksgrenadiers* (People's Infantry), were equipped and ready to go into the line; and by the beginning of November Hitler had, to the amazement of his generals, replaced his lost mobile reserve and sent 18 new divisions to the West.

The problem of where to mount his great offensive occupied a lot of Hitler's thinking, but one area had long attracted him—the heavily wooded hills where Luxembourg, Belgium, and Germany meet, known in Germany as the Eifel and in Belgium and Luxembourg as the Ardennes. It was an historic German invasion route, the scene of his great success in 1940. And—miraculously—it was the weakest-held section of the entire 450 miles of the Western Front.

That fact was decisive: once again it would be the Ardennes.

This time Hitler planned everything himself and although, for the sake of morale, the old but still much respected Field-Marshal Gerd von Rundstedt was persuaded to come out of retirement and assume nominal command, the Führer actually directed the battle from a new headquarters in the West.

Three armies—two armoured and one infantry—were joined to make Army Group B, commanded by Field-Marshal Model, an aggressive attacker and master of improvisation, who had prevented total defeat on the Eastern Front three times. The VI SS Panzer Army, which would spearhead the attack, was given to one of Hitler's oldest comrades, Josef 'Sepp' Dietrich, ex-sergeant-major in the regular German army, the Führer's personal bodyguard in the early street-brawling days of the Nazi Party, and former commander of the famous I SS Panzer Division, 'Leibstandarte Adolf Hitler' (Hitler's Bodyguard).

Moving alongside VI SS Panzer Army and adding weight to the left hook would be V Panzer Army commanded by another of Hitler's 'fighting generals' from the Eastern Front, Hasso von Manteuffel. The important task of throwing up a wall to cover the southern flank of the attack was given to the German VII Army commanded

by Erich Brandenberger, a general of the old school, unimaginative but dogged.

Hitler also decided to use the shattered German Parachute Corps once more to seize important crossroads behind the American lines and hold them open for his beloved SS Panzer divisions, and Colonel von der Heydte, a veteran of Crete, was ordered to get a force together. Also the Führer had one of his famous unorthodox ideas and sent for Otto Skorzeny, the man who had 'rescued' Mussolini. Skorzeny was ordered to train special units of German commandos dressed in Allied uniforms who would travel in captured vehicles ahead of the main force to seize bridges over the Meuse, the first big obstacle, and, as well, cause chaos behind the American lines by giving false orders, upsetting communications, and spreading rumours of great German successes.

An 85-mile sector of the front from Monschau in the north to Echternach in the south was chosen for the breakthrough. After a tremendous opening barrage, infantry in overwhelming strength would breach the American line in a dozen places through which the Panzers would pour in a classic Blitzkrieg, racing for the Meuse crossings before the Allies could regain their balance.

Once across the Meuse the second phase of the offensive, a double-pronged drive northwest to Antwerp, would begin. Army Group B's attack would be supported by one from General Student's XV Army in Holland, and when Antwerp and the Scheldt estuary had been taken the Allied forces in Europe would be cut in two and their four armies in the north—US 9th, US 1st, British 2nd, and Canadian 1st—could be destroyed. Then, Hitler thought, the Western Allies would be ready to make a separate peace, and Germany could switch all her forces to the East.

The German commanders in the field protested that the plan was far too ambitious. Old Field-Marshal von Rundstedt was scathing. 'Antwerp? If we reach the Meuse we should go down on our knees and thank God!'

But Hitler refused even to consider any of their alternative plans, insisting on his own and reminding them that their sole duty was to obey his orders. The field commanders' opposition and the tremendous logistic problems involved made the original date impossible and Hitler was forced to agree to several postponements. In the end he lost his patience, saying that generals are never ready to attack, and set a last unalterable hour, 0530 hours on Saturday December 16, 1944.

The final German strength was less than had been promised but more than the generals had expected, and their mood changed from deep pessimism to mild optimism. Without alerting Allied Intelligence, they had been able to move 20 divisions, including seven armoured, into the attack front which the Americans were holding with only six divisions, of which one was armoured.

The overall superiority in manpower was no more than five to two, which is about the minimum required for a successful attack. But the attacker chooses the ground as well as the time, and the main weight of the offensive—eight *Volksgrenadier* divisions and five Panzer divisions—was concentrated on 45 miles of the Ardennes held by two American infantry divisions, a squadron of reconnaissance cavalry, with the only reserve a single combat command of an untried armoured division.

In the north, this blitz front took in the

extreme right wing of 1st Army's 5th Corps, held thinly by the US 99th Infantry Division, six weeks in the line and yet to experience battle; and an inexplicably unguarded 2-mile gap between 5th Corps and General Middleton's 8th Corps front, the northernmost two-thirds of which was included in the mammoth breakthrough.

Next to the inter-corps gap, thinly stretched across a classic easy entry from Germany into Belgium known as the Losheim Gap (see map), were some 900 men of the 18th Cavalry Squadron who had not yet tied in with a newly-arrived division on their right. This was the 106th Infantry who, after a gruelling journey across France and Belgium, had taken over positions three days before on the forward or eastern slope of a high ridge known as the Schnee Eifel. Completely inexperienced and suffering from frostbite and 'trench foot' they were to prove easy meat for the attacking Germans.

The southern half of the blitz front, which was to be hit by V Panzer Army with three *Volksgrenadier* divisions, one parachute infantry division, and two Panzer divisions, was held by the 28th Infantry Division, holding US 8th Corps' centre. This veteran division had been badly mauled in the recent heavy fighting around Aachen, where it had lost 6,184 men, and had been sent to the quietest part of the Ardennes for rest and refitting.

Were five objectives possible?

The rest of Army Group B was to be committed on either side of the main thrust to destroy the American line and to supply flank protection for the advance. On 8th Corps' right General Patton's US 3rd Army was in the last stages of preparation for an all-out offensive through the Saar; on their left 5th Corps had begun, three days before the German attack, an attack north towards the Roer dams. Part of this attack entailed an unusual manoeuvre: the 2nd Infantry Division, greatly experienced and recently rested, had pushed an attack column through the middle of 99th Infantry Division and captured an important crossroads 4 miles inside Germany. The unexpected presence of this division and its supporting artillery was to help to upset VI SS Panzer Army's plans.

Army Group B would have to achieve five initial objectives, and achieve them quickly if there were to be any chance at all of reaching Antwerp. The first two objectives were the setting up of 'hard shoulders' at both ends of the assault front to secure the flanks and make sure that the attack could not be pinched out. Thirdly, Sepp Dietrich's crack SS Panzer divisions must quickly overrun the lightly held American line and race for the Meuse, securing the bridges within 24 or at the most 48 hours. Fourth, General von Manteuffel's right-hand armoured punch must move alongside the SS Panzer divisions and, even though their route was longer, keep up with them, and also capture the important road and rail centre of St Vith along the way. Fifth, Manteuffel's left-wing attack must first capture Bastogne, the equally vital communications centre in the south, and go on to seize bridges over a third section of the Meuse.

The long night of December 15, 1944, was one of the darkest and coldest of that dark, cold winter. By midnight everything was ready on the German side—some 200,000 men with more tanks, guns, and ammunition than for many months past, waited to start

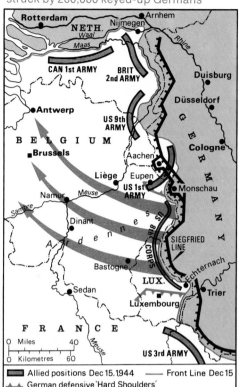

Allied positions Dec 15,1944 ——— Front Line Dec 15
▲▲▲ German defensive 'Hard Shoulders'
◀━━ Planned German counterattack

the biggest German offensive on the Western Front since 1940. Far to the rear Colonel von der Heydte's 1,250 paratroops, many about to jump for the first time, waited for trucks to carry them to the airfields. Skorzeny's men, in Allied uniforms and driving Allied vehicles, were lined up behind the leading tanks of the I SS Panzer Division, joking among themselves about it being too late to learn any more English and privately wondering if they would be shot if captured. The assault troops, many going into battle for the first time, tried to get some rest before the opening barrage. They had been thrilled by a multitude of stirring 'Orders of the Day'—from their own commanders, from the famous Field-Marshals von Rundstedt and Model and from the Führer himself. Many of them believed that they were about to take part in a great battle which would somehow miraculously win the war for Germany after all.

In the path of this mighty force were about 80,000 Americans, most of whom were sleeping peacefully, completely unaware of the storm that was about to break over them—for German security had been superb, Allied Intelligence sadly deficient. Some of these soldiers had not yet heard a shot fired in earnest; some had heard too many, and had been sent here so that their shattered nerves could recover. Most were thinking about their chance for leave at the many rest centres in the Ardennes or the promised Christmas festivities, a Christmas that many would never see.

Promptly at 0530 hours, the concentrated German artillery opened fire and almost all American positions were pounded heavily for periods from 20 minutes to an hour and a half. The startled Americans behind the front line tumbled out of their sleeping bags into shelters. At the forward outposts, where

the wire communications were quickly knocked out, the soldiers peered into the pre-dawn murkiness and asked each other what the hell had happened to this quietest of all fronts.

When the barrage stopped, hundreds of searchlights flicked on, reflecting off the low cloud to create 'artificial moonlight'. Moments later, before the dazed Americans could recover, German shock troops surged forward to make gaps for their tanks or to seize their own first-day objectives.

Tactically the most important of these was the securing of the flanks by setting up 'hard shoulders' at either end of the attack front. While not as dramatic as the Panzer thrusts these defence lines were absolutely vital, for without them the strong Allied forces north and south of the Ardennes could pinch out the offensive.

The northern 'hard shoulder' was to run from the town of Monschau along a ridge road to Eupen (see map). Sepp Dietrich decided first to attack on either side of Monschau, and after his other three infantry divisions had breached the American front lines and launched the SS Panzer divisions on their dash westwards, they would wheel right and continue the defence wall as far as Liège.

A first, fatal setback
The attack north of Monschau was halted at a roadblock before dawn by the 102nd Cavalry Squadron who, in the light of star shells, inflicted 20% casualties on the *Volksgrenadiers,* and stopped the assault dead. South of Monschau the *Volksgrenadiers* hit a battalion of the 99th Infantry Division in good defensive positions on high ground. As soon as the barrage stopped, German assault troops, closely packed, advanced steadily on to the American dug in positions. The result was not battle, but slaughter, yet the young Germans kept coming—in at least three verified instances their bodies fell into the American foxhole line. They could not possibly succeed for they were too few (the unexpected US 5th Corps attack towards the Roer dams, which had started three days before, tied down most of the German troops assigned to the attack around Monschau) and without armoured support. The assault was broken off and an attempt later in the day to get it rolling again was repelled.

At the end of the first day the plan to set up the 'hard shoulder' in the north had failed completely—and this was a failure that was to become increasingly serious for the Germans.

Some 85 miles to the south, General Brandenberger's tactics called for one of his four *Volksgrenadier* divisions to cross the Sauer river before dawn east of Echternach (the Sauer runs west to east here) and another to cross west of the town. After joining up south of Echternach they would then seize high ground behind the American artillery, so forcing the guns to pull back. Once they had done so, pontoon bridges could be put in over the Sauer and the heavy guns and equipment needed to set up the southern 'hard shoulder' could be brought across. At the same time, a third *Volksgrenadier* division would cross the river further up and, after overrunning an unexperienced American armoured infantry battalion, wheel left to continue the southern 'hard shoulder'.

The Echternach sector of the American front was held by 4th Infantry Division's 12th Infantry Regiment, still about 500 to

600 men under strength. The *Volksgrenadiers* attacking them would number about 12,000—a four to one advantage—but many were newly-raised 17-year-olds, and they had few vehicles, no tanks, and only a handful of self-propelled guns—which helped to even out the odds.

The Sauer runs fast in December, and the German assault troops in rubber boats found the crossing difficult; some had to try several locations before getting across, thus upsetting the timetable; but the opening barrage knocked out communications and deluged the forward posts with shells. Many were overrun before they had time to give the alarm and at first—as elsewhere along the Ardennes front—there was complete confusion. Villages were taken, lost, and re-taken with captors and prisoners changing rôles. In some places small bodies of American troops held out against the odds: 21 men turned a thick stone farmhouse into a fort and beat off all attacks for four days. Elsewhere, 60 Americans with only one machine-gun made a tourist hotel into a strongpoint, and held up the German advance long enough for relieving infantry to besiege the besiegers. But in many places the small American forces were simply overwhelmed.

The 60th Armoured Infantry Battalion, which had been given a small section of front a few days before for 'battle indoctrination', had about an hour's warning because the *Volksgrenadier* division sent against them was delayed by fog. Although greatly out-numbering the defenders, the Germans had no self-propelled guns, while the American armoured infantry—whose job is to protect its division's tanks—were fully equipped and wrought terrible damage on the German horse-drawn artillery and unarmoured transport. Although the American main line of resistance was penetrated several times the arrival of their reserves saved the situation and by nightfall the armoured infantry were still in position, blocking the *Volksgrenadiers'* attempt to join the Echternach attackers in forming a southern wall.

On this front, too, the Germans had failed to reach their main objectives. The American forward outposts had been overrun and the Germans were in force west of the Sauer, but they had failed to dislodge 4th Infantry Division's artillery, whose gunners were able to knock out the temporary bridges and prevent self-propelled guns or heavy mortars from being brought into play. Although the position of the American troops at the extreme southern flank of the Ardennes front was precarious, and would become more so before reinforcements arrived, the German advance had slipped behind schedule. Like the failure in the north, it was to have far-reaching effects on the battle.

Heady successes, serious setbacks
Along the line of the main attack the first 24 hours brought the Germans two main successes, one partial success, one serious failure, and three temporary setbacks which the plan could not afford.

The major success, like the major failure, took place on VI SS Panzer Army's front: a battlegroup spearheading I SS Panzer Division got through the gap between US 5th Corps and US 8th Corps and broke out into the unguarded rear areas. On the other hand XII SS Panzer Division and two divisions of *Volksgrenadiers,* who were to open gaps for the tanks, were held up all day.

The other major success was achieved by General Manteuffel's force north of the Schnee

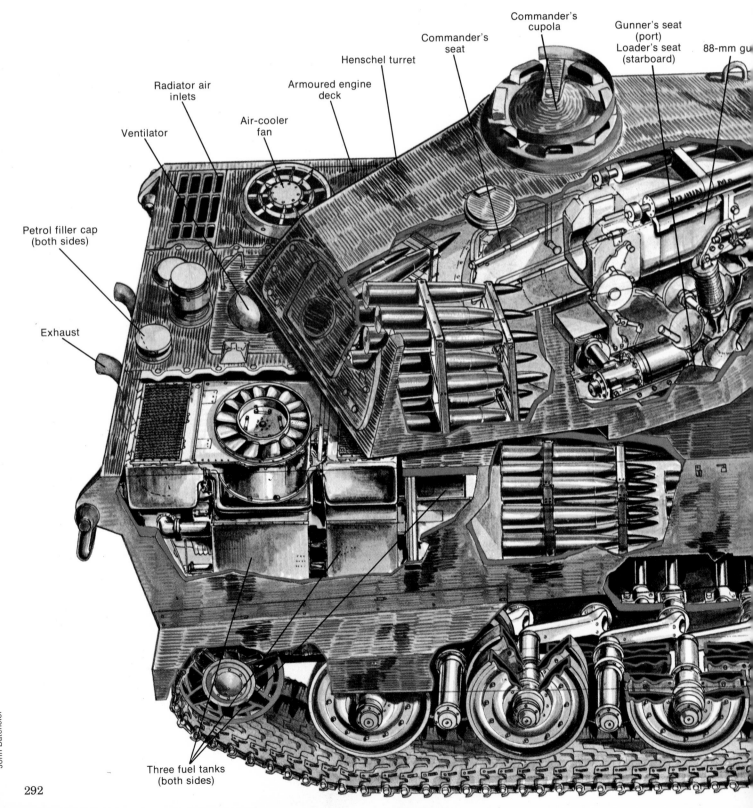

Radiator air
inlets

Air-cooler
fan

Ventilator

Armoured engine
deck

Henschel turret

Commander's
seat

Commander's
cupola

Gunner's seat
(port)
Loader's seat
(starboard)

88-mm gu

Petrol filler cap
(both sides)

Exhaust

Three fuel tanks
(both sides)

John Batchelor

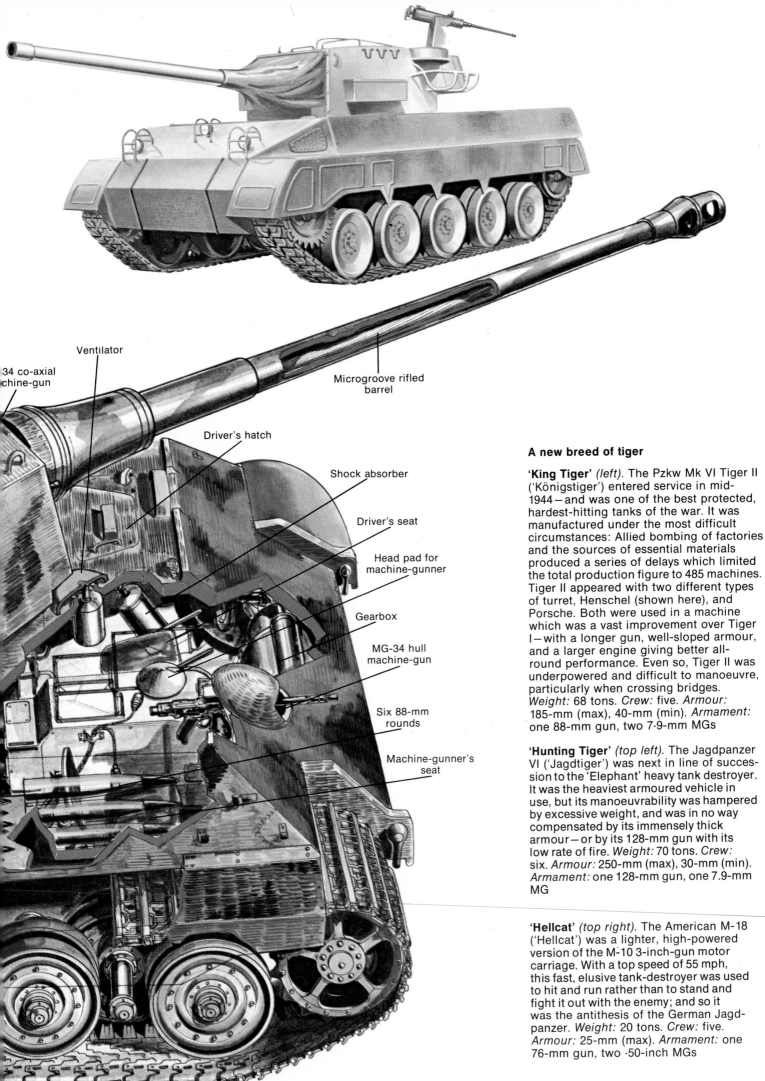

Ventilator

34 co-axial
chine-gun

Microgroove rifled
barrel

Driver's hatch

Shock absorber

Driver's seat

Head pad for
machine-gunner

Gearbox

MG-34 hull
machine-gun

Six 88-mm
rounds

Machine-gunner's
seat

A new breed of tiger

'King Tiger' *(left).* The Pzkw Mk VI Tiger II ('Königstiger') entered service in mid-1944—and was one of the best protected, hardest-hitting tanks of the war. It was manufactured under the most difficult circumstances: Allied bombing of factories and the sources of essential materials produced a series of delays which limited the total production figure to 485 machines. Tiger II appeared with two different types of turret, Henschel (shown here), and Porsche. Both were used in a machine which was a vast improvement over Tiger I—with a longer gun, well-sloped armour, and a larger engine giving better all-round performance. Even so, Tiger II was underpowered and difficult to manoeuvre, particularly when crossing bridges. *Weight:* 68 tons. *Crew:* five. *Armour:* 185-mm (max), 40-mm (min). *Armament:* one 88-mm gun, two 7·9-mm MGs

'Hunting Tiger' *(top left).* The Jagdpanzer VI ('Jagdtiger') was next in line of succession to the 'Elephant' heavy tank destroyer. It was the heaviest armoured vehicle in use, but its manoeuvrability was hampered by excessive weight, and was in no way compensated by its immensely thick armour—or by its 128-mm gun with its low rate of fire. *Weight:* 70 tons. *Crew:* six. *Armour:* 250-mm (max), 30-mm (min). *Armament:* one 128-mm gun, one 7.9-mm MG

'Hellcat' *(top right).* The American M-18 ('Hellcat') was a lighter, high-powered version of the M-10 3-inch-gun motor carriage. With a top speed of 55 mph, this fast, elusive tank-destroyer was used to hit and run rather than to stand and fight it out with the enemy; and so it was the antithesis of the German Jagdpanzer. *Weight:* 20 tons. *Crew:* five. *Armour:* 25-mm (max). *Armament:* one 76-mm gun, two ·50-inch MGs

293

Rundstedt, C-in-C Western Front: nominal commander of the Ardennes *Wacht am Rhein* offensive

Model, the 'Führer's fireman': C-in-C of Army Group B, comprising the three assault armies

Manteuffel: C-in-C of V Panzer Army, the 'left hook' of the Panzer assault through the Ardennes

Dietrich, top general of the Waffen-SS: C-in-C of VI SS Panzer Army, spearhead of the assault

▷ As they had been promised: infantry advancing past blazing US vehicles

Centre: A patrol dashes across a road littered with US guns

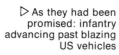

△ Directing the breakthrough: orders for the follow-up troops

▷ Scene of the Malmédy massacre, where SS troops shot 86 US POWs

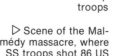

▷By December 18, the German spearheads had driven 25 miles in only 36 hours

Imperial War Museum

◁The offensive rolls on, past more abandoned US vehicles

▽ *Left:* A captured SS trooper; many were cut off in over-enthusiastic advances

Brown Bros

△ US soldiers await the crunch in Bastogne

◁ How it was in the early days: advance instead of retreat

Imperial War Museum

Imperial War Museum

Eifel, which swept through the strung-out positions of the 18th Cavalry Squadron in the Losheim Gap and reached the main road to St Vith less than 10 miles from that vital communications centre. But again, his centre thrust, intended to go round the south of the Schnee Eifel and join up with his right-wing attack, thus entrapping two regiments of newly-arrived infantry along the top of the hill, was held up all day only a mile or so from their start line.

General Manteuffel's main effort to reach the Meuse came from his left wing, where the élite XLVII Panzer Corps of one Panzer and two infantry divisions (plus a division of parachute infantry from Brandenberger's VII Army) planned to cross the Our, cut the main north/south highway, and seize bridges over the next river to the west (the Clerf) in the first 24 hours. This would enable them to take Bastogne the next day and also to get their Panzers on good roads to the Meuse.

His centre thrust also fumbled when a Panzer division and its supporting infantry division were unable to cross the Our in their sector at all and the armour had to be sent south to get over by another bridge. But the II Panzer Division, destined to advance further than any other troops in the Battle of the Bulge, got across the Our and moved up the wooded slopes to seize the main highway (known as 'Skyline Drive' to the heavily-shelled drivers of the lorries who used it to carry supplies to the American 9th Army in the north) thus achieving a partial success. Somehow the outnumbered and exhausted 28th Infantry Division was able to prevent them from crossing the Clerf for the whole of the second day, a gallant stand which bought the precious hours needed to reinforce Bastogne.

Although, at the time, neither side was able to see it, the pattern that emerged at the end of the first two days' fighting determined the outcome of the battle, and these events are worth examining a little more closely.

In VI SS Panzer Army confidence ran high, for it had not only the best and shortest route to the Meuse but had been given the most tanks, guns, and men. Two main armoured punches were planned: XII SS Panzer Division ('Hitler Jugend') was to lead the right-hand one and its great rival, I SS Panzer Division ('Leibstandarte Adolf Hitler') the left. Each waited behind a *Volksgrenadier* division which was to make the initial breakthrough; these four divisions were opposed by four *battalions* – less than half a division – of the green 99th US Infantry Division. But, because of the Roer dams attack going in just to the north, there was an exceptional concentration of American artillery on this front.

The German barrage here was the heaviest of all. A few days before, a US Intelligence report had said that the German front opposite one of 99th Infantry's battalions seemed to be very lightly held, adding that there were only two horse-drawn guns there. After an hour's non-stop shelling the battalion executive officer reported: 'They sure worked those horses to death.'

As soon as the shelling stopped, assault troops hit every American forward position in strength and most of the riflemen were killed or captured. But when the *Volksgrenadiers* tried to exploit this success they were hammered by heavy howitzer and artillery fire and went to ground. Some of the 'Hitler Jugend' Division, impatient at the delay, tried to advance their tanks alone,

but were stopped by large-calibre, high-explosive shells.

By dusk, about 1630 hours, the American survivors had formed strongpoints around their battalion command posts in the woods and, though reduced to half strength, somehow preserved a front. After only six weeks in the line these young soldiers had held up two élite SS Panzer divisions for an all-important 24 hours, the time needed to bring in other troops to hold the high ground behind the Elsenborn Ridge against which the 'Hitler Jugend' division was practically to destroy itself in the next few days before giving up and being moved to another part of the front.

But the leading battle group of the 'Leibstandarte Adolf Hitler' was commanded by one of Germany's toughest, most ruthless, and most daring SS Panzer leaders, Colonel Joachim Peiper, who demanded and got almost suicidal devotion from his men.

Disgusted at the failure of the *Volksgrenadiers* to open a breach for his battle group, he went forward and personally led his Panzers through the snarled-up rear areas, ordering them to run down anything that did not get out of their way. Breaking out into no-man's-land after dark, his spearhead lost five Panzers to old German mines. Carrying on all through the night, they seized the town of Honsfeld, far behind the American lines, at dawn on Sunday, December 17, capturing many vehicles and anti-tank guns and shooting down 19 unarmed American soldiers, the first of a number of atrocities perpetrated by these veterans from the bitter no-quarter fighting in Russia.

Peiper's vital breakthrough

In need of fuel, Peiper's men swung 2 miles off route into the 'Hitler Jugend' Division's zone and seized a large petrol dump at Büllingen, forcing 50 American soldiers to fill their tanks and then shooting them down in cold blood too, before swinging back on to their own route and pushing west as fast as possible.

Just after noon Peiper's men pierced an American column moving down from the north as reinforcements. This was part of the US 7th Armoured Division, on its way to St Vith. Only half an hour earlier Peiper's column would have run head on into their Armoured Combat Command and a great tank battle would have developed, but this had passed through and blind chance brought a field artillery observation battery of 125 men to the Malmédy crossroads at that precise moment. They could do nothing against the tanks and guns of a Panzer division and all were quickly captured. A couple of hours later, while standing in a field waiting to be marched back, these prisoners were machine-gunned by passing SS. Some were unconscious or feigned death but 86 died and the news of this massacre, reaching the Americans in front line positions that night by 'latrine telegraph', was responsible for a stiffening of the will to resist and an unwillingness to surrender.

Having apparently achieved a clean breakthrough, Peiper hoped to reach his objective – the bridge over the Meuse at Huy – by late that night or early the next morning. A few miles ahead of him lay Stavelot, and from there a good road ran almost due west 40 miles to the Meuse.

What happened next is something of a mystery still. His spearhead, racing on, was stopped when the leading half-tracks were knocked out; but this was no more than had

been expected; and German countermoves knocked out two American tanks and captured more prisoners. But the encounter bred caution in the leaders, and the battle group's advance guard did not get to the high ground across the river from Stavelot until dusk. There they saw hundreds of American vehicles and jumped to the conclusion that they had reached a heavily defended position.

In fact the only combat troops in Stavelot were a single battalion of engineers who were constructing a roadblock: there were no tanks or anti-tank guns at all. The vehicles were trucks engaged in moving fuel out of a huge dump a few miles away. The leading German tanks ran on to a newly-laid American minefield and the commanders who, after all, had been on the move for 36 hours and advanced 25 miles, must have decided that they had pushed their luck far enough for they greatly exaggerated the strength of the defences. Uncharacteristically, Peiper did not come up to see for himself but consented to a halt – probably realising that he must now wind up his tail anyway.

Whatever the explanation the stopping of Battle Group Peiper at Stavelot on the second night of the offensive was the turning point in VI SS Panzer Army's offensive, for although in the next week this strong force would remain the main threat on the northern front, lack of support and particularly lack of fuel prevented its breaking out to the west. American reinforcements from the 82nd Airborne Division, the 30th Infantry Division, the 3rd Armoured Division, and other units bore down heavily on Battle Group Peiper, which became isolated from the rest of I SS Panzer Division.

The unexpected stiff resistance of the US 99th Infantry Division in front of I SS Panzer Corps and the delay caused by the extensive minefields on that front brought about colossal traffic jams behind the German attack front as horse-drawn artillery, supply trains, bridging equipment, reserves, and huge siege guns all pressed forward trying to keep to their time-tables.

Skorzeny – master of confusion

Otto Skorzeny personally led his group through this tangle, bypassing clogged roads by cutting across fields (and losing his most experienced commander on an old German mine) and so was able to dispatch three of his disguised commando teams towards the Meuse crossings. One actually got to the bridge at Huy and 'guarded' it all day, doling out terrifying rumours to passing American units. Other teams blew up ammunition dumps and destroyed communications but the main result of the presence of German soldiers in American uniforms far behind the front was to set in motion the most elaborate measures to check on everyone's identity. All jeeps or staff cars were stopped and passengers asked the names of comic strip characters, the league positions of baseball teams, or details of the private lives of film stars. Often the more senior American officers did not know the correct answer and many spent a few hours in custody. All this, combined with the stories of German paratroops dropping everywhere, tied up troops who were desperately needed in the fighting.

In fact, like Skorzeny's operation, the parachute drop was something of a farce, for lack of fuel for the transport trucks stopped the paratroops on the first night and postponed their drop for 24 hours, when the element of surprise was lost and it was almost certain that American reinforcements would be moving through the drop zone.

Strong crosswinds scattered the aircraft and the paratroops came down at widely separated spots. Many of these young, courageous volunteers, jumping in the black, freezing night for the first time, came down in remote parts of the Ardennes, far from houses or roads. Some broke arms or legs on landing and although some were found by American search parties or local people others lay in the snow and slowly died. Bodies were still being found the following spring.

Only ten or 15 bombers found the drop zone and Colonel von der Heydte discovered that he had only about 350 men, little food, no blankets, no weapons larger than small mortars and machine-pistols, and no radios working. Just after first light the paratroops heard the noise of heavy trucks climbing towards them from the north and moments later trucks crammed with American infantry rolled through their position. This was the 1st Infantry Division, the most experienced in the American army, veterans of three beach assaults—Africa, Sicily, and Normandy. Now they were on their way to reinforce the 99th Infantry Division and the 2nd Infantry Division, now being pulled back from the Roer dams attack to screen 99th Infantry's withdrawal to the Elsenborn Ridge. 'The Big Red One' Division would arrive just in time to shore up the southern flank and help block VI SS Panzer Army's attack in which Hitler had such high hopes.

In the next few days Colonel von der Heydte had to watch two more American divisions, the 7th Armoured and the 30th Infantry, move into the attack zone without his being able to do anything about it. What Omar Bradley has described as America's 'secret weapon', mobility, was being brought into play.

After four days, out of rations and suffering severely from the intense cold, Colonel von der Heydte ordered his men to break up into small parties and find their own way back. He sent back his American prisoners and, with them, his own wounded with a request to the American commander to look after them. Two days later, exhausted and ravenous, he surrendered himself. It was the end of the once-great German Parachute Corps, whose exploits had won the admiration of soldiers everywhere.

On VI SS Panzer Army's left General von Manteuffel planned a double-pronged drive around the Schnee Eifel, which would first trap the green 106th Infantry Division's troops there and would then go on to take St Vith, whose road and rail communications were absolutely essential to the second phase of the German offensive.

Attached to the 106th Division and guarding its left flank were 900 men of the 18th Cavalry Squadron in village strongpoints across the Losheim Gap. At dawn they were hit by both Manteuffel's right-wing attack of reinforced *Volksgrenadiers* and Sepp Dietrich's left, a division of parachute infantry whose main axis ran from Germany to Manderfeld, the reconnaissance cavalry's headquarters.

The 18th Cavalry Squadron was part of the 14th Cavalry Group, whose commander, Colonel Mark Devine, went forward from Manderfeld to try to discover what was happening on his front. In some places the first German assaults had been beaten off,

but other small groups had been overwhelmed before they could do much more than radio for artillery support. Realising that this was a major attack and that his outposts were hopelessly outnumbered, Devine ordered those who were able to do so to disengage and fall back. He got through to his superiors at 106th Division HQ in St Vith and proposed a new flank defence line across the western end of the Losheim Gap to be followed by a counterattack as soon as his reserve squadron arrived. This was agreed to, for no one at divisional headquarters realised that both proposals were quite unreal in the light of the strength of the German attack.

Rumours, confusion—and panic

When Devine got back to his headquarters in Manderfeld about 1100 hours, he found it a shambles, with his staff frantically packing and trying to destroy their records. Floods of refugees had been pouring in with stories of terrible disasters and German successes. Their terror was unnerving. Panic swept through 14th Cavalry Group HQ and the staff piled into their vehicles with what personal possessions they could grab; and, in an attempt to destroy anything which might aid the Germans, they simply set fire to the whole town, destroying it completely. It was the beginning of a series of disorganised retreats which became a long nightmare, only ending some 60 hours and four commanding officers later, 25 miles to the rear, when the 14th Cavalry Group's survivors were attached to the 7th Armoured Division as part of the defence of St Vith.

When the cavalry broke off action and pulled back, Manteuffel's right wing raced through the Losheim Gap until it was halted by artillery near the village of Auw in front of St Vith. Here the commander of the 106th Infantry Division, General Alan Jones, only recently arrived on the Continent, was involved in his first battle. His main worry was the fate of his two regiments stuck out on the eastern side of the Schnee Eifel ridge. Wrongly believing that the 14th Cavalry was guarding his left flank, he sent one of his reserve battalions to stiffen his right flank and the other to engage Manteuffel's right wing, a mixed force of infantry and assault guns attacking the field artillery at Auw. These guns were then able to withdraw and take part in the all-important defence of St Vith itself, which took place over the next few days.

The southern prong of Manteuffel's attack around the Schnee Eifel had come under killing fire from 106th Division infantry on the southern slope of the hill, and after fierce hand-to-hand fighting in the streets of Bleialf, key to the road network there, the Germans had been halted less than 2 miles from their start line. Displeased, General Manteuffel ordered them to renew their attack at dawn, take Bleialf 'at all costs', and advance to join the northern prong, closing the trap on the two regiments of American infantry on the Schnee Eifel.

The 106th Division had lost little actual ground on the first day of the offensive and its inexperienced staff probably failed to realise the precariousness of their position. All through the night the Germans continued to move infantry and guns into the breaches they had made, in preparation for the next day's onslaught.

In answer to the 106th Division's request for reinforcements, 8th Corps gave it an armoured combat command, no longer needed for the Roer Dams attack, and during the evening of the 16th, promised that the 7th Armoured Division from the north was on its way and that its leading combat command would arrive at 0700 hours the next morning. This estimate was hopelessly out, for it had not taken into account either the winter road conditions or the traffic jams being caused by the disorganised headlong retreat of many rear troops. In fact the main body of tanks of the 7th Armoured did not arrive at St Vith until late on Sunday afternoon, too late to save the two regiments on the Schnee Eifel. It took the tanks five hours to cover the last 12 miles against a tide of panic-stricken staff and rear area troops.

By nightfall on December 17, some 8-9,000 American troops were surrounded in the Schnee Eifel. Two days later, without having incurred more than a few casualties or inflicted any serious damage on the encircling Germans who did not outnumber them but who did have tanks and self-propelled guns, they all surrendered. It was, as the official American history says, the most serious reverse suffered by American arms in the European theatre.

Jubilantly the Germans moved in for the kill at St Vith.

The central blow
The V Panzer Army's main effort, an attack by two Panzer corps in the centre, although destined to be the most successful of all, did not get off to the flying start planned. On the German right 58th Panzer Corps of a division of *Volksgrenadiers* followed by the 116th Panzer Division, planned to roll through a single regiment of the 28th Infantry Division (the 112th), holding trenches east of the Our river, and go flat out for the Meuse through the vacuum between Bastogne and St Vith, which it was expected the attacks on both those places would create.

South of this thrust XLVII Panzer Corps' XXVI *Volksgrenadier* Division would seize bridges over the Our for the armour of the élite II Panzer Division, and both infantry and tanks would smash through the centre of US 28th Infantry Division's front, held by their 110th Regiment, get across the Clerf river 6 or 7 miles further west, and go on to capture Bastogne. As an added precaution, one of General Brandenberger's divisions of parachute infantry would move alongside this attack, cutting the 110th Infantry Regiment off from the 109th further south.

It was a good plan and should have succeeded quickly, for the Germans numbered about 50,000 while the American defenders consisted of 14 companies of riflemen (about 3,250 combat troops) supported by artillery and howitzer positions, and one battalion of tanks. But, of course, only a part of the total German strength could be brought to bear at the beginning of the attack.

On 58th Panzer Corps' front the American defenders, being east of the Our, maintained intact bridges behind them capable of taking tanks and self-propelled guns. If these could be taken by surprise, the Panzers could get off to the flying start they needed to reach the Meuse.

To make sure of surprise General von Manteuffel ordered that this section of the front would not receive the pre-dawn opening barrage but, instead, white-clad *Volksgrenadiers* would quietly penetrate the rear areas of the American front line before dawn and, when the attack began, move swiftly to seize the two bridges.

Had the *Volksgrenadiers* on this front been more experienced or the defending infantry less so this plan might have succeeded, but the German division were a scratch lot of ex-garrison troops from Norway and Denmark, most of whom had never seen action. The first part of the plan worked—shock companies of *Volksgrenadiers* penetrated the American forward line during the night and, as soon as the barrage began—an hour later here than on the rest of the front—moved through the gaps in the long, deep, barbed-wire defences which the Americans had left open for moving up supplies at night.

The Germans achieved complete surprise. In one case they burst into a clearing just as a platoon was lined up for breakfast. The sudden fire of machine-pistols and exploding grenades killed a number of Americans and the rest broke. The white-clad shock troops moved swiftly towards the bridges—and here their inexperience was their undoing. Flushed with success they advanced openly on to defended pillboxes and manned trenches. The veterans of the US 112th Infantry Regiment, who had lost 2,000 out of 3,000 in the bitter Hurtgen Forest fighting the month before, picked the invaders off with rifle fire, sprayed them with machine-guns and, when they took refuge in gullies, plastered them with mortar fire. German casualties were very heavy here and elsewhere on this part of the front and by nightfall all the bridges were still in American hands.

The *Volksgrenadiers* had been badly mauled and the Panzer division had lost six tanks. Manteuffel's centre thrust was badly behind schedule and, in an attempt to catch up, the 116th Panzer Division was ordered to send a battalion of light tanks (Mk IVs) 5 or 6 miles south and cross the Our over a bridge which had been established by the XLVII Panzer Corps. The Mk IVs were then to turn north, come back along the American side of the Our, and take the bridges on 58th Panzer Corps' front from the rear.

The Panzer schwerpunkt

General Hasso von Manteuffel's main hope of reaching the Meuse lay with his XLVII Panzer Corps, the Wehrmacht's 'Number One Reserve' on the Western Front. For the Ardennes offensive this consisted of a first-class infantry division from the Eastern Front ('The Old XXVI', renamed the XXVI *Volksgrenadiers*) and the famous II Panzer Division, which had fought the Allies with spirit and courage all the way from Normandy to Germany. In reserve another crack division, Panzer Lehr, was to be thrown in to add weight to the *schwerpunkt*.

The XXVI *Volksgrenadiers* were given a particularly difficult rôle: they had to force the Our river, advance 7 or 8 miles and force the Clerf river, hold both these open for the armour to cross, and then follow the Panzers on foot 15 more miles to Bastogne, which it was then their task to take.

In order not to alert the Americans, *Volksgrenadier* shock troops were not allowed to cross the Our before the opening barrage but XXVI *Volksgrenadier's* commanding officer, Major-General Kokott, pointed out that he had been in the habit of putting men over the river at night and holding a line of outposts on the American side until dawn and not to do so would arouse sus-

At the tip of the 'Bulge': SS Colonel
Peiper with a scout team of his group. It
was Peiper's battle group which
committed the Malmédy massacre of US
POWs in the early days of the breakthrough

picion. He was given permission to continue this practice on the night before the attack and, taking advantage of the concession, slipped two of his three regiments over the Our and moved them silently up through the woods to the north/south highway, 'Skyline Drive', on which the American 110th Infantry Regiment had based its main line of resistance. This highway was one of XLVII Panzer's first objectives.

General von Manteuffel's main armoured punch, II Panzer Division, was to cross the Our at Dasburg, move rapidly up 4 miles through wooded country to the small town of Marnach on Skyline Drive, seize this, and then move another 3 miles and capture the town of Clervaux, principal crossing place of the Clerf and headquarters of the 28th Division's 110th Infantry Regiment. From here good roads ran to Bastogne and beyond.

The German schedule called for all the Clerf river crossings to be held by nightfall of the first day — less than 12 hours after the opening barrage. It would be a tight schedule and unit commanders were impatient to get their men moving.

The 28th Infantry Division's 110th Regiment, holding this 10 miles of the Ardennes front, had based its defences on a series of fortified villages held in company strength and backed up by artillery positions. It was realised that the Germans could not be prevented from crossing the Our, and the ground between Skyline Drive and the Our was virtually no-man's-land used by both sides for patrolling. In the event of an attack, which as elsewhere in the Ardennes was regarded as almost an academic problem, it was intended first to hold Skyline Drive, the principal tactical feature, and next to deny the Germans the Clerf river bridges.

Fierce US resistance

On this front as elsewhere the opening barrage knocked out wire communications but the first contact was made, not at the front line, but at Holzthum west of Skyline Drive, 5 miles from the Our and only 4 miles from an important Clerf bridge. The attackers, of course, were some of the XXVI Volksgrenadiers who had quietly moved up during the night. They were beaten off by the Americans who had been alerted by the opening barrage and word was flashed at 0615 hours to regimental headquarters at Clervaux enabling 110th Infantry's other strongpoints to prepare to resist attack.

Failing to clear Holzthum by direct assault the XXVI Volksgrenadiers tried to work round north but came under fire from an artillery battalion which caused them to go to ground. Annoyed, the German commander ordered an attack against the guns which were without infantry support but this too failed. Again and again the Volksgrenadiers attacked the villages of Holzthum and Consthum, which barred their way to the Clerf crossing, but were unable to get past. It was an unexpectedly stubborn defence and it cost these German troops, who had hoped to be the first to cross the Clerf, all the time advantage they had gained by their night crossing of the Our. Desperately they attacked the American artillery position but the gunners put their shells on one-second fuses and fired over open sights — in some cases parts of the shells blew back on the gun positions. Although the battery commander and 15 of his gun crews became casualties, the position was held.

Other positions on this part of the American front also put up unexpectedly fierce resistance. At Wahlhausen, a cluster of houses on top of a hill with an all-round view, an American observation post of a single platoon beat off attack after attack until their ammunition ran out. After dark the Germans shelled them with anti-aircraft guns and came on in force. The last message from Wahlhausen was a request for American artillery fire on top of them; only one man survived. The rest of the company to which this platoon belonged were in the village of Weiler near the German start line, and they too beat off successive waves of brave but largely inexperienced young Volksgrenadiers all day, and were not eliminated until nightfall. The troops who finally captured these two positions should by then have been across the Clerf.

General Kokott had ordered his assault troops to bypass the defended village of Hosingen on Skyline Drive but a company of riflemen and another of combat engineers sallied out and engaged the German columns on either side and drew them into a pitched battle for the village. This threw the German timetable out here, too, and the outnumbered Americans held out for two and a half days when, cut off and out of ammunition, the survivors surrendered.

The tough defence of the 110th Infantry Regiment's right flank stopped the XXVI Volksgrenadiers from getting across the Clerf until the third day and undoubtedly enabled Bastogne to be reinforced — and so later to resist all the German efforts to capture it.

The left half of the 110th Infantry Regiment's sector, based on Clervaux, also put up an unexpectedly fierce fight. At Marnach, midway between the Dasburg crossing and the key town of Clervaux, a company of American infantry held off the German assault all the first day, only going down when the tanks of II Panzer Division crashed into the little town. At Clervaux itself a particularly spirited defence held up the combined German armour and infantry for two days, the regimental commander himself remaining in his headquarters until the attackers had broken into the downstairs rooms. With survivors of his staff and some walking wounded he got out of an upstairs back door which led up the hill behind, but he was later captured.

The 28th Infantry Division's centre regiment, the 110th, lost about 2,750 men in two and a half days holding the Clerf crossings — but in doing so enabled Bastogne to be reinforced and later held, which in turn stopped General von Manteuffel from reaching the Meuse.

This then was the situation, after nearly 100 hours of continuous fighting in the Ardennes. On the northern flank the Elsenborn Ridge was securely held by four American infantry divisions and concentrated artillery — but it had been a near thing. The 99th Infantry Division was forced back by overwhelming infantry and tank attacks; the 2nd, breaking off its own offensive, had had to fight a desperate withdrawing action through the crumbling front. The 9th Division had moved in from Eupen to back up the Monschau position where no ground had been yielded despite wave after wave of attackers; and the veteran 1st Division had arrived just in time to hold the right of the ridge line against renewed SS Panzer attacks. Thus, with most of VI SS Panzer Army held almost at the start line and their

one success, Peiper's Battle Group (spearheading the 'Leibstandarte Adolf Hitler' Division) in a pocket, the main hope of a quick, unbroken advance to the Meuse in the north had failed. And with St Vith and Bastogne under attack but still in American hands, the original timetable had to be torn up.

'Our forces must now prepare to defend the territory we have already taken,' Field-Marshal von Rundstedt said as early as December 18. Although Hitler overruled him and ordered the Panzers to smash through regardless of casualties, even he was forced to face reality. On the 19th he cancelled the supporting attack from the German XV Army in the north.

The first crisis passes

But on the American side it was only after four days that some sort of order emerged from the confusion caused by the mass of small actions, the breakdown of communications, and the near panic in some of the rear areas. Now major decisions could be taken. Although at first General Bradley had thought the Germans were mounting a spoiling attack to stop General Patton's projected Saar offensive, he had immediately moved an armoured division into the attacked front from either side, the 7th from the north which saved St Vith, and the 10th from the south which got one combat command into Bastogne and another to the hard-pressed defenders around Echternach.

Also 9th Army's General Simpson voluntarily sent his 5th Armoured Division and his 30th Infantry to his old friend General Hodges' aid, and SHAEF's sole reserve, two airborne divisions, were also thrown into the battle. They had been resting and refitting at Rheims after nearly two months' fighting in Holland and were not supposed to be operational for another month: but after a wild 100-mile ride through the night the 101st came into Bastogne on December 19 and the 82nd arrived near the point of 'Liebstandarte' Division by the evening of the 18th.

Although the offensive was taking place entirely on the American front, Field-Marshal Montgomery moved part of his only reserve, 30th Corps, to backstop positions west of the Meuse.

When the full seriousness of the situation was realised at SHAEF on December 19, the offensive through the Saar was called off and General Patton was ordered to counter-attack the German left flank as soon as possible with two of 3rd Army's corps.

This, it was realised, would take time, and orders were given for Allied forces to fall back if necessary — but not further than the Meuse. General Eisenhower told General Bradley to 'choose the line he could hold most cheaply' and he asked Field-Marshal Montgomery to examine the possibility of giving up ground in Holland to shorten the line and amass a reserve.

While General Patton worked furiously to turn his whole front through 90°, and while Bastogne and St Vith waited for all-out assaults, General von Manteuffel drove his armour straight through the vacuum between these towns. This threatened to split the front in two, making it increasingly difficult for General Bradley to exercise control over both halves.

It was a situation which faced General Eisenhower with one of his most difficult command decisions of his entire military career.

BATTLE OF THE BULGE: THE CRISIS

Imperial War Museum

Ardennes, Belgium, December 16/21, 1944

While the hastily-deployed American defenders of St Vith and Bastogne fought desperately to stem the German tide in the Ardennes, another battle was being fought out in Allied headquarters. This involved the thorny subject of Montgomery's rôle in the Battle of the Bulge. It was clear to Eisenhower that Montgomery was in the best position to deal with the northern side of the Bulge until Patton was ready for his attack from the south—but Montgomery's approach aroused much surprise and resentment among the American generals. And while the Allied counterattacks hung in the balance, the Germans finally took St Vith, one of the vital obstacles in their path. Jubilantly, they moved in for the kill at Bastogne . . .

Above: US troops under shellfire near Houffalize

The bitter and costly battles for the Elsenborn Ridge, for the Schnee Eifel, for St Vith, for the Skyline Drive and Clerf, for the Sauer river crossings and Echternach—these did not decide the outcome of Hitler's winter counteroffensive. Yet taken together, these opening engagements drew much of the sting out of the total tactical and strategic surprise the Germans had scored, denying the German commanders the quick momentum they required if they were to achieve the strategic goal of Antwerp.

The grim fighting before the Elsenborn Ridge had jammed the northern shoulder of the German penetration, stalling the main effort of SS General Josef 'Sepp' Dietrich's VI Panzer Army. The battles on the Schnee Eifel and at St Vith had put the *verboten* sign on the vital roads that thread through St Vith, sharply restricting westward movement of the north wing of General Hasso von Manteuffel's V Panzer Army in the centre of the German line-up. These two stands together restricted Sepp Dietrich's Panzer columns to a corridor between St Vith and the Elsenborn Ridge only 4 miles wide.

The fight for the Skyline Drive and crossings over the little Clerf river at the town of Clerf had seriously slowed the V Panzer Army's main effort, scheduled to plunge swiftly through the centre of the Ardennes, taking the crucial road centre of Bastogne in the process, and seizing crossings of the Meuse river to protect the left flank of the VI Panzer Army. The determined American stand at crossings of the Sauer river and at Echternach at the southern base had similarly delayed General Erich Brandenberger's VII Army, which had to establish a solid shoulder extending far to the west if Manteuffel and Dietrich were not to be subjected to quick counterattack by a commander whom all the German generals respected—Lieutenant-General George S. Patton, Jr, commanding the US 3rd Army.

The stand at these forward positions also afforded time for the commander of the American 8th Corps, Major-General Troy S. Middleton—whose over-extended troops had borne the brunt of the German thrust—to dispose his reserves, however meagre, and contribute to the German delay. Of the two combat commands of the 9th Armoured Division that constituted the sole formal reserve, Middleton had sent one to St Vith. The other he had disposed on the roads behind the Clerf river leading into Bastogne. Also available were a few engineer combat battalions that Middleton turned from timber cutting and road building to reinforce various threatened sectors.

There were other reserves, though not formally designated as such, that would also have an impact, a kind of battlefield residue made up of headquarters companies, supply and service troops, and stragglers filtering back from broken or surrounded units. By turning to fight at critical road junctions, manning tanks pulled from repair shops, firing machine-guns for vital minutes while engineers demolished a bridge, these troops in hundreds of impromptu engagements had an effect in the sharply compartmented Ardennes terrain far out of proportion to their numbers.

That was what had happened, for example, at the town of Stavelot, in the deeply incised valley of the little Amblève river 15 miles south-west of the Elsenborn Ridge, where the one German force that had scored an unequivocal breakthrough in the early hours had become involved in a time-

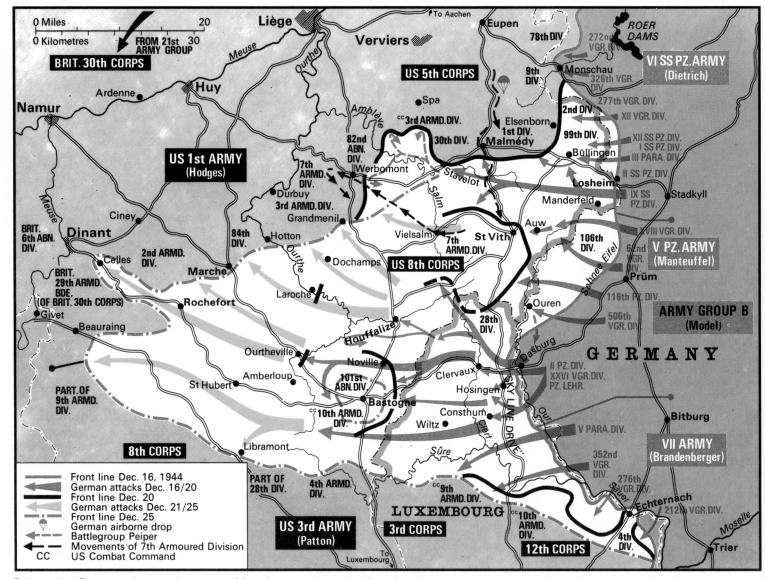

The map labels, reading across the image:

BRIT. 30th CORPS · 0 Miles 20 · 0 Kilometres 30 · FROM 21st ARMY GROUP · Liège · To Aachen · Eupen · ROER DAMS · 78th DIV. · 272nd VGR. DIV. · VI SS PZ. ARMY (Dietrich) · Verviers · 9th DIV. · Monschau · 326th VGR. DIV. · Meuse · Ourthe · Amblève · US 5th CORPS · 2nd DIV. · 277th VGR. DIV. · XII VGR. DIV. · Ardenne · Huy · Spa · 1st DIV. · Elsenborn · 99th DIV. · XII SS PZ. DIV. · Namur · CC 3rd ARMD. DIV. · 30th DIV. · Malmédy · Büllingen · I SS PZ. DIV. · III PARA. DIV. · US 1st ARMY (Hodges) · 82nd ABN. DIV. · Werbomont · Stavelot · Losheim · II SS PZ. DIV. · 7th ARMD. DIV. · Manderfeld · IX SS PZ. DIV. · Stadkyll · Durbuy · Salm · Auw · XVIII VGR. DIV. · BRIT. 6th ABN. DIV. · Dinant · Ciney · 3rd ARMD. DIV. · Grandmenil · Vielsalm · St Vith · 62nd VGR. DIV. · V PZ. ARMY (Manteuffel) · Celles · 2nd ARMD. DIV. · 84th DIV. · Hotton · 7th ARMD. DIV. · 106th DIV. · Schnee Eifel · Prüm · BRIT. 29th ARMD. BDE. (OF BRIT. 30th CORPS) · Marche · Dochamps · US 8th CORPS · 116th PZ. DIV. · ARMY GROUP B (Model) · Givet · Laroche · Ouren · 506th VGR. DIV. · Beauraing · Ourtheville · Houffalize · 28th DIV. · Dasburg · GERMANY · PART OF 9th ARMD. DIV. · Noville · Amberloup · 101st ABN. DIV. · Clervaux · II PZ. DIV. · XXVI VGR. DIV. · PZ. LEHR. · St Hubert · Bastogne · Hosingen · SKYLINE DRIVE · Bitburg · CC 10th ARMD. DIV. · Consthum · Wiltz · V PARA. DIV. · VII ARMY (Brandenberger) · Libramont · Clerf · 352nd VGR. DIV. · 8th CORPS · Sûre · 276th VGR. DIV. · PART OF 28th DIV. · 4th ARMD. DIV. · CC 9th ARMD. DIV. · LUXEMBOURG · CC 10th ARMD. DIV. · Echternach · 212th VGR. DIV. · Sauer · Moselle · US 3rd ARMY (Patton) · 3rd CORPS · 12th CORPS · 4th DIV. · Trier · To Luxembourg

Legend:
Front line Dec. 16, 1944
German attacks Dec. 16/20
Front line Dec. 20
German attacks Dec. 21/25
Front line Dec. 25
German airborne drop
Battlegroup Peiper
Movements of 7th Armoured Division
CC US Combat Command

Delays, the German planners knew, would be fatal for the Ardennes offensive—but the German flood was forced to stream between two vital American breakwaters: St Vith and Bastogne, holding out valiantly in the path of the advancing enemy. And the time taken to lever the Americans out of the St Vith horseshoe and besiege Bastogne crimped German operations

consuming fight. This was a task force commanded by *SS-Obersturmbannführer* Joachim Peiper of the I SS Panzer Division, which had plunged westward, murdering American prisoners in the process.

This delay alone would hardly prove fatal to Peiper, but little bands of die-hard defenders were waiting at other spots as well. An American major ordered Belgian troops manning a big fuel depot to pour petrol into a road cut, set it aflame, and deny Peiper access to the depot. A lone towed anti-tank gun at the next town delayed Peiper's tanks long enough for engineers to demolish two critical bridges. A brief break in heavy snow-clouds that had shielded the Germans since the start of the counteroffensive afforded American fighter-bombers a fleeting but sharp blow at the rampaging Panzers.

Yet without additional resources, these delays were temporary successes at best. If the overwhelming tide—some 200,000 men and more than a thousand tanks—that had surged into the Ardennes was to be fully and finally reversed, something other than that available to Middleton at the start—83,000 men and perhaps 300 tanks—had to be used.

Full realisation of what was happening in the Ardennes had been slow to come at head-quarters of Lieutenant-General Courtney S. Hodges' US 1st Army, located in the Hotel Britannique in the once fashionable water-ing place of Spa, whence the Kaiser had directed his armies in the First World War. Because the opening artillery bombardments had knocked out most telephone lines to forward units, reports from some sectors had been slow to emerge. Emanating mainly from the northernmost divisions, the first messages seemed to indicate only a local spoiling attack designed to thwart an American offensive against the Roer river dams near Monschau.

Local attack or not, the Supreme Allied Commander, General Dwight D. Eisenhower, and the commander of the 12th Army Group, Lieutenant-General Omar N. Bradley, who controlled the US 1st, 3rd, and 9th Armies, recognised immediately that Middleton would have to have help to meet it. That was what had started the 7th Armoured Division moving south from the 9th Army to bolster St Vith and the 10th Armoured Division from the 3rd Army to reinforce the southern shoulder near Echter-nach and Bastogne. General Hodges himself hastily pulled troops from unthreatened portions of the 1st Army's line farther north and sent them marching to help hold the Elsenborn Ridge, while Lieutenant-General William H. Simpson, commanding the 9th Army, sent two divisions hurrying south-ward to extend the northern shoulder to the west along the Amblève river.

As awesome reports continued to reach Hodges' 1st Army HQ on December 17, Hodges asked General Eisenhower for the Supreme Commander's reserve, which consisted of only two US airborne divisions that were recuperating from a bitter fight in Operation 'Market Garden' in the Netherlands. On Bradley's recommendation, Eisenhower agreed reluctantly to part with these two units—the 82nd and 101st Airborne Divisions—and gave the order that sent them on a wild, 100-mile night ride through sleeting rain. As finally determined, the 82nd was to form a cordon far to the west near the town of Werbomont to contain Peiper's tanks, while the 101st rushed to reinforce Bastogne.

By midnight of December 17, the second day, some 60,000 men and 11,000 vehicles were on their way to reinforce Hodges' 1st Army in the Ardennes. In the next eight days, three times those numbers would be on the move. The name of the game now was mobility, and that the Americans knew how to play.

Almost instinctively, everybody from Middleton up to the Supreme Commander had begun to act in keeping with doctrine long taught in American staff schools. The way to contain and eventually erase a salient created by a major offensive – as proved in the First World War – was first to hold the shoulders of the penetration. Firm shoulders would deny the enemy the room he required if major forces were to be committed. Counterattack from the flanks then might eliminate the restricted penetration. As modified only by a determination to deny the Germans the critical road net at Bastogne, that was how the American command went about facing its task.

Yet all the early moves were makeshift, designed to meet the immediate emergency. The broad, long-range decisions remained to be taken. These General Eisenhower faced as he gathered on December 19 in a damp old caserne in Verdun with key members of his staff. With him were Bradley, Patton, and Lieutenant-General Jacob L. Devers, the latter commanding the 6th Army Group, which controlled an American army and a French army forming the southern end of the Allied line.

He wanted to see, Eisenhower said at the first, only cheerful faces.

A new infantry division, he revealed, already had arrived in France and would be moved forward quickly. Three new divisions were to accelerate their shipping schedules from way-stations in Britain, and he would ask that divisions alerted for early movement from the United States ship their infantry regiments in advance direct to French ports. He also would ask authority for artillery units to use the radar-controlled 'proximity' fuse (a scientific advance formerly deemed so secret that it had been employed only by anti-aircraft units protecting ships at sea), which caused shells to burst with deadly effect while still in the air above the target.

The American offensives that had been underway north and south of the Ardennes, Eisenhower directed, were to be halted. Both Bradley and the commander of the 21st Army Group, Field-Marshal Bernard L. Montgomery, were to look to the possibility of limited withdrawals to gain reserves, but in no event were withdrawals to be made beyond the west bank of the Meuse river. Simpson was to extend his 9th Army southward to release divisions of the 1st Army around Aachen, while Devers' 6th Army Group was to extend northward to free the bulk of Patton's 3rd Army for counterattack.

Although the more obvious and desirable method of counterattack was to strike simultaneously from north and south close along the base of the German penetration, so preoccupied was Hodges with trying to contain the penetration that only Patton would be able to move swiftly. That being the case, Patton was to attack not along the base of the penetration but toward Bastogne. From there he was to continue north-eastward to another road centre at Houffalize, there to meet Hodges' troops coming down from the north. While not eliminating the penetration, that at least would contain it.

As for the cheerful faces that Eisenhower requested, Patton gave him ebullience. He could start his counterattack, Patton insisted – despite looks of incredulity on the faces of his colleagues – in just over 72 hours, early on December 22.

The meeting at Verdun had not long adjourned when Eisenhower's Chief of Intelligence, a British officer, Major-General Kenneth W. D. Strong, remarked that soon the German thrust would so split the 12th Army Group that all forces north of the pene-

tration should be transferred to Field-Marshal Montgomery's command. It was an explosive suggestion, for Eisenhower had so far resisted placing large bodies of American troops under foreign command and had specifically rejected an oft-recurring proposal that Montgomery be made overall ground commander on the Western Front.

The proposal nevertheless made sense – as even a shocked and hurt Bradley would have to admit – for direct telephone communications already had been cut, long-range radio was no substitute for the telephone, and the German salient made travel between Bradley's headquarters in Luxembourg City and those of Hodges and Simpson in the north circuitous at best. Since the counteroffensive opened, Bradley had met Hodges face to face only once; and confusion there was, not only from streams of stragglers and civilian refugees but in the command structure as well. Neither Hodges nor the corps commander, Middleton, could possibly maintain contact with all units on the broken, fluctuating front. To pull Bradley's headquarters out of Luxembourg City to a position west of the Meuse whence Bradley might control the entire front would be to flirt with panic among the civilian population and possibly to damage the morale of the troops as well.

Yet what was more important to Eisenhower – and this sweetened the pill for Bradley – was that giving Montgomery command north of the penetration would assure use of British reserves, which included an entire corps with four divisions and several armoured brigades. It was a step that would pay off as planned, for Montgomery promptly ordered his 30th Corps to move to reserve positions between Liège and Brussels and announced that the British would assume responsibility for the Meuse bridges from Liège to the big bend in the river at Namur.

Had Montgomery been an American, or even had he been a less self-assured, imperious personality, the shift in command would have been easier for American commanders to take. As it was, Montgomery on the 20th strode into the 1st Army's HQ (in the words of one of his own staff) 'like Christ come to cleanse the temple'. He ignored the 1st Army's detailed operations map to consult a small one of his own, on which he had plotted information provided by British liaison officers. He also declined General Hodges' invitation to lunch, turning instead to eat alone from a lunch box and Thermos – which, to be fair, was his normal practice.

Montgomery nevertheless approved the dispositions and measures Hodges had already taken. The incoming 30th Division, Hodges reported, had cut Peiper's supply line by retaking Stavelot; other troops of the 30th were battling Peiper at the tip of his penetration to cover assembly of the 82nd Airborne Division; a portion of the 3rd Armoured Division was on the way; and St Vith was holding, although the American position there had been compressed into a horseshoe-shaped salient maintaining only tenuous contact with other American forces to the rear.

While approving Hodges' moves, Montgomery nevertheless urged withdrawal from two positions that the Americans considered to be key: the Elsenborn Ridge and St Vith. It was a typical Montgomery manoeuvre, a step to 'tidy the battlefield' by removing what by any standards was a dangerous salient at St Vith and to soften what was an admittedly sharp northern corner of the German penetration at the Elsenborn Ridge.

Yet when Hodges and his staff reacted with shocked disbelief, Montgomery desisted.

Having gone along with the American determination, Montgomery went even farther, sanctioning a move already planned by Hodges to send the 82nd Airborne Division skirting the south flank of Peiper's penetration to push westward to the Salm river, which represented the rear of the St Vith horseshoe. Other than Peiper's task force, which American reinforcements were now effectively bottling up, tanks of the VI Panzer Army had yet to get over the Salm, so few were the roads available in the narrow corridor between the St Vith salient and the Elsenborn Ridge. To hold the Germans even temporarily at the Salm was to afford an avenue of escape for the troops in St Vith while at the same time providing cover for assembling a force for counterattack.

Montgomery wanted for counterattack, he told Hodges, the corps commander whom he deemed the 1st Army's most aggressive – Major-General J. Lawton Collins, who long ago had earned the nickname, 'Lightning Joe'. Pulled from the line near Aachen, Collins' 7th Corps was to be filled out with infantry and armoured divisions and readied for counterattack to hit the Germans once they had extended themselves in their quest for bridges over the Meuse.

Closing in on Bastogne

As Montgomery was moving to shore up the extended northern shoulder, combat commands of the US 9th and 10th Armoured Divisions were fighting a bitter delaying action in front of Bastogne, enabling the 101st Airborne Division to beat the Germans into the town. Yet from Bastogne all the way north to where the 82nd Airborne Division was assembling near Werbomont, no American line existed, leaving a gap more than 20 miles wide that included the town of Houffalize.

Having passed to the south of St Vith, two of General von Mantueffel's crack Panzer divisions – the II and the 116th – were hurtling almost without check into this gap. By nightfall of December 19 one column of 116th Panzer had reached Houffalize while reconnaissance troops had pushed 10 miles farther to the south-west toward a west branch of the Ourthe river. This joins the east-west main branch of the Ourthe at a point west of Houffalize, where the Ourthe makes a turn to the north-west for an eventual swing to the north.

Fortunately for the American cause, the troops forming for the defence of Bastogne had pushed their northern perimeter out as far as the town of Noville, almost half the distance to Houffalize, which left only one road leading west between Noville and Houffalize, that already taken by the 116th Panzer Division. The position at Noville blocked passage of the II Panzer Division.

Fortunately, too, General Middleton had rushed some of his conglomerate reserve – an engineer battalion, an independent tank destroyer battalion, even a Canadian forestry company – to destroy bridges and hold the west branch of the Ourthe. Before tanks of 116th Panzer could cross, the way was barred with outposts and demolished bridges.

Fortunately again, the II and 116th Panzer Divisions belonged to separate corps. Since the 116th had been scheduled to swing north-west after getting across the west branch of the Ourthe, the corps commander deemed he had no choice in the absence of a bridge but to recall his troops to Houffalize and resume his advance along the north bank of the main branch. In the counter-march he would lose 24 critical hours.

The II Panzer Division, meanwhile, battered against the defenders of Noville, finally pushing the Americans aside during the afternoon of December 20. This division belonged to the XLVII Panzer Corps, commanded by General Heinrich Freiherr von Lüttwitz, whose responsibility included Bastogne. Although Lüttwitz was preoccupied with taking the town, he had other troops to do it with, including the Panzer Lehr Division. While these troops probed the Bastogne perimeter, encircling the town in the process, Lüttwitz sent the II Panzer Division pushing on to the west.

That night (the 20th) the division's reconnaissance battalion got across the Ourthe at Ourtheville on a bridge that 116th Panzer had neglected to storm in the belief the Americans would destroy it, as they had all others. Yet the American demolitions unaccountably had failed, and the II Panzer Division got across the Ourthe dryshod.

The Meuse now lay only 23 miles to the west. But for a reason that seemed inexplicable at the time to the little bands of American defenders who still stood in the way, the II Panzer Division came to a halt.

In the north, in the meantime, the decision to send the 82nd Airborne Division skirting the south flank of Peiper's trapped tanks to push up to the Salm river behind the St Vith horseshoe proved to be exceptionally provident. Advancing without opposition, the airborne troops dropped off units along the way to face southward in the direction of Houffalize, thus affording some block should the 116th Panzer Division and accompanying infantry units swing northward. By the morning of the 21st, the rest of the paratroops were in position along the Salm, facing the west, where during the day the Germans were finally to wrest the town of St Vith from the 7th Armoured Division and the mixed units that had held it for over five days.

As nightfall came on December 21, the battle from the American viewpoint still was going badly:
● St Vith and its roads was now open to the Germans, with American withdrawal from the portion of the horseshoe still in their hands inevitable. Peiper was still dangerous, even though trapped;
● The situation on the southern shoulder of the German penetration was still fluid;
● The delaying forces in front of Bastogne were all but destroyed, leaving the lightly armed 101st Airborne Division, encircled in Bastogne, to muster such support as could be salvaged to defend against an entire German corps;
● One German Panzer division was across the Ourthe river 23 miles from the Meuse, another was at Houffalize presumably preparing to resume the trek westward;
● Ever since the start of the German attack on the 16th, fog and low overcast had denied all but the most daring (and usually unproductive) sorties by American fighter-bombers.

Yet, as is so often the case in battle, the other side saw the situation in another light.

As early as the third day, December 18, the German army group commander, Field-Marshal Walter Model, had come to the conclusion that the counteroffensive had fallen short. This may have been merely an initial reaction of surprise and frustration that the opening blows had failed to penetrate the

The price of violating the rules of war...

'Scarface' Skorzeny, Hitler's master commando. His men, dressed in American uniforms, spread chaos and confusion behind the US lines—but those who were caught paid the inevitable price before the firing squads

Südd Verlag

Imperial War Museum

Imperial War Museum

Imperial War Museum

American line as quickly as planned. Yet even Hitler had expressed at least tacit concern by cancelling a projected supporting attack by the XV Army against thinned American lines near Aachen. But that was before the II Panzer Division achieved its spectacular gain across the Ourthe river. So thrilled was the Führer with this development that he afforded Field-Marshal von Rundstedt two divisions from the general reserve to be employed as Rundstedt himself decided.

There were continuing problems on the German side nevertheless. The Americans at the northern corner on the Elsenborn Ridge still held, a rock against which the VI Panzer Army could but batter in vain, restricting Dietrich's armour to two of the four main roads intended for the advance westward, and one of those under heavy American artillery fire. That was why the remainder of the I SS Panzer Division was so slow to follow Peiper's lead, and why Peiper had been trapped. He eventually lost 39 tanks and the rest of his transport and equipment, with only 800 out of an original force of 2,000 men at last infiltrating back to safety.

Nor could Dietrich's other three SS Panzer divisions be brought to bear through this narrow passage: all efforts to do so produced traffic spill-over into the zone of the V Panzer Army around St Vith. At one point Field-Marshal Model personally helped direct traffic near St Vith and came upon General von Manteuffel doing the same thing. So critical was the jam that Field-Marshal von Rundstedt on the 21st ordered two of Dietrich's SS Panzer divisions transferred southward to Manteuffel, whose V Panzer Army henceforth would compose the German main effort. A shift southward of the boundary between the two armies, giving St Vith to Dietrich, was all part of the main plan.

For all the success of II and 116th Panzer Divisions in bypassing St Vith to the south and streaming westward between St Vith and Bastogne, the failure to capture these two road centres early in the fighting had sharply restricted Manteuffel's dash for the Meuse. And even after General von Lüttwitz's spearheads had drawn up to Bastogne on the 19th, he had been slow to launch a comprehensive attack because thawing roads leading up from the eastern river valleys slowed the arrival of supporting artillery.

Shortages of fuel crimped German operations everywhere, the most drastic shortage hitting II Panzer Division, preventing that front-running force from moving at all on the 21st. The shortages developed partly because the Germans had failed to capture any large American stocks, but also because awesome traffic jams plagued the steep, serpentine, icy roads behind the lines in the Eifel. One of Dietrich's Panzer divisions used up its fuel battering against the Elsenborn Ridge. When on the 21st Rundstedt ordered two of Dietrich's divisions to be transferred to Manteuffel, there would not—for 36 hours—be enough fuel to allow one of the divisions to move.

German commanders also had to keep looking over their left shoulders, for how long would it be before Patton would throw his 3rd Army against the German southern flank? How long, too, before the fog and overcast parted to enable the deadly American fighter-bombers to join the battle? Perhaps, despite the disagreements in the Allied command, the worst was over.

BATTLE OF THE BULGE: THE ALLIED COUNTERBLOW

Ardennes, Belgium, December 22, 1944/January 28, 1945

On December 22, the Allies still seemed on the edge of disaster—the Germans were still advancing towards the Meuse, still confidently demanding the surrender of Bastogne. But in reality, despite the disagreements which were rending the Allied command, the worst was over: incredibly stubborn American resistance had sapped the strength of the German drive and soon the US forces would begin their counterattack—unfortunately settling for the 'small solution' of squeezing the Germans out of the Bulge instead of amputating it cleanly. *Below:* American infantrymen advance towards beleaguered Bastogne

No one could have discerned it with any certainty at the time, but the day of December 22, 1944, saw the beginning of the climax of the battle in the Ardennes.

On that day, in a blinding snowstorm, General Patton made good his promise to counterattack. While rushing an infantry division into the line north-east of Luxembourg city to bolster a weakening American position at the southern base of the bulge, he threw another infantry division and the veteran 4th Armoured Division into a drive to break through to encircled Bastogne. The 3rd Army had withdrawn in the face of the enemy and executed a 90° shift in direction of attack with a speed unparalleled in military history.

On that day, too, the Germans surrounding Bastogne tightened their encirclement and delivered a surrender ultimatum, only to be left to ponder the meaning of the reply that came back in American slang: 'Nuts!'

Also on the 22nd, the Germans launched what they hoped would be the last leg on the drive to the Meuse—the II Panzer Division already across the west branch of the river and the 116th Panzer Division driving from Houffalize along the north bank of the main branch with plans to cross the river where it swings north near

Out of the east emerged what weathermen call a 'Russian high', bringing in the wake of the day's heavy snowfall sharply dropping temperatures that froze the ground, allowing tanks—both American and German—to manoeuvre freely, but also bringing weather that allowed aircraft to operate again.

Given the overwhelming Allied superiority in aircraft, the advantage of clear skies rested fully with the Allied side. As December 23 dawned, fighter-bombers and mediums would be out in force, wreaking havoc on German columns that heretofore had enjoyed virtual immunity to punishment from the air. Out in force, too, would be big C-47 transport aircraft, looking like pregnant geese against the sky and dropping multi-hued parachutes bearing critical supplies to the troops in beleaguered Bastogne.

For all the assistance from the air, by mid-day of December 23 a hasty line thrown up by the 84th Division beyond the Ourthe around Marche was in serious trouble. So was the American line between the Salm and the Ourthe, where the II SS Panzer Division attacked alongside the 116th Panzer Division. So devastating were the German strikes against the combat command of the 3rd Armoured Division that contingents of another infantry division ear-

American armour deploys during a counterblow against the 'Bulge'. Within ten days of the initial German thrust, the American forces were again on the offensive, but their efforts were much hampered by weather conditions like this

Hotton. General von Manteuffel was hoping to reinforce these two divisions, the II Panzer with the Panzer Lehr once the latter could shake loose from Bastogne, the 116th Panzer with the II SS Panzer Division, shifted from Dietrich's army.

Yet the Germans had lost too much time getting through Noville, waiting for fuel beyond the Ourthe, and countermarching to Houffalize to enjoy the same free wheeling they had experienced in earlier days: for the divisions scheduled to 'flesh out' Joe Collins' 7th Corps for counterattack were now arriving. First, a combat command of the 3rd Armoured Division, which Hodges committed astride the Houffalize-Liège highway to extend westward all the way to the Ourthe the southward-facing positions assumed by the 82nd Airborne Division between the Salm and the Ourthe. Second, the 84th Infantry Division, which in assembling behind the Ourthe near the town of Marche would lie full in the projected path of the II Panzer Division, north-westward from Ourtheville toward the Meuse. And before the battle south of the Meuse was over, the other two divisions joining Collins' corps also would enter the fight.

Another move began on the 22nd—American withdrawal from the St Vith horseshoe. Having lost 8,000 out of some 22,000 men, not counting the regiments of the 106th Division that had been trapped on the Schnee Eifel, the defenders of St Vith came back under orders from Montgomery. They were orders laced with the kind of accolade that had long ago endeared the Field-Marshal to the British Tommy: the heroic defenders of St Vith were authorised to withdraw 'with all honour . . . They put up a wonderful show'.

The last of them would make it before daylight on December 23, not to return to some warm, safe haven but to re-enter the line; for by this time the positions of the 82nd Airborne and 3rd Armoured Divisions between the Salm and the Ourthe were under heavy attack.

One final event on the 22nd would have an authoritative impact on the continuing battle. As darkness fell, chill winds began to blow.

marked to join Collins' counterattacking reserve were pulled into this fray, leaving only one division of armour from the counterattacking force still uncommitted. Once the remnants of the St Vith defenders were safely within American lines, Montgomery aided this fight by ordering the 82nd Airborne Division to withdraw from what had become a sharp corner at Vielsalm, along the Salm river west of St Vith.

Crisis there was between the Salm and the Ourthe; but to American commanders the most serious crisis was developing in what represented the tip of the bulge, beyond the Ourthe where the II Panzer Division bounced off the flank of the 84th Division and continued toward the Meuse. Here, by mid-day of the 23rd, the last of the units that Montgomery had hoped to assemble as a reserve, the 2nd Armoured Division, was arriving.

This development was destined to bring to a head a kind of covert contest of wills that since the day Montgomery had assumed command had been running between Montgomery and the commander of the US 1st Army, Courtney Hodges. As demonstrated by Montgomery's early wish to withdraw from St Vith and the Elsenborn Ridge, the British commander believed in a policy of rolling with the punches. The Americans, for their part, shocked at what a presumably defeated German army had done to them, were reluctant sometimes to the point of fault to give up any ground unless forced, particularly ground that American soldiers had bought with blood.

Montgomery's theory was that by holding the most economical line possible in the north and amassing a reserve in the process, he might force the Germans to overextend themselves, whereupon he would strike with Collins' 7th Corps. Montgomery was relatively unconcerned about the Germans reaching or even crossing the Meuse: by this time he had moved a British armoured brigade to cover the critical bridges on either side of the big bend at Namur. Furthermore, even should the Germans cross the Meuse, he had a reserve corps in position to annihilate them.

Possessed of no ready reserve, American commanders could hardly be so sanguine. As late as the 22nd, both Patton and Middleton were still concerned lest the Germans suddenly swing southwest in the direction of Sedan and the site of their triumph in 1940. Remembering 1914 and 1940, Paris had the jitters, and military police were enforcing a strict curfew in the French capital while guarding Eisenhower closely lest Otto Skorzeny's disguised raiders try to assassinate the Supreme Commander. Hodges and the staff of the 1st Army were still unconvinced that the Germans would not turn north to take Liège. Even the British were concerned enough to station guards and erect roadblocks on the outskirts of Brussels.

Having had close personal experience with the power of the German drive, Courtney Hodges remained most concerned of all. That he had been forced, contrary to Montgomery's plan, to keep committing incoming divisions as the Germans continued to work westward seemed to him under the circumstances the only way to run the fight. He saw the tip of Manteuffel's striking force embracing or soon to embrace four Panzer divisions—Panzer Lehr in the south, II Panzer and 116th Panzer in the centre, and II SS Panzer

The 'big' solution—severing the bulge completely—was rejected in favour of the 'small' solution: squeezing it out

1944 December 22: The Germans launch their last attempt to reach the Meuse. US forces withdraw from the St Vith area.
December 25: US 2nd Armoured Division attacks and turns back II Panzer Division 4 miles from the Meuse.
December 26: US 4th Armoured Division relieves Bastogne. Word reaches Hitler that Antwerp can no longer be reached.
December 30: A US attack north-east from Bastogne towards Houffalize is stalemated by a German attack on the corridor to Bastogne.

1945 January 3/4: The last German attack on Bastogne is defeated. The US counterattack begins.
January 8: Hitler authorises withdrawal to Houffalize.
January 16: US 1st and 3rd Armies link up at Houffalize.
January 20: General Patch's withdrawal from the north-eastern sector is complete.
January 22: The weather clears, allowing US pilots to take the air against German convoys.
January 28: The last vestige of the Bulge disappears.

in the north, while to the right of II SS Panzer, Sepp Dietrich was at last bringing his two remaining SS Panzer divisions to bear.

To Hodges, to withhold reserves while forces of such power were still on the move—even in view of radio intercepts indicating that the Germans were running short of fuel—was to flirt with disaster.

Without asking approval, the commander of the 2nd Armoured Division, Major-General Ernest Harmon, sent one of his combat commands southward on December 23 to investigate reports of German tanks passing south of Marche. Yet word came back of no contact except with British armoured patrols already working the area with no sign of the enemy.

Yet, in reality, the II Panzer Division had found free passage south of Marche and was toiling toward the Meuse at Dinant. (The only one of Skorzeny's disguised patrols to reach a Meuse bridge gained Dinant that night but was quickly captured by British guards.) By mid-afternoon of December 24—Christmas Eve—it was all too apparent to General Harmon that German tanks were present a few miles farther south in strength. He put in a call to Collins, his corps commander, for authority to turn the entire 2nd Armoured Division to the attack.

With Collins away from his headquarters, the 7th Corps' staff relayed the request to 1st Army HQ. Courtney Hodges was torn. Although still under Field-Marshal Montgomery's dictum to amass a reserve, and specifically to keep from getting the 2nd Armoured Division involved, Hodges' heart was with Collins and Harmon.

The word that came from Hodges was that Collins was 'authorised' to roll with the punch, to peel back to the north-west; but along with the failure specifically to order withdrawal, Hodges included no proviso denying attack. That was all the licence General Collins needed. That night he and Harmon mapped out an attack to begin early on Christmas Day, employing all of the 2nd Armoured Division.

Collins' decision represented the high-water mark of the German counteroffensive in the Ardennes. In conjunction with contingents

of British armour and American fighter-bombers enjoying another day in the sun, the 2nd Armoured Division on Christmas Day began to wipe out a II Panzer Division that at the height of its achievement had run out of gasoline at the town of Celles—only 4 miles from the Meuse and not quite 60 miles from the start line along the German frontier.

The Germans paid a price of more than 80 tanks. They left not only their spearhead but their ambition broken in the snow.

Bastogne relieved at last
There were two other events on Christmas Day equally disconcerting to the Germans. The first was in the north-west, where the US 3rd Armoured Division with help of infantry reinforcements brought to a halt an all-out attack by the II SS Panzer Division to break through between the Salm and the Ourthe, while on the west bank of the Ourthe other American troops dealt roughly with the 116th Panzer Division.

The second was at Bastogne.

Obsessed with the idea that the II Panzer Division was out on a limb, General von Manteuffel saw Bastogne as a boil that had to

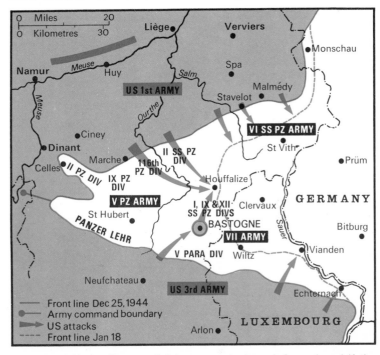

be lanced if the Panzer division were to be reinforced and if the entire German counteroffensive were not to be disrupted by Patton's counterattack. Rather than send the Panzer Lehr Division immediately to II Panzer's assistance, Manteuffel held on to it and ordered an all-out attack by Lüttwitz's XLVII Panzer Corps to be launched on Christmas Day to capture Bastogne. This time Lüttwitz was to hit a previously untested and presumably soft rear—or western—arc of the American perimeter.

Preceded by a heavy air bombardment of Bastogne the night before, the new attack posed such a threat that as the morning dawned many an American paratrooper shook hands with his buddies in a final gesture of salute. The farewells were premature. Before night came, the paratroops of the 101st with their pot-pourri of reinforcements had either held or quickly sealed off every penetration.

The next day, December 26, as dusk descended, an engineer battalion manning a portion of the southern fringe of the perimeter reported the approach of 'three light tanks, believed friendly'.

The 4th Armoured Division had arrived.

The siege was ended.

On this day after Christmas, the word reaching Hitler from Manteuffel, Model, and Rundstedt was that no chance whatever remained of reaching Antwerp. The only hope of salvaging any sort of victory from the Ardennes was to turn the V and VI Panzer Armies north to cross the Meuse west of Liège and come in behind Aachen. This presupposed the capture of Bastogne and a secondary attack from the north to link with the Panzer armies. Yet if these prerequisites were to be met, Hitler would have to abandon a new project he had been contemplating: a second counteroffensive in Alsace.

This was, in effect, a return to what Hitler earlier had labelled the 'Small Solution', a proposal his generals had championed when he first had broached the idea of a counteroffensive in the Ardennes. Deeming German resources too limited for taking Antwerp,

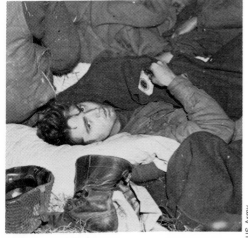
US wounded in makeshift conditions

Bastogne: 'bastion of the battered bastards of the 101st'...

POWs dig mass graves, also makeshift

A vital communications centre, Bastogne was the key to the Ardennes—and the target of an all-out German attack

they had wanted instead a limited attack to take the American supply base of Liège and cut in behind the 1st and 9th US Armies around Aachen. Hitler long ago had scorned the 'Small Solution'. Again he rejected it.

'We have had unexpected setbacks,' the Führer acknowledged, but that was 'because my plan was not followed to the letter'.

So stretched had the Americans become in Alsace in order to release Patton for counterattack, Hitler believed, that the second counteroffensive he contemplated there would score such gains as to turn Patton away from the Ardennes. Given the code name *Nordwind* ('North Wind'), the counteroffensive was to begin on New Year's Day.

Nor would Hitler accept the contention that Antwerp lay beyond reach. While agreeing that, once Bastogne was captured, the two Panzer armies might turn northward to clear the east and south banks of the Meuse, he saw this as no switch to the 'Small Solu-

tion' but as a temporary diversion to trap the American units that had rushed to the north shoulder of the bulge. This would prepare the way for renewing the drive on Antwerp.

On the Allied side, Bradley on Christmas Day and Eisenhower a few days later urged Field-Marshal Montgomery to turn the 1st Army quickly to the offensive in order to take some of the pressure off Bastogne and Patton's efforts to carve a viable corridor into the town. Montgomery responded that he expected the Germans to hit the 1st Army one more blow; but if that failed to come he would attack on January 3.

Montgomery's reluctance to attack annoyed the American commanders. The British field-marshal, they knew, had an entire corps in reserve. Although neither Bradley, Hodges, nor Patton asked commitment of British troops, they believed that so long as Montgomery had this reserve he need fear no further German thrust.

Another German blow in the north never came, primarily because

...and the rock which broke the German offensive

POWs: German casualties neared 100,000

The wrack of the receding German tide

Turret torn off by anti-tank fire, this shattered German tank symbolises the ferocity of the American defence of Bastogne

Patton's troops at Bastogne and on either side of the relief corridor that he opened on the 26th fought the V Panzer Army to a standstill. The battle reached a climax on December 30 when Patton, his forces around Bastogne swollen now to six divisions, tried to resume his attack north-east toward Houffalize. At almost precisely the same moment, General von Manteuffel launched another major attempt to cut the corridor into Bastogne and take the town.

Casualties on both sides mounted, and bitterly cold weather took an inevitable toll; but the American troops held firm, even after the Germans had driven a salient into the east side of the corridor. It was a struggle for survival such as Bastogne had not known even in the critical days of encirclement.

Threat to the 'Colmar Pocket'
As events strode to a climax at Bastogne, a crucible similarly demanding was beginning to develop for troops of the US 7th Army,

commanded by Lieutenant-General Alexander M. Patch, and some of their compatriots in General Jean de Lattre de Tassigny's French 1st Army, which together made up General Devers' 6th Army Group. Undermined by any standards of comparison with Bradley's 12th Army Group or Montgomery's 21st Army Group, Devers' forces had had to stretch already thin lines even thinner to absorb former positions of two of the 3rd Army's corps in order to release Patton for counterattack.

The new arrangement charged General Patch's 7th Army with 124 miles of front, the bulk of it along the German frontier facing the Saar industrial region, 40 miles of it along the Rhine to include the city of Strasbourg. From that point southward General de Lattre's French took over, containing what Allied troops called the 'Colmar Pocket', an expansive German bridgehead on the Rhine's west bank around the town of Colmar, a hold-out position that Devers' undermanned forces had yet been unable to eliminate and one that had posed a constant threat in General Eisenhower's mind ever since the counteroffensive had begun in the Ardennes.

Because General Patch's positions formed a right angle where the Franco-German border meets the Rhine, those American divisions in this extreme north-east corner of France would be threatened by entrapment should the Germans launch converging thrusts against them or should the Germans strike swiftly to deny the few passes through the Vosges Mountains, which stood behind them. Recognising that little of strategic importance lay in this low plain alongside the Rhine, General Eisenhower had told Devers at the meeting in Verdun to yield ground rather than endanger the integrity of his forces.

To withdraw all the way to the Vosges would nevertheless involve giving up Strasbourg, a city which the French looked upon symbolically as the capital of Alsace and Lorraine, the provinces lost to the Germans from 1870 to 1918 and again from 1940 until late 1944. To the French, to abandon Strasbourg was to relinquish a part of the soul of France.

Yet to defend 124 miles of front, including Strasbourg, the 7th Army had only seven divisions, plus the infantry regiments of three new divisions, only recently arrived from the United States in response to Eisenhower's call for assistance at the start of the Ardennes counteroffensive. Also available as a last resort were two divisions that Eisenhower had managed to cull from the line to recreate a Supreme Headquarters reserve; but these might at any time have to be sent into the Ardennes.

That left the stratagem of withdrawal in the event of a major German attack perhaps the only recourse.

That the Germans planned to attack either on New Year's Day or soon thereafter became clear to the 6th Army Group during the last week of December. The attack actually was to begin an hour before the first stroke of the New Year.

The American soldier, victor of Bastogne...

When Hitler had first proposed a counteroffensive in Alsace, the idea had been a heavy strike all the way to the American supply base of Metz, but even Hitler had to accept that this was too ambitious for the available resources. As in the Ardennes, the Führer himself planned the blow actually delivered – Operation *Nordwind*.

Attacking west of the Vosges Mountains, two divisions under the aegis of Army Group G (Generaloberst Johannes Blaskowitz) were to make a penetration, whereupon a reserve of two armoured divisions was to strike swiftly southward to seal from the rear the vital Saverne Gap, which separates the High Vosges in the south from the less imposing Low Vosges in the north. At the same time a supporting effort by three infantry divisions was to push down the spine of the Low Vosges. A few days later, a lone division was to cross the Rhine north of Strasbourg, while two divisions were to attack northward from the Colmar Pocket, link with the Rhine bridgehead (encircling Strasbourg in the process), then swing westward to the Saverne Gap.

The net effect would be to trap all American units east of the Low Vosges, the equivalent of five divisions, and those French troops guarding the northern periphery of the Colmar Pocket.

Sharply conscious of this possibility, General Eisenhower moved swiftly once the German attack began, and ordered General Devers to pull back from his north-eastern salient all the way to the Vosges, leaving only delaying forces on the low-lying plain.

That meant abandoning Strasbourg, a condition that prompted the head of the provisional French government, Charles de Gaulle, to send an emissary to Eisenhower's headquarters to express his dismay. Rather than relinquish the city, the word was, de Gaulle already had ordered General de Lattre to extend his lines north and take over the defence.

Struck by this defiance, Eisenhower's Chief-of-Staff, Lieutenant-General Walter B. Smith, threatened to cut off American supplies and equipment, without which the French army would be powerless – to which de Gaulle's man responded that the French were prepared to withdraw their troops from Eisenhower's command.

Although it sounded like an argument in a schoolyard, it was a serious confrontation. De Gaulle even went so far as to cable the American President and the British Prime Minister for support; but intercession proved unnecessary. When apprised by General Smith of the fervour of de Gaulle's objections and when apprised, too, by the end of the second day (January 2) of the success of Patch's troops in constraining the German main effort toward the Saverne Gap, Eisenhower withdrew the order. While directing the French to take responsibility for defending Strasbourg, he told General Devers to withdraw from the north-eastern salient only as far as the little Moder river, some 20 miles behind the existing lines.

By January 20 this withdrawal was complete. The Germans, meanwhile, had succeeded in establishing a Rhine bridgehead north of Strasbourg, advancing to within 8 miles of the city, and inducing near panic in the civilian population before commitment of a portion of General Eisenhower's reserve brought them to a halt. The attack northward out of the Colmar Pocket got within 13 miles of Strasbourg, but the French stopped it at the last bridge short of the city.

While Devers' 6th Army Group retained its integrity, Strasbourg stayed French. Having committed so much to the Ardennes, the Germans had simply been unequal to a second blow: ten under-

Thick fog and low clouds, combined with high winds, deprived the American armour and infantry of much-needed air support. Here men of the 82nd Airborne Division move through typical Ardennes Forest terrain

US Army

Although both Model and Rundstedt gave their endorsement, Hitler refused. The counteroffensive under the original concept of taking Antwerp and trapping Allied armies, he at last admitted, no longer had any chance of success; but he had arrived at definite ideas of how the bulge in the Ardennes might be turned to German advantage.

In creating the salient, Hitler reasoned, he had forced General Eisenhower to employ almost all his resources. That Eisenhower used élite airborne divisions to do the brutal defensive work of infantry was proof enough of that. By holding the bulge, he might keep the Allies widely stretched while pulling out some German units for spoiling attacks elsewhere—like Operation *Nordwind.* That way he might prevent the Allies from concentrating their forces in the north for a renewed offensive to cross the Rhine and capture the Ruhr industrial region.

Yet even this strategy begged the capture of Bastogne, for Hitler required the town both to anchor the southern flank of the bulge and to deny its nexus of roads to the Americans.

To American troops, Manteuffel's final offensive at Bastogne, aimed at severing the corridor into the town, appeared less a concerted attack than reaction by counterattack to Patton's efforts to drive on to Houffalize. Lasting two days—January 3 and 4—the German offensive delayed the drive on Houffalize; but it was too feeble either to pose any genuine threat to Bastogne or to thwart the American offensive entirely. What was more, it operated on borrowed time, for it opened on the same day that Field-Marshal Montgomery at last released Hodges' 1st Army to attack from the north.

The pattern of the drive to eliminate the bulge had been set at the Allied conference in Verdun on December 19 with the decision to send the 3rd Army to Bastogne. Although Patton insisted, once Bastogne was relieved, on shifting to the classic though venturesome manoeuvre for eliminating a deep penetration—cutting it off

...and of the whole Ardennes campaign

at its base—he found no support from either Hodges or Bradley. They were concerned about the limited roadnet at the northern base and about the effect of winter weather in the more sharply compartmented terrain along the German frontier. Montgomery conformed, moving parts of two British divisions to the tip of the bulge to enable General Collins to shift his 7th Corps slightly northward and drive from the north-west for Houffalize. Once the 1st and 3rd Armies met at Houffalize, both were to sweep, after the manner of synchronized windshield wipers, on to the German frontier.

In other words, they were going to push in the bulge rather than cut it off. It was—Field-Marshal von Rundstedt would observe after the war—the 'Small Solution'.

The nadir of winter
The snow was deeper than ever in the Ardennes, the temperatures lower, the fog thicker, the winds more penetrating when, early on January 3, General Collins sent two armoured divisions backed by infantry south-east toward Houffalize across ground featured by stretches of high marshland, dense patches of firs, and deep-cut streambeds. Only three of Sepp Dietrich's badly damaged divisions barred the way, including fragments of the mauled II Panzer Division. But that was enough, in view of the weather and the terrain, to slow the Allied advance to a crawl.

So murky was the atmosphere that not a single tactical aircraft could support the attack all day, and sorties by little artillery observation aircraft were possible for no more than an hour. It was a pattern that would undergo little change for a fortnight. On only three days would fighter-bombers be able to take to the air at all. Much of the time the men advanced through snow flurries, followed on the fourth day by a heavy snowfall that piled drifts in places to a depth of several feet.

Tanks stalled on icy hillsides in long rows. Trucks towing anti-tank guns or artillery pieces skidded, jack-knifed, collided, and blocked vital roads for hours. Two trucks towing 105-mm howitzers plunged off a cliff. Deliberate roadblocks formed by felled trees with anti-tank mines on the approaches could be eliminated only by

strength divisions were not enough. The fighting in bitter cold and snow nevertheless cost the Americans 15,600 casualties; the Germans, 25,000.

As the 6th Army Group was meeting its test in Alsace, the Germans managed two last spasms in a dying effort in the Ardennes. One came from the air, an extraordinary effort by the Luftwaffe. Early on New Year's Day, 700 German planes struck at Allied airfields in Belgium and the Netherlands. The blow took Allied airmen by surprise and cost 156 planes, most of them destroyed on the ground.

The second blow again was aimed at Bastogne, where General von Manteuffel had seen his offensive of December 30 collapse in the face of Patton's renewed attack. It was a blow of which Manteuffel himself disapproved. The time had long come, he believed, to abandon all attempts at maintaining the offensive in the Ardennes. Lest the troops in the tip of the bulge be trapped between Patton and what appeared to be a pending attack by the US 1st Army from the north, he appealed to Field-Marshal Model late on January 2 for permission to pull back to a line anchored on Houffalize.

These POWs, promised a quick victory in December, were humbled by defeat and capture in February

dismounted infantry making slow, sometimes costly flanking moves through deep snow. Bridges everywhere were demolished, the sites defended, so that, just as with the roadblocks, winter-weary infantry had to plod upstream or down to find an uncontested ford, then wade the icy stream to take the Germans in flank, finding in most cases that the foe at the last moment pulled back to fight again another day. The Germans occasionally counterattacked: five or six tanks, a company or a battalion of infantry at a time. Under these conditions, to advance 2 miles a day was a major achievement.

The 3rd Army had it as hard and more so, for the defences in the vicinity of Bastogne reflected the large concentration of German forces there for the various efforts to take the town. Bitterly cold, stung by biting winds and driven snow, nostrils frozen, Patton's troops saw little change in a pattern too long familiar. The Germans opposing them were old and dreaded foes—such units as the I, IX, and XII SS Panzer Divisions, the V Parachute, the Panzer Lehr. Accustomed too were the place names, the same towns and villages where little clots of tanks and infantry a fortnight before had thwarted the Germans in the race for Bastogne, although these were less towns and villages now than macabre monuments to the destructiveness of war.

Yet for all the rigour of the fighting, it became apparent on January 5 that the final crisis at Bastogne had passed. When Field-Marshal Model pulled out one of the SS Panzer divisions to go to the aid of the VI Panzer Army in the north, General von Manteuffel took it upon himself to pull another of the SS Panzer divisions from the line to form a reserve. Three days later, on January 8, Hitler himself authorised withdrawal from the tip of the bulge, not all the way back to Houffalize as Manteuffel had asked, but to a line anchored on a series of ridges 5 miles west of Houffalize.

This was the Führer's first grudging admission that the counteroffensive in the Ardennes had failed utterly. Dietrich's VI Panzer Army, he directed, was gradually to relinquish control of all but the SS Panzer divisions to Manteuffel's V Panzer Army, whereupon these four divisions were to assemble in the rear at St Vith. There they were ostensibly to guard against attacks near the base of the bulge: but in reality they were executing the first step in leaving

the Ardennes entirely. As Hitler's advisers in the East had long been warning, a powerful new Russian offensive was destined to begin any day. It would actually start on January 12, and Hitler on January 22 would order the VI Panzer Army to move with all speed to the Eastern Front.

Meanwhile, early on January 16, patrols of the US 1st and 3rd Armies met at Houffalize. Rent apart by the counteroffensive, the two armies had joined hands at the waist of the bulge, failing to trap many of the elusive foe but setting the stage for the return of Hodges' 1st Army to General Bradley's command. This General Eisenhower would order, effective the next day, at the same time retaining Simpson's 9th Army under Montgomery with an eye toward renewing an Allied offensive toward the Ruhr.

It would take another eight days to push in what was left of the bulge in a slow contest against weather and long-proven German ingenuity on the defence. Back to St. Vith, back to Clerf, back to Echternach, back to the Skyline Drive, back to many another spot where American infantrymen, surprised, frightened, but determined, had purchased a commodity called time.

On January 22 the clouds finally cleared dramatically. A brilliant sun came up, its rays dancing on a new snow cover. Pilots were early in the air, jubilant to find German vehicles stalled bumper to bumper waiting their turn to cross ice-encrusted bridges over the Our river into Germany. Astride the Skyline Drive, infantrymen cheered to see the carnage that both air and artillery wrought.

By January 28 the last vestige of the bulge in the Ardennes had disappeared.

The cost of the campaign

Of some 600,000 Americans who fought in the Ardennes—more than participated on both sides at Gettysburg—81,000 were killed, wounded, or captured, and the British incurred 1,400 casualties. The Germans probably lost 100,000 killed, wounded or captured.

Both sides lost heavily in weapons and equipment, probably as many as 800 tanks on each side, and the Germans 1,000 aircraft. Yet the Americans could replace their losses in little more than a fortnight, while the Germans could no longer make theirs good. The Germans nevertheless had managed to extricate almost all

THE GERMAN TANK-SMASHERS

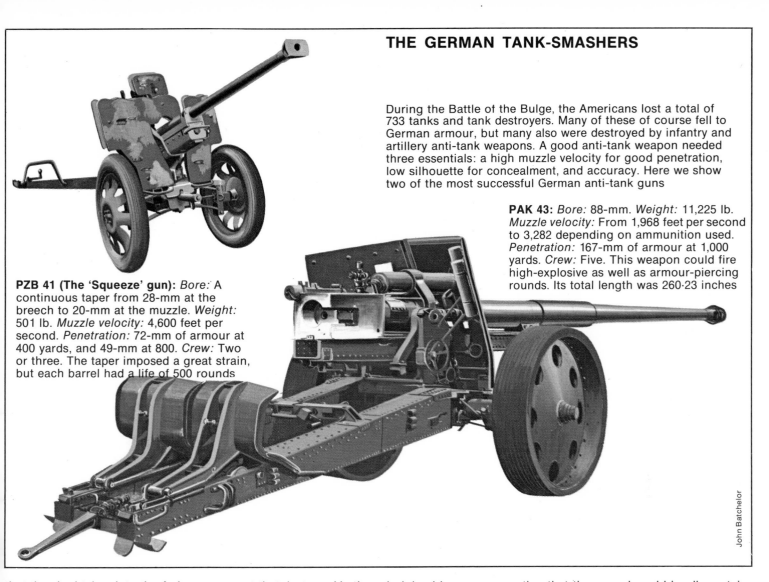

During the Battle of the Bulge, the Americans lost a total of 733 tanks and tank destroyers. Many of these of course fell to German armour, but many also were destroyed by infantry and artillery anti-tank weapons. A good anti-tank weapon needed three essentials: a high muzzle velocity for good penetration, low silhouette for concealment, and accuracy. Here we show two of the most successful German anti-tank guns

PAK 43: *Bore:* 88-mm. *Weight:* 11,225 lb. *Muzzle velocity:* From 1,968 feet per second to 3,282 depending on ammunition used. *Penetration:* 167-mm of armour at 1,000 yards. *Crew:* Five. This weapon could fire high-explosive as well as armour-piercing rounds. Its total length was 260·23 inches

PZB 41 (The 'Squeeze' gun): *Bore:* A continuous taper from 28-mm at the breech to 20-mm at the muzzle. *Weight:* 501 lb. *Muzzle velocity:* 4,600 feet per second. *Penetration:* 72-mm of armour at 400 yards, and 49-mm at 800. *Crew:* Two or three. The taper imposed a great strain, but each barrel had a life of 500 rounds

John Batchelor

that they had taken into the Ardennes except that destroyed in the fighting—a combination of weather, the 'Small Solution' of reducing the bulge, and German ingenuity had seen to that.

Not only did the Germans fail to come close to achieving their strategic objective of Antwerp: they fell short even of the interim objective of the Meuse. Although they had failed to wring from General Eisenhower any 'Backs to the Wall' order like that proclaimed by Sir Douglas Haig in 1918, they had provided the American command many an anxious moment. Yet neither Patton, Bradley, Eisenhower, nor even Hodges—once the first brutal impact of what had happened to his command had passed—had displayed any indication but that matters would be settled their way in the end. That the Germans under Hitler's tutelage should act irrationally and come out of their defences into the open would in the long run do nothing to aid their plight.

In deluding himself that the Wehrmacht of 1944 had the power to repeat the performance of 1940, Hitler had accomplished nothing other than to assure swift victory for the new Russian offensive and possibly delay for a few weeks a final offensive by the Allies. Yet in delaying that offensive he probably speeded the final act, for he retained fewer resources with which to oppose it.

The victor in the Ardennes was the American soldier—he who had given his Allies some sharp concern almost two years before at the Kasserine Pass but who had come a long way since that first battle experience in North Africa. Purportedly pampered, lacking in motivation, he had met the test when it came, giving his commanders—for all their Intelligence failure—time to bring their mobility and reserve power into play. Although Allied power would have told in the end in any case, the American soldier in the Ardennes made the outcome a certainty by his valour and determination at the Elsenborn Ridge, St Vith, Echternach, Clerf, Stavelot, Bastogne, Celles, and countless untold places.

Footnote to the battle

One unfortunate footnote to the battle remained. Perhaps as a reflection of a campaign that had begun in the British press to revive the old issue of making Montgomery overall ground commander, the Field-Marshal in a press conference on January 7

indulged in an exaggeration that the record could hardly sustain.

'As soon as I saw what was happening,' he said, 'I took certain steps myself to ensure that if the Germans got to the Meuse they would certainly not get over that river.' He was 'thinking ahead'. When 'the situation began to deteriorate . . . national considerations were thrown overboard' and 'General Eisenhower placed me in command of the whole northern front'. He had, he claimed, 'employed the whole available power of the British Group of Armies', bringing it into play gradually and then finally 'with a bang'. The operation was 'one of the most interesting and tricky I have ever handled'.

While denigration of American commanders was probably far from Montgomery's mind, his remarks had much the same effect, particularly after the Germans broke in on a BBC wavelength to imitate a British broadcast and give a distorted version of Montgomery's remarks. So upset was General Bradley that he told Eisenhower that rather than serve under Montgomery he would ask to be relieved. Patton said that if Bradley went, so would he.

Bradley saw Montgomery's remarks as a reflection on his own ability as a commander, yet Eisenhower had called in Montgomery only because he hesitated to shift Bradley's headquarters from Luxembourg city to a point farther west and because he wanted to ensure the use of British reserves if needed. While those reserves had been conveniently at hand, few of them had been employed, certainly in no such force as Montgomery intimated in saying he had committed 'with a bang' the 'whole available power of the British Group of Armies'. At most, an armoured brigade and parts of two divisions had briefly entered the fight.

That Montgomery had withheld undermanned British units consciously to save them for the coming offensive against the Ruhr was, in the American view, fully justified. But to have withheld them and then boast otherwise was unjustified.

It remained for that splendid orator, Winston Churchill, to heal the wound. In an address before the House of Commons, he paid full tribute to the American soldier and made abundantly clear that the fight for the Ardennes was an American battle and one, he believed, that would be regarded as 'an ever famous American victory'.

THE FIGHT FOR IWO JIMA

Pacific Theatre,
February 16/April 7, 1945

Before the Marines even set foot on
Iwo Jima the island citadel had been
given the heaviest bombardment of the
entire Pacific war. Yet the 36-day battle
for the island was the bloodiest in
Marine Corps history, a campaign that
cost the lives of more than 6,000
Americans and 22,000 Japanese. 'This
fight,' said Marine General Holland
Smith, 'is the toughest we've run across
in 168 years.' *Right:* The Marines hit
the beach and the ordeal begins. In the
background is Mount Suribachi, Iwo
Jima's dominating feature

US Marine Corps

Did Iwo Jima *have* to be taken by force? Could it not, like certain other Japanese-held strongholds in the Pacific, have been bypassed, cut off, and left 'to wither on the vine'? The answer is no, and for four good reasons, most of them dictated by Allied air strategy:

● First, heavy B-29 bomber losses over Japan emphasised the need for fighter escorts, and since the 2,800-mile round trip from US air bases in the Marianas to Japan and back was beyond the range of the fighters, a nearer staging point had to be captured.

● Second, Iwo Jima, with its two completed airbases and its proximity to Tokyo (660 nautical miles or three air hours) would itself make an excellent base for Allied bombers.

● Third, since Iwo Jima was traditional Japanese territory, administered by the Tokyo prefecture, its conquest would mean a severe psychological blow to the homeland, as well as a vital strategic outpost denied to the Japanese.

● Fourth, Iwo Jima was a necessary link in the air defences of the Marianas. So to isolate Iwo Jima would not be enough: it would have to be seized.

Preliminary planning for the invasion of Iwo Jima began as early as September 1943, and 13 months later, after the Marianas had been secured, Admiral Chester Nimitz informed Lieutenant-General Holland M. ('Howling Mad') Smith, one of the leading exponents of amphibious warfare and commander of all the Marines in the Pacific, that he would be in charge of an operation to take Iwo Jima. Handling the invasion itself would be Major-General Harry Schmidt's 5th Amphibious Corps, veterans of the Gilberts, the Marshalls, and the Marianas campaigns. Schmidt would control three divisions:

● The 3rd Marine Division (Maj-Gen G. B. Erskine), a veteran unit that had seen action on Guam, would be held offshore Iwo Jima as a floating reserve.

● The 4th Marine Division (Maj-Gen C. B. Cates) was also a battle-hardened unit, one that had been in on the Saipan and Tinian landings. It would take part in the initial assault along with the 5th Division.

● The 5th Marine Division (Maj-Gen K. E. Rockey), though yet untried in combat as a unit, was composed of 40% seasoned veterans.

Longest bombardment

Once the target had been selected, the Marines began a rigorous training programme for the invasion: practice landings were made on beaches as similar to Iwo's as possible, and a hill shaped much like Mount Suribachi, Iwo Jima's dominating feature (see map), was taken time and time again in mock assault. Meanwhile, as preparations continued, the air force had begun, on December 8, 1944, the longest and heaviest aerial bombardment of the whole Pacific war, a 72-day 'softening-up' by B-24s and B-25s. A few optimists thought that the island had been neutralised. Only the Marines who had to hit the beaches would be able to verify this.

The US navy, too, laid down its bombardments, which began in November 1944 and continued with intervals until February 16, 1945, when it began its pre-assault barrage. For three days US warships pounded the island from the sea in an attempt to pulverise, or at least neutralise, the Japanese guns capable of hitting the

Marine firepower

In the amphibious landings the worst moment of all was at the moment of contact with the shore, when the first wave of the landing force came under the fire of enemy beach defences with no heavy firepower of their own in support. The British met this problem with the DD swimming tank—but in the Pacific war the Americans preferred to improve on the well-tried 'Landing Vehicle, Tracked'—the Buffalo. Two armed versions helped the Iwo Jima landings, one armed with twin cannons for light support and one with a 75-mm howitzer for heavy support. The former was able to fire at ground targets while acting as a troop transport, while the howitzer version played the same role as the DD tank

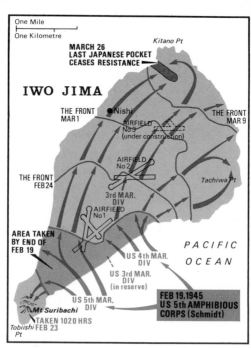

The course of the battle. The Marines landed on Iwo Jima without much opposition and within five days had conquered the southern part of the island, including Mount Suribachi. But the drive to the north was an agonising battle of attrition against an enemy who had sworn to kill ten Americans for each Japanese before dying. US casualties after the 36-day fight totalled almost 25,000

LVT(A) (Howitzer)
Weight: 13·7 tons. *Crew:* four. *Speed:* 20 mph on land, 7½ mph afloat. *Armament:* one 75-mm M-3 howitzer, two ·50-inch Browning machine-guns

LVT(A) (Twin Cannons)
Weight: 12·5 tons. *Crew:* six. *Troop capacity:* six. *Speed:* 20 mph on land, 7½ mph afloat. *Armament:* two 20-mm cannon, two ·50-inch Browning machine-guns

beaches. Like their counterparts in the air force, the navy too believed they had succeeded. Again, the verdict of the Marines would be the one that counted.

On February 17, two days before the actual invasion was scheduled to begin, LCI gunboats and rocket boats came close inshore to cover the frogmen clearing the beach approaches and checking beach and surf conditions. Suddenly, at 1100 hours, the Japanese, who felt certain that this was the invasion they had so long awaited, opened fire with their heaviest artillery. Some 170 casualties were suffered in this action, but the frogmen did return with a full report of beach and surf conditions. Moreover, by revealing their carefully concealed positions the massive coastal guns had marked themselves for certain destruction. They could have raised havoc on D-Day itself.

The morning of D-Day, February 19, found 450 vessels of the US 5th Fleet gathered offshore the tiny island—the largest collection of ships yet for a Pacific operation. And around and among these vessels swarmed the 482 LVT(A)s, packed with troops, that would carry the eight Marine battalions into action. The bombarding warships closed in to 1,000 yards and began firing. Then the air strikes began and the navy laid down a creeping barrage, the first time it was used in the Pacific. The first wave, 68 LVT(A)s, aligned itself for battle. Every few minutes one of these waves would begin the 4,000-yard dash to the shore and certain violence. If all went according to schedule, the first seven battalions of fighting Marines would be ashore within 45 minutes.

At 0902 hours the first wave of Marines hit the beach, the 5th Division on the left, the 4th on the right, and for the first few minutes reported only light resistance and scattered Japanese fire. Could the defences have been exaggerated? Had the preliminary bombardment really worked after all? It seemed too good to be true. Then, after 20 minutes, the deadly fire of all the Japanese weapons—all the artillery and mortars so carefully sited beforehand—opened up in a vicious barrage. Suddenly, the Marines, by now 200 to 300 yards inland, found themselves pinned down. Then the small-arms fire opened up—from underground pillboxes, from harmless looking sand hummocks, from apparently everywhere. The most costly operation in Marine history had begun in earnest.

Fatal Japanese mistake

The Japanese plan had been clever, but they had made one mistake, a fatal one: they had allowed the Marines to get ashore with all the equipment they would need. By 1030 hours elements of all eight assault battalions were ashore and the bigger LSMs were following up with tanks, bulldozers, and artillery. By the end of the day some 30,000 Marines had been landed and although their casualties had been high, very high, they knew they were there to stay: the entire neck of the island was now secure. By the end of the second day the Marines were at the foot of Suribachi. The next move was obvious.

For three days the Marines fought for control of Suribachi, and at 1020 hours on February 23 a 40-man patrol clawed its way to the summit and raised the American flag. But the fall of Suribachi by no means meant the fall of Iwo. The 4th and 5th

Divisions had now to turn north and face the first line of the main Japanese defence belt, and the savage days that followed were evidence of how carefully it had been prepared. The advance had been stopped cold: a battle of attrition, fought with bayonet, flamethrower, rifle, and grenade, had begun. Each time the Marines managed to penetrate one defence line they would find themselves facing another, seemingly more formidable than the last. Artillery was useless against these positions, and the terrain handicapped the tanks. To escape the Marine artillery barrages the Japanese would hug the US front lines as close as possible. So convincing was their camouflage that time after time they would deliberately allow the Marines to overrun their positions, holding their fire until the last possible moment not to give themselves away. By D+10 it had become clear that US strength was being bled off just as relentlessly as Japanese: casualties, and sheer exhaustion, had reduced many combat units to only 50% efficiency.

Not until D+18 (March 9) was a final breakthrough to the north-east shore of the island made by patrols of 3rd Division. But elsewhere on the island the 4th Division was forced to deal with a Japanese counterblow which, if not a formal Banzai charge, was definitely suicidal in nature: 650 Japanese were found dead in one area alone, and reports from other sectors brought the total to nearly 800. In no way had the

One month of the bloodiest fighting in US Marine history

Marine advance been blocked. From now on it was 'simply' a case of mopping up.

It was during this phase that the Marines discovered what the Japanese had been doing since they first occupied the island. Complex mazes of interwoven caves; networks of underground bunkers; ridges, gorges, ledges: the island was one vast lattice of defensive positions. In one area, 1,000 yards wide by 200 deep, 800 separate fortifications, pillboxes, and blockhouses were counted. Entire hills had been hollowed out and rebuilt to house hundreds of defenders, all of whom had sworn to kill ten Marines before dying. It was like nothing the Marines had ever encountered before.

An Intelligence officer of 4th Division described the action like this:
The enemy remains below ground in his maze of tunnels throughout our preliminary artillery fire. When the fire ceases he pushes OPs out of the entrances not demolished by our fire. Then, choosing a suitable exit, he moves as many men and weapons to the surface as he can, often as close as 75 yards from our front. As our troops advance toward this point he delivers all the fire at his disposal, rifle, machine-gun, and mortar. When he has inflicted sufficient casualties to pin down our advance he then withdraws through his underground tunnels most of his forces, possibly leaving a few machine-gunners and mortars. Meanwhile we have delivered a concentration of rockets, mortars, and artillery. Our tanks then push in, supported by infantry. When the hot spot is over-run we find a handful of dead Japs and few if any enemy weapons. While this is happening, the enemy has repeated the process and another sector of our advance is engaged in a vicious fire fight. And so the cycle continues.

It was not until D+25 that the Marines dared declare organised resistance on Iwo to have ceased, but even so, the actual mopping up lasted until D+34. On the night of March 25/26 the Marines witnessed the last convulsions of the desperate Japanese forces: a 300-man Banzai attack on a bivouac area. It had no effect.

Bloodiest prize in the Pacific

Iwo was the bloodiest prize in the Pacific, but its value had not been exaggerated. On March 4, twelve days before the island was declared secure, the first B-29 landed there. On April 7, 108 P-51 Mustangs left from Iwo for the first time to escort a daylight B-29 attack on Tokyo, and within three months of the island's fall more than 850 B-29s had made emergency landings there; without Iwo most of them would have been lost.

Yet the price of Iwo had been extraordinarily high, and whether the dead were Japanese or Americans they had died with the utmost violence. Of the 23,000 men defending Iwo only 1,083 were ever taken prisoner. As for the Americans, some 6,821 soldiers and sailors lost their lives in the struggle for the 8 square miles of Iwo: 24 Medals of Honor were won: 12,600 pints of blood were transfused: 2,650 men were classified 'casualties of combat fatigue'. It had been a fight with a fury unprecedented in the Pacific, and must have left America's military leaders with one haunting thought at least: if to conquer tiny Iwo it took a 72-day air bombardment, a three-day naval hammering, and 36 days of the best the Marines could offer, how long would it take to overwhelm Japan herself? And at what cost?

Far left: A wounded Marine is rushed to an aid station. But in the early days of the battle there were no safe areas, even for the wounded

D+1: Marines move up during the fight for an airfield— the *raison d'être* of the whole Marine invasion

D+4: Suribachi falls. This is one of several famous photos celebrating its capture

D+5: The drive to the north begins. In most areas the US tanks were handicapped by the terrain, and artillery was often quite useless against the carefully prepared defence positions

STRUGGLE FOR THE SEALANES

The Naval War to the End of 1940

The outbreak of war found the German navy still in the making but far from unprepared. To the tenuous Allied blockade of the Axis powers came the challenge of the Nazi surface raiders and the deadlier threat of the U-boats. The main aspects of the war at sea are described here together with the weapons and tactics developed in time to secure the vital convoy routes for the Allies

The war plans of the Royal Navy had been taking shape since 1936, when Hitler's march into the Rhineland had set the pattern of his future path of aggression. Even at that time, it was apparent to the British Chiefs-of-Staff that war would come, and in a memorandum to the Cabinet they assumed it would break out in the latter part of 1939.

As a result of the Rhineland occupation a supplementary naval estimate was introduced into the House of Commons in 1936 to build two new battleships, an aircraft-carrier, five cruisers, and a variety of smaller ships, to be followed in 1937 by estimates which included another three battleships, two more aircraft-carriers, seven cruisers, and a big increase in small craft.. And when the nation went to war in 1939, the first of these ships were beginning to join the fleet.

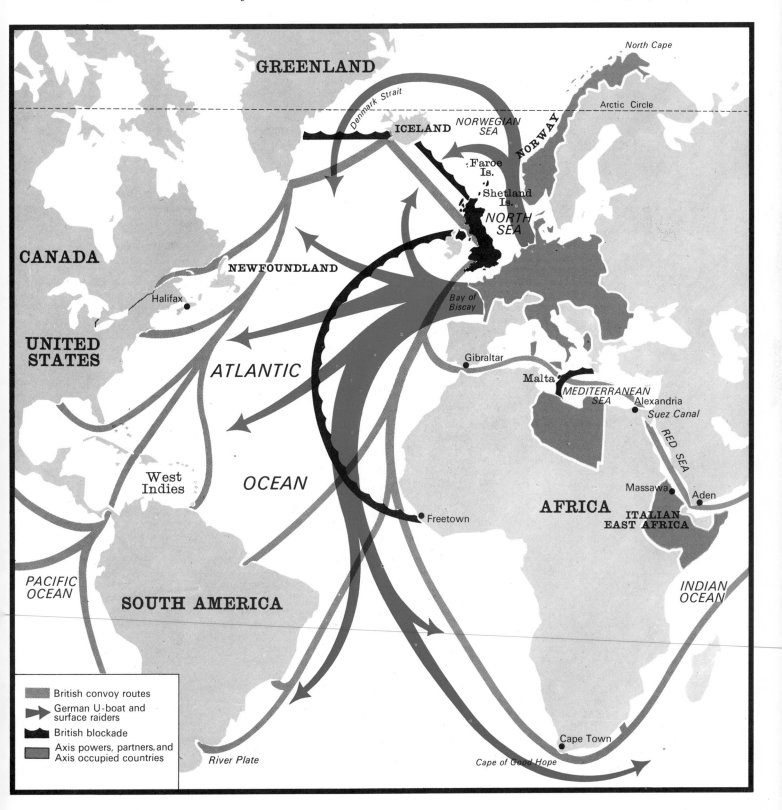

British convoy routes

German U-boat and surface raiders

British blockade

Axis powers, partners, and Axis occupied countries

The war plans, which were sent out from the Admiralty on January 30, 1939, represented the adoption of a defensive strategy. That this has to be so in the early stages of a war is a well-proved element in the exercise of sea power. The desire to rush into offensive action has so often been the prelude to local disaster that naval planning in the initial stages of a maritime war must always allow time for a sufficient force to be built up and trained for the offensive. Only when that stage has been reached can the true dividends of an offensive strategy be harvested.

The naval plan in 1939, which was based on the assumption that the war would be fought against both Germany and Italy from the start, fell into three broad parts. The first looked to the defence of trade in home waters and the Atlantic. This was fundamental to any national strategy, for supplies are the vital sinews of war. Second came the defence of trade in the Mediterranean and the Indian Ocean. It was obvious that, if Italy became an energetic enemy, her dominating geographical position in the Mediterranean would force all seaborne trade to use the longer route round the Cape of Good Hope, but it was hoped to contain her adequately with a strong fleet in the Mediterranean. The third broad part of the naval plan was the imposition of a blockade on Germany and Italy, and with the actual declaration of war was published the list of contraband liable to seizure at sea, even if carried in neutral ships.

To put the plan into operation, the main strength of the Home Fleet was concentrated in Scotland. Far to the north the cruisers of the Northern Patrol kept watch, waiting to intercept any enemy or neutral ship, whether inward or outward bound. From the Shetlands to the coast of Norway a line of search was mounted, partly by air patrols, partly by submarines. The Home Fleet, less a few units stationed elsewhere, lay at Scapa Flow, more than capable of meeting any surface threat which the enemy could mount at sea. At Rosyth lay the aircraft-carrier *Furious* and her attendant destroyers, while submarine flotillas were based at Dundee and Blyth to carry the naval war into German waters. A cruiser squadron and a destroyer flotilla lay in the Humber, while far to the south a force of battleships, aircraft-carriers, cruisers, and destroyers was based at Portland to hold the southern exit into the Atlantic.

In addition to the Home Fleet, the four home commands—Plymouth, Portsmouth, the Nore, and Rosyth—each had forces of destroyers, anti-submarine vessels, and minesweepers for convoy duties and local defence, under the command of the local commanders-in-chief. In the light of existing naval knowledge in 1939, all this formed a net strong enough and wide enough to catch any enemy ship attempting to force a way out or in.

In the Mediterranean, the agreement was that the French navy would hold the western basin in force. The British Mediterranean Fleet was therefore based on Alexandria, to operate in and dominate the eastern basin. To implement the blockade, the naval plan called for strong forces in the Gibraltar Straits and the Red Sea, where examination anchorages for all merchant ships entering the Mediterranean were set up.

The German battle plans

The German war plans were, of course, tailored to a fleet which was basically un-

ready for war. Shortly after coming to power, Hitler had told Admiral Raeder that he would not precipitate a general war until 1944, and it was on this assumption that Raeder had planned German naval expansion. When the war came in 1939, many of the ships which Raeder had hoped would be ready were still building or in the planning stage. Nevertheless, he still had a useful navy. The three pocket-battleships—nominally of 10,000 tons to keep within treaty limitations but secretly built to 13,000 tons—were immediately available. The battle-cruisers *Scharnhorst* and *Gneisenau*, which also exceeded their treaty limits, by 6,000 tons, were formidable opponents, and the big Hipper-class cruisers, some 4,000 tons overweight, were nearly ready. There were 56 U-boats, of which all but ten were operational, and their crews had been well trained, during the years when no U-boats were permitted, under the pretence that they were undergoing anti-submarine exercises.

The German battle instructions were issued to their fleet in May 1939. The plan envisaged a continuous series of operations in the North Sea to create as much nuisance as possible, mainly by attacks on shipping, and thus tying down large British forces to contain them. All the larger ships were due to cruise in the oceans in a heavy and sustained attack on merchant shipping. The U-boats were to operate against trade in the Atlantic and in the approaches to the main British ports. And to counterbalance the delay in the new heavy ships still under construction, a number of merchant ships were to be taken in hand for conversion into fast, heavily armed raiders.

In the German battle instructions, one ominous phrase was inserted: 'fighting methods will never fail to be employed merely because some international regulations are opposed to them.' It was a foreshadowing of the unrestricted submarine and raider warfare which, it had been hoped in Britain, had by now been outlawed for all time as an instrument of naval warfare.

The German navy made its war dispositions in good time. On August 21, 1939, the pocket-battleship *Graf Spee,* using darkness for her passage of the North Sea, slipped into the Atlantic unobserved. Three days later the *Deutschland,* another pocket-battleship, made a similar move, also undetected. Their supply tankers, *Altmark* and *Westerwald,* joined them there, their passages also being unobserved. Between August 19 and 29, 17 of the ocean-going type of U-boat were sent out to their Atlantic war patrol areas while seven of the smaller coastal type were dispatched to lay mines off the Channel ports. Six more were sent out to patrol the central North Sea.

The initial task of the Royal Navy was to draw a ring round the enemy, denying him the supplies which could only come over the seas. From the south of Norway, across and down the North Sea, and throughout the length of the Mediterranean, Allied sea power held the ring. Allied land and air power filled the Continental gaps. Only to the east, where Russia enjoyed a breathing space through her non-aggression pact with Germany, was a possible supply line left open. One result of this closing of the ring can be judged by the fact that, from the outbreak of war to the end of 1939, the Royal Navy seized 530,000 tons of supplies destined for Germany.

It was outside this ring, however, that the problems accumulated. Within hours of the

declaration of war the Donaldson liner *Athenia* was attacked by U-30 200 miles west of Hebrides, and was sunk with a loss of 112 lives. It is true that the captain of U-30 exceeded his instructions in sinking this ship, but her loss was taken in the British Admiralty as evidence that unrestricted submarine warfare was already in force. The provisional arrangements in the war plan for the defence of ocean trade, which was to have been by the patrol of focal points and the evasive routing of merchant ships, was abandoned, and it was decided to adopt the full convoy system as soon as it could be introduced.

Lack of escorts

It was at this stage that the Royal Navy began to feel acutely the pre-war lateness of the naval rebuilding programme. Such destroyers and other ships as were available as convoy escorts lacked the endurance to take them far out into the Atlantic, and until the new ships came along, a 'limit of convoy' had to be drawn at about 300 miles to the west. After that point, the ships in convoy dispersed and proceeded independently. Incoming convoys were escorted across the Atlantic by an anti-raider escort, usually an armed merchant cruiser, and then were picked up by the escort forces at the limit of convoy and escorted into British ports. Later, as the new ships became available, the convoy limit was pushed farther out into the Atlantic, but it was not until mid-1941 that the Royal Navy was able to provide an anti-submarine escort all the way across the Atlantic.

But even with these limitations, the shipping loss figures were fairly encouraging. Up to the end of 1939, U-boats had sunk 114 ships with a tonnage of 421,156, but nine U-boats had paid the price. Considering the attenuated strength of the escort forces, these figures were satisfactory. But that these results were ephemeral in the overall picture was always present in the British Admiralty's mind. It was known that Germany was embarking on a very substantial programme of U-boat construction, and that, by 1941 at latest, the number of operational submarines would be doubled or trebled, and that this number would be progressively increased as the war lengthened. There was no blinking the fact that, once the U-boat fleet was at full strength, merchant ship losses would be grievous.

In the meantime, an attempt to take the offensive against the U-boat led to disaster. Two hunting groups were formed, each consisting of an aircraft-carrier and four destroyers, to operate against U-boats in the western approaches. On September 14 the *Ark Royal* was narrowly missed by torpedoes from U-39. The escorting destroyers counterattacked, sank the U-boat, and captured her crew. But it had been a narrow shave.

Three days later the second hunting group was in action. The aircraft-carrier *Courageous* was sighted by U-29, which torpedoed and sank her with a loss of 519 lives, and lived to tell the tale. At that stage of the war aircraft-carriers were particularly valuable ships, since those ordered in 1936 and 1937 were not expected to be operational until 1941 at earliest, and the British Admiralty quickly decided that it was asking for trouble to risk them on that type of warfare. The *Ark Royal* was quickly withdrawn to take her proper place again with the Home Fleet.

Inside the Admiralty an organisation was growing to co-ordinate the war against the U-boat. Before the war an operational intelligence centre had been set up to deal with all intelligence received of an operational nature, to deduce its value, and to pass it out to the fleet.

On the submarine side a 'tracking room' was established into which came every piece of U-boat intelligence. Reports from agents in enemy countries, giving details of arrivals and departures, U-boat sightings by ships and aircraft, U-boat attacks, and, most prolific source of all, wireless bearings of every message transmitted at sea by a U-boat – all were channelled into the intelligence centre. The tracking room was connected by teleprinters to every wireless direction-finding station in the country, and within minutes of a U-boat using her wireless the bearings were coming in. By plotting the bearings on a chart, the U-boat's position was established.

Alongside the submarine tracking room was the 'trade plot', which showed the position, course, and speed of every convoy and independent ship at sea. By putting these two plots together, the position of any U-boat could be seen in relation to any convoy, and evasive action taken by signalling to the convoy to alter course if it were heading into danger of attack. Both the tracking room and the trade plot were manned day and night, and, as the war developed, a high degree of expertise in forecasting the movement of U-boats was built up.

Mine warfare

U-boats, however, by no means constituted the only danger to merchant ships. As early as the first week of war, some ships were being sunk or damaged by mines of a new type, quickly identified as 'magnetic influence' type, for which the British had no minesweeping countermeasure. It was not until November 23 that a German aircraft presented them with the answer. It dropped its mine in the mudflats off Shoeburyness, and at great personal risk it was dismantled by Lieutenant-Commander J. G. D. Ouvry, and revealed its polarity.

With that knowledge it became possible to develop a magnetic sweep which would explode the mines harmlessly and also to provide ships with a 'degaussing mantle' which enabled them to pass over the mines without actuating their firing gear. But by the end of November the magnetic mine had cost the British 46 ships of 180,000 tons, as well as a destroyer sunk and several warships damaged.

Another source of loss, and one much more difficult to counter, was the armed surface raider. It has been mentioned above that the Germans sent two pocket-battleships into the Atlantic, together with their supply tankers, before the outbreak of war. The first hint that they were at sea came to the Admiralty in the form of ships sunk or missing in waters far beyond those where the U-boats lurked. Gradually the picture was built up as more losses were reported, and the reaction of the Admiralty was to form hunting groups to cover the North and South Atlantic Oceans and the Indian Ocean. In addition, battleships and cruisers were sent across the Atlantic to Halifax to act as

While the horizon is clear, crew members sun themselves on the deck of a U-boat

raider escorts to successive convoys sailing to Britain.

The first success, and one that enormously boosted British morale, was the destruction of the pocket-battleship *Graf Spee* in the estuary of the River Plate. She had been tracked down by the positions of the ships she had sunk, and a brilliant piece of deduction by Commodore Henry Harwood had led to his hunting group being in position to intercept her as she moved towards the South American coast in search of other victims. She had sunk nine ships of some 50,000 tons before she was brought to action, a poor result in comparison with her overwhelming strength and fire-power. The cruise of the *Deutschland* was even less productive. She sank two ships in the North Atlantic before being called home.

The *Deutschland's* efforts in the Atlantic were followed in November by a more ambitious venture on the part of Admiral Raeder, who sent out the battle-cruisers *Scharnhorst* and *Gneisenau* on a combined cruise into the North Atlantic, with the object of dislocating the British patrol lines. It was a preliminary operation to give the two big ships some experience before letting them loose on the main trade routes. They sailed from Germany on November 21, but on the evening of the 23rd, just as they were breaking out into the Atlantic between the Faeroe Islands and Iceland, they were sighted and engaged by the armed merchant cruiser *Rawalpindi*. She, of course, was no match for a battle-cruiser, and was quickly sunk by the *Scharnhorst,* but not before she had sent out two wireless sighting reports.

Admiral Forbes, the Commander-in-Chief, at once sailed from Scapa Flow with the Home Fleet, and HMS *Newcastle*, the next ship to the *Rawalpindi* in the patrol line, closed the position and sighted the two battle-cruisers, but lost them again in a heavy rainstorm. Admiral Marschall, who commanded the two German ships, broke away at high speed and abandoned the operation, returning to Germany. The Home Fleet had little chance of catching the two battle-cruisers, for the distance was too great.

This whole operation raised some doubts in the British Admiralty's mind as to the degree of severity with which these German raiding ventures were to be carried out. It seemed inexplicable that, on sighting the *Newcastle,* these ships should not turn on her and send her to the bottom. Her 6-inch guns were no match for the 11-inch guns carried by the two battle-cruisers, and the fact that they turned back and ran for home hardly made sense in real naval warfare. At the time it was believed by the Admiralty and by Admiral Forbes that the *Rawalpindi* had been sunk by the *Deutschland,* but even this would not explain the sudden disengagement. She also carried 11-inch guns. This was an aspect of German naval warfare that was to recur throughout the war at sea, and one which caused constant surprise.

One other part of the initial German war plan went amiss in the early days. This was the design to employ forces in the North Sea to disrupt British shipping and tie down a sizable portion of the British fleet. On December 12 a force of five destroyers, covered by three cruisers, sailed to lay a minefield off the Northumberland coast. They were sighted on their return by the submarine *Salmon,* which torpedoed the cruisers *Leipzig* and *Nürnberg,* damaging them both. Two days later, as this force

approached the Danish coast, it was again attacked, this time by the submarine *Ursula.* The *Leipzig* escaped the torpedoes, but one of her escorting destroyers was hit and sunk.

Surprise at Scapa Flow

But the Royal Navy, too, was having its troubles. The biggest blow occurred early in the morning of October 14 when U-47, commanded by Lieutenant Prien, penetrated the defences of Scapa Flow and torpedoed and sank the battleship *Royal Oak*. The loss of the battleship herself was relatively unimportant in the context of the strengths of the opposing navies, but what was of concern was the realisation that the main operational base of the Royal Navy was vulnerable to submarine attack. Until its defences could be made secure by the use of more blockships in the entrances, the Home Fleet was forced to use Loch Ewe on the western coast of Scotland as an anchorage, even though it, too, was open to submarine attack. Indeed, only six weeks later, HMS *Nelson,* the fleet flagship, was damaged by a mine as she was entering Loch Ewe.

A balance sheet drawn up at the end of 1939 would have shown figures favourable to the Royal Navy. The main doubt in the mind of the British Admiralty before the war had begun was whether the threat to British trade poised by surface raiders could be held, and particularly were the three pocket-battleships held in dread. And here there was already a favourable balance, with only 15 British, Allied, and neutral merchant ships sunk and one of the three pocket-battleships lying on the sea bed in Montevideo Roads. The toll by the U-boats had not been unduly heavy: 114 ships of 421,000 tons had been sunk with a loss to the enemy of nine U-boats. Casualties from mines (79 ships of 262,000 tons) were severe, but with the discovery of the polarity of the German magnetic mine, it was believed that the back of this particular problem had been broken. On the debit side could be placed the loss of the *Royal Oak* and *Courageous,* one armed merchant cruiser, three destroyers, and one submarine. Taken as a whole, the picture was reasonably encouraging.

Yet in the longer view there was still much to worry the Admiralty in London. It had been believed before the war—and still was, since no evidence had come in to the contrary—that the British 'asdic' submarine detector, as fitted in all anti-submarine vessels, was a sufficient guarantee against any repetition of such merchant ship losses as had been experienced between 1914 and 1918, particularly when allied to the modern depth-charge, with its multiple depth settings. But evidence was already accumulating within the Admiralty of the size of the German U-boat building programme, and there were those who foresaw a time, judged at around a couple of years, when the defence could well be in danger of being swamped by sheer weight of numbers.

There was one other aspect of the submarine war which caused some uneasiness: a lack of sufficiently 'long-legged' escorts to provide merchant ship convoy for the whole length of passage. As matters stood at the beginning of 1940, there was, on the transatlantic passage alone, a gap of some 1,700 miles across which merchant ships were beyond the range of surface escort. It was an even longer gap on some of the other main trade routes.

As events turned out during the first six

months of 1940, these early doubts became real enough. The campaign in Norway in April and May of 1940, and the evacuation of the British Expeditionary Force from the Channel ports in May and early June of the same year, are well-known episodes from the history of the war, but a brief reference to them here is necessary to assess their influence on the overall picture of trade defence. During the Norwegian campaign ten destroyers and sloops were sunk and another 14 damaged. The evacuation of the BEF added six more destroyers and sloops sunk and a further 20 damaged.

This was a serious drain of those ships which, by their nature, were the best escorts for the defence of trade—but an even more serious gap in possible escort vessels was caused by the obvious corollary of the fall of France. The Germans were now poised on the Channel coast, and talk of invasion was in the air. This inevitably meant that many naval ships, and particularly destroyers, were tied up to watch for any enemy movement across the Channel, and this duty, which lasted for four months until the danger of invasion began to fade, inevitably led to further and serious shortages in the forces available for merchant ship escort.

The 'wolf-packs'

Bad as this was, there was worse to follow. In the last months of 1939 the enemy had attempted, though with little success, to organise attacks on convoys by groups of U-boats instead of by single boats. On a convoy being sighted and reported, U-boat headquarters would call in adjacent boats to press home the attack. From this beginning, it was not difficult to develop a more efficient method of the group attack. The U-boats were organised into operational 'wolf-packs', and when a convoy's course was reasonably well identified, the nearest pack was ordered to the vicinity by the U-boat headquarters. When the convoy was sighted, the U-boat concerned 'homed' the rest of the pack to the convoy by directional wireless signals. No attack developed until the whole pack had arrived.

With this tactic there was added the surface attack by night. A surfaced submarine presents only a tiny silhouette and is difficult to see even in the best conditions of visibility. They are also able to use their diesel engines on the surface and so are much faster than when submerged—indeed, their surface speed exceeded that of most British escort vessels. There was, therefore, very little hope of catching them even if they were sighted during the attack. Even more disastrous from the British point of view was the fact that a U-boat on the surface was virtually immune from discovery by 'asdic' detection.

This completely reversed the confidence with which, before the war, the Admiralty had contemplated an enemy attack on seaborne trade. The 'asdic' and the depth-charge were the twin foundations on which the whole theory of anti-submarine warfare had been firmly based, and these new German tactics completely outmanoeuvred them. The fitting of radar sets in escort vessels was the immediate and obvious answer, since radar would indicate the presence of a surfaced U-boat, but as yet there were no sets available, and another year was to elapse before enough became available to equip the escort fleet.

In the meantime, another duty lay before the Royal Navy. Almost as the evacuation of the BEF from Dunkirk and the Channel ports was taking place, other British troops were being landed in France in an attempt to form a line on which the advancing Germans could be successfully held. But in the rapidly crumbling situation ashore, any hope of stopping the German advance was slim indeed. It became even slimmer when it became apparent that the defeatist element in the French government was strongly in favour of negotiating with the Germans for an armistice.

The decision to bring home the remaining British troops in France, many of them landed only a few days earlier, was taken on June 15, using the ports of Cherbourg, St Malo, Brest, St Nazaire, and La Pallice. In the few days during which this operation was carried out, another 136,963 British troops were brought safely home, as well as some 38,500 Allies, of whom the majority were Polish.

The whole operation was carried out with only one loss, but that was a grievous one. Among other ships sent to carry troops home from St Nazaire was the liner *Lancastria*. She was lying out in the anchorage and had already taken more than 5,300 soldiers on board when she was hit during a heavy German air raid. Although she took some little time to sink, more than 3,000 of those on board lost their lives – mainly because, in the urgency of evacuation, there were insufficient lifebelts in the ship for all the extra men she was carrying.

With this final evacuation of British forces from France, coupled with the armistice which the French government signed with Germany, a completely new problem faced the Admiralty. The situation on which the original war plans had been drawn had now been shattered beyond recognition.

Taking stock, the Royal Navy had to face a situation in which the whole of the western coast of Europe, from the North Cape in Norway to the Spanish frontier in the Bay of Biscay, lay in the hands of the enemy. With the Norwegian ports and bases in his hands, Hitler could now command the eastern North Sea right up to the Arctic Circle. This gave him a wide corridor through which to pass his U-boats, his armed merchant raiders, and his blockade runners in the Atlantic. With similar facilities in the Bay of Biscay, U-boats could reach farther out into the Atlantic, and raiders and blockade runners could penetrate deep into ocean waters before they reached areas where British ships could seize them. This made the British Admiralty's task infinitely more difficult, for a ship is easily concealed in the immensity of the oceans.

A yet more potent threat to the nation's seaborne trade lay in German occupation of the airfields of western France, from which long-range Focke-Wulf 'Condor' aircraft could search the Atlantic for British convoys and report their positions to the waiting U-boats.

This particular problem was solved in a typically extempore fashion. A few merchant ships were fitted with catapults which could launch a Hurricane fighter, and one of these accompanied the more important convoys as they sailed within range of the Condors. When one of them was sighted, the Hurricane was catapulted into flight, shot down or drove off the intruder, and then ditched itself alongside a merchant ship so that the pilot could be picked up.

These catapult-aircraft-merchant ships or CAM-ships, as they were known, gave way in time to the MAC-ship (merchant-aircraft-carrier), in which a full flight deck was built over the top of a merchant ship, usually a tanker because of her length. The MAC-ships could carry up to about six fighters, which of course could land on again after operations and did not have to ditch alongside. And as time went on, the MAC-ships were replaced by auxiliary (or 'Woolworth') carriers, which embodied merchant ship hulls converted into full aircraft-carriers.

Strangulation of trade

While the battle of the skies was being fought by the Royal Air Force against German bombers and fighters intent on hammering Britain into submission, another battle was being fought in the coastal waters around Britain. Hitler's plan to defeat Britain lay not so much in invasion across the Channel, which was in fact to be his last resort if all else failed, but in the strangulation of trade.

In the wake of the advancing German armies came his motor torpedo-boats, known as E-boats, pushing their bases westward until they reached Cherbourg during the second half of June 1940. Their targets were the coastal convoys, combined with offensive minelaying before the ports of Britain. Heavy air attacks on convoys and ports also took their toll of ships. Although all these were hit-and-run attacks, they tied down a large number of British naval vessels, and it was to take some months of hard and incessant skirmishing before the enemy was held and the coastal trade could pass in comparative security.

Another naval task was the defence against seaborne invasion, which everyone in Britain expected during the summer and autumn of 1940. But this was nothing new; and the Royal Navy swung into its traditional defence, tried and proved through centuries of experience. It was based on the close watch of the invasion forces by flotilla vessels: in the old days by sloops, cutters, and gun-vessels; in 1940 by destroyers, motor torpedo-boats, and gunboats. Behind them, in the east and west coast ports, lay the immediate stiffening of the defence by ships of greater power: in the old days by frigates; in 1940 by cruisers. And behind them again lay the final safeguard of all – the immense strength of the battle fleet, which would be called south to action when the forces of invasion actually sailed.

Here, in 1940, across the waters of the English Channel stood the army of Hitler, as before it had stood the armies of Napoleon, of Louis XIV, of Philip II of Spain. Between them all and their dreams of conquest had stood the British navy. Between Hitler and his dreams it still stood. As the days and the weeks passed, as the invasion barges and the transports which had been taken from the inland waterways with so much dislocation of local trade still lay stationary at their moorings in the Channel ports, the Lords of the Admiralty could echo the words of the Earl of St Vincent, a First Lord of 150 years ago, that 'being a military question they must hesitate to express an opinion about invasion as such'. All they knew was that an invasion 'could not come by sea'.

In all the major fighting which had fallen to the Royal Navy so far – in the Norwegian campaign and in the evacuation from Dunkirk – one unmistakable new lesson had emerged: that ships at sea could not operate in waters dominated by enemy air power. The major naval weapon against the Axis powers – for Italy had joined the conflict on the fall of France – was still the blockade, and to keep this weapon in operation the ring of sea power around Europe still needed to be held. Now, however, it had to be drawn beyond the range of aircraft using the newly won airfields of Norway, Denmark, Holland, Belgium, and France. Britain, outflanked now to the south and east, had to guard well the north and west if she were not to be herself defeated. So, to the north, British sea power stretched out to Iceland and across the Denmark Straits to the coast of Greenland. In the west it reached from Northern Ireland out into the Atlantic, sweeping down in a wide arc to the south, to Gibraltar and Freetown. To complete the circle, the Mediterranean Fleet held the eastern waters of the Mediterranean from Malta to the western coast of Greece.

Within this tenuous circle were held the Axis powers. This was the barrier through which they had to break if they were to reach the raw materials of the rest of the world. It could not as yet be held strongly enough to prevent the surface raiders slipping through, nor could it ever stop the U-boats from reaching the outer oceans. But it could, and did, effectively stifle almost the whole of that seaborne trade without which the two dictators could not win their war.

This was a barrier which had to be held at all costs, for if final victory were to be won, the barrier had to serve a dual purpose. There was more to it than stopping the seaborne trade of Germany and Italy; while containing them in isolation, it had also to safeguard the slow build-up of British power and resources against the day when the national strategy could turn from the defensive to the offensive.

Behind its strength had to come the huge imports of oil, steel, tanks, guns, aircraft, and food without which the only future for Britain was defeat. And behind its strength, too, had to come the men, from the Dominions and colonies and, later, from the United States, who would add their strength to the armies which, one day, would carry the war back into Europe. And behind its strength must sail all those troops, weapons, and stores to hold the other vital theatres of war in the Middle East and, a year later, the Far East.

The task, in those summer months of 1940, appeared stupendous – and it was aggravated both by the loss of ships during the operations in Norway and at Dunkirk and by those which were now tied up in the anti-invasion duties. Where, in 1939, it had been possible to provide an average of two escort vessels for each convoy that sailed, now, in the summer of 1940, the average escort strength was down to 1·8 per convoy. The U-boats, now beginning to use French and Norwegian bases, were saving 1,000 miles or more on their passage to their patrol areas, and so were able to operate considerably farther out into the Atlantic, and well beyond the limit to which convoys could be escorted.

Two gleams of light shone fitfully into this dark prospect. The first was produced by the occupation by British troops of the Faeroe Islands and Iceland. Both were dependencies of Denmark, and on the invasion of that country by Germany in April 1940 had been quickly taken over by Britain to deny them to Hitler.

Iceland was extremely well placed to act

△ The sinking of one of Britain's oldest aircraft-carriers, the *Courageous*, torpedoed in the first fortnight of the war

as a base on the Atlantic convoy routes, a base from which escorts could operate to lengthen substantially the limit of convoy both from Britain and from the Canadian ports. There was no question of using it at once, for it takes time to develop the essential facilities of a naval base, but it would unquestionably pay substantial

dividends in the future.

The other gleam of light came from the negotiations between Churchill and Roosevelt over the release by the United States of 50 over-age destroyers in exchange for the lease of bases in Newfoundland and the West Indies. These destroyers, of the old 'flush deck and four-pipe' class, were hurriedly overhauled and re-equipped in US bases and taken into the British and Canadian navies. There they served to augment the already over-stretched escort force, at least temporarily until the new construction escort vessels began to join the fleet.

Return of the U-boats

The first six months of 1940 had been a relatively quiet time in the Atlantic on the U-boat front, due partly to the wild weather of January, in which U-boats found it very difficult to operate, and partly to the large-scale withdrawal of U-boats from the Atlantic to take part in the Norwegian campaign. But by June 1940 they were back on the Atlantic trade routes, not in any great strength as yet, as the building programme was only just beginning to bear fruit, but with a steadily increasing monthly total.

From their new Biscay bases, even the small 500-ton U-boats could now operate in areas as much as 600 miles out into the Atlantic, well beyond the limit of surface anti-submarine escort from Britain. There was little opposition to them out there, and the incoming and outgoing merchant ships were sitting ducks to their torpedoes. Closer in, they chose as their targets ships which—because of their speed—sailed independent of convoys, or ships which straggled from the convoys. These, too, were sitting ducks.

During September the U-boat command introduced the first serious wolf-pack attacks against British convoys. Two successive Atlantic convoys, SC-2 and HX-72, were attacked by a pack of ten U-boats north-west of Iceland, and 16 ships were sunk out of them. A month later an even more savage wolf-pack attack was launched.

Again the victims were two successive Atlantic convoys, SC-7 and HX-79, and a wolf-pack of eight U-boats, attacking them on four successive nights, sank 32 ships.

It was not unduly difficult to discover the answers to this form of attack. One of them, as mentioned above, was the fitting of radar in the escorts. Another was to discover a method of turning night into day more efficiently than by starshell from the escorts' guns. This was eventually provided by the scientists with the invention of 'Snowflake', a flare which lit up a large area of the ocean at once. But, like radar, this answer also lay in the future.

Another answer was the provision of air escort of convoys. This was a powerful deterrent to the U-boat, for aircraft ranging over the convoy area forced the shadowing U-boat to submerge and thus lose touch. And when fitted with ASV (airborne radar), escorting aircraft had an even wider range of effectiveness, for their sets could detect a surfaced U-boat in thick weather, and at a greater range, where the human eye would fail. But here again, at this stage of the battle, the necessary numbers of long-range aircraft did not exist in Coastal Command, and the protection from attack which they could provide was not available.

Yet another source of protection was deduced from the habits of the shadowing U-boat. In order to 'home' the remainder of the pack on to the convoy, the shadowing U-boat had to make a succession of wireless signals. While these might not be heard by the shore wireless direction-finding stations, because they were made on low power, they would normally appear as strong signals on board the escorts. If these ships, therefore, carried a direction-finding receiver, they could run down the bearing of the shadowing U-boat and expect to find her at the other end. This aid to U-boat destruction was, again, only embryonic in 1940, but it was from this date that steps were taken to produce suitable ship-borne direction-finding receivers. They eventually came into the escort fleet in July 1941.

All that remained, therefore, was to strive to extend the range of surface escort farther

Ullstein

out into the Atlantic, and to try to divert the convoys, by evasive routing, clear of those areas where the U-boat packs were thought to be lurking. This was the task of the U-boat tracking room in the Admiralty, using every piece of intelligence information that came in. The most prolific source of this intelligence was found to be the wireless bearings taken from shore stations of every signal made by the U-boats at sea.

Actual sighting reports made by the U-boats were quickly recognised as such from the form of the message itself, and convoys could be immediately warned that they were in danger. Sometimes a drastic alteration of course away from the U-boat would shake the shadower off. But although some of the best brains in the Navy were concentrated in the tracking room, the volume of intelligence coming in was not sufficient to enable them to do much more than grope in the dark. Later, as the raw material of intelligence improved both in quantity and quality, the tracking room was to achieve some spectacular successes. But that time was not yet.

Merchant ship sinkings

The losses of merchant ships caused by the U-boats through 1940 tell their own story. The two months of January and February had seen the loss of 85 ships totalling 290,000 tons. During March, April, and May, the U-boats had been largely withdrawn from the Atlantic to play their part in the Norwegian campaign, and during those three months only 43 ships of an aggregate of 140,000 tons were lost. But in June the U-boats were coming back and, moreover, beginning to operate farther afield in the Atlantic, and beyond the reach of the convoy escorts. June saw the loss to the U-boats rise to a figure of 58 ships with a total tonnage of 284,000. And the figures for the remainder of the year were equally grievous.

Losses such as these were beyond the replacement capacity of the British building yards, and although there was still as yet plenty of 'fat' in the total of pre-war tonnage afloat under the British flag, these figures clearly showed the writing on the wall. A

fair amount of merchant ship tonnage—particularly Norwegian and Dutch—had accrued to Britain with the German invasion of the western European countries in April and May, but even that could not allow anyone to contemplate the loss figure with anything but a feeling of apprehension. And as yet the peak of U-boat strength had not been even approached.

It was known in the British Admiralty that several hundred new U-boats were on order, and the existing operational strength was but a shadow of what was inevitably to come. Before the war, in his book on submarine warfare, Admiral Dönitz had put forward the estimate that 300 operational U-boats would be required to win a war against Britain. That meant a total force of some 900 submarines, to allow for losses, training, rest periods for crews, refits, and so on. This book had, of course, been read by many British naval officers, and none doubted the German capacity to build up to this figure. Moreover, the declaration by Hitler on August 17 of a total blockade of the British Isles, giving warning that neutral shipping would be sunk at sight, gave an added indication that the U-boat campaign was to be the means by which Germany expected to win her victory.

The loss to the enemy during 1940 was 22 U-boats, although the Admiralty at the time only knew of 16 confirmed cases; the remaining six were sunk by accident or unknown causes. But in view of the German building programme, this was not a satisfactory exchange rate. Taken over the whole year, it meant that for each U-boat lost, very nearly 100,000 tons of Allied shipping were sent to the bottom. Great Britain and her allies would need to do much better than that if the Atlantic battle, on which the outcome of the war depended, was to be won.

There was one great hope. During the year the limit of escorts had been pushed farther out into the Atlantic. As soon as the Iceland base became operational, an even larger step outwards could be made. And with the new construction of escort vessels now beginning to come forward, the time was not far distant when convoy could be estab-

lished right across the Atlantic from coast to coast. Convoys, the Royal Navy knew, had beaten the U-boat in 1917 and 1918. The Admiralty in London hoped, and expected, that they would do so again.

If U-boats had been the only cause of merchant ship losses, the problem of containment would not have been too great a

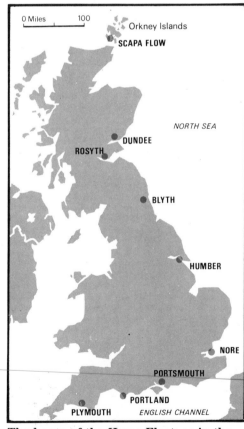

The bases of the Home Fleet; as in the First World War, the Scapa Flow anchorage was the main base. Here the bulk of the British battle fleet waited to counter any German attempt to break out into the North Atlantic. Portland was the base for the force blocking the Channel

327

task. But at the same time there were serious losses from other causes. German aircraft, operating mainly against the East Coast and English Channel coastal convoys, sank, during 1940, 192 ships of 580,000 tons. Mines throughout the year accounted for 201 ships of 510,000 tons, while the German E-boats claimed a further 23 ships of 48,000 tons. Although the great majority of these were comparatively small ships engaged in coastal trade, and thus more easily and quickly replaced by new construction, the total tonnage added to the overall loss was in excess of 1,000,000.

Return of the raiders

One other cause of loss gave an even greater degree of anxiety and apprehension to the Admiralty: the losses caused by armed merchant raiders—fast and heavily armed merchant ships sent out from Germany to operate individually in the distant oceans. The difficulty was to find them. It had been appreciated, when the raider hunting groups had been formed at the beginning of the war to deal with the pocket-battleships, that this was a most uneconomic use of ships. These groups had steamed many hundreds of thousands of miles, mostly to no avail, for by the time a hunting group could arrive in the vicinity of the last sinking report, the raider herself was by then many hundreds of miles away. And what was, perhaps, even worse than the actual merchant ship sinkings which the raiders achieved was the dislocation and disorganisation which their presence caused to the normal flow of seaborne trade.

What the Germans called the 'first wave' of the armed merchant raiders put to sea during the first half of 1940. The first out was the *Atlantis*, which left Germany on March 31. She was followed by the *Orion* (April 6), and the *Widder* (May 5). Two more, the *Thor* and *Pinguin*, broke through the Atlantic defences, such as they were, in June, and a sixth (the *Komet*), assisted by the Russians, made the Arctic passage to the north of Siberia to the Pacific in July and August. To prolong their periods of activity, a number of supply ships were also sent out, with which they could rendezvous when required.

Only on two occasions—and each time it was the same raider—was any contact made with them by a British warship. On July 28 the armed merchant' cruiser *Alcantara* encountered the *Thor* in the West Indies, off Trinidad. The British ship was outsteamed, outgunned, and outfought by the enemy, and as the *Alcantara* limped into port with serious damage, the *Thor* moved down into the South Atlantic to repair her damage and be replenished from a convenient supply ship.

A little over four months later, off the coast of South America, the *Thor* ran into another armed merchant cruiser, the *Carnarvon Castle*. The story was the same, and while the British ship was seriously damaged, the enemy suffered no injury and, after the action, made off into the blue. These two encounters were, in fact, the nearest the Royal Navy ever came during 1940 to sinking one of these elusive and dangerous ships. The damage they caused was widespread and serious. During the year, in the North and South Atlantic, Indian, and Pacific Oceans, these six ships sank 54 ships of an aggregate of 367,000 tons, but in addition they caused a considerable upheaval in the pattern of British seaborne trade through the delays in sailings and rerouting of merchant ships in the vicinity of their attacks. Some, too, were fitted as minelayers in addition to their usual gun and torpedo armament, and the minefields they laid were another cause of loss and delay.

It was not to be expected that the limited success of the first cruises of the *Deutschland* and *Graf Spee*, and the abortive attempt of the *Scharnhorst* and *Gneisenau* to break out in November 1939, would deter the enemy from further attacks on trade by warship raiders. In September 1940 the cruiser *Hipper* made an attempt to reach the Atlantic, but trouble in her engine-room caused her to abandon her planned sortie, and return home.

The next warship to make the attempt was the pocket-battleship *Scheer*. She left Germany on October 27, was not sighted by any British air patrols as she made her way up the Norwegian coast, and reached the Atlantic through the Denmark Straits undetected. On November 5 she sank a British merchant ship, which unfortunately failed to send a wireless report of the attack. Had she done so, it would have been possible to reroute a homeward-bound convoy from Halifax, which was steaming towards the position where the *Scheer's* attack had been made.

The convoy was HX-84, escorted by HMS *Jervis Bay*, an armed merchant cruiser which carried six 6-inch guns mounted on her upper deck. On the evening of November 5, only a few hours after the *Scheer's* earlier attack, the *Jervis Bay* sighted the pocket-battleship approaching the convoy at high speed from the northward. The result, even before the first gun was fired, was a foregone conclusion, for the armed merchant cruiser was not only outgunned, but also outranged by some 10,000 yards.

To save as many of the ships in the convoy as possible, Captain Fegen of the *Jervis Bay* ordered them to scatter to the south under cover of smoke. This they did, using the smoke-making apparatus with which they were all fitted, while Captain Fegen took the *Jervis Bay* into action with her huge adversary to provide as much time as possible for the ships in the convoy to get away. The *Scheer*, naturally, was undamaged during the action—the shells of the *Jervis Bay* could not even reach her—but the delay caused by Captain Fegen's defiance of the raider gave the convoy the chance it needed. By the time the *Jervis Bay* was sunk, the convoy was so scattered that the *Scheer* was unable to find more than five ships to sink, and one more to damage. The remainder escaped. For his gallantry and self-sacrifice on this occasion, Captain Fegen was awarded a posthumous Victoria Cross.

The epic of the *Jervis Bay* gave rise to another epic of skill and endurance, one which has few parallels in nautical history. The ship damaged by the *Scheer* after the sinking of the *Jervis Bay* was the tanker *San Demetrio*. She was hit and set on fire, and abandoned by her crew.

On the following day, some 18 hours after the attack, a handful of her crew, in an open boat under the command of her second officer, sighted her, still alight. They rowed alongside and climbed on board. Her decks were still hot from the fire on board, but they managed to rig some hoses and gradually got the fire under control. After working for several hours on the engines, they succeeded in getting one of them to function, and the ship began her long, slow journey

Depth-charges

Depth-charge mounted on a 'carrier' ready to be fired out in a wide arc from the ship's side, to port or starboard

The detonator hurls the depth-charge away from the ship; the 'carrier' drops away from the charge and is abandoned

A charge is dropped over a ship's stern from a chute where another charge is in place, ready to follow in a close pattern

Underwater explosions have a tremendous effect, due to the concentrated shockwaves. A near-miss could crack a U-boat's hull

A hunting escort-ship could fire wide or close patterns of charges, as the 'asdic' groped for the elusive 'ping' of a U-boat

FW200 Condor, the Luftwaffe's 'long arm'; a range of 2,210 miles (14 flying hours)

John Batchelor

to Britain. Without charts beyond a school atlas found on board, with no other navigational aid, and averaging a little less than 5 knots, these few men succeeded in bringing the *San Demetrio* home together with the greater part of her valuable cargo of oil.

After her attack on HX-84 the *Scheer* steamed south, away from the area in which she had so recently operated. She replenished her oil and ammunition from a supply ship and, after operating off the Azores, moved into the South Atlantic. Here she captured a British merchant ship loaded with foodstuffs, and deliberately allowed her to broadcast a raider report before sending a prize crew on board. The reason for this was to draw attention to her position in the South Atlantic and thus attract to the area any British hunting forces which might be engaged in anti-raider operations. This was to leave the coast clear in the north, where the cruiser *Hipper* was trying to make her second attempt to break out into the Atlantic.

The *Hipper* sailed from Germany on November 30, like the *Scheer* evaded the North Sea air patrols, and successfully broke through the Denmark Straits into the North Atlantic on December 7. She spent a few days in the North Atlantic searching for convoys to attack, but found none, as her captain did not realise that convoys were still at that date taking the northerly route across the Atlantic. As a result of her lack of success she proceeded south to investigate

the Sierra Leone route, and in the evening of December 24 gained touch with a convoy. She shadowed it throughout the night, hoping for fat pickings on the following day.

The convoy she was shadowing was, in fact, a troop convoy bound for the Middle East. These were always heavily guarded when at sea. As the *Hipper* approached on Christmas Day to attack, she was disconcerted to find it escorted by an aircraft-carrier and three cruisers. They had no difficulty in driving her off, but unfortunately lost sight of her in the low visibility. The *Hipper* was, in fact, slightly damaged during the exchange of gunfire. She decided to cut short her raiding cruise, and two days later arrived at Brest, on the French Biscay coast.

Next came the turn of the *Scharnhorst* and *Gneisenau*, acting as a squadron. Both had been fairly extensively damaged during the Norwegian campaign, and this was to be their first action since those days, having spent the intervening seven months in dock-yard hands. Their effort was abortive. The *Gneisenau* was damaged in heavy seas while steaming up the coast of Norway, and both ships thereupon reversed their course and returned to Kiel.

This 'second wave' of the warship raiders accounted for the loss of 17 ships of 97,000 tons, bringing the total losses of the year from all causes up to the formidable total of 1,059 ships of 3,991,641 tons. Of these, nearly 60% had been sunk by U-boats, the

majority of them on the vital North Atlantic trade route.

It is necessary for a moment to leave the Atlantic and take a quick look at the last link of the circle of sea power drawn around the Axis nations. When Italy joined Germany in hostilities during the last days of the fighting ashore in Europe, the naval position in the Red Sea at once gave some cause for alarm. Here, based on Massawa, the Italians had a force of nine destroyers, eight submarines, and an armed merchant raider.

The Red Sea was an essential link with British forces operating in the Middle East, and it was essential to hold this sea area if Germany and Italy were to be effectively denied access to the trade of the outside world and if British forces were to receive the replenishment in men, weapons, and stores they would need to conduct active operations.

As it turned out, the Italian naval threat never materialised. Three of the submarines were sunk and another captured intact within the first month of Italy joining the war; the destroyers took no action to attempt to harass British convoys in the Red Sea; and the spasmodic efforts of Italian aircraft to interfere with British shipping were unavailing. The Red Sea route remained firmly in British hands, and the circle of sea power remained unbroken.

The end of 1940 saw the situation at sea more or less in a state of balance. The Allies

Magnetic mine

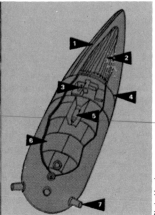

Chris Harrison

Lowered by parachute, the magnetic mine also had a contact fuse: if it hit a solid surface it was meant to explode like a bomb

As the mine sank, the rear parachute attachment was released: freed from the parachute, the mine would then rest on the sea bed

As a ship approached, the weak magnetic field set up would finally detonate the mine by closing the circuit with the magnetic needle

In shallow water, the explosion, directly below the ship's hull, was devastating. These mines caused heavy tonnage losses

1. 'Chute case (two halves)
2. Folded 'chute 3. Needle
4. Case join 5. Detonator
6. High explosive (approx 650 lb) 7. Anti-roll horns

had been defeated on the land, both in
Norway and France, but the sea defence still
held, even if stretched thin in some places.
Against the enemy occupation of naval
bases in Norway and France, with all that
they meant in extending the range of operations of the U-boats, Britain had occupied
Iceland and was equipping a naval and air
base there which, in the end, would prove
decisive in the ultimate decision of the
U-boat war. Against the rapid build-up in
numbers of the U-boat fleet, which was to
rise at one period to over 360 operational
boats, there was the certainty that, during
1941, end-to-end Atlantic convoy of merchant ships would be achieved, and the task
of the U-boats would be made much more
difficult and dangerous.

Only in one aspect of convoy warfare was
there some distress. It had been apparent
even in the First World War that submarines
hesitated to attack convoys which had air
as well as surface escort, even though at that
time there was no airborne weapon capable
of sinking a submarine. The same hesitation
was being experienced in 1940.

But air escort of convoys at sea called for
aircraft of long range and endurance – the
same aircraft particularly in demand for
the bombing offensive on Germany. RAF
Coastal Command, which under naval
direction provided the convoy air escort,
was starved of long-range aircraft, and the
convoys suffered severe losses as a result.
This was a problem which was not solved
until 1943, by which time the navy had
acquired enough auxiliary aircraft-carriers
to operate their own aircraft on the convoy
routes. Later still, American production of
long-range aircraft filled the gap, and released the aircraft-carriers for other duties.

As the year ended, there were hopeful
signs in a situation which still remained
dark from the British military defeats on
the Continent. Although now thrust far out
into the Atlantic, the sea defence of the
nation still held, and behind it the blockade
of Germany and Italy was virtually intact.
This was still the fundamental weapon
which, if it could be maintained, would in
the end lead to victory. The great danger
which now faced Britain was no longer
invasion from the Continent – the chance of
that had gone (if it ever really existed) –
but defeat in the war against the U-boats.

The whole future of the war now hung
upon that groping battle being fought in
the vastness of the oceans. It was to be a
race between the German U-boat building
programme and the time when it would be
possible to bring into operation a fully
integrated system of end-to-end surface and
air escort of convoys. Once that was in
operation, the defeat of the U-boats was
certain, although there was a long and
painful road still to travel.

Right: **A North Sea convoy of British
colliers and merchantmen**

By the end of 1942, the future course of
Allied strategy—every hope and every
plan—hung in the balance of a long,
bitter, groping battle fought out
between U-boat and convoy escort in
the grey battlefield of the Atlantic.
Throughout, the Allies were hampered
by their inability to concentrate all
their naval resources on this one battle.
But when victory came to them it was
with astonishing speed and completeness, only weeks after one of their most
disastrous reverses at sea

Securing the Sealanes

By the beginning of 1941 the difficulties and
complexities of the Battle of the Atlantic
were really starting to make themselves felt.
The severe merchant ship losses in 1940—
2,186,158 tons were sunk by the U-boats
alone—had in part been met by wartime
redeployment of peacetime shipping, but
from 1941 on there was no hope of meeting
further losses by this means. By this time
merchant shipping had been stretched to
its limit, and future losses could be made
good only by new construction.

There were several factors which were to
single out 1941 and 1942 as the years of
special peril in that swaying, groping battle
against the U-boats. The most immediate of
them was the rapid build-up in numbers of
the U-boats themselves, for the increased
building programme put in hand by Germany at the outbreak of war was, by 1941,
beginning to take effect. From the beginning
of 1941 to the middle of 1943, the rate of
building far exceeded the rate of loss, so
that each succeeding month saw more and
more U-boats in the Atlantic.

There were other factors in this battle
which also came to the aid of the U-boats.
An important one was the length of time a
convoy took to cross the Atlantic. Allowing
for diversions, weather, and other delays,
the average time of passage of an Atlantic
convoy throughout the whole of the war was
just over 15 days; convoys to and from Freetown took four days longer. These long
passages in effect presented the U-boats with
more targets as the merchant ships made
their laborious voyages across the ocean.

Another important factor was the short
sea endurance of British escort vessels. At
the outbreak of war, escort for convoys could
only be provided up to a distance of about
500 miles from the British coast; beyond
that the merchant ships were on their own.
The occupation of Iceland after the disastrous
land campaign of 1940 provided the opportunity of increasing the range of escort by
the provision of a refuelling base on the
island, but it was not until April 1941 that
the first base there was fully in commission.
Simultaneously, the Canadian navy de-

veloped bases in Newfoundland and eastern
Canada, and by the use of these bases the
range of surface escort was pushed ever
farther out into the Atlantic. By April 1941
it was as far as 35° W, a little more than
half-way; two months later the first convoy
with end-to-end surface anti-submarine
escort sailed across the Atlantic. But because of the shortage of escort vessels, the
average strength of escort was, in 1941, no
more than two ships per convoy. It was not
until the new long-range escorts, laid down
just before the war, began to join the fleet
that the strength of escort could be increased,
in 1942 and 1943, to more adequate numbers.

As important as the surface escorts were
those of the air, for of all the enemies of
the U-boat the one most feared was the aircraft. Their range of vision and speed of
attack were both vastly superior to those of
the surface escorts, and an aircraft circling
a convoy would force every U-boat within
attacking range to submerge, thus condemn-
ing them to their low underwater speed and
a much reduced range of vision. But here

again, as with the surface escorts, the problem was range and endurance. As yet there were no aircraft in Coastal Command with a range or endurance long enough to cover Atlantic convoys for more than a short period of their passage, even using Iceland and Newfoundland as additional bases. To try to fill the gaps with carrier-borne aircraft was out of the question, for the few aircraft-carriers in the fleet were all required for other operational duties. Perhaps even more important, in 1941 efficient airborne radar by which aircraft could locate U-boats on the surface was as yet still in the future, as was an efficient airborne weapon which could kill a submarine.

The odds, then, were still strongly in favour of the U-boat, and they remained in its favour throughout 1941 and 1942. These were the years of building up the Allied anti-submarine escort forces, both surface and air, in numbers, in training, in tactical doctrine, and in the provision of scientific aids to locate U-boats—a long and tedious road to travel, made longer and harder by the rapid increase in numbers of the U-boats and by the development of their pack tactics of attack.

Early in 1941 the first step along this road was taken by the removal of the headquarters of the Western Approaches command from Plymouth to Liverpool, and by the appointment of a commander-in-chief whose sole responsibility was to conduct the campaign against the U-boats. Into this new headquarters was integrated the headquarters of 15 Group, Coastal Command, so that both surface and air escort could be co-ordinated from one operations room. Duplicates of the U-boat and trade plots in the British Admiralty were set up in the Western Approaches operations room, and the two connected with direct telephone and teleprinter links between Whitehall and Liverpool.

Admiral Sir Percy Noble was appointed as Commander-in-Chief Western Approaches in February 1941. He was, perhaps, the first to appreciate that the key to victory in this campaign lay just as much in the training of the officers and men as in the number of available escorts. Anti-submarine training establishments were set up at Dunoon and Campbeltown, experimental work was carried out at Fairlie, and a sea training organisation was based at Tobermory. To this last establishment went all new escort vessels as they completed their acceptance trials. For a month they were engaged in arduous sea exercises designed to harden crews, who were largely new recruits, to accustom them to normal Atlantic weather conditions, and to give them a reasonably intimate knowledge of their own ship and her capabilities.

Specialist training followed the sea training, so that by the time the new ship became fully operational her complement had not only been toughened by the Tobermory training but had also acquired the necessary professional and technological skills. All this, however, took time, and it was not until mid-1943 that the total overall training could be considered adequate. Until that time, the operational need in the Atlantic for all and every escort had to take precedence.

Another decision by Admiral Noble was to organise all the escorts into groups. By allocating eight escort ships to a group, the C-in-C could count on an effective strength of five or six escorts for each group, leaving a margin for refits of ships, leave periods,

After the first 'Happy Time' of the U-boats, Allied losses fell off — but not for long

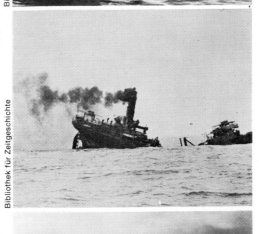

training, and other contingencies. The great value of the group system was that each escort captain quickly became familiar both with the other escorts in the group and with the group commander's methods.

It is in this reorganisation of the escort forces, and the emphasis on proper anti-submarine training, that the seeds of ultimate victory in the Atlantic were sown. Yet if it was one important thing to recognise the correct road to travel in search of victory, Britain's actual journey along that road was a vastly more difficult business. The priorities in naval building in 1940 and 1941 had to be balanced between the needs of the operational fleet for aircraft-carriers, cruisers, destroyers, and landing-craft of various shapes and sizes, and of the anti-submarine fleet for frigates, sloops, and corvettes for purely escort purposes. There could obviously be no absolute priority for escort vessels, and so there was no possibility of keeping even level with the rate of U-boat building in Germany, let alone overtaking it. Two and a half bitter years were to pass before the escort groups finally established their superiority in this vast campaign.

The tribulations of 1941, when Britain was still in the throes of reorganising her anti-submarine forces, were magnified by the establishment of German long-range bomber squadrons on the coasts of France and Norway. These consisted mainly of Focke-Wulf Condors able to operate up to 800 miles into the Atlantic. Their mission was two-fold. Primarily their task was to locate British convoys so that the U-boats could be directed to them, but a secondary role was to sink merchant ships proceeding independently or straggling from their convoys. And in their secondary role alone they came a very close second to the U-boats. While, in January 1941, U-boats sank 21 ships of 126,782 tons, the long-range bombers accounted for 20 of 78,517 tons. The figures for February were similar: 39 ships of 196,783 tons to the U-boats, 27 ships of 89,305 tons to the bombers.

The answer to the Focke-Wulf bombers came in many ways. One was to route the independently sailed merchant ships far to the north, beyond the range of the bombers based in Norway and France, and to bring in convoys along a narrow route patrolled by long-range fighters. Another was to press ahead with the mounting of anti-aircraft guns in the merchant ships themselves, manned by gun-crews of seamen and marines. A third was to fit catapults in the old seaplane-carrier *Pegasus* and use her, with naval fighters embarked, as an anti-aircraft escort for convoys.

A development of the *Pegasus* idea was to fit catapults in selected merchant ships and embark a Hurricane fighter, which could then be catapulted off whenever an enemy aircraft was sighted. On completion of its mission, the Hurricane was ditched alongside a friendly ship and the pilot rescued. It was through means such as these, and also through the reluctance of the Luftwaffe to work in harmony with the Kriegsmarine, that the attack of the long-range bombers on shipping was eventually beaten.

With the gradual extension of convoy across the Atlantic, the reign of the German U-boat 'aces' came to an end. These were the men who had distinguished themselves in the Atlantic battle by the actual tonnage of merchant shipping they personally had sunk. In the first 18 months of warfare, while the convoy system was still being built up and the ocean still carried a large proportion of independently routed merchant ships, the number of easy targets had presented many opportunities to skilled commanders to amass a considerable tonnage to their personal credit.

The U-boat commanders themselves referred to the first year and a half of the war as 'the happy time'. By February 1941 the three greatest of the U-boat 'aces' were Gunther Prien, who had sunk the *Royal Oak* in Scapa Flow and claimed over 150,000 tons of merchant shipping, and Joachim Schepke and Otto Kretschmer, both of whom claimed over 200,000 tons of Allied shipping sunk. All three of them had been decorated by Hitler with the Knight's Cross with Oak-leaves for their outstanding success, and all three were men from whom other U-boat commanders drew their inspiration. But by March all three had been eliminated from the battle. Prien, in U-47, was sunk on March 7 by the corvettes *Arbutus* and *Camellia* and the destroyer *Wolverine*; Schepke, in U-100, was sunk on March 17 by the *Walker* and *Vanoc*; and on the same night these same destroyers sank U-99, taking Kretschmer prisoner as he escaped

from his sinking U-boat. It was a heavy blow for Germany, for these three had been widely recognised in Germany as the cream of the U-boat commanders.

March 1941 saw the virtual end of the independent U-boat attack. As more and more merchant ships were brought into the convoy organisation, and as the range of convoy was extended farther across the Atlantic, the day of the individual U-boat was over. The British adoption and extension of convoy forced the U-boat command to work out new tactics, and it was from this situation that the pack attack at night was developed.

There was nothing basically new in this. A rudimentary form of pack attack had been evolved during the last year of the First World War, but had not been very successful because wireless signals, necessary for control of the pack, were still, relatively speaking, in their infancy. Tentative pack tactics had appeared in the Atlantic in 1940, but had not been developed because the individual U-boat operating in a fixed area was still finding sufficient targets to make its presence there well worth while. Those days, however, were now over for good, although in early 1942 the U-boats experienced another brief 'happy time'. This followed

the entry of the United States into the war, when a small number of U-boats concentrated on the eastern American seaboard and took a heavy toll of the unescorted shipping there. Six months later, when this shipping, too, was organised into convoys, these U-boats withdrew abruptly.

In the organisation of the pack attack, the U-boat command relied on one U-boat of the pack shadowing a convoy during daylight and homing in the remainder by directional wireless as night approached. All attacks were then made on the surface during the hours of darkness, when the tiny superstructure of the U-boat was well-nigh invisible to the defenders. With her high surface speed and her virtual invisibility, the advantages of night attack to the U-boat were considerable.

Yet the whole system had in it one element of weakness. The shadowing U-boat was forced to make a series of wireless signals reporting the convoy's position, speed, and alterations of course. These signals were invariably picked up by Allied directional-finding stations, and the bearings, when plotted in the British Admiralty's U-boat tracking room, revealed the position of the shadower.

For the Germans, the Battle of the Atlantic had two purposes and two phases. At first the Germans were trying to strangle Britain's lifelines across the Atlantic, but by 1942 the U-boats were fighting to prevent the establishment of an Allied invasion-force in Britain. Both phases were governed by the 'Black Gap' in mid-Atlantic, where Allied escorts could not protect the vital convoys. The occupation of Iceland in 1940 had been the first step towards closing the gap, but no positive counterattack could hurt the U-boats until long-range frigates and escort-carriers could shepherd the convoys all the way across. In the spring of 1943, with the Torch landings safely over, the attack on the U-boats began in earnest. The diagram below shows how the gap was closed, and depicts the major Atlantic convoy routes and U-boat bases

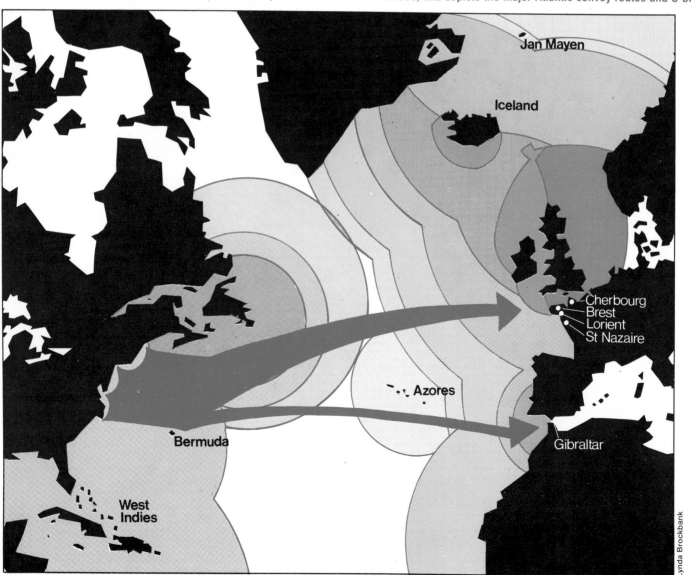

Sep 1939 May 1940

Jun 1940 Mar 1941

Apr 1941 Dec 1941

Jan 1942 Jul 1942

Aug 1942 May 1943

Jun 1943 Aug 1943

Sep 1943 May 1945

Jan Mayen

Iceland

Cherbourg
Brest
Lorient
St Nazaire

Azores

Bermuda

Gibraltar

West Indies

Lynda Brockbank

Yet even with this essential knowledge, there was still a very long road to travel before victory could come to the Allies in the Atlantic. There were, in the years 1941 and 1942, shortages in almost every aspect of the war against the U-boats – shortage of escort vessels, shortage of training time, shortage of adequate weapons, shortage of the technological advances required to deal with the modern German U-boat and her new tactics. But of all the shortages, the most chronic was that of long-range and long-endurance aircraft. It had already become apparent that the convoy which had both air and surface escort to protect it was virtually immune from attack. The problem was to devise a method whereby aircraft could always be on hand throughout the whole of a convoy's Atlantic passage.

To close the mid-Atlantic gap, which was as yet far beyond the range of any shore-based aircraft yet developed, the Admiralty in 1941 placed orders in America for a number of small escort carriers (virtually a Liberty ship hull fitted with a flying deck and hangar space). Yet even with American production methods it would be over a year before they could be expected to become operational. In the meantime, Coastal Command had to rely on a single squadron of very long-range Liberator aircraft which, originally composed of 20 aircraft, was very quickly reduced to a strength of ten by wastage and allotment to Ferry Command and BOAC. All attempts to increase the number, and to obtain long-range Lancaster bombers for the Atlantic battle, failed. The convoys and surface escorts were left to battle it out against the U-boats, handicapped as they were by the lack of one of the most powerful agents for success. Such air escort as did exist (700 miles from Northern Ireland and Western Scotland, 400 miles from Iceland, and 700 miles from Canadian bases) not only left a large gap in mid-Atlantic completely beyond reach of shore-based air escort, but was of itself spasmodic and in any case limited to daylight hours.

The Battle of the Oceans

It is difficult, over so immense a stage as the seas which both divide and join the Commonwealth, to appreciate the vast extent of the Battle of the Atlantic. The term itself is a restriction of the full encounter, for in effect the battle embraced far more than the North and South Atlantic oceans themselves. U-boats and armed raiders operated in the Indian Ocean, across which ran the main sea routes to India, Australia, and New Zealand, as important to global strategy as was the Atlantic. And for a long time the Arctic Ocean was the only available highway for supplies to Russia after the start of her great campaign, though later an alternative route was opened through the Persian Gulf. All of them called for protection from U-boat and raider attack, and what has come to be known as the Battle of the Atlantic was, more truly, a battle of the oceans.

In terms of voyages, this vast encounter ran into several hundreds of thousands of miles steamed each week; in terms of ships it could mean as many as 1,000 at sea on any one day throughout the whole of the war, all of them to be protected against attack by an enemy who could operate virtually unseen and unheard. This was the true yardstick against which the battle must be measured, an immense and ceaseless conflict waged over millions of square miles of ocean.

One other aspect of this battle needs to be mentioned. As early as 1941 the Chiefs-of-Staff were already laying their plans to move from the defensive to the offensive. All realised that when this time came, it would call for a vast Allied army based in Britain, with a huge logistic backing, poised for the assault on Europe which alone could lead to complete victory. Most of this great army, and most of its logistic backing, could only come from across the Atlantic, men and materials from the United States and Canada. Security of the Atlantic was vital for this vast movement, and only a clear-cut victory over the U-boats could guarantee such security. This Atlantic battle was the one vital cog in the whole machinery of the war, for failure there would inevitably bring defeat to the whole Allied cause. It was the one and only key which could unlock the door to final victory.

The merchant ship losses in 1941 were grievous. U-boats alone sank 432 ships of 2,171,754 tons, while aircraft claimed another 371 ships of 1,017,422 tons. Merchant and warship raiders added during the year to the total by 84 ships of 428,350 tons, while a further 111 ships of 230,842 tons were lost in enemy minefields laid around the British coasts. From all causes, the final loss for the year was 1,299 ships totalling 4,328,558 tons – an overall loss well beyond Allied building capacity to replace.

These figures give an accurate idea of the severity of the battle, but they were far surpassed by the figures for the following year. The U-boats alone exceeded the total losses for 1941 by very nearly 2,000,000 tons (6,226,215 tons), and the overall loss for the year was 7,790,697 tons, represented by 1,664 ships.

'The U-boat attack of 1942,' wrote Churchill, 'was our worst evil.' Indeed, in no other theatre of the war, save perhaps in the Pacific, was the outlook quite so black. And again it was the same story, the inability of the Allies, in the face of all their maritime commitments, to produce escort vessels and long-range aircraft fast enough to hold the U-boat growth. German ship production facilities were concentrated almost entirely on U-boats to the exclusion of almost every other type of vessel, and the speed with which they were produced can be measured by the steady increase in operational boats. Excluding those used for training and other purposes, the numbers of U-boats available for operations at sea rose from 91 in January 1942 to 196 in October of the same year, to 212 as the year came to its close, and to a peak of 240 in April 1943. And although during 1942 a total of 87 U-boats were sunk, including those lost through accidents in German home waters, the steady production of new boats far outweighed losses.

The entry of the United States into the war brought to the U-boat captains their second 'happy time'. For six months the US relied on sea and air patrols as the means of countering U-boat attacks, in spite of all British experience that convoy was the only method of holding in check the mounting ship losses. Admiral Dönitz, commander-in-chief of the U-boat area, sent five U-boats into the area on the declaration of war against the United States, increasing the number by stages to a total of 21. By June 1942, when the Americans eventually put all their ships into convoy, these U-boats had sunk no less than 505 vessels. This holocaust moved even Dönitz into song. 'Our submarines,' he exulted, 'are operating

close inshore along the coast of the United States of America, so that bathers and sometimes entire coastal cities are witnesses to that drama of war, whose visual climaxes are constituted by the red glorioles of blazing tankers.'

Dönitz and the German High Command had calculated that if an average of 800,000 tons of Allied shipping could be sunk each month, an Axis victory was certain. The overall rate of loss throughout 1942 was fractionally below 650,000 tons a month; but optimistic reports on estimated tonnage sunk made by the individual U-boat commanders led Dönitz to believe that his objective of 800,000 tons monthly was being achieved. Yet even 650,000 tons a month was a crippling rate for the Allies, far beyond their capacity for replacement, and it is true enough that, throughout these grim months of 1942, defeat in the Atlantic, and hence in the war as a whole, was a possibility that haunted the thoughts of all the war leaders.

Just as serious as the loss of essential imports which this rate of sinking made inevitable was the unforeseen cutback in the rate of building up forces in Britain for the assault on Europe, without which there could be no final victory over Germany. This build-up of forces had been given the codeword 'Bolero', and the plans hammered out by the Chiefs-of-Staff of Britain and the United States had called for a strength of five divisions of Canadian and United States troops in Britain by the end of 1942. As the year ended, 'Bolero' was so far in arrears that less than one division had arrived, and the overall plan was falling more and more into arrears. The whole future course of the war, every hope, every plan, hung in the balance poised over the Atlantic.

A new weapon for the Allies

During 1942, however, the anti-submarine frigates, ordered in 1939 and 1940, began to come forward from the builders' yards. These were ships which had the speed and endurance so vital in the Atlantic battle. One of the great problems of convoy escort had been the danger of allowing the existing escorts to hunt U-boats to their final destruction, more often than not a long and exacting operation. Their prime duty had always been to protect the merchant ships; but a convoy could not stand still in mid-Atlantic while its escorts were engaged in hunting and destroying. A great number of U-boats, located by radar and asdic, lived to fight again simply because the convoy escorts could not spare the time to hunt them to destruction. The merchant ships always had to come first.

The commissioning of the anti-submarine frigates, however, provided an answer to this problem. The growth in overall force represented by these frigates enabled Admiral Noble to build up support groups of ships, which could be directed to join the defences of any convoy threatened by a pack attack. While the normal escort group could continue with the convoy, providing the necessary close defence, the support group could engage in prolonged hunting operations, holding a detected U-boat with its asdics while the attacks were made. The first support group, under the command of Commander F. J. Walker, was at sea by the third week of September, 1942, but other events were to delay the full implementation of this new contribution to the Atlantic battle.

Almost simultaneously with the arrival of the frigates came the new ahead-throwing anti-submarine weapons; first the 'Hedgehog', a multi-barrelled mortar which threw 24 charges ahead of the attacking ship; and then the 'Squid', which threw a pattern of three full-sized depth-charges. The old method of attack, by dropping depth-charges over the ship's stern, had suffered from the great drawback that asdic contact with the U-boat was lost during the run-in, and the final stages of any attack had to be made by guesswork. The new weapons enabled asdic contact to be held throughout the attack and right up to the moment of depth-charge explosion, resulting in a far greater degree of accuracy.

By the late summer of 1942 the first of the new, small escort carriers, which had been ordered from the United States the previous year, was commissioned for service. She was the *Avenger,* and by the end of the year six more were serving in the fleet. These aircraft-carriers were to provide the final answer to the U-boat threat, their aircraft filling the Atlantic gaps which were still beyond the range of shore-based aircraft. It was in these gaps—in mid-Atlantic, off the north coast of Brazil, and around the hump of Africa—that the U-boats concentrated and continued to find convoys unprotected by air escort. Pack attacks on convoys in these areas were made in such strength as to swamp the surface escorts, and provided a rich harvest for the U-boats.

The stage, then, was set by the late autumn of 1942 to turn to the offensive in the Atlantic. With support groups to augment the surface escorts of threatened convoys, with carrier-borne aircraft to provide the essential air escort across the Atlantic gaps, with the new weapons of attack which enabled the full benefit of asdic contact to be held to the last moment, the prospects of success looked bright. And to Liverpool, in November 1942, came Admiral Sir Max Horton as commander-in-chief. He was a submarine officer of great distinction, and thus brought to his task an intimate knowledge of submarine warfare in all its aspects. He inherited from Admiral Noble an organisation in which most of the essential groundwork had already been done and a command whose forces were growing almost daily as the new ships ordered in 1940 and 1941 reached completion.

One other aspect of this Atlantic battle needs a mention. A part of the difficulties which beset the Allies in 1942, resulting in such heavy losses of shipping, had been caused by the withdrawal from Atlantic duties of the United States escort forces in June of that year. These vessels were needed partly for the Pacific war and partly to escort troop and logistic convoys for the projected assault on North Africa in November 1942.

By the end of the year the division of escort forces in the Atlantic was: Britain providing 50%, Canada 48%, and the United States 2%. Early in 1943, at a convoy conference held in Washington, the United States declared that they would have to withdraw completely from all trade convoy protection in the Atlantic. It was a decision which came at an awkward moment, with the battle at its height and the British and Canadian forces stretched to their utmost. The American decision, though it represented but a small part of the burden, had to be absorbed equally between Britain and Canada.

As the escort forces were poised, in the late autumn of 1942, to turn to the offensive against the U-boats, a new blow struck the Western Approaches command. Operation

'Torch', the invasion of French North Africa, was mounted in November, and both the escort carriers and the newly formed support groups were detached from the Atlantic convoy routes to provide protection for the troop convoys in which this expeditionary force was transported. This campaign was to last until May 1943, and until the end of March the Atlantic escort forces had to continue the battle still with no air cover over the three 'gaps', and still with no support groups to supplement the escort groups in the big battles which raged around the convoys.

As the year turned, the rate of loss in the Atlantic showed little change from the figures of 1942. Wild weather in the Atlantic during January produced difficulties for the U-boats in their operations, and the loss during the month was 203,000 tons. In February it rose to 359,000 tons; by March it was back to the high average rate of 1942, 627,000 tons of shipping being sunk in that month. It was during this month that the American decision to withdraw completely from the Atlantic was announced at the conference in Washington.

It was, in fact, while this conference was in session that one of the biggest and most disastrous convoy battles of the whole war was fought out in the Atlantic. Two convoys had been sailed from Halifax to Britain, one fast convoy of 25 ships and one slow one of 52. The fast convoy was sighted by a U-boat early in its passage, and before long a pack of eight U-boats was in contact. Over the next three days and nights they sank 12 merchant ships. Some hundred or so miles ahead, the slow convoy was also sighted and reported, and a pack of 12 U-boats concentrated against it. As the two convoys closed up, the two packs merged into one, swamping the defence and causing heavy loss. Out of these two convoys alone 21 ships of 141,000 tons were sunk.

What made this particular convoy battle even harder to bear was that only one U-boat was sunk by the escort forces. It was without question a serious defeat, remarkable even in a period in which there were few gleams of light to encourage the Allies in their desperate struggle.

Climax of the battle

Few could doubt, in March 1943, that the Atlantic battle had reached its climax, and that out of the operations of the next three or four months one side or the other must slide down into defeat. Admiral Dönitz was making his supreme effort, and out of an operational strength of 240 U-boats he concentrated no fewer than 112 in the North Atlantic. Flushed by success, and highly trained, the U-boat commanders were able, by the very nature of submarine warfare, to dictate the conditions in which they fought the battle. Almost without exception the U-boat packs were concentrated in those areas beyond the reach of air escort, and it was here that they reaped almost the whole of their grim harvest.

To the Atlantic, at the end of March, came the escort carriers, released at last from their duties with the Torch convoys. With them, too, came the support groups, so that at long last there existed in the Atlantic the possibility of hunting detected U-boats to their final destruction. And almost simultaneously, two other events made notable contributions to the battle. Using his authority as commander-in-chief of the US forces, President Roosevelt took a hand in the dis-

Admiral Sir Max Horton, successor to Noble

Admiral Karl Dönitz, Flag Officer U-boats

These three men were Germany's top scorers in the first 'Happy Time'

◁ Gunther Prien, of U-47, the man who sank the British battleship *Royal Oak* in Scapa Flow—he was lost in action in March 1941

◁ Joachim Schepke, of U-100; he was lost with his ship when he took too many liberties with a convoy's escort

◁ Otto Kretschmer, of U-99. He was Germany's 'top scorer' but was captured when U-99 was depth-charged and forced to the surface —the only one of the trio to survive the Battle of the Atlantic

U-BOATS SUNK 1941-43

number: 60, 40, 20, 0

1941   1942   1943

tribution of the very long-range Liberator aircraft being delivered from America. By the end of March, 20 of them were in operation in the North Atlantic; by mid-April the number had grown to 41. It was still far too few to cover the essential needs, but it was at least an earnest promise of better things to come.

The other great contribution came from the scientists. They designed a very short-wave radar set which could reflect from much smaller objects at sea and against which the German radar search receiver, as fitted in the U-boats, was of no avail. These centimetric radars were fitted to many of the surface escorts around the end of 1942 and beginning of 1943, and they led to many more contacts with attacking U-boats, with the added advantage that the U-boats had now no knowledge that they had been detected. The new radar was also being fitted in aircraft, but other priorities in the RAF made it slow to arrive in Coastal Command.

Early in May another considerable convoy battle was fought, providing the first real opportunity of testing out the value of the support group and continuous air escort in anti-submarine warfare. An outward bound convoy was delayed and to some extent scattered by a violent storm south of Greenland, an area which was known to contain a heavy concentration of U-boats. A pack of 12 U-boats concentrated around the convoy. This was the type of situation for which the support groups were formed, and two groups were ordered out from St John's, Nova Scotia, as the convoy approached the area. They were somewhat delayed by the storm which had scattered the convoy, and before they could arrive the U-boats had sunk five ships during night attacks, following this with four more sunk during the following day. One of the convoy's escorts, the corvette *Pink*, attacked and sank U-192.

The two support groups joined the convoy that evening, and for the first time U-boats came up against the full application of the new countermeasures. As the convoy was collected and re-formed after its battering in the storm, the U-boats renewed their attacks, but each one was detected and driven off before damage could be done to the merchant ships. HMS *Loosestrife* detected, chased, and sank U-638; the destroyer *Vidette* held U-125 with her asdic and sent her to the bottom with a hit from her Hedgehog, the *Oribi* rammed and sank U-531, and the sloop *Pelican* detected and held U-438 with her asdic and hunted her to final destruction. Aircraft operating over the convoy accounted for two more, U-710 being destroyed by a Coastal Command aircraft and U-630 by an aircraft of the Royal Canadian Air Force. But the cup of bitterness was not yet full for the U-boats, for U-659 and U-439 collided in the darkness and both were lost.

This was a severe defeat for the U-boats, but one defeat in a campaign does not necessarily mean victory for the other side. Yet the fate of the convoys which followed was to prove that this was, in fact, no flash in the pan. The next fast convoy lost three ships, but the cost to the enemy was three U-boats sunk. The slow convoy which made its passage at the same time had two ships sunk, while two U-boats were sunk by the escorts and others from the attacking pack were seriously damaged. Of the next pair of convoys, the result was even more dramatic. The slow convoy reached Britain with all its merchant ships in company, but in its path lay the sunken hulls of U-954, U-258,

U-209, U-273, and U-381. The fast convoy also arrived without loss, with U-752 joining her sisters on the bed of the Atlantic.

Perhaps more impressive still were the overall figures from April to July. In April, when the new and integrated system of surface and air escort was only just getting into its stride, the U-boats sank 245,000 tons of shipping and lost 15 of their number in the process. In May they sank 165,000 tons at a cost to themselves of 40 U-boats. In June the figures were 18,000 tons and 17 U-boats; and in July, 123,000 tons and 37 U-boats.

Nor was this the whole of the Atlantic story, for Coastal Command was conducting a separate offensive over the main U-boat transit areas to and from the Atlantic. Using the new centimetric radar, depth-charges set to explode at a shallow depth, and search-lights to illuminate U-boats detected at night, they sank a further 13 U-boats during April and May, taking full advantage of a tactical mistake made by Admiral Dönitz, who ordered his U-boats to proceed to and from their operational areas on the surface, and fight it out against attacking aircraft. Against the new weapons, they had small chance of success.

Against losses such as these it was hardly surprising that morale in the U-boats cracked. It was a staggering reversal of the trend of the battle in the Atlantic, and even more so in the realisation that it took no more than five weeks from the time the full offensive was mounted to drive the U-boats, at the very height of their power and success, to search for less hazardous waters in which to operate. For nearly three months after the decisive May battles, the Atlantic was empty of U-boats, and even when they did return, though never again in the same numbers, it was very noticeable that the individual U-boat commanders had lost their will to attack.

On the purely analytical plane, one could attribute this victory in the Atlantic battle to the influence of the support groups in anti-submarine warfare, to the provision of continuous air escort over the convoys, to the centimetric radar and the other new weapons provided by the scientists and technologists. A considerable element in the victory must go, too, to the expertise in the interpretation of U-boat Intelligence developed in the Submarine Tracking Room in the British Admiralty. Their handling of all forms of Intelligence, and in particular the directional bearings of U-boat wireless signals, enabled them to predict with considerable accuracy the build-up of U-boat concentrations in the Atlantic and to divert convoys from the main danger areas.

But the real victory went much deeper than this. It lay just as much in the skill and endurance of the men who manned the escort vessels and the merchant ships, in their refusal to acknowledge defeat in the dark years of 1941 and 1942, in their courage which fortified them to return again and again to that vast battlefield where the odds were weighted so heavily against them. Over the centuries there have been, in British naval history, victories which shine like jewels across the years: none can shine more brightly than that achieved in this long, bitter, groping battle fought across the oceans.

In the concept of overall strategy in the European theatre, the winning of the Battle of the Atlantic was always recognised as the essential prerequisite of ultimate victory. When the German armies overran most of

Europe in 1940 and 1941, it was British sea power, fortified by the navies of the Dominions and of such allies as had ships to contribute, that alone stood between the Axis and the domination of the world. Sea power, with its flexibility and natural resilience, held the ring around Germany and Italy, denying to the enemy the riches of the world which lay across the oceans. The U-boat campaign was the chosen, indeed the only, weapon of the Axis to break the ring. How nearly it succeeded can be read in the figures of Allied shipping losses in 1941, 1942, and the first three months of 1943. But with the clear-cut victory which emerged in May 1943, not only was the ring still unbroken, but now it could contract, closing in every day until even the coastal waters of Germany became too dangerous for her shipping to use.

With the Atlantic battle won, an endless stream of convoys, securely guarded and virtually immune from loss, crossed the Atlantic, bringing to Britain the troops, the guns, the tanks, the supplies needed to launch in 1944 the direct attack on German-held Europe. With the road now open, the whole future course of the European campaign lay clear and inevitable. To Britain, to North Africa, to Russia, to Malta, an endless stream of men, weapons, and supplies came and gathered against the day of the final assaults. All were carried by sea, and their safe arrival at their destinations proclaimed the planned offensive. The victories which lay so surely in the future, in which the armies and the air forces of the Allies were to shatter the resistance of the enemy, were all made possible by the full opening of the sea routes across the world.

So history repeated itself, for in all war experience it is the winning of the maritime war which precedes the land victory. By mid-1943 the maritime war had been won and the main task of the navies of the Allies had been accomplished; now it was the task of the armies and the air forces to go in and win the final victory.

A long and groping battle

1941 February: Admiral Sir Percy Noble appointed C-in-C Western Approaches.
March: The leading German U-boat aces— Prien, Schepke, and Kretschmer—are eliminated.
April: The Allied refuelling base in Iceland begins operation.
June: First Allied convoy with end-to-end surface escort crosses the Atlantic.
December: The United States enters the war: a second 'happy time' for the U-boats begins.

1942 June: US escort forces are withdrawn from Atlantic duties.
September: The first British support group begins operation.
November: Admiral Sir Max Horton takes over as C-in-C Western Approaches.

1943 March: In a running battle with the escorts of convoys HX-229 and SC-122, U-boat packs sink 21 ships for the loss of only one submarine. But at the end of the month the escort carriers and support groups return from the Torch operation.
April: U-boats sink 245,000 tons of shipping for the loss of 15 submarines.
May: During attacks on five convoys, 20 U-boats are sunk. During the whole month 165,000 tons of shipping are sunk—for the loss of 40 U-boats.
June: The U-boat toll mounts: for only 18,000 tons sunk, 17 U-boats are destroyed. For the first time, the balance favours the Allies.

'The Battle of the Atlantic was the dominating factor all through the war. Never for one moment could we forget that everything elsewhere depended on its outcome' Churchill

For the Allies, the Battle of the Atlantic was not only a race to develop new and more advanced equipment than the enemy, but it was also a struggle to build even the basic minimum of aircraft and ships to provide an adequate escort for all convoys. Before the war, the escort programme and Coastal Command had been the 'Cinderellas' of the defence budget, and the chronic shortage of ships and aircraft was not something which could be rectified at once, when all other branches of the services were crying out for new equipment. It was not until the middle of 1942 that a massive building programme—much of which was undertaken in Canada—meant that the ships to provide a shore-to-shore escort became available in adequate numbers, and the RAF began to receive aircraft specially designed for the anti-submarine patrol role—instead of having to make do with old equipment which lacked the necessary range and duration. But once the escort forces had received the vital ships and aircraft, equipped with the new anti-submarine weapons, the 'happy time' of the U-boats was quickly ended

HMS Starling: an escort sloop of the modified *Black Swan* class. This class, the first of which were laid down before the outbreak of war, proved to be a most efficient escort design, combining good AA and anti-submarine armament with adequate speed and seaworthiness. **Displacement:** 1,350 tons. **Dimensions:** $299\frac{1}{2} \times 38\frac{1}{2} \times 8\frac{3}{4}$ feet. **Speed:** 20 knots. **Armament:** Six 4-inch and 12 20-mm anti-aircraft guns. **Complement:** 192

HMS Clematis: a corvette of the *Flower* class. This class was ordered before the war as part of the massive rearmament programme, and the design was based on the whale catcher. The ships proved to be too small to fulfill the ocean escort role adequately, in spite of being excellent sea-boats. **Displacement:** 925 tons. **Dimensions:** $205 \times 33 \times 11\frac{1}{2}$ feet. **Armament:** One 4-inch gun, one multiple pom-pom. **Complement:** 85

HMS Towey: a frigate of the *River* class. This was the first of the new ocean escort classes, larger and faster than the corvettes and designed for mass production. The subsequent *Loch* and *Bay* classes were developments of this design. **Displacement:** 1,370 tons. **Dimensions:** $301\frac{1}{4} \times 36\frac{1}{2} \times 9$ feet. **Speed:** 20 knots. **Armament:** Two 4-inch guns, ten 20-mm anti-aircraft guns. **Complement:** 140

HMS Biter: one of the escort carriers which were brought into service to bridge the 'mid-Atlantic gap' in land-based air cover. They were built on merchant ship hulls and had wooden flight-decks. **Displacement:** 8,200 tons. **Dimensions:** $492\frac{1}{4} \times 66\frac{1}{4} \times 23\frac{1}{4}$ feet. **Speed:** $16\frac{1}{2}$ knots. **Armament:** Three 4-inch and 15 20-mm anti-aircraft guns, 15 aircraft. **Complement:** 555

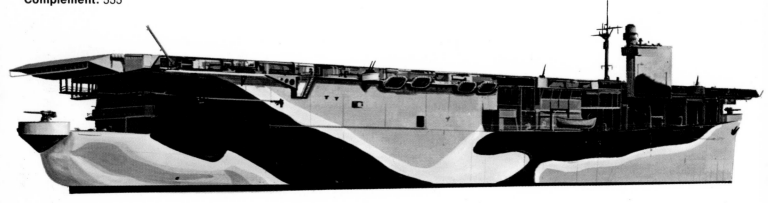

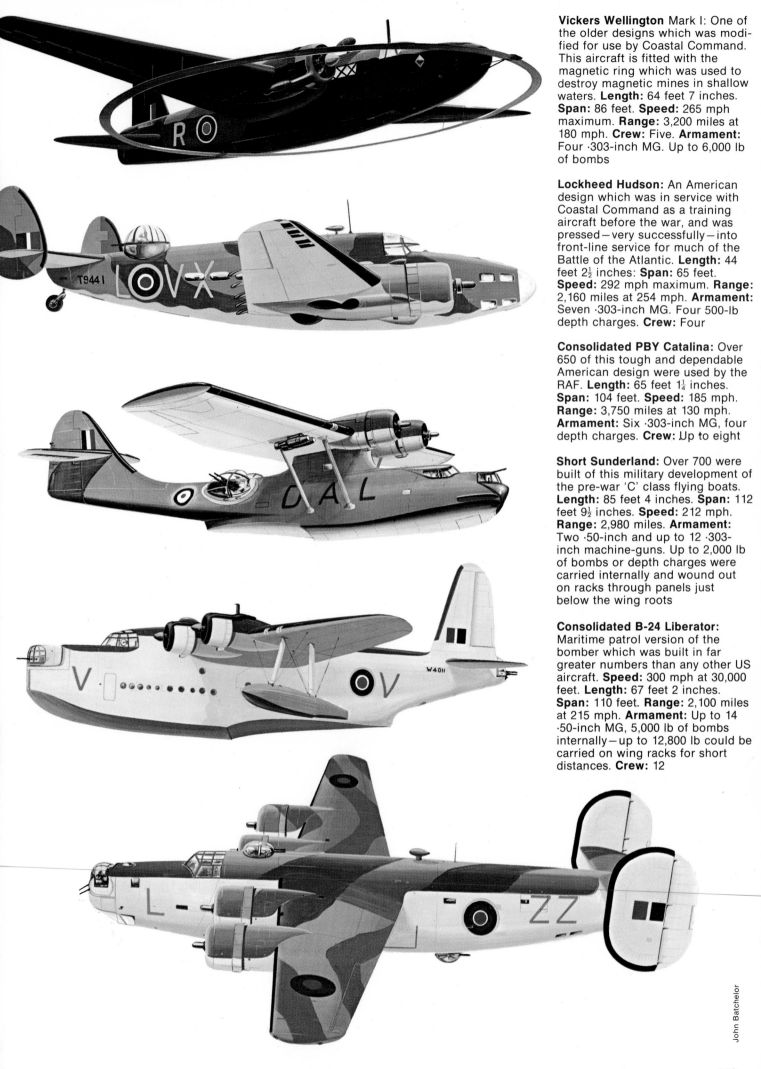

Vickers Wellington Mark I: One of the older designs which was modified for use by Coastal Command. This aircraft is fitted with the magnetic ring which was used to destroy magnetic mines in shallow waters. **Length:** 64 feet 7 inches. **Span:** 86 feet. **Speed:** 265 mph maximum. **Range:** 3,200 miles at 180 mph. **Crew:** Five. **Armament:** Four ·303-inch MG. Up to 6,000 lb of bombs

Lockheed Hudson: An American design which was in service with Coastal Command as a training aircraft before the war, and was pressed—very successfully—into front-line service for much of the Battle of the Atlantic. **Length:** 44 feet 2½ inches: **Span:** 65 feet. **Speed:** 292 mph maximum. **Range:** 2,160 miles at 254 mph. **Armament:** Seven ·303-inch MG. Four 500-lb depth charges. **Crew:** Four

Consolidated PBY Catalina: Over 650 of this tough and dependable American design were used by the RAF. **Length:** 65 feet 1¼ inches. **Span:** 104 feet. **Speed:** 185 mph. **Range:** 3,750 miles at 130 mph. **Armament:** Six ·303-inch MG, four depth charges. **Crew:** Up to eight

Short Sunderland: Over 700 were built of this military development of the pre-war 'C' class flying boats. **Length:** 85 feet 4 inches. **Span:** 112 feet 9½ inches. **Speed:** 212 mph. **Range:** 2,980 miles. **Armament:** Two ·50-inch and up to 12 ·303-inch machine-guns. Up to 2,000 lb of bombs or depth charges were carried internally and wound out on racks through panels just below the wing roots

Consolidated B-24 Liberator: Maritime patrol version of the bomber which was built in far greater numbers than any other US aircraft. **Speed:** 300 mph at 30,000 feet. **Length:** 67 feet 2 inches. **Span:** 110 feet. **Range:** 2,100 miles at 215 mph. **Armament:** Up to 14 ·50-inch MG, 5,000 lb of bombs internally—up to 12,800 lb could be carried on wing racks for short distances. **Crew:** 12

John Batchelor

KOREA-
the Air War

The air war over Korea was the first jet versus jet
war of the 20th Century. It showed how the heavy
bombers of the Second World War had become
obsolete, but the ground attack fighters could still
hit transport and tactical targets. The high speed
fights between the American Sabres and the
Communist MiG-15s demonstrated that tactical
skill could still give an edge in
jet dog fights.

By the autumn of 1943 there was no longer any doubt that Japan was going to lose the war in the Pacific. One by one the conquests she had made in her lightning offensives of 1942 were slipping from her grasp, overwhelmed by the ever-growing military strength of the United States. It was only a question of time.

In November 1943, President Roosevelt, Prime Minister Winston Churchill and General Chiang Kai-shek met in Cairo to discuss the future of the Far East after the eventual collapse of Imperial Japan. Among other things, it was agreed that Korea, which had been a province of Japan since 1910, should once more become a free and independent state.

The Allied leaders in Cairo, however, had overlooked one very significant factor. Their decisions had been reached without any consultation with the Soviet Union, who at that time was not at war with Japan. When Russia finally declared war in the Far East in August 1945, her actions precipitated a chain of events which were to tear the carefully laid Allied plans to shreds.

One of the first Soviet acts after the surrender of Japan in September 1945 was to occupy the northern half of Korea, while United States forces occupied the southern half. As a temporary measure, designed to speed up the surrender of the Japanese forces in Korea, the two powers agreed that their respective zones of occupation should be divided by the 38th Parallel of latitude. No agreement was reached, however, on the question of Korean independence, and in September 1947, following the complete breakdown of talks, the US Government laid the problem of Korea's future before the United Nations General Assembly.

Over the next three years Korea became a major pawn in the growing struggle between East and West. The rift between the country's two halves grew steadily wider, with the opposing ideologies digging in on either side of the 38th Parallel. The Soviet-dominated north steadfastly rejected all demands for free elections; in the end, voting was held only in the south, supervised by the United Nations, and in August 1948 the Republic of Korea was established under the presidency of Dr Syngman Rhee. A month later the Communist Democratic People's Republic was formed in the north, at Pyongyang.

The two republics faced each other across the Parallel, each claiming domination over the whole country and each backed by the political, economic and military might of a great nation. Border incidents multiplied steadily as military equipment flowed into the north from the Soviet Union, but in the belief that there would be no major Communist threat in the foreseeable future, the Americans withdrew their forces from the south in the summer of 1949. The Republic of Korea, they considered, was outside the US defensive perimeter in the Pacific.

It was a fatal mistake, for the Americans had failed to appreciate the extent of Soviet expansionist plans in the Pacific area—plans in which the possession of South Korea formed a corner-stone. Not only would the overrunning of South Korea eliminate a vital American foothold on the Asian mainland; it would also, the Kremlin

An F-80 Shooting Star escorts a B-29. The US Air Force bomber had been hit during a raid and its damaged engine is visible in the foreground

believed, give a boost to anti-American factions in Japan.

The Communist invasion of South Korea began at 0400 in the morning of Sunday, June 25, 1950, the armour and infantry battering their way across the Parallel and dislocating the lightly armed Republic of Korea (ROK) forces that opposed them. The attack achieved almost complete surprise, and it was five hours before the United States forces in Japan received news of it and were placed on the alert.

American reaction to the news, at first, was one of confusion. Apart from a plan to evacuate US nationals by air, there was no provision for American intervention in the event of hostilities in Korea. The substantial striking power of the Far East Air Forces could only be released on the authority of the C-in-C Pacific, General Douglas MacArthur, and securing that authority would take time.

It was not until June 27, with the North Koreans advancing rapidly and the

situation deteriorating fast, that General Earle E. Partridge, commanding the US Fifth Air Force in Japan, was ordered to begin the evacuation of American personnel from Korea. A small armada of US transport aircraft at once started a shuttle service between the South Korean airfields of Kimpo and Seoul—both of which had already been under Communist air attack—and Japan. Fighter cover, on MacArthur's orders, was provided by F-80 Shooting Star jets and F-82 Twin Mustangs. It had been rightly expected that the North Korean Air Force would attempt to interfere with the transports, and at noon on the 27th five Yak-7 fighters were sighted over Seoul, heading for Kimpo. They were intercepted by F-82s of the 68th and 339th Squadrons, which shot down three of the enemy aircraft in the first air battle of the Korean War. That afternoon the Communists tried again, this time with eight Ilyushin Il-10 fighter-bombers. The Il-10s were caught to the north of Seoul by the F-80s of the 35th Fighter-Bomber Squadron, and after a brief one-sided fight the wreckage of four of the Communist machines was blazing on the ground. The other four turned and ran for their base at

Heijo, near Pyongyang. There were no further attacks during the remaining two days of the airlift.

At the beginning of their offensive, the North Koreans possessed a total of 132 combat aircraft, all of them Russian-built. The force included 62 Il-10 ground-attack aircraft and about 70 Yakovlev Yak-3, Yak-7 and Yak-9 fighters, as well as a few Lavochkin La-7s. It far outnumbered the tiny ROK Air Force, which in June 1950 had only 60 aircraft, all of them trainers. The North Korean pilots, who were Russian-trained, were keen, aggressive and self-confident; their main drawback was that they lacked experience, and this cost them dearly in action against the Americans, many of whom were veterans of the Second World War.

Nevertheless, the North Koreans managed to inflict some damage whenever they succeeded in slipping through the American fighter screen. While the F-80s and F-82s were defending the airlift, for example, four Yak-9s attacked Suwon airfield on June 28, destroying an American F-82 and a B-26 light bomber on the ground. Later that afternoon more enemy fighters attacked a C-54 transport that was landing at the

same field, severely damaging it. Six more attacks were made on Suwon the next day, but this time the F-80s were in the area and two Communist aircraft were destroyed.

On this same day—June 29—the Far East Air Forces' bombers were at last authorised to fly in support of the reeling South Koreans. While B-26s and heavy B-29s attacked North Korean airfields and bridge targets, F-80s and F-82s bombed and strafed Communist troop concentrations along the Han River. The ROK forces continued to give ground, however, and it was clear that air intervention alone could not stop the Communist offensive. On the morning of June 30, therefore, President Harry S. Truman authorised General MacArthur to commit land forces to the battle, and units of the 24th US Infantry Division began to move over from Japan. A few hours later General George E. Stratemeyer, commanding FEAF, ordered General Partridge to establish Fifth Air Force combat units on South Korean airfields.

The rapid deployment of US combat aircraft to Korea resulted in the speedy establishment of American air superiority over the battlefield. As American attacks on their main airfields mounted, the North Koreans were forced to disperse their aircraft on makeshift forward airstrips near the front, and from these well-camouflaged sites they carried out a series of low-level hit-and-run attacks in July. The North Korean air offensive, however, was nearing its end; the USAF and US Navy mounted heavy strikes against the North Korean airfields, including those captured by the enemy in their drive south, and by July 20 they had destroyed 60 Communist aircraft on the ground and in the air.

Meanwhile, on July 7, the United Nations Security Council had voted to set up a unified Allied command in Korea to resist Communist aggression. The Russians could have vetoed this decision, but their delegate was absent from the Council when the vote was taken. During the weeks that followed, combat units drawn from several nations began to arrive in Korea; Australia, South Africa and Britain all contributed air units, although in fact Mustangs of the Australian No. 77 Squadron and Fireflies and Seafires from the British carrier HMS *Triumph* had been flying strikes against Korean targets since July 3, before the UN decision was reached.

By the end of August, following an assessment of reconnaissance photographs, it was estimated that the strength of the North Korean Air Force had been reduced to 20 aircraft. Battered by continual fighter-bomber attacks, the North Koreans began to fall back, and by mid-October the UN forces were on the offensive everywhere. It was then that the situation began to change dramatically.

On October 14, unidentified aircraft bombed the UN airfield at Kimpo under cover of darkness. The next morning, American aircraft carrying out a reconnaissance along the Yalu River came under heavy anti-aircraft fire from Chinese batteries on the other side, and three days later a B-29 reconnaissance aircraft reported a heavy concentration of Chinese Communist aircraft at Antung, just across the river. On November 1, UN aircraft striking at airfields in the north were attacked by Red Chinese Yak fighters, and

an F-80 was shot down by Chinese AA fire.

That same afternoon, a flight of Mustangs patrolling the river was attacked by six fast, swept-wing jets that came down on them from Manchuria. The Americans escaped, but they knew that from now on they would have to fight hard for mastery of the air. The enemy aircraft had been identified as Russian MiG-15 jet fighters.

On November 2 the first Chinese 'volunteer' forces crossed into North Korea, and air battles along the Yalu grew in intensity during the days that followed. The UN pilots were at a clear disadvantage in that they were forbidden to cross the river into Chinese territory; this meant that the Chinese fighters could climb to altitude over Manchuria, dive across the river at high speed, make a fast attack on any UN aircraft they found, then cross the river to safety once more.

Nevertheless, the experience of the UN pilots counted for a lot; this was shown on November 8, when Chinese MiGs and American F-80s clashed in history's first jet-versus-jet battle. Although the F-80s were technically outclassed, their pilots prevented the MiGs from breaking through to attack a formation of B-29 bombers, and one enemy fighter was shot down by Lieutenant Russell J. Brown of the 51st Fighter Intercepter Wing. However, B-29s flying lone reconnaissance missions began to suffer heavily at the hands of the MiGs in the Yalu area, and from now on most sorties of this type were carried out by RF-80 photo-reconnaissance jets.

It was an alarming situation. The MiG-15 was superior to any of the Allied types it encountered, and posed a dangerous challenge to UN air superiority. Only the superior skill of the UN pilots saved them from crippling losses. By the beginning of December 1950 the Chinese People's Air Force (CPAF) had received about 100 MiGs; it also possessed 150 piston-engined fighters, 175 Il-2 and Il-10 ground-attack aircraft, and 150 twin-engined light bombers. It was virtually an extension of the Soviet Air Force; its instructors, combat leaders and senior technical personnel were all Russian.

To counter the MiG threat, the Americans rushed the 4th Intercepter Wing, equipped with North American F-86A Sabre jets, to Korea via Japan in December 1950. The Sabres carried out their first patrol along the Yalu on December 17 and shot down one MiG. Since the Sabre pilots had to make the long flight north from their bases at Kimpo or Taegu, which reduced the time they could spend in the combat area to a matter of minutes, they were forced to patrol at low speed in order to conserve fuel, which placed them at a distinct disadvantage. The MiG pilots exploited this weakness by attacking from above at near-sonic speed, making their escape before the Sabres had time to react.

The Americans learned their lesson quickly. They reduced their patrol time still further, and adopted new tactics which involved sending four flights of Sabres into the combat area at high speed, each flight separated by a three-minute interval. The tactics worked; in an air battle between eight Sabres and 15 MiGs on December 22, the Americans shot down six Communist aircraft for the loss of one of their own number.

In January and February 1951, however,

lack of maintenance facilities in Korea compelled the Sabres to be withdrawn to Japan for overhaul, and for several weeks the UN crews in their Mustangs, F-80s and B-29s had a hard time. For the first time in the war the Communists were able to establish a measure of air superiority, and they retained it for some time even when the Sabres returned and began operating from Suwon. By this time the Chinese had 75 MiGs based on Antung, and in April large formations of enemy fighters attacked UN bombers striking at targets near the Yalu. Although Sabres provided top cover for the bombers and F-84 Thunderjets acted as close escort, many MiGs invariably succeeded in diving through the Sabre screen on to the bomber formations, where the slower Thunderjets were unable to cope. On April 12 there was a massive dog-fight when 50 MiGs attacked a force of 39 B-29s, escorted by Sabres and F-84s; three bombers were shot down and six more badly damaged, while the Sabres claimed four MiGs destroyed and six damaged. The Thunderjets, fighting for their lives, scored no kills.

The Americans emerged from the battle of April 12 severely shaken. The Communist pilots had fought with amazing tenacity, and it was not until much later that the reason for it was learned. In the spring of 1951, Soviet, Polish and Czech pilots were beginning to arrive in Manchuria for a three-month tour of combat duty. Whole Soviet fighter squadrons were attached to CPAF air divisions, their Russian markings painted out and replaced by Chinese insignia.

By the end of June 1951 over 300 MiGs were based on the three airfields of Antung, Ta-ku-shan and Ta-tung-kou, across the Yalu, and more airfields were being built at a rapid rate. It was also estimated that the Communists had another 150 MiGs in reserve in China, and against this formidable force the United Nations had only 44 Sabres in Korea, with a further 45 available in Japan. Fortunately for the UN ground-attack 'workhorses', the Mustangs, F-80s, and F-84s, the MiGs seldom appeared over the battlefield itself, being content to patrol the Yalu; those that did

venture as far south as Pyongyang, equipped with long-range fuel tanks, preferred to remain at high altitude, where they enjoyed a slight performance advantage over the Sabres. On the few occasions when they did make a low-level 'bounce' they could usually be outflown by F-80 and F-84 pilots, and on several occasions MiGs were also destroyed by piston-engined fighters such as the Hawker Sea Furies of the British Fleet Air Arm.

More major air battles flared up in September 1951, when the MiGs operated in formations up to 75 strong. In October they came up in strength to intercept formations of B-29s which had been detailed to attack new Communist airfields in North Korea. In four weeks the MiGs flew over 2,500 missions and presented a serious challenge to UN air superiority yet again; the Americans lost 15 aircraft, but they claimed the destruction of 32 MiGs. Nevertheless, the determined attacks pressed home by the enemy had prevented the bombers from knocking out their targets, and at the end of October—for the first time—25 MiGs began operating from the North Korean base at Uiju.

The October battles had resulted in a tactical victory for the Communists, and it had a marked effect on the planners of US Air Defense Command. Within a fortnight, an additional 75 Sabres were on their way to Korea; they were new-model F-86Es, and they became operational with the 51st Fighter Wing in January 1952. During that month the 51st shot down 25 MiGs, and from that moment the situation began to ease considerably. Frequent air battles continued during February and March 1952, but the Communists had now ceased to appear in large numbers and instead were operating in formations of 12 aircraft or less. Then, in May, came a new development; the MiGs, with the help of a recently completed radar network, began a period of intensive night operations. On the night of June 10, during their first successful radar-controlled interception, the MiGs destroyed three out of four B-29s over North Korea; the old bombers' main ally, cover of darkness, had been brutally torn aside.

Despite their new techniques, however,

the Communists failed in their bid to wrest air superiority from the United Nations—although they had come perilously close to achieving that goal in 1951. Even so, while the UN pilots retained superiority over North Korea during 1952, the Communist air build-up in Manchuria went on; by the beginning of December they had 1,500 combat aircraft north of the Yalu, including 950 MiGs. It was then that Allied reconnaissance revealed a new threat: 100 new jet bombers, lined up on two Manchurian bases. They were twin-jet Ilyushin Il-28s, Russia's first operational jet bombers, and if the Communists had decided to use them offensively they could have ranged as far afield as Japan with impunity at night. But they never were used; their presence in Manchuria was purely a show of strength, and although they were sighted several times by UN pilots, they always kept well north of the river.

During 1951 and the early part of 1952 much of the United Nations' fighter-bomber effort had been devoted to attacks on road and rail targets in North Korea, but in the spring of 1952 FEAF planners decided to switch the emphasis to other target systems, preferably those in which China and the Soviet Union had an interest. The feeling was that the destruction of such targets would influence the North Koreans' Russian and Chinese masters into hastening the peace negotiations at Panmunjom. The problem was that worthwhile strategic targets were scarce; the exception was North Korea's hydro-electric power system, but the US joint Chiefs of Staff had been reluctant to authorise attacks on these plants. With the armistice talks moving towards total deadlock in the spring of 1952, however, it was decided that additional military force would be required to break the stalemate, and approval was given for the hydro-electric strikes to go ahead.

The first such attack took place on June 23, 1952 against the big power station at Suiho. Protected by 84 Sabres, 70 Douglas Skyraiders and Grumman Panthers from the US aircraft carriers *Boxer*, *Princeton* and *Philippine Sea* hammered the gener-

ator plant, and as they flew away 79 F-84s and 45 F-80s unloaded their bombs on the target in turn. The attack was a complete success, and the plant was wiped out. Large numbers of MiGs were sighted taking off from Antung, but they flew away in Manchuria, doubtless believing that the armada of fighter-bombers was on its way to hit their bases. Later that day more Navy and Air Force fighter-bombers struck at the hydro-electric plants at Choshin, Kyosen and Fusen, causing severe damage. That night, quite literally, the lights went out all over North Korea.

The hydro-electric strikes were followed by a sustained air pressure campaign against a wide variety of targets in the north. On July 11, 1952 almost every operational UN combat unit was involved in 'Operation Pressure Pump', a series of heavy attacks on 30 military targets within Pyongyang, the North Korean capital. The attacks began at 1000 hours in the morning with a massive assault by Panthers and Corsairs of the US Navy's Task Force 77 and the 1st Marine Air Wing, Mustangs of the small ROK Air Force, Sea Furies and Fireflies from the British carrier HMS *Ocean*, and Thunderjets of the Fifth Air Force. After dark, the attacks were continued by B-29s; 1,254 sorties were flown in all, and every target was either destroyed or badly damaged. The UN lost three aircraft. The attacks on Pyongyang were repeated, in even greater strength, on August 29. Other heavy raids were carried out on industrial targets, including chemical plants. At night, communications and troop concentrations were hit by B-26s, which unloaded incendiary bombs in relays on targets marked by special 'pathfinder' crews.

The job of knocking out industrial targets in north-eastern Korea was assigned to the Navy pilots of Task Force 77, often working close up to the Soviet border. On September 1, Panthers, Corsairs and Banshees from the carriers *Essex*, *Princeton* and *Boxer* hit the synthetic oil refinery at Aoji in the biggest naval air strike of the war, and a fortnight later more carrier aircraft from the *Bon Homme Richard* and *Princeton* struck at supply depots and bar-

racks in the town of Hoeryong, right on the Soviet frontier.

During further naval air strikes, in November, the Soviet Air Force made its only open attempt to interfere with UN air operations over Korea. On November 18, 1952, while Task Force 77's jets were once again hitting Hoeryong, a large formation of MiGs was sighted assembling near Vladivostok. A few minutes later a number of MiGs were seen approaching the Task Force from the north; they bore no national markings, but there was no doubt as to their identity. They were intercepted by Grumman Panther jets, which shot down one and drove the rest away. Details of this fight were not made public until years later, because of the political implications.

The early months of 1953 saw more intense air fighting over the Yalu. An improved version of the Russian jet fighter, the MiG-15bs, had now appeared in Manchuria, and the Sabre pilots found it a formidable opponent. For the first time the Communist pilots often stayed to fight, even though the odds were against them, and they showed a higher degree of teamwork. Nevertheless the UN pilots retained their superiority; in January 1953, for example, they claimed the destruction of 37 MiGs for the loss of a single Sabre.

In the night sky over the north, however, it was a different story. From November 1952 onwards the effectiveness of the Communist night-fighters increased considerably and the B-29 squadrons suffered heavy losses. The Americans sent F3D-2 Skynight and F-94 Starfire all-weather fighters on intruder missions over the north to cover the bomber streams at night, and the Skynights shot down two enemy fighters in November, but these operations presented no real solution to the night-fighter menace. Their biggest value was as a morale-booster for the bomber crews; it was comforting to know that friendly fighters were in the vicinity, even though they could not be seen.

In May 1953, with the armistice talks once more bogged down, heavy bombing attacks were launched against another target system: North Korea's network of irrigation dams. The first such attack was

flown on May 13, when 59 Thunderjets hit a 2,300-foot earth and stone dam on the Potong River 20 miles north of Pyongyang. The dam was totally destroyed, and the resulting flood caused widespread damage to rice crops, roads and railways. Several more attacks were carried out during the next three weeks, but not all were so successful; the solidly packed structures proved amazingly resistant to high explosives.

In June 1953 there was a significant development in the air battles over the Yalu. Suddenly, almost overnight, the skill of the Communist pilots showed a marked decline. To the Sabre pilots it seemed that the Reds were scraping the barrel; the MiGs often took no evasive action at all when attacked, and their pilots sometimes bailed out before a shot was fired at them. The inference was plain: the Russians had pulled out of the air battle, leaving the Chinese and North Koreans to fend for themselves. Sensing that the war was drawing to a close, the UN fighter pilots went all out during these last weeks to score as many victories as possible; they destroyed 77 enemy fighters in June alone, with 50 more damaged. Thirty-two MiGs were destroyed in July, before the jets met in combat for the last time on the 22nd. Five days later, on July 27, 1953, the long-awaited armistice finally brought the Korean War to a close.

In three years of air fighting, United Nations had destroyed over 1,000 enemy aircraft, 790 of them MiG-15s. Allied losses were 139 machines, 78 of them Sabres. It had been a conflict in which skill and teamwork, together with superior training standards based on a wealth of combat experience, had paid massive dividends.

Both sides had learned a lot from the Korean air war. It had a dramatic effect on the organisation and equipment of both the Soviet Union and the United States; the martyrdom of the Second World War vintage B-29 Superfortress, of which the Russians had a copy—the Tupolev Tu-4—in widespread service, gave impetus to the rapid development of heavy jet bombers on both sides of the Iron Curtain. Combat

Left: A series of pictures showing a MiG 15 under attack by a Sabre piloted by 2nd Lt Edwin Aldrin. The series shows the pilot ejecting from his aircraft. *Right:* A US Air Force F-86 Sabre of the 51st Fighter-Interceptor Wing drops its wing tip fuel tanks before going into action against MiG fighters. The 51st flew cover for the bombers of the 5th Air force when they attacked North Korean targets

US Air Force

experience in Korea also accelerated the development of a new generation of air superiority fighters; in the United States the Lockheed Aircraft Corporation developed the F-104 Starfighter, while Russia's answer was the MiG-21. Also from Lockheed came the revolutionary, high-flying U-2 — America's solution to the problems of strategic reconnaissance that had manifested themselves in Korea.

In other fields, too, the Korean War had revolutionised military thinking. One of them was battlefield support, it was in Korea that helicopters were first used in this role in large numbers, and their vulnerability led to the development of new, fast helicopter gunships that were to be

used with such success more than a decade later in Vietnam.

As far as the US Navy was concerned, the Korean episode confirmed that the fast attack carrier was still the most vital naval unit in modern warfare — a belief that was once again confirmed by Vietnam. The performance of the naval aircraft used in Korea, however, had given rise to serious misgivings, and the years that followed saw US naval air units re-equipped with more modern attack aircraft, the most important of which were the Douglas Skyhawk and the McDonnell Phantom. The latter, in fact, was designed to fill the requirement for a multi-role combat aircraft, capable of carrying out all the tasks,

from air superiority fighter to close-support, for which a wide variety of types had been needed in Korea.

Most important of all, the Korean War showed that the Communists would not have risked aggressive action if the Allied forces in the Far East — and for that matter throughout the world — had been stronger. It led, directly, to the birth of the nuclear deterrent: the western world's biggest insurance for peace over the past two decades. At the same time it proved conclusively that a major war could still be fought without recourse to nuclear weapons; a fact that was to lead to a drastic revision of strategic thinking in the context of East-West relations.

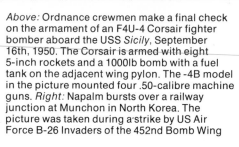

Above: Ordnance crewmen make a final check on the armament of an F4U-4 Corsair fighter bomber aboard the USS *Sicily*, September 16th, 1950. The Corsair is armed with eight 5-inch rockets and a 1000lb bomb with a fuel tank on the adjacent wing pylon. The -4B model in the picture mounted four .50-calibre machine guns. *Right:* Napalm bursts over a railway junction at Munchon in North Korea. The picture was taken during a strike by US Air Force B-26 Invaders of the 452nd Bomb Wing

National Archives

Popperfoto

Dien Bien

Phu

The French airborne occupation and fortification of the valley of the Nam Yum at Dien Bien Phu was regarded by many military experts as an ideal blocking move against Viet Minh forays into Laos. No one believed that they would be able to haul medium artillery through the jungle and having done this keep a major army and its guns supplied. Not only did the Viet Minh win the logistic struggle but they went on to win the battle at Dien Bien Phu.

Popperfoto

349

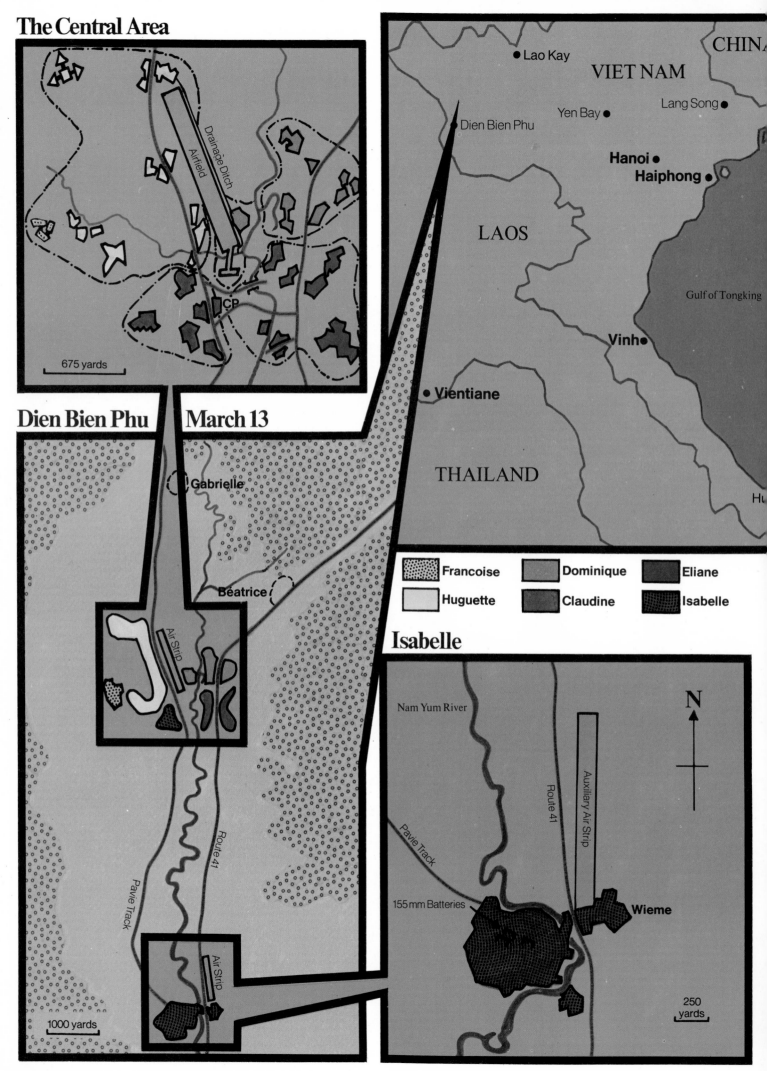

The Central Area

675 yards

Dien Bien Phu   March 13

Gabrielle

Béatrice

Air Strip

Air Strip

Route 41

Pavie Track

1000 yards

CHINA

VIET NAM

Lao Kay

Yen Bay

Lang Song

Hanoi

Haiphong

LAOS

Gulf of Tongking

Vinh

Vientiane

THAILAND

Dien Bien Phu

Hu

| Francoise | Dominique | Eliane |
| Huguette | Claudine | Isabelle |

Isabelle

N

Nam Yum River

Route 41

Pavie Track

Auxiliary Air Strip

155 mm Batteries

Wieme

250 yards

350

By the autumn of 1953 the war in Indo-China had already been dragging on for seven years. It had been born in the vacuum created between the withdrawal of the defeated Japanese and the return of the French colonial rulers, who—in the eyes of their Eastern subjects—had suffered an even more humiliating defeat at the hands of fellow orientals less than five years previously. A comparable vacuum had not occurred in countries such as Burma and the Philippines where British and American forces, bearing with them early prospects of independence, had expelled the Japanese. A combination of French intransigence towards de-colonialization, the corruptness of local rulers, and military aid from Red China had progressively imposed the stamp of orthodox Communism upon what had begun, typically enough, as a nationalist, anti-colonial revolt. The political leader of the Viet Minh (League for the Independence of Vietnam) was now 63-year-old Ho Chi Minh, who claimed to have learned the meaning of revolution when in Paris in the 1920's. His military lieutenant was a 43-year-old doctor of political economy and former history master, General Vo Nguyen Giap, who had waged guerrilla war against the Japanese and now employed it against the French whom he had every reason to hate. For not only had he been imprisoned in French gaols, his sister had been executed by the French and his wife, sentenced to hard labour for life, had died in a French prison.

The war had so far cost France over 11,000 nationals killed, together with another 12,000 Foreign Legionnaires and African troops and 14,000 Indo-Chinese. Over 120,000 were either wounded or missing. Since the politicians refused to send national servicemen to Indo-China, it was the cream of the French regular cadres that bore the brunt; every three years consumed an entire class of Saint-Cyr officers. Six hundred billion francs were spent on the war each year—far more than the capital value of France's remaining commercial installations there. Eighteen successive governments had come and gone in the Fourth Republic and none had found a way of ending the war. France's current Premier was Joseph Laniel, a weaver from Calvados known to his associates simply as 'poor Joseph', whose ministry has been described by one French historian as 'manufactured, like his speeches, with scissors and paste'. In Indo-China the war was run, with little direction from Paris, by an army as anxious to redeem the honour it still held to be tarnished from 1940 as it was to crush the Viet Minh. It had been constantly denied the men and equipment it demanded and only Marshal de Lattre de Tassigny with his immense stature had succeeded in bullying extra resources from the over-strained French economy. He had devoted these resources chiefly to the construction of a miniature Maginot Line of block-houses guarding Hanoi and the Red River delta. On de Lattre's death in December 1951 General Raoul Salan became commander-in-chief

The fortified base at Dien Bien Phu. It was neither an offensive base, nor a real defensive position and once the Viet Minh had mobilised their regular units and their armies of coolie porters they were able to strangle it

Popperfoto

The confident days of January 1954, Colonel de Castries at the wheel of a jeep with M. Marc Jacquet, Secretary of State for the Associated States, one of the many visitors

in Indo-China and was in turn succeeded by General Henri Navarre on May 29, 1953.

An uncommunicative figure with a strange affinity for cats, Navarre was outspoken in declaring, however, on taking up his command: "I shall not make the same mistakes as my predecessors." His boast was to be fulfilled—certainly no other French commander had erred on quite so grandiose a scale. One of his first appointments was to promote a giant brigadier, René Cogny, to command the key northern sector. In the south, around Saigon, the war had deteriorated to one of ambush and attrition; while in the north the French defensively based on de Lattre's blockhouses had the delta fairly well under control. But, farther inland, it seemed to Navarre as if Giap might be mounting a serious threat to the kingdom of Laos. Apart from this threat the French generally held the initiative throughout Indo-China, and Giap appeared indecisive. During the summer of 1953 more French troops had become available, and tens of thousands of Vietnamese recruits were joining the French Union forces (though Adlai Stevenson had observed pessimistically that, in contrast with South Korea, none smiled when he inspected them). In addition United States military aid was pouring in. On the other hand, with the end of the Korean War in sight, it appeared that Red China would shortly be free to concentrate her resources on aiding the Viet Minh.

Towards the end of 1953 Navarre began to formulate a strategy aimed both at relieving the threat to Laos and at inflicting a major defeat upon the Viet Minh before Chinese aid could become effective.

He would lure General Giap (whom his predecessor, Salan, had dismissed with Saint-Cyrien superciliousness 'as a non-commissioned officer learning to handle regiments') into the kind of copy-book set-piece battle taught at Western staff colleges ever since Napoleon, and then crush him by superiority of equipment and fire-power.

On November 21 a strong French paratroop force led by three generals dropped on the isolated village of Dien Bien Phu ('the big administrative centre on the frontier'), deep in Viet Minh country and astride Giap's main communications with China. Navarre's plan was to bait the trap by establishing a powerful and aggressive garrison there. The attraction of Dien Bien Phu lay in the fact that it possessed an airstrip (built by the Japanese) and occupied the largest valley in the area, which appeared too big to be easily sealed off. But it was under 100 miles from the Chinese border, and almost 200 from the French bases round Hanoi, so that supply aircraft would be operating at extreme range. Over the exceedingly rugged intervening terrain, land communications with Hanoi were non-existent, so that the Dien Bien Phu garrison would have to be sustained entirely by air. Aerial reconnaissance had been carried out during the dry season, thus no account had been taken of the heavy rainfall at Dien Bien Phu; or of the fact that fog often filled the basin between the surrounding hills. Moreover, it appears that Navarre had been warned categorically by his air transport chief, Colonel Nicot, that his service would not be in a position to maintain a permanent flow of supplies to the garrison. Despite these factors, and without going into the logistics of the operation too thoroughly, Navarre was confident that he could achieve his ends. He knew that Giap had artillery but hitherto he had used nothing bigger than Japanese and Chinese 75-mm field-guns, and he had never marshalled more than a few scattered light anti-aircraft weapons with which to harass dropping operations. Finally, Navarre's Intelligence officers estimated that Giap's primitive supply system over the tortuous jungle trails would be incapable of provisioning any force attacking Dien Bien Phu with more than 25,000 shells for its guns or with sufficient rice.

Right from the beginning, the cryptic Navarre never seems to have made it clear to Cogny, his subordinate in control of Dien Bien Phu, that he intended it to become a fortress designed to withstand a regular siege. Cogny conceived of it more as a base for guerrilla operations against Giap's rear links although heavy enemy concentrations in the area made it an improbable choice as an anchor for such light, mobile forces. Navarre disposed of a total of 100 battalions, though all but 27 of these were absorbed in the static defences of the de Lattre Line protecting the Red River delta. Nevertheless, with his professional soldier's low esteem for the potential of Giap's irregulars, he further divided his forces by attempting a simultaneous large-scale operation in south Vietnam. Thus only nine battalions remained for Dien Bien Phu; whereas it would probably have required at least 50 to safeguard so large a perimeter as that delineated by the chain of hills dominating Dien Bien Phu's wide valley.

This then was the situation when the first paratroops launched 'Operation Castor' on November 21, 1953. By Christmas a series of costly failures had made it clear to the French that Dien Bien Phu could not be used as a base for offensive operations as General Cogny had hoped. The French then undertook a second battle, designed to dislodge the enemy from dangerous look-out points on the surrounding heights from which the whole valley, and its essential airstrip, could be kept under constant observation. In the first attack, misdirected French artillery fire killed 15 Algerians. By mid-February 1954 this second battle had also been lost, with the garrison abandoning the crucial heights. On the 17th Cogny gave the order that attacks out of Dien Bien Phu were henceforth to be limited only to 'light reconnaissance'. The fact that simultaneously two Viet Minh columns were striking in both north and south Laos clearly revealed that Dien Bien Phu had already forfeited any usefulness as a base for active counter-insurgent operations. From now on its role would be purely defensive.

Meanwhile, General Giap had willingly accepted Navarre's challenge. With superhuman efforts some 50,000 coolies, living off a few pounds of rice a day and wheeling specially strengthened bicycles that could carry 450lb cargoes, were methodically moving up a siege train of over 200 guns. Many of them were American 105-mm medium pieces, captured by the Chinese, and heavier than anything yet used by Giap. Using the utmost ingenuity and industry, Giap's gunners burrowed through the crests of the hills wrested from the French so that the muzzles of the guns poked out of small tunnels directly down onto the French garrison, presenting targets almost impossible to hit. When the defenders were asked what would happen if the Viet Minh installed their artillery

on the slopes facing Dien Bien Phu, the response was that this had never been done since Napoleon.

While Giap was slowly mustering his siege forces, the French could still have used their air mobility to withdraw the garrison, and, having pinned down the bulk of Giap's forces, gain a tactical victory elsewhere. But Navarre, confident in the superiority of his arms over a guerrilla force in a pitched battle, was determined to sit it out at Dien Bien Phu. The French engineers estimated that 36,000 tons of materials would be required to fortify Dien Bien Phu. But a Dakota could only fly in three tons per trip and such a total would take five months to supply. In the end a total of some 4,000 tons was provided – and that consisted mainly of barbed wire. So while Giap's men burrowed into the surrounding hills, the French did little to make Dien Bien Phu more tenable. By the time the Viet Minh commander was ready to attack, the fortified area of Dien Bien Phu spread over an area roughly 12 miles by six. The central zone, containing the headquarters and based on three of the original four dropping zones, was surrounded by Huguette, Dominique, Eliane and Claudine strongpoints. To

the north was the fortified zone of Gabrielle, with Anne-Marie and Béatrice to the north-east and north-west; further away to the south was Isabelle. Most of the fortified zones were built on the small natural hills in the valley. But the standard of the defences was poor. "The trenches were often dug only to knee level," a survivor stated after the battle, "there were no shelters, no blockhouses, nothing." Even the latrines were un-sandbagged. Worse still, the guns and mortars were not properly dug in, and, glinting in their open firing positions, were strikingly visible to the Viet Minh on the hills. Colonel Piroth, the one-armed artillery commander at Dien Bien Phu, had refused offers of extra artillery. "I have more than I need," he declared, adding, "We know to the nearest gun what they have got. We shall win because we have some 155s with plunging fire." When questioned by the visiting minister of defence, René Pleven, about the threat of Viet Minh artillery, another colonel retorted "We shall fight as at Verdun". With all its Pyrrhic glory, Verdun 1916 seems to have been never very far from French minds at Dien Bien Phu, and it was certainly the horrors and carnage of

Verdun that were to be evoked there.

On March 13, as 28 Viet Minh infantry battalions, comprising 37,500 men, braced themselves for battle, Giap opened his bombardment. Simultaneously numerous explosive charges were detonated so as to deceive Piroth's gunners as to the location of the Viet Minh guns, which, in their underground positions, proved to be almost invulnerable both to gunfire and air strikes.

Terrible destruction was wreaked almost immediately on the ill-prepared French positions, including the destruction of two Dakotas and a fighter on the airstrip. In Béatrice two 105-mm guns were destroyed and the commander killed, and in the evening the Viet Minh infantry moved in. After savage fighting, Béatrice was captured with the loss of 75 per cent of the defending Legionnaires, less than 200 men regaining the main French lines. The next day the 5th Vietnamese Parachute Battalion was dropped in to reinforce the French troops. That evening eight battalions of the Viet Minh 308th Division attacked Gabrielle – defended by a battalion of Algerian riflemen. It was all but overrun during the night, and a counter-attack launched by the French at dawn allowed a

The early days at Dien Bien Phu; in the foreground napalm laden Bearcat fighters of the 'Saintonge' group, in the distance two Dakotas being readied for takeoff

mere 150 Algerians to escape before the French withdrew. The fanaticism of Giap's men, who used the still-living bodies of their own casualties as duck boards to cross the French minefields, had a disturbing effect on the Algerian defenders. French morale was very low. The same day Piroth, who had guaranteed that no enemy cannon would 'be able to fire three rounds before being destroyed', was so overcome by remorse that he blew himself up with a hand-grenade. By March 31, 'Isabelle', a quarter of a square mile, in which 18,000 men fought permanently in waist-deep swamp water, was isolated from the main garrison. During the rest of March many of the Thai, North African and Vietnamese troops deserted, some crossing to the Viet Minh and some becoming 'internal deserters' living in holes along the banks of the Nam Yum river. Here they remained until the end of the siege, refusing to take any part in the fighting. On the night of the 30th Dominique and Eliane were attacked. A four-day battle followed in which the French scored some isolated successes and inflicted appalling casualties on the attackers. At the end both sides were exhausted, and the Viet Minh forced to regroup their forces.

Conditions for the defenders now became increasingly appalling. They were particularly bad for the wounded, for whom there were hopelessly inadequate medical supplies and hospital space, and too few doctors and matters were worsened by Giap's deliberate refusal to take back his own wounded. But the defenders, paratroops, Legionnaires, Algerians and Indo-Chinese detachments, fought back with extraordinary courage and endurance. By April 5 Giap's men – representing half of the total Viet Minh forces – had already suffered some 10,000 casualties, and morale showed signs of ebbing as the Tricoleur still waved at Dien Bien Phu.

Although the French at home were by and large sick to death with the war in Indo-China, those on the spot tended to regard Dien Bien Phu, spiritually, as something of a requital of honour; but if the heroism of the troops more than made up for the humiliations of 1940, the same could hardly be said of their senior commanders, some of whom, worse than the Bourbons, seem to have learned nothing and forgotten everything. The remark by an outstanding American historian of the war in Vietnam, Bernard Fall, that they (and the politicians in Paris) spent their time writing memoranda 'concerned with covering themselves more against personal responsibility than against enemy attacks' has a nasty ring of the Third Republic about it. By mid-March unappeasable hatred had grown between the cat-like Navarre and the bull-like Cogny, in a style all too reminiscent of Lords Lucan and Cardigan in the Crimea. Working in the same building, they communicated only by memoranda or via intermediaries, and Navarre never seems to have made his intentions properly clear to any of the executants.

Colonel de Castries, the actual commander at Dien Bien Phu, who was assisted until well on in the battle by an attractive female secretary, though certainly not lacking in courage, displayed a patrician distaste from another age for mud and blood. After his chief of staff had broken down and had been flown out, de Castries was not often seen outside his command post. According to Colonel Jules Roy, author of *The Battle of Dienbienphu,* de Castries, a thrice-wounded cavalryman, "timidly used his reserves to stop gaps or mend holes, not to strike. In reality he could not get them together because there were no shelters large enough to contain them."

The quartermaster's branch was a mess, and air supply inept; partly, it seems, because a certain national arrogance impeded the French from benefiting from United States experience. On the other hand, the French air force was undoubtedly deceived by its American colleagues (as indeed they deceived themselves in the 1960s) as to the efficacy of interdiction bombing against an Asiatic enemy in Korea. Soon Giap's guns made the vital airstrip at Dien Bien Phu unusable.

Now the second of the major French miscalculations began to exert its lethal

influence. From China, Giap had massed a formidable array of anti-aircraft weapons. Transport pilots flying into his murderous flak 'envelope' compared it unfavourably with wartime experiences over Germany. Losses, hard to replace from the French air forces slender resources, mounted steadily. Day by day the Viet Minh dug out trenches to the French strongpoints, gradually encircling them in preparation for the final assault. Although Dien Bien Phu still held out with incredible heroism and continued to receive small paratroop reinforcements, there was now no hope of escape for the beleaguered garrison.

Conceivably more and better tactical air support could have saved Dien Bien Phu, and at least have ensured a more durable peace in Indo-China. (As a comparison it is worth noting that whereas during the 167 days of siege at Dien Bien Phu air sorties totalled 10,400, in 1966 the weekly American total often exceeded 25,000.) In 1954 the only source which could have provided this extra air cover was the United States, and France pleaded repeatedly for assistance. Admiral Radford, the US Chief of

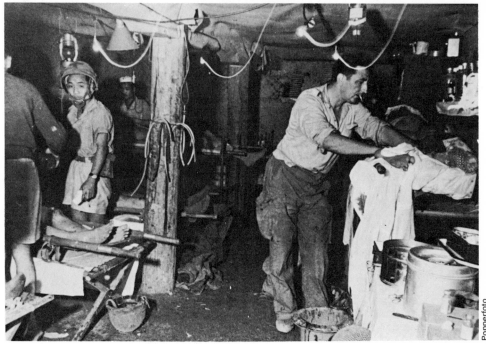

Top left: An M101 A1 105-mm howitzer in its gun pit. Though the ammunition bays are dug in, the gun and crew are exposed to plunging fire from the surrounding hills. *Left:* The crowded resuscitation ward in the underground hospital at Dien Bien Phu. *Above:* Reinforcements jump into the beleaguered fort during a daylight drop

Staff, was distinctly favourable, but secretary of state John Foster Dulles was badly misinformed on Dien Bien Phu, and until the end was unable to appreciate the issues at stake. Against a shocking background of muddle and machinations he constantly encouraged the French to fight on beyond their means, while misleading them as to the extent of direct support the United States might be expected to provide *in extremis*. He is reported to have talked wildly about dropping "one or two atom bombs" on Giap and, contingent on British acquiescence, a heavy air strike from American carriers was actually planned for the end of April. But Eden, bent on a course of non-intervention, was determined that Indo-China was to go to the negotiating table at the Geneva Conference the following month, and had made this clear to the Americans all along.

By May 1 the Viet Minh were ready to launch an all-out attack on the remaining French positions. In the face of overwhelming numbers the strongpoints were quickly swamped. On May 6, Giap brought up Russian Katyusha rockets to administer the *coup de grâce*. As a final illusion, the embattled defenders at first took the noise of the rockets to be that of a French relief column. Typical of the persistent French heroism in the last hours was that of a tank commander who had plaster casts removed from both arms broken earlier in the battle, so that he could man the one remaining operational tank. On May 7, with men dying at their posts from the effects of 55 days of constant bombardment, little sleep or food, Dien Bien Phu was overwhelmed. It never surrendered. Only about 3,000 men out of a total of 16,544 survived the siege and subsequent captivity. Over 3,000 died in the battlefield area and some 10,000 on the gruelling trek to, and in, the prison camps. Giap's army suffered 8,000 dead and 15,000 wounded. Instead of the 25,000 shells that French Intelligence assessed was all Giap's transport could bring up, 350,000 had fallen on the garrison; including 12,000 despatched to the Viet Minh by inaccurate French air drops.

The day after the fall of Dien Bien Phu the agenda of the Geneva Conference turned to Indo-China. As a result, France under Pierre Mendès-France (the government of 'poor Joseph' Laniel having been swept away on the backwash) withdrew entirely from Indo-China. Partition created the Communist state of North Vietnam, triumphant and strong in victory, and the weak independent fragments of South Vietnam, Cambodia, and Laos. Six months later the standard of revolt against France was hoisted in Algeria, many of whose troops had fought with valour at Dien Bien Phu and had seen France humbled by an army of Asiatic peasants. Dien Bien Phu was to cost France not only Indo-China but the rest of her empire as well.

TET

The VietCong and North Vietnamese offensive in January 1968 came as an almost complete surprise to the US forces in South Vietnam. Up to then they had asserted that they were winning the war. Ironically the Allied counter-offensive following Tet destroyed the VietCong hold in the South and was a major defeat for the North. Yet despite this victory the Press and public in the United States turned Tet into an American defeat. It was a defeat which ultimately led to the defeat of the South.

The second Indo-Chinese War began in the late 1950s about four years after the French withdrawal from their Far Eastern colonies. Vietnam had been divided at the Geneva conference of May-July 1954. North of the 17th Parallel the Communist Viet Minh had established the Democratic Republic of Vietnam, while to the south a new non-Communist state had been set up. Elections were to be held on July 20, 1956 to re-establish the national unity of the State of Vietnam and the Democratic Republic.

The elections never took place. To the north the DRVN established a firm hold over the country, while to the south the Communist cadres that had remained intact after the French withdrawal began to grow restive as they saw the date of the promised elections come and go without either side attempting to hold them.

By 1958 the VietCong (as the southern Communist cadres were known) had begun a programme of assassinations and attacks on low-level administrators and government outposts. The increased military activity of the VietCong attracted the attention of both the United States and North Vietnam. The North decided that the South might become too independent, and in May 1959 the Central Committee of the Vietnamese Communist Party resolved that ". . . the struggle for reunification will now have to be carried out by all appropriate means other than peaceful".

Following this pronouncement, the North began to develop the land route within Laotian and Cambodian territory that became known as the Ho Chi Minh trail.

The fighting in the South increased and the government grew more autocratic. The United States, who had supplied arms to the French in the late 40s and early 50s, continued this policy, and by November 1961 they also had 948 advisers serving in the country. The number of advisers increased rapidly from 2,646 in January 1962 to 16,732 in October 1963. In 1962 American-piloted helicopters arrived in the South. Despite this assistance, the political and military situation continued to deteriorate.

The United States felt increasingly frustrated and saw as the source of the trouble the support and assistance given by the North. A series of provocative manoeuvres in 1964 along the North Vietnamese coast by the US 7th Fleet drew North Vietnamese torpedo boats into attacking the USS *Madox* and the United States had an excuse for bombing the Northern naval bases. By the end of the year the North had sent their first organised military unit down the Ho Chi Minh trail.

Mortar attacks on the compounds of American advisers at Pleiku killed nine advisers and produced retaliatory raids on the North. On February 13, 1965 President Johnson authorised operation Rolling Thunder, the air attack on North Vietnam. On March 8, 3,500 US Marines landed at Danang to protect the city and airbase.

On March 11 the VietCong launched their summer offensive and once again hammered the ARVN (Army of the Republic of Vietnam) troops. After increasing

pressure, the US 173rd Airborne Brigade and an Australian battalion emerged from their enclaves to conduct a search-and-destroy operation on June 27-30, 1965. On June 17 President Johnson authorised reinforcements, bringing the strength of US forces from 75,000 to 125,000. A month later this was raised to 184,000.

United States, Australia, New Zealand, Thailand, South Korea and the Philippines committed forces to the South, but despite massive operations in the South and the bombing of the North, the strength of the VietCong (VC) and North Vietnamese (NVA) troops continued to rise. By January 2, 1967 General William Westmoreland, commanding the Military Assistance Command Vietnam (MACV), estimated that enemy strength stood at nine divisional HQs, 34 regimental HQs and 152 combat battalions.

Using the massive fire power and mobility at his disposal, Westmoreland launched his troops on a series of major search and destroy operations. On January 8, 1967 some 15,000 US and ARVN troops cleared the 'Iron Triangle' in War Zone D, north-west of Saigon. They uncovered an underground city of bunkers, tunnels, living and sleeping rooms and even a 60-bed hospital. In Operation Junction City, between February 22 and April 3, 25,000 troops killed 1,179 NVA for the loss of 50 American soldiers.

The lesson that the Americans were failing to learn was that the North and the VietCong could take casualties which were unacceptable by Western standards. They were slowly winning the war by propaganda rather than conventional means. The Americans, however, were opti-

A US Marine festooned with M72 rocket launchers waits beside a wounded friend. *Overleaf:* US Marines take cover during a bombardment of the Khe Sanh base

Popperfoto

Above: US Military Police with the bodies of Viet Cong sappers killed in the American Embassy in Saigon on the first day of Tet.
Left: Military Police bring in a wounded VC sapper captured during the fighting in Saigon on 31st January

mistic. In his annual report at the end of 1967 Westmoreland stated, "The friendly picture gives rise to an optimistic outlook for CY1968 (Calendar Year 1968). In CY67 the logistics base and increased forces permitted Allied Forces to assume a fully offensive posture. With ground forces, TAC-air, B-52s, and Naval gunfire support ships working together, continuous pressure was applied against the enemy. An improved intelligence system frequently enabled Allied Forces to concentrate and pre-empt enemy military initiatives."

In mid-January 1968 a North Vietnamese division had begun to manoeuvre around the US base at Dak To in the Central Highlands. Westmoreland reinforced the base and drove back the enemy units. At the same time the NVA 325th Division and the 304th moved closer to the 3rd Battalion 26th Marines in their base at Khe Sanh. The Americans and the world Press decided that Khe Sanh was being chosen by the North as the Dien Bien Phu of the United States. This impression was strengthened by the presence of the 304th Division, which had participated in the defeat of the French at Dien Bien Phu. It was estimated that the North had deployed six infantry regiments, two artillery regiments, an unknown number of light tanks and support and service units. From captured documents the Americans later discovered that their aim was to bleed the Americans in a long siege. The opening moves of this operation were a series of patrol clashes and attacks on the outposts around the base. On January 22 the Americans initiated Operation Niagara, a massive air support operation to attack the North Vietnamese concentration areas and communications – this was later extended to close support for the garrison.

By mid-January Westmoreland had

installed 6,000 Marines at Khe Sanh and several other brigades north of Hue, making a total of 40,000 supporting troops. Whether he had fallen for a plan to draw off American troops from the populated areas, as General Vo Nguyen Giap, the commander of the Northern forces, had said, is debatable. The North would have liked a victory, but they were preparing to divert American attention, hopefully inflict casualties and then launch an offensive which would stun public opinion in the United States and galvanise the South into open rebellion.

The date chosen for this attack was January 30, 1968, the Tet holiday. Tet is the beginning of the lunar new year and is celebrated by a three-day holiday. Families gather at home, there are fireworks and meals with traditional foods like sugared palm, homemade breads and rice wine. The movement of relatives and the sound of the fireworks would provide a cover for the infiltration of NVA units into the cities.

Planning had begun as far back as July 1967, and an American report stated that the NVA and VietCong had strengthened city forces by "assigning experienced officers to the city units and giving these cadre priority in their choice of personnel. Additional sapper companies and battalions were activated and equipped with sufficient weapons. Special-action units were also strengthened. Operating units conducted a crash training program at bases located in and out of South Vietnam. Sapper tactics were stressed. Supposedly, the battlefield was prepared; yet evidence indicates that thorough planning and control were lacking."

However, the Winter-Spring Offensive, as Hanoi had dubbed the operation, could not have been better timed. A truce had been arranged between the North and the South and it had come into effect at 1800 on January 29. In addition to elements of the ARVN being on leave with their families at home, the Americans had also adopted a policy of removing the US presence from Vietnamese cities which had been given the coy code name of Moose. The signs of an impending offensive had

Rex Features

Rex Features

Above: An NVA soldier armed with an AK47 in a foxhole in a garden in Hue. *Far left:* US marines double down a road in Hue. On the left is a banner erected during the celebrations for the Tet lunar festival. The man nearest the camera is armed with an M72 rocket launcher. *Left:* Two NVA soldiers on guard in Hue

been noted by General Frederick C. Weyand, commander of III Corps, and he had put his troops on maximum alert. However, in Saigon there were only 300 US troops ready for immediate action. Westmoreland was unable to believe that the NVA and VietCong could undertake an operation on such a large scale.

John Parrish, a doctor serving with the US Marines at Phu Bai near Hue, visited friends in the city: "There seemed to be an increased number of men on the streets. They walked among the women and children, but they did not seem to be accompanying any of them. They moved with an air of purpose and expectation that seemed more serious than that of a holiday spirit.

"A Vietnamese man in civilian clothes stared hatefully from the rear standing rail of an old Vietnamese bus bumping along in front of our jeep. His look was one of contempt. His body acted as a shock absorber to hold his stare knifing directly towards me. . . . It soon became evident that this man was only a more obvious member of a large, unfriendly audience. The usual accepting, pseudo-friendly or disinterested crowds lining the highway were spotted with unfamiliar, poorly-hidden glances of curiosity, hate and study."

The first Tet attacks struck at 0015 on

Above: A US Marine fires his M 16 rifle during fighting in Hue on February 4th. *Left:* ARVN troops operate a simple ferry over the Perfume River on February 6th. *Below:* A US Marine fires his M 60 machine gun during fighting in the suburbs of Hue

January 30 at Nha Trang. The same night, attacks were made on 11 other cities in the II Corps area and against military installations and airfields. Documents captured by the Americans showed that the NVA and VC units in this area had not received orders for a one-day postponement of the attack. The main offensive fell on the night of January 30-31, hitting an additional 18 cities throughout the country. In all, 27 of the 44 province capitals were attacked.

However, the attack which caused the biggest sensation was the battle for Saigon.

At 0300 on the 31st, 19 VC sappers blasted their way through the outer walls of the US embassy in Saigon. They killed two of the military police on duty and fired at the armoured doors of the embassy with rocket launchers. They failed to break down the doors and took cover in the grounds where they pinned down the 'reaction force' of six Marines and then held off a helicopter assault by men of the 101st Airborne Division until daylight. By 0900, however, daylight allowed the Americans to see their enemy, and soon the sappers, distinctive in their bright check shirts, lay dead – their blood spattered over the white gravel and fountains in the embassy gardens. Press coverage was dramatic, there were pictures of the American ambassador, Elsworth Bunker, walking through his garden with the bodies making an unsightly intrusion into the ordered background. The last battle of the military police was recorded as they shot it out with the VC sappers, and George Jacobson, mission co-ordinator, was photographed leaning from his window, pistol in hand.

While this was happening, elements of 11 NVA and VC battalions, ranging in size between 300 to 400 men, had penetrated Saigon. They entered the grounds of the Presidential palace, captured the government radio station and even broke through the heavily guarded perimeter of Tan Son Nhut airbase and engaged in fire fights with elements of the 1st Infantry Division. Together with the 25th Infantry Division and ARVN units, the 1st Infantry Division drove off these attackers with heavy casualties.

With the dawn, the Americans and South Vietnamese reacted violently. Strikes by helicopter gun ships and bombers burned down the radio station and destroyed a model cotton mill and the only low-income housing project ever built in the city. The VC and NVA, however, went to ground in the old Chinese quarter of Cholon and the Phu Tho racetrack and held out for two weeks, sniping and disappearing before the South Vietnamese troops could react.

In the town Americans who were living outside the barracks and diplomatic compounds hid or fought off attacks with small arms. A mere half-mile from the embassy they saw VC political cadres moving from house to house declaring the complete victory of the National Liberation Front. Street 'trials' were held, and Vietnamese who worked for the Americans or were known to be pro-Government were executed. These executions were never seen by the Press, but there was world-wide horror when Saigon's police chief shot a NVA officer, captured in the street fighting, and chose to do this in the middle of the street in front of television cameras.

Fighting elsewhere was equally intense.

In Dalat NVA troops dug in around the central market-place and held out against a series of disorderly counter-attacks. In My Tho and Ben Tre the South Vietnamese forces barricaded themselves into their compounds and left the NVA and VC troops to hoist their flags over the poorer quarters of the city. Thousands of Montagnard refugees fled from Kontum City and Ban Me Thuot when their camps were caught in the cross-fire.

At Quang Tri three regiments of the NVA 324th Division were met by a stubborn ARVN and Regional Forces defence. At the same time the US 1st Brigade of the 1st Cavalry Division (Airmobile) counter-attacked the enemy's rear and trapped them between two fires.

Though the fighting in Saigon and the destruction of the cities made spectacular television news, they were nothing compared with the long fight for Hue.

At 0349 on January 31 rockets and heavy mortar fire hit selected targets within the city to the north and south of the river. The NVA attacked with seven to 10 battalions of infantry. Two battalions drove into the walled portion of the city or Citadel. The mission of the NVA 802nd Battalion was to overrun the 1st ARVN Division Headquarters, while the 800th Battalion was to seize the southern portion of the city.

At 0400 the 800th reached the airfield, where they hit the reaction force of the 1st Division, the Black Panther Company. In the fire fight that followed, the NVA were diverted south and the Black Panther pulled back to assist the HQ staff of 1st Division in their defence against the 802nd Battalion. While this fighting was going on the NVA 806th Battalion had established a strong blocking force on the north-west corner of the city astride Route 1, covering the most likely avenue of reinforcement.

By dawn the NVA had occupied the entire Citadel except for the 1st Division HQ compound. Outside the city, however, the ARVN establishments remained intact. Across the Perfume River the MACV compound had been attacked by elements of the 4th NVA Regiment. This walled compound housed the American advisers to South Vietnamese units in and around Hue. Well armed and motivated, they repulsed the attacks while only suffering light casualties. However, they could not prevent the NVA 804th and K4B Battalions from occupying all of the city south of the river.

To the east of the city the NVA 810th Battalion was deployed as a blocking force, while the 1st Battalion 4th NVA Regiment had established a block astride Route 1 to stop reinforcements from the south. This was the situation by the evening of January 31.

The North Vietnamese were to feed reinforcements into the battle in and around the city, so that by the end a force of about 10,000 men participated in the fight for Hue.

John Parrish was returning from Hue as the attack was developing when he met the Marines from A Company 1st Battalion, 1st Marines, who had been sent to the aid of the MACV compound. "The lead truck of the convoy motioned us off the road to make way. The second truck motioned us to turn around and follow. The turret gunner of the tank motioned us to

get the hell out and pointed toward Phu Bai."

For Parrish, as a doctor, this was to be the beginning of days and nights of harrowing work as the casualties from the city were evacuated to the nearest hospital available. In the end the doctors were ordered to take six hours' sleep, but Parrish said that, despite their fatigue, they suffered from insomnia.

The forces sent to the relief of the MACV compound were followed by 1st Battalion, 1st Marines Command Group, and G Company, 2nd Battalion 5th Marines. A platoon of tanks and two M42 self-propelled 40-mm guns arrived with this second group. These tanks fought with the Marines until February 17, though one was destroyed and they all took hits by rockets and damage to their optical equipment.

On February 1-3 three additional Marine companies, a battalion and a regimental command group were brought into the MACV compound by trucks and helicopters. By February 4 Marine strength stood at one tank platoon, five rifle companies, two battalion command groups and one regimental command group. An attempt to cross the Perfume River (Sang Huong) was repulsed by the NVA.

Outside the city the 3rd Brigade 1st Cavalry Division sealed off the approaches from the north and west. On February 9, while 5th Battalion 7th Cavalry maintained the blocking position, the 2nd Battalion 12th Cavalry entered the village of Bon Tri and encountered a well dug-in regimental-size enemy complex. For three days US artillery, air strikes and naval gunfire pummelled the positions. On February 12 the 2nd Battalion had to break contact without any substantial change in the situation. The 5th Battalion took over, but it too was unable to dislodge the enemy. It remained for the 2nd Battalion again to pick up the assault on February 21 and finally secure the village.

Back in the city, the Marines continued operations to extend the perimeter and secure the landing craft ramp north-east of the MACV compound for resupply. The NVA troops had effectively isolated the northern part of the city by blowing the six-span girder bridge. It was necessary for the 1st Battalion 1st Marines to drive two companies south along Route 1 as far as the Phu Cam River. The 2nd Battalion 5th Marines, with three companies, then moved west along the south bank of the Perfume River to clear as far as the Phu Cam River. By February 10 the 2nd Battalion had reached its initial objective and turned south along the Phu Cam River to clear the far bank and link up with the 1st Battalion.

The area to the south of the river was declared secure on February 10, although operations continued to the south-west and east of Hue. Attention now shifted to the north bank, where the ARVN were fighting for the citadel.

By daylight on January 31 it had become clear to the commanding general 1st ARVN Division that substantial reinforcements were needed. He issued orders to his 3rd Regiment, the 1st Airborne Task Force,

US Marines run up the Stars and Stripes on the dawn of 24th February at the Imperial Palace, Hue. Fighting ended two days later on the 26th

and the 3rd Troop, 7th Cavalry to move to the Citadel. The cavalry and two of the airborne battalions had to fight their way past a road block set up about 400 yards north of the citadel, and though they lost four M113 personnel carriers, they reached the 1st Division compound from the north.

More reinforcements came on February 1-2 when the 9th Airborne Battalion and the 4th Battalion of the 2nd Regiment were airlifted into 1st Division Headquarters from Quangtri and Dong Ha. Simultaneously the 2nd and 3rd Battalions of the 3rd Regiment moved east from the division training centre along the Perfume River and made an unsuccessful attempt to enter the south-west corner of the Citadel. They were later moved by water around the city and penetrated the 1st Division compound on February 7.

The ARVN 1st and 4th Battalions had been operating to the east of Hue when the enemy offensive began. They were both surrounded and had to fight their way back to the city. The 1st Battalion arrived on February 1 and the 4th followed on February 5 after it had fought continuously for four days and been reduced to a mere 170 men.

With three battalions the 1st ARVN Division began a limited offensive on February 1. Initially the drive was to clear the area to the west in the direction of the airstrip, but as more battalions became available operations were undertaken to the south by the airborne task force. The drive to capture the west wall of the Citadel became the responsibility of the 3rd Regiment.

Little headway was made between February 7 and 11. By now the ARVN forces were under strength (a battalion had an average strength of 200 men), but the NVA were able to reinforce the Citadel through the west wall.

On February 11 a company of the 1st Battalion 5th Marines, reinforced by a platoon of tanks and several Ontos vehicles, arrived by landing craft at the 1st ARVN Division compound. The following day the rest of the battalion arrived and was assigned to the south-eastern area of the city, where they relieved the 1st Airborne Task Force.

In the first phase of their attack the 1st Battalion 5th Marines moved south on two axes parallel to the east wall of the Citadel. Heavy rocket and small arms fire pinned down the attack after some initial progress. A two-company force was sent down the wall of the Citadel to flush out the enemy, and then the advance continued. Despite naval gunfire and air strikes, progress was slow, and it was necessary to systematically destroy each enemy position. By February 22 the wall had been secured.

During the final phase of this action the fire from the old Imperial Palace, on the right flank, had become very heavy. The American command was reluctant to use air strikes and artillery against the palace on political and historic grounds. The 1st ARVN Reconnaissance Company was repositioned to give flank security, and on February 12 the 1st and 5th Battalions Vietnamese Marines arrived with six 105-mm howitzers and were deployed to attack the last enemy strongpoints in the south-western corner of the Citadel.

Outside the city the actions fought by

the US 1st Cavalry Division had achieved their mission which had been to deny the enemy access to Hue, interdict routes of egress from Hue and locate and destroy enemy units west of the city.

On February 16 intelligence learned that the commanding officer in the Citadel had been killed by artillery. His second-in-command had requested permission to withdraw but had been refused by his political leaders.

On the night of February 23-24 the 2nd Battalion 3rd ARVN Regiment conducted a surprise attack westward along the south-eastern portion of the Citadel. They overcame well-defended barriers, including claymore mines, and reached the flagpole in the Imperial Palace grounds. At 0500 on the 24th they hauled down the Viet-Cong flag and raised the South Vietnamese flag. At 1515 the Black Panther Company and 2nd Battalion 3rd ARVN Regiment entered the Palace and secured it by 1700.

At 0500 the following day the last enemy

position was seized after an artillery barrage. With its capture the Citadel was declared secure and the battle of Hue was over. During the battle the Americans deployed three direct support batteries, a medium battery and, near the end, an 8-in battery. Between February 3 and 26 they fired 52,000 rounds. In addition 7,670 rounds of 5-in to 8-in naval shells were fired and 600 tons of bombs and napalm were dropped. It was estimated that the US Army and Marines and the ARVN killed 5,000 NVA and VietCong, captured 16,000 weapons and half a million rounds of ammunition. American and Allied losses were 2,144 killed during the 30-day siege.

Though the fighting had ended in Hue, the siege of Khe Sanh still continued in the north. It was not to end until April 6, when the advanced guards of a relief force reached the Marine base. Before that the Army, Marines and Air Force had destroyed a number of small attacks between February 29 and March 1. The

most significant attack fell on the 29th, when three ground assaults were made at 2130, 2330 and 0315. They were all stopped short of the wire by artillery fire and small arms fire. The Forward Air Controllers of the Marine garrison had also developed the 'arc-light' raid, (radar directed bombing by B-52s) to a 'mini arc light' in which Grumman Intruders could be called in, armed with 28 500-pound bombs. The arc-light tactic was taken further to the 'micro arc light' which used fewer bombs and covered a smaller area, but was on call within 10 minutes, in contrast to the 'mini arc light' which took roughly 45 minutes.

Bombing was co-ordinated with artillery fire from within the Khe Sanh perimeter and also from the Army fire base at the 'Rockpile', where four batteries of 175-mm guns were deployed. The Marines themselves had three batteries of 105-mm howitzers, one battery of 4·2-in mortars and one battery of 155-mm howitzers. With these guns they were able to work out

A C-130 Hercules transport air drops supplies to the Marine combat base at Khe Sanh on January 23rd. This resupply operation was one of the few occasions when it was thought wiser to parachute stores rather than risk landing an aircraft on the airstrip where a C-130 had burned out after being hit by Viet Cong ground fire

US Marine Corps

an elaborate artillery and bombing pattern which they called the 'artillery box'.

The B-52s would bomb the approach to the target area, cutting off reinforcements or retreat, the army artillery would fire a barrage which blocked the flanks, and the Marine artillery would fire a smaller box within the bigger box. As the Army fire moved towards the centre of the box, the Marine fire moved towards the Khe Sanh perimeter. Any NVA soldier who survived this barrage would run on to the perimeter defences of Khe Sanh.

Besides the artillery box the artillery fired time-on-target shoots from nine batteries, separate battalion time-on-target missions, battery multiple-volley

individual missions and battery harassment and interdiction missions. By the end of the siege 158,981 rounds of all calibres were fired. In addition there was a daily average of 45 B-52 sorties and 300 tactical air strikes. In the 70 days of the air operations 96,000 tons of bombs were dropped in the battle area—this was nearly twice the tonnage dropped by the Army Air Corps in the Pacific during 1942 and 1943.

On March 31 the Marine Corps and Army began Operation Pegasus, a 15-day air assault aimed at ending the siege. Backed by an elaborate fire support and air strike programme, the 1st Cavalry Division with the 1st Marine Regiment and the ARVN 3rd Airborne Task Force began a push from Ca Lu to reopen Route 9 to Khe Sanh. By April 14 the road had been opened and the siege had officially ended. Besides capturing 557 individual weapons, 207 crew-served weapons and two antiaircraft guns they also found tons of food and ammunition and vehicles ranging from PT76 light tanks to motor scooters. The NVA lost 1,304 killed and 21 captured. To this must be added the 1,602 confirmed killed NVA and estimates of between 10,000 and 15,000 killed by air and artillery in the jungle during the siege. Marine losses were 256 killed.

The follow-up operation in Au Shau valley does not fall under the title of the Tet offensive. It was the drive against the withdrawing NVA forces and yielded more captured arms and materiel, as well as greater enemy losses.

Stand and Fight

The casualties suffered by the NVA and VC forces were vast. By the end of February, when the fighting had begun to wane, it was estimated that they had lost 38,794 killed and 6,991 captured. The Americans had 1,536 killed and 7,764 wounded, with 11 missing. The ARVN had 2,788 killed and 8,299 wounded, with 587 missing. To the Americans in Vietnam Tet had also been a pleasing revelation that the despised ARVN and even the National Police were prepared to stand and fight. The losses had been great, but the NVA and VC losses were among their best troops and most highly motivated men. Even executions and political preaching in captured areas had not produced the national uprising they had hoped for, and after Tet the VC was virtually a finished force.

Though the Tet offensive was won in Vietnam, it was lost in the United States. The protest movement became more vociferous, and then on March 31, in a broadcast to the nation, President Johnson announced that he would not seek another term of office and would devote his remaining time in office to the pursuit of peace negiotiations. Bombing in the North was to be limited to interdiction in the south and west, apparently on the understanding that Hanoi would not take advantage of this cessation to increase the rate of infiltration.

This was the beginning of the negotiations which were to lead to the withdrawal of the United States from South-East Asia. Their departure was followed by increased pressure by the North and then by attacks in March 1975 which resulted in the capitulation of Saigon on April 30, 1975. The North had lost the Tet offensive, but ultimately won the war.

YOM KIPPUR

WAR

The Arab Israeli war of 1973 showed that the Egyptians could launch and sustain a major military operation — but it also showed the remarkable flexibility of the Israeli forces who counterattacked and won.

On Saturday October 5, 1973 the forces of Egypt and Syria, after long and careful preparation, mounted a full-scale offensive against Israel.

In the south the general idea was to hold an extensive exercise in the area immediately west of the Suez Canal beginning on October 1 and move from this, without a pause, straight into the assault.

The Canal was to be crossed, territory on the east bank consolidated, and from this base Sinai would be invaded by two armies deploying over 1,000 tanks, including the most modern Soviet models. There followed one of the greatest tank battles of history, one in which the pendulum of fortune swung dramatically from one side to the other. It ended in a manoeuvre which will be studied and admired as long as military history is read, while the final swing of fortune resulted in the defeated carrying off at least part of the spoils of victory.

The years since the Six Day War of 1967 had been spent in improving the morale and training of the Egyptian Army. In 1973 the Egyptian infantry, especially the commandos, proved very good, but their tank crews and pilots were still no match for their Israeli counterparts.

Accordingly, the Egyptians were lavishly re-equipped with surface-to-air weapons; 62 batteries of semi-static SA-2 (Guideline) and SA-3 (Goa), fully mobile SA-6 (Gainful) on tracked vehicles for the support of the divisions in the field, and man-portable SA-7 (Grail) missiles were supplied by the Soviet Union, as well as a whole array of conventional AA artillery equipment from medium calibre to multi-barrelled automatics mounted on armoured tracked vehicles like the ZSU 23. With these they hoped to protect their forming-up areas and the bridgehead in Sinai from which they proposed to launch their main offensive from interference by the Israeli Air Force.

Similarly, on the ground a formidable anti-tank armament was built up. The infantry were issued with the improved RPG-7 rocket launcher with night-sights and the portable version of the AT-3 ('Sagger') wire-guided anti-tank missile; the armoured corps acquired the BRDM-2 armoured personnel carrier mounted with batteries of six Sagger launchers – again, provided by the Soviet Union. The artillery had the smooth-bore 85-mm recoilless anti-tank gun and the dual-purpose field 122-mm howitzer with a powerful anti-tank projectile. The new Soviet T-62 tanks with their 115-mm smooth-bore guns of revolutionary design were untried but reputedly more than a match for any tank in the world.

The Egyptian engineers, equipped with new Soviet military bridging (manoeuvrable, and easily repaired when hit by slipping in a new section), assiduously practised the complex drill of crossing a water obstacle in the face of the enemy. The task was made uniquely difficult by the fact that during the years of conflict each side had built along many sections of the Suez Canal enormous earth ramparts, 160 feet high in places on the Egyptian bank, almost half that height on the Israeli, which had to be captured and breached before armour and artillery could cross. The Egyptian Army carried out this operation with a skill of which any first-rate army in the world would have been

Paris Match

proud. It also achieved complete tactical surprise.

To explain the Israeli government's late reaction to the unmistakable indications of an impending Arab offensive would require a lengthy analysis of complex and interlocking military and political factors. Basically, however, the Israelis, for political reasons, were tied to a passive defence: they had to await aggression. To mobilise their army unnecessarily was alarmist, terribly costly and disruptive of their national life. It was feared, moreover, that premature mobilisation or even the initial move of their standing army to battle stations might actually provoke conflict. But to delay either might jeopardise their entire scheme of defence, because the balance of forces in being was so greatly in favour of the Arabs that the country could rapidly be overrun beyond the point of recovery. But, above all, Israel had to fight on two fronts: a formidable army was also poised on the Syrian frontier. This last factor was to dominate the fighting along the Canal until October 13, drawing in the bulk of reservists and keeping the Israeli armed forces at full stretch in the north.

The Israeli frontier defences consisted of 16 fortified frontier posts sited along or behind the rampart, each manned by some 30 men with the task of watch and ward and of taking the initial shock of any crossing in strength. Behind these were two parallel lines of defence prepared in advance, one close to the Canal and one further back. Along each were ready-prepared 'ramps' for tanks – elevated

firing sites protected by earth parapets. (These play a great part in Israeli defence tactics, for the rapid deployment of an impregnable gun-line in front of an advancing force.) This was the so-called 'Bar Lev line', named for the former Israeli Chief of Staff. Behind it was a single armoured division with one brigade forward covering the whole line and two in reserve, commanded by the brilliant Major-General 'Albert' Mandler, the victor of the the Golan Heights battle in 1967.

It was an economical plan, but only workable if the timings were exactly right, as it confined the initial defence of the Canal line to some 460 reservist infantry in the strong points, and 100 tanks over a 100-mile front, reinforced to 300 on full alert.

By October 4 the intelligence reports left no doubt that war was a certainty, but for most of October 5 and 6 – the solemn day of prayer and atonement known as Yom Kippur – the Israeli government wavered, delaying not only full mobilisation but even the forward move of the Bar Lev covering force to its battle stations.

At 1415 on the 6th, while the garrisons were at prayer, though alerted, a tremendous bombardment broke out; the Egyptian Air Force attacked the reserve areas, tanks and guns appeared on the Egyptian rampart to fire down directly on to the strong points, and commando infantry crossed along the whole length of the Canal in assault boats. They by-passed the strong-points, which continued to fight desperately once they had recovered their wits, and penetrated to the as yet unoccupied stop-lines of tank 'ramps'. Behind them

Popperfoto

Left: Two Egyptian soldiers pose on the Suez Canal, in the background the Egyptian flag flies over a strong point of the Bar Lev Line. The soldier on the left is armed with an AK47 rifle while his comrade has an Egyptian made Port Said sub-machine gun. *Above:* Israeli soldiers, survivors of the attack on the Bar Lev Line, are paraded in Egypt. The capture of Israeli troops was a major triumph for the Egyptians

engineers breached the Israeli rampart with water-hoses and bulldozers and prepared 10 bridges for the crossing of the main force. Before long the leading elements of five infantry divisions were in position on the east bank, 10 bridges had been thrown across, and the tanks of the armoured brigades which form part of Egyptian infantry divisions had begun to join their infantry. Waiting behind, and ready to form up for the main break-through, were three 'mechanised' divisions, each consisting of two brigades of mechanised infantry and a tank brigade, and two armoured divisions of two tank brigades and one of mechanised infantry. The whole force was deployed in two armies, the Second in the north and the Third in the south, with a boundary at the point where the Canal joins the north shore of the Great Bitter Lake.

Simultaneously with the Canal crossing a force of commandos in helicopters was despatched to seize the vital Giddi and Mitla passes, through which Israeli reinforcements for the Bar Lev line must move.

This first phase went well for the Egyptians. Delayed by the vacillations in Tel

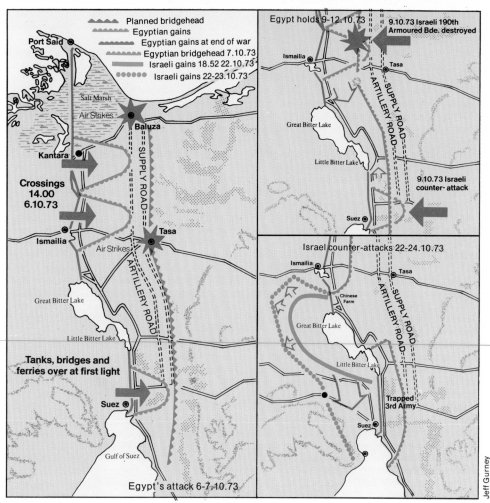

Planned bridgehead
Egyptian gains
Egyptian gains at end of war
Egyptian bridgehead 7.10.73
Israeli gains 18.52 22.10.73
Israeli gains 22-23.10.73

Port Said

Salt Marsh
Air Strikes
Baluza

Kantara

**Crossings
14.00
6.10.73**

Ismailia

Tasa
Air Strikes

Great Bitter Lake

Little Bitter Lake

**Tanks, bridges and
ferries over at first light**

Suez

Gulf of Suez

Egypt's attack 6-7.10.73

Egypt holds 9-12.10.73
9.10.73 Israeli 190th Armoured Bde. destroyed
Ismailia
Tasa

Great Bitter Lake

Little Bitter Lake

9.10.73 Israeli counter-attack

Suez

Israel counter-attacks 22-24.10.73
Ismailia
Tasa

Chinese Farm

Great Bitter Lake

Little Bitter Lake

Trapped 3rd Army

Suez

Jeff Gurney

Above: An Israeli combat group near El Kentara, it includes a Centurion tank and an M-48, in the background is an M4 half track equipped as a mobile command post. Right: A column of M113 APC's passes a White half track on the road to the Canal

Aviv, Mandler's division did not move until the evening, and on arrival in the dark at its pre-planned positions found itself ambushed by strong forces of Egyptian infantry. A hail of RPG-7 rockets took a deadly toll, and in the morning, when the situation was pieced together by the horrified Israeli staff, it was seen that a third of the tanks had been lost, along with all central control. Small parties of Mandler's tanks, some alone or in pairs, fought on desperately, the strong-points were under attack by assault troops and the air was crackling with their radio requests for air and artillery support. By Sunday evening many of the strong-points had fallen and Mandler had lost more of his tanks—two-thirds by nightfall. The only gleam of cheer for the Israelis was the failure of the Egyptian helicopter attack on the passes and the interception of a Marine brigade in amphibious tanks and APCs on the eastern shore of the Great Bitter Lake by Israeli tanks, who massacred it.

All Sunday, while the Egyptians brought over their tanks, the Israelis fought a heroic battle for time while reservists were rushed down to them. The brigades were sorted out and the command structure reorganised into a three-divisional front under the southern army commander, Major-General Samuel Gonen. Major-General Adan's division took over in the north. (Israeli divisions have no fixed composition but take over control of brigades as ordered—and it should be noted that all 'brigades' are armoured, unless otherwise described, and are named after their commanding generals.) Major-General Sharon took over the central sector. He was an ex-parachutist, a brilliant leader, pugnacious and unbiddable, and given to carefully calculated impulses. He was, inconveniently, senior to the Army Commander. Mandler side-stepped to take control in the south. However, although the position looked more stable, Israel's tribulations were not yet over. In war it is difficult to recover from a bad start, and the muddles created breed yet more.

Gonen's plan was for Mandler to hold on in the south, while Adan penetrated the Egyptian front near Al Kantara, turned south and rolled up the Egyptian Second Army from its left. Sharon' was to hold himself ready to go to Mandler's assistance or exploit Adan's attack, as circumstances dictated. Unfortunately for Adan, things went badly wrong, possibly through over-hasty orders (although Israelis are accustomed to act on the briefest of instructions) and lack of accurate intelligence about the Egyptian positions. When counter-attacking, commanders always have this difficult choice between adequate preparation and striking the enemy quickly before he has had time to consolidate his gains. Adan's brigades turned south too early and missed the flank of the Second Army, which was concentrated in a narrow strip five miles wide under the cover of its missile umbrella. Finding no enemy, he wheeled west and was committed to a frontal attack against positions bristling with anti-tank weapons.

Adan's brigades were without their infantry and artillery components, the effective counter to anti-tank units; unwarned or ignorant of the fate of Mandler's division, they charged in hell-for-leather and were shot to pieces by Saggers and RPG-7 launchers fired by well-concealed and well-dug-in infantry. One complete battalion of the 190th Brigade was destroyed and its CO taken prisoner. (It was this event which caused a good deal of uninformed speculation about the future of the tank. The guided missile has unquestionably altered the balance of land warfare, but tanks used unsupported have always been at the mercy of a strong defence. The Israelis were not to repeat this tragic error.) Not only did Adan's counter-attack fail but, due to contradictory orders, Sharon's division took no part in the battle. The Egyptians continued to build up, because though the few Israeli aircraft detached from the land and air battle raging in the north repeatedly

braved the intense missile and AA gunfire along the Canal to attack the bridges, the Egyptian engineers were able, with equal devotion, to repair them. The 8th was another bad day for Israel.

Gonen, his immediate attempt to push his opponent back to the Canal having failed, ordered his divisions to avoid further loss and go over to the defensive until his forces could be built up for a large, properly co-ordinated counter-offensive. This was an audacious plan to cross the Canal and invade Egypt, prepared long in advance of the war. The Israeli high command, despite the situation on both fronts and the severe strain under which it was working, was already discussing when to launch this operation.

It was helped forward in some measure by the obstreperous Sharon, who was temperamentally unsuited to a passive defence. Following the tradition of the Israeli armed forces, which is never to desert a comrade, on the 9th, in defiance of orders, he began a series of forays to locate and rescue the survivors of the garrisons of the strong-points, who had been told to escape but were trapped among the Egyptian units. In one remarkable, typical exploit a brigade commander in his tank, two lieutenant-colonels and a small party of tanks and half-tracks penetrated the Egyptian lines, and while the brigade commander, fighting with his single tank, drove off a platoon of infantry, the remainder picked up 30 men, packed them all on the top of one tank and sent them to safety while they covered the withdrawal. There followed a certain amount of sharp fighting from which one useful piece of intelligence emerged. One of the alternative crossing points for the Israeli counter-offensive was where the Canal meets the north shore of the Great Bitter Lake, and there proved to be a wide unguarded gap between the Second and Third Egyptian Armies.

The command situation in the south now became difficult, as, apart from Sharon's disobedience of Gonen's orders, Gonen himself was at risk of dismissal (unfairly, since the cause for the Israeli setbacks lay in the initial government decisions). However, in an army like that of Israel, which is politically conscious and whose leadership is based on intense personal relationships, it would have been bad for morale to sack two commanders. Sharon stayed, and the sagacious Bar Lev, now a government minister, was drafted back into the Army from his desk to act as a 'supremo', with Gonen retained as a sort of director of operations. It worked, although later, when the Defence Minister and the Chief of Staff came down to the southern front as well, it looked as if the war was being run by a committee.

The Egyptians in the meantime pressed on with the orderly development of their plan. Their next phase was what Montgomery used to call the 'dog-fight' – a battle of attrition with many local, limited-objective attacks, while their break-out divisions crossed over and poised themselves for the break-out phase. They lost the dog-fight.

An Israeli M3 half track arrives at the empty Bar Lev Line during the counter thrust in the second week of the Yom Kippur war. M3 APCs are being replaced by M113s

The Israelis are not only very quick on the uptake but able to modify their tactics in mid-battle, which the best of armies find difficult. The co-operation of all three arms was restored, the correct counter to un-armoured anti-tank operators being co-ordinated infantry action and sup-pressive machine-gun and artillery fire. Each Israeli tank battalion has organic to it 16 US fully tracked APCs carrying infantry. These were re-equipped with as many as four or five machine-guns apiece, the crews ordered to ride with their heads outside the armour keeping a look-out, observe the track of the incoming Saggers, which fly rather slowly, and smother the points of origin with fire. The tanks were told to be more circumspect, and practise what they had already been taught in the way of group-control fire by sections (troops) and companies (squadrons), which greatly increases the chance of hitting a nominated target. In spite of great courage and skill shown by the Egyptian infantry, who would stalk tanks, or advance by night and dig in close to a flank or even in the Israeli rear, no progress was made, and the Egyptians lost more tanks than they could afford, in spite of being able to dispose of 1,550, not counting reserves.

Nevertheless, they decided to go on with the break-out, not least because of the appeals of their Syrian allies, who were in danger of complete defeat. On the morning of October 14 strong forces advanced on a wide front against the unbroken Israeli defence. One infantry division, with its organic 120 tanks reinforced by another tank brigade, struck east and north-east. In the centre an armoured division (250 tanks), reinforced by another tank brigade, struck due east, and two more tank brigades in the south made directly for the Giddi and Mitla passes. A fourth division made up of an infantry brigade, a mechan-ised brigade and a tank brigade moved along the coast of the Gulf of Suez also with the passes as its objective, hoping to take

the defence in the left flank.

This exactly suited the Israeli book. They wanted the bulk of the Egyptian combat troops well east of the Canal, depending on their slender threads of communication across the ten bridges for supply. (Using projected British Second World War figures, assuming the Egyptian formations to be at full strength, that every soldier in Sinai had to have drinking water – a very heavy commodity – brought to him from Egypt, and that all formations were fighting at 'intense' rates, conjecturally some 10,000 tons of munitions and supplies had to be brought forward over the Canal every day of the offensive.) With the bridges behind them cut and the Israelis established in their administrative areas, the Second and Third Armies could be starved out.

The Egyptians were probably correct in not throwing their rigid plan aside and mounting a full-scale offensive as soon as the extent of their success on the 7th and 8th were perceived, as their staff and commanders lacked the calibre for rapid improvisation and the control of fluid operations, but they paid dearly for their delay. Nor did they utilise effectively their powerful assets. Their air force remained supine, and when it did appear later it was badly beaten. (During the whole war, aerial combat losses, disregarding surface-to-air weapons, were 172 on the Arab side, five on the Israeli). By the 14th victory in the north had freed the Israeli air force for operations in the Canal area, and although some attempt was made to move at least part of the enormous array of AA guns and missiles forward into Sinai, they had little effect on the course of the battle.

There was also some unexplained and terrible defect in the training of the Egyptian tank crews, judging by relative losses. Israeli tank gunnery alone during the break-out knocked out 262 Egyptian tanks for very few of their own, and the Israelis picked up enough of the modern T-62 tanks with their revolutionary 115-mm gun to re-equip a whole brigade. In short, the battles of October 14 proved an Egyptian disaster, two tank brigades being destroyed and the offensive capability of

A victor's grin from an Israeli paratrooper as he rides in his half track personnel carrier. Israel's airborne forces have always been the elite force in her army

the rest seriously reduced. When the news filtered back, the high command was badly shaken. In Tel Aviv, by contrast, on the evening of the battle General Elazar, the Chief of Staff, gave the formal order to mount the offensive into Egypt, with H-hour 1700 hours the following day. Sharon, reinforced by a parachute brigade (Matt) in a ground motor-infantry role, was to drive a corridor through the Egyptian positions, clear the tactical road net the Israelis had constructed behind their rampart, establish a bridgehead over the Canal at Dervesoir (just north of the Great Bitter Lake), ferry tanks across and then build a pontoon bridge. This was to be followed by the Israeli engineers' *pièce de résistance*, a monstrous preconstructed bridge on rollers which was to be towed across the desert along a special road, aimed straight at the crossing point, by a team of bulldozers and tanks. When the corridor was secure and the bridgehead deep enough, Sharon was to attack north while two armoured divisions under Major-General Magen, who had taken over after Mandler had been killed, and Adan would turn left to cut off the Third Army in the south.

The main axis exploited the gap between the two armies, but Israeli intelligence knew that north of the chosen corridor there was a well-organised defensive position on the high ground in the area, and in the long deserted Japanese experimental farm (whose notices in ideograms were mistaken for Chinese by the Israeli troops: hence the name of 'Chinese Farm'). This was to prove much stronger than any estimate, as it turned out. Sharon's plan in more detail was to use one of his armoured brigades (Tuvia) north of this area to isolate it, to take it in reverse, and use another (Amnon) to help Matt's paratroopers to clear the corridor and reduce the Chinese Farm.

What followed was a 'soldier's battle': assault boats arrived at the wrong rendezvous; reliable bridge machinery broke down; darkness, and unexpected enemy resistance dislocated the pre-arranged plan; but order was restored by the initiative and sheer valour of private soldiers and junior officers. This was backed by the coolness and nerve of Generals Bar Lev and Gonen, who never wavered. Once committed, they felt the operation must go on, and all talk of pulling Matt's men back from the fingertip hold they had secured on the west bank was firmly resisted. The bold decision to cross without waiting for a secure corridor to be opened, but while the fighting was actually going on, meant that when the Egyptian resistance finally cracked, the 'expanding torrent'—the Israelis are great disciples of Liddell Hart— could flow across at once.

It was, however, a gamble which might have ended disastrously in the face of an opponent who reacted more quickly. The local Egyptian commanders were brave enough, but everything they did was too late, while the high command refused to believe that the Israelis were in earnest; a 'television exercise', they said, when the first reports came in. They committed a fatal error in not liquidating the bridgehead in the early hours of the battle.

The first Israeli setback was that no sooner had the road to the crossing point been cleared than a sortie from the Chinese Farm cut it again, and although Matt was over according to schedule and by 0700 on the 16th tanks had been rafted over to him, there was later an agonising period of 36 hours when the build-up in the bridgehead was halted while the battle of the corridor was fought and won.

The fighting in and around the Chinese Farm was as ferocious as any recorded in military history and as dense as any in terms of troops per square mile. The farm itself was strongly held by infantry lavishly stocked with anti-tank missiles and by dug-in tanks. Just to the north of it were spread out the administrative vehicles of the Egyptian 16th Infantry Division, and among them were crowded the tanks and more vehicles of all kinds from the 21st Armoured Division, which had retired behind the infantry to lick its wounds after the battle of the 14th. Into this area, about five by 10 miles, there pressed, on the night of the 15th, Tuvia's brigade eastwards with an axis north of the farm and Amnon's brigade, which moved along the shore of the Great Bitter Lake and then north to the rear, or west, of the Farm, while Matt's parachute infantry began a bitter, and for the moment losing, battle with the defenders of the Farm's southern perimeter.

A terrific battle began as the sun set and continued through the night, with tanks firing point-blank at each other or at the parachutists, a constant hail of RPG-7s from the Chinese Farm and a rain of artillery fire falling indiscriminately on friend and foe alike. It is probable that the Egyptians had no real idea of what was happening and that the first onslaught to clear a corridor was taken simply as a counter-attack, for Matt's brigade, threading its way through this extraordinary battle, was able to achieve his part of the plan largely unmolested. Having mislaid his assault boats and found them again, he achieved an unguarded stretch of the west bank, and by the morning had a bridgehead three miles wide into which more of his supporting tanks were being ferried. He was, however, cut off.

The Israelis had built a network of roads leading to the Canal specifically for this purpose, and it was essential to clear two, an up and a down route, for the bridges and later for the mass of tanks and APCs waiting to cross. (The number of combat troops involved was roughly the same as in the whole British Army.) After the initial failure, which so alarmed the Israeli Chief of Staff and Defence Minister that there was talk of withdrawal, there followed a long and complicated series of actions where failure and success rapidly alternated and attacks from every direction were met or launched. On October 17 the pontoon bridge was at last brought up and thrown across the Canal.

On the same day the supine Third Army at last sent the 25th Armoured Brigade north along the east shore of the Great Bitter Lake; too late, like all the Egyptian moves. It was met by General Adan who trapped it against the water, destroying 86 of its 96 tanks, along with all its vehicles, for the loss of four of his own.

Meanwhile, over on the west bank, Sharon, fuming because for the moment no more tanks were being sent over to him, was making his presence felt, and the Egyptians suddenly realised that they had been

deluding themselves and that this was no propaganda raid, but that they were in deadly danger. A tremendous air and artillery bombardment was directed into the bridgehead area and at the pontoon bridge. Neither proved of any avail. The Egyptian Air Force finally emerged, but was repulsed by the Israeli pilots and the gun-fire was apparently largely blind, i.e. 'predicted', or fired off the map.

On the 18th the persistence of Amnon and Tuvia was at last rewarded, Tuvia's tanks finally clearing the corridor completely and Amnon's crushing the last defenders of the Chinese Farm. That day the portable bridge, having been damaged and repaired under heavy artillery fire by

Popperfoto

the Israeli engineers, was trundled into position, and the main force, amid great confusion, traffic jams and shocking scenes of destruction—dead men and burning tanks and vehicles stretched for mile upon mile—surged over to deliver the final blow.

There was tactical success. Sharon, after more heavy fighting against the dogged Egyptian infantry, captured the Egyptian rampart for a firing position and having reached the outskirts of Ismailiya was demanding to be loosed against Damietta and the coast to round up the whole enemy force in the north. Magen and Adan, fighting against strong opposition from units brought back over the Canal, drove forward, taking the Genefa Hills which

commanded the Third Army's rear areas, mopped up the SA batteries (one of which actually tried a horizontal shot with an SA-2) and reached Suez, where an over-confident gallop into the town led to a unit being trapped and mauled. From first to last, the Egyptian infantry's stubbornness in defensive fighting never wavered, but both armies east of the Canal were doomed, and there can be little doubt that any further attack by the Egyptians to restore the position west of the Canal would have been smashed, so great was the ascendancy of the Israeli tank crews. Then the two great powers, whose clients the belligerents were, stepped in to avoid too great a victory for one or too great a

An Israeli tank crewman talks with Egyptian prisoners while his comrade guards them in the shadow of an anti-tank ditch. In the background an American built M-48 tank armed with a British 105-mm gun rumbles past a mobile command post of two jeeps. An Israeli flag flutters from the radio antenna on one of the jeeps which is armed with an FN machine gun

humiliation for the other, and at 18.52 on October 22 a cease fire was imposed. Fighting, however, continued for two days, during which the Israelis made considerable additional gains. Despite these, in the peace settlement that followed the Egyptians received part of the territory they had so signally failed to regain by force of arms.

379

INDEX

Page numbers entered in italics indicate photographs. Warships are listed in italics and by class while code names are qualified by weapon type or operation.